৭৯ *Giving Well, Doing Good*

Philanthropic and Nonprofit Studies

Dwight F. Burlingame and David C. Hammack, editors

Giving Well, Doing Good

&

READINGS FOR THOUGHTFUL
PHILANTHROPISTS

EDITED BY

Amy A. Kass

INDIANA UNIVERSITY PRESS
BLOOMINGTON & INDIANAPOLIS

This book is a publication of

Indiana University Press
601 North Morton Street
Bloomington, IN 47404-3797 USA

http://iupress.indiana.edu

Telephone orders   800-842-6796
Fax orders   812-855-7931
Orders by e-mail   iuporder@indiana.edu

Library of Congress Cataloging-in-Publication Data

Giving well, doing good : readings for thoughtful philanthropists / edited by Amy A. Kass.
    p. cm.—(Philanthropic and nonprofit studies)
    Includes bibliographical references and index.
    ISBN 978-0-253-35048-0 (cloth : alk. paper)—ISBN 978-0-253-21955-8 (pbk. : alk. paper) 1. Charity. 2. Charities. 3. Endowments. 4. Gifts. I. Kass, Amy A.
    BJ1533.P5K37 2008
    361.7—dc22   2007024504

1   2   3   4   5   13   12   11   10   09   08

What is the meaning of this dance of sisters in a circle, hand in hand? It means that the course of a benefit is from hand to hand, back to the giver; that the beauty of the whole chain is lost if a single link fails, and that it is fairest when it proceeds in unbroken regular order. . . . Their faces are cheerful, as those of human beings who give or receive benefits are wont to be. They are young, because the memory of benefits ought not to grow old. . . . [I]n benefits there should be no strict or binding conditions, therefore the Graces wear loose flowing tunics, which are transparent, because benefits love to be seen.

FROM SENECA'S DESCRIPTION OF THE THREE GRACES, IN *DE BENEFICIIS*

CONTENTS

THREE Bequests and Legacies | 149

ACKNOWLEDGMENTS

This volume grew directly out of the nation-wide series of "Dialogues on Civic Philanthropy" that I facilitated, during 2005–2006, with people active in the world of American philanthropy. I wish first to acknowledge, with deep gratitude, the generous support of the organizations that made those conversations possible: Hudson Institute's Bradley Center for Philanthropy and Civic Renewal, the Council on Foundations, the Association of Small Foundations, the Achelis and Bodman Foundations, the Bill and Melinda Gates Foundation, the Pettus-Crowe Foundation, the Conference of Southwest Foundations, and the Georgia State Humanities Council. But the seeds for this book were planted much earlier. Indeed one might say that it represents a second sprouting, as it develops more pointedly and fully—and especially for philanthropists— the themes identified in my earlier anthology *The Perfect Gift*, the work for which was generously supported by Lilly Endowment, Inc., both through its Project on Civic Reflection and its predecessor, the Tocqueville Seminars for Civic Leadership.

Funding is rarely forthcoming without advocates and projects seldom succeed without advisors, and I have been blessed with both. In particular, I am most grateful for the attention and encouragement of the following individuals: Irene Crowe, benefactress par excellence, whose interest in and enthusiasm for this project sustained me, start to finish, in more ways than I can name; William Schambra, who dared first to encourage and whole-heartedly support conversations that went against the grain of policy-driven Washington, D.C.; Joanne Scanlan, who gave unstintingly of her time and wisdom, orienting me to the many ways of philanthropy-land; Tim Walter, whose own thoughtful and successful leadership sustained my belief that thoughtfulness *is* necessary for success; and Kenneth Weinstein and Herbert London, who gave my endeavors a most hospitable home at the Hudson Institute. I am also indebted to the too-numerous-to-mention-by-name participants in, and advisors to, the dialogues I have facilitated in Washington, D.C. and across the country for honestly sharing their genuine concerns and searching questions about philanthropy today; my own thinking owes much to these gifts. And last, but also first, I wish to thank Elizabeth Lynn, whose vision for the practice of civic reflection and whose eagerness to extend its reach encouraged me to go out and meet the aforementioned people.

The many conversations so crucial to the development of this volume, as well as the index that appends it, owe very much to the care, creativity, perspicuity, and unqualified goodwill of Krista Shaffer, one of Hudson Institute's hidden treasures. The range of selections herein collected was broadened and deepened thanks to the ingenuity and good sense of Kevin Laskowski. My ability to obtain permission to reprint many of the selections owes much to the financial support of the Earhart Foundation and the interest of Montgomery Brown. Finally, I am especially grateful to my associate, Ruth Martin, whose discerning eye, able pen, and finely tuned sensibilities mark everything in this volume that can be deemed worthy and good.

Above all, as always, I am most grateful to Leon, whose encouragement and support through windy weather made it possible for me to complete this project.

INTRODUCTION

This anthology explores the enterprise of philanthropy—its assumptions, its aspirations, and its achievements. Addressed to current and prospective donors, trustees and professional staff of foundations, and leaders of nonprofit organizations, it seeks to illuminate fundamental questions about the idea and practice of philanthropy, questions of great importance to philanthropy's future. It aims especially to promote more thoughtful discourse about practical issues facing the philanthropic sector and to point a way toward a philanthropic practice that is more responsible, responsive, and civic-spirited, and above all successful—fulfilling for givers, useful for recipients, beneficial for all.

Philanthropy and American Society

Philanthropy in the United States is flourishing. Every year millions of Americans donate large amounts of money, time, and energy in organized efforts to promote numerous civic goods. The scale of giving is unprecedented, as are the range of activities that receive philanthropic support. At the same time, however, American philanthropy also faces unprecedented challenges, in part the result of its ever-growing importance and the changes that have accompanied its success. Both the promise and the perils of philanthropy's present and future may be better appreciated if we sketch first an outline of philanthropy's past, showing the emergence of some of its key features and potential tensions: religious versus secular, local versus national (or even global), charitable relief versus social reform, volunteer or amateur versus professional, private versus governmental.

America's philanthropic beginnings, traceable back to colonial times, were religiously inspired. In his 1710 pamphlet *Bonifacius* ("Doing Good"), Cotton Mather, the leading clergyman in the Massachusetts Bay Colony, summoned fellow citizens to create voluntary associations in the service of social betterment: "Neighbors, you stand Related unto One another; And you should be full of Devices, That all the Neighbors may have cause to be glad of your being in the Neighborhood." The spirit of philanthropy derived from the Christian obligation of charity ("love of neighbor"), and its early practice revolved around local churches.

But the practice of philanthropy soon spread to other venues as voluntarism acquired more secular engines, fueled especially by the rationalist optimism of the Enlightenment. The quintessential new philanthropist was, of course, Benjamin Franklin, whose early "Dogood Papers"—clearly a response to *Bonifacius*—sought to re-found the philanthropic spirit on purely secular ground. Later, as a young tradesman in Philadelphia, Franklin started the "Junto," a club of civic-spirited young artisans, whose deliberations launched a vast array of public philanthropic projects, including, among others, the paving, cleaning, and lighting of public streets; the creation of a lighthouse, a volunteer fire department, a fire insurance association, a hospital, and a circulating library; and the founding of the American Philosophical Society for Useful Knowledge as well as an Academy for the Education of Youth (forerunner of the University of Pennsylvania). By the early nineteenth century, American philanthropic activity and voluntary associations were in full flower. They captured the attention of Alexis de Tocqueville, whose magisterial *Democracy in America* praises as quintessentially American (in contrast to European) the impulse to set up churches, hospitals, schools, universities, orphanages, and countless other such organizations throughout the land. In towns and cities, large and small, these associations, now comprising the "nonprofit sector," became—and have remained—the pillars of rich civic life.

At the end of the nineteenth century, philanthropy stood on the threshold of major growth and transformation, a consequence of the expansion of the American economy, as people of great wealth looked for new ways to deploy the enormous sums they had accumulated. The early decades of the twentieth century witnessed the emergence of philanthropy on a national scale, with the rise of the first large foundations—among them, the Russell Sage Foundation (1907), the Carnegie Corporation of New York (1911), the Rockefeller Foundation (1913), and, later, the Ford Foundation (1936). These large foundations differed from earlier philanthropic enterprises not only in their abundant resources but also in their purpose. Rather than fund responses to local needs or sponsor "palliatives," they hoped to use their wealth to attack the "root causes" of social ills.

The next innovations involved new roles for government and for (paid) philanthropic professionals. It is hard in the age of the welfare state to imagine it, but until the 1960s philanthropic activity in America ran largely on private money and depended mainly on unpaid volunteers; voluntary associations were still the center of beneficent works and deeds. To be sure, hospitals, schools, museums, symphonies, and other service-providing nonprofit institutions were—and still are—supported also by contributions from state and local governments, as well as by income earned from those who use their services (making these institutions subject to pressures from the market). But the federal government stayed out of philanthropic ventures. Indeed, the emerging large foundations explicitly saw themselves as providing what the federal government would not: the vision and the wherewithal to manage the social, educational, and scientific needs of an advanced industrial nation. The federal government cooperated in the growth of private philanthropy only indirectly, encouraging the proliferation of foundations through the federal tax code, which excluded charitable contributions from income subject to federal taxation.

After World War II, the federal government's role began to change. Security considerations and international competition in science and technology (especially with the Soviets, and after Sputnik) brought the federal government into supporting higher education and scientific research. The civil rights and anti-poverty movements led to a raft of federal legislation and activity, culminating in the Great Society programs of the 1960s. With federal funding flowing freely, government support of nonprofit activities soon equaled and, eventually, surpassed private donations. The explicit goal of this massive federal initiative was to effect social change, especially for victims of poverty and discrimination; under the protection of federal legislation, many minority groups established nonprofit organizations to advance their own causes. But the influx of federal funding had unanticipated and unintended consequences for the ways and means of philanthropic organizations. Programs were reformatted to meet federal goals and guidelines; nonprofit boards lost some of their independence, as their organizations became subject to public review and national legislation; many nonprofit organizations shifted from volunteer to paid professional staff; and the interests and influence of individual donors were curtailed by new restrictions and competition.

Notwithstanding these changes, private philanthropy still occupies a central place in American civic life, generating civic energy and promoting civic renewal. As in the past, the extraordinary generosity of American philanthropy—institutional and independent, communal and personal—sustains schools and hospitals, research laboratories and churches, museums and operas, magazines and radio stations, and myriad activities to feed, clothe, house, train, and succor the needy and the dispossessed. Of perhaps equal significance, philanthropic activity continues to mobilize the energy and dedication of hundreds of thousands of our fellow citizens as active participants in promoting robust and responsible civic life. In these respects, the current state of philanthropy could hardly be more encouraging.

Philanthropic Activity, Present and Projected

American philanthropy is, in fact, booming. In 2004, nearly 1.4 million nonprofits registered with the Internal Revenue Service.[1] Nearly half of American adults volunteer their time.[2] In addition, the nonprofit sector employs almost 10 percent of our total workforce—double that of 25 years before.[3] Perhaps most significant, the number of active grant-making foundations—especially small, medium-sized, and community foundations—continues to rise dramatically.

According to the Foundation Center, they numbered nearly 68,000 in 2004, more than double their number in 1991 and triple that of 1981. Their total assets are also rising, as is the amount of foundation money directed toward charities. Foundations gave away an estimated $33.6 billion in 2005, and foundation giving has nearly tripled since 1995.[4]

Active grantmaking by foundations is, however, but a small part of America's philanthropic largesse, estimated as only 11.5 percent of total giving in 2005. Individual Americans, meanwhile, gave 76.5 percent (or $199.07 billion) of all charitable funds.[5] And in times of crisis, the generosity of Americans has, in recent years, outdone itself. The personal and communal outpouring following 9/11 was extraordinary. So too were the responses to the natural disasters of 2005—the Asian tsunami, the Pakistan earthquake, and the Gulf Coast disasters caused by hurricanes Katrina and Rita. Yet even these manifestly heroic contributions to disaster relief in emergencies are dwarfed by the steady, mundane, and largely unheralded generosity of the American people in support of ordinary charitable causes. Indeed, individual giving for the three disasters of 2005—currently estimated at $5.83 billion—represents less than 3 percent of what Americans typically donate to charities and churches every year.[6]

Projections for the coming decades suggest that philanthropic giving will rise, very likely massively. According to a highly respected wealth simulation model, developed by Paul Schervish and John Havens, the next 50 years will see ever-increasing and unprecedented philanthropic activity, owing to record intergenerational transfers of many newly made fortunes. By a conservative estimate, $41 trillion is expected to change hands through inheritance,[7] and much of this money will find its way into new philanthropic activity, dwarfing that of today and likely transforming how philanthropy is practiced.

Other changes are also making their influence felt. Billionaire Warren Buffett has recently announced the transfer of 85 percent of his wealth to philanthropic causes, strong evidence for researchers' claim that, despite reductions in estate taxes, our wealthiest Americans are not trying to maximize the transfer of wealth to their personal heirs but looking for larger and deeper purposes for their material means.[8] We are also witnessing the rise of a new breed of philanthropists, "venture philanthropists"—young, successful entrepreneurs who bring expectations gleaned from business to bear on their philanthropic ventures—as well as "philanthropreneurs"—those whose philanthropic and business ventures merge as they seek to harness the marketplace for charitable purposes (and sometimes profit). In recent years, there have also been large increases in "values-driven" philanthropy, especially among members of evangelical churches. In addition, new technologies that drive down costs of starting and maintaining foundations make it likely that small, as well as mega, foundations will continue to proliferate. Finally, the rise of the Internet has massively expanded the networks in which people enmesh themselves, creating a new "gift economy" of exchange of services and enabling many more philanthropists, and on a global scale, to leverage funds and collaborators for their pet projects. For all these reasons, philanthropy's future role in American life seems likely only to increase.

Growing Concerns and Suggested Remedies

Yet despite—and perhaps because of—these new and promising developments, all is not well with philanthropy, especially in the world of foundations. Critics—including some insiders—express growing concerns about unmet needs, unresponsive donors, doubtful effectiveness, irresponsible practices, and inadequate accountability. The foundation boom has gone hand-in-hand with increasing professionalization—the reliance on specialized experts to develop, implement, evaluate, and promote projects—with the consequence of ever-increasing administrative expenses. Thanks to the professionalization and bureaucratization of foundations, access to funds has become more complicated, threatening philanthropy's hitherto much praised ability to be more nimbly and immediately responsive than big government. Success in securing grants often goes not to the best proposals or the most needy organizations but to the most skilled competitors, who, knowing the secrets of grantsmanship, deftly tweak their programs to appear to comply with foundation priorities. Nationwide, more than 90 percent of grant proposals to foundations are turned down; many small nonprofit associations, including faith-based and minority institutions, go underfunded, understaffed, and, according to some, systematically unrecognized, working hard just to make ends meet and often handicapped by inexperience with new information technologies. Finally, the growing reliance on Internet networking, for all its efficiency, raises new concerns about the impact of such "virtual relationships" on genuine civic engagement and face-to-face philanthropic activities.

Philanthropy's problems have become substantive as well as procedural. The philanthropic sector has been drawn into controversies about the state of our culture and about philanthropy's role in fostering controversial educational and cultural change. Battles over "the culture wars" or "political correctness," as well as serious disagreements about whether certain philanthropic activities are in fact achieving their desired goals, have put foundations on the defensive and increasingly at the center of public attention and controversy. Today more than before, one hears about donors discontented with the uses made of their benefactions, and some large gifts to prestigious universities have been withdrawn for such reasons. In addition, heightened concern for our national security has had some worrisome repercussions for philanthropy, with increased private anxiety and public scrutiny over where money is being spent. The relative invisibility of foundations is a thing of the past; today they are objects of intense public, even governmental, attention.

Especially significant has been the public outcry over, and Congress' direct response to, several well-publicized egregious examples of irresponsible managerial practices in the foundation world, including self-dealing, nepotism, and cronyism. Once before, in the 1970s and 1980s, after Congress enacted the Tax Reform Act of 1969,[9] foundations and charities reorganized their structures and professionalized their practices in order to meet the more rigorous demands for public accountability. Today, although no new regulatory legislation has yet been enacted, the very fact of public scrutiny has ushered in a period of intense and critical self-examination, as the philanthropic sector is again making efforts to improve accountability and insure probity.

Not everyone in the world of philanthropy believes that major change is needed. Many organizations—including the Association of Small Foundations, Independent Sector, and the Alliance for Charitable Reform (spearheaded by the Philanthropy Roundtable)—have been lobbying against any new legislative strictures. Others, however, have seen in the recent scandals an opportunity for much needed reform. Suggestions include more vigorous self-regulation, updated and strengthened statutory and regulatory standards, and increased resources devoted to oversight by the IRS, state attorneys general, and the philanthropic sector itself.[10] Proponents of reform argue that better regulations regarding accountability and stricter standards of enforcement—whether self-imposed or directed by Congress—will inspire more public trust. They also suggest that new and improved codes of ethics can articulate ideals toward which philanthropic practice should strive and offer rough guidelines to govern more specific conduct.

But if one takes a large view of the field, it is clear that new codes, rules, and regulations will not be enough, not even to accomplish their purpose of improving professional integrity. Such strictures abstract from the rich context of moral choice, ignore the motives and passions that lead people to give, and fail to reach the moral sensibilities and habits of the heart of particular agents. They also pay little if any attention to the big practical question: how to get people to practice what is preached. Most important, by focusing only on the prevention of misconduct, they ignore a much more fundamental need, namely, assessing how philanthropy, once freed of misconduct, should be conducted: what does it mean *to give well* and *to do good* in the twenty-first century? New codes and regulations cannot address the growing interest in larger questions about the future of American philanthropy—questions about goals and purposes, relations between donors and recipients (grantors and grantees), wisdom in legacies and bequests, assessment of success, public accountability, and philanthropic leadership.

The new opportunities and new challenges for philanthropy invite a self-conscious return to these questions. Indeed, with philanthropy on the threshold of an exciting new era, it is especially fitting that present and future philanthropists reflect more deeply on the whys and wherefores of their activities. The readings in this volume have been selected because of their power to stimulate such reflection. They are informed by and organized around the following basic themes and questions.

Themes and Questions of This Anthology

1. *Goals and Intentions:* American philanthropy has long been devoted to a variety of ends, including direct alleviation of suffering, promoting social change, advancing social justice, developing and sustaining civic life, enhancing education and culture, and correcting social ills through research into their "root causes" and efforts to counter them with public policy. Although philanthropists commonly appeal to serving "the public good" or promoting "the general welfare," they often differ widely on the meaning of these ideals and how best to promote them. There is indeed little agreement even about the most basic question, "What *is* philanthropy?" and how it is related to "charity." And despite a general historic shift in institutional giving, from more specific goals (for example, ending yellow fever) to broader social goals (for example, promoting civic society), the social goods that are being served have become less clear.

What are the goals of philanthropy as practiced today? How are they related to the goals of governmental programs and public policy, or to the activities of voluntary associations, including religious institutions? What is the relation between philanthropy and charity? Above all: *What should today's philanthropy aim to do? Should its energies be directed mainly toward securing the floor—removing obstacles such as poverty and disease, somatic and psychic—or toward lifting the ceiling—promoting excellences such as learning and the fine arts? Should the major targets today be equality and social justice? Freedom and self-governance? Moral and spiritual renewal? Something else?*

2. *Gifts, Donors, Recipients; Grants, Grantors, Grantees:* Champions of democratic participation have long been in favor of giving potential recipients and beneficiaries a greater role in the grant-making process. But whether it is reasonable to try to do so depends in no small part on what exactly one understands a grant to be. Grantor-grantee relations will be affected, often profoundly, by the operative understanding of "grantor" and "grantee" and by the fundamental meaning of "a grant."

For example, when the federal government first began sponsoring research, it realized that, in order to get what it wanted, it would also have to support the kind of research that universities wanted to do. This gave rise to a dual system of relationships, one based on contracts, the other on grants. Over time, however, the distinction seems to have become blurred. Is a grant really a contract? Or is it more like a gift?

If philanthropic practice is to become more democratic, as well as more effective and more accountable, the crucial elements of philanthropic exchange require clarification. *What is the meaning of a grant? How is it similar to or different from a gift? From a contract? What sorts of relationships and obligations does a grant imply for givers and receivers? How should grant- or gift-making decisions be rendered?*

3. *Bequests and Legacies:* The ability of established foundations to make grants depends in large part on the bequests of founders and major donors. Family foundations, increasingly important actors in American philanthropy, are born largely from bequests made and legacies left by parents and other ancestors. In recent years, much public attention has been directed to measures needed to encourage more such gifts (for example, the debates about the pros and cons of eliminating the estate tax). Less attention has been paid to what is arguably even more important: what is required to give and receive such gifts wisely and well.

Although bequests and legacies that are explicitly directed beyond the family may avoid the pitfalls of intergenerational strife, an equally vexing issue may arise here as well, connected to the deference owed to—and claimed for—the intent governing the donor's bequest. Hence, every kind of bequest and legacy may well require not only greater clarity about expectations but also prior preparation if the expectations are to be realized. *What is the relationship between a bequest and legacy? What should guide people who make a bequest? What should guide heirs and trustees? How should we prepare the next generation?*

4. *Effectiveness:* There has long been much interest in getting better and more reliable—more measurable—information about the effectiveness of grants or gifts, be they from private charity, foundations, or government. And for good reasons: No one wants to do harm in the name of doing good; no one thinks that good intentions are an acceptable excuse for bad results; everyone realizes that ignorance in the name of doing good can undermine doing real good, and no one condones the arrogance of such ignorance. But although everyone wants good results, people differ on the *meaning* of a good result, or even on whether results can accurately be measured or assessed in a timely or useful way. No wonder there are today more than one hundred conflicting approaches to measurement and evaluation.

But the difficulty of assessment is more than methodological. For it is one thing to gauge whether grant recipients are performing the particular activities that they said they would; or whether they are proceeding according to their proposed plan; or whether the available resources are being effectively managed; or even whether recipients have delivered the promised concrete results. It is quite another, and more difficult, thing to discern what sort of an impact a grant really has, whether it has really made a difference for good, and if so, how, where, when, and to whom. *What is effective philanthropy? How should we judge its success? What attitudes, dispositions, or measures are conducive to effective philanthropy?*

5. *Accountability:* Everyone today seems to agree that philanthropy should be more accountable and responsive to some overseeing authority. As one observer puts it, "it is time to put the response back into responsibility." But there is little agreement regarding the authority to which philanthropy should respond.

Who should be the arbiter of what is—and what is not—in the "public good"? Likewise, everyone seems to agree that grantors as well as grantees ought to explain what they are doing and why. But, again, it is unclear what sort of account is warranted, as well as to whom it should be addressed.

These matters become especially urgent (and far more complicated) once we look beyond the ethics of managerial conduct to consider also the purposes and contents of grants, or more generally, to the interests and goals of philanthropists. Are there limits on what responsible philanthropy should be free to promote—especially in a post-9/11 world? The federal government grants special privileges to the nonprofit sector, notably in matters of taxation. Do these privileges carry special responsibilities, not merely for administrative integrity but also for the character of organizations and activities that philanthropy supports? Transparency is surely a good thing, but one must still wonder whether the activities of philanthropy can be made transparent without jeopardizing the very freedom that foundations treasure. Account-giving is also a good thing, but one may wonder what sort of account-giving might justify the civic privileges that philanthropy enjoys. *For what should philanthropy be responsible? To whom should philanthropy be accountable? How should we educate for responsibility?*

6. *Philanthropic Leadership:* Many foundation leaders agree that one can learn quickly much of what one needs to know to keep a foundation out of trouble. There is far less agreement, however, about what it takes or means positively to lead well. Some believe that no professional training is necessary. Indeed, they claim that a cadre of professionally trained leaders would not only be a positive disadvantage to the field in general, but also a strong disincentive for anyone who might otherwise be interested in entering it. Yet "philanthropy training," especially in the form of nonprofit management programs, as well as "leadership training" are growing industries.

Is philanthropy a profession? Is there a body of knowledge that its leaders should master? Are there specific skills, attitudes, or virtues required for excellent leadership in philanthropy, and do they differ from those required for other forms of leadership (for example, statesmanship or religious leadership)? Is effective leadership in philanthropy dependent upon (or separable from) one's ideological beliefs and commitments? Are nonprofit management or leadership programs helping or hindering the development of excellent leaders? *What should we expect of philanthropic leaders?*

The Readings

The questions raised above are difficult, complex, and unlikely to be settled once and for all. Different people will approach and answer them differently. For this reason especially, this anthology has been prepared with the widest possible view of philanthropy, one that hopes to speak to all persons who now—or who might soon—regard themselves as practicing philanthropy. It does not presuppose that there is one right answer to any of the questions it raises, nor does it take sides in any current disagreements in the field. As there are many mansions in the house of philanthropy, there is no need to divide the house. For all who live under its roof—be they donors, grantors or professionals in philanthropy, or leaders of nonprofits—share (or *should* share) certain common attributes: a benevolent disposition, thoughtfully expressed, in concrete deeds, freely chosen, for some public (as opposed to merely personal) ends. Philanthropists of every stripe can benefit from reflecting more deeply on what it means—for their own preferred form of giving—to give well and to do good.

In approaching fundamental questions of the sort raised here, we can get valuable help from reflecting on fundamental texts. Accordingly, many of the readings collected in this anthology are taken from "classic" texts, written by major thinkers and writers, and from essays written by experienced practitioners in philanthropy, both old and new. There are selections from poets such as Shelley and Wordsworth, philosophers such as Plato and Maimonides, novelists such as Dostoevsky and Ellison, short story writers such as Bierce and Le Guin, civic leaders such as Lincoln and DuBois, and leaders in philanthropy such as Frederick Gates and Paul Ylvisaker. The texts have been chosen not because they are part of a canon, or because they represent a particular position or portion of humanity, but because they are especially effective in posing basic issues and offering alternative answers. Roughly half of the selections are from imaginative literature, chosen because they encourage us to identify and think with characters faced with concrete decisions of the sort that anyone engaged in philanthropic activity is obliged to ponder.

As a university teacher for more than thirty years, I have found readings like those collected here to be the best companions for thought and the richest materials for enlarging horizons, stimulating the imagination, and challenging intellectual complacency. I also have some strong evidence for the value of using this approach with donors, foundation executives and staff, leaders of nonprofit organizations, and other people interested and engaged in civic life. Over the past ten years I have been leading discussion seminars, involving such participants and using these and similar readings, designed to encourage more reflective and civic-spirited philanthropy. In 2005–2006, I convened six "Dialogues on Civic Philanthropy," held nation-wide, involving people variously engaged in the philanthropic enterprise, each hosted by a regional or national philanthropic group.[11] Though the conversations ranged broadly, each dialogue focused primarily on one of the six themes of this anthology. The primary purpose of these conversations was to enable practitioners in philanthropy, in the company of their peers, to clarify the questions they were wrestling with, and to deepen their reflections in search of better answers. Yet the Dialogues also enabled *me* to see more clearly the central concerns of practitioners and to include in this volume readings that speak directly to them.

All of my seminars assume that civic feelings and ideas can be renewed, the understanding deepened, and the heart enlarged by self-reflective discussion. According to comments received from seminar participants, this is exactly what has happened. Many have found, with the help of texts like those in this volume, a more nuanced and imaginative vocabulary for understanding the complex problems of philanthropy, and rich sustenance for their hunger for critical self-scrutiny. Some have encouraged their own institutions and colleagues to extend and support such conversations in the future. The one unanimous conclusion from the dialogues is the desirability of more dialogues of a similar sort.

Drawing on my experience in these seminars, I have selected readings based on three main criteria: Will the reading encourage and enable readers to become more thoughtful—to dig deeper and to care more? Will it provide readers with a more robust ethical vocabulary for doing so? Can its benefits be obtained both in private study and in organized seminars?

As any teacher knows, even the best texts generally do not teach themselves. We are frequently lazy readers who pass off what is puzzling or unfamiliar, and, arguably even worse, fail to see the depth in what is, by contrast, familiar and congenial. Moreover, when a subject is especially close to us, or when a text challenges our practices or beliefs, our prejudices often get in the way of understanding. Accordingly, in arranging this anthology, I have introduced each reading with some observations and questions designed to make for more active and discerning reading. I have done this with some mixed feelings, concerned about getting between author and reader or imperiling your understanding of texts written by subtler and greater minds by imposing my own limited understanding and personal concerns. I encourage you to use the introductions if you find them helpful, but to treat them with the proverbial grain of salt.

The readings in each of the six sections have been ordered around selected sub-themes, and the rationale is explained in the general introductions to each chapter. Nevertheless, as with any anthology, readers are free to pick and choose what they will. I heartily encourage you to indulge your preference. In spirit and purpose, as emphasized above, this anthology is not one-size-fits-all. Its purpose is to help all who care about philanthropy—both seasoned laborers and neophytes in the philanthropic vineyard, as well as would-be philanthropists—better understand their own professional or personal giving practices.

The British economist Walter Bagehot once mordantly observed: "The most melancholy of human reflection, perhaps, is that on the whole, it is a question whether the benevolence of mankind does more harm than good." It is the assumption of this volume that deep and serious reflection concerning the themes of this volume will make it more likely that the philanthropy of the future will both give well and do good.

Notes

1. According to the Urban Institute's National Center for Charitable Statistics.

2. See the Independent Sector's *Giving and Volunteering in the United States* (2001).

3. See the Independent Sector's *Nonprofit Almanac* (2002).

4. See *Foundation Yearbook* (2006).

5. See *Giving USA* (2006).

6. See *Giving USA* (2006).

7. In 2002 dollars. John J. Havens and Paul G. Schervish, "Why the $41 Trillion Wealth Transfer Is Still Valid: A Review of Challenges and Questions," *The Journal of Gift Planning* (2003).

8. See Paul G. Schervish, John Havens, and Albert Keith Whitaker, "Leaving a Legacy of Care," *Philanthropy* (Jan/Feb 2006).

9. This law obliged foundations to give away annually a minimum fraction of their assets (now 5 percent). It also imposed on foundations a 4 percent excise tax on investment income, barred them from owning more than 20 percent of any one business, and stipulated requirements for disclosing all their financial transactions.

10. See Rick Cohen, "Hearings and Roundtables: NCRP Brings Philanthropic Accountability Standards to Capitol Hill," *Politics of Philanthropy* (2004).

11. These dialogues were generously supported by the Bradley Center for Philanthropy and Civic Renewal, the Council on Foundations, the Association of Small Foundations, the Achelis and Bodman Foundations, the Bill and Melinda Gates Foundation, the Pettus-Crowe Foundation, the Conference of Southwest Foundations, and the Georgia State Humanities Council. They were hosted, in turn, by the Council on Foundations in Washington, D.C., the Northwest Area Foundation in St. Paul, Minnesota, The Foundation Center in New York City, Southern California Grantmakers in Santa Monica, California, the Conference of Southwest Foundations in Dallas, Texas, and jointly by the Georgia State Humanities Council and the Southeastern Council on Foundations in Atlanta, Georgia. Transcripts of proceedings are available at www.civicphilanthropy.net. The dialogues were similar in form to earlier seminars that I conducted, first under the auspices of the "Tocqueville Seminars for Civic Leadership" through The University of Chicago, and later via the "Project on Civic Reflection," a still robust and influential project, headquartered at Valparaiso University, using readings collected in my earlier anthology, *The Perfect Gift: The Philanthropic Imagination in Poetry and Prose*. The Tocqueville seminars were generously supported by the Lilly Endowment, as is the ongoing Project on Civic Reflection.

Giving Well, Doing Good

ONE

Goals and Intentions

Most people in philanthropy today readily recognize that "philanthropy" has become an umbrella term under which many philosophies and practices take cover. As Rick Cohen puts it, in his essay in this chapter, modern "philanthropy almost defies singular characterization much less prescription. [It] is a multihued potpourri with multiple concerns and purposes." But despite its many ways, philanthropy's goals and intentions—its purposes—are not a haphazard laundry list dictated by current problems or future prospects, or governed by mere whim. Philanthropy is a serious enterprise not only because it can do both good and harm, but also because philanthropists self-consciously and deliberately consider which goods they should pursue. In determining what good they aim to do—what impact they want to have—all philanthropists, tacitly or explicitly, must ask themselves fundamental questions: What do I think is good? What do I think is important? What do I think is urgent?

The readings included in this chapter reflect the varying answers people give to these questions. Not surprisingly they display our most treasured, and often conflicting, aspirations: for freedom, justice, equality, dignity, excellence, happiness, love, and community. They point to the important decisions givers must make in choosing their interests, methods, and recipients. The ordering of the selections follows a guiding dialogic thread, each addressing the general question:

What should today's philanthropy aim to do?

Almost every discourse about American philanthropy refers to Alexis de Tocqueville's *Democracy in America,* especially its discussion "On the Use that the Americans Make of Association in Civil Life." Tocqueville regarded the tendency of Americans to associate voluntarily, for everything from re-pairing streets to building hospitals, as the backbone of our republic. Voluntary associations, he observed, are helpful for individuals, otherwise weakened by isolation and limited resources, and are crucial for building, renewing, and perpetuating civic life. They are, in effect, "schoolhouses" of democracy, through which ordinary citizens learn not only to organize and govern themselves, but also to appreciate the freedom that enables them to do so, and thus, to want to safeguard their independence against the encroachments of government.

Some people refer to Tocqueville, however, only to criticize his picture of American civic life as antiquated and, for all practical purposes, radically insufficient. With many neighborhoods in decay, and ordinary civility and public trust in short supply, they question whether voluntarism—citizens' willingness to make common cause and neighbors' willingness to care for neighbors—is still a viable philanthropic model. Wouldn't our rights and well-being be better safeguarded, they argue, if government were more vigorous? Such is the implicit argument of Carol Sue Franks' "Whatever Happened to Chris Olsen?"

Dostoevsky's tale of "The Grand Inquisitor" sharpens the debate between freedom and self-governance, on the one hand, and concern for our own and others' welfare, on the other, by imagining a "philanthropic" regime in which everyone is equally cared for and content, but no one, save the Grand Inquisitor himself, is free.

The relevance of Dostoevsky's tale to today's philanthropic sector is driven home by Rick Cohen's essay, "Philanthropy and the Role of Social Justice," in which he argues that "unless the nation chooses to turn the responsibility of self-governance over to philanthropic philosopher kings and queens" (that is, grand inquisitors), philanthropy *must* enable "those most affected by the challenges of our society to weigh in on the solutions." But like the Grand Inquisitor, Cohen too aims at social justice, and his argument challenges us not only to think about his view of justice, but also whether, if realized, a society restructured in its image would, in fact, be different from the Inquisitor's.

By most accounts, justice lies in equality, injustice in inequality. But to the protagonist of Mark Helprin's "Perfection," equality is an illusion, and justice, however important and worthy an end, is seldom realizable in our lifetime. Rather, the "mechanism of the world"—incomprehensible to humans and recalcitrant to our manipulation—renders men equal by its own godly consonance. Human agency should be used rather to strive for human excellence, not because we can directly rectify injustice, but because efforts to do so help correct the cosmic imbalance between good and evil.

In "The Talented Tenth," W. E. B. DuBois also makes an argument for encouraging and supporting human excellence but on altogether different grounds. Interested more in culture and civilization than in social justice, he focuses on the crucial role to be played by the best and the brightest and on the importance of institutions of higher learning that succor them. Education produces leaders, he contends, and leaders lift up their communities and civilization.

In contrast to DuBois' "top-down" approach to social change, Anna Faith Jones propounds a "bottom-up" approach. In "Doors and Mirrors: Reflections on the Art of Philanthropy," she argues that philanthropy should help communities help themselves by enabling them to build connections that support, respect, and empower individuals. More concerned about human dignity than human excellence, Jones champions the benefits vital communities provide their members rather than the benefits the talented few bring to their communities. Reading Jones and DuBois back to back, we are invited to reflect on whether these two visions of social change, community, and individual empowerment are complementary or contradictory.

Frederick Gates, speaker of the "Address on the Tenth Anniversary of the Rockefeller Institute," is a quintessential proponent of modern American philanthropy and the endowed research institute, one of its favorite sons. Gates applauds the mission of research—seeking and increasing knowledge of universal value—as well as its likely by-products—"new moral laws and new social laws, new definitions of what is right and wrong in our relations with each other."

In his encyclical *Deus Caritas Est* ("God Is Love"), Pope Benedict XVI, by contrast, cautions that the only thing of persistent and universal value is love. Making no distinction between charity and philanthropy, he recalls us to old moral and social ways, arguing for the importance—indeed, the indispensability—of personal care and concern.

Nearly all of the previous readings see philanthropy in the service of providing relief or promoting some form of progress or social change. Our final selection, Bruce Cole's "The Urgency of Memory," speaks instead about the need to conserve historical memory, cultural legacies, and civic self-understanding. As important as Tocqueville's "science of association," Cole implies, is the need to cultivate the art of preservation, if we are to assure the survival of civilization in a "forward-looking people" prone to amnesia.

ALEXIS DE TOCQUEVILLE

"On the Use that the Americans Make of Association in Civil Life"

In the early 1830s, French aristocrat and social theorist Alexis de Tocqueville traveled to America in order to observe democracy in its "greatest development" and to learn what "to fear or hope from its progress." Many people still turn to his analysis, recorded in his magisterial work, Democracy in America, *to explain, and indeed to justify, many democratic policies and practices. Tocqueville devotes this famous chapter of his work to America's "voluntary associations," the ancestors of our modern foundations and nonprofits. In it, he draws our attention to the manifold ways in which Americans of all "ages, conditions, and minds" voluntarily unite, the multiple reasons they do so, and the efficacy of such reciprocal action by neighbors upon one another. Individuals in democratic times, as he points out, may be too weak to satisfy their own needs and interests, and thus are strengthened and personally benefited by working in concert with others. But Tocqueville claims the stakes are much higher: "[T]he science of association is the mother science, the progress of all the others depends on the progress of that one." Only by cultivating the habit of associating, only by immersing themselves in larger public concerns, can private individuals become self-governing citizens. And, only by this means, he insists, will we "remain civilized or become so."*

Philanthropy guided by Tocqueville will attend first and foremost to building up civil or civic life, by enabling and encouraging neighbors to form associations and to help neighbors in myriad ways. Yet some philanthropists question the usefulness of such modest measures. As one foundation leader recently observed, "[W]e no longer have the luxury of assuming that small acts of generosity can meet the needs of today—or tomorrow. . . . We must make the distinction between funding soup kitchens (charity) and figuring out why we need soup kitchens in the first place—and then making them unnecessary (philanthropy)."[1] Are such small associations for local action obsolete? Do we turn our backs on them at our peril? Is philanthropy thus understood and thus practiced mere "charity"?

I do not wish to speak of those political associations with the aid of which men seek to defend themselves against the despotic action of a majority or against

---

1. Ed Skloot, "Is Distinguished Philanthropy Still Possible?" (speech delivered to the Annual Conference of the Minnesota Council on Foundations, Minneapolis, Minnesota, December 13, 2002).

the encroachments of royal power. I have already treated this subject elsewhere. It is clear that if each citizen, as he becomes individually weaker and consequently more incapable in isolation of preserving his freedom, does not learn the art of uniting with those like him to defend it, tyranny will necessarily grow with equality.

Here it is a question only of the associations that are formed in civil life and which have an object that is in no way political.

The political associations that exist in the United States form only a detail in the midst of the immense picture that the sum of associations presents there.

Americans of all ages, all conditions, all minds constantly unite. Not only do they have commercial and industrial associations in which all take part, but they also have a thousand other kinds: religious, moral, grave, futile, very general and very particular, immense and very small; Americans use associations to give fêtes, to found seminaries, to build inns, to raise churches, to distribute books, to send missionaries to the antipodes; in this manner they create hospitals, prisons, schools. Finally, if it is a question of bringing to light a truth or developing a sentiment with the support of a great example, they associate. Everywhere that, at the head of a new undertaking, you see the government in France and a great lord in England, count on it that you will perceive an association in the United States.

In America I encountered sorts of associations of which, I confess, I had no idea, and I often admired the infinite art with which the inhabitants of the United States managed to fix a common goal to the efforts of many men and to get them to advance to it freely.

I have since traveled through England, from which the Americans took some of their laws and many of their usages, and it appeared to me that there they were very far from making as constant and as skilled a use of association.

It often happens that the English execute very great things in isolation, whereas there is scarcely an undertaking so small that Americans do not unite for it. It is evident that the former consider association as a powerful means of action; but the latter seem to see in it the sole means they have of acting.

Thus the most democratic country on earth is found to be, above all, the one where men in our day have most perfected the art of pursuing the object of their common desires in common and have applied this new science to the most objects. Does this result from an accident or could it be that there in fact exists a necessary relation between associations and equality?

Aristocratic societies always include within them, in the midst of a multitude of individuals who can do nothing by themselves, a few very powerful and very wealthy citizens; each of these can execute great undertakings by himself.

In aristocratic societies men have no need to unite to act because they are kept very much together.

Each wealthy and powerful citizen in them forms as it were the head of a permanent and obligatory association that is composed of all those he holds in dependence to him, whom he makes cooperate in the execution of his designs.

In democratic peoples, on the contrary, all citizens are independent and weak; they can do almost nothing by themselves, and none of them can oblige those like themselves to lend them their cooperation. They therefore all fall into impotence if they do not learn to aid each other freely.

If men who live in democratic countries had neither the right nor the taste to unite in political goals, their independence would run great risks, but they could preserve their wealth and their enlightenment for a long time; whereas if they did not acquire the practice of associating with each other in ordinary life, civilization itself would be in peril. A people among whom particular persons lost the power of doing great things in isolation, without acquiring the ability to produce them in common, would soon return to barbarism.

Unhappily, the same social state that renders associations so necessary to democratic peoples renders them more difficult for them than for all others.

When several members of an aristocracy want to associate with each other they easily succeed in doing so. As each of them brings great force to society, the number of members can be very few, and, when the members are few in number, it is very easy for them to know each other, to understand each other, and to establish fixed rules.

The same facility is not found in democratic nations, where it is always necessary that those associating be very numerous in order that the association have some power.

I know that there are many of my contemporaries whom this does not embarrass. They judge that as citizens become weaker and more incapable, it is necessary to render the government more skillful and more active in order that society be able to execute what individuals can no longer do. They believe they have answered everything in saying that. But I think they are mistaken.

A government could take the place of some of the greatest American associations, and within the Union several particular states already have attempted it. But what political power would ever be in a state to suffice for the innumerable multitude of small undertakings that American citizens execute every day with the aid of an association?

It is easy to foresee that the time is approaching when a man by himself alone will be less and less in a state to produce the things that are the most common and the most necessary to his life. The task of the social power will therefore constantly increase, and its very efforts will make it vaster each day. The more it puts itself in place of associations, the more particular persons, losing the idea of associating with each other, will need it to come to their aid: these are causes and effects that generate each other without rest. Will the public administration in the end direct all the industries for which an isolated citizen cannot suffice? And if there finally comes a moment when, as a consequence of the extreme division of landed property, the land is partitioned infinitely, so that it can no longer be cultivated except by associations of laborers, will the head of the government have to leave the helm of state to come hold the plow?

The morality and intelligence of a democratic people would risk no fewer dangers than its business and its industry if the government came to take the place of associations everywhere.

Sentiments and ideas renew themselves, the heart is enlarged, and the human mind is developed only by the reciprocal action of men upon one another.

I have shown that this action is almost nonexistent in a democratic country. It is therefore necessary to create it artificially there. And this is what associations alone can do.

When the members of an aristocracy adopt a new idea or conceive a novel sentiment, they place it in a way next to themselves on the great stage they are on, and in thus exposing it to the view of the crowd, they easily introduce it into the minds or hearts of all those who surround them.

In democratic countries, only the social power is naturally in a state to act like this, but it is easy to see that its action is always insufficient and often dangerous.

A government can no more suffice on its own to maintain and renew the circulation of sentiments and ideas in a great people than to conduct all its industrial undertakings. As soon as it tries to leave the political sphere to project itself on this new track, it will exercise an insupportable tyranny even without wishing to; for a government knows only how to dictate precise rules; it imposes the sentiments and the ideas that it favors, and it is always hard to distinguish its counsels from its orders.

This will be still worse if it believes itself really interested in having nothing stir. It will then hold itself motionless and let itself be numbed by a voluntary somnolence.

It is therefore necessary that it not act alone.

In democratic peoples, associations must take the place of the powerful particular persons whom equality of conditions has made disappear.

As soon as several of the inhabitants of the United States have conceived a sentiment or an idea that they want to produce in the world, they seek each other out; and when they have found each other, they unite. From then on, they are no longer isolated men, but a power one sees from afar, whose actions serve as an example; a power that speaks, and to which one listens.

The first time I heard it said in the United States that a hundred thousand men publicly engaged not to make use of strong liquors, the thing appeared to me more amusing than serious, and at first I did not see well why such temperate citizens were not content to drink water within their families.

In the end I understood that those hundred thousand Americans, frightened by the progress that drunkenness was making around them, wanted to provide their patronage to sobriety. They had acted precisely like a great lord who would dress himself very plainly in order to inspire the scorn of luxury in simple citizens. It is to be believed that if those hundred thousand men had lived in France, each of them would have addressed himself individually to the government, begging it to oversee the cabarets all over the realm.

There is nothing, according to me, that deserves more to attract our regard than the intellectual and moral associations of America. We easily perceive the political and industrial associations of the Americans, but the others escape us; and if we discover them, we understand them badly because we have almost never seen anything analogous. One ought however to recognize that they are as necessary as the first to the American people, and perhaps more so.

In democratic countries the science of association is the mother science; the progress of all the others depends on the progress of that one.

Among the laws that rule human societies there is one that seems more precise and clearer than all the others. In order that men remain civilized or become so, the art of associating must be developed and perfected among them in the same ratio as equality of conditions increases.

CAROL SUE FRANKS

"What Ever Happened to Chris Olsen?"

Debates over big versus small government and public services versus private initiatives did not end with Tocqueville's assessment of American democracy. Especially in the past forty years, the debate has raged within and between the nonprofit and political sectors regarding who should shoulder the responsibility and foot the bill in providing Americans with valuable social services. In her award-winning essay, teacher Carol Sue Franks helps us understand why. With sensitivity, simplicity, and finally outrage, Franks draws our attention to the plight of one man, "civil and polite" Chris Olsen, who fell between the cracks of our society, a society in which anonymity and alienation appear to her to be the norm. Insufficiently sustained by economic opportunity, family concern, government aid, or neighborly charity, this man in his early fifties suddenly succumbed to the heart disease he had long endured. A few months after losing his job, a few weeks before receiving state heath insurance, he was unable to bridge the gap, to make his means or medication "last a little longer."

At the start of her essay, Franks states that Chris Olsen's death reminded her of her own purpose. Though she never directly identifies what that is, we infer that her concern for her neighbor, not adequately satisfied by giving alms, transformed her into an advocate for public assistance. Very likely, she would have philanthropy use its resources to do the same: advocate for more and better government-sponsored service initiatives for people on the edge of poverty. But is that where the story she tells points? Both the lines of Donne with which she prefaces the essay, and the outrage with which she ends it, summon us to see our fate as inseparable from our neighbor's. What kind of philanthropic activity best attends this insight? Who should shoulder the responsibility for and extend a hand to our needy neighbors?

> Every man is a piece of the continent, a part of the main. If a clod be washed away by the sea, Europe is the less, as well as if a promontory were, as well as if a manor of thy friend's or of thine own were. Any man's death diminishes me because I am involved in mankind; and therefore never send to know for whom the bell tolls; it tolls for thee.
>
> John Donne (Meditation 17, 1624)

Chris Olsen is dead. He didn't want to die. I don't know if he thought much about his purpose in life, but he has made me aware again of my own.

On January 9, 2004, Portland, Oregon, was encrusted in an icy snow so hard that no one, no matter how large, could break through it to walk. Somehow an ambulance backed into the east side of the apartment complex, where I have lived for over a decade. I couldn't see who was being loaded into the back, but when the ambulance drove away, the siren wasn't blaring and the lights weren't flashing. That meant that there was no hurry. The passenger was dead.

I don't know my neighbors very well. The apartments are low budget and nondescript. Let me illustrate what I mean by nondescript. Two or three years after I moved in, I came home one night, cold sober, and pulled into the apartment complex to the west of mine. I parked my car in what I thought was my space—in front of a juniper hedge. I went to a door that I thought was mine, put the key in the deadbolt, and tried to open the door. My key didn't work. At that moment, I noticed that the apartment number—same style, same positioning—wasn't mine. I pulled my key from the deadbolt and fled.

As I fled, I heard the apartment door open, and a young man's voice barked at me through the darkness, "Who are you?!"

I froze. In the United States, many city dwellers have guns for just such occasions.

"You're never going to believe this," I began, "but I live in the apartment to the east and . . ."

He laughed. "I've put my key in your deadbolt, too."

That's what I mean by nondescript. In such apartments, turnover is high. Only two or three of my neighbors have been here as long as I. My purpose in life has nothing to do with acquiring better housing. Mine suffices.

On January 10, I learned that the dead neighbor was Chris Olsen, a man in his early fifties who had, in fact, lived in the apartment complex longer than I. Over the years, Chris and I had chatted by our mailboxes from time to time, mostly about weather and cats (a mutual love), but sometimes about bigger things—his allergies and heart trouble, my father's death, his night work at a printing office. He never mentioned family, just whatever cat had moved in on him at the time, always a savvy street cat, who could teach me to follow it to Chris's door to ring the doorbell so Chris would let it in. His cats were always smart—survivors.

I speculated that the couple who lived next to me and asked Chris to baby-sit their toddler were somehow related to him. Chris ate lots of meals there, and the little boy adored Chris, addressing him as Uncle Chris. After Chris died, I was surprised to learn that the people next door were good neighbors to Chris, nothing more. Just good neighbors. Better than I.

Chris was an odd man, perhaps what people used to call a savant—someone with noticeable patches of brightness and dullness. He took pride in living on his own, paying his rent on time, being kind to children and other neighbors, and caring for whatever half-feral cat that had claimed him at the time. He was computer savvy and had worked at the same job for over twelve years. He didn't have a driver's license, but he could read. Sometimes, as he looked through his mail, he read to me. I think he wanted to show me that he could read. A few times he read something to me and asked me what it meant. We chatted amicably about his junk mail.

Chris must have walked or bussed to work, though I never saw him leave or come home. Sometimes, I saw him shambling like a large toddler to the Plaid Pantry, a twenty-four-hour convenience store two blocks west of the apartments. Chris wasn't noticeably large, perhaps 5'9" and 190 pounds—boxy, but not obese, but his movement spoke of marginal motor skills.

At one of our mailbox chats, I learned that he had once been mugged and robbed on his way to the convenience store; another time, his apartment had been broken into and his computer stolen. In the spirit of small talk, I told him about the window peeper I'd had—and my 1985 Toyota that had been stolen in 1995. Generally, we had little crime in our complex, but no one was affluent. Chris and I never talked about poverty. And we never talked about God or religion. Or purpose. Chris had that emotional intelligence and recognizable goodness that made children and stray cats love him. I respected him.

On the other hand, Chris was, by anyone's standards, odd. One late-fall day, five years or so before his death, I had the sad duty of going to his apartment door to tell him that his current cat, a long-haired, tuxedo tom that Chris had named Pooter, had been struck by a car on Division Street, which ran east and west in front of our apartments, and was lying dead under the junipers. I tried to be tactful, but Chris's grief was instant and deep. Despite the fall chill, Chris shuffled barefoot in his short, blue terrycloth robe across the parking lot to the junipers to fetch Pooter. As he walked, stunned, he talked, "Oh no. Oh no. Oh no. Maybe it's not Pooter. Maybe it's some other cat. Oh no. Maybe he's not dead. Oh no. Oh no. Oh no." I was sorry I hadn't simply disposed of Pooter's body.

As Chris bowed over Pooter, the blue robe crept too high in back and fell open in front, fully exposing his genitals to me and to a few onlookers who had gathered. Chris petted Pooter's black-and-white fur and let his tears drip onto the stiffening cat. The man that I had guessed was related to Chris joined us. "Close your robe and stand up, Chris," he growled.

Chris stood, clutching his cat to his heart, and somehow managed to close his robe. His grief had made him oblivious to a small matter like public nudity, a nudity that was, to those who knew him, asexual. He carried the dead cat into his apartment and closed the door behind him.

A few days later, Chris thanked me for letting him know about Pooter, and he insisted on showing me a memorial he had erected in his apartment. On his printer, he had produced a large photo, poster-sized, of Pooter. The poster was on the wall above a long, narrow table. The table held a variety of small incense burners, a crucifix, and a white ceramic bowl, probably Pooter's dish. There was also a large boot box on the table. I didn't ask Chris what was in it. I couldn't smell anything dead, and Chris's apartment was clean, if cluttered. My eyes held briefly on the crucifix. Perhaps St. Francis would take care of Chris's cat. "Pooter would like this," I said. Chris smiled serenely.

At other times, when my apartment was too hot, I'd open my secluded front door so the air would move. Many times over the years, I'd be startled to turn toward my door only to see Chris—inside my apartment—crouched on his hands and knees, wearing his faded blue jeans and worn tee-shirt, his thick glasses sliding down his nose, looking under my daybed for my cat Jeremiah—just to say hello to her. Generally, because I wasn't expecting to see a middle-aged man crouched on my floor, I'd holler, "Jesus!"

"I'm sorry," Chris would always say. "I didn't mean to scare you." He always meant it, genuinely. But, sometimes only days later, he'd startle a "Jesus!" out of me again.

Chris was like that: simple with patches of brightness.

In November of 2003, two months or so before he died, Chris had come into hard times. After over twelve years of steady work, he had been laid off. Despite the term "laid off," Chris knew the lay-off was permanent. At our mailboxes, Chris told me the bad news. He added, "I've lost my health insurance, too."

I understood. Like Chris, I could be laid off. Like him, I take pride in supporting myself, in doing my job well. Some 15 years ago, as I entered the Department of English where I teach, the department chair told me, in passing, that he had gone through the adjunct teaching applications and 75 people were waiting for my position. He didn't mean anything by his statement. He just saw me and, on impulse, said it, because he thought I might be interested. I know I'm fungible; that is, at some level, I'm just like any other quarter that goes into the pay phone. I have been an adjunct at my current job for twenty-three years, a teacher for thirty-four. Still, I feel unsure of my employment future. I think that Chris had felt surer of his. Like Chris, I've lived, from time to time, without health insurance; unlike Chris, I don't have a long-term, pre-existing health problem that makes employers shy of hiring me. If I ever become seriously ill, I don't believe my employers will renew my teaching contract. As many writers have suggested, including Benjamin Cheever (*Selling Ben Cheever,* 2002), "Job security [in the United States] is a thing of the past." When our jobs go, our health insurance goes. Chris needed his heart medication.

"Are you eligible for the Oregon Health Plan?" I asked. I thought perhaps he didn't know about the option; in 1994, Oregon's Governor John Kitzhaber (M.D.) pioneered the first state health care system in the country, part of his effort to cover some of the forty-five million Americans without health coverage (American Academy of Family Physicians, 2000).

"Not until the end of January. I'm cutting back on my heart medicine, so it should last me until then." Chris was one of those waiting for eligibility.

"Does your new cat trigger your asthma?" I was somewhat acquainted with his little gray tom, a flea-bitten and unneutered street cat, who had already trained me to ring Chris's doorbell.

"No," Chris said, "cats are about the only thing I'm not allergic to."

I should have pushed the issue, but, at that time, I still thought the man who told Chris to close his robe was family. And I knew that the man's wife was a pediatric nurse. I recalled seeing Chris leave their home with leftover food, probably food that he shared with his cat.

For lots of reasons, the current theory of neighbors caring for neighbors is flawed. People need public assistance—food, clothing, shelter, and work that doesn't cost them their pride, something the Roosevelts understood. Chris had pride; he'd earned it. He'd been a steady employee and tenant as long as I'd known him. He was civil and polite, gentle with children and with his pets. Chris could no more afford to support the stray that depended on him than his neighbors could afford to pay for the medication and food he needed. While the wheels of the health-care process were grinding along, Chris was dying.

After Thanksgiving, turkeys went on sale at the local supermarket. For less than seven dollars, I bought a 21-pound turkey, baked it, trimmed an ounce or two off one side, and told Chris that Jeremiah and I were "turkeyed out." "Could you and your kitty," I asked him, "use a fresh baked turkey?"

"We sure could."

My gift felt puny. Not enough to cover his needs. Here's another problem with the current political policy of replacing social services with neighborly charity: the wealthier one is, the less likely one is to be inconvenienced by a neighbor's neediness. If someone in a wealthy neighborhood goes belly up, that family discreetly disappears into a poorer neighborhood. In short, the least capable of lending financial assistance shoulder the greatest part of public assistance. Even had I known that Chris was only weeks from a fatal heart attack, I couldn't have bought his medicine for him. The most I could do was to provide a bit of food. Chris was unwilling to declare to his neighbors the depth of his need. He had pride. English has lots of words for those who ask for charity: free loaders, spongers, down-and-outers, beggars. As people fall farther, losing their homes and moving under bridges, the names become harsher: indigents, bums, ne'er-do-wells. We have not enough words for public assistance, too many words for the people who need it.

In mid-December, Chris returned my roaster, shiny clean. "If you bake another turkey and can't use it all, be sure to think of us."

"I will," I promised.

Before I got to another turkey, a cold front moved into Portland. When I wasn't snowed in, I was in my office, where I had access to a computer, writing. When I write, I am filled with purpose. Sometimes, I worked all night. Since my old cat had died in late July, nothing drew me home except eating, sleeping, and bathing. I forgot about Chris.

On the morning of January 9, from what I have pieced together since, Chris had a heart attack, dialed 911 for an ambulance, and managed to unlock his apartment door. The ambulance arrived too late to save him. His scruffy cat watched as Chris was put in the ambulance. When the cat got underfoot, trying to stay with Chris, the manager of the apartments put the cat in Chris's apartment and locked it in. In the process, the manager was badly scratched.

On the morning of January 10, a Saturday, I stood by Chris's door and talked to the landlady, who is a retired, first generation German immigrant, and her manager, a young man who works two other jobs. They could find no next of kin, no one to claim Chris's body. Even the couple who had befriended Chris knew nothing of his family. The landlady said that Chris had been unable to pay his rent for the last three months. "I told him not to worry," she said, "that he could make it right when he went back to work. But, of course, he was worried." She had tried to find his family on the Internet, but there were too many "Chris Olsens." She had tried to call his former employer, but the print shop was closed for the weekend. "We'll try to reach them again on Monday."

The manager added, "I don't know what we're going to do about his belongings. It's like a garbage scow in there. And I'm not tangling with that cat again."

Half-heartedly, I spoke, "I'll take the cat home if you don't need a second pet deposit." I didn't have the hundred dollars.

"That would be great!" the landlady said. "I was going to take it home rather than having it put down, but we have a dog that doesn't care for cats."

None of us knew the cat's name, just its personality. It was a ruffian. The manager said, "I've seen it take down a squirrel."

"Maybe that's why both of its ears are torn," I recalled.

The landlady let me into Chris's apartment. "Garbage scow" was an understatement. Cat urine was only one of many dreadful smells. The floor was covered with clutter too busy to identify. I found the cat in Chris's bedroom. It recognized me and let me carry it to my apartment.

I wasn't quite ready for another cat. By fall, I thought that I might have money for another pet deposit, neutering, shots, litter, food—in short, luxury items. When I had tried to picture my next cat, I often thought of two kittens— perhaps a white one and a gold one, or maybe an Abyssinian (they like water) or a Siamese (they're keenly intelligent). I hadn't pictured anything like this ragged-eared tom. He was the antithesis of my last cat, an urbanite, a spoiled calico who used my toilet, drank from a crystal goblet, and disdained anything messy. This fellow was a thug, a street cat who scoffed at a litter box, drank from gutters, and ate like a pig, splattering half-and-half cream (his first luxury item) on my walls and snuffling his food around his dining area. He wasn't quite ready for a new human; he wasn't quite ready for civilization.

Chris died on Friday, January 9, of a massive coronary. Five days later, the landlady found a nephew in Walport, a short distance from Portland, to claim Chris's body and handle his "estate." As the nephew, a bright, pleasant man, excavated Chris's estate, I talked with him. He and his wife were relieved not to have to take Chris's cat, "We have three already," he said.

Standing at the door, I looked again at the horrible mess of Chris's apartment, the dwelling of a man who had given up trying to fend for himself—and even for his cat. He could give his cat shelter and love, but little food, no litter box, no health care. Still, the cat had been satisfied to stay with Chris under those conditions. And he had tried to get in the ambulance with Chris. The cat knew Chris better than any of us did.

I've since named the cat Hank, and he has installed himself in my heart. Cats can do that fast. On April 1, two to three months after Chris's death, Hank told me something big about Chris. We walked together to the manager's apartment to deliver our rent check. Hank stopped on Chris's doorstep, looked up at me, and paused briefly to see if I would ring the doorbell.

"Chris is gone," I said. "You're my cat now."

Chris's death diminishes us. Chris had kept hope as long as he could. His needs were simple: he needed his job back, so he could pay his rent and electricity, buy food, and take care of his cat. He needed medication for his asthma and his heart. He needed good neighbors. He wanted to live. All of this, he was denied. First came unemployment; then the resulting poverty wore him down. Then his heart gave out.

Recently, I read a book by David K. Shipler, *The Working Poor: Invisible in America* (New York: Alfred A. Knopf, 2004). For the last five or six years, Shipler has been looking into the lives of the "working poor" in the U.S. in order to "unravel the tangled strands of cause and effect that led to their individual predicaments." He prefaces his book as follows:

> Most of the people I write about in this book do not have the luxury of rage. They are caught in exhausting struggles. Their wages do not lift them far enough from poverty to improve their lives, and their lives, in turn, hold them back. The term by which they are usually described, "working poor," should be an oxymoron. Nobody who works hard should be poor in America.

Shipler concludes his profile of the lives of the working poor in the United States by observing, "Workers at the edge of poverty are essential to America's prosperity, but their well-being is not treated as an integral part of the whole. . . . It is time to be ashamed." It is, in fact, time to be outraged.

Used with permission from The Power of Purpose Awards, Sponsored by the John Templeton Foundation.

FYODOR DOSTOEVSKY

"The Grand Inquisitor"

The famous discourse "The Grand Inquisitor" is presented as a "poem" in The Brothers Karamazov *by the great Russian novelist Fyodor Dostoevsky (1821–1881). It is created by Ivan Karamazov and narrated to his younger brother Alyosha, the former as skeptical as the latter is devout. In Ivan's "poem," set in sixteenth-century Seville, Jesus Christ returns to console human beings during the most terrible days of the Spanish Inquisition. The Grand Inquisitor—an old cardinal of ninety years—recognizing Him from afar, has Him arrested and imprisoned. Alone, in the dark stillness of the night, the cardinal visits the prisoner. The "poem" is the old man's apologia, in which he explains why he, far more than Jesus, is the true philanthropist, the true friend and savior of humanity.*

The Grand Inquisitor frames his denunciation of Jesus around Jesus' rejection of the temptations Satan posed in the desert (as reported in Matthew 4:1–11)—to turn stones into bread, to cast Himself from the Temple and be saved by the angels, and to rule over all the kingdoms of the world. He argues that Jesus' lofty insistence on freedom, his refusal to embrace "miracle, mystery, and authority," severely burdened and misjudged the urgent needs and fondest desires of most human beings. Rather than save us, he concludes, Jesus doomed us to suffer. The Grand Inquisitor, by contrast, bases his rule on the assumption that few of us can, or ever really want to, rule ourselves, and he provides us instead not only with creature comforts and safety but with an earthly presence—firm authority—on whom to lean. While the few rulers and leaders remain free, the many do not. Yet social equality appears to be achieved and, above all, the many are happy. Jesus listens throughout in silence, but when the old man finishes, He "softly kissed him on his bloodless aged lips." What does the kiss mean? Is there necessarily a tension between freedom and happiness? Between freedom and social equality? In an earlier conversation with his brother, Ivan claims that it is "possible to love one's neighbor abstractly [that is, to love humanity as such], and even occasionally from a distance, but hardly ever up close." Does this characterize the Grand Inquisitor's philanthropic attitude? Is the Grand Inquisitor's philanthropy a gift or a curse?

". . . My story is laid in Spain, in Seville, in the most terrible time of the Inquisition, when fires were lighted every day to the glory of God, and

> In the splendid *auto da fé*
> The wicked heretics were burnt.

Oh, of course, this was not the coming in which He will appear according to His promise at the end of time in all His heavenly glory, and which will be sudden 'as lightning flashing from east to west.' No, He visited His children only for a moment, and there where the flames were crackling round the heretics. In His infinite mercy He came once more among men in that human shape in which He walked among men for three years fifteen centuries ago. He came down to the 'hot pavement' of the southern town in which on the day before almost a hundred heretics had, *ad majorem gloriam Dei* ["For the greater glory of God"], been burned by the cardinal, the Grand Inquisitor, in a magnificent *auto da fé,* in the presence of the king, the court, the knights, the cardinals, the most charming ladies of the court, and the whole population of Seville.

"He came softly, unobserved, and yet, strange to say, everyone recognized Him. That might be one of the best passages in the poem. I mean, why they recognized Him. The people are irresistibly drawn to Him, they surround Him, they flock about Him, follow Him. He moves silently in their midst with a gentle smile of infinite compassion. The sun of love burns in His heart. Light, enlightenment, and power shine from His eyes, and their radiance, shed on the people, stirs their hearts with responsive love. He holds out His hands to them, blesses them, and a healing virtue comes from contact with Him, even with His garments. An old man in the crowd, blind from childhood, cries out, 'O Lord, heal me and I shall see Thee!' and, as it were, scales fall from his eyes and the blind man sees Him. The crowd weeps and kisses the earth under His feet. Children throw flowers before Him, sing, and cry 'Hosannah.' 'It is He—it is He!' all repeat. 'It must be He, it can be no one but Him!' He stops at the steps of the Seville cathedral at the moment when the weeping mourners are bringing in a little open white coffin. In it lies a child of seven, the only daughter of a prominent citizen. The dead child lies hidden in flowers. 'He will raise your child,' the crowd shouts to the weeping mother. The priest, coming to meet the coffin, looks perplexed, and frowns, but the mother of the dead child throws herself at His feet with a wail. 'If it is Thou, raise my child!' she cries, holding out her hands to Him. The procession halts, the coffin is laid on the steps at His feet. He looks with compassion, and His lips once more softly pronounce, 'Maiden, arise!' and the maiden arises. The little girl sits up in the coffin and looks round, smiling with wide-open wondering eyes, holding a bunch of white roses they had put in her hand.

"There are cries, sobs, confusion among the people, and at that moment the cardinal himself, the Grand Inquisitor, passes by the cathedral. He is an old man, almost ninety, tall and erect, with a withered face and sunken eyes, in which there is still a gleam of light, like a fiery spark. He is not dressed in his gorgeous cardinal's robes, as he was the day before, when he was burning the enemies of the Roman Church—at that moment he was wearing his coarse, old, monk's cassock. At a distance behind him come his gloomy assistants and slaves and the 'holy guard.' He stops at the sight of the crowd and watches it from a distance. He sees everything; he sees them set the coffin down at His feet, sees the child rise up, and his face darkens. He knits his thick gray brows and his eyes gleam with a sinister fire. He holds out his finger and bids the guards take Him. And such is his power, so completely are the people cowed into submission and trembling obedience to him, that the crowd immediately make way for the guards, and in the midst of deathlike silence they lay hands on Him and lead Him away. The crowd instantly bows down to the earth, like one man, before the old inquisitor. He blesses the people in silence and passes on. The guards lead their prisoner to the close, gloomy vaulted prison in the ancient palace of the Holy Inquisition and shut Him in it. The day passes and is followed by the dark, burning 'breathless' night of Seville. The air is 'fragrant with laurel and lemon.' In the pitch darkness the iron door of the prison is suddenly opened and the Grand Inquisitor himself comes in with a light in his hand. He is alone; the door is closed at once behind him. He stands in the doorway and for a long time, for a minute or two, gazes into His face. At last he goes up slowly, sets the light on the table and speaks.

"'Is it Thou? Thou?' But receiving no answer, he adds at once, 'Don't answer, be silent. What canst Thou say, indeed? I know too well what Thou wouldst say. And Thou has no right to add anything to what Thou hadst said of old. Why, then, art Thou come to hinder us? For Thou has come to hinder us, and Thou knowest that. But dost Thou know what will be tomorrow? I know not who Thou art and care not to know whether it is Thou or only a semblance of Him, but tomorrow I shall condemn Thee and burn Thee at the stake as the worst of heretics. And the very people who have today kissed Thy feet, tomorrow at the faintest sign from me will rush to heap up the embers of Thy fire. Knowest Thou that? Yes, maybe Thou knowest it,' he added with thoughtful penetration, never for a moment taking his eyes off the Prisoner."

"I don't quite understand, Ivan. What does it mean?" Alyosha, who had been listening in silence, said with a smile. "Is it simply a wild fantasy, or a mistake on the part of the old man—some impossible *qui pro quo* ["one for the other," mistaken identity]?"

"Take it as the last," said Ivan, laughing, "if you are so corrupted by modern realism and can't stand anything fantastic. If you like it to be a case of *qui pro quo,* let it be so. It is true," he went on, laughing, "the old man was ninety, and he might well be crazy over his set idea. He might have been struck by the appearance of the Prisoner. It might, in fact, be simply his ravings, the delusion of an old man of ninety, approaching his death, overexcited by the *auto da fé* of a hundred heretics the day before. But does it matter to us after all whether it was a *qui pro quo* or a wild fantasy? All that matters is that the old man should speak out, should speak openly of what he has thought in silence for ninety years."

"And the Prisoner too is silent? Does He look at him and not say a word?"

"That's inevitable in any case," Ivan laughed again. "The old man has told Him He hasn't the right to add anything to what He has said of old. One may say it is the most fundamental feature of Roman Catholicism, in my opinion at least. 'All has been given by Thee to the Pope,' they say, 'and all, therefore, is still in the Pope's hands, and there is no need for Thee to come now at all. Thou must not meddle for the time, at least.' That's how they speak and write too—the Jesuits, at any rate. I have read it myself in the works of their theologians. 'Hast Thou the right to reveal to us one of the mysteries of that world from which Thou hast come?' my old man asks Him, and answers the question for Him. 'No, Thou has not; that Thou mayest not add to what has been said of old, and mayest not take from men the freedom which Thou didst exalt when Thou wast on earth. Whatsoever Thou revealest anew will encroach on men's freedom of faith; for it will be manifest as a miracle, and the freedom of their faith was dearer to Thee than anything in those days fifteen hundred years ago. Didst Thou not often say then, "I will make you free"? But now Thou hast seen these "free" men,' the old man adds suddenly, with a pensive smile. 'Yes, we've paid dearly for it,' he goes on, looking sternly at Him, 'but at last we have completed that work in Thy name. For fifteen centuries we have been wrestling with Thy freedom, but now it is ended and over for good. Dost Thou not believe that it's over for good? Thou lookest meekly at me and deignest not even to be wroth with me. But let me tell Thee that now, today, people are more persuaded than ever that they have perfect freedom, yet they have brought their freedom to us and laid it humbly at our feet. But that has been our doing. Was this what Thou didst? Was this Thy freedom?'"

"I don't understand again," Alyosha broke in. "Is he ironical, is he jesting?"

"Not a bit of it! He claims it as a merit for himself and his Church that at last they have vanquished freedom and have done so to make men happy. 'For now' (he is speaking of the Inquisition, of course) 'for the first time it has become possible to think of the happiness of men. Man was created a rebel; and how can rebels be happy? Thou wast warned,' he says to Him. 'Thou hast had no lack of admonitions and warnings, but Thou didst not listen to those warnings; Thou didst reject the only way by which men might be made happy. But, fortunately, departing Thou didst hand on the work to us. Thou has promised, Thou has established by Thy word, Thou hast given to us the right to bind and to unbind, and now, of course, Thou canst not think of taking it away. Why, then, hast Thou come to hinder us?'"

"And what's the meaning of 'no lack of admonitions and warnings'?" asked Alyosha.

"Why, that's the chief part of what the old man must say."

" 'The wise and dread spirit, the spirit of self-destruction and nonexistence,' the old man goes on, 'the great spirit talked with Thee in the wilderness, and we are told in the books that he "tempted" Thee. Is that so? And could anything truer be said than what he revealed to Thee in three questions and what Thou didst reject, and what in the books is called "the temptation"? And yet if there has ever been on earth a real stupendous miracle, it took place on that day, on the day of the three temptations. The statement of those three questions was itself the miracle. If it were possible to imagine simply for the sake of argument that those three questions of the dread spirit had perished utterly from the books, and that we had to restore them and to invent them anew, and to do so had gathered together all the wise men of the earth—rulers, chief priests, learned men, philosophers, poets—and had set them the task to invent three questions, such as would not only fit the occasion, but express in three words, three human phrases, the whole future history of the world and of humanity—dost Thou believe that all the wisdom of the earth united could have invented anything in depth and force equal to the three questions which were actually put to Thee then by the wise and mighty spirit in the wilderness? From those questions alone, from the miracle of their statement, we can see that we have here to do not with the fleeting human intelligence, but with the absolute and eternal. For in those three questions the whole subsequent history of mankind is, as it were, brought together into one whole, and foretold, and in them are united all the unsolved historical contradictions of human nature. At the time it could not be so clear, since the future was unknown; but now that fifteen hundred years have passed, we see that everything in those three questions was so justly grasped and foretold, and has been so truly fulfilled, that nothing can be added to them or taken from them.

"'Judge Thyself who was right—Thou or he who questioned Thee then? Remember the first question; its meaning, though not the exact words, was this: "Thou wouldst go into the world, and art going with empty hands, with some promise of freedom which men in their simplicity and their natural unruliness cannot even understand, which they fear and dread—for nothing has ever been more insupportable for a man and a human society than freedom. But seest Thou these stones in this parched and barren wilderness? Turn them into bread, and mankind will run after Thee like a flock, grateful and obedient, though forever trembling, lest Thou withdraw Thy hand and deny them Thy bread." But Thou wouldst not deprive man of freedom and didst reject the offer, thinking, what is that freedom worth, if obedience is bought with bread? Thou didst reply that man lives not by bread alone. But dost Thou know that for the sake of that earthly bread the spirit of the earth will rise up against Thee and will strive with Thee and overcome Thee, and all will follow him, crying, "Who can compare with this beast? He has given us fire from heaven!" Dost Thou know that the ages will pass, and humanity will proclaim by the lips of their sages that there is no crime, and therefore no sin; there is only hunger? "Feed men, and then ask of them virtue!" That's what they'll write on the banner, which they will raise against Thee, and with which they will destroy Thy temple. Where Thy temple stood will rise a new building; the terrible tower of Babel will be built again, and though, like the one of old, it will not be finished, yet Thou mightest have prevented that new tower and have cut short the sufferings of men for a thousand years; for they will come back to us after a thousand years of agony with their tower. They will seek us again, hidden underground in the catacombs, for we shall again be persecuted and tortured. They will find us and cry to us, "Feed us, for those who have promised us fire from heaven haven't given it!" And then we shall finish building their tower, for he finishes the building who feeds them. And we alone shall feed them in Thy name, declaring falsely that it is in Thy name. Oh, never, never can they feed themselves without us! No science will give them bread so long as they remain free. In the end they will lay their freedom at our feet, and say to us, "Make us your slaves, but feed us." They will understand themselves, at last, that freedom and bread enough for all are inconceivable together, for never, never will they be able to share between them! They will be convinced, too, that they can never be free, for they are weak, vicious, worthless and rebellious. Thou didst promise them the bread of Heaven, but, I repeat again, can it compare with earthly bread in the eyes of the weak, ever sinful and ignoble race of man? And if for the sake of the bread of Heaven thousands and tens of thousands shall follow Thee, what is to become of the millions and tens of thousands of millions of creatures who will not have the strength to forego the earthly bread for the sake of the heavenly? Or dost Thou care only for the tens of thousands of the great and strong, while the millions, numerous as the sands of the sea, who are weak but love Thee, must exist only for the sake of the great and strong? No, we care for the weak too. They are sinful and rebellious, but in the end they too will become obedient. They will marvel at us and look on us as gods, because we are ready to endure the freedom which they have found so dreadful and to rule over them—so awful it will seem to them to be free. But we shall tell them that we are Thy servants and rule them in Thy name. We shall deceive them again, for we will not let Thee come to us again. That deception will be our suffering, for we shall be forced to lie. This is the significance of the first question in the wilderness, and this is what Thou has rejected for the sake of that freedom which Thou has exalted above everything. Yet in this question lies hid the great secret of this world. Choosing "bread," Thou wouldst have satisfied the universal and everlasting craving of humanity individually and together as one—to find someone to worship. So long as man remains free he strives for nothing so incessantly and so painfully as to find someone to worship. But man seeks to worship what is established beyond dispute, so that all men would agree at once to worship it. For these pitiful creatures are concerned not only to find what one or the other can worship, but to find something that all would believe in and worship; what is essential is that all may be *together* in it. This craving for *community* of worship is the chief misery of every man individually and of all humanity from the beginning of time. For the sake of common worship they've slain each other with the sword. They have set up gods and challenged one another, "Put away your gods and come and worship ours, or we will kill you and your gods!" And so it will be to the end of the world, even when gods disappear from the earth; they will fall down before idols just the same. Thou didst know, Thou couldst not but have known, this fundamental secret of human nature, but Thou didst reject the one infallible banner which was offered Thee to make all men bow down to Thee alone—the banner of earthly bread; and Thou hast rejected it for the sake of freedom and the bread of Heaven. Behold what Thou didst further. And all again in the name of freedom! I tell Thee that man is tormented by no greater anxiety, than to find someone quickly to whom he can hand over that gift of freedom with which the ill-fated creature is born. But only one who can appease their conscience can take over their freedom. In bread there was offered Thee an invincible banner; give bread, and man will worship Thee, for nothing is more certain than bread. But if someone else gains possession of his conscience—oh! then he will cast away Thy bread and follow after him who has ensnared his conscience. In that Thou wast right. For the secret of man's being is not only to live but to have something to live for. Without a stable conception of the object of life, man would not consent to go on living, and would rather destroy himself than remain on earth, though he had bread in abundance. That is true. But what happened? Instead of taking men's freedom from them, Thou didst make it greater than ever! Didst Thou forget that man prefers peace, and even death, to freedom of choice in the knowledge of good and evil? Nothing is more seductive for man than his freedom of conscience, but nothing is a greater cause of suffering. And behold, instead of giving a firm foundation for setting the conscience of man at rest forever, Thou didst choose all that is exceptional, vague and enigmatic; Thou didst choose what was utterly beyond the strength of men, acting as though Thou didst not love them at all—Thou who didst come to give Thy life for them! Instead of taking possession of men's freedom, Thou didst increase it, and burdened the spiritual kingdom of mankind with its sufferings forever. Thou didst desire man's free love, that he should follow Thee freely, enticed and taken captive by Thee. In place of the rigid ancient law, man must hereafter with free heart decide for himself what is good and what is evil, having only Thy image before him as his guide. But didst Thou not know he would at last reject even Thy image and Thy truth, if he is weighed down with the fearful burden of free choice? They will cry aloud at last that the truth is not in Thee, for they could not have been left in greater confusion and suffering than Thou has caused, laying upon them so many cares and unanswerable problems.

" 'So that, in truth, Thou didst Thyself lay the foundation for the destruction of Thy kingdom, and no one is more to blame for it. Yet what was offered Thee? There are three powers, three powers, alone, able to conquer and to hold captive forever the conscience of these impotent rebels for their happiness—those forces are miracle, mystery and authority. Thou hast rejected all three and hast set the example for doing so. When the wise and dread spirit set Thee on the pinnacle of the temple and said to Thee, "If Thou wouldst know whether Thou art the Son of God then cast Thyself down, for it is written: the angels shall hold him up lest he fall and bruise himself, and Thou shalt know then whether Thou art the Son of God and shalt prove then how great is Thy faith in Thy Father." But Thou didst refuse and wouldst not cast Thyself down. Oh! of course, Thou didst proudly and well, like God; but the weak, rebellious race of men, are they gods? Oh, Thou didst know then that in taking one step, in making one movement to cast Thyself down, Thou wouldst be tempting God and have lost all Thy faith in Him, and would have been dashed to pieces against that earth which Thou didst come to save. And the wise spirit that tempted Thee would have rejoiced. But I ask again, are there many like Thee? And couldst Thou believe for one moment that men, too, could face such a temptation? Is the nature of men such, that they can reject miracle, and at the great moments of their life, the moments of their deepest, most agonizing spiritual difficulties, cling only to the free verdict of the heart? Oh, Thou didst know that Thy deed would be recorded in books, would be handed down to remote times and the utmost ends of the earth, and Thou didst hope that man, following Thee, would cling to God and not ask for a miracle. But Thou didst not know that when man rejects miracle he rejects God too; for man seeks not so much God as the miraculous. And as man cannot bear to be without the miraculous, he will create new miracles of his own for himself, and will worship deeds of sorcery and witchcraft, though he might be a hundred times over a rebel, heretic and infidel. Thou didst not come down from the Cross when they shouted to Thee, mocking and reviling Thee, "Come down from the cross and we will believe that Thou art He." Thou didst not come down, for again Thou wouldst not enslave man by a miracle, and didst crave faith given freely, not based on miracle. Thou didst crave for free love and not the base raptures of the slave before the might that has overawed him forever. But Thou didst think too highly of men therein, for they are slaves, of course, though rebellious by nature. Look round and judge; fifteen centuries have passed, look upon them. Whom hast Thou raised up to Thyself? I swear, man is weaker and baser by nature than Thou hast believed him! Can he, can he do what Thou didst? By showing him so much respect, Thou didst, as it were, cease to feel for him, for Thou didst ask far too much from him—Thou who has loved him more than Thyself! Respecting him less, Thou wouldst have asked less of him. That would have been more like love, for his burden would have been lighter. He is weak and vile. What though he is everywhere now rebelling against our power, and proud of his rebellion? It is the pride of a child and a schoolboy. They are little children rioting and barring out the teacher at school. But their childish delight will end; it will cost them dear. They will cast down temples and drench the earth with blood. But they will see at last, the foolish children, that, though they are rebels, they are impotent rebels, unable to keep up their own rebellion. Bathed in their foolish tears, they will recognize at last that He who created them rebels must have meant to mock at them. They will say this in despair, and their utterance will be a blasphemy which will make them more unhappy still, for man's nature cannot bear blasphemy, and in the end always avenges it on itself. And so unrest, confusion and unhappiness—that is the present lot of man after Thou didst bear so much for their freedom! Thy great prophet tells in vision and in image, that he saw all those who took part in the first resurrection and that there were of each tribe twelve thousand. But if there were so many of them, they must have been not men but gods. They had borne Thy cross, they had endured scores of years in the barren, hungry wilderness, living upon locusts and roots—and Thou mayest indeed point with pride at those children of freedom, of free love, of free and splendid sacrifice for Thy name. But remember that they were only some thousands, and gods at that; and what of the rest? And how are the other weak ones to blame, because they could not endure what the strong have endured? How is the weak soul to blame that it is unable to receive such terrible gifts? Canst Thou really have come only to the elect and for the elect? But if so, it is a mystery and we cannot understand it. And if it is a mystery, we too have a right to preach a mystery, and to teach them that it's not the free judgment of their hearts, not love that matters, but a mystery which they must follow blindly, even against their conscience. So we have done. We have corrected Thy work and have founded it upon *miracle, mystery* and *authority.* And men rejoiced that they were again led like sheep, and that the terrible gift that had brought them such suffering, was, at last, lifted from their hearts. Were we right teaching them this? Speak! Did we not love mankind, so meekly acknowledging their feebleness, lovingly lightening their burden, and permitting their weak nature even sin with our sanction? Why hast Thou come now to hinder us? And why dost Thou look silently and searchingly at me with Thy mild eyes? Be angry. I don't want Thy love, for I love Thee not. And what use is it for me to hide anything from Thee? Don't I know to Whom I am speaking? All that I can say is known to Thee already. I can see it in Thine eyes. And is it for me to conceal from Thee our mystery? Perhaps it is Thy will to hear it from my lips. Listen, then. We are not working with Thee, but with *him*—that is our mystery. It's long—eight centuries—since we have been on *his* side and not on Thine. Just eight centuries ago, we took from him what Thou didst reject with scorn, that last gift he offered Thee, showing Thee all the kingdoms of the earth. We took from him Rome and the sword of Caesar, and proclaimed ourselves sole rulers of the earth, though hitherto we have not been able to complete our work. But whose fault is that? Oh, the work is only beginning, but it has begun. It has long to await completion and the earth has yet much to suffer, but we shall triumph and shall be Caesars, and then we shall plan the universal happiness of man. But Thou mightest have taken even then the sword of Caesar. Why didst Thou reject that last gift? Hadst Thou accepted that last counsel of the mighty spirit, Thou wouldst have accomplished all that man seeks on earth—that is, someone to worship, someone to keep his conscience, and some means of uniting all in one unanimous and harmonious anthill, for the craving for universal unity is the third and last anguish of men. Mankind as a whole has always strived to organize a universal state. There have been many great nations with great histories, but the more highly they were developed the more unhappy they were, for they felt more acutely than other people the craving for worldwide union. The great conquerors, Tamerlane and Genghis Khan, whirled like hurricanes over the face of the earth striving to subdue its people, and they too were but the unconscious expression of the same craving for universal unity. Hadst Thou taken the world and Caesar's purple, Thou wouldst have founded the universal state and have given universal peace. For who can rule men if not he who holds their conscience and their bread in his hands? We have taken the sword of Caesar, and in taking it, of course, have rejected Thee and followed *him*. Oh, ages are yet to come of the confusion of free thought, of their science and cannibalism. For having begun to build their tower of Babel without us, they will end, of course, with cannibalism. But then the beast will crawl to us and lick our feet and spatter them with tears of blood. And we shall sit upon the beast and raise the cup, and on it will be written, "Mystery." But then, and only then, the reign of peace and happiness will come for men. Thou art proud of Thine elect, but Thou hast only the elect, while we give rest to all. And besides, how many of those elect, those mighty ones who could become elect, have grown weary waiting for Thee, and have transferred and will transfer the powers of their spirit and the warmth of their heart to the other camp, and end by raising their *free* banner against Thee. Thou didst Thyself lift up that banner. But with us all will be happy and will no more rebel nor destroy one another as under Thy freedom. Oh, we shall persuade them that they will only become free when they renounce their freedom to us and submit to us. And shall we be right or shall we be lying? They will be convinced that we are right, for they will remember the horrors of slavery and confusion to which Thy freedom brought them. Freedom, free thought and science, will lead them into such straits and will bring them face to face with such marvels and insoluble mysteries, that some of them, the fierce and rebellious, will destroy themselves, others, rebellious but weak, will destroy one another, while the rest, weak and unhappy, will crawl fawning to our feet and whine to us: "Yes, you were right, you alone possess His mystery, and we come back to you, save us from ourselves!" Receiving bread from us, they will of course see clearly that we take the bread made by their hands from them, to give it to them, without any miracle. They will see that we do not change the stones to bread, but in truth they will be more thankful for taking it from our hands than for the bread itself! For they will remember only too well that in the old days, without our help, even the bread they made turned to stones in their hands, while since they have come back to us, the very stones have turned to bread in their hands. Too, too well they know the value of complete submission! And until men know that, they will be unhappy. Who is most to blame for their not knowing it? Speak! Who scattered the flock and sent it astray on unknown paths? But the flock will come together again and will submit once more, and then it will be once for all. Then we shall give them the quiet humble happiness of weak creatures such as they are by nature. Oh, we shall persuade them at last not to be proud, for Thou didst lift them up and thereby taught them to be proud. We shall show them that they are weak, that they are only pitiful children, but that childlike happiness is the sweetest of all. They will become timid and will look to us and huddle close to us in fear, as chicks to the hen. They will marvel at us and will be awestricken before us, and will be proud at our being so powerful and clever, that we have been able to subdue such a turbulent flock of thousands of millions. They will tremble impotently before our wrath, their minds will grow fearful, they will be quick to shed tears like women and children, but they will be just as ready at a sign from us to pass to laughter and rejoicing, to happy mirth and childish song. Yes, we shall set them to work, but in their leisure hours we shall make their life like a child's game, with children's songs and in-nocent dance. Oh, we shall allow them even sin, they are weak and helpless, and they will love us like children because we allow them to sin. We shall tell them that every sin will be expiated, if it is done with our permission, that we allow them to sin because we love them, and the punishment for these sins we take upon ourselves. And we shall take it upon ourselves, and they will adore us as their saviors who have taken on themselves their sins before God. And they will have no secrets from us. We shall allow or forbid them to live with their wives and mistresses, to have or not to have children—according to whether they have been obedient or disobedient—and they will submit to us gladly and cheerfully. The most painful secrets of their conscience, all, all they will bring to us, and we shall have an answer for all. And they will be glad to believe our answer, for it will save them from the great anxiety and terrible agony they en-dure at present in making a free decision for themselves. And all will be happy, all the millions of creatures except the hundred thousand who rule over them. For only we, we who guard the mystery, shall be unhappy. There will be thou-sands of millions of happy babes, and a hundred thousand sufferers who have taken upon themselves the curse of the knowledge of good and evil. Peacefully they will die, peacefully they will expire in Thy name, and beyond the grave they will find nothing but death. But we shall keep the secret, and for their hap-piness we shall entice them with the reward of heaven and eternity. Though if there were anything in the other world, it certainly would not be for such as they. It is prophesied that Thou wilt come again in victory, Thou wilt come with Thy chosen, the proud and strong, but we will say that they have only saved themselves, but we have saved all. We are told that the harlot who sits upon the beast, and holds in her hands the *mystery,* shall be put to shame, that the weak will rise up again, and will rend her royal purple and will strip naked her 'loath-some' body. But then I will stand up and point out to Thee the thousand mil-lions of happy children who have known no sin. And we who have taken their sins upon us for their happiness will stand up before Thee and say: "Judge us if Thou canst and darest." Know that I fear Thee not. Know that I too have been in the wilderness, I too have lived on roots and locusts, I too prized the freedom with which Thou hast blessed men, and I too was striving to stand among Thy elect, among the strong and powerful, thirsting "to make up the number." But I awakened and would not serve madness. I turned back and joined the ranks of those *who have corrected Thy work.* I left the proud and went back to the humble, for the happiness of the humble. What I say to Thee will come to pass, and our dominion will be built up. I repeat, tomorrow Thou shalt see that obedient flock who at a sign from me will hasten to heap up the hot cinders about the pile on which I shall burn Thee for coming to hinder us. For if anyone has ever deserved our fires, it is Thou. Tomorrow I shall burn Thee. *Dixi* ["I have spoken"].'" . . .

[Ivan resumes.] ". . . When the Inquisitor ceased speaking he waited some time for his Prisoner to answer him. His silence weighed down upon him. He saw that the Prisoner had listened intently and quietly all the time, looking gently in his face and evidently not wishing to reply. The old man longed for Him to say something, however bitter and terrible. But He suddenly approached the old man in silence and softly kissed him on his bloodless aged lips. That was all his answer. The old man shuddered. His lips moved. He went to the door, opened it, and said to Him: 'Go, and come no more . . . come not at all, never, never!' And he let Him out into the dark squares of the town. The Prisoner went away."

"And the old man?" [Alyosha asked.]

"The kiss glows in his heart, but the old man adheres to his idea."

From *The Brothers Karamazov* by Fyodor Dostoevsky, translated by Constance Garnett (New York: Macmillan, 1915).

RICK COHEN

"Philanthropy and the Role of Social Justice"

In this essay, Rick Cohen, former executive director of the National Committee for Responsive Philanthropy and current National Correspondent for the Non-profit Quarterly, *presents what he regards as the most urgent priorities for America's foundations: To ratchet up support to community-based, constituent-led nonprofits, to fund advocates and watchdogs of government and corporate policy and behavior, and to democratize their own governance. They should, in short, promote "social justice philanthropy," which consists, accordingly, of "part public policy advocacy, part socio-economic redress, and part grassroots democracy." Unlike charity, Cohen suggests, which attends to the immediate needs of disadvantaged groups, social justice philanthropy should aim at redressing "the less than just social and economic system" that insufficiently provides for those needs. But Cohen readily acknowledges that foundation wealth is the creature of the very system he would have it change. Hence, he concludes, "Therein lies the social justice challenge for philanthropy": how to get "privileged, wealthy donors, trustees, and foundation staff . . . to spur and support" basic social and economic change. Is this the "social justice" challenge for philanthropy? Is "social justice," as Cohen implies, the same as "social equity"? Should advocates of social justice insist, as Cohen does, on the distinction between charity and philanthropy?*

ℰᴏ

Populated by philanthropic institutions of multiple shapes and designs, institutional philanthropy almost defies singular characterization much less prescription. American philanthropy is a multihued potpourri with multiple concerns and purposes. But that said, some purposes may be better than others, and aiming at achieving "social justice" may be best of all.

Though "social justice" philanthropy is one of those phrases widely used and largely left undefined, it is best described as grantmaking that revives and unleashes the forces of grassroots democracy aimed at representing and giving voice to the constituencies that do not fare well in our economy and society. Now *au courant,* the term and its practice have both historic roots and philosophical moorings, as well as practical applications.

All philanthropy, but especially that concerned with social justice, should take its bearings from the report issued in the mid-1970s in which the Filer Commission (The Commission on Private Philanthropy and Public Needs) called on philanthropy to focus on the crucial social issues and public needs of the nation today and tomorrow. Influenced by the advocacy of nonprofit leaders, who banded together under the rubric of the "Donee Group," it suggested that philanthropy deserves the public's trust regarding its stewardship of tax exempt resources only insofar as it succeeds in addressing real and urgent public needs.

Two things follow: First and foremost all philanthropic foundations must recognize that they exist and function based entirely on a license granted by the public. Contrary to the way in which all too many foundation executives and trustees—from small family foundations to institutional behemoths—act and think, foundations are not wholly private instruments of individual elee-mosynary inclinations. The money at their disposal is not theirs. Rather, they function as temporary stewards of their philanthropic endowments, entrusted by the citizenry to deploy their resources for the public good. The Council on Foundations' Steve Gunderson describes this as more than charity, but "philanthropy seek(ing) to solve those problems that create the need for charity."[1] If they operate accountably and responsibly, foundations serve as the institutions that connect and harness private philanthropy to avenues for addressing the public good.

Second, philanthropy must chart a path for itself that responds to the demands of our society today, rather than linger over visions of what might have existed at some apocryphal view of philanthropic correctness in the past.

How can we gauge the relevance of philanthropy to today's social problems? When the former executive director of the New York Foundation, Madeline Lee, was asked at the 1997 convocation of a nonprofit association to address what role philanthropy should play in the future, without reference to schools of philosophy, she simply enumerated the major issues affecting New York City: national budget deficits, cutbacks in services to the poor, the inferior quality of education delivered by New York City schools, inadequate voter turnout, and threats to nonprofit and public rights to free speech. Lee might or might not describe herself as a "social justice grantmaker," but her common sense approach in determining philanthropy's goals provides a clue to the ways and means of social justice philanthropy and its critical role for foundation grantmaking.

As Lee's response implies, social justice philanthropy is part public policy advocacy, part socio-economic redress, part grassroots democracy. Indeed, most self-identified "social justice grantmakers" draw from a list much like Lee's—now increasingly emphasizing issues of racial equity—and work on all three fronts. But behind the definition-by-itemization tendencies of some social justice grantmakers, a still more cogent, rooted definition is discernable. Though a utopian concept of a completely egalitarian society may guide some grantmakers, the society in which we live—one in which inequalities gave rise to the very wealth that made foundations possible—requires a more practical definition of

---

1. Steve Gunderson, "Leading to Change: The Risk of Leadership" (speech delivered to "Leadership Grand Rapids 20th Anniversary," Grand Rapids, Michigan, May 18, 2006).

social justice philanthropy. To this end, John Rawls' two principles of justice may serve us well: the first calls for all people to have "equal right to the most extensive system of basic equal liberties"; the second, the distributive justice principle, acknowledges the reality of social and economic inequalities that are morally justifiable if they "work to the benefit of the least advantaged" in our society.[2]

There is a simple elegance in resting social justice philanthropy on these two Rawlsian principles. It requires philanthropy to support greater and more equally distributed liberties, opportunities, and wealth, and to direct its attention to those populations that are most disadvantaged, through organizations that represent them with authenticity and legitimacy.

The large disparities in our society, especially racial inequities, were made evident in the wake of Hurricane Katrina's natural and man-made catastrophes. Philanthropic foundations prepared to take their bearings from "real and urgent public needs" have won an especially relevant lesson: Since rebuilding the Gulf Coast is to function as an experiment, let it be an experiment for ethics, probity, and the revival of the nonprofit sector's ability to call government and corporations to account.

Concerned about how it fulfills its own mission of responsibility to the American public, the nonprofit sector should be equally motivated to bolster the mission-capacity of government at all levels, else no amount of monies funneled to the Red Cross or any other charity will make a difference in the long run. Foundations can and should do less charity and more philanthropy. The wish of some foundation leaders that the foundation sector had been faster with money devoted to Katrina relief confuses charity and philanthropy—or substitutes foundation resources for government expenditures. In the transition to reconstruction, that too is not the role of foundations, it is the role of government. But what philanthropy can and should do is fund the watchdogs who will scrutinize the probity of the government, corporate, and nonprofit players who will be entrusted with the implementation of reconstruction plans.

The philanthropist Alan Rabinowitz describes what he calls "social change philanthropy" as facilitating "the changing of societal institutions so they don't produce the very problems that 'charity' tries to alleviate."[3] These formulations address the reality of working within the structures of our socio-economic system, including institutional philanthropy, and endorse working to reduce disparities in power, opportunity, wealth, and privilege. They do not require systemic change, and they do not relegate direct charitable assistance to a lower, less justice-oriented dimension than policy advocacy. Both assistance and advocacy can be pursued under the rubric of social justice philanthropy, but foundations are especially well-positioned to ratchet up support for community-based

2. John Rawls, *A Theory of Justice* (Cambridge, Mass.: Belknap Press of Harvard University Press, 1971).

3. Alan Rabinowitz, *Social Change Philanthropy in America* (New York: Quorum Books, 1992).

groups that organize and advocate for attention to and change in government and corporate policy and behavior.

With 1.4 million potential nonprofit grantees for social justice grantmakers to choose from, what constitutes distributive justice becomes as problematic within the nonprofit sector as it is in society. One of the pernicious misinterpretations of research done on conservative foundations in 1997 by the National Committee for Responsive Philanthropy (NCRP)[4] was that the broad mass of philanthropy should stop frittering its money away on lots of small organizations and focus its capital on a handful of national think tanks, which would, in turn, frame the issues and shape the messages for the nation's populace. Cynthia Gibson's recent analysis of 836 national advocacy organizations raises serious questions about the legitimacy of such delegations of authority. What efficacy or authenticity can these organizations boast, she argues, if they "represent" constituencies who have little say in the organizations' priorities, programs, and activities?[5] This kind of top-down, elite dominance—in which organizations do the thinking for communities, claiming to know the solutions for constituents' problems better than the constituents themselves—helps to perpetuate rather than overcome inequities.

As social justice grantmaking ought to be concerned about the legitimacy of the nonprofits that speak for disadvantaged communities, so it should be concerned with making foundations themselves open, permeable, and more responsive to their target constituencies. It's not their money, but foundation trustees administer the funding as if it were, for the most part ignoring societal pressures for breaking the near exclusivity of class and race control at the top echelons of foundations. Philanthropy ought to catch up with the rest of society by opening itself to direct participation in decision making by those nonprofits purportedly served by foundations.

Strikingly, the foundations that have done the most, albeit still in baby steps, toward involving constituents in their grantmaking decisions have been, in terms of big dollars, the health conversion foundations.[6] Why? These foundations are products of a public process, usually the intervention of constituencies whose stake in nonprofit health insurer and hospital assets would be entirely lost were it not for the intervention of community-based advocates and state attorneys general trying to save something from the conversion

---

4. Sally Covington, *Moving a Public Policy Agenda* (National Committee for Responsive Philanthropy, 1997).

5. Cynthia M. Gibson, "In Whose Interest: Do National Nonprofit Advocacy Organizations Represent the Under-represented?" *The Nonprofit Quarterly* (Summer 2006).

6. Among the plentiful examples are the community advisory board established for the Maine health conversion foundation created from the merger of BCBSME and Anthem Insurance, New Mexico's Con Alma Health Foundation, the Foundation for a Healthy Kentucky, and the Foundation for Seacoast Health in New Hampshire.

process. Community advisory boards and other mechanisms for substantive community input into foundation grantmaking priorities have had some positive effects on conversion foundations. But foundations can do much better than an occasional community advisory board process, or using grantee satisfaction surveys as substitutes for real input into grantmaking.

Foundation grantmaking is a relatively small part of nonprofit finances compared to government funding and individual giving. Foundations typically cite their 10 percent slice of nonprofit revenues as a defense against too much scrutiny and criticism. But foundation resources are distinctively different, both as philanthropic rather than charitable dollars, and as funding ventures potentially more flexible and more risk-oriented than what a government agency will support or an individual donor will contemplate. A grantmaking regime based on principles of distributive justice should lead both grantmakers and nonprofits to formulations that do more than simply attach foundation dollars to attractive issues and "isms" deemed to benefit disadvantaged groups—rather philanthropy must recommit itself to supporting the democratic instincts of community-based, constituency-responsive and constituency-led organizations, and provide them with the capital to bring community perspectives to the halls of power. Without philanthropic support, community voices are drowned out in our current din of high-priced lobbying. Social justice philanthropy cannot be reasonably pursued if the groups representing socio-economically disadvantaged populations, due to a reluctance of funders to support their public policy advocacy, "speak with a whisper that is lost on the ears of inattentive government officials, while the advantaged roar with a clarity and consistency that policy-makers readily hear and routinely follow."[7]

A legitimate complaint about the advocates of social justice philanthropy is that the groups they support sometimes sound and act self-marginalizing, working at the fringe of the sector, supporting niche "identity" groups, and focusing on causes defined by their distance from conventional institutions, interactions, and processes. Foundations feel free to allocate these groups, which they see as marginal players, small dollops of grant funds, satisfied by having supported social justice but not having dipped into the bulk of their resources to provide sustainable, multi-year support. Private foundations in particular have hardly begun to leverage the bulk of their assets toward adequately capitalizing the nonprofit sector, much less the slice of nonprofits addressing social justice concerns. Yet the foundation world, joined by some cowering nonprofits, justifies protection of its 5 percent pay-out rate—a spending floor that functions as a spending ceiling. In doing so, it behaves self-indulgently and self-protectively, fighting like any other sector to protect itself from demands that it do more and accomplish more and feather its own nest less. Nonprofits

---

7. Task Force on Inequality and American Democracy, "American Democracy in an Age of Rising Inequality" (American Political Science Association, 2004).

on the front-lines, addressing the nation's most urgent needs, are struggling for survival, many teetering before their own financial apocalypses, while foundations are ensuring their own interests. If philanthropy is to achieve the goal of social justice, future philanthropy should stop sitting on its assets, mobilize its capital more effectively and aggressively on behalf of the nonprofit delivery system in this nation, and use its tax-exempt, balance-sheet wealth, in addition to its grantmaking, to address the urgent public needs of this nation and more particularly the social justice needs of our society.

It is now somewhat popular to be identified as a social justice grantmaker. Independent Sector and the Foundation Center collaborated on a project to find that 11 percent of foundation grantmaking now goes to social justice causes. But automatically classifying grants that address specific issues and topics (such as various identity-group issues) as, by default, "social justice grantmaking" misses the point. In the framework suggested here, the definition of social justice grantmaking is not tied to niche issues. It is, again, grantmaking that revives and unleashes the forces of grassroots democracy aimed at representing and giving voice to the constituencies that do not fare well in our economy and society. Funding and strengthening grassroots organizations is not a romantic, "let a thousand flowers bloom"-into-irrelevance strategy. Providing the opportunity for those most affected by the challenges of our society to weigh in on the solutions, rather than watch from the sidelines, is crucial to our democratic process, unless the nation chooses to turn the responsibility of self-governance over to philanthropic philosopher kings and queens. Therein lies the social justice challenge for philanthropy—how privileged, wealthy donors, trustees, and foundation staff can translate their largesse earned from a less than just social and economic system to spur and support a grassroots social justice dynamic.

Adapted from "What Can and Should Philanthropy Do in the Future?" written for the Dialogues on Civic Philanthropy, "Goals and Intentions" (March 17, 2005). By permission of the author.

MARK HELPRIN

From "Perfection"

Many in philanthropy, guided by the noble desire to right wrongs and correct injustices, assume such ends can be achieved or engineered by human hands. In his short story, "Perfection," contemporary American author Mark Helprin offers an alternative understanding of justice and how to "win" it.

Helprin's story takes its bearings from the trials and ultimate triumph of the 1956 New York Yankees. The story is set in the spring of that year, when, despite their mighty lineup—including Mickey Mantle and Yogi Berra—the Yankees were foundering. Through a series of events, a young Yeshiva boy, Roger Reeves, resolves to "save" them. Though he is small in stature, slight in build, and hitherto utterly unfamiliar with most everything outside the beliefs and traditions of Jewish orthodoxy, including baseball, Roger miraculously wins a coveted place on the team, and at every at-bat hits the ball out of the park. Before Roger returns to his Yeshiva, Casey Stengel, the Yankees' manager, urges him to give a seminar to the team explaining his success. Roger's explanation (reprinted below) says little, at least ostensibly, about how to win baseball games, but it speaks volumes about why we might strive to do so.

Drawing from the wells of his religious tradition, Roger attributes his remarkable achievement to the "everpresent will of God for balance and perfection." Human beings, he implies, cannot by themselves right the terrible wrongs or remedy the many injustices in the world. But the aspiration and effort to do good—to achieve human excellence in any form—repairs the imbalance, acting as a cosmic counterweight to evil or "imperfection." Is Roger's conception of perfect justice a rebuke, or inspiration, to philanthropy? For you baseball fans, has there ever been a catch, a hit, or a steal of home perfect enough to make you believe it contributed to the redress of evil? (By the way, the Yankees went on that year to win the World Series, which included, stunningly, Don Larsen's perfect game. A mere accident?)

℘

[Casey Stengel to Roger] . . . "Tell us what you do know."

"Okay," said Roger, "but I'm telling you, I don't know anything."

That was not quite true. He had begun to think about the game. For example, he liked very much that the ball was an object descending from heaven, and he thought of it, therefore, not as an object to be captured for the glory of the captor but as a gracious gift that brought with it in train a bit of the loveliness of the sky.

For the seminar, the Yankees went to their secret practice field at Lake Honkus, near Mohonk, in the Shawangunks. The Yankees had bought a secluded estate and set up a baseball field on what had been a cow pasture, where they could practice in secret their surprise plays and coded signals. The lodge where they stayed was filled with wrought iron, Indian blankets, and buffalo heads. In fact, in Roger's room, he and a moose had a staring contest for at least an hour.

The next morning, Roger and the Yankees put away a huge breakfast, during which Roger discovered that the maple syrup the Yankees used on their pancakes was kosher, and made an interesting sauce for pickled herring. Then they went outside and sat on benches facing a portable blackboard. The weather was wonderfully cool and clear at Lake Honkus. Stengel brought Roger up to the front, stood him next to the blackboard, gave him a piece of chalk, and said, "Kid, we're totally secure."

Roger looked at the Yankees, who looked at him expectantly. What could he possibly say that would enable them to hit a ball out of the park or jump twenty feet in the air?

"From baseball I know nothing," he began, "but what's a lock?"

"What's a lock?" Mantle echoed.

Roger nodded.

"You mean like a lock on a door," Larsen asked, "or a lock in a canal?"

"Both," said Roger.

"A door lock is a metal thing with a lot of really smart junk in it," Berra said.

"Okay," said Roger, "and the lock of a canal?"

"A chamber for raising and lowering boats, with water from the river or canal to run it."

"Yes," said Roger.

Time passed. The Yankees stared at Roger. More time passed. Then Roger said, "Both illustrate the mechanism of the world."

The Yankees inched forward. No clinic had ever begun like this.

"God is perfect," Roger said. "His creation is perfect. It doesn't seem so to us—we who suffer and die, who must live with sadness and terror—because we can't see it in its entirety. If we could, we would see that it is in perfect balance. The counterweight for which we long—to right wrongs and correct injustices— is sometimes far away from us in space, time, or both. But, taken as a whole, from far enough afield, all is in balance, all is just.

"Good. What does this have to do with baseball and locks? As set out in the teachings of Rabbi Pepper of Biloxi and Rabbi Goldfinch of Barnevelt, the modern-day disciples of Rabbi Yoel ben Isaac of Zamosc and his grandson Rabbi Yoel ben Uri (whose last names I will not say), each a *baal shem,* and their descendants, et cetera, in God's eyes, in fact, and in truth, all souls, absent the deficit of sin, are equal. For example, a wise and brilliant king has no higher rank in the view of the Almighty than a beggar who has not even the comprehension to speak his own name. At the final judgment, both souls can glow equally in the same circle of continuous light."

The Yankees nodded slightly. They understood; they had all deeply loved those who were far from perfect.

"Okay," said Roger. "So here is the question that Yoel ben Isaac put forth and Yoel ben Uri answered. If these souls occupy the same level at the end, equally beloved of God, and if God's creation is perfect, how can an imbalance exist in their lives on earth? How can one suffer all the miseries of this life, and the other know all the glories, if in the end every account is to be reconciled and they come to the same reward? In a perfect universe, how can such a shortfall exist? How can God allow it?"

Not even the entire Yankee lineup could answer this question, though they strained to do so. Roger again challenged them. "Tell me, how can God allow it? Do you know?" He surveyed them. They didn't. "I'll tell you, then. It's simple. He doesn't. What is equal in the end is equal also in the beginning and in the middle. There is no deficit even on this earth, even in the smallest picture, the tightest section of view. But how can this be? The king and the beggar live vastly different lives. Ah! That's what you think. That's what may be apparent. But it isn't true. Why? Because," he said to the Yankees, their eyes unblinking, "the mechanism of creation is like a lock."

The Yankees waited. How was it like a lock, both kinds?

"Both kinds. The metal lock has a cylinder that, for the door to open, must turn. This cylinder has a row of holes drilled in it, in which rest pins. In the barrel inside of which the cylinder turns and is encased, is a line of holes spaced exactly like their counterparts in the cylinder, with its own set of pins. In the locked position, the pins from the barrel fall into the holes in the cylinder and prevent it from turning, because they cross and block the interface. When the key is put in, it raises the pins exactly to the points—at a different level in each hole—where the barrel pins are above the line and the cylinder pins are below it. If all the pins were raised indiscriminately, sometimes the cylinder pins would block the interface, and sometimes the barrel pins would. If they were not raised at all, the barrel pins would block the interface and, thus, the rotation. To allow the turning, each pin must be raised according to what it requires. Some are raised more, some less, which is why the key is jagged. In the end, its unevenness makes a perfect equality that allows the lock to open.

"And a lock that lifts or lowers a boat is a mechanism that gets its power from the urge of all water to find its own level. Only that way can things flow, rivers run, and the world function—when the disparate forces of the universe are conjoined, and rest easy in an equality of perfection. Every force that exists is held in balance by a counterpart with which it must be united, and with which it is united, even if the connection be not apparent to us.

"Like the pins in a lock, the beggar and the king are lifted by God variously and invisibly, but equally, even in this world, so that the perfection will not be broken, for, by definition, the perfection *cannot* be broken. They ride unseen waves and are held aloft by unseen supports. Were they not so lifted, the world would not work.

"Only those who have suffered can know the strength of the compensation they acquire. The emissary that comes to them is all-embracing, and though some may deny or mock this, it is many times more real than the world itself, for next to this working of perfection the world itself seems only a tinsel of the imagination. God compensates even in this world. He must. He does. And the reception of His compensation, like a quantity of physics, is the certain though insubstantial thing we call holiness. Those who would deny it would do so simply from lack of having received it. Perhaps the king, gifted in other ways, has no knowledge of holiness, while for the beggar with no gifts, it is overflowing. You may wonder what this has to do with baseball."

They nodded.

"It seems clear to me," he said, as a breeze brought resinous air from a thick pine forest that bordered the practice field as evenly as a crewcut. "I have been able to do what I did because my arm was guided, my strength supplied, my speed achieved, by the everpresent will of God for balance and perfection. Perhaps a Phoenician ship listed too much to port, thousands of years ago; or it was too cloudy, for too long, over a glacier in the Himalaya; or a woman's heart was broken for a day by her suitor in Montana. I don't know. I do know that it is important to know that such balances exist, and that, if I didn't know it, I wouldn't have the heart to continue."

"Can we hook into this stuff?" Berra asked.

"Not if all you want to do is win games," Roger answered.

"But wait a minute," Berra demanded. "Let's say someone cheated in Chinese checkers a thousand years ago in Peru. If I could hook into that, I could run twenty feet back to the plate even though Zelinka is just an inch from it, and put him out, right?"

"No," said Roger. "It doesn't necessarily work that way, and God is not fond of games."

"Even baseball?"

"Even baseball."

"Why?"

"Games can become, because of their closed set of rules, an independent universe, a distraction from the seeking of perfection. If they are taken as a universe in themselves, what a meager universe that is. This offends God, who worked for six whole days to make the universe we have. Can you imagine what would come of the work of an omnipotent being for six whole days? What is the infinity of detail, the infinity of extent, the infinity of connectedness, and the infinity of surprise, times six?"

"It doesn't apply to baseball?" Stengel asked, not quite sure of exactly what *it* was.

"If your object is merely to play baseball, it doesn't."

"What's your object, then, Roger?" Mantle asked.

"Because of the imperfection I have seen, I live for the hope of restoration. That's all I live for, even if it be a sin."

"What imperfection?" Stengel asked.

Roger's expression was incomprehensible to the Yankees as anything but some sort of nervous ailment, because boys his age who are not afflicted with a crippling disease do not show on their faces the pain of old men. "I was born during the war," he said, to answer the question, "in a place called Majdanek. I knew nothing else. The physical privation of this place, the terror of the selections and the frequent killing of people around me, seemed natural. Until I was three, I existed in the aura of my parents' love. I don't know what they did to keep us alive, but I know that whatever it was it was done for me. I stop abruptly when I begin to imagine what they must have suffered, especially my mother. For this I pray with love and gratitude, every day. I wish it were they who had lived and I who had died, although that would have taken from them what they wanted most.

"Just before the liberation, when I was three, we were marched out and made to stand at the edge of a pit. In the pit were thousands of bodies. Bulldozers had compressed and shaped them. They were as white as snow, and beneath them was a lake of blood. Even among the crushed forms and severed limbs, some people remained alive, though not for long.

"My mother and father told me that they loved me. They tried to shield me with their bodies. When the firing began, the force of the machine-gun bullets caught them and the other adults and they were hurled into the pit as if a wind had blown them away. The firing had been over the heads of the children, who stood on the rim untouched and unable to move. The guns were not lowered, because bullets were scarce.

"A soldier came by and picked me up by both ankles. My head hit the ground, and then he swung me around like an ice skater swinging his partner. I remember the blood rushing to my head, and the world blurring into blue and white. Even as I was twirled, the soldiers were laughing. After I was released, for a moment, I flew. Undoubtedly, I passed over my mother and father, and though I thought I was going to fly forever, I fell into the center of the pit, face-to-face with a dead woman upon whom I had fallen, whose mouth was open.

"I thought I was dead, too, until the bulldozers drove over us. The sound of bones breaking was like the sound of burning kindling. Many times, the bulldozer drove right over me, but though I was too frightened to move, I found myself each time between the treads. Then I was caught in a wave of tumbling bodies that, pushed by the blade, washed up at the edge. The bulldozer no longer came near me. I lay quietly as it worked, and then slept.

"After nightfall, I was awakened as I was wetted with gasoline. Choking on it, I climbed over the rim and walked into the darkness. I thought that this was death and that I was dead, but when I looked back and saw the huge blaze of the fire in which my mother and father were burning, I knew that I was still alive. I knew the difference. I wanted to die, I wanted very much to die, but, not knowing how, I lived.

"That is the imperfection I have seen," he said, "and all I want from the world is some indication or sign that, forward in time, or where time does not exist, there is a justice and a beauty that will leap back to lift the ones I love from the kind of grave they were given."

W. E. B. DUBOIS

"The Talented Tenth"

In this essay, W. E. B. DuBois (1868–1963), educator, author, civil rights activist, and famed African American leader, vigorously advocates supporting higher education for the best and brightest, "The Talented Tenth." Though he is especially interested in the effect that succoring such elites will have on the advancement of his own people—hence his focus on black colleges—one can, he insists, generalize: "[I]t is, ever was, and ever will be from the top downward that culture filters. The Talented Tenth rises and pulls all that are worth the saving up to their vantage ground. This is the history of human progress."

Philanthropy has long voted with its feet for the general view espoused here. For centuries, high culture, especially in the visual arts and music, has been patron driven. And charitable support for colleges and universities—higher learning—continues to be prodigious.[1] But support for excellence—especially in democratic times, especially when the disjunction between haves and have-nots looms large—has always been questioned: How do we identify the "talented tenth"? Is it ever possible to know ahead of time that people so supported or so educated will become the "leaders of thought" or the "missionaries of culture" that DuBois envisioned? How do we determine which thinking or what culture should be supported?

The Negro race, like all races, is going to be saved by its exceptional men. The problem of education, then, among Negroes must first of all deal with the Talented Tenth; it is the problem of developing the Best of this race that they may guide the Mass away from the contamination and death of the Worst, in their own and other races. Now the training of men is a difficult and intricate task. Its technique is a matter for educational experts, but its object is for the vision of seers. If we make money the object of man-training, we shall develop money-makers but not necessarily men; if we make technical skill the object of education, we may possess artisans but not, in nature, men. Men we shall have only as we make manhood the object of the work of the schools—intelligence, broad sympathy, knowledge of the world that was and is, and of the relation of men to it—this is the curriculum of that Higher Education which must

---

1. According to *Giving USA 2006*, 14.8 percent ($38.56 billion) of all charitable contributions in 2005 aided education, a portion of the pie second only to religion, which received 35.8 percent.

underlie true life. On this foundation we may build bread winning, skill of hand and quickness of brain, with never a fear lest the child and man mistake the means of living for the object of life. . . .

. . . Who are to-day guiding the work of the Negro people? The "exceptions" of course. And yet so sure as this Talented Tenth is pointed out, the blind worshippers of the Average cry out in alarm: "These are exceptions, look here at death, disease and crime—these are the happy rule." Of course they are the rule, because a silly nation made them the rule: Because for three long centuries this people lynched Negroes who dared to be brave, raped black women who dared to be virtuous, crushed dark-hued youth who dared to be ambitious, and encouraged and made to flourish servility and lewdness and apathy. But not even this was able to crush all manhood and chastity and aspiration from black folk. A saving remnant continually survives and persists, continually aspires, continually shows itself in thrift and ability and character. Exceptional it is to be sure, but this is its chiefest promise; it shows the capability of Negro blood, the promise of black men. Do Americans ever stop to reflect that there are in this land a million men of Negro blood, well-educated, owners of homes, against the honor of whose womanhood no breath was ever raised, whose men occupy positions of trust and usefulness, and who, judged by any standard, have reached the full measure of the best type of modern European culture? Is it fair, is it decent, is it Christian to ignore these facts of the Negro problem, to belittle such aspiration, to nullify such leadership and seek to crush these people back into the mass out of which by toil and travail, they and their fathers have raised themselves?

Can the masses of the Negro people be in any possible way more quickly raised than by the effort and example of this aristocracy of talent and character? Was there ever a nation on God's fair earth civilized from the bottom upward? Never; it is, ever was and ever will be from the top downward that culture filters. The Talented Tenth rises and pulls all that are worth the saving up to their vantage ground. This is the history of human progress; and the two historic mistakes which have hindered that progress were the thinking first that no more could ever rise save the few already risen; or second, that it would be better for the uprisen to pull the risen down.

How then shall the leaders of a struggling people be trained and the hands of the risen few strengthened? There can be but one answer: The best and most capable of their youth must be schooled in the colleges and universities of the land. We will not quarrel as to just what the university of the Negro should teach or how it should teach it—I willingly admit that each soul and each race-soul needs its own peculiar curriculum. But this is true: A university is a human invention for the transmission of knowledge and culture from generation to generation, through the training of quick minds and pure hearts, and for this work no other human invention will suffice, not even trade and industrial schools.

All men cannot go to college but some men must; every isolated group or nation must have its yeast, must have for the talented few centers of training where men are not so mystified and befuddled by the hard and necessary toil of earning a living, as to have no aims higher than their bellies, and no God greater than Gold. This is true training, and thus in the beginning were the favored sons of the freedmen trained. Out of tile colleges of the North came, after the blood of war, Ware, Cravath, Chase, Andrews, Bumstead and Spence to build the foundations of knowledge and civilization in the black South. Where ought they to have begun to build? At the bottom, of course, quibbles the mole with his eyes in the earth. Aye! truly at the bottom, at the very bottom; at the bottom of knowledge, down in the very depths of knowledge there where the roots of justice strike into the lowest soil of Truth. And so they did begin; they founded colleges, and up from the colleges shot normal schools, and out from the normal schools went teachers, and around the normal teachers clustered other teachers to teach the public schools; the college trained in Greek and Latin and mathematics, 2,000 men; and these men trained full 50,000 others in morals and manners, and they in turn taught thrift and the alphabet to nine millions of men, who today hold $300,000,000 of property. It was a miracle— the most wonderful peace-battle of the 19th century, and yet to-day men smile at it, and in fine superiority tell us that it was all a strange mistake; that a proper way to found a system of education is first to gather the children and buy them spelling books and hoes; afterward men may look about for teachers, if haply they may find them; or again they would teach men Work, but as for Life—why, what has Work to do with Life, they ask vacantly. . . .

. . . [The college-bred Negro] is, as he ought to be, the group leader, the man who sets the ideals of the community where he lives, directs its thoughts and heads its social movements. It need hardly be argued that the Negro people need social leadership more than most groups; that they have no traditions to fall back upon, no long established customs, no strong family ties, no well defined social classes. All these things must be slowly and painfully evolved. The preacher was, even before the war, the group leader of the Negroes, and the church their greatest social institution. Naturally this preacher was ignorant and often immoral, and the problem of replacing the older type by better educated men has been a difficult one. Both by direct work and by direct influence on other preachers, and on congregations, the college-bred preacher has an opportunity for reformatory work and moral inspiration, the value of which cannot be overestimated.

It has, however, been in the furnishing of teachers that the Negro college has found its peculiar function. Few persons realize how vast a work, how mighty a revolution has been thus accomplished. To furnish five millions and more of ignorant people with teachers of their own race and blood, in one generation, was not only a very difficult undertaking, but very important one, in that, it placed before the eyes of almost every Negro child an attainable ideal. It brought the masses of the blacks in contact with modern civilization, made black men the leaders of their communities and trainers of the new generation. In this work college-bred Negroes were first teachers, and then teachers of teachers. And here it is that the broad culture of college work has been of peculiar value. Knowledge of life and its wider meaning, has been the point of the Negro's deepest ignorance, and the sending out of teachers whose training has not been simply for bread winning, but also for human culture, has been of inestimable value in the training of these men. . . .

The problem of training the Negro is to-day immensely complicated by the fact that the whole question of the efficiency and appropriateness of our present systems of education, for any kind of child, is a matter of active debate, in which final settlement seems still afar off. Consequently it often happens that persons arguing for or against certain systems of education for Negroes, have these controversies in mind and miss the real question at issue. The main question, so far as the Southern Negro is concerned, is: What under the present circumstance, must a system of education do in order to raise the Negro as quickly as possible in the scale of civilization? The answer to this question seems to me clear: It must strengthen the Negro's character, increase his knowledge and teach him to earn a living. Now it goes without saying that it is hard to do all these things simultaneously or suddenly and that at the same time it will not do to give all the attention to one and neglect the others; we could give black boys trades, but that alone will not civilize a race of ex-slaves; we might simply increase their knowledge of the world, but this would not necessarily make them wish to use this knowledge honestly; we might seek to strengthen character and purpose, but to what end if this people have nothing to eat or to wear? A system of education is not one thing, nor does it have a single definite object, nor is it a mere matter of schools. Education is that whole system of human training within and without the school house walls, which molds and develops men. If then we start out to train an ignorant and unskilled people with a heritage of bad habits, our system of training must set before itself two great aims—the one dealing with knowledge and character, the other part seeking to give the child the technical knowledge necessary for him to earn a living under the present circumstances. These objects are accomplished in part by the opening of the common schools on the one, and of the industrial schools on the other. But only in part, for there must also be trained those who are to teach these schools—men and women of knowledge and culture and technical skill who understand modern civilization, and have the training and aptitude to impart it to the children under them. There must be teachers, and teachers of teachers, and to attempt to establish any sort of a system of common and industrial school training, without first (and I say first advisedly) without first providing for the higher training of the very best teachers, is simply throwing your money to the winds. School houses do not teach themselves— piles of brick and mortar and machinery do not send out men. It is the trained, living human soul, cultivated and strengthened by long study and thought, that breathes the real breath of life into boys and girls and makes them human, whether they be black or white, Greek, Russian or American. Nothing, in these latter days, has so dampened the faith of thinking Negroes in recent educational movements, as the fact that such movements have been accompanied by ridicule and denouncement and decrying of those very institutions of higher training which made the Negro public school possible, and make Negro industrial schools thinkable. It was: Fisk, Atlanta, Howard and Straight, those colleges born of the faith and sacrifice of the abolitionists, that placed in the black schools of the South the 30,000 teachers and more, which some, who depreciate the work of these higher schools, are using to teach their own new experiments. If Hampton, Tuskegee and the hundred other industrial schools prove in the future to be as successful as they deserve to be, then their success in training black artisans for the South, will be due primarily to the white colleges of the North and the black colleges of the South, which trained the teachers who to-day conduct these institutions. There was a time when the American people believed pretty devoutly that a log of wood with a boy at one end and Mark Hopkins at the other, represented the highest ideal of human training. But in these eager days it would seem that we have changed all that and think it necessary to add a couple of saw-mills and a hammer to this outfit, and, at a pinch, to dispense with the services of Mark Hopkins.

I would not deny, or for a moment seem to deny, the paramount necessity of teaching the Negro to work, and to work steadily and skillfully; or seem to depreciate in the slightest degree the important part industrial schools must play in the accomplishment of these ends, but I do say, and insist upon it, that it is industrialism drunk with its vision of success, to imagine that its own work can be accomplished without providing for the training of broadly cultured men and women to teach its own teachers, and to teach the teachers of the public schools.

But I have already said that human education is not simply a matter of schools; it is much more a matter of family and group life—the training of one's home, of one's daily companions, of one's social class. Now the black boy of the South moves in a black world—a world with its own leaders, its own thoughts, its own ideals. In this world he gets by far the larger part of his life training, and through the eyes of this dark world he peers into the veiled world beyond. Who guides and determines the education which he receives in his world? His teachers here are the group-leaders of the Negro people—the physicians and clergymen, the trained fathers and mothers, the influential and forceful men about him of all kinds; here it is, if at all, that the culture of the surrounding world trickles through and is handed on by the graduates of the higher schools. Can such culture training of group leaders be neglected? Can we afford to ignore it? Do you think that if the leaders of thought among Negroes are not trained and educated thinkers, that they will have no leaders? On the contrary a hundred half-trained demagogues will still hold the places they so largely occupy now, and hundreds of vociferous busy-bodies will multiply. You have no choice; either you must help furnish this race from within its own ranks with thoughtful men of trained leadership, or you must suffer the evil consequences of a headless misguided rabble. . . .

Men of America, the problem is plain before you. Here is a race transplanted through the criminal foolishness of your fathers. Whether you like it or not the millions are here, and here they will remain. If you do not lift them up, they will pull you down. Education and work are the levers to uplift a people. Work alone will not do it unless inspired by the right ideals and guided by intelligence. Education must not simply teach work—it must teach Life. The Talented Tenth of the Negro race must be made leaders of thought and missionaries of culture among their people. No others can do this work and Negro colleges must train men for it. The Negro race, like all other races, is going to be saved by its exceptional men.

From *The Negro Problem: A Series of Articles by Representative Negroes of Today* (New York: James Pott and Co., 1903).

ANNA FAITH JONES

"Doors and Mirrors: Reflections on the Art of Philanthropy"

"Teach a man to fish, feed him for a lifetime"; "God helps them who help themselves"; "Give those who desire to rise the aids by which they may rise." From Lao Tzu to Benjamin Franklin to Andrew Carnegie, sages have sung the praises of helping people to help themselves. Although—but perhaps also because—this concept has long been a staple of philanthropic self-description, it is easy to neglect or just plain forget. Such was the case at the Boston Foundation until the mid-1980s, when Anna Faith Jones assumed its helm as president and CEO.

For thirty years the Foundation had been helping community-based agencies leverage government monies and services. But when such an agenda became no longer feasible, Jones helped steer the Foundation back into the impoverished communities it served—quite literally: they went directly to the poor and asked them what they experienced, cared about, and required. Having thus engaged its potential grantees not as objects of charity but as subjects capable of speaking out on their own behalf, the Foundation used its funds to leverage the power of the community to help itself: to energize its people, to work together, and to become their own advocates. They thus succeeded in breaking down the have/have-not barrier, not by redistribution of resources so much as by relationship—not only between grantmaker and grantees, but also and most importantly, between and among the grantees themselves. In short, the Boston Foundation opened doors and held up mirrors, in which they and the grantees could discover themselves in relation to their communities. Their approach seems so straightforward and self-evident. Why is it so rarely practiced?

One evening a few years ago I spoke at the opening of an art exhibit at the Boston Public Library. Sponsored by Dorchester Community Center for the Visual Arts, and underwritten by a grant from the Boston Foundation, the exhibit included many works by professional artists and other adults, but much of it was by children and teens completely new to art. These young people, from a part of Boston that includes some of the city's poorest and most troubled neighborhoods, had worked over a period of several months with trained artists to create life-size portraits of themselves that they had painted on hollow-core doors a local lumber company had contributed to the program.

The results were striking. Under the lights in the library, in the hush that daytime institutions take on after hours, the paintings stood in groupings in the four-story atrium of this great public building. All over six feet tall, the images were full of bold splashes of color—reds, oranges, blacks, golden-greens—that seemed bursting with energy.

As I stepped up to the podium and looked out at those doors—nearly a hundred of them standing in that high, light-filled space—and as I looked from those radiant images to the smiling faces of the audience of families and friends gathered in support of the artists, I could see, I could feel, what it is that art does for individuals and for a community.

There, in those paintings, were the young people of Dorchester, presenting themselves to the world as they saw themselves. Simultaneously bold and innocent, the self-portraits conveyed a very different view of this community's young people than the one we see in headlines and on the evening news, where Dorchester represents the "inner city," a place of drugs and gangs and violence. These youngsters had freed themselves from other people's definitions to stand on their own, in their uniqueness and particularity, as large as life and as vibrant. They had discovered how to use art—not as experts, but as serious practitioners—to explore and celebrate their own identities, to create something that would tell the rest of us who they really were.

That sea of doors remains as an image in my mind today. Some of the doors stood alone, but many of them were hinged together, not only supporting each other but also intensifying the impact of each, so that the whole added up to more than the sum of the parts: a vivid metaphor for the way our individual lives are enhanced when we feel respected and supported by our communities.

The Boston Foundation's grant to the Dorchester Community Center for the Visual Arts was just one of many thousands made to nonprofit organizations engaged in everything from health care to housing to job training to education during the more than twenty-five years I spent as part of the foundation. Yet it captures the essence of what we were trying to do as a community foundation: build connections within the community that we saw as essential to freeing individuals to become themselves.

It seems to me that this is the primary mission of philanthropy in America, as it is the mission of the country itself: to make it possible for individuals to emerge from the constraints of history, from lives defined by poverty, by age or gender, by physical disability, by racial or ethnic discrimination, or by any other condition limiting the development of their innate potential. If philanthropy does a great deal of important work in this country today, none is more fundamental or more significant, in my view, than this work for individual freedom. It is the basis of our democracy.

What we tried to do at the Boston Foundation during my years there was to effect that freedom for individuals by leveraging the power of the community. We realized that no amount of "giving" could do for the community what the community could do for itself. We came to reject the notion that solutions could be superimposed on communities by outsiders. The grant to the Dorchester arts organization was minor in itself; its success depended on the impressive power locked within even the most economically deprived communities to lift individuals above their circumstances and transform their lives. With this small grant we tapped into the power present in the natural enthusiasm of children to express themselves; the power present in the desire of community elders, like the experienced artists who participated in this project, to share their knowledge; and the power that resounded in the applause at the end of my remarks that night, which lifted people to their feet—the remarkable power, the profoundly transformative power, of a community to recognize and celebrate the accomplishments of its individual members.

In a moment like that one at the Boston Public Library, it is clear that the money involved in philanthropy is, in an important way, secondary. It is essential as a means for fostering change, that is true, but it is not the change agent itself. Consumed as we all are with money in this business—the raising of it, the disbursing of it, and the often agonizing decisions that this involves—it is easy to forget that in the end this work is not about money. It is about people. Neither a community foundation like the Boston Foundation nor other, much larger philanthropic institutions have the power to change society. Only people have that power. A philanthropic organization attempting to bring about fundamental social change can do so only by getting the resources to the people who can make that change.

Because this is true, the relationship between philanthropic organizations and the people they try to help is of fundamental importance. It follows naturally, then, that successful grantmaking is based essentially on the ability of the grantee and grantor to communicate. Ultimately this is a process of getting to know one another. It is a responsibility shared by both parties, and we have to work at it. While we may automatically treat representatives of prestigious institutions with a great deal of respect, unfortunately the same does not always hold true in our relationships with those groups struggling on the fringes of society. Poor people in this country are too often seen as the objects of philanthropy rather than as the agents of change. The image we have of the poor makes a difference in what we do, and how well we do it. And the problem starts with seeing the poor as "them." This is an old issue, but a crucial one, and how to get beyond it remains an important challenge.

Remember the famous remark of the cartoon character Pogo: "We have met the enemy and they are us." At the Boston Foundation, we had a similar awakening, not so comic, but certainly parallel in that it brought us face to face with a startling reality. What we found out anew was that, in a critical way, the poor too are "us."

To tell you how we came to understand this basic truth and what the experience taught us, let me begin with a little background about the Boston Foundation and its purposes.

From its inception in 1915, the Boston Foundation had provided funds to charitable organizations throughout the metropolitan area to help the poor and needy. In effect, the foundation was Boston's "United Way" for several decades before the United Way itself came along. Every year it made modest operating grants to dozens of charities in Boston, and these charities provided social services throughout the community. During the Great Depression, when the demands on their services threatened to swamp these independent charities and their counterparts throughout the country, the federal government stepped in, and, in a new way in American history, the community as a whole assumed broad responsibility for the well-being of the citizenry.

In the 1950s and 1960s, as federal funding for social programs expanded, the role of the Boston Foundation changed. Increasingly, it was able to play a catalytic role, helping community-based agencies attract federal funding and adapt federal programs in areas of need, taking chances on experimental programs until they could fend for themselves, and providing the funds that would launch new efforts. In the 1970s, for example, the Boston Foundation provided funds to start several of the city's community health centers, an innovation that became a national model. In the early 1980s, it took the lead in new approaches to developing low-income housing, and these approaches were also widely imitated. Foundations like ours were playing a new part now, not just responding to the community's needs, but becoming a laboratory for social change and improvement.

But in the mid-1980s, when I became the head of the foundation—and I have to note here that the timing was exquisite—America was in full retreat from the goals and ideals of the Great Society programs. Those efforts of the 1960s and 1970s were deemed failures, and it became the practice to attribute poverty not to social and historic circumstances, but to the personal failings of individuals. To some of us, it seemed that the "war on poverty" had turned into something resembling a war on the poor.

In those years of the mid-1980s, the federal government took a giant step backward in its commitment to helping the needy. At the Boston Foundation, we felt the rug was being pulled out from under us. As cuts and more cuts were announced in Washington, we watched the principal source of social funding slowly diminish. Our grantees clamored for us to fill the gap, but we simply did not have the resources. Even accompanied by thousands of other "points of light," we could not begin to make up for the cuts in federally supported programs to aid the poor. With our minimal resources we struggled to find a new way to help.

At first we focused on what we understood to be the key areas of poverty. We provided what help we could, for instance, to mothers with small children, who were the first to suffer from the worst of the cuts. But soon we realized that our pockets were not nearly deep enough to change things through this kind of help. We needed to apply some new and creative thought to addressing the whole problem of poverty and to how, in the current era, we might be more effective in doing so.

We then did something so obvious, so straightforward, and so self-evident that we wondered afterward why it had not occurred to us earlier. We reached out directly to the poor and asked them what *they* needed, what *they* wanted. We convened a series of community hearings in which we asked several hundred Boston residents—primarily poor and low-income adults and youth, male and female, from a wide variety of racial and ethnic groups—to share with us their personal stories of the obstacles and indignities they faced in their struggle for economic mobility.

These meetings were not always easy, and we had moments of wondering what we had wrought. But listening to those voices from the community was an enlightening and indelible experience. In meeting after meeting, voices raised in anger and frustration also struck chords of dogged determination and tenacious faith and hope—in God, in family, and in the promise of our country's democratic way of life.

The people who so generously came to us and shared their experiences were hardly recognizable in relation to the representations of the poor and distressed neighborhoods we were hearing about in the media. They were as different from those stereotypes as the children of Dorchester showed themselves to be when they were given the opportunity to paint true images of themselves.

What we heard repeatedly in those meetings was a plea for dignity and respect, for opportunity, and for the chance to participate fully in the life of the community. When we asked what this meant, the participants said good jobs, decent housing, education for their children, and a habitable community in which they could feel respected and included. Most of all, these citizens wanted a say in getting these things for themselves. What they wanted, it was utterly clear, was no different from what the rest of us want. When we looked very hard at "these people," at their basic needs and deepest aspirations, at their goals in life and their hopes for their children, it was like looking in a mirror. The people we saw were remarkably like ourselves.

What did this mean for the Boston Foundation and how we conducted our business?

In practical terms, it meant dramatically changing our funding pattern. It meant redirecting our resources toward organizations more organically connected with the communities they serve, organizations with more community people on boards and staff, directly shaping and implementing policy. It meant drawing into the decision-making arena teenagers, elderly people, single mothers, the disabled, the jobless, the poor. Even if these people are struggling on the margins of society, even if their very problem seems to be their powerlessness, these are the people whose engagement and participation are most critical to successful social change. Such change cannot be imposed by politicians, or experts, or academics, or even well-intentioned persons such as those who run important philanthropic institutions.

In a democracy, social change occurs only through a process that is itself democratic, a process that involves people acting on their own behalf. We know this from the labor movement in this country, when people working twelve-hour days found time to organize for change. We know it from the women's movement, when women took to the streets and went to jail for the right to participate in society as voters. And we know it from the civil rights movement, when domestic workers, schoolchildren, obscure religious congregations—people from the so called powerless fringes of society—stood up for themselves and insisted on change.

At the Boston Foundation, we went about refocusing our funding in the community based on this renewed sense of who we were and who "the poor" were; we took care to direct our funds in a way that would energize people to come together around issues important to them, to work with their neighbors, to learn the process of advocating for themselves, to get their hands on the reins of their own lives, and to take control of their own destinies in the rebuilding of their own communities.

If we ask ourselves what philanthropy can do, what it ought to do, how it ought to do it, I believe this is the answer. And I believe this very deeply. Whether we work through indigenous institutions, churches, or other community organizations, or simply with a group of concerned citizens, I believe the best work we as community foundations, in particular, can do is to give the gift of respecting, believing in, and working with people, where they are, to help strengthen their capacity to change and improve their own lives.

The nineteenth-century novelist George Eliot believed that successful communities depend on the ability of individuals to imagine in others a center of self equivalent to their own. The relationship we have with ourselves ultimately determines the direction of our lives. Philanthropy that aims to improve society must be rooted in that same fundamental identification with others, including those who may be leading very different lives. I think it is that belief that helps people discover how to take action in their own behalf.

The experiences of my own past are focused by these themes of identification and empowerment. I grew up in Washington, D.C., when it was a segregated city. My family lived on the campus of Howard University—my father was its president for many years—and the community there was something of a world unto itself, where black people occupied positions of authority and black leaders of the time came to study and to speak. In those days, Howard's classrooms held students who would become major figures in the civil rights era, and it was possible to sense their energy and determination even then. But we knew that beyond the enclosing walls of the university lay another world entirely, one in which we were rarely welcome. There were department stores in which we would not be waited on. There were theaters and restaurants from which we were simply excluded.

As one of the early black colleges, Howard had a lifeline to the federal government, which provided the bulk of its financial support. But that support was far from automatic; the budget request presented to Congress each year was always challenged by elected officials opposed to the kind of social progress the school represented. The core funding from the federal government was absolutely crucial to the university, success in securing it was no mean feat, and equally important to the school's survival was the public commitment that this money represented. That commitment was enhanced in important ways by support from high-ranking government officials, including President Roosevelt himself.

One gesture of that support stands out among my very earliest memories, and the full significance of it became clear to me only in subsequent tellings of the story by my parents. In the late thirties, the university put up a new chemistry building, and FDR accepted the invitation to speak at the dedication. My father then made a special request of the president: that he let the students see that he was crippled. The young people at Howard were struggling with a huge social disability, my father argued, and if they could see the president of the United States struggling with a disability himself, it would help them to see what they themselves might overcome.

When he arrived at Howard, FDR let himself be lifted from his car in full view of the audience gathered for the dedication. And then, with great difficulty, he made his way to the speakers platform. It was a gesture that must have cost Roosevelt a good deal. He had never made it before in his public life, as Doris Kearns Goodwin notes in *No Ordinary Time,* and would repeat it only one other time, at a hospital for wounded and crippled soldiers, during the war. For the audience at Howard that gesture seemed to erase the barrier between the privileged and the excluded; for a moment, there was that sense of fellow feeling that marks a community of shared understanding. It was a great gift. "If I can do this," he seemed to say, "think what you can do."

That belief in the innate power of all human beings, regardless of status, to act most effectively to develop their own potential—that's the critical thing, in my view. That belief was vital to my vision of the philanthropic mission of a community foundation, and it was vital to my own personal development. What the federal government provided, however unwittingly, through its support of the university, and what FDR validated in his visit to the campus that day, was not simply "help" for a group of people clearly in need of assistance; it was a recognition and support of the latent power of such a community to take charge of its own destiny.

Looking at Howard University in those early days, some people saw an institution operating on the remotest margins of society, an institution for permanent outsiders, run by a man whose own father had grown up in slavery. Others saw Howard, and all of black America in those days, as a deprived but potentially powerful community. For those of us within that community, there was no question that the ultimate hope for the future lay within the circle of our own community, in its institutions, and in the spirit of African Americans themselves.

For me, this community, these people, were a bastion against the ugliness of racism all around us. There was present a kind of strength that is bred in the bone, an inner strength borne of the knowledge of shared sufferings and shared beliefs. At moments, this power was something one felt as an almost physical experience.

I remember one of those moments very clearly. I can see myself now, as a very young girl, standing in an immense crowd of people, old and young, black and white, in front of the Lincoln Memorial. It was twilight and we were listening to the voice of Marian Anderson, the famous contralto. Denied the right to hold her concert in Constitution Hall by the Daughters of the American Revolution, she had won permission from the Department of the Interior to sing on the steps of the Lincoln Memorial. As her rich voice floated over us in the shadow of that powerful and symbolic statue of Abraham Lincoln, the crowd was hushed by the soaring beauty of the music and united by an overwhelming and collective sense of justice done in the face of senseless discrimination.

I look back on that experience as one of the defining moments of my life. It was on those same steps that Martin Luther King Jr. stood to proclaim his dream thirty years later. And there was that same stirring, the same sense of the spirit, the same sense of people melded into one by an experience. There is immense energy in people united in mutual understanding and shared commitment. At such moments the important "connective tissue" of community is realized. Rebuilding and strengthening the potential of this connection is the very essence of democratic community building.

It is when philanthropy reaches into and supports this fundamental power of people in a community that it can be most effective in bringing about social change. And from my own experience I know that there is no group of people in our society today who lack the ability to transform their own communal life. What philanthropy can do is to put a bit of ground under people's feet. And then, let them go. Ultimately we need to see ourselves engaged in a mutual learning and growing process with people in community—a relationship of partners working toward a more just and humane society.

FREDERICK T. GATES

"Address on the Tenth Anniversary of the Rockefeller Institute"

Frederick T. Gates (1853–1929), a Baptist minister and early champion of medical reform, was the chief philanthropic advisor to John D. Rockefeller Sr. and mentor to John D. Rockefeller Jr. He prodded the former to fund the Rockefeller Institute for Medical Research (now Rockefeller University) and served as its founding director. The Institute exclusively devoted itself to understanding the underlying causes of disease—and not by accident. As Rockefeller stated and Gates insisted, "the best philanthropy is constantly in search of finalities—a search for cause, an attempt to cure the evils at their source." To identify and cure ills—medical and social—at their "root" became the major aim of the Rockefeller Foundation (established 1913) and shaped the attitudes and practices of many other large foundations for decades to come. Indeed, many still regard the prototypical American foundation as one that attacks "root causes."

At the Institute's tenth anniversary celebration, in 1911, Gates praises the "values of research" as "universal as the love of God" and as "beneficial in its purpose." Medical research is poised, he says, to find and propagate "new moral laws and new social laws, new definitions of what is right and wrong in our relations to each other." Gates is prescient, if excessively ebullient: In this era of globalization, more than ever the value of research is "universal." Medical advances not only affect social as well as physical bodies (consider, for example, how international medical interventions reshape local communities); they also compel us to rethink matters of "right and wrong" (for example, in the debates over stem cell research or genetically modified organisms). Indeed, if our contemporary Gates—Bill Gates—carries out his promise to channel the majority of his foundation's prodigious resources into medical research and global health, and if others follow suit, philanthropy will bring about massive changes in our moral and social landscape, not all of them intended. Yet this issue of unintended consequences invites questions about the overall outcome of philanthropy that seeks to combat "root causes," and on a massive scale. Does it do more good than harm? How can we be sure? Is such scientific giving (what Gates called "wholesale philanthropy") unquestionably better than charity (Gates' "retail giving")? How enthusiastic should we be about large-scale social engineering or unlimited biomedical research?

ℰ

. . . It is to me the greatest honor and privilege of my life, indeed, the greatest significance of my life, if it have any significance at all, to have been connected, even though in a subordinate and external way, with the history of this Institute, to have been a sort of hewer of wood and drawer of water to this modern temple of Jehovah, and particularly to you, who are the life of the Institute itself, and to Dr. Flexner, your presiding genius. I say it has been the greatest privilege of my life; but I ought to make one exception. My eldest son, the apple of my eye, is on the staff of Dr. Meltzer, and is thus permitted to work along with you in your high vocation. That interior service of my son I regard as of far higher dignity than any external service such as mine.

Some years ago, as I was walking down Broadway one morning, I had the good fortune to have as companion the President Emeritus of [Harvard] the oldest and, in some ways, the greatest of our American universities, made greatest in those ways by him; a man full of years, as you know, with a breast laden with wisdom, an author of distinction, a patriot, a statesman, a man who for nearly eighty years has been pondering the great problems of humanity and of human life. We happened to be talking about the Institute, and I ventured to confess to him that to me this Institute was the most interesting thing in the world. Nothing, said I, is to me as exciting, so fascinating as the work that the Institute is doing. Dr. Eliot stopped, turned to me, and said, in the fullness of his wisdom and experience: "I myself feel precisely so. The Rockefeller Institute is to me the most interesting thing in this world."

That, gentlemen, was significant. Of course Dr. Eliot could know little, if anything, of the technique of your work. Certainly it was not the technique that interested him; it was those great underlying general considerations, which give peculiar greatness and value to your work, and which make an irresistible appeal to a layman, even though he can know nothing of the technicalities of your daily studies. If I have any claim at all on your attention tonight, I have wondered if it might not be found in opening up to you, who are professional men, technicians, the heart of a layman for a little, about your great vocation. Why is it, for illustration, that the founder of this Institute, who is a layman, has done this great thing? The doing of it was not suggested to him by any technician nor by any professional man. The thought itself originated in the heart of a layman, and it has been throughout supported and enlarged by laymen—laymen who think it the most interesting possible theme for study and thought and for the play of imagination. Why is it so?

It is so for one thing, if one stops to think about it just a moment, because the values of research are universal values. Picture in your thought for a moment this round globe on which we live. Trace its hemispheres and its continents. They are all limited and bounded by their shores, and they are inhabited by nations which have their own fixed boundaries, and their separate speech, and their unique histories. The nations have their racial antagonisms and their peculiar ideals and their distinctive literatures. There is very little indeed in the world that is universal, common to us all. Authors, the greatest of them, can speak in a single language only and are little heard in other tongues.

Statesmen and generals are confined in their influence to single nations, the empire of kings is limited. But here is an institution or in this medical research is a work whose value touches the life of every man that lives. Think of that! Is there not something within us, an instinct of humanity, which cannot be fenced in by the boundaries of a merely national patriotism, a sympathy which transcends national boundaries and which finds complete expression only when it identifies us with all humanity? Who has not felt the throbbing of desire to be useful to the whole wide world? Here at least is a work for all humanity, which fully satisfies and fills that glorious aspiration.

I do not exaggerate. This work is as universal in its values as the atmosphere which surrounds the globe and presses down with fifteen pounds of weight on every square inch of it, a work whose values go to the palace of the rich and the hovel of the poor, a work alike for the babe in the cradle and for tottering age, a work which penetrates everywhere. The discoveries of this Institute have already reached the depths of Africa with their healing ministrations. You announce a discovery here. Before night your discovery will be flashed around the world. In thirty days it will be in every medical college on earth. In sixty days it will be at the bedsides of the best hospitals, and from those hospitals it will work its way to every sick room in the world that is visited by a competent physician. Universal diffusion may sometimes take years, but with the progress of civilization and the deeper wearing of present grooves, diffusion will come more rapidly. So your work in the scope of its values is as universal as the love of God.

I say as universal in its scope as the love of God. I add, and as beneficial in its purpose. Mere universality would not, of course, be of itself very significant. Disease, too, is universal. But this is a healing ministration, to prevent or destroy disease. It is rescue from disease, and so it is the most intimate, the most precious, the superlative interest of every man that lives. It touches his health, his life, and the lives of his most dearly beloved. It does not affect the mere externals of life, the appointments, the circumstances, the business, the accomplishments of life. Your vocation goes to the foundations of life itself. It deals with the innermost heart of every man that lives. It deals with his life and its well being. For what is health? Health is happiness; health itself is happiness. God has so made us in His beneficence that man when he is in perfect health, with all his functions working perfectly and in harmony, cannot but be happy in the mere exercise of the functions of abounding health. Look at a child, in the exuberance of its health. It has no great thoughts. It can read no great books. It has no mighty enterprise to fill its life and inflame its imagination. It cannot be thrilled with eloquence, with art, or with music. It is just healthy, and being in perfect health it is radiantly happy in the unconscious exercises of its beneficent functions.

So the values of medical research are the most universal values on earth, and they are the most intimate and important values to every human being that lives. Why, then, should it not be the most interesting thing in the world to us and to all men?

And then think of its permanency as well! You work not for today, but for ever; not for this generation, but for every generation of humanity that shall come after you. Thus your work is multiplied by infinity. Has it not often occurred to us that after all science is about the only thing that is destined to live forever in this world? Humanity in its progress, moving forward majestically from age to age, carries with it, nevertheless, just as little useless baggage as is possible. The generations as they succeed each other take from the past and hand on to the future only the things that are proven to be permanently useful. The useless thing is thrown into the limbo of oblivion and left behind, whether it be the history of kings or empires, whether it be literatures or inventions, philosophies or religions—all go as soon as they are proved to be useless. But there is one thing that humanity has always got to live with, and that is old Nature and her laws in this world. Whatever you learn about nature and her forces and prove and incorporate into your science will be carried forward, though all else be forgotten. Humanity, as I said, must always live in this world with her forces and their reactions on mankind. These forces are not going to change. Humanity cannot afford to leave your work behind, whatever else it leaves behind. Humanity must carry it forward; and it will. What you do can never be lost.

I hesitate to speak of another thing that makes this Institute highly interesting to me, because you will say that this, at least, is a more personal idiosyncrasy. You will say that it is a reminiscence of the days when I was a minister, interested in theology. You will smile if I say to you that I often think of this Institute as a theological seminary, presided over by the Rev. Simon Flexner, D.D. [Doctor of Divinity] (Laughter and applause) But I tell you, friends, if there be over us all the Sum of ALL and that Sum conscious—a Conscious, Intelligent Being, and that Being has any favorites on this little planet, I must believe that those favorites are made up of that ever enlarging group of men and women who are most intimately and in very truth studying him and his ways with man. That is your work. To you He is whispering His secrets. To you He is opening up the mysterious depths of His Being. There have been times when as I looked through your microscopes, I have been stricken with speechless awe. I felt that I was gazing with unhallowed eyes into the secret places of the Most High. I say if God looks down on this world and has any favorites, it must be the men who are studying Him, who are working every day, with limited intelligence and in the darkness—for clouds and darkness are round about Him—and feeling their way into His heart.

You smiled just now when I spoke of our honored guest as the Rev. Simon Flexner, D.D. Why did you smile? Friends, it was only because your ideas of religion are the traditional and ecclesiastical ideas of the past, but I am now talking about the religion, not of the past, but of the future, and I tell you that as this medical research goes on you will find out and promulgate as an unforeseen by-product of your work new moral laws and new social laws, new definitions of what is right and wrong in our relations with each other. You will educate the human conscience in new directions and new duties. You will make it sensitive to new distinctions. You will teach nobler conceptions of our social relations and of the God who is over us all. You may be doing work here far more important than you dream for the ethics and the religion of the future. Theology is already being reconstructed in the light of science, in the light of what you and others are doing in research, and that reconstruction is one of the most important of the services which scientific research is performing for humanity.

These, then, are some of the ways in which a layman looks at your work. What I have said thus far applies to all medical research; but let me now speak a word in conclusion more particularly of our own Institute. I have the advantage of some of you. You look over yonder at those splendid buildings—soon to be more splendid and more numerous—and think of them as forming the Institute. They and the workers there, which are in fact the Institute, limit your conceptions of it. But I had the good fortune to be in at an earlier day. I am acquainted with what I may call the prenatal history of the Institute, when there were no buildings and when none of you had ever seen each other or dreamed of being here. I remember the time when the Institute existed simply as a dream in the minds of Mr. Rockefeller and his staff, unknown to all the world outside of his office . . . [L]et me tell you just a word about that. We did not know anything of any of you. We had never heard of Dr. Flexner. I, at least, had never heard of Dr. [William H.] Welch [reforming dean of the Johns Hopkins University School of Medicine and founding Chair of the Board of the Rockefeller Institute]. We knew very little indeed about medicine, but some few things, after all, we did know for certain. Down there at the office we had read Dr. [William] Osler's "Principles and Practice of Medicine." We did have a dim idea as to what it meant, for we had read it with a medical dictionary at our side. We did intelligently and clearly see that there was a tremendous need of medical research. We knew that Pasteur had put forth and established the germ theory of disease. We knew that at that time some half dozen or dozen of the disease germs had been isolated. We knew that there were one or two specifics, and we also knew that there were sixty or seventy more diseases that were certainly germ diseases of which the germs had not been yet even discovered. We knew that they must be discovered; we knew that specifics must be found for them all.

As we reflected upon the situation our horizon enlarged. It dawned upon us with tremendous power that Pasteur had discovered a new hemisphere, that he was a new Columbus, and that as certainly as Columbus he had opened up nothing less than a new era for the whole human race. We saw that the duty of thoughtful and intelligent men was fully to explore and open up that continent which Pasteur had discovered. That is what we saw. It did not take much imagination to see that, and we could guess a good deal, too, even with our lay minds.

We could guess that that continent had great river systems, and if exploration could only discover the mouths of those rivers science could work her way along up these rivers, finding tributary rivers and rivulets and rills, forming the controlling, the fundamental principles of the science of medicine, and that we could through these rivers and their tributaries probably explore considerable areas of country, with its fauna and its flora. We could easily guess that there would be found great continental divides, with their lofty mountain ranges, like the Alleghenies and the Rockies, and that these mountain ranges would have passes that human curiosity would thread, or that the great ranges would ultimately be tunneled, with immense labor and cost. We knew also that the old continent, the old world of medicine, was after all very little known, that until very late times little accurate scientific exploration had been done in any department of medicine. Or, turning directly to the human body, we then knew that there was a very considerable number of rooms in this wondrous palace in which we live, into which the healing hand of the surgeon had never yet been admitted, rooms which had never been unlocked to the human eye, and we dared even to guess that Carrels[1] and Meltzers and others might arise who would open up the human system to surgery in its every room.

And now to carry forward my figure. Just as after Columbus had discovered the new continent, all the more civilized and enterprising nations began to send exploring expeditions thither, so we thought that all the nations, and particularly America, should fit out ships and send out exploring expeditions into this new continent of medicine and into the old one as well. As so we fitted out our ship and put Captain Flexner on board (laughter).

But I want to say here for your comfort, or more likely for your amusement, that we did not cherish any extravagant dreams. I want to assure you that not only did we think, but we actually said—s-a-i-d, said—to each other that very likely this Institute would never discover a single important medical fact. I say that we said it to each other, out loud; in fact, we wrote it down. But we also said that even if we knew for certain that our enterprise would never add anything to medical knowledge, we would nevertheless do this thing. Why? In the first place, because we believed that the mere announcement of the establishment of this Institute, the bringing together of the faculty, the conducting of the work, would call public attention to the importance of research, and that very likely many thoughtful men of wealth would think it a good thing for them to start out in the same line on their own account, and that as a result there would probably be added to the various medical schools of the country departments of investigation and research, suitably endowed; and that a good many families of

---

1. Alexis Carrel was a French surgeon and biologist associated with the Rockefeller Institute from 1906 to 1939. A Nobel prize winner, Carrel is even better known as the author of the bestselling book "Man the Unknown" (*L'homme, cet inconnu*, 1935), in which he advocates eugenics and the use of gas chambers to "euthanize" criminals and the criminally insane.—Ed.

wealth, having had grievous experience with some particular mysterious or fatal trouble, would endow research for that particular disease. We foresaw that much and foresaw, as we all now know, quite truly. Ten years have passed, and already there are many departments of research, many great and splendid funds for research. They are springing up on every side. Our conclusion was correct, that if our particular baby never amounted to anything we might reasonably count on many others, and that among them all there would be great discoveries, and medical science would be notably advanced.

We were right about that, but we never dreamed in the highest flights of our imagination of the brilliant results which you have attained. We never dreamed that within ten years would be gathered here a group of men who would have discovered fundamental medical facts hitherto unguessed, that would form a galaxy of fixed stars in the firmament forever. Never did we dream it. But such is now the fact. We have lived to see men coming here practically unknown and rising in this brief time to imperishable fame; renown as imperishable as the stars. Their names will be associated with the history of medicine as long as medical history is written. We have lived to see the time when kings and emperors, great societies and foreign institutions, have vied with each other to honor themselves by honoring you. If you had made only one of the many important discoveries that are credited to the Institute, I can say to you from the founder tonight and from the men who have been associated with him, that he would feel and all would feel abundantly repaid for every dollar of money and every moment of thought that has ever been put into this institution, though it were never to achieve anything else.

I cannot forbear a brief mention of a great moral value that medical research is conferring. The time was—we can all remember it—when medicine was under such difficulties and in such darkness that the enthusiastic young men who committed themselves to medicine pretty soon found themselves, too many of them, in one of two categories, either confirmed pessimist, disappointed and chagrined, or else mere reckless pill slingers for money. This Institute and others like it have conferred dignity and glory upon medicine. They have awakened the medical profession to a proud and healthy consciousness of the dignity of their vocation. They have created or are creating out of the chaos of the past a true science of medicine. They are giving to every physician a new sense of pride and dignity in his calling. They are making him realize that his life is devoted to a great science, that he himself may be and ought to be an observer, a close and reverent student at the bedside of the sick, that it is possible for him to heal and that he has a great and worthy function in life. The elevation of the medical profession, the high character of the young men who are now being drawn into it because it is becoming a science, the dignity that this work of research is giving to the medical profession—that, of itself, if research had nothing else to offer, would be a most worthy result.

I conclude with a single word, but for that word I have said all the other words. That word is this: The spirit of this great Institute, the inspiration of it, the directing force of it, that spirit which, more than any other single agency, has wrought these great and beneficent results, is an embodied spirit. It has a local habitation and a name, and that name is Simon Flexner.

We are met together primarily to speak of the honored guest of the evening, but I am sure you will join with me and sympathize with my feeling if I preface what I say with an appreciative word of the founder. It has been my privilege for more than twenty years to be associated with the founder personally, in some of those years very intimately associated; and those years of intimate personal relationship have wrought in me an ever increasing appreciation and reverence for the greatness of his character and the nobility of his aims. He is not given to display of any kind, least of all to exploiting of himself, but, ladies and gentlemen, Mr. Rockefeller is a very great man. He has not one only, but many great titles to distinction, and that world wide. He has broken several world records; they are not likely to be broken again. If he were placed in a group of say twenty of the greatest men of affairs of today, he would be the most modest, retiring, and deferential man of them all, but before these giants had been with him for long, the most self-confident, self-assertive of them would be coming to him in private for his counsel. He has done many things which entitle him to the reverence and gratitude of the generation in which he lives, and that reverence and that gratitude, I am glad to say, is beginning to be shown in increasing volume. But he is one of the few great men, I am persuaded, whose fame will increase with the years instead of diminishing. His renown will be greater in future generations than it is in this, as the world in retrospect comes to know the value of his services. Among many titles to the gratitude of posterity, I count his worthiest title, the title that will carry his name widest over the earth and deepest into the future, to be the founding of this Institute for Medical Research.

Reprinted in *Making the Nonprofit Sector in the United States,* edited by David C. Hammack (Bloomington: Indiana University Press, 1998), pp. 321–328.

POPE BENEDICT XVI

From Deus Caritas Est *("God Is Love")*

Deus Caritas Est *("God Is Love") is the first encyclical, or pastoral letter, of Pope Benedict XVI. In the second half of the document, excerpted below, the Pope considers the meaning and importance of Christian charity, or caritas. The word "caritas" is sometimes translated as "charity," other times as "love," thereby reminding us, as the Pope does, of the relation between charitable giving and charitable disposition. Charity, he insists, is essentially an expression of love, not primarily an instrument of social justice, as politics should be, or an outcomes-oriented service provider. He downplays the need for professional expertise and highlights the need for humanity and heartfelt concern. Though people require material aid, often a more important service of charity is "refreshment and care for their souls." As the Pope states so simply, "man needs, and will always need, love."*

Drawing the lessons from the Pope's encyclical, one commentator pointedly indicated its challenge to contemporary mainstream philanthropy:

> *There is no substitute for the rich diversity of charitable activities and agencies that is a defining characteristic and glory of American society, and there is no substitute for the personal giving and volunteering that the social critic Alexis de Tocqueville (a Catholic layman) recognized as the engine of charitable activism in the United States. Giving ourselves to others in works of charity is important for the giver as well as the receiver. Retail charity at the personal level is crucial for the individual and crucial for society. It can't be replaced by a wholesale form of philanthropy that, aiming to change 'unjust social structures,' often ends up turning men and women into mere numbers.[1]*

Is this challenge justified? If so, can the purpose of charity, as the Pope understands it, have any real relevance to the purposes of organized philanthropy today? Can love serve as a guide for philanthropy as it seeks to meet the enormous challenges ahead?

Justice and Charity

Since the nineteenth century, an objection has been raised to the Church's charitable activity, subsequently developed with particular insistence by Marxism: the poor, it is claimed, do not need charity but justice. Works of charity—almsgiving—are in effect a way for the rich to shirk their obligation to work for

---

1. George Weigel, "The Blessings of Charity: A Papal Challenge to Conventional Wisdom," *Philanthropy Magazine* (March 2006).

justice and a means of soothing their consciences, while preserving their own status and robbing the poor of their rights. Instead of contributing through individual works of charity to maintaining the status quo, we need to build a just social order in which all receive their share of the world's goods and no longer have to depend on charity. There is admittedly some truth to this argument, but also much that is mistaken. It is true that the pursuit of justice must be a fundamental norm of the State and that the aim of a just social order is to guarantee to each person, according to the principle of subsidiarity,[2] his share of the community's goods. This has always been emphasized by Christian teaching on the State and by the Church's social doctrine. . . .

[But t]he Church cannot and must not take upon herself the political battle to bring about the most just society possible. She cannot and must not replace the State. Yet at the same time she cannot and must not remain on the sidelines in the fight for justice. She has to play her part through rational argument and she has to reawaken the spiritual energy without which justice, which always demands sacrifice, cannot prevail and prosper. A just society must be the achievement of politics, not of the Church. Yet the promotion of justice through efforts to bring about openness of mind and will to the demands of the common good is something which concerns the Church deeply.

Love—*caritas*—will always prove necessary, even in the most just society. There is no ordering of the State so just that it can eliminate the need for a service of love. Whoever wants to eliminate love is preparing to eliminate man as such. There will always be suffering which cries out for consolation and help. There will always be loneliness. There will always be situations of material need where help in the form of concrete love of neighbor is indispensable. The State which would provide everything, absorbing everything into itself, would ultimately become a mere bureaucracy incapable of guaranteeing the very thing which the suffering person—every person—needs: namely, loving personal concern. We do not need a State which regulates and controls everything, but a State which, in accordance with the principle of subsidiarity, generously acknowledges and supports initiatives arising from the different social forces and combines spontaneity with closeness to those in need. The Church is one of those living forces: she is alive with the love enkindled by the Spirit of Christ. This love does not simply offer people material help, but refreshment and care for their souls, something which often is even more necessary than material support. In the end, the claim that just social structures would make works of charity superfluous masks a materialist conception of man: the mistaken notion that man can live "by bread alone" (*Mt* 4:4; cf. *Dt* 8:3)—a conviction that demeans man and ultimately disregards all that is specifically human.

---

2. The principle of subsidiarity holds that government should undertake only those initiatives which exceed the capacity of individuals or private groups.—Ed.

We can now determine more precisely, in the life of the Church, the relationship between commitment to the just ordering of the State and society on the one hand, and organized charitable activity on the other. We have seen that the formation of just structures is not directly the duty of the Church, but belongs to the world of politics, the sphere of the autonomous use of reason. The Church has an indirect duty here, in that she is called to contribute to the purification of reason and to the reawakening of those moral forces without which just structures are neither established nor prove effective in the long run.

The direct duty to work for a just ordering of society, on the other hand, is proper to the lay faithful. As citizens of the State, they are called to take part in public life in a personal capacity. So they cannot relinquish their participation "in the many different economic, social, legislative, administrative and cultural areas, which are intended to promote organically and institutionally the *common good*." The mission of the lay faithful is therefore to configure social life correctly, respecting its legitimate autonomy and cooperating with other citizens according to their respective competences and fulfilling their own responsibility. Even if the specific expressions of ecclesial charity can never be confused with the activity of the State, it still remains true that charity must animate the entire lives of the lay faithful and therefore also their political activity, lived as "social charity."

The Church's charitable organizations, on the other hand, constitute an *opus proprium,* a task agreeable to her, in which she does not cooperate collaterally, but acts as a subject with direct responsibility, doing what corresponds to her nature. The Church can never be exempted from practicing charity as an organized activity of believers, and on the other hand, there will never be a situation where the charity of each individual Christian is unnecessary, because in addition to justice man needs, and will always need, love. . . .

The Distinctiveness of the Church's Charitable Activity

. . . [I]t is very important that the Church's charitable activity maintains all of its splendor and does not become just another form of social assistance. So what are the essential elements of Christian and ecclesial charity?

Following the example given in the parable of the Good Samaritan, Christian charity is first of all the simple response to immediate needs and specific situations: feeding the hungry, clothing the naked, caring for and healing the sick, visiting those in prison, etc. The Church's charitable organizations, beginning with those of *Caritas* (at diocesan, national and international levels), ought to do everything in their power to provide the resources and above all the personnel needed for this work. Individuals who care for those in need must first be professionally competent: they should be properly trained in what to do and how to do it, and committed to continuing care. Yet, while professional competence is a primary, fundamental requirement, it is not of itself sufficient. We are dealing with human beings, and human beings always need something more than technically proper care. They need humanity. They need heartfelt concern. Those who work for the Church's charitable organizations must be distinguished by the fact that they do not merely meet the needs of the moment, but they dedicate themselves to others with heartfelt concern, enabling them to experience the richness of their humanity. Consequently, in addition to their necessary professional training, these charity workers need a "formation of the heart": they need to be led to that encounter with God in Christ which awakens their love and opens their spirits to others. As a result, love of neighbor will no longer be for them a commandment imposed, so to speak, from without, but a consequence deriving from their faith, a faith which becomes active through love (cf. *Gal* 5:6).

Christian charitable activity must be independent of parties and ideologies. It is not a means of changing the world ideologically, and it is not at the service of worldly stratagems, but it is a way of making present here and now the love which man always needs. The modern age, particularly from the nineteenth century on, has been dominated by various versions of a philosophy of progress whose most radical form is Marxism. Part of Marxist strategy is the theory of impoverishment: in a situation of unjust power, it is claimed, anyone who engages in charitable initiatives is actually serving that unjust system, making it appear at least to some extent tolerable. This in turn slows down a potential revolution and thus blocks the struggle for a better world. Seen in this way, charity is rejected and attacked as a means of preserving the *status quo*. What we have here, though, is really an inhuman philosophy. People of the present are sacrificed to the *moloch* of the future—a future whose effective realization is at best doubtful. One does not make the world more human by refusing to act humanely here and now. We contribute to a better world only by personally doing good now, with full commitment and wherever we have the opportunity, independently of partisan strategies and programs. The Christian's program—the program of the Good Samaritan, the program of Jesus—is "a heart which sees." This heart sees where love is needed and acts accordingly. Obviously when charitable activity is carried out by the Church as a communitarian initiative, the spontaneity of individuals must be combined with planning, foresight and cooperation with other similar institutions.

Charity, furthermore, cannot be used as a means of engaging in what is nowadays considered proselytism. Love is free; it is not practiced as a way of achieving other ends. But this does not mean that charitable activity must somehow leave God and Christ aside. For it is always concerned with the whole man. Often the deepest cause of suffering is the very absence of God. Those who practice charity in the Church's name will never seek to impose the Church's faith upon others. They realize that a pure and generous love is the best witness to the God in whom we believe and by whom we are driven to love. A Christian knows when it is time to speak of God and when it is better to say nothing and to let love alone speak. He knows that God is love (cf. *1 Jn* 4:8) and that God's presence is felt at the very time when the only thing we do is to love. He knows—to return to the questions raised earlier—that disdain for love is disdain for God and man alike; it is an attempt to do without God. Consequently, the best defense of God and man consists precisely in love. It is the responsibility of the Church's charitable organizations to reinforce this awareness in their members, so that by their activity—as well as their words, their silence, their example—they may be credible witnesses to Christ.

. . . Saint Paul, in his hymn to charity (cf. *1 Cor* 13), teaches us that it is always more than activity alone: "If I give away all I have, and if I deliver my body to be burned, but do not have love, I gain nothing" (v. 3). This hymn must be the *Magna Carta* of all ecclesial service; it sums up all the reflections on love which I have offered throughout this Encyclical Letter. Practical activity will always be insufficient, unless it visibly expresses a love for man, a love nourished by an encounter with Christ. My deep personal sharing in the needs and sufferings of others becomes a sharing of my very self with them: if my gift is not to prove a source of humiliation, I must give to others not only something that is my own, but my very self; I must be personally present in my gift.

BRUCE COLE

"The Urgency of Memory"

In one of his earliest public speeches, the Lyceum Address, Abraham Lincoln took as his subject the perpetuation of our political institutions. Delivered in 1838, a time of civil unrest and impending crisis, Lincoln was most immediately concerned about the rash of violent actions, perpetrated by unruly mobs, which was spreading through much of the country. But his greater concern was the difficulty in safeguarding our free institutions, now that the burden of preserving them had fallen to a generation that did not create them. Lincoln worried about the future of our way of life once the powerful influence of still living memories— of the American Revolution—faded with the people and circumstances that produced and experienced them. As he noted, "the silent artillery of time" would do "what invading foemen could never do."

In this selection, Bruce Cole, art historian and current chairman of the National Endowment for the Humanities, harkens back to Lincoln's theme. Taking his bearings from the events of September 11, 2001, he focuses on our urgent need to preserve civic and cultural institutions and especially to arm ourselves against the dangers of "American amnesia." And he points to the ways in which the humanities—arts and letters—and, in particular, his government agency, can help. Private philanthropy has long been active in conservation efforts to preserve nature and the environment, as well as in efforts to endow and preserve certain cultural institutions—museums, operas, orchestras, and the like. Should it also address Lincoln's and Cole's concerns? Is this too broad a reach for conservation-minded philanthropy?

Good morning. It is an honor and pleasure to be here today.

It's been said that a picture is worth a thousand words; as an art historian, I ardently believe this is true. And so I freely confess that nothing I say here today is as meaningful, as momentous, or as memorable as the sight of what lies nearby. We are on hallowed ground.

The magnitude of the horrific events of September 11 is still being realized, the aftershocks still felt. But even in an age of uncertainty there are truths to be discovered, lessons to discern, and hope to share.

Today, I'd like to talk to you about the centrality of the humanities to democratic and civic life; the danger of American amnesia; and the possibilities of recovering our memory and protecting the best of our culture.

Importance of the Humanities

In times of crisis, the humanities and the arts are often praised as sources of consolation, comfort, expression, and insight, but rarely seen as essential, or even high priorities. But they are much more than that. Indeed, the humanities help form the bedrock of civic understanding and civil order.

The range of the humanities disciplines is wide; their impact deep. The classics and archeology show us from whence our civilization came. The study of literature and art shape our sense of beauty. The knowledge of philosophy and religion give meaning to our concepts of justice and goodness.

The NEH was founded in the belief that cultivating the best of the humanities had real, tangible benefits for civic life. Our founding legislation declares that "democracy demands wisdom." America must have educated and thoughtful citizens who can fully and intelligently participate in our government of, by, and for the people. The NEH exists to foster the wisdom and knowledge essential to our national identity and survival.

Indeed, the state of the humanities has real implications for the state of our union. Our nation is in a conflict driven by religion, philosophy, political ideology, and views of history—all humanities subjects.

Our tolerance, our principles, our wealth, and our liberties have made us targets. To understand this conflict, we need the humanities.

The values implicit in the study of the humanities are part of why we were attacked. The free and fearless exchange of ideas, respect for individual conscience, belief in the power of education . . . all these things are anathema to our country's enemies. Understanding and affirming these principles is part of the battle.

The attack on September 11 targeted not only innocent civilians, but also the fabric of our culture. The terrorists struck the Twin Towers and the Pentagon, and aimed at either the White House or Capitol dome—all structures rich in meaning, and bearing witness to the United States' free commerce, military strength, and democratic government. As such, they also housed many of the artifacts—the manuscripts, art, and archives—that form our history and heritage.

In the weeks following the attack, the NEH awarded a grant to Heritage Preservation, an organization which conducted a survey of the damage to our cultural holdings. They found that the attack obliterated numerous art collections of great worth. Cantor Fitzgerald's renowned "museum in the sky" is lost, as well as priceless works by Rodin, Picasso, Hockney, Lichtenstein, Corbusier, Miro, and others. Archaeological artifacts from the African Burial Ground and other Manhattan sites are gone forever, as are irreplaceable records from the Helen Keller archives. Artists perished alongside their artifacts. Sculptor Michael Richards died as he worked in his studio on the 92nd floor of Tower One. His last work, now lost, was a statue commemorating the Tuskegee Airmen of World War II.

Of course, the loss of artifacts and art, no matter how priceless and precious, is dwarfed by the loss of life. Each life that was snuffed out that day was itself a work of art and a historical record. Each person who died on September 11 meant the world to others. I often fear that the scholarly tendency to over-theorize under-estimates the importance of the individual. One of the clearest lessons of that awful day is that individuals matter—their decisions, their courage, their sacrifices, their hopes, their lives. They—not theories—are the stuff of history.

Today, it is all the more urgent that we study American institutions, culture, and history. There is much we have lost, but there is much we have learned. Defending our democracy demands more than successful military campaigns. It also requires an understanding of the ideals, ideas and institutions that have shaped our country.

This is not a new concept. America's founders recognized the importance of an informed and educated citizenry as necessary for the survival of our participatory democracy. James Madison famously said, "the diffusion of knowledge is the only true guardian of liberty." The humanities tell us who we are as a people and why our country is worth fighting for.

They are part of our homeland defense.

Dangers of Amnesia

All great principles and institutions face challenges, and the wisdom of the humanities, and the principles of democratic self-government, are not immune. We are standing along the periphery of a horrendous attack from without on our way of life and government. But we face a serious challenge to our country that lies within our borders—and even within our schools: the threat of American Amnesia.

One of the common threads of great civilizations is the cultivation of memory, Lincoln's "mystic chords of memory, stretching from battlefield and patriot grave to every living heart and hearthstone all over this great land." Many of the great works of antiquity are transliterated from oral traditions. From Homer to *Beowulf,* such tales trained people to remember their heritage and history through story and song, and passed those stories and songs throughout generations. Old Testament stories repeatedly depict prophets and priests encouraging people to remember, to "write on their hearts" the events, circumstances, and stories that make up their history.

We are in danger of forgetting this lesson. For years, even decades, polls, tests and studies have shown that Americans do not know their history, and cannot remember even the most significant events of the 20th century.

Of course, we are a forward-looking people. We are more concerned with what happens tomorrow than what happened yesterday.

But we are in danger of having our view of the future obscured by our ignorance of the past. We cannot see clearly ahead if we are blind to history.

Unfortunately, most indicators point to a worsening of our case of American amnesia.

I'll give just a few examples. One study of students at 55 elite universities found that over a third were unable to identify the Constitution as establishing the division of powers in our government, only 29 percent could identify the term "Reconstruction," and 40 percent could not place the Civil War in the correct half-century.

The recent National Assessment of Education Progress test found that over half of high school seniors couldn't say who we fought in World War II. And lest you think I'm picking on students—and hey, I'm a former professor—a nationwide survey recently commissioned by Columbia Law School found that almost two-thirds of all Americans think Karl Marx's dogma, "From each according to his ability, to each according to his needs," was or may have been written by the founding fathers and was included in the Constitution.

Such collective amnesia is dangerous. Citizens kept ignorant of their history are robbed of the riches of their heritage, and handicapped in their ability to understand and appreciate other cultures.

If Americans cannot recall whom we fought, and whom we fought along-side, during World War II, it should not be assumed that they will long remember what happened here on September 11.

And a nation that does not know why it exists, or what it stands for, cannot be expected to long endure. We must recover from the amnesia that shrouds our history in darkness, our principles in confusion, and our future in uncertainty.

Recovering Our Memory

Our nation's future depends on how we meet these challenges. We all have a stake, and a role to play, in recovering America's memory. There are several things we can do to alleviate our serious case of American amnesia.

At the NEH, we have recommitted ourselves to the core functions of the agency, including the preservation, protection, and exhibition of historical and cultural artifacts. We reaffirmed the central role of scholarship in all our activities.

We believe an important part of the NEH's role is to ensure the survival of seemingly obscure knowledge. Scholarly editions, Presidential papers, preserved copies of historic newspapers, and lexicons of ancient tongues all deserve—and will receive—the same enthusiastic support we give to television documentaries seen by millions.

We are also preparing to launch a new initiative to bolster the study and understanding of American history. In the coming months and years, I want the NEH to help lead a renaissance in knowledge about our history and culture. Understanding ourselves is the first step to understanding our place in the world.

In this age of uncertainty, we can draw from the humanities' deep well of wisdom. For perspective, guidance, and even consolation, we can look to arts and letters.

But these resources are not available to everyone. Too many Americans, especially young people, have been deprived of the tools of citizenship and the building blocks of the good and examined life.

This is a challenge we need to meet and best. We cannot expect that a nation which has lost its memory will keep its vision. We cannot hope that forgetting the past will enhance our focus on the future. And we cannot neglect the great democratic imperative: to give each succeeding generation a brighter light, a broader perspective, and an enriched legacy with which to face the future.

A speech delivered at the Art in an Age of Uncertainty conference, New York University, June 7, 2002.

TWO

Gifts, Donors, Recipients; Grants, Grantors, Grantees

Richard Cavanagh, former Executive Dean of Harvard University's John F. Kennedy School of Government, reports having noted upon his arrival a category in its accounting system called "Gifts, Grants, Contracts." Bewildered, he turned to Harvard's head of finance for illumination. "What are these? What is the difference among them?" he asked. He received the following explanation: "A contract is something where you have to perform in order to get that particular pot of money. A grant is something where you have to perform if you ever hope to get another grant. And a gift is something where you make a best effort to perform so long as the donor is alive." This description, however humorous, is endorsed by others well beyond Harvard's groves. But while the differences may pale by comparison with the similarities—money is money is money, and performance is necessary regardless—for most people in philanthropy today the differences are real. More important, they have consequences for the relations between givers and receivers. If such relations are to be improved, philanthropic leaders argue, we need to clarify and deepen our understanding of the very thing that passes between us. This chapter is a response to that demand.

Philanthropy's various traditions and practices have spawned a far more variegated vocabulary than any accounting system, or chapter heading, can handle: On the one side, in addition to givers or grantors, there are donors, funders, and benefactors, to name a few; on the other, there are receivers, grantees, donees, fundraisers, and beneficiaries. And the "coin" that passes between them, although usually referred to as gifts, grants, or contracts, has multiple additional names: donations, bequests, benefactions, covenants, investments, sponsorships, and disbursements head the list but don't exhaust it. To some degree, overlapping usage discourages stringent distinctions and definitions. Yet the terms we use and, even more, our awareness of the meaning and expectations we ascribe to them, can reveal—and may invite revision of—our fundamental attitudes and assumptions about the philanthropic process and its actors.

The readings collected in this chapter invite this sort of scrutiny. Grouped under two closely related but separable topics, we begin with those that address the question:

What is the meaning of a grant or gift?

Our first two selections, by Aristotle, "On Benefactors and Beneficiaries," and from Seneca, *De Beneficiis* ("On Benefits"), prompt us to think about the "coin" of the philanthropic realm, and hence about all philanthropic practice, in terms long ignored, namely, as "benefactions" or "benefits," or literally, as "good deeds."

The next readings draw on more contemporary usage, yet challenge familiar understandings. Craig Dykstra's essay on "What Is a Grant?" considers the meaning of a grant by comparing it to investments and gifts. S. I. Hayakawa's "The Story of A-Town and B-ville" asks us to reflect on competing vocabularies as competing ideologies, while "A Hand Up, Not a Handout" by Muhammad Yunus challenges the ideology of charity itself.

Last in this grouping, George Moore's story "Alms-Giving" presents the charitable exchange in its simplest form—as a decision to give. While the story's protagonist is pulled in different directions by his heart and his head, his choice is ultimately informed mainly by the relationship he establishes with his recipient, not by prior understanding of the thing that is passed between them. The story thus points directly to our next topical grouping:

What sorts of relationships and obligations does a grant/gift imply for givers and receivers?

Maimonides' "Eight Levels of *Tzedakah* (Giving)" offers a hierarchically arranged catalogue of possible donor-recipient relations, which invites us not only to locate ourselves on his "ladder" but also to defend the position(s) we occupy.

In "Gift and Gratitude in Ethics," Paul F. Camenisch states that gifts and gift-giving entail moral imperatives, prompting us to reflect on whether our own giving relations are in fact freighted with "rights and duties, benefits and costs."

Arna Bontemps' short story "Woman with a Mission" reveals how receiving benefits can incur heavy costs, and invites reconsideration of the virtues and vices of more explicitly contractual relations. By contrast, Bruce Holland Rogers' light-hearted story "A Patron of the Arts" reminds us of the joys—and risks—of the personal philanthropic relation, especially when pursued imaginatively with a sense of wonder and adventure.

Jacques Barzun's "The Folklore of Philanthropy" examines the more mediated relationships between foundations and their grantees, holds up to light common practices that exacerbate tensions, and offers radical proposals for reform—for example, doing away with grant applications altogether. Pablo Eisenberg shares many of Barzun's concerns but, in "Penetrating the Mystique of Philanthropy: Relations between Fund Raisers and Grant Makers," turns his attention to the reform of "the receiving end" of grantmaking—why it is necessary and what it will take.

Psychiatrist Roy W. Menninger's essay "Foundation Work May Be Hazardous to Your Mental Health" addresses the psychological pitfalls—the "occupational dangers"—of giving, asking for, and receiving money. The following short story, Henri Barbusse's "The Eleventh," gives us a good glimpse of such "occupational dangers" through the eyes of a fresh recruit to philanthropic practice.

The next two readings highlight, in more political than personal terms, the relations between the rich and poor. The excerpt from Alexis de Tocqueville's *Memoir on Pauperism* considers the relationship created by "individual almsgiving" in contrast to "legal [or, government] charity," and argues in favor of individualized practice. By contrast, in the short excerpt from *The Rights of Man,* Thomas Paine asserts that a just society will make support of the poor a matter of right, not one of "grace and favor."

Finally, in "Foundation Grants and the Grantor/Grantee Relationship," Sara Engelhardt looks at recent trends in grantee selection and their implications for grantor/grantee partnerships.

ARISTOTLE

"On Benefactors and Beneficiaries"

In this brief but rich selection, Greek philosopher Aristotle (384–322 BC) takes up the relation between benefactors (literally, good-doers) and beneficiaries. Excerpted from his Nicomachean Ethics, *it appears in the context of his discussion of friendship and its relation to self-love. Why, Aristotle wonders, do benefactors seem to love their beneficiaries more than the reverse? In answering, he offers two competing analogies: the relation between creditors and debtors and that between craftsmen and their crafted products (or poets and their poems). Most people, he suggests, think that benefactors are like creditors, whose concern for their debtors stems from their desire to be repaid. But, he argues, they are more like craftsmen or poets, for their beneficiaries, like the craftsman's products or poet's poems, both make manifest and embody their work (or deed or activity) as benefactors. Hence, the benefactor lives in the recipient. Though benefaction may take the form, for example, of giving money, its full meaning lies not in the object given but in the act of benefaction itself. For the benefactor to expect something in return would be tantamount to transforming an exercise of his generous activity into an impersonal transaction of utilitarian exchange. In addition, Aristotle suggests that the benefactor enjoys the pleasure of nobility, which is more lovable than the pleasure of gain. Is such nobility or virtue alive and well in modern philanthropy? Are our grants or donations more like "loans" or more like "poems"? Do grantors live in their grantees?*

৪১

Benefactors seem to love their beneficiaries more than the beneficiaries love those who have benefited them. As this seems unreasonable, it should be investigated. Now for the majority, the explanation is plain: beneficiaries (like debtors) owe, but benefactors (like creditors) are owed. In the case of loans, debtors wish that their creditors would die, but creditors will even take care of the safety of their debtors. Similarly, so it is thought, benefactors wish their recipients continued existence so that they will receive back favors, whereas the recipients do not care to make a return. Now Epicharmos probably would say that those who say such things are looking at life from the seamy side; but it seems to be human. For the many do not remember kindnesses, but seek rather to receive well than to do well.

But it would seem that the cause is more natural, and, in fact, the case of the benefactor is different from that of the creditor. For creditors feel no affection for their debtors; they wish only for their safety, and then only so that the debts will be paid. In contrast, benefactors love and are fond of those they have treated well, even though they are neither useful to them now nor likely to become so later on.

The same thing also happens with craftsmen; for every craftsman loves his own work more than he might be loved by that work were it to become alive. This is especially true, perhaps, with poets, for they love exceedingly their own poems, loving them as children. This is in fact also the case with the benefactor, for the beneficiary is the work of the benefactor; thus, the benefactor is fond of him more than "the work" [that is, the beneficiary] is of its maker. The cause of this is that being is desirable and loveable for all, and we are most emphatically when we are-at-work, when we are in activity (in living and acting). But any deed is, in a sense, the doer-at-work. So he loves his work, because he also loves being. . . .

At the same time, in addition, the benefactor also has the nobility of his action, so that he rejoices in the person for whom the action was done. For the recipient, however, there is nothing noble in the benefaction, but, at most, something profitable; and the profitable is less pleasant and loveable than the noble. Now for the doer, his deed abides, for the noble is long lasting, but for the recipient, the useful passes away. Pleasant are the activity of the present, the hope of the future, and the memory of the past; but pleasantest is the pleasure of actively being-at-work, and it is similarly also the most loveable. . . .

Moreover, all love more those things that come-to-be laboriously, for example, those making their own wealth love it more than those inheriting it. Yet it seems that receiving-well is trouble-free, whereas doing-well is troublesome. (On account of this, also, mothers love their children more than fathers; for their genesis is more labored for mothers, and they know that they are their own.) It would seem that also this is true of benefactors.

From book IX, chapter 7 of *Nicomachean Ethics* by Aristotle. Translated from Greek by Leon R. Kass.

SENECA

From De Beneficiis *("On Benefits")*

Given the mounting pressures for public accountability and the demand for effectiveness, it is little wonder that many in philanthropy today regard grantmaking as more of a contractual than a gift-giving transaction. For grants understood as contracts allow grantmakers to enforce and monitor specific outcomes. An attractive boon, they claim. Ancient Roman stoic philosopher Seneca (4 BC to 65 AD) thinks otherwise. In his treatise De Beneficiis *("On Benefits"), written as a discussion with his friend Liberalis, Seneca states outright: "The book-keeping of benefits is simple: it is all expenditure." A "benefit," Seneca suggests, is, as its name announces, a "good deed." Although it may take the form of money, credit, a favor, or advice, he argues that its meaning "exists only in the mind" of the giver, that is, in the spirit or intention with which the object is tendered. Are "benefits" closer, then, to gifts than they are to grants? Would—could—grants still be grants if they were so understood? Do we lose benefits in moving towards increasingly enforceable expectations?*

Among the numerous faults of those who pass their lives recklessly and without due reflection, my good friend Liberalis, I should say that there is hardly any one so hurtful to society as this, that we neither know how to bestow or how to receive a benefit. . . . As it is, virtue consists in bestowing benefits for which we are not certain of meeting with any return, but whose fruit is at once enjoyed by noble minds. So little influence ought [the anticipation of return] have in restraining us from doing good actions, that even though I were denied the hope of meeting with a grateful man, yet the fear of not having my benefits returned would not prevent my bestowing them . . .

. . . The book-keeping of benefits is simple: it is all expenditure; if any one returns it, that is clear gain; if he does not return it, it is not lost, I gave it for the sake of giving. No one writes down his gifts in a ledger, or like a grasping creditor demands repayment to the day and hour. A good man never thinks of such matters, unless reminded of them by some one returning his gifts; otherwise they become debts owing to him.

It is a base usury to regard a benefit as an investment. Whatever may have been the result of your former benefits, persevere in bestowing others upon other men; they will be all the better placed in the hands of the ungrateful, whom shame, or a favorable opportunity, or imitation of others may some day cause to be grateful. Do not grow weary, perform your duty and act as becomes a good man. Help one man with money, another with credit, another with your favor; this man with good advice, that one with sound maxims. . . .

. . . These, however, are but the outward signs of kindnesses, not the kindnesses themselves. A benefit is not to be felt and handled, it is a thing which exists only in the mind. There is a great difference between the subject-matter of a benefit, and the benefit itself. Wherefore neither gold, nor silver, nor any of those things which are most highly esteemed, are benefits, but the benefit lies in the goodwill of him who gives them. The ignorant take notice only of that which comes before their eyes, and which can be owned and passed from hand to hand, while they disregard that which gives these things their value. The things which we hold in our hands, which we see with our eyes, and which our avarice hugs, are transitory, they may be taken from us by ill luck or by violence; but a kindness lasts even after the loss of that by means of which it was bestowed; for it is a good deed, which no violence can undo. For instance, suppose that I ransomed a friend from pirates, but another pirate has caught him and thrown him into prison. The pirate has not robbed him of my benefit, but has only robbed him of the enjoyment of it. Or suppose that I have saved a man's children from a shipwreck or a fire, and that afterwards disease or accident has carried them off; even when they are no more, the kindness which was done by means of them remains. All those things, therefore, which improperly assume the name of benefits, are means by which kindly feeling manifests itself. In other cases also, we find a distinction between the visible symbol and the matter itself, as when a general bestows collars of gold, or civic or mural crowns upon any one. What value has the crown in itself? or the purple-bordered robe? or the fasces? or the judgment-seat and car of triumph? None of these things is in itself an honor, but is an emblem of honor. In like manner, that which is seen is not a benefit—it is but the trace and mark of a benefit.

What, then, is a benefit? It is the art of doing a kindness which both bestows pleasure and gains it by bestowing it, and which does its office by natural and spontaneous impulse. It is not, therefore, the thing which is done or given, but the spirit in which it is done or given, that must be considered, because a benefit exists, not in that which is done or given, but in the mind of the doer or giver. How great the distinction between them is, you may perceive from this, that while a benefit is necessarily good, yet that which is done or given is neither good nor bad. The spirit in which they are given can exalt small things, can glorify mean ones, and can discredit great and precious ones; the objects themselves which are sought after have a neutral nature, neither good nor bad; all depends upon the direction given them by the guiding spirit from which things receive their shape. That which is paid or handed over is not the benefit itself, just as the honor which we pay to the gods lies not in the victims themselves, although they be fat and glittering with gold, but in the pure and holy feelings of the worshippers.

From book I of *De Beneficiis* by Seneca. Translated from Latin by Aubrey Stewart.

CRAIG DYKSTRA

"What Is a Grant?"

Craig Dykstra, educator, author, and vice president for religion at Lilly Endow-
ment Inc., here directly addresses the question at hand: What is the meaning of a
grant? Or, in his terms, "What kind of human transaction or engagement is taking
place when a grant is made?" He considers grants by way of contrasting two near
relatives, investments and gifts. An investment is expected to reap a profit for the
investor. A grant, by contrast, creates a "common good asset"—an intellectual, hu-
man, or social "profit" for others. A gift is (or should be) free of expectation—its
meaning lies in its expression of affection or appreciation. Though Dykstra ac-
knowledges that such gift-giving is neither common nor appropriate in grantmak-
ing, still, he argues, a grant "can and should have at least a hint of the character of
a gift." Given in the right spirit, grants "convey appreciation for the grantee's actual
and potential contribution" and recognize "mutual engagement between the
grantor and the grantee in a larger common enterprise and a shared vision of the
good." In passing, Dykstra notes that most grants, unlike gifts, have contracts at-
tached to them, but he avoids suggesting that a grant is a contract. Which, if any,
of these competing vocabularies—grant as investment, gift, contract—would you
use to describe the human transaction that is the making and receiving of a grant?

ℰ

Awhile back, Kathleen Cahalan . . . asked me this question: "What is a grant?"
As evaluation coordinator for the Religion Division [at Lilly Endowment Inc.]
for several years, she had seen a great many grant proposals and met with a
large number of the Endowment's religion grantees. So there had to be something more to her question than the obvious. She was asking, I thought, a
deeper question. Something like, "What kind of human transaction or engagement is taking place when a grant is made?" or "What meaning is involved in
making and receiving a grant?"

An Investment

In the previous issue of this newsletter, I suggested one answer. I said that making a grant is an act of making an investment and linked that term to its Latin
root, "investire," which means to clothe. In this sense, to invest means to protect
something, to clothe it in some way that will help it survive and even thrive.

There is another, more obvious way to talk about a grant as an investment.
When used in the more familiar context of economics, the word investment
refers to the employment of one kind of asset (money, for example) to create
another kind of asset (say, a new business or a home). Some process is always

involved in the transformation of the one kind of asset into the other, a process that always involves work. Money is used by someone to do some kind of work that creates something new that did not exist before.

That, in fact, is a very good description of what foundations are often trying to do when they make grants. They give money to a wide variety of institutions so the people who work in them can create things of value that, without their labor, would not exist. These people work to create important new ideas, well-educated students, new social networks, more effective social services and so forth—or, to use the latest (but very helpful) jargon, intellectual, human, and social capital. . . .

Common Good Assets

People usually make investments in the hope of gaining a return. Businesses invest because they want to make a profit. Individuals invest because they want to increase their personal wealth or to create a larger and more secure retirement fund. Is that what is happening when a foundation makes a grant? Not really. By law, a foundation is a "non-profit" organization, which means it is prohibited from making profits. So the "return" we hope for from making grants is not growth in our own financial assets. Rather, our aim in making grants is to generate a charitable good, or what we might call a "common good asset."

Several years ago, Michael Sherraden wrote an important book entitled *Assets for the Poor.* He argued that American welfare policy was built entirely on the assumption that what poor people need is *income;* that is, a steady stream of small doses of assistance that provides just enough for them to survive for another day. Sherraden argued that that is a perverse premise. Instead, he said, we should be helping the poor build *assets* of their own that they can use progressively to build up a sustainable and expanding infrastructure for their own lives. Assets rather than income are what create the foundation for freedom, personhood, community, and well-being.

A grant is an "investment" when it works this way with its recipients, whoever they may be. A grant is an investment when it creates assets that can be used over and over again to build up the physical, economic, intellectual, moral, cultural and even spiritual capital human beings and communities need to live humane and even flourishing lives. In our work in the Religion Division, we are trying to invest in building up the assets (excellent pastoral leadership, strong seminaries, insightful intellectual resources) that are indispensable if the religious lives of American Christians are actually to be deepened and enriched.

Gift-Giving

What, then, about giving a grant? Isn't a grant an act of charitable *giving*? Can a grant be a *gift*? I do think a grant is in some ways a gift, but of an unusual kind.

The best gifts, true gifts, have no expectations attached to them. As a gift, it is simply a sign of appreciation, affection or even love. The most important thing about a gift is that it carries this kind of symbolic freight. Thus a gift—what the gift is, how it is given, to whom it is given—must always be thought through with great care, so that what it "says" or "conveys" or "means" is appropriate to the person you are giving to and, above all, to the relationship between giver and receiver. Similarly with one's response to a gift. The main response a gift-giver wants is recognition of what the gift means and a sense that that meaning is mutually shared and enjoyed.

Charitable giving can have the character of a gift if the giving is done really well, if it is done with the giver having no expectations whatsoever of some kind of return on the charitable contribution. Charitable giving is *gift*-giving if one is giving simply to alleviate some pain or meet some need without gaining for oneself a social or psychological return that elevates one above the recipient. This is a terrifically difficult human action to accomplish. Indeed the philosopher Simone Weil thought it so difficult to do that it was, literally for her, a miracle of grace whenever it happened (see *Gravity and Grace*). But, praise God, charitable gifts in this sense are sometimes actually given. And sometimes grants may be pure charity of that kind as well.

A Grant Is Not a Gift

Most often, however, a grant is not a gift in this sense, because it is given with expectations attached. The grantor expects the grantee to do something specific with the money, and to produce various kinds of "common good assets" by means of it. All of which the grantor and grantee agree upon when the grant is "negotiated." Gifts are never negotiated; grants are. Gifts never have "contracts" attached to them; most grants do. People are not (or at least should not be) expected to "report back" on gifts; they are on grants.

As a "grantmaker" I would be deeply disappointed if a grantee expressed deep gratitude for a grant but then did nothing with it. And if a person thought a grant was a sign of affection, he or she would have badly misinterpreted its meaning. (One might, of course, feel some degree of affection for a grantee, but that is not why a grant is made. Indeed, giving a grant is a very bad way to express affection. Giving gifts out of your own resources is the way to do that.)

Still, in spite of all this, a grant can and should have at least a hint of the character of a gift, in the sense that grants (as opposed to sheer quid pro quo contracts) convey appreciation for the grantee's actual and potential contribution to the common good and are thus a sign of gratitude for the mutual engagement between the grantor and the grantee in a larger common enterprise and a shared vision of the good. In the best of circumstances, grants can—and should—be given in that spirit. And in that spirit, one hopes that, in response, the grantee might convey some "recognition of what the grant means and a sense that that meaning is mutually shared and enjoyed."

From *Initiatives in Religion* 8, no. 2 (Summer/Autumn 2000). Published by the Religion Division, Lilly Endowment. By permission of the author.

S. I. HAYAKAWA

"The Story of A-Town and B-ville"

S. I. Hayakawa (1906–1992), a psychologist, educator, author, and U.S. senator from California (1977–1983), is most widely known for his work on the meaning of language, or semantics. In this selection, an excerpt from his popular book Language in Thought and Action, *Hayakawa invites us to consider competing vocabularies as competing ideologies. A-Town and B-ville are in trouble: recession has hit hard, and in each town one hundred families have lost their source of income. Both towns take action: The first provides "relief" for its citizens, making the assistance difficult to secure in order to ward off the undeserving. B-ville provides the same amount to its indigent, but as deserved "insurance claims" disbursed from the community's resources. The towns' decisions produce very different results. Is this surprising?*

If we apply his account to the world of philanthropy, Hayakawa would be suggesting that the very terms we use to discuss our transactions—grants, benefits, donations, contracts, gifts, investments, etc.—have encased in them not only our fundamental attitudes toward and expectations of others but also our self-understanding. Is he right? Does it, for example, make any difference if we refer to those we serve as "the poor" or as "my brothers," or to philanthropic funds as "public" or "private" monies? If you called the "grant" you recently made a "gift," would it take on a fundamentally different meaning? If so, for whom?

&

Once upon a time, said the Professor, there were two small communities, spiritually as well as geographically situated at a considerable distance from each other. They had, however, these problems in common: both were hard hit by a recession, so that in each of the towns there were about one hundred heads of families unemployed.

The city fathers of A-town, the first community, were substantial and sound-thinking businessmen. The unemployed tried hard, as unemployed people usually do, to find jobs; but the situation did not improve. The city fathers had been brought up to believe that there is always enough work for everyone, if you only look for it hard enough. Comforting themselves with this doctrine, the city fathers could have shrugged their shoulders and turned their backs on the problem, except for the fact that they were genuinely kindhearted men. They could not bear to see the unemployed men and their wives and children starving. In order to prevent hardship, they felt that they had to provide these people with some means of sustenance. Their principles told them, nevertheless, that if people were given something for nothing, it would demoralize their character. Naturally this made the city fathers even more unhappy, because they were faced with the horrible choice of (1) letting the unemployed starve, or (2) destroying their moral character.

The solution they finally hit upon, after much debate and soul-searching, was this. They decided to give the unemployed families "relief payments" of two hundred dollars a month. (They considered using the English term "dole," but with their characteristic American penchant for euphemism, they decided on the less offensive term.) To make sure that the unemployed would not take their unearned payments too much for granted, however, they decided that the "relief" was to be accompanied by a moral lesson; to wit: the obtaining of the assistance would be made so difficult, humiliating, and disagreeable that there would be no temptation for anyone to go through the process unless it was absolutely necessary; the moral disapproval of the community would be turned upon the recipients of the money at all times in such a way that they would try hard to get "off relief" and "regain their self-respect." Some even proposed that people on relief be denied the vote, so that the moral lesson would be more deeply impressed upon them. Others suggested that their names be published at regular intervals in the newspapers. The city fathers had enough faith in the goodness of human nature to expect that the recipients would be grateful, since they were getting something for nothing, something which they hadn't worked for.

When the plan was put into operation, however, the recipients of the relief checks proved to be an ungrateful, ugly bunch. They seemed to resent the cross-examinations and inspections at the hands of the "relief investigators," who, they said, took advantage of a man's misery to snoop into every detail of his private life. In spite of uplifting editorials in A-town Tribune telling them how grateful they ought to be, the recipients of the relief refused to learn any moral lessons, declaring that they were "just as good as anybody else." When, for example, they permitted themselves the rare luxury of a movie or an evening of bingo, their neighbors looked at them sourly as if to say, "I work hard and pay my taxes just in order to support loafers like you in idleness and pleasure." This attitude, which was fairly characteristic of those members of the community who still had jobs, further embittered the relief recipients, so that they showed even less gratitude as time went on and were constantly on the lookout for insults, real or imaginary, from people who might think that they weren't as good as anybody else. A number of them took to moping all day long; one or two even committed suicide. Others, feeling that they had failed to provide, found it hard to look their wives and children in the face. Children whose parents were "on relief" felt inferior to classmates whose parents were not "public charges." Some of these children developed inferiority complexes which affected not only their grades at school, but their careers after graduation. Finally, several relief recipients felt they could stand their loss of self-respect no longer and decided, after many efforts to gain honest jobs, that they would earn money by their own efforts even if they had to rob. They did so and were caught and sent to the state penitentiary.

The depression, therefore, hit A-town very hard. The relief policy had averted starvation, no doubt, but suicide, personal quarrels, unhappy homes, the weakening of social organizations, the maladjustment of children, and, finally, crime, had resulted. The town was divided in two, the "haves" and the "have-nots," so that there was class hatred. People shook their heads sadly and declared that it all went to prove over again what they had known from the beginning, that giving people something for nothing inevitably demoralizes their character. The citizens of A-town gloomily waited for prosperity to return, with less and less hope as time went on.

The story of the other community, B-ville, was entirely different. B-ville was a relatively isolated town, too far out of the way to be reached by Rotary Club speakers and other dispensers of conventional wisdom. One of the aldermen, however, who was something of an economist, explained to his fellow aldermen that unemployment, like sickness, accident, fire, tornado, or death, hits unexpectedly in modern society, irrespective of the victim's merits or deserts. He went on to say that B-ville's homes, parks, streets, industries, and everything else B-ville was proud of, had been built in part by the work of these same people who were now unemployed. He then proposed to apply a principle of insurance: if the work these unemployed people had previously done for the community could be regarded as a form of "premium" paid to the community against a time of misfortune, payments now made to them to prevent their starvation could be regarded as "insurance claims." He therefore proposed that all men of good repute who had worked in the community in some line of useful endeavor, whether as machinists, clerks, or bank managers, be regarded as "citizen policyholders," having "claims" against the city in the case of unemployment for two hundred dollars a month until such time as they might again be employed. Naturally, he had to talk very slowly and patiently since the idea was entirely new to his fellow aldermen. But he described his plan as a "straight business proposition," and finally they were persuaded. They worked out in detail, to everyone's satisfaction, the conditions under which citizens should be regarded as policyholders in the city's social insurance plan, and decided to give checks for two hundred dollars a month to the heads of each of B-ville's indigent families.

B-ville's "claim adjusters," whose duty it was to investigate the claims of the citizen "policyholders," had a much better time than A-town's "relief investigators." While the latter had been resentfully regarded as snoopers, the former, having no moral lesson to teach but simply a business transaction to carry out, treated their clients with businesslike courtesy and got the same amount of information as the relief investigators had, with considerably less difficulty. There were no hard feelings. It further happened, fortunately, that news of B-ville's plans reached a liberal newspaper editor in the big city at the other end of the state. This writer described the plan in a leading feature story headed "B-VILLE LOOKS AHEAD. Adventure in Social Pioneering Launched by Upper Valley Community." As a result of this publicity, inquiries about the plan began to come to the city hall even before the first checks were mailed out. This led, naturally, to a considerable feeling of pride on the part of the aldermen, who, being boosters, felt that this was a wonderful opportunity to put B-ville on the map.

Accordingly, the aldermen decided that instead of simply mailing out the checks as they had originally intended, they would publicly present the first checks at a monster civic ceremony. They invited the governor of the state, who was glad to come to bolster his none-too-enthusiastic support in that locality, the president of the state university, the senator from their district, and other functionaries. They decorated the National Guard armory with flags and got out the American Legion Fife and Drum Corps, the Boy Scouts, and other civic organizations. At the big celebration, each family to receive a "social insurance check" was marched up to the platform to receive it, and the governor and the mayor shook hands with each of them as they came trooping up in their best clothes. Fine speeches were made; there was much cheering and shouting; pictures of the event showing the recipients of the checks shaking hands with the mayor, and the governor patting the heads of the children, were published not only in the local papers but also in several metropolitan picture sections.

Every recipient of these insurance checks had a feeling, therefore, that he had been personally honored, that he lived in a wonderful little town, and that he could face his unemployment with greater courage and assurance, since his community was behind him. The men and women found themselves being kidded in a friendly way by their acquaintances for having been "up there with the big shots," shaking hands with the governor, and so on. The children at school found themselves envied for having had their pictures in the papers. All in all, B-ville's unemployed did not commit suicide, were not haunted by a sense of failure, did not turn to crime, did not manifest personal maladjustments, did not develop class hatred, as the result of their two hundred dollars a month....

At the conclusion of the Professor's story, the discussion began:

"That just goes to show," said the Advertising Man, who was known among his friends as a realistic thinker, "what good promotional work can do. B-ville's city council had real advertising sense, and that civic ceremony was a masterpiece ... made everyone happy ... put over the scheme in a big way. Reminds me of the way we do things in our business: as soon as we called horse-mackerel tuna-fish, we developed a big market for it. I suppose if you called relief 'insurance,' you could actually get people to like it, couldn't you?"

"What do you mean, 'calling' it insurance?" asked the Social Worker. "B-ville's scheme wasn't relief at all. It *was* insurance."

"Good grief, man! Do you realize what you're saying?" cried the Advertising Man in surprise. "Are you implying that those people had any *right* to that money? All I said was that it's a good idea to *disguise* relief as insurance if it's going to make people any happier. But it's still relief, no matter what you *call* it. It's all right to kid the public along to reduce discontent, but we don't need to kid ourselves as well!"

"But they *do* have a right to that money! They're not getting something for nothing. It's insurance. They did something for the community, and that's their prem—"

"Say, are you crazy?"

"Who's crazy?"

"You're crazy. Relief is relief, isn't it? If you'd only call things by their right names . . ."

"But, confound it, insurance is insurance, isn't it?"

P.S. Those who have concluded that the point of the story is that the Social Worker and the Advertising Man were "only arguing about different names for the same thing," are asked to reread the story and explain what they mean by (1) "only" and (2) "the same thing."

From *Language in Thought and Action*, 4th edition, by S. I. Hayakawa. 1978. Reprinted with permission of Heinle, a division of Thomson Learning: www.thomsonrights.com. FAX 800-730-2215.

MUHAMMAD YUNUS

"A Hand Up, Not a Hand Out: Why Not Microloans for Katrina Victims?"

Muhammad Yunus, considered the godfather of microfinance, won the 2006 Nobel Peace Prize, in concert with the Grameen Bank he founded, for developing microcredit "into an ever more important instrument in the struggle against poverty." The Grameen Bank, like other micro-credit institutions, allows the poor to borrow money—a practice usually denied them by traditional banks. As Yunus states in the essay below: "One of our most successful tools for rebuilding businesses is not government handouts, but rather, small loans . . ."—a hand up, in other words, not a handout. And he recommends the same practice as the best help for the victims of Hurricane Katrina. Is such a method a distinct and preferable alternative to government assistance—or to philanthropy? Consider the S. I. Hayakawa selection above: Would A-town or B-ville—could New Orleans or Biloxi—fare better with microcredit?

Microfinance is an emerging field, and there is ongoing debate and experimental effort to determine whether it should continue to be run on philanthropic funding, or whether it should emerge as a fully commercial profit-making enterprise. As one practitioner in the private sector said: "I want to treat someone as a client, not like a beneficiary of a donation. Because when we have someone that we psychologically think of now as a client we say, 'How are we going to satisfy them?' If you're just going to give money, it's very different."[1] Is it more— or less—humane to regard the poor as 'clients' rather than as applicants or supplicants? To provide financial services rather than grants or charity?

ℒ

America's government and people brought charity to a new level last year in their response to Hurricane Katrina. The rebuilding has been particularly difficult, however, because it has involved lives as well as bricks and mortar. Many victims had been desperately poor all their lives. Helping them to self-sufficiency has proved just as difficult, if not harder, than putting homes and businesses back up again.

Having many very poor citizens, and more than its share of natural disasters, Bangladesh—my own country—has a great deal of experience facing both these challenges. We have a per capita gross national income of $440, with half

---

1. Robert Annibale, quoted in "Millions for Millions" by Connie Bruck, *The New Yorker*, 30 October 2006.

the population living below the poverty line. We've little to start with, and much of that is repeatedly snatched away. In 1998, floods covered much of the country for over two months, affecting 30 million people; and a single cyclone killed 300,000 in 1970. Despite these catastrophes, more of our people are climbing out of poverty.

So at the risk of sounding presumptuous: What can the U.S. learn from Bangladesh about post-disaster economic recovery? Like many other countries, even Bangladeshis were quick with a handout after Katrina, giving the U.S. $1 million for the victims. But Americans might be surprised to learn that one of our most successful tools for rebuilding businesses is not government handouts, but rather, small loans packaged with practical business and social advice.

Microfinance is one of the biggest success stories of the developing world, and proponents like me believe it could be just as successful in helping the poor in wealthy countries such as the U.S. The basic philosophy behind microfinance is that the poor, although spurned by traditional banks because they can't provide collateral, are actually a great investment: No one works harder than someone who is striving to achieve life's basic necessities, particularly a woman with children to support. Sadly, it is also true that in catastrophic circumstances, very little of the cash so generously given ever gets all the way down to the very poor. There are too many "professionals" ahead of them in line, highly skilled at diverting funds into their own pockets. This is particularly regrettable because very poor people need only a little money to set up a business that can make a dramatic difference in the quality of their lives.

I started the Grameen Bank 30 years ago by distributing about $27 (no typo here!) worth of loans among 40 extremely poor Bangladeshis. Since the bank officially opened in 1983, it has loaned $5.7 billion in microfinance. Today, Grameen has 6.6 million borrowers in Bangladesh alone, borrowing $500 million a year in loans that average just over $100 each. The loans are entirely financed by borrowers' deposits and the bank recovers 98.85% of all money loaned. Notably, Grameen Bank has been profitable in all but three years since its launch. Our largely poor customers save $1.008 for every dollar they borrow, so the poor are truly funding the poor.

The bank supports businesses such as small services, stores, direct sales, furniture-making, cell phone stations and milling, all of which support the local economy. And it works. More than half of our borrowers have moved out of poverty, mainly through their own efforts. Most importantly, when you lend money to disadvantaged people, it gives them a sense of pride, rather than the humiliation they may feel over a handout. And just as helpful as the money is the guidance they get from the bank. Training and connecting poor, inexperienced workers to a reliable and ethical lending and savings service is a huge advantage for them that only gets stronger after a disaster. This is particularly true of women, who are often constrained by social and financial barriers.

Grameen communities have also made tremendous strides on health and social issues, such as sanitation, and pushed aside discriminatory practices such as bridal dowries.

The impact of microfinance is spreading world-wide. As of December 2004, 3,100 microcredit institutions reported reaching 92,270,289 clients, 66,614,871 of whom were among the world's poorest when they took their first loan. Assuming five persons per family, the loans to the 54.8 million poorest clients affected some 330 million family members by the end of 2004.

Microfinance has worked so well that it has become a major instrument of reconstruction in post-tsunami Asia as well. A Sri Lankan conglomerate, Ceylinco, partnered with Grameen to provide small loans to 10,000 tsunami victims. These range from $300 to $10,000 and carry an interest rate of 6%, less than half the rate for similar small loans in Sri Lanka. The loans have a one-year grace-period, and Ceylinco takes no collateral, thereby heaping all the risk onto itself. But the company felt this was still a wise investment.

Because some countries that rely heavily on microfinance also happen to be disaster-prone, Grameen now has special disaster loan funds (DLFs) to help meet the urgent need for cash after a catastrophe. These funds also aim to offset the microlender's own losses. The funds were established in Bangladesh after the record flooding of 1998, which affected 20% of the population. Similar funds were set up in Central America in the wake of Hurricane Mitch, and in Poland after the floods of 1997. The DLFs are financial reserves and usually derived from the initial donor grant to the micro-credit lender.

Many people ask, Why not just give free cash, especially under such dire circumstances? In Bangladesh, we've learned that when aid is free, not only do the poor get the least of it, but everyone inflates their needs. While some handouts are clearly necessary in such times, we focus on lending small amounts of money. This lets us keep costs down and rebuild funds for the next disaster. Most importantly, our Grameen banks are ready to act at a moment's notice. They can respond to a disaster without waiting for anyone's permission, immediately becoming like humanitarian agencies by suspending loan payments, and providing cash, food and medicines. Once rebuilding starts, the bankers keep detailed records of the money lent, and people are allowed to repay bit by bit.

That is the strategy we followed after the 1998 flooding, which covered 50% of Bangladesh's land and affected customers at about 70% of our branches. More than 700 Grameen borrowers or their family members were killed and just over half (a million borrowers) were affected by the flooding. That represents a small percentage of the overall population affected, but the Bank and its staff were there right away to help with immediate needs. Later, microlenders helped people restructure their loans or gave out new loans on more favorable terms.

Microlending has already helped millions reach a better life through their own initiative. It has also given them valuable skills as well as crucial financial back-up in case they ever face a natural disaster like Katrina. So it might be time to think about another type of support for Katrina's victims: the micro-loan. As our small, flood-battered country has learned, giving someone a hand up doesn't always require a handout. The most important thing is to help people get back to work while letting them hold on to their self-respect. Micro-loans can do just that.

From *The Wall Street Journal,* 14 October 2006, Editorial Page. Reprinted from *The Wall Street Journal.* Copyright © 2006 Dow Jones & Company. All rights reserved. With permission of Vidar Jorgensen.

GEORGE MOORE

"Alms-Giving"

One often hears the meaning of the choices that donors make discussed in terms of the faculty used in their making: Gifts, it is said, come from the heart, grants from the head. Gifts are associated with "altruism, compassion, generosity, impulse, and gratitude," grants with "strategy, competition, investment, capacity, and impact."[1] In real life, as most of us are aware, things are seldom so clearly bifurcated. In this short story, Irish author and art critic George Moore (1852–1933) focuses on a transaction between an individual (his unnamed first person narrator) and a blind beggar. The narrator wrestles, heart against head, in deciding when, or if, to give to the beggar. What makes this seemingly simple choice so complex? Should it be so complicated? At the very end of the story, the narrator admits to himself, "the blind beggar has taught me a great deal, something that I could not have learnt out of a book, a deeper truth than any book contains." What does he learn? Is it a lesson all givers—including grantsmen—should heed?

༄

As I searched for a penny it began to rain. The blind man opened a parcel and I saw that it contained a small tarpaulin cape. But the several coats I wore made it difficult to find my change; I thought I had better forego my charity that day, and I walked quickly away.

"Eight or nine hours a day waiting for alms is his earthly lot," I said, and walking towards the river, and leaning on the parapet, I wondered if he recognized the passing steps—if he recognized my steps—and associated them with a penny? Of what use that he should know the different steps? If he knew them there would be anticipation and disappointments. But a dog would make life comprehensible; and I imagined a companionship, a mingling of muteness and blindness, and the joy that would brighten the darkness when the dog leaped eagerly upon the blind man's knees. I imagined the joy of warm feet and limb, and the sudden poke of the muzzle. A dog would be a link to bind the blind beggar to the friendship of life. Now why has this small blind man, with a face as pale as a plant that never sees the sun, not a dog? A dog is the natural link and the only link that binds the blind beggar to the friendship of life.

Looking round, I could see that he was taking off his little cape, for it had ceased raining. But in a few weeks it would rain every day, and the wind would

---

1. See, for example, Sara Engelhardt, "Foundation Grants and the Grantor/Grantee Relationship," reproduced later in this chapter.

blow from the river in great gusts. "Will he brave another winter?" I asked myself. "Iron blasts will sweep through the passage; they will find him through the torn shirt and the poor grey trousers, the torn waistcoat, the black jacket, and the threadbare overcoat—someone's cast-off garment. But he may have been born blind, or he may have become blind; in any case he has been blind for many years, and if he persists in living he will have to brave many winters in that passage, for he is not an old man. What instinct compels him to bear his dark life? Is he afraid to kill himself? Does this fear spring from physical or from religious motives? Fear of hell? Surely no other motive would enable him to endure his life."

In my intolerance for all life but my own I thought I could estimate the value of the Great Mockery, and I asked myself angrily why he persisted in living. I asked myself why I helped him to live. It would be better that he should throw himself at once into the river. And this was reason talking to me, and it told me that the most charitable act I could do would be to help him over the parapet. But behind reason there is instinct, and in obedience to an impulse, which I could not weigh or appreciate, I went to the blind man and put some money into his hand; the small coin slipped through his fingers; they were so cold that he could not retain it, and I had to pick it from the ground.

"Thankee, sir. Can you tell, sir, what time it is?"

And this little question was my recompense. He and I wanted to know the time of day. I asked him why he wanted to know the time, and he told me because that evening a friend was coming to fetch him. And, wondering who that friend might be, and hoping he might tell me, I asked him about his case of pencils, expressing a hope that he sold them. He answered that he was doing a nice bit of trading.

"The boys about here are a trouble," he said, "but the policeman on the beat is a friend of mine, and he watches them and makes them count the pencils they take. The other day they robbed me, and he gave them such a cuffing that I don't think they'll take my pencils again. You see, sir, I keep the money I take for the pencils in the left pocket, and the money that is given to me I keep in the right pocket. In this way I know if my accounts are right when I make them up in the evening."

Now where, in what lonely room does he sit making up his accounts? But, not wishing to seem inquisitorial, I turned the conversation.

"I suppose you know some of the passers-by."

"Yes, I know a tidy few. There's one gentleman who gives me a penny every day, but he's gone abroad, I hear, and sixpence a week is a big drop."

As I had given him a penny a day all the summer, I assumed he was speaking of me. And my sixpence a week meant a day's dinner, perhaps two days' dinners! It was only necessary for me to withhold my charity to give him ease. He would hardly be able to live without my charity, and if one of his other patrons were to do likewise the world would be freed from a life that I could not feel to be of any value.

So do we judge the world if we rely on our reason, but instinct clings like a child and begs like a child, and my instinct begged me to succor this poor man, to give him a penny every day, to find out what his condition was, and to stop for a chat every time I gave him my penny. I had obeyed my instinct all the summer, and now reason had intervened, reason was in rebellion, and for a long time I avoided, or seemed to avoid, the passage where the blind man sat for eight or nine hours, glad to receive, but never asking for alms.

I think I forgot the blind man for several months. I only remembered him when I was sitting at home, or when I was at the other side of the town, and sometimes I thought I made myself little excuses not to pass through the passage. Our motives are vague, complex and many, and one is never quite sure why one does a thing, and if I were to say that I did not give the blind man pennies that winter because I believed it better to deprive him of his means of livelihood and force him out of life than to help him to remain in life and suffer, I should be saying what was certainly untrue, yet the idea was in my mind, and I experienced more than one twinge of conscience when I passed through the passage. I experienced remorse when I hurried past him, too selfish to unbutton my coat, for every time I happened to pass him it was raining or blowing very hard, and every time I hurried away trying to find reasons why he bore his miserable life. I hurried to my business, my head full of chatter about St. Simon's Stylites, telling myself that he saw God far away at the end of the sky, His immortal hands filled with immortal recompenses; reason chattered about the compensation of celestial choirs, but instinct told me that the blind man standing in the stone passage knew of no such miraculous consolations.

As the winter advanced, as the winds grew harsher, my avoidance of the passage grew more marked, and one day I stopped to think, and asked myself why I avoided it.

There was a faint warmth in the sky, and I heard my heart speaking to me quite distinctly, and it said:

"Go to the blind man—what matter about your ten minutes' delay; you have been unhappy since you refrained from alms-giving, and the blind beggar can feel the new year beginning."

"You see, sir, I have added some shirt buttons and studs to the pencils. I don't know how they will go, but one never knows till one tries."

Then he told me it was smallpox that destroyed his eyes, and he was only eighteen at the time.

"You must have suffered very much when they told you your sight was going?"

"Yes, sir. I had the hump for six weeks."

"What do you mean?"

"It doubled me up, that it did. I sat with my head in my hands for six weeks."

"And after that?"

"I didn't think any more about it—what was the good?"

"Yes, but it must be difficult not to think, sitting here all alone."

"One mustn't allow one's self to give way. One would break down alto-gether if one did. I've some friends, and in the evening I get plenty of exercise."

"What do you do in the evenings?"

"I turn a hay-cutting machine in a stable."

"And you're quite contented?"

"I don't think, sir, a happier man than I passes through this gateway once a month."

He told me his little boy came to fetch him in the evening.

"You're married?"

"Yes, sir, and I've got four children. They're going away for their holidays next week."

"Where are they going?"

"To the sea. It will do them good; a blow on the beach will do them a power of good."

"And when they come back they will tell you about it?"

"Yes."

"And do you ever go away for a holiday?"

"Last year I went with a policeman. A gentleman who passes this way, one of my friends, paid four shillings for me. We had a nice dinner in a public house for a shilling, and then we went for a walk."

"And this year are you going with the policeman?"

"I hope so, a friend of mine gave me half-a-crown towards it."

"I'll give you the rest."

"Thankee, sir."

A soft south wind was blowing, and an instinct as soft and as gentle filled my heart, and I went towards some trees. The new leaves were beginning in the high branches. I was sitting where sparrows were building their nests, and very soon I seemed to see further into life than I had seen before. "We're here," I said, "for the purpose of learning what life is, and the blind beggar has taught me a great deal, something that I could not have learnt out of a book, a deeper truth than any book contains." . . . And then I ceased to think, for thinking is a folly when a soft south wind is blowing and an instinct as soft and as gentle fills the heart.

From *The Untilled Field* by George Moore (Philadelphia, 1903).

MOSES MAIMONIDES

"Eight Levels of Tzedakah (Giving)"

Spanish-born scholar and physician Moses Maimonides (1135–1204), also known as "RaMBaM," is still regarded as one of Judaism's most revered rabbis and philosophers (or "sages"). This famous selection, excerpted from the final chapter of Hilchot Matanot Ani'im ("Laws Concerning Gifts to the Poor"), appears in a tractate called the Sefer Zera'im ("The Book of Seeds"),[1] which is part of the Mishneh Torah ("Retelling of the Torah," that is, of the first five books of the Hebrew Bible). In it, Maimonides takes his bearings from practices in the Jewish community nearly nine hundred years ago and draws on Judaism's traditional teachings. Thus, he speaks of giving in terms of tzedakah (from Hebrew root tzedek, meaning equity or justice) as opposed to charity or philanthropy, conveying the view that giving to the poor is fueled more by a sense of fairness or justice than by mercy, conscience, love or compassion, and, even more importantly, that its overarching purpose is the rectification of social imbalance.

But does Maimonides' concern for righteousness or justice also account for the variety of relations between givers and receivers that he depicts, as well as his hierarchical ordering of them? Does, for example, taking someone by the hand (the highest level on his "ladder") do more to repair social injustice than giving to someone anonymously (the next to highest level)? Is it better—more just—to give anonymously, for example, to the United Fund, than to give grudgingly (the lowest rung) to someone you know? Or, in the end, is all charitable giving equally just or good? More generally, do the relations here depicted, or their ordering, have any relevance for organized philanthropy, that is, relations between grantors and grantees?

ɬə

1. There are eight levels of *tzedakah*, one better than the next. A high level, of which none is higher, is where one takes the hand of an Israelite and gives him a gift or loan, or makes a partnership with him, or finds him employment, in order to strengthen him until he needs to ask help of no one. *Concerning this it says, "And you will give*

---

1. For Maimonides, giving to the poor is regarded as one instance of distributing growing things. Indeed, in Jewish thought more generally, ownership is tantamount to custodianship. In biblical times, for example, farmers were required to leave crops standing in the corners of their fields for the poor, who would also be entitled to any crops that fell in the course of harvesting. This arrangement provided for the needy, but it also necessitated the able-bodied poor to engage in the harvesting of the corners and the gathering of the fallen crops. This helps explain, at least in part, why the topic of this selection appears in the tractate *The Book of Seeds.*—Ed.

strength to the resident alien, so he may live among you,"[2] *as if to say, strengthen him until he will not falter or need.*

2. Below this is one who gives *tzedakah* to the poor, not knowing to whom he gives, while the poor person does not know from whom he takes. *For this is [fulfillment of a] commandment for its own sake.*[3] *And for such there was a Chamber of Secrets in the Temple, whereunto the righteous would contribute secretly, and wherefrom the poor of good families would draw their sustenance in equal secrecy. Close to such a person is he who contributes directly to the alms fund.*

    One should not, however, contribute directly to the alms fund unless he knows that the person in charge of it is trustworthy, is a Sage, and knows how to manage it properly . . .

3. Below this, the giver knows to whom he gives, and the poor person does not know from whom he takes. *For example: the rabbinic sages who went in secret, tossing coins in the door openings of the poor. In this case, it is proper and good [to do this] if the alms officers do not behave precisely [i.e., conduct themselves as they should].*

4. Below this, the poor person knows from whom he takes, and the giver does not know: *as per example of the greatest of the sages who would bundle small change in their sheets, and throw them over their shoulders, in sight of the poor, who took, so they would have no shame.*

5. Below this, one puts into another's hand before [the latter] asks.

6. Below this, one gives another after [the latter] asks.

7. Below this, one gives another less than is appropriate, in a pleasant manner.

8. Below this, one gives begrudgingly (sorrowfully, reluctantly, or with regret).

From *Hilchot Matanot Ani'im* ("Laws Concerning Gifts to the Poor") by Moses Maimonides. Translated from Hebrew by Judah Mandelbaum.

---

2. Lev. 25:35.—Ed.

3. See Deut. 15:4, 7, 9, 11; 24:12, 14, 15; Lev. 14:21; 19:10, 15; 23:22; 25:35, 39, 47; Exod. 22:25; 23:3, 6, 11.—Ed.

PAUL F. CAMENISCH

From "Gift and Gratitude in Ethics"

In this very brief excerpt, theologian Paul F. Camenisch captures the moral rela-
tionship that is established by any act of giving. Elsewhere he emphasizes the re-
ciprocal character of the relationship: "Each party will have rights and duties,
benefits and costs arising from the relation." Though the giver initiates the rela-
tionship, the recipient must consent and accept its obligations "to be a full par-
ticipant in the way of life of which gift is a part." What does it mean for a
recipient to be thus obliged? (Does anonymous giving deny the fulfillment of this
moral relationship? When is it right to refuse a gift?) Are the "rights and duties"
that attach themselves to grantmaking different from those described here?

A gift is not a windfall, a boon from the blue. It is something of value given to
one unearned and undeserved by another agent at some cost to that agent and
for the benefit of the recipient. Like other human acts there is behind that act
some motive or intention. Gift comes to be gift and to be given through the
will of the giver. It is given for some reason(s). And in accepting the gift, the recipient cannot strip it of its connection with the donor's will and intention,
with the donor's reason(s) for giving it. To accept the gift is on some level to
consent to that total complex reality and to consent to become a part of it.

From "Gift and Gratitude in Ethics," in *Journal of Religious Ethics* 9 (Blackwell, 1981),
pp. 1–34. Reprinted with permission of Blackwell.

ARNA BONTEMPS

"A Woman with a Mission"

Arna Bontemps (1902–1973), noted African American poet, author, anthologist, and librarian, was a major figure of the Harlem Renaissance. In this short story, he models the relation between a patroness and her beneficiary. Mrs. Rainwater is "a woman with a mission." Ardently believing that "the refined races lost something vital, an essential vitamin, a certain mystic power," she is determined to search out and support the elusive "microbe," wherever it might be found. At first, her "love" and investment ran to American Indians; now, it goes to the artistic training of "Negroes." Young, impoverished, and an aspiring vocalist, Leander Holly becomes her protégé. But with time, Mrs. Rainwater's stringent "unwritten code" for her young geniuses begins to cloy, and Leander tries to manipulate it to his own advantage, rationalizing his actions thus: "She wants to make a slave of me . . . like any other old miser—she's not giving something for nothing." To be sure, Mrs. Rainwater does want something: "How can I keep others from taking the credit for the talents I have sponsored?" she plaintively cries, when she realizes that she has been betrayed. But is she enslaving her protégé? Is she really a miser? Should we simply decry the "contractual" model here depicted?

The circumstances under which Mrs. Eulalie Rainwater discovered the strange genius were almost incredible.

"Fancy," she exclaimed, languishing upon a heap of rich cushions in her sun parlor. "Just fancy, darling. It's the most astonishing thing that ever happened to me. Positively overwhelming. Take these dishes away, Lottie, I can't eat another bite. Excitement at my age—"

Lottie, the brown girl, nodded and reached for the tea things. As a maid her position was distinctly exceptional in Mrs. Rainwater's Larchmont home. For Lottie herself was somewhat of a discovery too where the wealthy old woman was concerned, though indeed a minor one. A little thing always leads to a bigger one, however; and since Lottie represented the starting point of Mrs. Rainwater's artistic interest in Negroes, her value could not be overestimated now that the genius was in hand.

"Have a cigarette?"

"Yes, please." The girl stood before her with the tray.

"He has a finer voice than Roland Hayes, and he's as charming and unspoiled as Robeson. But he must be brought along very carefully. The wrong influences might ruin everything."

"He'll have temptations," Lottie agreed discreetly. "There'll be opportunities to sing in Harlem night clubs and possibly with revues like the *Blackbirds*."

"He mustn't think of it," Mrs. Rainwater said emphatically. "To prostitute a voice like Leander Holly's would be a ringing crime. It would wreck all my plans for him at one stroke. I couldn't allow it under any conditions."

Lottie went into the kitchen. Somehow she could not help feeling glad with Mrs. Rainwater—glad and tremulous at once, in fact; for Lottie knew even better than the old white-haired woman what unhappy possibilities lay ahead of the young singer. But Mrs. Rainwater was so sweet, so good, so perfect in her relations to the young people she "encouraged" that the girl was not able to entertain a genuine foreboding. The little fairy world that revolved around that tender old goddess was not real anyhow, Lottie thought; one could never be convinced that it was not a dream. Naturally, earthly hazards and earthly dangers couldn't enter. It was as safe as any other make-believe place.

At first Mrs. Rainwater's love had run to American Indians. She estimated that she had helped nearly a thousand artists and students who showed her projects involving this romantic group. As a result of her encouragement and her investments, she could point to several creditable books of folk lore, a distinguished body of paintings, a bit of fiction and music, and scores of scholarly works dealing with skull measurements and the like. Most of the latter had never been published, being of doubtful interest to the larger reading public, but Mrs. Rainwater preserved each one in a fire-proof vault. Now in her declining years, partly because of ennui and partly because the former field was nearly exhausted, she had turned to the Negro.

It was odd that she had not considered him earlier, yet she could well account for the tardy recognition. Her interest in the more primitive American groups was not an ordinary interest. Mrs. Rainwater had a philosophy: she was a woman with a mission. It was in her bosom like a patriotic duty, like a religion.

The refined races have lost something vital, an essential vitamin, a certain mystic power. Fortunately for America (and for her theory) this touch was still to be found in the United States. The Navajos had it moderately, but the Negroes possessed it in abundance. Her search for it was like isolating a difficult microbe. This much was definite: the thing was most evident in artistic expression. There were strange lost currents that these people touched when they sang, when they wrote poetry, even when they told stories.

"It is a precious heritage, a treasure from the jungle," she explained. "We must get our hands on it at any cost."

"Funny," Lottie always said. "Funny I never thought of that."

"Why, of course you didn't, you poor dear. Just another child playing with diamonds."

Mrs. Rainwater did not make the mistake of revealing all that was in her mind. Even to Lottie she did not tell everything. Her plans were her own. The girl was several times tempted to ask, "Well what are you going to have us do with this spiritual gift when we've pinned it down?" But the old woman easily read her thoughts.

"I have important designs for you youngsters, but you mustn't ask me what they are now. Just let us hold everything in strict confidence. No strangers must enter our circle, Lottie. You must help me explain it to Leander. It is such a private matter, so delicate and yet so weighty, that I tremble to think how I'll convey all its implications to that extraordinary young man."

"I think he'll understand," the girl remarked.

The frail gray woman sat for hours on her sun porch. Stacks of the newest books were nearby, but she seldom touched them now. She felt as crisp and insecure as a dry leaf on a bough. Leander Holly's genius filled her sky with big contending winds. She was arranging for his future voice training; she was definitely making it possible for him to live without economic distress. That much was accomplished. But how could she safeguard him from dangerous Harlem influences, from the Tisdale crowd, for example?

Well, one thing that would help was to have him move across to Jersey. There he'd be safe from the night life. He would have time to practice and an opportunity to see the green earth occasionally. And that degraded dilettante, Tisdale (the opprobrium was her own), would be less likely to ensnare the youth. Mrs. Rainwater reached for a sheet of linen note paper. She would engineer that move at once.

The discovery was now nearly a year in the past, but it remained as vivid as yesterday. It had been such a masterpiece of detection. Mrs. Rainwater never liked to have a genius presented to her; she never liked to have one seek her or make an appeal. She distrusted all such comers. A curious instinct told her that valuable gems are to be found only in unexpected places.

Naturally her heart thumped and her breath came short when, following a red cap through the Grand Central station and down the platform to her train, she suddenly heard a silvery voice singing *Du Bist Du Ruh*. A Negro tenor was singing the German words.

"Oh." The old woman trembled. Her doll-blue eyes turned to heaven, like the eyes of an ancient prophetess. She might have expected to see white doves circling overhead, but the singing was quite enough. She put one hand to her breast and again uttered that throbbing little word, "Oh."

Leander paused with the leather bags as if waiting for her to catch up. Actually he was wondering if she heard his song through the hum of the crowd, wondering if he had modulated the tone so as to sound innocent and unintentional and yet still managed to be heard.

"What number did you say your seat was, ma'am?"

"Oh." Her thoughts were far away. Then, with excitement, "Yes, yes. Here is my ticket. See?"

"Thank you."

"And what is *your* number?"

He pointed to his button.

In her seat she managed to say, "Do you like German songs?"

"Quite well," he said. "Next to spirituals."

He was small for a red cap, slight and brown and clean. His manners were easy and gracious, and Mrs. Rainwater would have asked a few more questions, but the train was leaving.

"I know your chief," she said. "Ezra High. The chief of the red caps. Will you tell him Mrs. Rainwater said to telephone her tonight?"

"I surely will."

He began singing again as he walked through the train. It was a little self-conscious, a trifle showy, but Mrs. Rainwater understood. Primitive. Unspoiled. She was certain that he did not *feel* self-conscious, that he did not mean to be ostentatious. And of course he knew nothing of her. It would be absurd to think that the poor boy was seeking to attract a patron under circumstances like this. Mrs. Rainwater convinced herself on that point and settled back into the seat with folded hands and set purpose.

The boy swung off the train just as it got in motion and hurried up to the red caps' locker room. Inside the door he slapped his palms together, sailed his cap across the room, and cut a few brief pigeon wings. Something like an imprisoned bird quaked and fluttered in his breast.

Ezra High, an old West Indian mulatto, watched him with amused eyes.

"Did you see her?" he asked.

"See her!" The boy was beside himself. "Everything is peaches. She heard me and asked my number. Then she told me to have you call her tonight."

"She'll see you through if she takes a fancy to you," the chief said. "That's all she's been doing for thirty years. I worked for her husband. He owned the Rainwater Line—coast steamers. And I mean he left her plenty. She's sponsored hundreds of young college folks. This Negro fever is something new, though. She must have read that book called *The New Negro*."

"Lordy, it ain't true," Leander said. "It must be a mistake. You don't mean she might see me through the conservatory—music lessons and all that?"

"She always allowed the others about two hundred a month outside of extras, trips, presents, and whatnot."

Leander put his hand on the old fellow's shoulder.

"I can't tote no more leather today, chief. I got castles to build."

That night the plot was completed, and the next evening Leander went to Larchmont to sing for Mrs. Rainwater. The old woman sat rapt throughout a performance in which the boy sang about a dozen songs accompanied by Lottie. While he was doing a group of spirituals, she wept softly. Her eyes, so blue and moist they suggested the eyes of a baby, turned to the ceiling again and again. Mrs. Rainwater's heart was too full; it was overflowing.

Lottie made cocktails, and the three drank in silence. A little later the old woman drew Leander aside.

"You have a rare gift," she said faintly. "A very rare gift."

"Thank you."

There was a pause.

"Are you getting the best possible training?"

"The best I can afford," he told her.

"Yes, yes. Of course you are, poor boy. Well I have something to suggest for your development, but I'd rather put it in a note. I'll write you a letter tomorrow. Your people have something precious, a spiritual heritage from the jungle that informs your art with a quality that America needs. It would be a calamity to have it lost, wasted."

She was almost whispering the words. It was told as if it were the revelation of a secret. Leander was entranced. He glanced at luxury around him and knew beyond doubt that he had been ushered into a dream world.

He returned to Harlem with Lottie and spent half the night discussing the amazing old woman with the girl who had been her maid for several years. He learned what Mrs. Rainwater gave and what she *expected*. There was an unwritten code to which all her young geniuses were required to subscribe. There was her theory about spiritual currents among primitive people; he would have to respect that. There was the odd obsession she had for writing letters. She generally sent one a day—in her own hand—to the people she happened to be sponsoring at the moment, and she always expected a good, fond answer. She never trusted conversation. To be authentic the entire discourse had to be repeated in the calm meditation of a personal letter. Then there was the matter of secrecy. Leander would be under oath to hold in confidence all Mrs. Rainwater's words, her gifts. She always spoke of those who told as traitors. She was forever admonishing them not to betray her.

These last words seemed rather strong to Leander. He could not understand why she should be so sharp in upbraiding the overjoyed young people who only recounted her goodness and generosity, but he was willing to conform, no matter what the restrictions. Still he did find it hard to imagine the gentle old woman in a huff.

The boy sang boldly as he walked up Edgecombe Avenue to the row of apartment houses on the hill. A milkman's wagon rumbled in the quiet street.

The move to Jersey did not displease Leander. It was indeed a small concession to make in return for the large gifts he had received. Coming thus at the end of a year's patronage and explained in a small, solemn note, the request seemed utterly reasonable. So while he found the little cities of Jersey dreary as compared to Harlem, he was able to convince himself that Mrs. Rainwater's decision was made in his interest. He settled down in Montclair and devoted his time to vocal exercises and daily letters to what he soon began to call (in his mind) the "throne."

This last chore was at first like punching a time clock, and more disagreeable. The letters Mrs. Rainwater expected constituted a sort of spiritual diary, something like a confessional. Leander found that the ones she enjoyed most were those in which he praised her mystic insight and told her how her wisdom had filled his life with meaning by revealing the great unnoticed forces that stirred his soul. She would take no thanks for her financial aid, but she could not hear enough of this other praise. And Leander developed a formula that made writing reasonably easy after the first six months.

Mrs. Rainwater decided that to be consistent with her treatment of geniuses Lottie should move to Montclair also. Lottie had storytelling gifts. She would probably never make a writer of consequence but she could collect bright sayings of Negroes. That would make a worthy project. Her list might grow so long that it could be indexed and become a reference compendium. Bright sayings of Negroes—the idea was fascinating. Lottie might be given more leisure for this work, and Montclair was just the place for her. There she could be an asset to Leander, playing accompaniments for him and helping to keep him away from Harlem's lights.

For this the boy was genuinely thankful. Lottie's room was just around the corner and he found her good company. And he soon learned to his complete astonishment and delight that the girl was as ready for a let up as he was. They were just a pair of wooly-headed urchins straying on celestial streets. Each had been homeless and nearly destitute before the good angel found them, and each looked upon himself as a clever imposter in the role of genius. They laughed at the studied guile by which they maintained their positions. After all, they were just ordinary young people. Their talents—well, they wouldn't fuss with her about that.

"Whenever I want a present," Lottie said, "I give her one first. Like last week. I'd been hinting how I needed a fur coat. I made sure she had it well in mind; then I let it drop for a few days. All of a sudden I lit on the right medicine. I found a phonograph record of the African Zulu singers that toured England. I paid a dollar for it and had it sent by mail. Two days later the fur coat came. She likes to have you make her little 'artistic' presents. That gives her an excuse to lay out the cash on you."

"Thanks," Leander laughed. "I need a good Gladstone bag. I'll send her that little voodoo drum I have."

"It's just the thing, but you don't have to stop at a Gladstone bag. You can just as easily get a wardrobe trunk and an overcoat in the bargain."

That night the two left their cages and ran over to Harlem for a few dances at the Savoy. Afterwards they went to an odd little place where there was food and drink and the entertainment was informal. The manager, an old friend, asked for a song and Leander obliged with a popular number. When he had finished, a handsome white haired man invited the singer to meet some downtown visitors. At his own table again, Leander introduced the man to Lottie.

"Mr. Tisdale—"

"How do you do."

When he was gone, Lottie touched Leander's knee.

"That's the one," she whispered. "He's the one Mrs. Rainwater calls the 'degraded dilettante.' They're old enemies."

"Yes? I liked him," Leander said.

"Don't tell her that. Lordy, she'd die."

"That's foolish."

"Foolish I know, but it's gospel. They're both interested in Negroes, but they got different ways of showing it. He likes to help singers and musicians by introducing them to managers, getting them chances to entertain in places where the pay is good. He's helped painters to sell pictures, and he's even gotten stories published for some of the writers who couldn't get started by themselves. You know what the old lady thinks of that. Commercialism. She says he's no true friend, that he's just preying on talented young black folks. According to her, his interest is just a passing fancy."

The room was very dim. The dancing was the slow orgiastic kind one finds in the den-like places that stay open till morning. Music was provided by a piano and a drum. Leander drank. Presently the small room took on a rosy glow. The loose-jointed dancers, humped at the shoulders and melting into their partners, delighted him more and more with their antics. But he was not satisfied to watch.

"Come on, gal," he said. "Let's rassle."

The drummer's cymbals clashed. His stick went into the air, touched the ceiling. His grinning upturned face was a rigid Congo mask.

Lottie hummed the melody softly as she danced. It seemed to Leander like the purring of a warm cat on his chest. The shadows of the room fell about him like pendulums of jungle vines. Dry, imaginary leaves crackled under his feet. Was this, he wondered, the primitive heritage that the old lady, Mrs. Rainwater, was trying to have him recapture? Hardly, he told himself. Hardly.

Meanwhile the telephone rang frantically in the hallway of the house where Leander had his room. The old black landlady, getting out of bed in her flannel night gown and stocking cap, answered petulantly.

"No, ma'am. Leander Holley ain't in yet. No'm, he ain't."

And when the boy returned at seven o'clock in the morning, he found a note. Mrs. Rainwater, it seemed, had called him at ten o'clock the night before, shortly after he left for Harlem. Failing to find him home, she had called again at every hour till three. Finally, she had left a message. Would Leander please call her as soon as he returned?

Mrs. Rainwater's voice, as calm and charming as ever, seemed nevertheless strange to Leander this morning.

"To Harlem with Lottie?" she said.

"Yes," he told her lightly. "The jungle beast in me raised his head and roared."

But she was not amused.

"I'd like to talk with you today."

"I'll come in the afternoon," he said respectfully. "Yes, ma'am."

Leander slept a few hours, but he was far from rested when he went to Larchmont. His head felt large, and his eyes burned, and his voice was husky. In addition, he was excited and apprehensive. He knew Mrs. Rainwater was displeased with his little jaunt, and he was not sure that she did not have a scolding in store. And when the Filipino butler let him in, Leander knew at once that all was not well in the Rainwater home. The atmosphere was charged. The boy felt more alien than ever before in the elegant surroundings. He walked with fear and trembling on the glassy floors.

Mrs. Rainwater was waiting in the sun parlor. She was rigid, as coldly beautiful as an old silver image. No blood ran in her veins, no passions stirred. The two exchanged casual words. Then Leander put the match to the powder.

"Where is Lottie?" he asked.

"She's gone home." The old woman's toe twitched ever so little. "I'll have to explain. I have put confidence in you youngsters, Leander. I have rested large hopes in you, your artistic development. Naturally I shouldn't want to be betrayed."

"Betrayed?"

"That's it exactly. At least *you* haven't gone that far yet. Lottie didn't tell me the truth about that frolic of yours last night. She said she wasn't with you. I've had to discipline her. She's probably on her way to Philadelphia by now. Relatives of some sort, I think."

Leander could not speak. For a moment he saw his little golden world withdrawing, vanishing like an early moon behind foothills. He felt sick at the thought of such a loss. He wanted to cry. But in a moment he had another thought. Was it really because of Lottie's falsehood that she had been fired? Might it not have been to teach *Leander* a lesson—to let him know that the rules under which he now served were severe?

Resentment rose in him. She wants to make a slave of me, he thought. She wants me to get permission when I leave home. She's like the rest, like any other old miser—she's not giving something for nothing. Only her manners are different. She is refined.

"She didn't mean any harm—"

"Don't tell me that, Leander."

"Honestly, I suggested—"

"You suggested it, surely. But Lottie knew better. I've talked so much with her. She knew my attitude toward that licentious night life. It will cloud your ideals, throw you into contact with destructive influences. You met Tisdale?"

"Yes."

"See? That's what I mean. If you had only told me of your plans—"

"I'm sorry," he said. "I didn't think. I'm really sorry." He said it with conviction.

"Hm. Well—"

Leander couldn't get the episode out of his mind. If he had only told *her*—so that was it. He was to consult her, to get her approval when he wanted to leave his room. More and more resentment filled his mind. The loss of the tiny golden world became less and less a thing of dread. God, she regards me as a slave, he kept telling himself. I must have sold myself. For three days he did not touch a piano, did not sing a note. For the first time in a year he failed to go for his singing lesson at the appointed time.

"The devil with it," he said, and instead he spent the day walking in the country.

In the mail he found a note from Philadelphia, along with Mrs. Rainwater's letter. Lottie would be glad to have him come down—they might have another whirl together—but, of course, he knew the dangers. She was herself an object lesson to him. A single misstep might mean his losing the kingdom. Generous people like Mrs. Rainwater were not found every day. But if he did want to take a chance, she had something that might interest him. A well-established Negro quartet in that city had just lost its first tenor. The group was preparing for promising engagements in vaudeville (thanks to Tisdale, who was helping them) when a misfortune robbed them of one singer. Tisdale had recommended Leander to the manager.

Curiously, Mrs. Rainwater's letter dealt with the same subject, but in a different vein.

"Mr. Tisdale is seeking your address," it said. "He wants to tempt you into a vulgar quartet venture of some sort. Have nothing whatever to do with it."

The old woman knew everything, Leander thought. It was almost mystic the way she got reports. He sat down and worked out a clever plot. He wrote Mrs. Rainwater a note in which he promised to have nothing to do with the quartet or with anything in which Mr. Tisdale was even remotely connected. He used all his most trusted blandishments to soothe the woman's feelings. Then in a postscript he remarked that he was running down to Philadelphia—simply for a change of air, a jaunt. He'd be back in two or three days. He *knew,* he said, she would approve, so he was not waiting for an answer.

In Philadelphia he purchased a lovely old bottle and sent it to her. He also wrote a letter each day while there: but when he returned he found no mail in his room, and consternation took him. He had offended the kind old woman, he thought. She was not angry or she would have written a sharp letter. She was just hurt, wounded. Leander's heart melted, and he hastened over to Larchmont with contrition on his lips, with words of apology ready.

Mrs. Rainwater had all his little absurd presents tied in a strong paper bundle that suggested an impending journey to the rubbish heap if he failed to call. She was standing when he entered the sun parlor.

"I didn't think you'd hope to fool me," she said.

"I—"

"It was positively brazen. That syrupy letter. The effrontery of it. Running down there, letting Tisdale and Lottie string you along—and to think that you would attempt to throw dust in my eyes. Traitors—"

"You can do what you please about it," Leander said pettishly. "You don't have to go on helping—"

"Do as I please!" And then, to his utter dismay, Mrs. Rainwater stomped her small frail foot. "How can I recall those vocal lessons? How can I keep others from taking the credit for the talents I have sponsored. What can I do about that overcoat you're wearing?"

Leander's face burned. His hands became moist.

"I didn't ask for anything," he protested.

"You didn't directly—no, but you betrayed me into believing you had a soul."

He went out. On the quiet streets of the exclusive neighborhood he felt frightened. He had a strange presentiment that presently small, hostile children would come from behind those fine houses and pelt him with stones. He hurried.

At a corner drug store he entered a telephone booth and called Philadelphia. To Lottie he said, "Tell them that the quartet proposition will be O.K. I'll be down tomorrow."

From *The Old South: "A Summer Tragedy" and Other Stories of the Thirties* (New York: Dodd, Mead, and Co., 1973). Reprinted by permission of Harold Ober Associates Incorporated. Copyright © 1973 by Alberta Bontemps, Executrix.

BRUCE HOLLAND ROGERS

"A Patron of the Arts"

The relatively exclusive, and critical, focus on inequities in the relationship between donor and recipient obscures what scholar Paul Schervish has called "the most fundamental sociological fact about philanthropy: namely, that philanthropy is a social relation of giving and getting between donors and recipients, directly mobilized and governed by strength of character and a moral compass, born of identification with another as a radical end like oneself." In a far more playful way, American short-story writer Bruce Holland Rogers drives home the same point, by positively modeling what others decry. In this story, the first-person narrator indicates how he "became one of the principal patrons of the Montreal poet Donat Bobet and how it became [his] custom to dine with him, every now and then." Though the social relation between the two is founded in "pretend," it seems to be just this pretence that enables the two men, each in his own way, to give to and get from the other. Were you to meet the extraordinary Donat Bobet, in similar circumstances, might you be inclined to befriend him? As a foundation program officer, might you be inclined to recommend support for him? At the end of the story, Donat names his benefactor both a "patron of the arts" and an "artist." Is there artistry in patronage? Is philanthropy an art form?

It was my custom, after work, to go to a particular café on Rue Queen. There, I always had a *café au lait* and a *tarte aux pommes* while I read *Le Devoir*, beginning with the opinion page. The waiter knew what to bring me the moment I sat down. I always left exactly the same tip.

One spring day—the first almost-warm day after a difficult winter—I felt one of those dissatisfactions that can arrive suddenly, like unpleasant weather. I had put on weight during the winter. I was still a bachelor, with no prospects in sight. I was a year older than I had been the previous spring.

What I needed was a change. As I followed my usual path from the office, I resolved to have my *café au lait* at a different café.

I walked along Rue Saint-Paul, looking for a suitable place. I saw several that were unsuitable—too much for tourists, too brightly lit, too dim. This one was too close to the traffic, and that one was too much in the wind. I continued. One café had an awning that was badly soiled—little details can tell you a lot about a place. If they don't clean their awning, what can the kitchen be like? I grew tired. I began to regret my adventure. But then, at last, I found a place that would almost do. If I altered my standards just a bit to allow for the artificial flower on each table, the café would suit me.

As I have said, the day was almost warm, warm enough that there were tables and chairs outside. But there was still wind, enough to have driven all the patrons indoors. I went inside only to make sure that I had the waiter's attention, then I sat at the table that was least exposed to wind but still in the sun. I opened *Le Devoir* to the opinion page, and I was halfway through the section when the waiter brought me my *café au lait* and *tarte aux pommes*, and I asked for the bill at once. It came to a little more than at my customary café, enough that I did not think I would come here again. I would leave a nice tip, though. It was an opportunity to use up all the change in my pocket.

A man's voice nearby loudly declared, "*Mesdames et messieurs,* thank you! Thank you!"

I looked up from my paper. Beyond the farthest table stood a man dressed in an ill-fitting black suit and a red cap. He was looking at me, but then his gaze roamed from table to table, as if there were a great multitude of customers and he were looking into the eyes of each person. "I thank you," he said again. "Please . . ." He gestured as if asking for applause to cease. "I am, as many of you know, Donat Bobet. Today's recital will be brief . . ." he held up his hands. "Please, I am sorry, it must be brief today. Two poems only, today. The first is a poem by Alain Bosquet. It is called, 'No Need.'"

The waiter stuck his head out of the door to ask me, "Is he bothering you?"

Had I been planning on becoming a regular at the café, I might have answered in the affirmative. However, as the purpose of coming here was to have a one-time adventure, I said, "Not at all." I folded my newspaper.

"Don't give him any money," said the waiter. And to Monsieur Bobet he said, "If you come among the tables and chairs, it's trespassing!"

"Please," said Bobet. "Please hold your applause until the end."

The waiter went back inside. The poem was a short one about how the designs of animals were sufficient to their needs. An elephant's trunk meant that it needn't stoop, a giraffe's height meant it needn't fly, a chameleon's skin meant it needn't run away, and a turtle's shell meant that it need not find a home. In conclusion, a poet's poems meant that a poet did not need to understand. Or perhaps it was that a poet didn't need to be understood. As he recited the final line, Donat Bobet made a grand flourish with his hand. He swept the cap from his head and bowed. He said, "Thank you! Thank you everyone! You are too kind."

"I'm not sure I understand it."

"A question?" Bobet cupped a hand to his ear, as if he had just barely heard my voice among the throng of loud admirers.

Absurdly, I raised my voice. "I don't understand it!"

"Ah, well," said Bobet, "understanding isn't everything, is it?" He put his cap back on his head. "Here, for example, is one that you are quite sure not to understand. It is called, 'Afloat on the Saint-Laurent.'" He proceeded then to recite a long poem about the great monuments of Europe floating up the *fleuve,* toward Lake Ontario. The Brandenburg Gate, the Arc de Triomphe, the Nelson obelisk, among others, all floated in from the sea, against the current. Among them were busts and statues from Athens, from Prague, from Oslo. When they got to the lake, there they stayed, bobbing on the waves and interfering forever with shipping. At the end, Donat Bobet repeated his grand flourish. He bared his head and bowed. He said, "Thank you! Thank you all so very much. Modesty prevents me from telling you the author of that particular poem. Thank you."

I clapped politely. I picked up my paper and stood.

"As you leave, *mesdames et messieurs,* I would be most grateful for your patronage. Anything at all will help. I mean that quite earnestly. A penny is nothing to you, but to a poet a penny is a portrait of the queen!"

I remembered the waiter's warning not to give the poet anything, but it would be less awkward to settle a few coins on him than to walk by without doing so.

I considered the change I had left on the table for the waiter. There were some pennies there, and quarters, and a dollar coin. But a penny donation was insulting, no matter what Bobet had just said. In any case, it didn't seem right to take from the waiter who had been protective of my solitude, even if I had declined his protection. I opened my wallet and produced a five.

When I handed the bill to Donat Bobet, he looked me in the eyes and said, "Thank you." As I started to walk away, he produced a pen and began to make marks on the bill. He was defacing the portrait of Laurier. He was making the old prime minister smile.

I had gone but a short distance from the café when I heard a shout. "Monsieur! Monsieur!" It was Bobet, running after me, waving the bill. "Fifty! Did you mean to give me so much?"

"Fifty?" I said. We both knew full well what I had given him. But he showed me the five-dollar note. Not only was Wilfrid Laurier smiling, but Bobet had inked in a 0 after each 5. CINQ had been revised to CINQUANTE, and FIVE to FIFTY.

I frowned. "That's no joke. It's one thing to draw on a smile—"

"Fifty!" Bobet said. "Sir, you are a true patron of the arts! I am so grateful! Please, you must dine with me, at my expense. Please! I'll make such a meal. Fifty! I will transport your tastebuds to Indochina! You must say yes! Please say you will do me this honor!"

The waiter had warned me not to give this fellow money, and perhaps Bobet always attached himself to donors. Perhaps he was operating some sort of confidence game. But, of course, I had no confidence in him, so how could he take advantage of me? I could walk away if things took a turn I didn't like. I had no better plans. Day after day, I worked with reasonable, sober people. Hadn't I resolved to have an adventure today? "All right. I consent. But you mustn't try to pass that bill off as the real thing. Not while I'm along."

"My apartment is in this direction," he said, turning me around. "We must stop for a few things along the way. Oh, what a feast we will have!"

We went into a little grocery store. I thought, *Ah, here's his game. He'll try to get me to pay for a week's provisions!* But Bobet's shopping consisted of a pound of ground chicken and a lime. His five dollars would cover that. As we stood in line, Bobet considered a bouquet of flowers for $6.99. He inspected three different bouquets, then put each one of them back. The cashier rang up the ground chicken, the lime . . . At the last moment, Bobet reached for one of the bouquets. "After your generosity," he said, "I can afford it!"

He gave the cashier his five dollars and a smile. She hardly looked at the bill, but stood waiting for the rest.

"Well?" said Bobet.

"You're still short," said the cashier.

"My word!" said Bobet. "By how much?"

The cashier looked at the total. "Six dollars and seventeen cents?"

Bobet shook his head. "The price of luxurious living!" He looked at me. "I am not accustomed to spending so freely. I'm afraid your donation went to my head. I suppose we can do without the flowers."

Flowers. Was that all he would try to take me for? I was grateful that he hadn't insisted to the cashier that he had given her fifty dollars. I opened my wallet. I gave him ten. He paid, accepted the cashier's change, and then did not pocket the money as I expected. He gave the change to me. "I am so embarrassed," he said. "I am behind the times. I thought fifty would carry us much further. But no matter. We will still have our feast!"

We walked together up Rue Saint-François-Xavier. I didn't see how he could afford to live in this neighborhood. Then we took a side street and came to a building with cracks in the old stone walls. Several of the windows were painted over. Bobet opened the lobby doors with a key, then stood still.

"Oh, what am I thinking?" he said. "We need wine. I'm sorry. Would you do me the favor of picking some up? There is an SAQ nearby." He told me how to walk to the liquor store.

I went out and bought the wine. I bought a nice Chardonnay, since I expected that I might drink it alone. Bobet did have a key to that tumble-down building, but what of it? He might have stolen it. He might have run to the end of his game with me. I wasn't positive that the man actually lived anywhere but on the street.

When I returned, though, I found his name behind the cracked glass of the apartment directory.

"Third floor," he said when I buzzed. "Mine is the apartment with the magnificently ornate carved doors. You'll know them when you see them. The other apartments . . . Well, my neighbors don't keep their places up as I do."

I found the stairs. The stairwell was lit with a naked bulb. There were certainly no ornately carved doors on the second floor. The doors and hallways were dirty yellow. I wondered if they had been painted in the last century.

I did not see any unusual doors on the third floor, either. Just the same yellow paint, the same dented doorknobs. Finally, at the end of the hallway, a door that was just like all the others had something written on it, like graffiti. It said, "Magnificent ornately carved doors of an oriental motif."

It made me smile. I knocked.

Bobet came to the door wearing an apron. "Dinner is well underway!" he said. "Shall we open the wine to let it breathe?"

"It's a Chardonnay," I said. "We can drink it at once."

"But come in, come in!" He waved me inside and took the wine from me. "Please, have a look around."

Just inside the door, the walls of the brief hallway were marked with big squares and rectangles, each with more graffiti in the same hand that had labeled the front door. Inside one rectangle was written, "The Bog in the Forest, by Fedor Vassiliev." Next to that was one that said, "The Pond at Montgeron, Claude Monet." The apartment was nothing more than a hallway leading to a single room with a table and chairs in one corner, a stove in another, and a bed in the third. Here the imaginary paintings were "By Alexander Mordvinov, View of the Grand Canal in Venice, Midday," "Garden at Giverny, Claude Monet."

"As you can see," Bobet said as he worked at the stove, spoon in hand, "I have a passion for the Russians."

"And Monet," I observed.

"Monet, of course! Monet is a god! I would love to have one of his haystacks . . ."

"You still have some wall space," I said.

"But not the money," Bobet said. "Not yet." He laughed. "Although now that I have met a wealthy patron . . ."

On the floor, inside another rectangle, were the words, "Persian carpet of black, gold, red, and white, in a fine geometric pattern." The simple wooden chair against one wall said, "Overstuffed armchair. Red."

I sat in the red chair. I smiled. In truth, I felt a bit as if I truly were a wealthy patron of the arts. I rubbed my belly. There was a much slimmer me inside there, underneath the winter fat. Actually, it was several winters of fat. Bobet was furiously stirring three pans on the stove. I said, "It smells good." And it did. Whatever he was doing with the ground chicken smelled rich and exotic.

The flower bouquet sat in the middle of the table in a mason jar labeled "cut crystal." The biggest window in the room looked onto the alleyway, but written on the pane were the words, "view of the Saint-Laurent." Bobet opened the wine and poured it into two glasses. "Come, come!" he said.

I rose from the overstuffed armchair. Bobet served our dinners on unmatched but elegant china plates. Each plate held a mound of rice which, judging from the bits of peas and carrots, had been an element of an earlier meal. I overlooked that. The ground chicken had been divided into thirds, each cooked in its own spices. A flower garnished each plate.

We ate. I detected lemon grass and red pepper in one portion, lime and coriander in another. In the third, I tasted a bit of garlic, and perhaps a hint of ginger. All three were marvelous.

I relaxed. I looked about the room. "Is that incense burner really an antique?" It was made of folded aluminum foil. Written on one relatively unwrinkled surface were the words, "Tang dynasty bronze."

"Oh, yes," said the poet. "I inherited it. My family had money at one time." He lifted his wineglass. "To art and artists," he said.

"But I am no artist."

"My friend, you most certainly are," said Donat Bobet. "What is more, you are a rich patron, a man admired for his taste and generosity. I salute you!"

I took up my wine glass. With my free hand, I imitated the flourish Bobet had made with his hand when he finished reading a poem. I said, "I thank you!"

We drank. In time, we finished the bottle. At some point, I asked, "So how much do you need, to keep all of this up?"

"Oh," he said, "an occasional gift of fifty, just as you gave me today . . ."

That is how I became one of the principal patrons of the Montreal poet Donat Bobet and how it became my custom to dine with him, every now and then.

JACQUES BARZUN

"The Folklore of Philanthropy"

The House of Intellect, *by noted American writer, educator, and cultural historian Jacques Barzun, was a bestseller at the time of its publication in 1959, profoundly influencing debate about culture and education for years to come. This excerpt helps explain why. In it, Barzun turns his critical and prescient eye on foundation giving practices, many of which have indeed become (folk)lore in the intervening decades. Though his immediate concern is how such practices adversely affect those who labor in the name of Intellect, his observations resonate with those made by people who have been on the 'asking' end of a grant. For example: What small, floundering nonprofit has not been victimized by the "tendency of the foundation to prefer large demands to small, [or] clear social undertakings to dim private ones—in a word, projects to persons"? Or, what struggling organization, knowing the philanthropic tastes of foundation "x," has been able to suppress the "urge to stultify itself at the expense of honesty"? At the end of his chapter, Barzun makes a radical suggestion: End the businesslike "impartiality" of foundation decision-making—of which the grant application is chief ornament—in favor of "direct judgment" by a few who can "know and choose men and ideas at a glance." Is this a vote for or against the democratization of grantor-grantee relations? Would this alleviate or exacerbate the corrupting elements of the current grantmaking process? Is there a better way of overcoming these elements?*

છે

The now characteristic behavior of the modern foundations was determined soon after they were established. One can readily imagine the awesome weight of responsibility that descended on the men who were first given millions of dollars with which to do something for the good of the nation. What should they do? What could they do? Everybody's eyes were on them, everybody's hand was stretched out. The beggar, one surmises, was ready as always to curse the professed Christian who passed him by. Does not the Christian depend for his salvation on the beggar? No beggars, no Christian charity. Does not the foundation depend on takers of money for its continued existence as a charitable institution? No applicants, no tax exemption. So from the outset the tendency of the foundation was to prefer large demands to small, clear social undertakings to dim private ones—in a word, projects to persons.

Holding in check any likelihood of indiscriminate largesse was the ever-present sense of responsibility. There was the annual report to think of, in which the grants would undergo public scrutiny. Even before the annual report, the relation of the executives to the trustees put a premium on projects with an attractive exterior. The trustees' review might go only a little deeper than the public's, but for that very reason, projects must be defensible from the surface outward. Their briefly stated aims and skeleton budgets must commend themselves to the average educated man of business.

Among the applicants themselves the criticism of favored projects might be sharper, but this would not matter if impartiality seemed to rule the distribution—equal-handedness to North and South, to large and small institutions, to old and new, to home and foreign missions, to health, to education, and to welfare. It was important, also, not to compete with any going concern, especially commercial enterprises such as trade publishers of books and magazines; not to encroach on individual rights by anything like a contract requiring work for value received; and not to weaken initiative by helping those who would not help themselves. These motives led to rules which still govern foundation awards, irrespective of their effects on education and Intellect.

To particularize: 'impartiality' has meant the support of institutions ostensibly in a class with others, but actually weaker. The principle of concentrating resources has never been acknowledged or deliberately followed. If it has come into play at all, it is only because the leading institutions, embracing more units, could not help receiving more support. And this support, given to projects rather than to the institution, has nearly everywhere had the result of weakening the structure and scattering the intellectual forces of the establishment. Today, the chief beneficiaries are alarmed to see the damage done to their fabric. The levers of destruction were the matching grant and the short-term allowance for 'original' ideas, which I shall discuss farther on. As for the projects themselves, they were hampered by the rule that denies money for publishing. When their results are in hand, scholars must spend time and energy to secure commercial publication or beg a subsidy from some agency that can use the book or brochure for its own interested ends.

Finally, the show of freedom from obligation has been mutually deceptive. Projectors have known how desirable it is to be copious in the production of forecasts, interim reports, and summaries of results; and yet the foundations have never exercised any authority, such as their knowledge might warrant, to insist on even so elementary a need as the readability and compactness of the conclusions offered to the intellectual community. This negligence has meant that innumerable 'studies' have crowded the library shelves and enlightened only their makers. In short, abdication of power has occurred on both sides— the foundations wanting no responsibility and the researchers no audience. This was to be expected. The foundations have been great amplifiers of the dominant traits of our intellectual life, rather than artisans of a new conception of it.

As foundations grew in number, they tended to specialize, explicitly or by custom. But apart from this limitation and those implied by the rules I have described, access to the reservoirs of charity was kept entirely free. Anyone could apply for any purpose and would receive a courteous answer on thick paper. From being a public trust the foundations were soon forced into the position of a public office, which meant that they had to develop a bureaucracy. The work of sorting out from the mass of plausible and mad projects the deserving cases devolved usually on young men drawn from academic life. They were first attracted to the grueling work by the importance of the trust and its influence for good, and secondarily, perhaps, by the executive mode of life, which seemed an improvement on the academic mode of shabby-genteel. The talent required consisted of administrative ability coupled with the diplomacy of the personnel manager, both of which implied interests broader than the specialist's.

Most of the traditions created by these tireless young men were unconscious adaptations of ideals current in the national life; a few were deliberate policies framed by the trustees out of their experience of business and public relations. For example, the practices that grew up about the framing and judging of projects reflected the common inclination toward the measurable, and this not in a crude sense, but on the contrary, a complex, often fantastic sense. Likewise, the lust for novelty, the 'creative' and the exotic found the dispensers of money ever sanguine, not to say progressively infatuated. But the aesthetic attitude joined to the taste for the tangible produced a bias toward natural and social science, on the one hand, and toward the performing arts, on the other. The regard for humanistic scholarship was also high, but the scholar's needs, most characteristic of Intellect, seemed to defy the established order of thought. The humanities gave rise to no projects properly so called, were not expensive enough, and promised few social benefits. Their work remained invisible. To support it was like gambling sums too small to be exciting on horses altogether too dark.

The recipients of foundation grants naturally did not criticize these assumptions—only particular decisions under them—and to this day the general public has but a vague idea of foundation procedures and their effects. Indeed, it is but fair to add that the effects are only now becoming clear to the officials and petitioners themselves, though the new currency of terms such as 'projectism' shows a growing awareness.

In trying here to make that awareness both deeper and more general, I am not, of course, aiming darts at any particular foundation or foundations, nor have I any of their officials in mind, save as Platonic archetypes. I have naturally disguised details while keeping strictly to the philosophic truth of the case.

It says much for the acceptance of foundation folklore that we all know what a project is: it is something neatly clamped in a folder, not too thin and not too bulky, and typed preferably on an electric typewriter. The last page consists of figures, headed 'Estimated Budget' and divided into three- or five-year slices. The project is in truth a literary form, like the Shakespearean sonnet, and its correct composition is an art not vouchsafed to everyone. There is a language appropriate to projects, a tone which veils the diversity of minds, an indefinable fitness to the particular proposal and the promise it holds forth. Just as there is the love sonnet and the meditative sonnet, so there is the problem project and the survey project. Each must follow style and fashion; the idea must be turned in such a way that it shall make the project different from all others, yet 'in line with current programs' and at the same time 'widely applicable' if successful. Thus a psychologist who might like to know whether modern composers can actually hear the counterpoint they write would have to present his project either as a device for predicting future success in music students, or else as a measurement scale for rating with precision the great contrapuntists of the past, thus 'making obsolete the crude, subjective criticism still in use.' If the example seems satirical, it is nevertheless true to the mythology of research and the desire for a universal submission to scientific method, both of which weigh heavily on all projects.

In every branch of learning and in every center of research, some persons are found capable of converting a thoughtful piece of curiosity into a project so that it will appear ideal—or, as is said, 'a natural'—for foundation support. Other people, also able but without this knack, must have their projects 'processed,' and still others learn the trick. The consequence is a strong urge in many a man to stultify himself at the expense of what used to be called intellectual honesty. The scholar or scientist salves his conscience with the thought that he will turn the proceeds to good use. He hopes to do 'his own work' behind the shelter of phrases denoting expected attitudes; to do fundamental research though proposing foundational research.

For he knows that if he does not use the accepted language his most commonplace ideas will seem wild or barren. They will shock and not be receivable. It would be rude, for instance, to say that you 'expect to finish the work in three years.' You must say: 'It is anticipated that the project will be satisfactorily completed within a three-year period.' It would be egotistical to suggest that 'an answer to the ancient and perplexing question, What are the rational principles of translation, must interest every scholar and educated reader, and I mean to have a try at it.' You must write: 'The project here submitted to the Modern Age Foundation is in line with similar projects which it has endorsed before in its valuable program of people-to-people understanding and cooperation, and it is hoped that by deploying on the crucial procedural focus of the translation problem the specialized competence and distinct approach of a team of experts from varied areas under the close supervision of the undersigned, a contribution may be made to a problem currently of urgent immediacy and global importance.'

Nothing, in effect, is closer to the stance of projectism than the attitude shown in the dedicatory epistles of earlier centuries, in which a patron was similarly wooed by flattery, circumlocution, and conventional promises. There is this difference, of course, that the flattery of the modern is not directed at a living person but at the effigy of itself that the particular foundation has hoisted aloft. And this impersonality is reciprocal. The foundation by its ethics takes no interest in the persons of the suppliants, but only in that self-same effigy. Princely patronage, in becoming institutionalized, has thus bred a centaur-like abstraction: a beggar on horseback, if you will, in which it is the horseback (so to say) that drives and chooses the road. This is why it is correct to speak of projec*tism,* more powerful than beggars or bureaucracy.

At first sight, one might think that stated goals and a disregard of persons would best serve the great abstraction of Intellect. The fact is that intellectual ambition and power still reside in individuals and nowhere else. Teamwork may discover but not invent. The most characteristic, because the oldest, features of Intellect continue to occur in the subjects least susceptible to collectivization. It is in the foundations' gingerly handling of those subjects, notably the humanities and the highest type of theoretical science, that one sees how incompatible are foundation lore and Intellect. The foundations have been embarrassed in consequence. I have had visits from half a dozen representatives of foundations earnestly inquiring into the mystery: how to serve the humanities. These men were perturbed by what seemed to them irregular about pure scholarship and their distress is instructive. It shows, on the one hand, the desire to do right and serve all interests; and on the other, the oblivion that has overtaken the rules of Intellect. Although foundation officials tend to use their trustees much as in Dickens Mr. Spenlow used as an excuse for refusals his supposedly hardhearted partner Mr. Jorkins, whom no one ever saw, it is not the trustees by themselves who are to blame, nor even the influence of business habits. It is the temper of distrust toward persons, our refuge-seeking in the 'objective,' which is fostered by our schools and universities, our political institutions and public prints, our ideas of philanthropy and our pride in the impersonality of science.

Fifty years ago, William James said that the social value of a college education was to tell a good man when you saw one. From the way he said it, one infers that this simple truth already seemed a paradox. It is now a heresy. You do not tell a good man when you see one: you ask him to fill out a blank. You ask him to collect letters of recommendation; you send out forms on which distrait persons put check marks opposite the names of qualities and virtues and guess at percentages of merit. The guesses help or hinder the applicant's chances and bear as little relation to life—let alone to objectivity or the nature of Intellect—as the inert heap of letters of recommendation. The truth of this is acknowledged in practice. Short of proved criminal tendencies or dementia praecox, every candidate turns out to be able, responsible, co-operative, and well trained. The astonishing variety of mankind nowhere appears in these documents; rather, the population of the country turns out to consist wholly of paragons, for letters that hint of a defect are a species of death warrant and hence are seldom written.

Around leading personalities, it is true, judgments collect and create a reputation independent of the paper file. But this comes late in the day, usually when it is no longer needed; and reputation is hard to establish after middle life, especially if the person is not a native and yet already on the scene. I remember a foreign scholar, whose works were well known and whose residence in this country for some ten years had made him many distinguished admirers. He wanted after his retirement to finish a three-volume work in an important branch of philosophy. The combined efforts of a dozen or more high-placed American scholars were unavailing to obtain for this man the supplement to his pension which would have given him three or four years of peace of mind to finish his work. Every foundation was interested; innumerable letters were filed. But when it came to the disbursement of twelve thousand dollars, half a century's alienation from intellectual man interposed its veto.

Do we see here a subtle manifestation of the envy I described as part of dogmatic equality? Just as in welfare charity the social worker does not want to see the beneficiary rioting in pleasure, so in intellectual charity the unavowed feeling seems to be: 'Why should he revel in the joys of research and writing—superior and independent—while the rest of us carry on this important but unrefreshing paper work?' We do not, it is true, begrudge youth that same freedom, and as we shall see, freeing a man for a mission occurs every day. But the Fulbright student or scholar is an 'ambassador,' so that he is not indulging himself in the pure luxury of doing only what he most wants to do, uncommitted, unclassified, unlectured at.

What strengthens the suspicion that these emotions exist and affect the giver's judgment of the petitioner is the delight that all keepers of money evidence when they are asked to pay, not for a man working, but for equipment, clerical help, microfilm, travel to research centers, and incidental expenses. When such things are required in order to pursue intellectual work, what relief, what joy! We are being virtuous and sensible too. The bill will be large. We are spending *enough* money and not frittering it away piecemeal on intellectuals. It is this yearned-for security that has given first place in foundation fancy to the conference.

The conference has the advantage of maximizing at once high purposes and down-to-earth costs. One hundred learned men brought to one spot for a stated cause are known to produce a foundation effect directly proportional to the square of the distance traveled, multiplied by the cube of the mimeographed matter given off. And for these *exciting* results nothing is paid but railroad fares and hotel bills, taxi drivers and stenotypists. This is not caricature: I have myself been offered a quarter of a million dollars without formality—over the counter, so to speak—to organize a world conference on a particular topic which at the time was thought momentous. All I had to do was to give up everything I was doing and start inviting notables from all over—I would know who they were and the magic of the subject plus an offer of expenses would draw them like a magnet. My intellectual contribution was to divide the subject and assign congenial topics and hotel rooms. When I declined and proposed a more lasting use of the money, for a related purpose yet not one furthering any ends of my own, I was told that the suggestion would be taken under advisement. . . .

One reason why my counterproposal was never heard of again was that it violated—as I knew in advance—the chief tenet of foundation lore: instead of being a new creation, my idea only buttressed an existing enterprise; and instead of being observation, a study of others' work, it would directly aid those already working. The principle of compulsory newness is an offshoot of school creativity and utopianism. I have heard an official call his foundation's grants the 'venture capital of social change.' He was devout in the belief that his chosen projects were helping remake the country and the world; the recipients of funds were evangelists, though being scientific they were without a gospel, and the foundation had only the dogma of rationalized habit. Like other foundations this one represented its projects as original in conception, pioneering in purpose, and epoch-making in promise. Applicants hampered by sober ideas must impart to them an apocalyptic glow, and men engaged in recognizable activities need not apply. In truth, most foundations decided from the start that whatever schools, colleges, and universities were already doing was of no interest. This purely academic work would go on in its old-fashioned way and be paid for out of old-fashioned endowments. No one engaged in the central duties of a going concern could be foundation fodder; but obviously, any such person should be encouraged to take a look at his performance, in the expectation that when he saw it as it really was he would do something else.

In this we see the vestiges of sound instinct. Nearly everything is susceptible of improvement, and money should certainly be offered for things never before done. But the instinct is polluted by creative pride and secretly stirred by the ancestral repugnance to schoolwork. That the result denies the value of tradition and experience in human affairs, particularly the affairs of Intellect, does not bother men whose patterns of thought tend to be formed by analogy, not so much with science, as with scientific research, that is, the external preparations for science. The studies subsidized imply, for example, that a college does not know by inspection when it needs more books or teachers. This must be 'studied' and 'found out' by comparison and exchange of ideas. . . .

This is not to say that all studies sponsored by foundations have been of small use. But when useful, the utility has been confined almost entirely to those making the study. Neither the institutions of learning nor the intellectual public could possibly assimilate as much 'knowledge' as they are offered in this form; first, because our channels of intelligence are clogged or broken down, and second, because despite their aping of science, the reports of studies are almost always too large and too vague.

By contrast, the effect of foundation grants on our seats of learning has been simple and may be shortly stated: inflation and strain. By pouring money into projects, studies, and institutes—all new and superimposed on existing purposes—the foundations have steadily added to the financial and administrative burdens of universities, while creating on the rim of the central structure vested interests whose allegiance is to the outside source of funds, not to the institution they happen to belong to. The unity and sense of loyalty of large companies of scholars have thus been undermined. Again, by encouraging individuals with a knack for project-making, the foundations have entrenched the idea that the prestige of a grant, free funds, and the comforts of adequate equipment and a private secretary come only to the intellectual promoter. Oh, to be the director of a project and lead an airport existence! To stay on the spot and teach or meditate is the sign of the unenterprising if not the mediocre. . . .

. . . A foundation only expresses with large means the charitable urge of private persons. And they, lacking the support of a tradition for intellectual giving, follow such habits as they have acquired in other occupations. They give to what they love or approve, and would be quite surprised to be told that this is as wrong as the nepotism they would scorn to commit. They are 'for' peace or 'for' science, or they 'believe in' foreign exchanges or the small liberal arts college or mass psychiatry, and so they indulge these illicit passions when they ought to be considering what it is that the country (or the art, the institution, the person) requires of them—of their thought and of their purse.

This is not to cast blame on these amateur givers as individuals but only to point out what effects follow a culture's losing all knowledge of the nature and conditions of intellectual life. The conditions are even more important to know than the nature of the innumerable arts and sciences that make up the whole. A society that understood the conditions and maintained them could reap the products without worrying about what took place in between. Our mania for fiddling with processes and qualifications and neglecting plain prerequisites is seen in the attempt to produce art by mass procurement—establishing a program at an institution, or offering fellowships to applicants, with the hope that 'in a ten-year period' some works shall be produced. All this generates is paper work, committees, and quantities of respectably unimportant work. There are only two ways in which to go about adding to the stock of great art: make an outright gift to a proved master, young or old, without project-forging and reference-hunting; or free an already active artistic center from commercial necessity, again without strings, promises, *or hopes.*

These two ways, unfortunately, require excellence of judgment and the willingness to use it. We are betrayed by our cultivated inability to know and choose men and ideas at a glance, the way the jewel expert knows a diamond. Such men exist—the teachers or colleagues of those from whom we may expect good work. It follows that we could reduce enormously the waste of time and effort by giving, not a fellowship or grant directly to the applicant, but to an instructor or sponsor the privilege of awarding it. The list of awarders' names, changing from year to year, would not be hard to compile. The best men would most frequently receive the right to nominate, would draw the best students, would know in any year who among them deserved the prize. The objection to this can be foreseen: the scheme would make for partiality and jealousy. Quite so. But that partiality, of one fine mind for another, is what is meant by an intellectual tradition. As for jealousy, it is a regrettable fault, but we cannot abolish it by tactfulness, and we shall never have excellence unless we are willing to distinguish it in public from mediocrity.

Instead of this direct judgment, fallible but apt, we rely on what we like to think is a more democratic choice, because it is made by a committee from among unlimited applications. In fact, democracy is foiled by the inevitable 'preliminary screening,' done by some trusted assistant, who necessarily works by rule of thumb upon the external appearances of the record. In a short time, every alert applicant knows the 'line' to take for success in the first stage as well as for the later interview. By this as by other roads, our young intellect is brought to see his career as a subdivision of public relations. One might indeed generalize and say that wherever the style and procedure cost large sums, Intellect is submerged and judgment warped to advertisers' standards.

The money of philanthropy should smell of its object, not its origin; which does not mean being Puritanical about its use. The intellectual life is expensive and it deserves solid comfort, but if due relations obtained, foundation offices would not look like the headquarters of a billion-dollar trust where the student's overcoat and hat seem a blemish, and where the long meditations of young executives are guarded by murmuring vestals trained to be kind to scholars. If minds were concentrated on the work, there would be fewer releases and reports, illustrated newsletters, and syrupy expositions of educational problems. The note of sensual competition would be absent, as would the tone of the middleman who, with a little co-operation from all parties, will make anything as pleasant and plausible as anything else—this month, next year, for you, for me, for basic research, for applied research, strongly with the current, sweetly provocative, a conservative man, a pioneer armed with precedents, emancipated in spirit, respectful of the *status quo*, against sin.

Philanthropy, in sum, is manipulation for the general good, anxiously contrived, timidly eager for approval, and therefore seeking love and publicity. The fact that by now every agency of Intellect without exception must praise itself in print in order to survive is no sign of commercialism in its leaders or in culture; greed is not the motive; the motive is fear of isolation through privilege, and especially fear of the appearance of privilege, coupled with profound distrust of its own judgment.

PABLO EISENBERG

"Penetrating the Mystique of Philanthropy: Relations between Fund Raisers and Grant Makers"

Pablo Eisenberg is a long-time anti-poverty activist, community advocate, non-profit and foundation watch-warden, and educator. Though he explicitly criticizes foundation practices, his prime concerns here are the attitudes and practices not of donors but of donees. By accepting the premise that they are "unequal partners in the philanthropic process," Eisenberg argues, donees "have helped to create [and perpetuate] the monster [they] so greatly resent." It is up to them, then, to de-mystify the "mystique of philanthropy." Though Eisenberg calls for collective action—without which, he insists, reform will never be possible—the specific reforms he advocates require the active participation of individuals. For the deepest obstacle to reform, he implies, is the donee's own self-understanding vis-à-vis his or her donor. At the core of his advice is the admonition to "be true to yourself": remember your strengths, remember your importance, and make them both known, in person, to donors. Surely, this is a worthy thing to hope for. But is it practical? Would it be sufficient—is it possible—to overturn the so-called "Golden Rule of Grantsmanship": he who has the gold makes the rules?

෴

For most of us who work for community organizations, there is a mystique about foundations and corporations and the way they give away their money. This air of mystery and awe is a major reason we have such a hard time raising money from them. We are not familiar with their history and how they operate. We know few if any of their board members. We are not likely to meet them or their professional staff at the local supermarket or anywhere else where we work and socialize. When we do meet, it is almost always about a proposal we have submitted to them for funding.

Since they have the money we desperately need, we naturally view our relationship with them as inherently unequal, an imbalance of power. We also know or have heard about their "establishment" priorities, their relative lack of accountability and the problems encountered by organizations similar to ours in getting a fair hearing. And we are aware that charitable giving, unlike the political and judicial systems, does not provide any legal avenues for appeal. A foundation or corporate donor's decision is final.

These perceptions and experiences have combined to create a picture of philanthropy that is deadly in its impact on so many of our organizations. It is a portrait of an elite group of givers to whom respect and obedience must be given by a host of petitioners asking for philanthropic handouts. It is like the worshipers in ancient Greece pleading with the Delphic Oracle for good fortune.

While the attitudes and actions of those who give money have helped shape this nature of philanthropy, those of us on the receiving end—the donees—must share some of the responsibility for perpetuating the mystique of philanthropy. By accepting the premise that donees are unequal partners in the philanthropic process, we have helped to create the monster we so greatly resent.

In general, we have traded our rights as donees for the hope that by being cautious we might win over the donors. We have sought to be loved and adopted rather than respected. In seeking safety, we have not gained either the respect or love of contributors. Nor have we helped close the wide gulf of communication and understanding that separates us from the giver community.

By approaching fund raising apprehensively and passively without confidence we do not attack the problem of raising money in an organized and strategic way as we would an important community problem. We appear uncertain, frequently leaving the donors with the impression that we are disorganized, undependable and weak. How many times have we seen some of the toughest organizers, who sport several institutional scalps on their belts, turn to Jell-o when faced with a foundation?

Until we stop acting as beggars in the philanthropic game, we will not be able to eliminate this mystique. The first step is to adopt an attitude that says, "We are at least as good as the donor." This should not be an assertion of arrogance but a recognition of our own qualities and strengths.

We must remember that donors need us as much as we need them if their giving is to be of high caliber. Many of us are more experienced and skilled in our fields than our colleagues in philanthropy. Many have had the kind of learning experiences in poor communities that most donors will never have. Given that many corporate and foundation people want to do a good job, they often view productive relationships with donees as an important part of their work. By assuming we are equals, we can be treated as equals. If we can have solid working relationships with local politicians, Congressmen, union officials, and nonprofit colleagues, we can enjoy similar contact with philanthropoids.

Part of the beggar's mentality is to think in terms of what the donors want, not what we need to fulfill our objectives. Since foundations and corporations have varied priorities, we have often tried to be all things to all people, cutting and tailoring our interests and programs to fit those of the donors. In many cases, the result has been dismal. Either we undermined our mission or initiated programs for which we were ill suited. And donors are seldom fooled by our flexibility.

A donee community less submissive, more determined to maintain its integrity and more aggressive in its posture with donors would lead to greater respect and receptivity for our cause in the philanthropic world.

If we look at ourselves with confidence and at donor institutions more realistically, we will find that the task of requesting and receiving money will become easier and less stressful.

The proposal, for example, should loom less ominously. For many, it has become part of the philanthropic mystique, filled with expectations of excellence that cannot be met. We become paralyzed when we try to write the perfect proposal. The proposal should be considered for what it is, no more and no less: the means by which we state why we need the money and what we will do with it. It is not meant to be a jewel of prose.

Although most foundation and corporate professionals understand the limitations of proposals, they often do not have the background, experience, or motivation to judge or be excited by the activities of nonestablishment organizations. For this reason, we cannot afford to let them evaluate us by our proposals alone. We need to see them in their offices, get them to know us as individuals and persuade them to visit our organizations. By meeting personally with donors, we can help break down the barriers between donor and donee that have fueled the mystique of philanthropy.

The inaccessibility, lack of accountability and bad manners of many foundations and corporations are trademarks of philanthropy that many of us have resented and criticized for years—unfortunately mostly among ourselves. Few of us have actively fought back to demand accountability, fair access, due process in grantmaking procedures and equitable treatment in decision making. We have accepted unreturned phone calls, unwillingness to meet applicants, rudeness, arrogant behavior, decisions without explanation and double standards with a complacence that we would not tolerate in our dealings with other sectors and people.

This pattern of behavior, although it has improved somewhat in recent years, will not change unless we decide to do something about it. In other words, we need to insist on the attention of donor staff directors and trustees, monitor the activities of the giving world more closely, and be prepared to appeal to the public in extreme cases. Of course we also must make sure that we meet the standards we set for donors—too often we are as unaccountable as those we criticize.

Some people worry that challenging donors will lead to anger and retribution. The experiences of those organizations that have challenged donors do not bear out such anxieties. A few may have been hurt in the short run, but most have gained the respect and additional support of philanthropic institutions. We who are mistreated by donors have very little to lose and everything to gain by refusing to accept unfair procedures and practices.

But we can't do it alone; we need to act collectively. In certain cities and states, coalitions of nonprofits can be formed to monitor donor institutions and push for public accountability.

If we do not start to work together on fundraising, we will never reform philanthropy, and those organizations that are the best financed and can afford to take the most risks are frequently the ones not willing to rally on behalf of colleague organizations. We will have to do a better job in pushing ourselves and our reluctant friends to join in a common effort. Only then will we be able to put to bed the mystique of philanthropy and open new opportunities for future funding.

From *The Nonprofit Quarterly* (Fall 1999). Reprinted with permission of *The Nonprofit Quarterly*.

ROY W. MENNINGER, M.D.

"Foundation Work May Be Hazardous to Your Mental Health: Some Occupational Dangers of Grantmaking (and Grantreceiving)"

Roy W. Menninger, M.D., current chair of Menninger Trustees, was for twenty-six years the president and CEO of The Menninger Foundation, a national psychiatric hospital. In this article, adapted from a speech presented at the 1981 annual conference of the Council on Foundations, Menninger applies his prodigious psychiatric understanding and skill, as well as his experience as a fundraiser, to the activities of giving, asking for, and receiving money. In particular, he calls attention to the "darker sides," to the unavoidable or "occupational dangers," of grantmaking and grant-receiving—the temptation to exploit the power position of the donor or the dependent position of the seeker. Menninger regards both sides of the equation as ineluctably intertwined with each other and, hence, as equally culpable for what goes right or wrong in their relationship. "There has to be a genuine quid pro quo *between giver and receiver," he insists. "Each must feel that the decision to give is justified and worthy, with a worthwhile* psychological contract *the result" (emphasis added). And he calls for both parties to be more involved in, more concerned about, and more committed to the relationship. Given Menninger's own psychiatric moorings his advice is not unexpected. But what does it mean? What sort of involvement, concern, and commitment would it take to develop a meaningful "psychological contract"?*

Asking for money is a difficult business and one that stirs up a variety of feelings. At times the qualities of honesty and sincerity that ought always to be at the heart of the process seem to slip away, making it seem that fund-raising is a bit of a con job. This feeling has little to do with the purposes for which the money is sought; rather it reflects the complex nature of the transaction between seeker and donor.

Some of the psychological aspects of the giving and receiving transaction are familiar to many of us, but they are not commonly discussed or shared with others, even our close colleagues. Even talking about them is embarrassing and seems unprofessional, as though giving voice to our thoughts would demonstrate some kind of personal inadequacy. Many of us manage these thoughts and feelings by saying nothing and pretending that the problems, if there are any, belong to someone else. But of course, when the less attractive, less acceptable aspects of the giving/receiving transaction are forced underground, they are more than likely to return later in some more destructive form.

Money stirs up considerable ambivalence in most of us. It is a metaphorical freight car laden with a variety of beliefs and fantasies. To some extent these are idiosyncratic, but they are also culturally determined and reinforced. We have all kinds of fantastic notions about what money means and what more money could further mean. Most simply, money is thought of as a means to do or get something. But other motivations, which are commonly unexpressed and perhaps not even acknowledged, are no less important. We see money as a way of buying love, or appreciation, or approbation. We can see it as a way out of dependency and a means of becoming autonomous. Money can be power to control others, or to get revenge.

We use numbers representing dollars to characterize ultimate value. The phrase "net worth" states the value of the individual. And we honestly do believe that the larger that number, the "more valuable"—and somehow "better"—the individual is. By an insidious transformation we convert quantity into quality. On reflection most of us do acknowledge that there is no necessary relationship; indeed we can often see inverse relationships between quantity of money and quality of life, whether we're talking about individuals or institutions.

Yet we persist in the fantasy that money "makes the difference." As I examine projects as a member of a review committee for another organization, the covert message is very strong. "If you simply give us the money, we'll figure out what to do with it. Don't ask us for the plan first; we don't need one. We'll work it out as we go along." Along with the common view that money is necessary, goes the fantasy that money alone is sufficient.

Many people think that a generous application of money can substitute for carefully thinking through a problem, and that enough money can make the problem go away. There have been signs of this point of view in earlier social programs of government, and many of us have seen a pattern of substituting a financial demand for thought within our own organizations. Having enough money makes it easy to avoid the tough task of figuring out where one is going and what one is trying to do.

Many of us do-gooders seem to feel that idealism and good intentions are their own justification, and therefore, we should not be required to be effective or accountable; some of us feel that a saintly performance and motivation on earth is enough to get points in heaven.

Money can be a problem in other ways. It often distorts relationships. Look at what happens to our relationship with our own teenagers when we are hit up for another handout for the third time in a week, or consider how money can be a bribe for grandparents trying to buy the love of a grandchild. Money, when it is used to buy and control relationships, ultimately demeans them, albeit unintentionally.

Reasons for Giving

Reasons for giving come from several sources. They're not always conscious; one can discern, if one looks carefully, several lower levels of motivation even in the most altruistic acts of giving.

The first level is the narcissistic level. A donor gives money for honor and glory—for the name on the building, or even the whole institution. Here is a wish—often a transparent one—for the visible evidence of one's commitment. This kind of giving fights the anonymity many of us find disturbing in life and intolerable in prospect after death. The narcissistic level of giving also reflects a great need for love and recognition. Giving often masks a fearful preoccupation that one is unlovable or unwanted for oneself alone, as if only by generosity can one gain a sense of worth. The self-esteem of such a donor is actually quite low. But precisely because giving can increase one's sense of worth, it also confounds the basic question: would people love me if I had no money at all? This is a point of concern that people who've never had money have trouble understanding and accepting.

The second level of giving is moralistic and conscience-driven, with guilt as the motivation. Sometimes the guilt stems from having more that others, or for the way in which the money was earned, or simply for having it at all. Some people feel guilty for living, and their wish to give money may be an effort to appease this very distressing feeling—to buy it off by gifts to others.

This level of giving reflects the moral or religious view that giving is a duty. "It is expected of me; I have to." (Sometimes the "having to" refers to the IRS.) But giving, when seen as an obligation, does bring its own reward—lessening feelings of embarrassment, shame, guilt and fear.

The third level—which might be described as the most mature form of giving—is a way of participating in the life of others, or an expression of gratitude. Here the key element is the other, the recipient; not the self, the giver. The giver wishes to be, and becomes a genuine participant who shares in an achievement by facilitating it. This giving also has the reward of a beneficent return, although the benefits are primarily for others rather than oneself.

We all like to think that what we do is altruistic giving. Why, then, emphasize some less attractive sides of giving? Because giving is never pure. The most altruistic and most noble giving also contains elements of narcissism and guilt, and even gifts which seem blatantly self-aggrandizing include an altruistic element. The point is to recognize that elements of each level play a part in every gift-receiving transaction, and that the relative strength and importance of each will affect the transaction itself.

Donors and recipients need to feel that the decision to give is justified, and that the transaction concludes with a worthwhile psychological contract. Discussions between both parties about the purpose of the money may really be a process of mutual testing where the giver tries to determine what form his rewards for giving will take. At the same time, the receiver "psychs-out" the giver as he tries to determine what kind of reward the giver really needs. This may be self-glorification, release from guilt, a chance to participate in someone else's important work—or all three. The fact that the same proposal can be described in three different ways proves the point.

For example, I am carrying on a conversation with a wealthy widow from Dubuque; purpose, money. I am very eager to know what form of reward she will most appreciate. In describing the purpose for which the gift will be used I may emphasize the possibilities of naming the facility for the donor if I sense the reward is self-glorification. Or I can speak about the moral obligation we collectively have to the mentally ill, if I think the key is guilt. I might also dwell on the opportunity to participate in the development of a new approach to mental illness, thus appealing to the altruistic urge to give.

This is, of course, an oversimplification. I don't mean to suggest that the process of trying to understand the psychology of the giver is crass, manipulative or hypocritical, although of course it may be. But even altruistic givers are motivated by reasons linked to their unique psychological needs. None of us ought to forget that giving is bilateral; those who seek to be given to must also be prepared to give in some psychologically meaningful way to the giver.

The psychological trappings of the transaction may in fact be of greater influence in the donor's decision to give than the practical details of the proposal itself. We all know of proposals, nothing but blue-sky, which were set forth with such conviction and enthusiasm that the donor responded with the funds, feeling that this opportunity to participate was just what he'd been looking for all these years. "He's such a marvelous person with such a strong sense of where he's going and what he's all about! I certainly don't understand what he has in mind . . . but I love him!"

Sometimes a very well-thought out, well-developed and meticulously detailed plan is put forward by a reticent research-oriented person whose presentation is (though not by intention) dull. Only under exceptional circumstances will a donor overlook the missing promise of psychological reward.

Sometimes the very dedication of the seeker, if he overidentifies with his cause to the point of narcissism, can be a problem for the donor. The seeker has become so convinced of the greatness of his purpose that he believes few other things are, or could be, as significant. So absorbed can the seeker be in this conviction that he and the project seem one. This is not unusual; all of us are only partially separable from the things we believe in. The trouble comes when the seeker in effect says, "Love me, love my dog," and expects the donor to accept his commitment without question. For the donor with a strong need to be a "nice guy," but some doubts about the project, the seeker's narcissism is unsettling. And a donor who finds it difficult to approach the project (and its salesman) rationally may be forced to withdraw, even though he wants to be helpful.

Such is the nature of human communication that every communication (including much that is non-verbal) contains clues to the relationship itself—what it is, how one or the other would like it to be, what it must become in the future. A communication of matters of substance always conveys something else as well: information about the parties' hopes or fears for the relationship. This is not to say that the content of a proposal is of no importance (although sometimes that is clearly the case), but to suggest that the psychological basis of the transaction also bears attention, and warrants an effort of understanding by both parties.

Psychological Aspects of Giving

The average man-in-the-street thinks giving money away is a simple, straightforward proposition. He assumes that philanthropy is easy and pleasant. Certainly it is not work; you will even make friends. But as you know so well, the reality is that it is exceedingly hard work. It's difficult to make really good decisions. You know you don't have all the information you'd like; you are not at all sure you even have the right information. There are surprises, sometimes unpleasant ones; there are contests of value, swings of preference, paralyzing ambivalences, pet peeves and hobbyhorses. Indeed, you will probably be making enemies at least as often (if not more often) than friends. "This business of benevolence," as Andrew Carnegie called it, is anything but a straightforward proposition.

Benevolence had proved far more difficult than he had dreamed when he glibly wrote in his *Gospel of Wealth* about "the man of wealth becoming a trustee for his poorer brethren, bringing to their service his superior wisdom, his superior ability to administer, doing for them better than they could or would for themselves." Before long, Carnegie was disenchanted with "the supremely difficult art of spending large sums of money in undertaking to be of permanent advantage to the public." The public, he discovered, recognized no experts in philanthropy; there were only men with money, and other men trying to get it away from them. He was to say repeatedly that he had not worked one-tenth as hard at acquiring money as at divesting himself of it. By 1906 he was so sick of the game that he wrote, "the final dispensation of one's wealth preparing for the point of exit is, I've found, a heavy task. You have no idea of the strain I've been under." And he went on to say, "Millionaires who laugh are very, very rare indeed."[1]

I think one of the most difficult tasks in the psychology of giving must be how to decide among the many "goods" which come to the door seeking help. With more than a million organizations and countless individuals seeking help, (and now, profound reductions in federal support for human service programs)

---

1. Joseph Frazier Wall, *Andrew Carnegie* (New York: Oxford University Press, 1970), pp. 880–881.

the opportunities for generosity are myriad. One is responsible for a wise choice, yet the guidelines for decision are not always clear.

The process of deciding is fraught with complications. Who sets the criteria for choice? Who has what kind of power to decide what? With individuals, or even small foundations, this is relatively easy, since only one or two people do it all: investigation, presentation, decision. But in larger foundations it is often not clear who has what role: is it the donor who decides, even from the grave? What if his concepts are now so anachronistic, or specific (who wants buggy whips anymore?) as to exclude 99% of the proposals?

Perhaps the Board decides. The Board is full of good intentions but it is all too aware of its fiduciary responsibilities, saddled with its own pet projects and hobbyhorse interests, yet uncomfortably dependent upon a staff for information, evaluation and even recommendation.

What about the staff? This group has taken pains to learn about the proposals and, in fact, may know more about some of the projects than do the seekers themselves. Staff members sometimes find it hard to remain properly humble when they believe they are probably brighter, and certainly wiser, than either the board or the seekers. Succumbing to the seductions of the God complex is a real occupational hazard. Having money to give away and the power to decide whom to give it to is intoxicating, and foundations can be irritating examples of the "narcissism of the righteous."

Any organization where several parties are engaged in the decision-making process has the ingredients for various degrees of tension and disagreement. The broader the range of the value systems represented in the organization, the greater the likelihood of conflict. But unfortunately foundation staff and trustees do not often discuss these differences in value and viewpoint, since to do so seems to invite open conflict, and is not a part of "the way we do things." This is a prospect that many people will do anything to avoid, even at the risk of chronic sub-surface conflict, low morale, passive resistance and procrastination, as well as inefficient operations that conspire to make foundation giving less imaginative and of less consequence than it ought to be.

The process of giving puts special burdens and obligations on individuals who come into the philanthropy business motivated by a desire to do good. I see this in my own field; many of us in mental health share a strong need to make the world a better place. We carry into our work a tremendous inner conviction about how important the tasks are and how important it is for us to do them. People who feel this commitment are generally pretty conscientious men and women. Society should be grateful, since such people work harder, longer and for less than one would think reasonable. They're a great social benefit, to be sure, but at what personal cost? Chronic depression; a pervasive sense of doubt about one's effectiveness or sense of self-worth; obsessional worrying and behavior that sometimes makes decisions almost impossible; an enormous need to be liked and to be seen as helpful by others. People like this sometimes have a recurring problem of over identifying with the grantee. Some reach the point where the conflicting pressures can no longer be handled and overreact in the opposite direction, at which stage they seem curt, cold, and withdrawn.

A high risk of burnout afflicts conscientious people who are so strongly motivated to provide service to others. They have a much higher need for appreciation and fulfillment than they are often willing to recognize. Most conscientious people, for example, have a terrible time taking a vacation. They feel indispensable. They feel guilty about leaving. They feel they do not deserve to be good to themselves, that personal pleasures are not nearly as important as working to help these suffering people or those vital projects. To believe that one is stronger, and indispensable, is a kind of negative arrogance—and it isn't true anyway.

Sooner or later, the backlash comes. The personal needs that have been pushed to the back burner become painfully obvious. People are open systems, with a need to take in as much as they give out. When the system is radically out of balance, the inevitable result is psychological bankruptcy, or burnout.

Most people can carry on at high levels of effort for the short run, and even need to work this way at intervals. But without a recouping effort of some sort (I don't mean just a vacation, but some kind of psychologically satisfying input) one stands at high risk of burnout. That applies to all of us—not just the workers in the trenches, but the executives and even the Board members.

Psychological Aspects of Asking and Receiving

Asking for money isn't easy either. For me, becoming a fund raiser has been a very painful process. At bottom I, and I think others, often find the process an affront to one's sense of integrity. No matter how significant the project or prestigious the institution conducting it, the pursuit of funds often puts the seeker in the role of having to appeal to another for help, a position that sometimes feels like begging. The role is uncomfortably reminiscent of the dependent position all of us were in as children. Asking for money is a disturbing downward shift from a more adult role of coequality. Asking implies need, of course; it's the obvious reason for asking. But need also implies inadequacy, and having to ask someone to meet this need exposes one as well to feeling patronized and even depreciated.

I still vividly remember when I was in medical school, and would go with my father to cocktail parties, where they'd give him a chance to tell his story about our little shop on the prairies of Kansas. He was very articulate in his cornfed country style; he could raise money without ever using the word or directly asking for it. I don't know how he did it; only that he had a marvelous sense of himself and was comfortable at it. But I used to get almost physically ill as I watched him at what I thought was a demeaning work, hardly fit for a doctor. I'd get angry at him, and say "How can you have spent years becoming a doctor and then

a psychiatrist, only to turn into a boomer!" He didn't take well to those comments! And here I am twenty years later, doing the same thing! In retrospect, I
think he was bothered by the same feeling I imply: a sense of having forsaken the
great heritage of medicine, for a role as a drummer and mendicant.

A successful shift—he was able to make it; I am struggling with it—involves some new thinking about one's roles and talents, the tasks to be done,
and most important, the meaning of the work one is raising the money to do.
Even so, the sense that one is selling oneself, with all the negative and debasing
connotations of the word, is never vanquished. The terms we use to describe
the process are revealing.

The notion of "getting money" seems active and aggressive, while "receiving money" implies a polite form of passive acceptance. Seekers use various
images according to the different ways they look at the grant seeking business.
So we regard it as a form of combat—an aggressive struggle in which the seeker
must be victorious by grinding down the giver. Some will see it as a game with
winners and losers and a score to keep. In a game, of course, it's fair to use
tricks and surprise tactics.

Others make the business of giving and receiving money sound like a se-
duction or a love affair; the language they use and the seeking process itself, has
faintly erotic overtones. Eroticism may even take on an aggressive character; in
the strain to persuade, the love words give way to more vulgar terms. There is
flattery, fawning, the desire to be liked and likeable (proved by being given to
and depended on) as if being attractive were the ultimate key to acceptance.

Lastly, there are those who simply regard fundraising as a straightforward
business transaction of proposing, negotiating, buying, selling and trading.
The selling aspect reminds me of the Arab sheik who returns home from the
United States. A fellow sheik asks him, "Well, what impressed you most about
the Americans?" "Their salesmen," he replies, strapping on his skis.

One seldom sees any of these one-dimensional approaches in pure culture, especially among sophisticated fundraisers. They are caricatures, although there is usually something of each in most seeker-donor engagements.
In small doses, they add charm and challenge to the exchange. But each sums
up certain attitudes and expectations seeker and donor have toward each other,
attitudes that obviously affect the evolving relationship between them.

I think it's important for givers and for foundation staff to realize that asking for money carries with it difficult feelings for the asker, no matter how sophisticated he seems. These feelings can give rise to hypocritical or offensive
behavior, ranging from fawning, gushy praise to inappropriately aggressive
and challenging postures. Sometimes the feelings will be covered up by bra-
vado or disdain. One often sees in seekers particularly in the face of a turn-
down, a contempt for the giver—a real sourgrapes attitude. This is a way to
discharge the contempt and shame one feels for oneself by displacing it onto
the giver, along with some negative comments about what kind of a foundation

they are, anyway! The point is that there is always some ambivalence contained in the dependent status of seeking money.

Conclusions

We all need to be aware of some of the darker sides of human views of money and of giving and receiving if we are to keep from exploiting the power position of the donor or the dependent position of the seeker. On both sides of this equation, all of us are affected by power and need, as well as by the less attractive aspects of money. We are all part of the problem.

This is part of the process of giving, intrinsic to the transaction itself. It is not possible to avoid these darker sides by conscious intention. No matter how righteous one is, no matter how good a person (indeed, maybe because one is all those things), one is inevitably a part of the problem of the giving/receiving relationship. Acknowledging this is the beginning of a healthier approach to a complicated business. These feelings can be managed much more effectively if they can be identified. If one can put a name to them, recognize them and begin to understand their part in the process, they cease to exert a kind of influence that seems magical, covert and incomprehensible.

We all find it difficult to ask for money, and I suspect many of us are also ambivalent about giving. I believe that these feelings can be adequately handled only in the context of a genuine relationship.

The giving/receiving process is fundamentally a relationship, one which deserves to be respected in its own right. Both giver and receiver must work to create the basis for mutual respect and appreciation. If this is not true, the whole thing is a sham. Put otherwise, there has to be a genuine *quid pro quo* between giver and receiver. Each must feel that the decision to give is justified and worthy, with a worthwhile psychological contract the result. Because it is based on relationship, a great deal turns on the qualities of the interaction, and the extent to which the donor is willing to be involved. The reluctance to enter into such a relationship reduces these interactions to their barest denominator—of being crass, manipulative or mechanistic, or, put simply, plain seductions or aggressive acts.

It is the refusal to be involved in, concerned about, and committed to the relationship that contributes to some of the less attractive aspects of the philanthropic business.

"Foundation Work May Be Hazardous to Your Mental Health: Some Occupational Dangers of Grantmaking (and Grantreceiving)" by Roy W. Menninger, M.D. (Washington, D.C.: Council on Foundations, 1981). Reprinted with permission of the Council on Foundations and the author.

HENRI BARBUSSE

"The Eleventh"

Despite efforts to improve relations between givers and recipients, many a young, idealistic donor or grantmaker still fears becoming hardhearted. Does this necessarily come with the terrain? Maybe so, suggests this short story by Henri Barbusse (1873–1935), French journalist, editor, and author. On the first day of each month, at exactly nine o'clock, ten poor people—no more, no less—are admitted to the hospitality of a luxurious palace-hospital. No questions are asked. Only one rule obtains: the ten must leave when the month expires and never return. During their month's stay, they enjoy the life and privileges of the regular residents of this earthly paradise. The young employee charged with opening the door each month is initially honored to do so. But gradually he becomes haunted by the eleventh person in whose face he is obliged to shut that door. "[H]e seemed to me the most pitiable case, and I felt that I was myself smitten in the person of the one condemned," he laments. The young assistant finally quits, concluding that he was "taking part in an abominable injustice." Was he? Has he overreacted? What would you do in his place? More generally, how do you stay committed to giving, as an individual or via a foundation, when you are confronted with difficult choices and your own doubts?

The Master, who had a pale head with long marble-like hair, and whose spectacles shone in solemnity, came to a standstill on his morning round opposite my little table at the door of Room 28, and condescended to announce to me that I was henceforth appointed to let in the ten poor people who every month were admitted to the hospitality of the House. Then he went on, so tall and so white among the assiduous flock of students that they seemed to be carrying a famous statuette from room to room.

I stammered the thanks which he did not hear. My 25-year-old heart felt a happy pride in reflecting that I had been chosen to preside in one of the noblest traditions of the House in which, a humble assistant, I was wandering lornly among wealthy invalids.

On the first day of every month the luxurious palace-hospital became the paradise of ten vagabonds. One of its outer doors was opened to admit the first ten who came, whoever they were, wherever they had fallen from or escaped. And for a whole month those ten human derelicts enjoyed the entire hospitality of the comfortable institution, just as much so as the Master's most valuable patients, as much as the archdukes and multi-millionaires. For them, too, were the lofty halls whose walls were not only white, but glistening, the huge corridors like covered streets, which in summer or in winter had the coolness or the mildness of spring. For them also, the immense garden beds set among green velvet, like bunches of flowers so enlarged by magic that one walked among them. For them equally, the outer walls, far off but impassable, which shield one against wide-open Space, against rambling roads, against the plains which come to an end no more than the sky. For thirty days the refugees busied themselves only with doing nothing, only worked when they ate, and were no longer afraid of the unknown or of the coming day. They who were remorseful learned to forget things, and they who were bereaved, to forget people.

When by chance they met each other, they simply had to turn their heads away hurriedly. There was not in all the House, by order of the Master, a mirror in which they would have found their bad dream again. At the day's end came the dormitory, peaceful as a cemetery, a nice cemetery, where one is not dead, where one waits—where one lives, but without knowing it.

At eight o'clock on the first day of the following month all ten of them went away, cast back into the world one by one, as into the sea. Immediately after, ten others entered, the first ten of the file which, since the night before, had been washed up against the wall of the house as upon the shores of an island. The first ten, no more, no less, no favors, no exceptions, no injustices; one rule only—they who had already been were never again admitted. The arrivals were asked nothing else—not even for the confession of their names.

And on the first day of the month, as soon as nine o'clock had sounded, exactly together from the Anglican church and the Catholic chapel of the House, I opened the little Poor-door.

A crowd of beings was massed against the door-wing and the wall. Hardly had the former turned in the shadow when the tattered heap rushed forward as though sucked in.

My helper had to throw himself forward to enforce a little order upon the greedy invasion. We had to detach by force, to tear away from the mass each one of the besiegers, who were pressed side by side and elbow to elbow, fastened to each other like fantastic friends. The eighth entered, the ninth, the tenth.

And then the door was quickly closed, but not so quickly that it prevented me from seeing, only a step from me, him upon whom it closed, the eleventh, the unlucky one, the accursed.

He was a man of uncertain age; in his grey and withered face lack-luster eyes floated. He looked at me so despairingly that he seemed to smile. The touch of that extraordinary disappointment made me start, of that face that was mute as a wound. I glimpsed in a flash—the time that the door took to shut—all the effort he had made to get there, even if too late, and how much he too deserved to come in!

Then I busied myself with the others; but a few minutes later, still affected by the distress I had read on the face of the outcast, I half opened the door to see if he were still there. No one. He and the three or four others—uncertain rags that had fluttered behind him—had gone to the four winds of heaven, carried away along the roads like dead leaves. A little shiver went through me, a shiver almost of mourning for the conquered.

At night, as I was falling asleep, my thoughts went again to them, and I wondered why they stayed there till the last moment, they who arrived only when ten had already taken their places at the door. What did they hope for? Nothing. Yet they were hoping all the same, and therein was a mean miracle of the heart.

We had reached the month of March. On the last day of the old month, towards nightfall, a rather frightened murmur crept from the side of the high road, close to the door. Leaning over a balcony, I could make men out there, stirring like insects. These were the suppliants.

The next morning we opened to these phantoms whom the magical story of the house had called across the world, who had awakened and unburied themselves from the lowest and most awful of depths to get there. We welcomed the ten who first came forward; we were obliged to drive back into life the eleventh.

He was standing, motionless, and offering himself from the other side of the door. I looked at him, and then lowered my eyes. He had a terrible look, with his hollow face and lashless eyelids. There breathed from him a reproach of unbearable artlessness.

When the door divided us forever, I regretted him, and should have liked to see him again. I turned towards the others, swarming in gladness on the flagstones, almost with resignation, wondering at my own firm conviction that the other, sooner than these, ought to have come in with us.

And it was so every time. Every time I became more indifferent to the crowd of admitted and satisfied, and devoted my gaze still more to him who was refused salvation. And every time he seemed to me the most pitiable case, and I felt that I was myself smitten in the person of the one condemned.

In June, it was a woman. I saw her understand and begin to cry. I trembled as I furtively scanned her; to crown all, the weeper's eyelids were blood-red as wounds.

In July, the appointed victim was incomparably regrettable by reason of his great age; and no living being was so compassionable as he who was repulsed the month after, so young was he. Another time, he who had to be snatched from the group of the elect besought me with his poor hands, encircled with the remains of frayed linen, like lint. The one whom Fate sacrificed the following month showed me a menacing fist. The entreaty of the one made me afraid, and the threat of the other pitiful.

I could almost have begged his pardon, the "eleventh" of October. He drew himself up stiffly; his neck was wrapped high in a grayish tie that looked like a bandage; he was thin, and his coat fluttered in the wind like a flag. But what could I have said to the unfortunate who succeeded him thirty days later?

He blushed, stammered a nervous apology, and withdrew after bowing with tragic politeness—piteous remnant of an earlier lot.

And thus a year passed. Twelve times I let in the vagrants whom the stones had worn out, the workmen for whom all work was hopeless, the criminals subdued. Twelve times I let in some of those who clung to the stones of the wall as on to reefs of the sea coast. Twelve times I turned others away, similar ones, whom I confusedly preferred.

An idea beset me—that I was taking part in an abominable injustice. Truly there was no sense in dividing all those poor folk like that into friends and enemies. There was only one arbitrary reason—abstract, not admissible; a matter of a figure, a sign. At bottom, this was neither just nor even logical.

Soon I could no longer continue in this series of errors. I went to the Master, and begged him to give me some other post, so that I should not have to do the same evil deed again every month.

From *We Others: Stories of Fate, Love, and Pity* by Henri Barbusse, translated by Fitzwater Wray (New York: E. P. Dutton and Co., 1918).

ALEXIS DE TOCQUEVILLE

From Memoir on Pauperism

In this brief selection, excerpted from one of his more obscure writings, Memoir
on Pauperism *(first published in 1835 but not translated into English until
1968), French social theorist Alexis de Tocqueville (1805–1859) examines the social context and consequences of "individual alms-giving" as opposed to "public
alms-giving" or "legal charity." Hands-down, he concludes, the first is preferable
to the second. Though he was probably one of the earliest public intellectuals to
argue that government aid to the poor may do more harm than good, he was
also sensitive, with the coming of the Industrial Revolution, to the insufficiency
of private alms-giving. Elsewhere in the* Memoir *Tocqueville notes: "[I]ndividual
charity seems quite weak when faced with the progressive development of the industrial classes and all the evils that civilization joins to the inestimable goods it
produces. It was sufficient for the Middle Ages . . . when its task was less difficult;
could it be sufficient today when the burden is heavy and when its forces are so
weakened?" Collective suspicion of government giving, as well as reliance on it,
has only grown since Tocqueville's time. Thus the question he bequeaths to us is
a very live one: Is there any way of infusing government giving with the spirit
and powers that individual agency has?*

But this [that poor laws legalize humiliation] is still not all: individual alms-
giving established valuable ties between the rich and the poor. The deed itself
involves the giver in the fate of the one whose poverty he has undertaken to
alleviate. The latter, supported by aid which he had no right to demand and
which he may have had no hope of getting, feels inspired by gratitude. A
moral tie is established between those two classes whose interests and passions so often conspire to separate them from each other, and although divided by circumstance they are willingly reconciled. This is not the case with
legal charity. The latter allows the alms to persist but removes its morality.
The law strips the man of wealth of a part of his surplus without consulting
him and he sees the poor man only as a greedy stranger invited by the legisla-
tor to share his wealth. The poor man, on the other hand, feels no gratitude
for a benefit that no one can refuse him and that could not satisfy him in any
case. Public alms guarantee life but do not make it happier or more comfortable than individual alms-giving; legal charity does not thereby eliminate
wealth or poverty in society. One class still views the world with fear and
loathing while the other regards its misfortune with despair and envy. Far

from uniting these two rival nations, who have existed since the beginning of the world and who are called the rich and the poor, into a single people, it breaks the only link which could be established between them. It ranges each one under a banner, tallies them, and, bringing them face to face, prepares them for combat.

From *Memoir on Pauperism* by Alexis de Tocqueville, English translation copyright © 1968 by Seymour Drescher, 60–61. By permission of Ivan R. Dee, Publisher.

THOMAS PAINE

From The Rights of Man

Thomas Paine (1737–1809) was a prominent political writer and agitator, best known to Americans as the author of Common Sense, *the popular pamphlet which helped spur and support the American Revolution. In his most influential book,* The Rights of Man, *published 1791–1792, Paine calls for sweeping reforms of English governance, including its tax system, especially as it relates to the poor. In this excerpt, he lays out a plan, not unlike social security, by which the aged poor will receive a return on their taxes upon reaching the age of fifty. Importantly, Paine insists the support is not "charity" which the government might provide, but a "right" that the government is bound to secure. What does it mean—does it make a difference—to call such assistance a right, rather than charity? Does it change the relations between rich and poor—or citizens to each other—to do so?*

In a passage not included below, Paine states: "Public money ought to be touched with the most scrupulous consciousness of honor. It is not the produce of riches only, but of the hard earnings of labor and poverty. It is drawn even from the bitterness of want and misery. Not a beggar passes, or perishes in the streets, whose mite is not in that mass." Though he is here rebuking the idle extravagance of government expenditure, many a foundation considers its endowment "public money." Is it? Are charitable funds rightfully "owed" the public? Does it change the relations between grantors and grantees to believe so?

෫ə

I now proceed to the case of the aged.

I divide age into two classes. First, the approach of age, beginning at fifty. Secondly, old age commencing at sixty.

At fifty, though the mental faculties of man are in full vigor, and his judgment better than at any preceding date, the bodily powers for laborious life are on the decline. He cannot bear the same quantity of fatigue as at an earlier period. He begins to earn less, and is less capable of enduring wind and weather; and in those more retired employments where much sight is required, he fails apace, and sees himself, like an old horse, beginning to be turned adrift.

At sixty his labor ought to be over, at least from direct necessity. It is painful to see old age working itself to death, in what are called civilized countries, for daily bread.

To form some judgment of the number of those above fifty years of age, I have several times counted the persons I met in the streets of London, men, women, and children, and have generally found that the average is about one in sixteen or seventeen. If it be said that aged persons do not come much into the streets, so neither do infants; and a great proportion of grown children are in schools and in work-shops as apprentices. Taking, then, sixteen for a divisor, the whole number of persons in England of fifty years and upwards, of both sexes, rich and poor, will be four hundred and twenty thousand.

The persons to be provided for out of this gross number will be husbandmen, common laborers, journeymen of every trade and their wives, sailors, and disbanded soldiers, worn out servants of both sexes, and poor widows.

There will be also a considerable number of middling tradesmen, who having lived decently in the former part of life, begin, as age approaches, to lose their business, and at last fall to decay.

Besides these there will be constantly thrown off from the revolutions of that wheel which no man can stop nor regulate, a number from every class of life connected with commerce and adventure.

To provide for all those accidents, and whatever else may befall, I take the number of persons who, at one time or other of their lives, after fifty years of age, may feel it necessary or comfortable to be better supported, than they can support themselves, and that not as a matter of grace and favor, but of right, at one-third of the whole number, which is one hundred and forty thousand, as stated in a previous page, and for whom a distinct provision was proposed to be made. If there be more, society, notwithstanding the show and pomposity of government, is in a deplorable condition in England.

Of this one hundred and forty thousand, I take one half, seventy thousand, to be of the age of fifty and under sixty, and the other half to be sixty years and upwards. Having thus ascertained the probable proportion of the number of aged persons, I proceed to the mode of rendering their condition comfortable, which is:

To pay to every such person of the age of fifty years, and until he shall arrive at the age of sixty, the sum of six pounds *per annum* out of the surplus taxes, and ten pounds *per annum* during life after the age of sixty. The expense of which will be,

Seventy thousand persons, at £6 *per annum* . . .   £420,000
Seventy thousand ditto, at £10 *per annum* . . .   700,000
                                                     £1,120,000

This support, as already remarked, is not of the nature of a charity but of a right. Every person in England, male and female, pays on an average in taxes two pounds eight shillings and six pence *per annum* from the day of his (or her) birth; and, if the expense of collection be added, he pays two pounds eleven shillings and sixpence; consequently, at the end of fifty years he has paid one hundred and twenty-eight pounds fifteen shillings; and at sixty one hundred and fifty-four pounds ten shillings. Converting, therefore, his (or her) individual tax in a tontine, the money he shall receive after fifty years is but little more than the legal interest of the net money he has paid; the rest is made up from those whose circumstances do not require them to draw such support, and the capital in both cases defrays the expenses of government. It is on this ground that I have extended the probable claims to one-third of the number of aged persons in the nation.—Is it, then, better that the lives of one hundred and forty thousand aged persons be rendered comfortable, or that a million a year of public money be expended on any one individual, and him often of the most worthless or insignificant character? Let reason and justice, let honor and humanity, let even hypocrisy, sycophancy and Mr. Burke, let George, let Louis, Leopold, Frederic, Catherine, Cornwallis, or Tippoo Saib, answer the question.

From *The Rights of Man, Part Second, Combining Principle and Practice* (1894 edition) by Thomas Paine.

SARA L. ENGELHARDT

"Foundation Grants and the Grantor/Grantee Relationship"

As president of The Foundation Center since 1991, and as a staff member of the Carnegie Corporation of New York for over twenty years prior, Sara Engelhardt has come to know and appreciate the unique importance of foundations in American civic life. But well aware of the tough decisions that grantmakers regularly have to make, and the competing "right" ways of making them, she knows and appreciates, too, as she makes clear here, how bewildering such decisions—and the foundations that make them—can seem to nonprofit organizations, and how they can endanger good relations between grantors and grantees. Yet in concluding this short essay, Engelhardt in effect issues a warning: "If [foundations] are to continue to play [a] unique role, we must remember that their value to our society lies in their partnership with grantees, however imperfect, not in the value of their endowments." Does the understanding that Engelhardt proffers of the difference between grants and gifts, or the multiple ways she mentions of how foundations choose their grantees, indicate how tensions between grantors and grantees might be eased? Are such "partnerships" really possible?

How Does a Grant Differ from a Gift?

We usually think of grants[1] as firmly rooted in the gift relationship, but a grant's special characteristics make the relationship between giver and receiver fundamentally different. The main difference is that while gifts are generally made from personal resources, a grant is made from funds held in trust for public benefit. The public's "ownership" of the money—both before and after it is given—creates a community of interest around the grant that profoundly affects it. Significantly,

- The grant is a matter of public record; it cannot be anonymous, as gifts may be.
- It carries an obligation to use it for a public purpose.
- Numerous interested parties may hold the giver and the receiver accountable: the IRS, state attorneys general, the governing boards of

---

1. In this essay, I'm discussing grants made by private foundations to nonprofit organizations. Only some of these dynamics pertain to foundation awards to individuals and to grants made by public charities or governments.

the grantor and the recipient, and the intended beneficiaries of the grant, among others.

If we think of a gift as coming from the heart, a grant is given with the head. The gift of money *into* a foundation by an individual or a family may have qualities of heart, but foundation grants reflect a formality of planning, documentation, and reporting that is more readily connected to the head. A gift is often associated with altruism, compassion, generosity, impulse, and gratitude, even love—words laden with the emotional connotations. Grants are more likely to suggest strategy, competition, investment, capacity, and impact.

The worth of a gift is frequently found in the act of giving, not in its tangible value. In contrast, the worth of a grant is never in the transaction but in how the grant is used. Unfortunately, because it's so difficult to judge the effectiveness of a grant in promoting the public interest, the transactional relationship between grantor and grantee tends to bear much of the burden of expectation and critique focused on foundations.

The Dynamics of the Grantor/Grantee Relationship

Grantmaking foundations exist to give money away. Without grantees they cannot fulfill their mission and they have no legal legitimacy. This dependence of foundations on nonprofits might ideally create a partner relationship, and indeed, foundations often refer to grantees as their "partners." Nonetheless, the Golden Rule of Grantsmanship—he who has the gold makes the rules—means that grantees never really call the shots. The grantor's rules determine the grantee selection process, which in turn shapes the grantor/grantee relationship once the grant is made.

The three predominant systems for selecting grantees use either defined programs, existing relationships, or desired outcomes to drive the process. Program-driven foundations create a competitive process to find the best possible grantees in their areas of interest, an approach that may require substantial resources. This model is widely recognized as the standard foundation practice. However, a majority of foundations (albeit the smaller and younger ones) avoid the competitive dynamic and the expense by not accepting applications but rather "pre-selecting" their grantees. The latest system to emerge is outcome-driven grantmaking. It is often used by the new "venture philanthropy" foundations and is increasingly adopted by older, established foundations that want a more "strategic" approach to grantmaking. Despite the benefits of all three grantmaking styles, the grantor/grantee relationships that result have their critics.

No matter how thorough and fair the competitive process used by program-driven foundations, they inevitably turn down excellent nonprofits with a social purpose aligned with theirs. To protect their decision-making objectivity, these foundations' relationships with their grantees are often transitory and guarded. The system is stressful to individuals at the foundation with front-line relationships with grantees, and it can be downright bewildering to grantees. It may also be behind some of the current public displeasure with foundations—charges that they are inefficient and fickle, demands that they pay out more of their funds to help the causes they care about, and concerns that they cannot demonstrate sufficient social impact to justify their freedom to operate as they choose.

Grantees in the "pre-selected" process are likely to be educational, cultural, or healthcare institutions with ties to the donor's family or organizations to which board members contribute in other ways, as well. Here, the relationships with grantees may be personal and enduring, perhaps resembling gift-giving more than grantmaking. These foundations are a target of public officials, who consider them prime vehicles for abuse precisely because of the personal relationships. Others consider them wasteful because of the cost of maintaining a foundation. In many cases, though, subsequent donor gifts or bequests build these into mainstream foundations with more traditional grantmaking practices, so curtailing them would drain a key pipeline for future grants.

Given the problems with these grantmaking models, it's no surprise that over the past twenty-five years, many program-driven foundations have narrowed their focus, begun issuing RFPs [Requests for Proposals] that prescribe outcomes and even the means for achieving them. A number of foundations have very publicly entered into long-term, comprehensive relationships with a few grantees. And venture philanthropists with foundations champion this approach, pointing to such advantages as efficiency, the ability to focus on outcomes and effectiveness, and the potential for foundation money to build lasting capacity in the nonprofit sector, rather than to support isolated projects or short-lived change.

While this last approach creates more of a grantor/grantee partnership than the others, some observers have begun to point out the hazards to the grantee in the relationship. In the interest of gaining support or maintaining a relationship, a nonprofit may stray off mission or cede its autonomy in governance to the grantor. Its tried-and-true method of ameliorating a social problem may be subverted to a foundation's unproven theory of change. Some suggest that this approach reduces grantees to mere foundation contractors. Others worry that the grantees may be put at risk by having too narrow a base of support.

As reservoirs of funds for public benefit, foundations have a wide perspective on our society and the nonprofit organizations within it that drive social progress. Although their combined resources are small relative to the government and commercial sectors, they have the autonomy, flexibility, and permanence to work in concert over the long term with our other social institutions to take on some of the most difficult challenges we face. Through their diverse grantmaking purposes and strategies, they help create a force for opportunity, experimentation, dissension, and achievement that enables civil society to reinvent and revitalize itself. If they are to continue to play this unique role, we must remember that their value to our society lies in their partnership with grantees, however imperfect, not in the value of their endowments.

Written for the Dialogues on Civic Philanthropy, "Grants, Grantors, Grantees" (July 21, 2005). By permission of the author.

THREE

Bequests and Legacies

In his treatise *On Benefits,* in the midst of a discussion of the giving and receiving of benefits, Seneca begs his reader's indulgence in order to "glance at
a matter which," he says, "does not belong to our subject." The "matter" that commands his attention—the three goddesses of ancient mythology known as the
Graces—turns out not to be tangential, either to Seneca's concerns or to ours,
especially as we begin to reflect on the meaning and importance of bequests
and legacies.

Seneca begins by asking "why the Graces are three in number, why they
are sisters, why hand in hand, and why they are smiling and young, with a
loose and transparent dress." He answers:

> Some writers think that there is one who bestows a benefit, one who receives it,
> and a third who returns it; others say that they represent the three sorts of bene-
> factors, those who bestow, those who repay, and those who both receive and repay
> them. . . . What is the meaning of this dance of sisters in a circle, hand in hand? It
> means that the course of a benefit is from hand to hand, back to the giver; that the
> beauty of the whole chain is lost if a single link fails, and that it is fairest when it
> proceeds in unbroken regular order. . . . Their faces are cheerful, as those of hu-
> man beings who give or receive benefits are wont to be. They are young, because
> the memory of benefits ought not to grow old. . . . [And, since,] in benefits there
> should be no strict or binding conditions, therefore the Graces wear loose flowing
> tunics, which are transparent, because benefits love to be seen.

The three Graces, according to Seneca, embody in their circular dance the
full course of benefaction. Utterly crucial are the relations of giving and receiving both to the past and to the future. More precisely, the full meaning of giving
and receiving requires seeing also the relation of both to returning—how a

benefit, once received, is, literally, re-membered in the future. Thus, Seneca's lovely gloss on the three graceful maidens points us directly to bequests and legacies, that aspect of philanthropy that has most deliberately to do with re-paying the past and paying forward into the future—that links past and future "hand in hand."

A legacy, like a bequest, refers to "money or property bequeathed to an-other by will"—to bequeath, from the Old English *becwethan,* literally means, "to declare" or "to express in words" the disposition of one's money or prop-erty by will. But although the terms "legacy" and "bequest" are etymologically related, in ordinary usage we tend to distinguish them, often regarding a be-quest as but a part of a legacy. When people speak of their legacies—inherited or wished for—they often speak more about the beliefs, attitudes, practices, and teachings they hold most dear than about the things that money can buy or endow. For example, when a group of donors and professionals in philan-thropy was recently asked, "Who do you want to be in a hundred years?" not a one expressed a desire to be remembered for the monetary bequests they in-tend one day to make. It is, then, unclear whether any bequest, however ex-pressed or intended, can secure its author's legacy. In light of this, we begin our chapter with readings that help us to address this question:

What is the relation between a bequest and a legacy?

Percy Bysshe Shelley's "Ozymandias" casts doubt on the possibility of turning a bequest into a lasting legacy by showing how Time—the unstable medium of all our labor—can make a mockery of even the most masterful of human ac-complishments and intentions.

Michael Benedum's "Codicil to His Last Will and Testament" exemplifies the bequest that becomes its author's legacy as both monetized gift and biogra-phy. Whereas Benedum articulates himself both in will (act) and in testament (speech), the father in the tale that follows, from *Nathan the Wise* by Gotthold Lessing, creates from true intention false words and wealth—with appropri-ately ambiguous consequences.

Phil Cubeta's case study, "Bequests as Legacies: Devising Philanthropic Strategies," invites us to consider how—and whether—a family, vexed with com-peting interests, can shape a common legacy. An open philanthropic dialogue, Cubeta suggests—with its many actors vying for various "goods"—is the best hope for legacy-building.

Cubeta's scenario reminds us that intergenerational dialogue, whether tacitly embedded in our decisions or explicitly expressed in conversation, is an ongoing process of determining what we owe the past and what we owe the fu-ture. Such concerns take on special urgency when we accept a bequest or con-sciously take pen in hand to craft our wills, a fact that frames the next large question in this chapter:

What should guide those who give and those who receive bequests?

A selection from E. M. Forster's *Howards End* encourages examination of the relation between money and non-pecuniary values, especially critical to any donor seeking to promote the latter by means of the former.

The first scene of Shakespeare's *The Tragedy of King Lear* provokes reflection on whether and how one's own parental preferences ought to direct the bequests one leaves to one's children, while the selection from Henry James's *The Portrait of a Lady* invites reflection on the reverse: whether and how children's preferences should guide or direct parents' gifts.

"Donor Intent"—and its fulfillment or nonfulfillment—is the focus of the two essays that conclude this section: Julius Rosenwald's "Principles of Public Giving" and Waldemar Nielsen's "The Ethics of Philanthropy and Trusteeship." Each offers a different argument regarding what should guide, over time, the expression and interpretation of donor intent. But each, in its own way, gives evidence that it is trust above all that binds generations in the philanthropic process. This observation leads directly to the last general topic of the chapter:

How should we prepare the next generation?

Joseph Lumarda's personal account "Life Lessons: Making a Trust-ee" directly takes up the issue of trust by inviting us to think about whom we trust, with what we entrust them, and how to educate the trust-ees of future generations.

In his essay "Promethean Legacy: Receptive Giving, Generous Receiving," Albert Keith Whitaker uses the ancient story of Prometheus and his son Deukalion to help us understand why it might be especially difficult for children to "receive inheritances generously," or for parents to "give them receptively." Elizabeth Goudge's "Christmas with the Children" describes a grandfather's attempt to instill just such generosity of spirit in his grandchildren, by enlarging the giving-and-receiving of gifts on Christmas day to include turning, and returning, to those less fortunate.

Sociologist Robert Wuthnow, in "(Not) Talking about Money," points to yet another major obstacle in preparing the next generation to give, receive, or return—we don't talk to them about money. Returning again to the relation between monetary and other values, he urges us to reintegrate our everyday financial concerns with our higher aspirations. "Selections from Ethical Wills," edited by Susan Turnbull, suggest how to "talk" to our children about important values beyond monetary assets—even from beyond the grave.

John Maynard Keynes, in the chapter's last selection, "Economic Possibilities for Our Grandchildren," anticipates a time without financial concerns, and so advocates the conscious cultivation, in ourselves and our (grand) children, of "the arts of life." Thus, remembering Seneca's wonderful image, we are invited to wonder: Is philanthropy, as the dancing Graces suggest, such an art?

PERCY BYSSHE SHELLEY

"Ozymandias"

This masterful poem by English Romantic poet Percy Bysshe Shelley (1792–1822) was written in 1818, supposedly as part of a game or contest with a friend to see if both could compose a sonnet on the theme of the ruined monument erected to himself by Pharaoh Ramses II (also known as Ozymandias). Though allegedly just "tossed off," it is no accident that the poem remains one of his most widely read. For in it Shelley turns his prodigious lyric powers to an abiding human concern, one particularly pressing for any prospective donor: "What of us lives on?" Or more modestly put, "What can we hope will live on?"

The "action" of the poem is easy enough to grasp: The speaker meets a traveler who tells him of a broken statue in the desert commemorating the King of Kings, "Ozymandias." But the form of the poem, as well as its content, jar us out of complacency. For example, those familiar with the traditional sonnet form will quickly realize that Shelley uses it in an untraditional and, hence, destabilizing way. This is echoed by the evident ambiguity of the sonnet's central metaphor: How are we to understand the shattered, ruined statue? Or the wasteland in which it stands? Or its arrogant, passionate expression? Or its monomaniacal inscription ("Look on my Works, ye Mighty, and despair!")? Why doesn't Ozymandias live on in his former glory? Is it because he is human? Is it because of the type of human he was? Or, turning again to us, do the bequests we make, or the legacies we desire, also create insuperable obstacles to their fulfillment?

I met a traveller from an antique land,
Who said—"Two vast and trunkless legs of stone
Stand in the desert. . . . Near them, on the sand,
Half sunk a shattered visage lies, whose frown,
And wrinkled lip, and sneer of cold command,
Tell that its sculptor well those passions read
Which yet survive, stamped on these lifeless things,
The hand that mocked them and the heart that fed;
And on the pedestal, these words appear:
My name is Ozymandias, King of Kings,

Look on my Works, ye Mighty, and despair!
Nothing beside remains. Round the decay
Of that colossal Wreck, boundless and bare
The lone and level sands stretch far away."

Reprinted in *Shelley's Poetry and Prose* (Norton Critical Edition), edited by Donald H. Reiman and Sharon B. Powers (New York: W. W. Norton, 1977), p. 103.

MICHAEL L. BENEDUM

Excerpts from the "Codicil to His Last Will and Testament"

Michael Late Benedum (1869–1959), known as the "Great Wildcatter" for his work prospecting new sources of oil across four continents, amassed a fortune ranking him among the one hundred wealthiest Americans of his day. But if Churchill's dictum—"we make a living by what we get, but we make a life by what we give"—is correct, Benedum's many bequests may well be the most significant aspect of his legacy. For as his codicil makes clear, Benedum carefully designed his will to reflect the beliefs and values he espoused in his lifetime. Through it, he literally bequeaths (from a root meaning "to speak out" or "to express") his self-understanding and his world-view. Many a philanthropic advisor would no doubt be delighted to hear of Benedum's alignment of his bequests and the things he holds dear. But thanks to Benedum's self-conscious articulation of this alignment, we are alerted to an often unarticulated concern: Monetized gifts can surely promote one's legacy, but can they assure the spiritual intangibles we most treasure?

The disposition of a not inconsiderable estate is never an easy assignment.

It has been a thorny & laborious problem for me because, recognizing my frailty & inadequacy, I have not been able to lose sight of the awesome responsibility involved.

If I could have looked upon my material goods as personal property, belonging to me alone, my task would have been immeasurably lighter. But I have never regarded my possessions in that light. Providence gives no fee simple title to such possessions. As I have seen it, all of the elements of the earth belong to the Creator of all things, and He has, as a part of the Divine Purpose, distributed them unevenly among His children, holding each relatively accountable for their wise use and disposition.

I have always felt that I have been only a trustee for such material wealth as Providence has placed in my hands. This trusteeship has weighed heavily upon me. In carrying out this final responsibility of my stewardship, I have sought to utilize such wisdom and understanding of equity as the Creator has given me. No one with any regard for his responsibility to his God and his fellow man should do less. No one can do more.

As I have seen it, life is but a proving ground where Providence tests the character and mettle of those He places upon the earth. The whole course of mortal existence is a series of problems, sorrows & difficulties. If that existence be rightly conducted, it becomes a progress towards the fulfillment of human destiny. We must pass through darkness to reach the light.

Throughout my adult life, day by day & year by year, I have been instilled with the conviction that wealth cannot be measured in terms of money, stocks, bonds, broad acres or by ownership of mine and mill. These cannot bear testimony to the staple of real excellence of man or woman. Those who use a material yardstick to appraise their wealth and foolishly imagine themselves to be rich are objects of pity. In their ignorance and misanthropic isolation, they suffer from shrinkage of the soul.

All of us aspire to a higher and better life beyond this, but I feel that the individual who seeks to climb the ladder alone will never find the way to Paradise. Only those who sustain the faltering ones on the rungs above and extend a helping hand to the less fortunate on the rungs below, can approach the end with the strength of sublime faith and confidence.

At the end of life each of us must face the great teacher that we call death. Stern, cold & irresistible, it walks the earth in dread mystery and lays its hands upon all. The wealth of empires cannot stay its approach. As I near my rendezvous with this common leveler of mankind, which takes prince and pauper alike to the democracy of the grave, I do so with resignation to the will of God, and with faith in His eternal justice.

Life has been sweet to me . . . sweet in the loved ones that have been mine, sweet in the friends who have surrounded me & rewarding in the opportunities that have come my way. I could not leave this earth with any degree of happiness and satisfaction if I felt that I had not tried to bring some of these joys to those less fortunate than I have been.

We know not where seed may sprout. In the poorest and most unregarded child who seems to be abandoned to ignorance and evil, there may slumber virtue, intellect and genius. It is our duty to sow and to nurture, leaving it to others to harvest the fruits of our efforts.

While I am conscious that my love for the land that gave me birth has been an influence in guiding the disposition of my estate, there are other practical reasons why I have favored my native state of West Virginia. It is not that I am unmindful or unappreciative of my adopted home of Pennsylvania, but rather that I have sought to appraise and balance the needs of each and the available potential for supplying those needs.

I cannot close my eyes to the realistic consideration that Pittsburgh and Pennsylvania abound in riches, having a citizenship in which men of great wealth are more common than rare. West Virginia is in a less fortunate position. There can be no question but that its needs are much greater than those of my adopted home. Consequently, in making specific provisions for West Virginia institutions, I have done so in good conscience, with a sense of equity & with recognition of a responsibility to distribute my estate in a way that will bring the greatest good to the greatest number. This decision was not made lightly or impetuously.

Conscious that in this Codicil to my Last Will & Testament, I am figuratively speaking from the grave, and that the great book of my account with the Creator has been closed beyond change or amendment, I submit my soul to His tender mercy, and my memory to the generosity & compassion of my fellow man.

Signed by
Michael L. Benedum
on the 15th day of June 1957

Courtesy of the Claude Worthington Benedum Foundation.

GOTTHOLD E. LESSING

From Nathan the Wise

German philosopher and author Gotthold Ephraim Lessing (1729–1781) was known in his time as a "learned antiquarian, an incomparable writer, and a terrible controversialist." No doubt Lessing's play Nathan the Wise, *first published in 1779, contributed to his reputation. Not only was it one of the earliest pieces of literature to celebrate religious tolerance; it did so by depicting Jews in a favorable way. Although the tale excerpted here, as told in its context in Lessing's play, is intended to convey a lesson about religion, it spurs one to think even more about the relation between wealth and love, and between both of those goods and legacy. The wealth of the father—a precious ring—is meant to be passed to his "dearest son," making him, by virtue of possessing it, loved ("dear") alike by God and all men, and "lord of all the race." As a manifestation of the father's love, the ring is intended to promote a way of life, a legacy of peace and harmony. For years the legacy is maintained. But there eventually comes a father, who, loving each of his three sons equally, breaks tradition for affection's sake: he triplicates the ring, bestows on each son, "singly and apart," his special blessing, gives each his wealth, and dies. Peace and harmony come to an abrupt end, as each brother wrangles with the next about who has "the true original genuine ring." As partisans of equality, we can certainly sympathize with the latter-day father's plight. Yet his decision destroys the legacy. Does it also create a new legacy? Should he—could he—have done differently? Is giving wealth ever sufficient to convey and sustain love?*

Nathan:

. . . In hoar antiquity there dwelt
In eastern lands a man who had received
From a loved hand a ring of priceless worth.
An opal was the stone it bore, which shot
A hundred fair and varied hues around,
And had the mystic power to render dear
Alike to God and man whoever wore
The ring with perfect faith. What wonder, then,
That eastern man would never lay it off,
And further made a fixed and firm resolve
That it should bide for ever with his race.

For this he left it to his dearest son,
Adding a stringent clause that he in turn
Should leave it to the son he loved the most,
And that in every age the dearest son,
Without respect to seniority,
By virtue of the ring alone should be
The lord of all the race . . .
And thus the ring came down from sire to son,
Until it reached a father of three sons
Each equally obedient to his will,
And whom accordingly he was constrained
To love alike. And yet from time to time,
Whene'er the one or other chanced to be
Alone with him, and his overflowing heart
Was not divided by the other two,
The one who stood beside him still would seem
Most worthy of the ring; and thus it chanced
That he by kindly weakness had been led
To promise it in turn to each of them.
This state of matters lasted while it could,
But by-and-by he had to think of death,
And then this worthy sire was sore perplexed.
He could not brook the thought of breaking faith
With two dear sons to whom he'd pledged his word;
What now was to be done? He straightway sends
In secret for a skilled artificer,
And charges him to make two other rings
Precisely like the first, at any cost.
This the artificer contrives to do.
And when at last he brings him all three rings
Even the father can't say which is which.
With joyful heart he summons then his sons,
But singly and apart, bestows on each
His special blessing, and his ring—and dies . . .
Scarce was the father dead, each several son
Comes with his ring and claims to be the lord
Of all his kindred. They investigate,
Recriminate, and wrangle—all in vain—
Which was the true original genuine ring
Was undemonstrable— . . .
The sons now sued each other; each of them
Swore to the judge he had received his ring
Straight from his father's hand—as was the fact—

And that, too, after he had long enjoyed
His father's promise to bequeath the ring
To him alone—which also was the truth;
Each vowed the father never could have proved
So false to him; and rather than believe
A thing like this of such a loving sire,
He was constrained—however loath he was
To think unkindly of his brethren—
To charge them both with some nefarious trick,
And now he would unmask their treachery
And be avenged for such a cruel wrong.
. . . The Judge pronounced—Unless you bring your sire,
And place him here before the judgment-seat,
I must dismiss your suit. Think you I'm here
For solving riddles?—or perhaps you wait
Until the genuine ring declares itself.
Yet stay—you said the genuine ring contains
The magic power to make its wearer loved
More than all else, in sight of God and man;
This must decide the case—the spurious ring
Will not do this—say, which of you is he
The other two most love?—what, no reply?
Your rings would seem to work reflexively,
Not on external objects; since it seems
Each is enamored of himself alone.
Oh, then, all three of you have been deceived,
And are deceivers too; and all three rings
Are spurious alike—the genuine ring
Was lost, most likely, and to hide its loss,
And to supply its place, your father caused
These three to be made up instead of it.
. . . And then the Judge resumed—
Belike ye would not relish my advice
More than the judgment I have now pronounced;
In that case, go—but my advice is this:
Accept the case precisely as it stands;
If each of you in truth received his ring
Straight from his father's hand, let each believe
His own to be the true and genuine ring.
Perhaps your father wished to terminate
The tyranny of that special ring
'Mid his posterity. Of this be sure,
He loved you all, and loved you all alike,

Since he was loath to injure two of you
That he might favor one alone; well, then,
Let each now rival his unbiased love,
His love so free from every prejudice;
Vie with each other in the generous strife
To prove the virtues of the rings you wear;
And to this end let mild humility,
Hearty forbearance, true benevolence,
And resignation to the will of God,
Come to your aid,—and if, in distant times,
The virtues of the genuine gem be found
Amid your children's children, they shall then,
When many a thousand years have rolled away,
Be called once more before this judgment-seat,
Whereon a wiser man than I shall sit
And give his verdict—now, begone. Thus spake
That sapient Judge.

From Act II, Scene vii of *Nathan the Wise* by Gotthold Lessing, translated by Patrick Maxwell, edited by George Alexander Kohut (New York: Bloch, 1917).

PHILIP B. CUBETA

"Bequests as Legacies: Devising Philanthropic Strategies"

Philip Cubeta is chief of staff and (self-described) "charitable cheerleader" for a financial services group. Using "the case of the forest primeval," which he creates here, Cubeta invites us to engage with him for a moment in his trade—to devise a philanthropic strategy that will both direct the bequests of a wealthy family and promote its legacy. The case on which we are to cut our advisory-teeth is, however typical, far from easy. Quickly evident are the extreme differences within the family, which differences leave Meg, the recently widowed mother and "key decision maker" of the family, seriously questioning what will (or could) be her legacy. Cubeta offers us guidance regarding what must be thought about, and, although the path is far from clear, he remains (as his self-description forewarns) rather cheerful: "Meg's love for both her children promises a hopeful outcome," he says. Is Cubeta's cheerfulness well founded? Can you devise a strategy that will enable Meg to emerge from the thicket sanguine about her family's legacy? Is it more important for Meg to secure family harmony, or to pursue her own interests and values? More generally, how significant are philanthropic bequests, and the process by which we make them, in determining our legacies?

෴

> In the middle of our life's walk
> I found myself in a dark wood
> for the straight road was lost.
> —Dante

The Case of the Forest Primeval

Sarah, age 36, and her brother, Bill, are heirs to a fortune made in the forestry industry in Northern California. Their family now has holdings of approximately $55 million, including raw land with first growth redwood trees, but most of the family wealth is now in gas and oil stock in a family owned company, run by Bill.

Each year the family has a meeting with their family officer, Alex, to plan the family's giving in the light of their overall goals and objectives. Sarah is an environmentalist who has been trying without success to have at least $7 million worth of the old growth lands contributed to the Trust for Public Land. Her father had consistently refused. Sarah's dad recently died, leaving Sarah's mother, Meg, as the key decision-maker. Bill's philanthropic, business, and political interests converge. Along with donations to conservative political candidates, he contributes large sums each year to a libertarian think tank in Washington, D.C., that lobbies for tax breaks for businesses, income tax relief, estate tax repeal, tort reform, and regulatory rollbacks, particularly for the oil and gas industry.

Meg's sympathies are divided. Her heart leans to Sarah and the environment, but her head leans to Bill's strategic philanthropy. He tells her what her husband did, that the weak perish and the strong survive. The best rise to the top. The best way to help others is to maximize net profit. The family's responsibility is to grow the business that creates jobs. The best way to do that is to align all the family resources, including its political clout, its family foundation, its charitable contributions, its business entities, its PR efforts, and the various thinkers it can hire, to drive a single coherent agenda. As a compromise Bill offers a series of public service announcements from the family foundation aimed at the environmental community touting prudent forestry through selective logging. He suggests that Sarah be the family spokesperson. She angrily refuses. Meg steps in and suggests that it might be a good time to break for lunch.

Meg, after the group disperses with little progress made, wonders what will be her legacy. To whom has she given what, as a mother? What values have she and her husband passed on? How can she create some semblance of family harmony? As the majority owner of the family resources how will she allocate them between her children and the family foundation or foundations? She has a pretty good idea of what her deceased husband would do, but he and she never did agree on politics and money, and yet they loved one another and supported one another's efforts. Meg smiles, wondering, "What next? Do I see an attorney? A priest? A family therapist?"

What Should Guide the Family?

Rather than finding solutions, let me just point out the issues for consideration.

Values: We can say that the client/donor/citizen's "values" should guide the giving. Of course in diverse society, values are what may divide us into warring camps. Values are what wedge issues, civil wars, and revolutions, as well as markets, are made from. Values are soft issues with hard edges. "Family values" may be the cause of family feuds, or contention within the family itself.

Goals: We can say that giving should be strategically aimed at specific goals. Bill would agree, and so might Sarah, though they would disagree about the specific goals that the family should pursue. But secretly, Sarah has reservations. She sees that Bill is so driven by goal logic that he is no longer the brother she remembers. Ever since he went to Harvard for that MBA he has been a logical machine reducing all he touches to the dehumanizing calculus (as she sees it) of costs and benefits. In the process he has lost, in her opinion, his soul, or part of it. To Bill, Sarah's goals are wishy-washy and non-specific. She wants to save the forest, be a good person, be seen as a leader in her tight little environmental group, but she has no long-term plan for maximizing the family's interests. She won't discuss options for managing the forest to balance conservation with productivity. To her it is a sacred commitment to "Mother Earth," and how can he argue with dogmatism?

Financial, Tax, and Legal: All the strategies (foundations, wills, trusts, investments) considered by the family will have their own internal logic. Each will have current and projected financial, tax, and legal implications. While strategies are means, not ends, the means are so complex that managing them can become a full time job. The head of the family office, Alex, is a JD, CPA and is frustrated with Sarah's "touchy-feely" idealism. She does not understand tax law or financial strategies, much less the game of political influence. She seems to operate in a vacuum, wanting to be Saint Sarah, the innocent victim sacrificed. Bill, on the other hand, as an MBA, grasps both means and ends and wields both with a clear eye on the bottom-line. Alex is far happier with Bill's focus on means, ends, and results. Bill has doubled the family's net worth in five years. Sarah ought to be grateful, she spends it fast enough.

Needs of Others and the Community: "What does the family owe to the community," Sarah asks, "and to the planet? What does the family owe to future generations? What does the family owe to God's creation in the forest primeval of which the family is the steward?" Bill and Alex (the family officer) twist in their chairs, having to listen to this granola-inspired claptrap. The gas company is under indictment for polluting the groundwater in Arkansas, and the possibility of a class action suit looms. There are more pressing matters than squirrels running around in the redwoods. Elections are in the offing; a family friend is in the running for governor. At the federal level legislation and judicial action is pending to quash the lawsuits. The think tank, founded by Meg's husband twenty years ago, has changed the terms of the debate about the public interest. They are gearing up to promote freedom and public benefits via private ownership. A grassroots group or two is being organized with family funding through discreet intermediaries, to promote increased citizen responsibility through private philanthropy rather than taxes. Unless the chips fall just right, the family may find its asset base shrinking. "The needs of the community," thunders Bill, "are best served by growth and strength of our companies. If we take our eye off the ball, thousands are going to be thrown out of work."

Closing Thoughts

Legacy planning is "the unlicensed practice of the liberal arts." The philanthropic consultant enters these personal and family dramas at his or her own risk as a bit player or minor character, but one who, like the Fool in the courts of power, may play a pivotal role. In the deep and sometimes treacherous dialogues of civic philanthropy no one can claim to be "value-neutral," "value free," or completely disinterested. In the words of Bob Dylan, we all "gotta serve somebody." We can serve ourselves, our clients, our customers, our constituents, our company, our political group, but we can also use the conversation of giving to transcend or moderate *partis pris,* maintaining our own views, but rising above our differences, not to reach consensus, but to support the fragile open spaces of democracy in which we come together to have an open dialogue about public ends and private means. In these hazardous conversations we hash out for ourselves what it means to be a person, a parent or child, a brother or sister, a citizen, a donor and a spiritual being, or a thinker. The "should" that hides in our question about what should guide donors is the mystery of the good, or the just, that we contest within a shared commitment to the open society.

My sympathies are with Sarah, but Bill's commitment to freedom is an open invitation to a deeper conversation about how his ideals might best be served. Meg's love for both her children promises a hopeful outcome. Alex works for the family, and can carry out whatever solutions best fit the vision and values that emerge from family debate. The advisor who enters that conversation can come to it as a faithful servant, a representative of one family member or another, a facilitator, or as what? A fallible citizen contesting the "should" by his or her own lights, not to impose his or her own views, but to help the donor reach a thoughtful and reasoned course of action by the donor's own lights, all things considered in this dark wood. In the end it is Meg's money, her life, her children, and our society. As citizens, we all have a stake in the conversation.

Written for the Dialogues on Civic Philanthropy, "Bequest and Legacies" (November 29, 2005). By permission of the author.

E. M. FORSTER

From Howards End

British author E. M. Forster (1879–1970) was an especially acute observer of the "monied" class. In his novel Howards End, *he contemplates class relations, especially as they burdened human ties (his epigraph to the novel sounds a plaintive cry, "Only connect"). In the selection below, the upper-class well-educated Schlegel sisters, Helen and Margaret, have just made the acquaintance of Leonard Bast—a poor clerk with rich inner resources. That night, with other similarly situated young women, they discuss Mr. Bast in counterpoint to a hypothetical bequest: How best give away one's money? Are the "Mr. Basts" of the world deserving? How might they be aided?*

Margaret argues that schemes of patronage are not nearly as valuable as sums of money: "give Mr. Bast money, and don't bother about his ideals." In a curious turn of phrase, she names cash the "warp of civilization." Money, in other words, is what gives the world its structure—but not its meaning. As her sister later asks, what, then, is the woof? Margaret's metaphor asks us to consider the relation between money—cash value—and worth—what we value. Should a donor's bequest attempt to pass down values with its monetary value? Or, should money be allowed to provide, as Margaret suggests, its own education?

ℰ

The sisters went out to dinner full of their adventure, and when they were both full of the same subject, there were few dinner-parties that could stand up against them. This particular one, which was all ladies, had more kick in it than most, but succumbed after a struggle. Helen at one part of the table, Margaret at the other, would talk of Mr. Bast and of no one else, and somewhere about the entree their monologues collided, fell ruining, and became common property. Nor was this all. The dinner party was really an informal discussion club; there was a paper after it, read amid coffee-cups and laughter in the drawing-room, but dealing more or less thoughtfully with some topic of general interest. After the paper came a debate, and in this debate Mr. Bast also figured, appearing now as a bright spot in civilization, now as a dark spot, according to the temperament of the speaker. The subject of the paper had been, "How ought I to dispose of my money?" the reader professing to be a millionaire on the point of death, inclined to bequeath her fortune for the foundation of local art galleries, but open to conviction from other sources. The various parts had been assigned beforehand, and some of the speeches were amusing. The hostess assumed the ungrateful role of "the millionaire's eldest son," and implored her expiring parent not to dislocate society by allowing such vast sums to pass out of the family. Money was the fruit of self-denial, and the second generation had a right to profit by the self-denial of the first. What right had "Mr. Bast" to profit? The National Gallery was good enough for the likes of him. After property had had its say—a say that is necessarily ungracious—the various philanthropists stepped forward. Something must be done for "Mr. Bast": his conditions must be improved without impairing his independence; he must have a free library, or free tennis-courts; his rent must be paid in such a way that he did not know it was being paid; it must be made worth his while to join the Territorials; he must be forcibly parted from his uninspiring wife, the money going to her as compensation; he must be assigned a Twin Star, some member of the leisured classes who would watch over him ceaselessly (groans from Helen); he must be given food but no clothes, clothes but no food, a third-return ticket to Venice, without either food or clothes when he arrived there. In short, he might be given anything and everything so long as it was not the money itself.

And here Margaret interrupted.

"Order, order, Miss Schlegel!" said the reader of the paper. "You are here, I understand, to advise me in the interests of the Society for the Preservation of Places of Historic Interest or Natural Beauty. I cannot have you speaking out of your role. It makes my poor head go round, and I think you forget that I am very ill."

"Your head won't go round if only you'll listen to my argument," said Margaret. "Why not give him the money itself. You're supposed to have about thirty thousand a year."

"Have I? I thought I had a million."

"Wasn't a million your capital? Dear me! we ought to have settled that. Still, it doesn't matter. Whatever you've got, I order you to give as many poor men as you can three hundred a year each."

"But that would be pauperizing them," said an earnest girl, who liked the Schlegels, but thought them a little unspiritual at times.

"Not if you gave them so much. A big windfall would not pauperize a man. It is these little driblets, distributed among too many, that do the harm. Money's educational. It's far more educational than the things it buys." There was a protest. "In a sense," added Margaret, but the protest continued. "Well, isn't the most civilized thing going, the man who has learned to wear his income properly?"

"Exactly what your Mr. Basts won't do."

"Give them a chance. Give them money. Don't dole them out poetry, books and railway-tickets like babies. Give them the wherewithal to buy these things. When your Socialism comes it may be different, and we may think in terms of commodities instead of cash. Till it comes give people cash, for it is the warp of civilization, whatever the woof may be. The imagination ought to play upon money and realize it vividly, for it's the—the second most important thing in the world. It is so slurred over and hushed up, there is so little clear thinking—oh, political economy, of course, but so few of us think clearly about our own private incomes, and admit that independent thoughts are in nine cases out of ten the result of independent means. Money: give Mr. Bast money, and don't bother about his ideals. He'll pick up those for himself."

She leant back while the more earnest members of the club began to misconstrue her. The female mind, though cruelly practical in daily life, cannot bear to hear ideals belittled in conversation, and Miss Schlegel was asked however she could say such dreadful things, and what it would profit Mr. Bast if he gained the whole world and lost his own soul. She answered, "Nothing, but he would not gain his soul until he had gained a little of the world." Then they said, "No they did not believe it," and she admitted that an overworked clerk may save his soul in the superterrestrial sense, where the effort will be taken for the deed, but she denied that he will ever explore the spiritual resources of this world, will ever know the rarer joys of the body, or attain to clear and passionate intercourse with his fellows. Others had attacked the fabric of society—property, interest, etc.; she only fixed her eyes on a few human beings, to see how, under present conditions, they could be made happier. Doing good to humanity was useless: the many-colored efforts thereto spreading over the vast area like films and resulting in an universal grey. To do good to one, or, as in this case, to a few, was the utmost she dare hope for.

Between the idealists and the political economists, Margaret had a bad time. Disagreeing elsewhere, they agreed in disowning her, and in keeping the administration of the millionaire's money in their own hands. The earnest girl brought forward a scheme of "personal supervision and mutual help," the effect of which was to alter poor people until they became exactly like people who were not so poor. The hostess pertinently remarked that she, as eldest "son," might surely rank among the millionaire's legatees. Margaret weakly admitted the claim, and another claim was at once set up by Helen, who declared that she had been the millionaire's housemaid for over forty years, overfed and underpaid; was nothing to be done for her, so corpulent and poor? The millionaire then read out her last will and testament, in which she left the whole of her fortune to the Chancellor of the Exchequer. Then she died. The serious parts of the discussion had been of higher merit than the playful—in a men's debate is the reverse more general?—but the meeting broke up hilariously enough, and a dozen happy ladies dispersed to their homes.

Helen and Margaret walked the earnest girl as far as Battersea Bridge Station, arguing copiously all the way. When she had gone they were conscious of an alleviation, and of the great beauty of the evening. They turned back towards Oakley Street. The lamps and the plane trees, following the line of the embankment, struck a note of dignity that is rare in English cities. The seats, almost deserted, were here and there occupied by gentlefolk in evening dress, who had strolled out from the houses behind to enjoy fresh air and the whisper of the rising tide. There is something continental about Chelsea Embankment. It is an open space used rightly, a blessing more frequent in Germany than here. As Margaret and Helen sat down, the city behind them seemed to be a vast theatre, an opera-house in which some endless trilogy was performing, and they themselves a pair of satisfied subscribers, who did not mind losing a little of the second act.

"Cold?"

"No."

"Tired?"

"Doesn't matter."

The earnest girl's train rumbled away over the bridge.

"I say, Helen—"

"Well?"

"Are we really going to follow up Mr. Bast?"

"I don't know."

"I think we won't."

"As you like."

"It's no good, I think, unless you really mean to know people. The discussion brought that home to me. We got on well enough with him in a spirit of excitement, but think of rational intercourse. We mustn't play at friendship. No, it's no good."

"There's Mrs. Lanoline, too," Helen yawned. "So dull."

"Just so, and possibly worse than dull."

"I should like to know how he got hold of your card."

"But he said—something about a concert and an umbrella—"

"Then did the card see the wife—"

"Helen, come to bed."

"No, just a little longer, it is so beautiful. Tell me; oh yes; did you say money is the warp of the world?"

"Yes."

"Then what's the woof?"

"Very much what one chooses," said Margaret. "It's something that isn't money—one can't say more."

From chapter 15 of *Howards End* by E. M. Forster (New York: G. P. Putnam's Sons, 1910).

WILLIAM SHAKESPEARE

From The Tragedy of King Lear, *Act I, Scene i*

William Shakespeare (1564–1616), English poet extraordinaire, takes up the troubling, sometimes tragic, business of making a bequest in The Tragedy of King Lear. By the end of the play's first scene (excerpted below), the seeds of the tragedy are firmly planted. Lear, King of Britain, convenes his court for the purpose of formally announcing the division of his kingdom and declaring whom he has chosen to marry his youngest and dearest daughter Cordelia. Though still strong, Lear is well aware of his age. He intends, so he claims, to arrange now for the peaceful transfer of his kingdom, by divesting himself of rule, legal possession of territories, and all cares of state—in short, by surrendering all his power. We know, from the first exchange in the play, that he has already decided what benefaction he intends to bestow on each daughter. Nevertheless, Lear proceeds publicly as if the division depends on his daughters' affection for him, and he unabashedly calls on each daughter to tell him how much she loves him, thereby hoping that all will see the rightness of his decision to leave the fairest portion to Cordelia. Goneril and Regan willingly comply, each exaggerating to outdo the other. But Cordelia cannot bring herself to do so and refuses to "play the game." And so, the tragedy ensues. What—who—is primarily responsible for the debacle? How—why—do things go so far wrong? Could the tragedy have been averted? Though none of us has kingdoms to bequeath, people with several children, one of whom is better than the other(s) in heart and mind, inevitably confront similar situations. What would—what will—you do? How will you get everyone to accept it?

✠

Act I. Scene i. *A Room of State in* KING LEAR's *Palace.*

[*Enter* KENT, GLOUCESTER, *and* EDMUND.]

Kent. I thought the king had more affected the Duke of Albany than
    Cornwall.
Glo. It did always seem so to us; but now, in the division of the kingdom, it
    appears not which of the dukes he values most; for equalities are so
    weighed that curiosity in neither can make choice of either's
    moiety.... —The king is coming.

[*Sennet. Enter* LEAR, CORNWALL, ALBANY, GONERIL, REGAN,
CORDELIA, *and* Attendants.]

Lear. Attend the Lords of France and Burgundy, Gloucester.
Glo. I shall, my liege.

[*Exeunt* GLOUCESTER *and* EDMUND.]

Lear. Meantime we shall express our darker purpose.
　　　Give me the map there. Know that we have divided
　　　In three our kingdom; and 'tis our fast intent
　　　To shake all cares and business from our age,
　　　Conferring them on younger strengths, while we
　　　Unburden'd crawl toward death. Our son of Cornwall,
　　　And you, our no less loving son of Albany,
　　　We have this hour a constant will to publish
　　　Our daughters' several dowers, that future strife
　　　May be prevented now. The princes, France and Burgundy,
　　　Great rivals in our youngest daughter's love,
　　　Long in our court have made their amorous sojourn,
　　　And here are to be answer'd. Tell me, my daughters,
　　　Since now we will divest us both of rule,
　　　Interest of territory, cares of state,—
　　　Which of you shall we say doth love us most?
　　　That we our largest bounty may extend
　　　Where nature doth with merit challenge. Goneril,
　　　Our eldest-born, speak first.
Gon. Sir, I love you more than words can wield the matter;
　　　Dearer than eyesight, space, and liberty;
　　　Beyond what can be valu'd, rich or rare;
　　　No less than life, with grace, health, beauty, honour;
　　　As much as child e'er lov'd, or father found;
　　　A love that makes breath poor and speech unable;
　　　Beyond all manner of so much I love you.
Cor. [*Aside.*] What shall Cordelia speak? Love, and be silent.
Lear. Of all these bounds, even from this line to this,
With shadowy forests and with champains rich'd,
　　　With plenteous rivers and wide-skirted meads,
　　　We make thee lady: to thine and Albany's issue
　　　Be this perpetual. What says our second daughter,
　　　Our dearest Regan, wife to Cornwall? Speak.
Reg. I am made of that self metal as my sister,
　　　And prize me at her worth. In my true heart
　　　I find she names my very deed of love;
　　　Only she comes too short: that I profess
　　　Myself an enemy to all other joys
　　　Which the most precious square of sense possesses,
　　　And find I am alone felicitate
　　　In your dear highness' love.
Cor. [*Aside.*] Then, poor Cordelia!
　　　And yet not so; since, I am sure, my love's
　　　More richer than my tongue.

Lear. To thee and thine, hereditary ever,
    Remain this ample third of our fair kingdom,
    No less in space, validity, and pleasure,
    Than that conferr'd on Goneril. Now, our joy,
    Although our last, not least; to whose young love
    The vines of France and milk of Burgundy
    Strive to be interess'd; what can you say to draw
    A third more opulent than your sisters? Speak.
Cor. Nothing, my lord.
Lear. Nothing?
Cor. Nothing.
Lear. Nothing will come of nothing: speak again.
Cor. Unhappy that I am, I cannot heave
    My heart into my mouth: I love your majesty
    According to my bond; no more nor less.
Lear. How, how, Cordelia! mend your speech a little,
    Lest you may mar your fortunes.
Cor. Good my lord,
    You have begot me, bred me, lov'd me: I
    Return those duties back as are right fit,
    Obey you, love you, and most honour you.
    Why have my sisters husbands, if they say
    They love you all? Haply, when I shall wed,
    That lord whose hand must take my plight shall carry
    Half my love with him, half my care and duty:
    Sure I shall never marry like my sisters,
    To love my father all.
Lear. But goes thy heart with this?
Cor. Ay, good my lord.
Lear. So young, and so untender?
Cor. So young, my lord, and true.
Lear. Let it be so; thy truth then be thy dower:
    For, by the sacred radiance of the sun,
    The mysteries of Hecate and the night,
    By all the operation of the orbs
    From whom we do exist and cease to be,
    Here I disclaim all my paternal care,
    Propinquity and property of blood,
    And as a stranger to my heart and me
    Hold thee from this for ever. The barbarous Scythian,
    Or he that makes his generation messes
    To gorge his appetite, shall to my bosom
    Be as well neighbour'd, pitied, and reliev'd,
    As thou my sometime daughter.

Kent. Good my liege,—
Lear. Peace, Kent!
    Come not between the dragon and his wrath.
    I lov'd her most, and thought to set my rest
    On her kind nursery. Hence, and avoid my sight!
    So be my grave my peace, as here I give
    Her father's heart from her! Call France.
    Who stirs?
    Call Burgundy! Cornwall and Albany,
    With my two daughters' dowers digest the third;
    Let pride, which she calls plainness, marry her.
    I do invest you jointly with my power,
    Pre-eminence, and all the large effects
    That troop with majesty. Ourself by monthly course,
    With reservation of a hundred knights,
    By you to be sustain'd, shall our abode
    Make with you by due turn. Only we shall retain
    The name and all th' addition to a king;
    The sway, revenue, execution of the rest,
    Beloved sons, be yours; which to confirm,
    This coronet part betwixt you.

[*Giving the crown.*]

Kent. Royal Lear,
    Whom I have ever honour'd as my king,
    Lov'd as my father, as my master follow'd,
    As my great patron thought on in my prayers,—
Lear. The bow is bent and drawn; make from the shaft.
Kent. Let it fall rather, though the fork invade
    The region of my heart: be Kent unmannerly
    When Lear is mad. What wouldst thou do, old man?
    Think'st thou that duty shall have dread to speak
    When power to flattery bows? To plainness honour's bound
    When majesty falls to folly. Reserve thy state;
    And, in thy best consideration check
    This hideous rashness: answer my life my judgment,
    Thy youngest daughter does not love thee least;
    Nor are those empty-hearted whose low sound
    Reverbs no hollowness.
Lear. Kent, on thy life, no more.
Kent. My life I never held but as a pawn
    To wage against thine enemies; nor fear to lose it,
    Thy safety being the motive.

Lear. Out of my sight!

Kent. See better, Lear; and let me still remain
    The true blank of thine eye.

Lear. Now, by Apollo,—

Kent. Now, by Apollo, king,
    Thou swear'st thy gods in vain.

Lear. O vassal! miscreant!

[*Laying his hand on his sword.*]

Alb. & Corn. Dear sir, forbear.

Kent. Do;
        Kill thy physician, and the fee bestow
        Upon the foul disease. Revoke thy gift;
        Or, whilst I can vent clamour from my throat,
        I'll tell thee thou dost evil.

Lear. Hear me, recreant!
        On thine allegiance, hear me!
        Since thou hast sought to make us break our vow,—
        Which we durst never yet,—and, with strain'd pride
        To come betwixt our sentence and our power,—
        Which nor our nature nor our place can bear,—
        Our potency made good, take thy reward.
        Five days we do allot thee for provision
        To shield thee from diseases of the world;
        And, on the sixth, to turn thy hated back
        Upon our kingdom: if, on the tenth day following,
        Thy banish'd trunk be found in our dominions,
        The moment is thy death. Away! By Jupiter,
        This shall not be revok'd.

Kent. Fare thee well, king; sith thus thou wilt appear,
        Freedom lives hence, and banishment is here.
        [*To* CORDELIA.] The gods to their dear shelter take thee, maid,
        That justly think'st, and hast most rightly said!
        [*To* REGAN *and* GONERIL.] And your large speeches may your deeds
            approve,
        That good effects may spring from words of love.
        Thus Kent, O princes! bids you all adieu;
        He'll shape his old course in a country new. [*Exit.*]

[*Flourish. Re-enter* GLOUCESTER, *with* FRANCE, BURGUNDY, *and*
Attendants.]

Glo. Here's France and Burgundy, my noble lord.

Lear. My Lord of Burgundy,
        We first address toward you, who with this king

Hath rivall'd for our daughter. What, in the least,
Will you require in present dower with her,
Or cease your quest of love?

Bur. Most royal majesty,
I crave no more than hath your highness offer'd,
Nor will you tender less.

Lear. Right noble Burgundy,
When she was dear to us we did hold her so,
But now her price is fall'n. Sir, there she stands:
If aught within that little-seeming substance,
Or all of it, with our displeasure piec'd,
And nothing more, may fitly like your Grace,
She's there, and she is yours.

Bur. I know no answer.

Lear. Will you, with those infirmities she owes,
Unfriended, new-adopted to our hate,
Dower'd with our curse, and stranger'd with our oath,
Take her, or leave her?

Bur. Pardon me, royal sir;
Election makes not up on such conditions.

Lear. Then leave her, sir; for, by the power that made me,
I tell you all her wealth.—[*To* FRANCE.] For you, great king,
I would not from your love make such a stray
To match you where I hate; therefore, beseech you
To avert your liking a more worthier way
Than on a wretch whom nature is asham'd
Almost to acknowledge hers.

France. This is most strange,
That she, who even but now was your best object,
The argument of your praise, balm of your age,
The best, the dearest, should in this trice of time
Commit a thing so monstrous, to dismantle
So many folds of favour. Sure, her offence
Must be of such unnatural degree
That monsters it, or your fore-vouch'd affection
Fall into taint; which to believe of her,
Must be a faith that reason without miracle
Could never plant in me.

Cor. I yet beseech your majesty—
If for I want that glib and oily art
To speak and purpose not; since what I well intend,
I'll do 't before I speak—that you make known
It is no vicious blot nor other foulness,
No unchaste action, or dishonour'd step,

That hath depriv'd me of your grace and favour,
But even for want of that for which I am richer,
A still-soliciting eye, and such a tongue
That I am glad I have not, though not to have it
Hath lost me in your liking.
Lear. Better thou
Hadst not been born than not to have pleas'd me better.
France. Is it but this? a tardiness in nature
Which often leaves the history unspoke
That it intends to do?—My Lord of Burgundy,
What say you to the lady? Love is not love
When it is mingled with regards that stand
Aloof from the entire point. Will you have her?
She is herself a dowry.
Bur. Royal King,
Give but that portion which yourself propos'd,
And here I take Cordelia by the hand,
Duchess of Burgundy.
Lear. Nothing: I have sworn; I am firm.
Bur. I am sorry, then, you have so lost a father
That you must lose a husband.
Cor. Peace be with Burgundy!
Since that respects of fortune are his love,
I shall not be his wife.
France. Fairest Cordelia, that art most rich, being poor;
Most choice, forsaken; and most lov'd, despis'd!
Thee and thy virtues here I seize upon:
Be it lawful I take up what's cast away.
Gods, gods! 'tis strange that from their cold'st neglect
My love should kindle to inflam'd respect.
Thy dowerless daughter, king, thrown to my chance,
Is queen of us, of ours, and our fair France:
Not all the dukes of waterish Burgundy
Shall buy this unpriz'd precious maid of me.
Bid them farewell, Cordelia, though unkind:
Thou losest here, a better where to find.
Lear. Thou hast her, France; let her be thine, for we
Have no such daughter, nor shall ever see
That face of hers again, therefore be gone
Without our grace, our love, our benison.
Come, noble Burgundy.

[*Flourish. Exeunt* LEAR, BURGUNDY, CORNWALL, ALBANY,
GLOUCESTER, *and* Attendants.]

France. Bid farewell to your sisters.

Cor. The jewels of our father, with wash'd eyes
　　Cordelia leaves you: I know you what you are;
　　And, like a sister, am most loath to call
　　Your faults as they are nam'd. Love well our father:
　　To your professed bosoms I commit him:
　　But yet, alas! stood I within his grace,
　　I would prefer him to a better place.
　　So farewell to you both.

Reg. Prescribe not us our duties.

Gon. Let your study
　　Be to content your lord, who hath receiv'd you
　　At fortune's alms; you have obedience scanted,
　　And well are worth the want that you have wanted.

Cor. Time shall unfold what plighted cunning hides;
　　Who covers faults, at last shame them derides.
　　Well may you prosper!

France. Come, my fair Cordelia.

[*Exit* FRANCE *and* CORDELIA.]

Gon. Sister, it is not little I have to say of what most nearly appertains to us
　　both. I think our father will hence to-night.

Reg. That's most certain, and with you; next month with us.

Gon. You see how full of changes his age is; the observation we have made of it
　　hath not been little: he always loved our sister most; and with what poor
　　judgment he hath now cast her off appears too grossly.

Reg. 'Tis the infirmity of his age; yet he hath ever but slenderly known
　　himself.

Gon. The best and soundest of his time hath been but rash; then, must we look
　　to receive from his age, not alone the imperfections of long-engraffed
　　condition, but, therewithal the unruly waywardness that infirm and
　　choleric years bring with them.

Reg. Such unconstant starts are we like to have from him as this of Kent's
　　banishment.

Gon. There is further compliment of leave-taking between France and him.
　　Pray you, let us hit together: if our father carry authority with such
　　dispositions as he bears, this last surrender of his will but offend us.

Reg. We shall further think of it.

Gon. We must do something, and i' the heat.

[*Exeunt.*]

From *The Complete Works of William Shakespeare*, edited by W. J. Craig (London: Oxford University Press: 1914).

HENRY JAMES

From The Portrait of a Lady

Henry James (1843–1916), American-born short story writer, novelist, and critic, spent most of his adult life traveling in Europe. For many years he concerned himself with the impact of the older civilization of Europe on American life, and to this period belongs his novel The Portrait of a Lady, *the source of this selection. The story's "Lady" is Isabel Archer—a high-spirited young American— around whom revolve the Touchetts, an American family settled in England—Daniel, an ailing, old banker, his hard-hearted wife, and Ralph, his invalid son. Isabel has been "taken up" by Mrs. Touchett, her estranged aunt, and brought to England. Though left poor by her imprudent father, she harbors unconventional aspirations and insists on her independence, refusing both offers of matrimony and insinuations of patronage. For these reasons and then some, her cousin Ralph comes to admire Isabel.*

In this passage Ralph asks his dying father to alter his will so that Isabel might receive half of the inheritance left for him, readily acknowledging, even as he does so, the snares and traps for Isabel that are likely to ensue. Ralph also insists that the bequest be made in his father's name, so that Isabel will not know her true beneficiary. Why does the business-savvy Daniel Touchett accede to Ralph's plan— which he thinks "immoral"? What guides his decision? Similarly situated, would you do the same? Is Ralph an enlightened receiver, or has he "scandalously" taken advantage of his father's wishes and much diminished state?

છે

On the day following [the famous doctor] Sir Matthew Hope reappeared at Gardencourt, and now took a less encouraging view of the old man [Mr. Touchett], who had grown worse in the twenty-four hours. His feebleness was extreme, and to his son, who constantly sat by his bedside, it often seemed that his end must be at hand. The local doctor, who was a very sagacious man, and in whom Ralph had secretly more confidence than in his distinguished colleague, was constantly in attendance, and Sir Matthew Hope came back several times to Gardencourt. Mr. Touchett was much of the time unconscious; he slept a great deal; he rarely spoke. Isabel had a great desire to be useful to him and was allowed to watch with him several times when his other attendants (of whom Mrs. Touchett was not the least regular) went to take rest. He never seemed to know her, and she always said to herself—"Suppose he should die while I'm sitting here"; an idea which excited her and kept her awake. Once he opened his eyes for a while and fixed them upon her intelligently, but when she went to him, hoping he would recognize her, he closed them and relapsed into unconsciousness. The day after this, however, he revived for a longer time; but on this occasion Ralph was with him alone. The old man began to talk, much to his son's satisfaction, who assured him that they should presently have him sitting up.

"No, my boy," said Mr. Touchett, "not unless you bury me in a sitting posture, as some of the ancients—was it the ancients?—used to do."

"Ah, daddy, don't talk about that," Ralph murmured. "You must not deny that you're getting better."

"There will be no need of my denying it if you don't say so," the old man answered. "Why should we prevaricate just at the last? We never prevaricated before. I have got to die some time, and it's better to die when one is sick than when one is well. I am very sick—as sick as I shall ever be. I hope you don't want to prove that I shall ever be worse than this? That would be too bad. You don't? Well then."

Having made this excellent point he became quiet; but the next time that Ralph was with him he again addressed himself to conversation. The nurse had gone to her supper and Ralph was alone with him, having just relieved Mrs. Touchett, who had been on guard since dinner. The room was lighted only by the flickering fire, which of late had become necessary, and Ralph's tall shadow was projected upon the wall and ceiling, with an outline constantly varying but always grotesque.

"Who is that with me—is it my son?" the old man asked.

"Yes, it's your son, daddy."

"And is there no one else?"

"No one else."

Mr. Touchett said nothing for a while; and then, "I want to talk a little," he went on.

"Won't it tire you?" Ralph inquired.

"It won't matter if it does. I shall have a long rest. I want to talk about you."

Ralph had drawn nearer to the bed; he sat leaning forward with his hand on his father's. "You had better select a brighter topic," he said.

"You were always bright; I used to be proud of your brightness. I should like so much to think you would do something."

"If you leave us," said Ralph, "I shall do nothing but miss you."

"That is just what I don't want; it's what I want to talk about. You must get a new interest."

"I don't want a new interest, daddy. I have more old ones than I know what to do with."

The old man lay there looking at his son; his face was the face of the dying, but his eyes were the eyes of Daniel Touchett. He seemed to be reckoning over Ralph's interests.

"Of course you have got your mother," he said at last. "You will take care of her." "My mother will always take care of herself," Ralph answered.

"Well," said his father, "perhaps as she grows older she'll need a little help."

"I shall not see that. She will outlive me."

"Very likely she will; but that's no reason—" Mr. Touchett let his phrase die away in a helpless but not quite querulous sigh and remained silent again.

"Don't trouble yourself about us," said his son. "My mother and I get on very well together, you know."

"You get on by always being apart; that's not natural."

"If you leave us we shall probably see more of each other."

"Well," the old man observed with wandering irrelevance, "it cannot be said that my death will make much difference in your mother's life."

"It will probably make more than you think."

"Well, she'll have more money," said Mr. Touchett. "I have left her a good wife's portion, just as if she had been a good wife."

"She has been one, daddy, according to her own theory. She has never troubled you."

"Ah, some troubles are pleasant," Mr. Touchett murmured. "Those you have given me for instance. But your mother has been less—less—what shall I call it? less out of the way since I have been ill. I presume she knows I have noticed it."

"I shall certainly tell her so; I'm so glad you mention it."

"It won't make any difference to her; she doesn't do it to please me. She does it to please—to please—" And he lay a while trying to think why she did it. "She does it to please herself. But that is not what I want to talk about," he added. "It's about you. You will be very well off."

"Yes," said Ralph, "I know that. But I hope you have not forgotten the talk we had a year ago—when I told you exactly what money I should need and begged you to make some good use of the rest."

"Yes, yes, I remember. I made a new will—in a few days. I suppose it was the first time such a thing had happened—a young man trying to get a will made against him."

"It is not against me," said Ralph. "It would be against me to have a large property to take care of. It is impossible for a man in my state of health to spend much money, and enough is as good as a feast."

"Well, you will have enough—and something over. There will be more than enough for one—there will be enough for two."

"That's too much," said Ralph.

"Ah, don't say that. The best thing you can do, when I'm gone, will be to marry."

Ralph had foreseen what his father was coming to, and this suggestion was by no means novel. It had long been Mr. Touchett's most ingenious way of expressing the optimistic view of his son's health. Ralph had usually treated it humorously; but present circumstances made the humorous tone impossible.

He simply fell back in his chair and returned his father's appealing gaze in silence.

"If I, with a wife who hasn't been very fond of me, have had a very happy life," said the old man, carrying his ingenuity further still, "what a life might you not have if you should marry a person different from Mrs. Touchett. There are more different from her than there are like her."

Ralph still said nothing; and after a pause his father asked softly—"What do you think of your cousin?"

At this Ralph started, meeting the question with a rather fixed smile. "Do I understand you to propose that I should marry Isabel?"

"Well, that's what it comes to in the end. Don't you like her?"

"Yes, very much." And Ralph got up from his chair and wandered over to the fire. He stood before it an instant and then he stooped and stirred it mechanically. "I like Isabel very much," he repeated.

"Well," said his father, "I know she likes you. She told me so."

"Did she remark that she would like to marry me?"

"No, but she can't have anything against you. And she is the most charming young lady I have ever seen. And she would be good to you. I have thought a great deal about it."

"So have I," said Ralph, coming back to the bedside again. "I don't mind telling you that."

"You *are* in love with her, then? I should think you would be. It's as if she came over on purpose."

"No, I am not in love with her; but I should be if—if certain things were different."

"Ah, things are always different from what they might be," said the old man. "If you wait for them to change you will never do anything. I don't know whether you know," he went on; "but I suppose there is no harm in my alluding to it in such an hour as this: there was some one wanted to marry Isabel the other day, and she wouldn't have him."

"I know she refused Lord Warburton; he told me himself."

"Well, that proves there's a chance for somebody else."

"Somebody else took his chance the other day in London—and got nothing by it."

"Was it you?" Mr. Touchett asked, eagerly.

"No, it was an older friend; a poor gentleman who came over from America to see about it."

"Well, I am sorry for him. But it only proves what I say—that the way is open to you."

"If it is, dear father, it is all the greater pity that I am unable to tread it. I haven't many convictions; but I have three or four that I hold strongly. One is that people, on the whole, had better not marry their cousins. Another is that people in an advanced stage of pulmonary weakness had better not marry at all."

The old man raised his feeble hand and moved it to and fro a little before his face.

"What do you mean by that? You look at things in a way that would make everything wrong. What sort of a cousin is a cousin that you had never seen for more than twenty years of her life? We are all each other's cousins, and if we stopped at that the human race would die out. It is just the same with your weak lungs. You are a great deal better than you used to be. All you want is to lead a natural life. It is a great deal more natural to marry a pretty young lady that you are in love with than it is to remain single on false principles."

"I am not in love with Isabel," said Ralph.

"You said just now that you would be if you didn't think it wrong. I want to prove to you that it isn't wrong."

"It will only tire you, dear daddy," said Ralph, who marveled at his father's tenacity and at his finding strength to insist. "Then where shall we all be?"

"Where shall you be if I don't provide for you? You won't have anything to do with the bank, and you won't have me to take care of. You say you have got so many interests; but I can't make them out."

Ralph leaned back in his chair with folded arms; his eyes were fixed for some time in meditation. At last, with the air of a man fairly mustering courage—"I take a great interest in my cousin," he said, "but not the sort of interest you desire. I shall not live many years; but I hope I shall live long enough to see what she does with herself. She is entirely independent of me; I can exercise very little influence upon her life. But I should like to do something for her."

"What should you like to do?"

"I should like to put a little wind in her sails."

"What do you mean by that?"

"I should like to put it into her power to do some of the things she wants. She wants to see the world for instance. I should like to put money in her purse."

"Ah, I am glad you have thought of that," said the old man. "But I have thought of it too. I have left her a legacy—five thousand pounds."

"That is capital; it is very kind of you. But I should like to do a little more."

Something of that veiled acuteness with which it had been on Daniel Touchett's part the habit of a lifetime to listen to a financial proposition still lingered in the face in which the invalid had not obliterated the man of business. "I shall be happy to consider it," he said, softly.

"Isabel is poor then. My mother tells me that she has but a few hundred dollars a year. I should like to make her rich."

"What do you mean by rich?"

"I call people rich when they are able to gratify their imagination. Isabel has a great deal of imagination."

"So have you, my son," said Mr. Touchett, listening very attentively but a little confusedly.

"You tell me I shall have money enough for two. What I want is that you should kindly relieve me of my superfluity and give it to Isabel. Divide my inheritance into two equal halves and give half to her."

"To do what she likes with?"

"Absolutely what she likes."

"And without an equivalent?"

"What equivalent could there be?"

"The one I have already mentioned."

"Her marrying—some one or other? It's just to do away with anything of that sort that I make my suggestion. If she has an easy income she will never have to marry for a support. She wishes to be free, and your bequest will make her free."

"Well, you seem to have thought it out," said Mr. Touchett. "But I don't see why you appeal to me. The money will be yours, and you can easily give it to her yourself."

Ralph started a little. "Ah, dear father, *I* can't offer Isabel money!"

The old man gave a groan. "Don't tell me you're not in love with her! Do you want me to have the credit of it?"

"Entirely. I should like it simply to be a clause in your will, without the slightest reference to me."

"Do you want me to make a new will then?"

"A few words will do it; you can attend to it the next time you feel a little lively."

"You must telegraph to Mr. Hilary then. I will do nothing without my solicitor."

"You shall see Mr. Hilary to-morrow."

"He will think we have quarreled, you and I," said the old man.

"Very probably; I shall like him to think it," said Ralph, smiling; "and to carry out the idea, I give you notice that I shall be very sharp with you."

The humor of this appeared to touch his father; he lay a little while taking it in.

"I will do anything you like," he said at last; "but I'm not sure it's right. You say you want to put wind in her sails; but aren't you afraid of putting too much?"

"I should like to see her going before the breeze!" Ralph answered.

"You speak as if it were for your entertainment."

"So it is, a good deal."

"Well, I don't think I understand," said Mr. Touchett, with a sigh. "Young men are very different from what I was. When I cared for a girl—when I was young—I wanted to do more than look at her. You have scruples that I shouldn't have had, and you have ideas that I shouldn't have had either. You say that Isabel wants to be free, and that her being rich will keep her from marrying for money. Do you think that she is a girl to do that?"

"By no means. But she has less money than she has ever had before; but her father gave her everything, because he used to spend his capital. She has nothing but the crumbs of that feast to live on, and she doesn't really know how meager they are—she has yet to learn it. My mother has told me all about it. Isabel will learn it when she is really thrown upon the world, and it would be very painful to me to think of her coming to the consciousness of a lot of wants that she should be unable to satisfy."

"I have left her five thousand pounds. She can satisfy a good many wants with that."

"She can indeed. But she would probably spend it in two or three years."

"You think she would be extravagant then?"

"Most certainly," said Ralph, smiling serenely.

Poor Mr. Touchett's acuteness was rapidly giving place to pure confusion. "It would merely be a question of time then, her spending the larger sum."

"No, though at first I think she would plunge into that pretty freely; she would probably make over part of it to each of her sisters. But after that she would come to her senses, remember that she had still a lifetime before her, and live within her means."

"Well, you *have* worked it out," said the old man, with a sigh. "You do take an interest in her, certainly."

"You can't consistently say I go too far. You wished me to go further."

"Well, I don't know," the old man answered. "I don't think I enter into your spirit. It seems to me immoral."

"Immoral, dear daddy?"

"Well, I don't know that it's right to make everything so easy for a person."

"It surely depends upon the person. When the person is good, your making things easy is all to the credit of virtue. To facilitate the execution of good impulses, what can be a nobler act?"

This was a little difficult to follow, and Mr. Touchett considered it for a while. At last he said—

"Isabel's a sweet young girl; but do you think she is as good as that?"

"She is as good as her best opportunities," said Ralph.

"Well," Mr. Touchett declared, "she ought to get a great many opportunities for sixty thousand pounds."

"I have no doubt she will."

"Of course I will do what you want," said the old man. "I only want to understand it a little."

"Well, dear daddy, don't you understand it now?" his son asked caressingly. "If you don't we won't take any more trouble about it, we will leave it alone."

Mr. Touchett lay silent a long time still. Ralph supposed that he had given up the attempt to understand it. But at last he began again—

"Tell me this first. Doesn't it occur to you that a young lady with sixty thousand pounds may fall a victim to the fortune-hunters?"

"She will hardly fall a victim to more than one."

"Well, one is too many."

"Decidedly. That's a risk, and it has entered into my calculation. I think it's appreciable, but I think it's small, and I'm prepared to take it."

Poor Mr. Touchett's acuteness had passed into perplexity, and his perplexity now passed into admiration.

"Well, you *have* gone into it!" he exclaimed. "But I don't see what good you are going to get of it."

Ralph leaned over his father's pillows and gently smoothed them; he was aware their conversation had been prolonged to a dangerous point. "I shall get just the good that I said just now I wished to put into Isabel's reach—that of having gratified my imagination. But it's scandalous, the way I have taken advantage of you!"

From chapter 18 of *The Portrait of a Lady* by Henry James (The Harvard Classics, 1917).

JULIUS ROSENWALD

"Principles of Public Giving"

Julius Rosenwald (1862–1932) rose to wealth through his dealings with Sears, Roebuck, and Company, and established the Julius Rosenwald Fund in 1917 to advance "the well-being of mankind." Much of his giving was directed to helping black communities help themselves. To this end, for example, he contributed, through matching grants, to the development of more than five thousand "Rosenwald schools" devoted to black education in the rural south, and provided seed money for YMCAs and YWCAs in black neighborhoods in many cities. Rosenwald's most notable (and still controversial) contribution to the practice of philanthropy was his insistence that endowments be self-expiring. In this essay, he offers due reason: "While charity tends to do good, perpetual charities tend to do evil." His evidence is, in part, provided by history, as transformations in the manner and mechanics of living render many charities obsolete; in part by a concern that restrictions on funds (that is, spending from income, not principal) unduly limits the ability of recipient organizations to take risks, experiment, or invest in a timely manner; and in part by his view that advisory boards, strapped with perpetual obligations, become frigid cautious bureaucracies, who, thinking always of the future, lose sight of the interests and needs of their contemporaries. Instead, he argues, potential donors should suppress the desire for immortality, trust the future to future generations, and, above all, be guided by the needs of their own time. Does this mean abandoning one's own legacy?

୫ର

There are few colleges in the land today which are not striving for 'adequate endowment.' Museums, orchestras, operas, homes for the aged, hospitals, orphanages, and countless other charitable and remedial organizations, are aiming at the same goal. It was recently estimated that more than two and a half billion dollars were given to various endowments in this country in the last fifteen years. The sum is vast, equal to the total national wealth a hundred years ago, but institutions continue to solicit more and greater endowments, and men of wealth are encouraging them with ever-increasing gifts.

All of this giving and receiving is proceeding without much, if any, attention to the underlying question whether perpetual endowments are desirable. Perhaps the time has come to examine, or rather reexamine, this question, for it is not a new one in the long history of philanthropy.

I approach this discussion neither as an economist nor as a sociologist, but simply as an American citizen whose experience as a contributor to charitable causes and as a trustee of endowed institutions has given him some insight into the practical side of the problem. My only purpose is to raise the question of how best we may aid in the advancement of public welfare.

We can learn much from British experience, which has been more varied as well as longer than our own. Monasteries, in the earlier centuries, received such enormous grants that Edward I and his successors undertook to limit their possessions. Despite these efforts, it is estimated that shortly before Henry VIII secularized the monasteries between one-third and one-half of the public wealth of England was held for philanthropic use. This first great struggle between the living State and the dead hand indicated, as Sir Arthur Hobhouse has pointed out, that the 'nation cannot endure for long the spectacle of large masses of property settled to unalterable uses.'

This experience was reflected in laws intended to restrict charitable bequests in perpetuity, but the endowment of charities of all kinds continued until there was hardly a community in all England without its local fund. So obvious had abuses become that a Parliamentary Commission was created to inquire into the situation. Its preliminary report, published in 1837, filled thirty-eight folio volumes and listed nearly thirty thousand endowments with a combined annual income of more than £1,200,000.

Those who view endowments uncritically might think the condition of English charities fifty years ago happy in the extreme, for less than 5 percent of the population lived in parishes without endowed charities, all sorts of human needs had been provided for by generous donors, and funds were increasing rapidly. But Mr. Gladstone, who certainly was a humanitarian, rose in the House of Commons to say that the three commissions which had investigated the endowed charities 'all condemned them, and spoke of them as doing a greater amount of evil than of good in the forms in which they have been established and now exist.'

The history of charities abounds in illustrations of the paradoxical axiom that, while charity tends to do good, perpetual charities tend to do evil. James C. Young, in a recent article, 'The Dead Hand in Philanthropy,' reports that some twenty thousand English foundations have ceased to operate because changing conditions have nullified the good intentions of the donors; and a large number of American funds, many of them of comparatively recent origin, have likewise become useless.

When I was a boy in Springfield, Illinois, the covered wagons, westward bound, rolled past our door. The road ahead was long and full of hardships for the pioneers. They were hardy and self-reliant men and women, but many of them were so inadequately equipped that if misfortune overtook them, as it frequently did, they were almost certainly doomed to suffering, and perhaps death.

The worst hardships and dangers of the Western trail had passed in my boyhood, but there was still use, then, for the Bryan Mullanphy fund, established in 1851 for 'worthy and distressed travelers and emigrants passing through St. Louis to settle for a home in the West.' A few years later the trustees could with difficulty find anyone to whom the proceeds of the fund might be given. Some years ago, for lack of beneficiaries, the income had piled up until the fund totaled a million dollars. I have not followed its later fortunes, but, unless the courts have authorized a change in the will, that money is still accumulating, and will accumulate indefinitely. The Mullanphy gift was a godsend in its brief day. The man who gave it found one of the most urgent needs of his time and filled that need precisely. He made only one mistake: he focused his gift too sharply. He forgot that time passes and nothing—not even the crying needs of an era—endures. He deserves to be remembered as a generous-hearted man who realized, perhaps better than anyone else in his generation, that a wealth of pioneer blood and energy was being dissipated in the creation of our American empire. If he is remembered at all, it is more likely as the creator of a perpetuity which lost its usefulness almost as soon as it was established.

Mullanphy's mistake has been made not once but countless scores of times. It has been made by some of the wisest of men. Benjamin Franklin in drawing his will assumed that there would always be apprentices and that they would always have difficulty when starting in business for themselves in borrowing money at a rate as low as 5 percent. In addition, he assumed that a loan of three hundred dollars was enough to enable a young mechanic to establish himself independently. With these assumptions in mind, Franklin set up two loan funds of a thousand pounds each. One was for the benefit of 'young married artificers not over the age of twenty-five' who had served their apprenticeships in Boston, and the other for young men of similar situation in Philadelphia. The accumulated interest as well as the principal was to be lent out for a hundred years. By that time, Franklin's calculations showed, each thousand pounds would have amounted to £135,000. One hundred thousand pounds of each fund was then to be spent. The Boston fund was to be used in constructing 'fortifications, bridges, aqueducts, public buildings, baths, pavements or whatever may make living in the town more convenient for its people and render it more agreeable to strangers.' In Philadelphia, he foresaw that the wells which in his day supplied the city with water would become polluted; accordingly, he proposed that Philadelphia's fund should be used for piping the waters of Wissihicken Creek into the city. Fortunately, Boston provided herself with pavements, and Philadelphia herself with a water supply, without waiting for Franklin's money. Great as his intellectual powers were, he had miscalculated at every point. The class he proposed to benefit gradually became nonexistent; therefore the funds failed to accumulate as rapidly as he had anticipated. At the end of a hundred years, instead of the $675,000 he had expected in each fund, there were only $391,000 in Boston and $90,000 in Philadelphia, and meanwhile the good works which he had chosen as the grand climax of a career devoted to good works had long been provided.

Benjamin Franklin was a wise man, and so was Alexander Hamilton; yet it was Hamilton who drafted the will of Robert Richard Randall, who in the first years of the last century left a farm to be used as a haven for superannuated sailors. A good many years ago the courts were called upon to construe the word 'sailor' to include men employed on steamships. Even so, the fund for Snug Harbor, I am assured, vastly exceeds any reasonable requirement for the care of retired seafarers. The farm happened to be situated on Fifth Avenue, New York. Today it is valued at thirty or forty million dollars.

I have heard of a fund which provides a baked potato at each meal for each young woman at Bryn Mawr, and of another, dating from one of the great famines, which pays for a half a loaf of bread deposited each day at the door of each student in one of the colleges at Oxford. Gifts to educational institutions often contain provisions which are made absurd by the advance of learning. An American university has an endowed lectureship on coal gas as the cause of malarial fever. In 1727, Dr. Woodward, in endowing a chair at Cambridge, England, directed that the incumbent should lecture for all time on his *Natural History of the Earth* and his defense of it against Dr. Camerarius. It did not occur to the good doctor that his scientific theories might eventually become obsolete; yet, with the passing of years and the progress of scientific knowledge, the holder of the chair had to admit his inability to comply with the founder's instructions and at the same time execute Dr. Woodward's plain intent—namely, to teach science. The list of these precisely focused gifts which have lost their usefulness could be extended into volumes, but I am willing to rest the case on Franklin and Hamilton. With all their sagacity, they could not foresee what the future would bring. The world does not stand still. Anyone old enough to vote has seen revolutionary changes in the mechanics of living, and these changes have been accompanied and abetted by changing points of view toward the needs and desires of our fellow men.

I do not know how many millions of dollars have been given in perpetuity for the support of orphan asylums. The Hershey endowment alone is said to total $40,000,000 and more. Orphan asylums began to disappear about the time the old-fashioned wall telephone went out. We know now that it is far better for penniless orphans, as for other children, to be brought up under home influence. The cost of home care for orphans is no greater than the cost of maintaining them in an orphanage. But the question is not one of cost, but of the better interest of the children. Institutional life exposes them needlessly to contagion, and is likely to breed a sense of inferiority that twists the mind. The money which the dead hand holds out to orphan asylums cannot be used for any other purpose than maintaining orphan asylums; it therefore serves to perpetuate a type of institution that most men of good will and good sense no longer approve.

To protest twenty-five years ago that orphans were not best cared for in asylums would have been considered visionary; fifty years ago it would have been considered crack-brained. There is no endowed institution today which is more firmly approved by public opinion than orphanages were within the lifetime of any man of middle age. Let that fact serve as a symbol and a warning to those who are tempted to pile up endowments in perpetuity.

There is another and to my mind no less grievous error into which many givers still are likely to fall. They conceive that money given for philanthropic purposes must be given, if not for a limited object, then at least in perpetuity: the principal must remain intact and only the income may be spent. The result has been, as many a trustee knows, that institutions have become 'endowment poor.' Though they have many millions of dollars in their treasuries, the trustees can touch only the 4 or 5 percent a year that the money earns. There is no means of meeting an extraordinary demand upon the institution, an extraordinary opportunity for increasing its usefulness. Research suffers; museums are unable to purchase objects that never again will be available; experiments of all sorts are frowned upon, not because they do not promise well, but because money to undertake anything out of the ordinary cannot be found, while huge sums are regularly budgeted to carry on traditional and routine activities. And nothing serves more successfully to discourage additional gifts than the knowledge that an institution already possesses great endowments.

As a trustee of the University of Chicago, I know how difficult the problem is. Opportunities for purchasing libraries or for extending the work of some department into new fields are continually coming before us, and though we have endowments of $43,000,000 we have frequently been unable to authorize the use of even a few thousands for some object which would add much to the University's resources and usefulness, to say nothing of its prestige. We may not even convert the principal of our endowments into books or men, which are the real endowment of any university.

A number of years ago the University started collecting more endowment. I did not contribute to the fund, but instead turned over a sum of which the principal may be exhausted. That fund, I am assured, has been of considerable service. It has been used for such diverse purposes as the purchase of the library of a Cambridge professor; for paying part of the cost of Professor Michelson's ether drift experiments; for reconstructing the twelve-inch telescope at Yerkes Observatory; for a continuation of research in glacial erosion in the state of Washington, and for research in phonetics. If the fund had been given as permanent endowment, it is obvious that some of the objects could not have been achieved. The men who desired to undertake experiments and research might have been forced to postpone their investigations; the books purchased might have been scattered among a dozen libraries, never to be reassembled. It is true that money disbursed now will not yield income to the University fifty years hence, but it is also true that fifty years hence other contributors can be found to supply the current needs of that generation.

I am convinced that the timidity of trustees themselves is often responsible for their inability to spend principal. Donors would in many cases be willing to give greater discretion to trustees in such matters if they were asked to
do so. A notable example in point is the consent by Mr. Carnegie, more than
ten years ago, to the current use of funds which he had given originally for endowment to Tuskegee Institute. At a time when this school was in desperate
need of money, I proposed at a meeting of the board of which Honorable Seth
Low was chairman and Theodore Roosevelt was a member that we request
Mr. Carnegie to permit us to spend not only the interest but also a small portion of the principal of his gift. My suggestion was at first frowned upon. Finally the board agreed, and a letter, dated January 24, 1916, was sent to Mr.
Carnegie by Mr. Low which read in part as follows:

> I am writing to submit to you a suggestion which has been made to me by one or
> two of my fellow trustees of the board of Tuskegee Institute. Mr. Rosenwald, in
> particular, who is a generous supporter of the Institute, feels very strongly that a
> permanent endowment fund is less useful than a fund the principal of which can
> be used up in fifty years, his idea being that every institution like a school ought
> to commend itself so strongly to the living as to command their interest and
> support. . . . In accordance with this suggestion, I am writing to ask whether you
> would be willing to permit the trustees to use, each year, at their discretion, not
> more than 2 percent of the principal of the fund which you so generously gave
> some years ago toward the endowment of the Institute. It is always possible that
> within the lifetime of the next generation industrial training for the negro race
> will be assumed by the state or national government. Should any such change or
> any unforeseen change in conditions take place, a fund so firmly tied up in perpe-
> tuity that the principal cannot be touched, except possibly through an act of the
> legislature, might be a disadvantage rather than an advantage.

To this Carnegie's secretary, Mr. John A. Poynton, replied on February 23,
1916, giving Mr. Carnegie's approval to the suggestion in the following terms:

> Mr. Carnegie has given careful thought to the proposal that your trustees be per-
> mitted to use each year a portion of the principal of the fund which he contrib-
> uted toward endowment. In establishing his foundation Mr. Carnegie has favored
> the plan of giving the trustees and their successors the right to change the policy
> governing the disposition of the principal as well as interest when to them it
> might seem expedient, believing it impossible for those now living to anticipate
> the needs of future generations. Mr. Carnegie would be happy to have the trustees
> of Tuskegee assume a similar responsibility in connection with the fund which he
> contributed toward the endowment of that institute, and asks me to say that he is
> willing to have a small percentage of the principal used annually for current ex-
> penses if three fourths of the members of your board should decide in favor of
> such a plan.

Here is evidence that Mr. Carnegie might have relaxed the terms of his other
gifts had he been asked to do so. It was not the donor but the trustees who were
timid. (I have seen trustees act in much the same way in matters of financial

administration. Men accustomed to investing a large part of their private fortunes in sound common stocks have felt that as trustees they must invest only in first mortgages or bonds. Of late a good many boards of trustees have enjoyed a change of heart, to the vast benefit of the institutions they serve. But that is a digression.) In some of the institutions with which I am best acquainted, funds given with no strings attached have been added to the perpetual endowment as a matter of course. It is a noteworthy fact, though not as widely known as it should be, that the Rockefeller foundations are not perpetuities. If any of them today are wealthier than at their establishment, it is not because the trustees are not free to spend principal when the occasion rises. As a matter of fact, I am told these boards have expended about seventy-five million dollars of their capital or special funds, and it is probable that at least two of them will disburse all of their principal funds within another decade or two.

I am opposed to gifts in perpetuity for any purpose. I do not advocate profligate spending of principal. That is not the true alternative to perpetuities. I advocate the gift which provides that the trustees *may* spend a small portion of the capital—say, not to exceed 5 to 10 percent—in any one year in addition to the income if in their judgment there is good use at hand for the additional sums. Men who argue that permission to spend principal will lead to profligate spending do not know the temper of trustees and the sense of responsibility they feel toward funds entrusted to them; nor do they appreciate the real difficulties which face donors and trustees of foundations in finding objects worthy of support. I am prepared to say that some of the keenest minds in this country are employed by foundations and universities in seeking such objects; yet, when a real need is discovered, it often cannot be met adequately, simply because of restrictions placed on funds in hand.

The point has been raised that great institutions must have perpetual endowments to tide them through hard times when new money may not be forthcoming. Those are precisely the times when it is most important to have unrestricted funds which will permit our institutions to continue their work until conditions improve, as they always do. A great institution like Harvard ought not to have to restrict its activities merely because its income for one reason or another has been temporarily curtailed. The spending of a million or two of principal at such a time is not imprudent. Sound business sense, indeed, would commend it.

I am thinking not only of university endowments, but also of the great foundations established to increase the sum of knowledge and happiness among men. Too many of these are in perpetuity. It is an astonishing fact that the men who gave them—for the most part, hard-headed business men who abhorred bureaucracy—have not guarded, in their giving, against this blight. I think it is almost inevitable that as trustees and officers of perpetuities grow old they become more concerned to conserve the funds in their care than to wring from those funds the greatest possible usefulness. That tendency is evident already in some of the foundations, and as time goes on it will not lessen but increase. The cure for this disease is a radical operation. If the funds must exhaust themselves within a generation, no bureaucracy is likely to develop around them.

What would happen, it might be asked, if the billions tied up in perpetuities in this country should be released over a period of fifty or one hundred years? What would become of education and of scientific research? How could society care for the sick, the helpless, and the impoverished? The answer is that all these needs would be as well provided for as the demands of the day justified. Wisdom, kindness of heart, and good will are not going to die with this generation.

Instead of welcoming perpetuities, trustees, it seems to me, would be justified in resenting them. Perpetuities are, in a measure at least, an avowal of lack of confidence in the trustees by the donor. And it is a strange avowal. The trustees are told that they are wise enough and honest enough to invest the money and spend the income amounting to 4 to 5 percent each year; but they are told in the same breath that they are not capable of spending 6 to 10 or 15 percent wisely.

If trustees are not resentful, it is because they know that donors of perpetuities are not thinking in those terms. Sometimes perpetuities are created only because lawyers who draft deeds of gifts and wills have not learned that money can be given in any other way. More often, probably, perpetuities are set up because of the donor's altogether human desire to establish an enduring memorial on earth—an end which becomes increasingly attractive to many men with advancing years.

I am certain that those who seek by perpetuities to create for themselves a kind of immortality on earth will fail, if only because no institution and no foundation can live forever. If some men are remembered years and centuries after the death of the last of their contemporaries, it is not because of endowments they created. The names of Harvard, Yale, Bodley, and Smithson, to be sure, are still on men's lips, but the names are now not those of men but of institutions. If any of these men strove for everlasting remembrance, they must feel kinship with Nesselrode, who lived a diplomat, but is immortal as a pudding.

There has been evolution in the art of giving, as in other activities. The gift intended to meet a particular need or support a particular institution in perpetuity was once generally approved, but is now outmoded. There are evidences that all perpetuities are becoming less popular, and I look forward with confidence to the day when they will become a rarity. They have not stood the test of time.

To prove that I practice what I preach, it may not be out of place to say that every donation that I have made may be expended at the discretion of the directors of the institution to which it is given. The charter of the foundation which I created some years ago provides that principal as well as income may be spent as the trustees think best. This year, as the management of this fund was being reorganized, I was anxious to make sure that the trustees and officers would meet present needs instead of hoarding the funds for possible future uses. I have stipulated, therefore, that not only the income but also all of the principal of this fund *must* be expended within twenty-five years of my death. This I did in the following letter to the board of trustees, approved and accepted by the board at its meeting in Chicago on April 29, 1928:

> I am happy to present herewith to the trustees of the Julius Rosenwald Fund certificate for twenty thousand shares of the stock of Sears, Roebuck and Company.
>
> When the Julius Rosenwald Fund was created and sums of money turned over, it was provided that the principal as well as the income might be spent from time to time at the discretion of the Trustees, and it was my expectation from the beginning that the entire principal should be spent within a reasonable period of time. My experience is that trustees controlling large funds are not only desirous of conserving principal, but often favor adding to it from surplus income.
>
> I am not in sympathy with this policy of perpetuating endowment, and believe that more good can be accomplished by expending funds as trustees find opportunities for constructive work than by storing up large sums of money for long periods of time. By adopting a policy of using the fund within this generation we may avoid those tendencies toward bureaucracy and a formal or perfunctory attitude toward the work which almost inevitably develop in organizations which prolong their existence indefinitely. Coming generations can be relied upon to provide for their own needs as they arise.
>
> In accepting the shares of stock now offered, I ask that the Trustees do so with the understanding that the entire fund in the hands of the Board, both income and principal, be expended within twenty-five years of the time of my death.

I submitted this letter, in advance, to a wide circle of men and women experienced in philanthropy and education, anticipating a good deal of dissent. There was almost none. Twenty years ago when I, among others, spoke in this vein, our ideas were considered visionary; today they are receiving an ever wider approval.

I believe that large gifts should not be restricted to narrowly specified objects, and that under no circumstances should funds be held in perpetuity. I am not opposed to endowments for colleges or other institutions which require some continuity of support, provided permission is given to use part of the principal from time to time as needs arise. This does not mean profligate spending. It is simply placing confidence in living trustees; it prevents control by the dead hand; it discourages the building up of bureaucratic groups of men, who tend to become overconservative and timid in investment and disbursement of trust funds. I have confidence in future generations and in their ability to meet their own needs wisely and generously.

Originally published in *The Atlantic Monthly* 143 (May 1929).

WALDEMAR NIELSEN

"The Ethics of Philanthropy and Trusteeship; The Carnegie Foundation: A Case Study"

Waldemar Nielsen (1917–2005), author of The Big Foundations *and other writings about American philanthropy, is credited with pushing foundations into the limelight—and into a new era of self-contemplation. In this selection, Nielsen reviews the nearly century-long history of the Carnegie Corporation in order to explore the "ethical possibilities of philanthropy and trusteeship."*

Andrew Carnegie was a remarkably motivated donor, famous for his meditation on philanthropy, "Gospel of Wealth," and for his unusual depth and breadth of interest in charitable causes and practices. As Nielsen states, he "should have done as well as a donor could possibly hope in setting up a new foundation." But the history of the Carnegie Corporation has been far from smooth and uncomplicated. Where does the fault lie? With Carnegie? With the judgment of his entrusted heirs? In the fact that the endowment is perpetual? Or should we withhold blame and, rather, take seriously Carnegie's own view in favor of institutional perpetuity: "As in all human institutions, there will be fruitful seasons and slack seasons. But as long as it exists, there will come, from time to time, men into its control and management who will have vision and energy and wisdom, and the perpetual foundation will have a new birth of usefulness and service." Have the fruits of the Carnegie Corporation's more productive boards redeemed its lesser harvests? Were Carnegie, miraculously, to reappear, do you think he would have been so forgiving of the uneven sproutings of his charitable seed?

I want to illustrate the ethical possibilities of philanthropy and trusteeship by analyzing a specific and very instructive case, namely, the large and respectable foundation—one of the best in the U.S. today—created by Andrew Carnegie. Very large foundations such as Carnegie's (some two hundred hold assets ranging from $100 million to several billions of dollars) control a large portion of the total assets of all the nearly thirty thousand grant-making foundations in the country. This control makes their influence and visibility disproportionately great.

Because of the scale of their assets, and because of their professional and technical capabilities, they can work in fields of advanced science and on complex problems of national and even international scope. They can influence whole categories of cultural, social, and scientific institutions, and they can influence the policies of governments.

They wield money and, consequently, power. Because of this money and power, once the original donor has departed from the scene, competition (polite or rowdy) for control of that power frequently emerges.

The troubling question then arises: Who, over the longer term, will tend to acquire control over such institutions? Who will keep faith with the donor's vision and intentions after he or she is gone?

In theory, power and control flow from the donor, who sets the general course and character of the institution, to the trustees, who set policies and priorities within that broad guidance, to the chief executive and the professional staff, who formulate and execute programs to accomplish those directives.

In reality, foundations depart from this theoretical pattern so frequently and widely that we should regard it as, if not quite a myth, then at least a great simplification.

To take some obvious examples, such major donors as Henry Ford, Howard Hughes, and John MacArthur left their trustees no real policy or program guidance other than legal boilerplate language. So the donor in such cases made himself virtually a nonfactor from the start. At the other extreme, donors such as Buck Duke, in setting up his Duke Endowment, not only specified its general purpose but also the unalterable list of permitted grantees and the percentage of income it should give to each. In between these extremes, donors have made many shadings, from broad and ambiguous guidance to narrow and precise restrictions.

The powers given the board as "trustees" of the donor after the donor's departure rest on three familiar premises: namely, that they will serve the donor's purposes and intent faithfully; they will act in a disinterested and responsible spirit; and they will bring to bear in their policy-making a broad and informed view of the changing needs and opportunities in the sphere of the foundation's programs.

In this textbook conceptual structure, the trustees decide ultimate policy and the staff and officers, including the president, fulfill this policy as subordinates to them.

So much for the theory. In real cases, not a static hierarchy but dynamic and shifting patterns of influence and control usually direct a foundation. In the very large foundations, if the donor did not impose real guidance from the start, or if donor and family influence greatly dissipates after a generation or two, the board of trustees and the chief executive officer and staff contend with each other for power and control of the institution. The dominance of the one or the other ebbs and flows, with sometimes great and unpredictable effects on the foundation's programs and effectiveness.

Examining one actual and important "best case" offers the most helpful way to gain a sense of the longer-term prospects for the performance of a donor foundation in accordance with the donor's intent.

Andrew Carnegie and the Carnegie Corporation offer a particularly instructive real-life instance. Carnegie, one of the greatest American donors, held an almost unparalleled belief and interest in philanthropy: He had fully developed a philosophy of the charitable responsibilities of the rich, articulated in his famous "Gospel of Wealth" and other writings. Throughout his life he gave generously and by the end he had committed virtually all of his great fortune to philanthropy.

An exceptionally entrepreneurial and experienced donor, he had created a series of outstanding philanthropic institutions during his lifetime, from the Carnegie Institute and the libraries project to his Foundation for the Advancement of Teaching and his Endowment for International Peace. He personally wrote statements of policies and objectives for these creations in prose that offered models of clarity and practicality.

A man of extraordinary breadth of interests in education, science, culture, and international affairs, he also had a remarkably wide acquaintance with outstanding leaders in many fields of American life—from government and business to intellectuals, scholars, and scientists. In the formation of his various philanthropies he brought his own extensive experience in creating and developing new organizations to bear as well as his wide range of acquaintances in nonprofit fields. He assembled as boards of trustees not mere sets of old business cronies but rather groups of distinguished and strong individuals from public life.

His own wealth and prestige enabled him to attract such leaders to his philanthropies, and he trusted them to carry out their responsibilities. He made the classic statement of confidence in the fidelity and capability of foundation trustees: "as in all human institutions, there will be fruitful seasons and slack seasons. But as long as it [the foundation] exists there will come, from time to time, men into its control and management who will have vision and energy and wisdom, and the perpetual foundation will have a new birth of usefulness and service."

Thus this man, his competence and experience as a donor almost unparalleled, should have done as well as a donor could possibly hope in setting up a new major foundation. To his new "Corporation" he bequeathed the huge remainder of his estate at the end of his life.

How in fact did his hopes and plans turn out after his death in 1919?

The story, covering more than seventy years, breaks into some four chapters—the Betrayal; the Slump; the Muddle; and the Renaissance—with the final chapters yet unwritten.

Carnegie named to the board of his Corporation the heads of the five principal philanthropic institutions he had previously created, plus his financial and personal secretaries. Even though advisers told him that the situation of the institutional trustees contained inherent conflicts, since they would both distribute and benefit from the funds, he ignored that advice. (It was not until 1946 that the foundation dropped these ex officio trustees from the board.) He also reserved to himself the right to administer the foundation as long as he lived, which he did from 1911 until 1919. During that period, the board met only once a year merely to ratify decisions he had already made. So despite his protestations of confidence in his trustees, as long as he was alive he behaved egocentrically if not dictatorially.

Almost as soon as he died, these confusions and contradictions produced serious problems. He left a foundation (confusingly called the "Corporation") with almost no qualified staff and with a board dominated by built-in grantees. Within three years they had appropriated nearly $40 million in grants without benefit of long-range planning or serious consideration of the impact of the spending spree on the foundation's future. (Because the charter required that the foundation pay grant commitments only from the foundation's income [then some $6 million a year] and not from capital, this spree restricted its programs for the next fifteen years.) Not surprisingly, the bulk of this money went to institutions represented on the foundation's board.

Was this a betrayal by the board? Did Carnegie provoke it by his own conduct and his questionable choices of eminent but compliant and conflicted trustees? Certainly the trustees made a self-interested grab of money for their own institutions. But since Carnegie himself created these, the trustees did not divert funds to unauthorized purposes. Still, though not unlawful, was it at least greedy?

Soon thereafter, the Corporation's two most influential and ambitious trustees at the time radically redirected the substance, spirit, and general thrust of its programs. Henry Pritchett, head of the Carnegie Foundation for Advancement of Teaching and former president of the Massachusetts Institute of Technology, and Elihu Root, a prominent attorney, former Secretary of War and of State, and a Nobel Laureate, envisaged the foundation not as a mere dispenser of benefactions but as a private instrument to foster "reforms." Their general approach used the foundation to create powerful nongovernmental agencies of scientists and experts to counter what they regarded as dangerous populist influences threatening "traditional American values" and the power of the established Anglo-Saxon elite.

In carrying out their new grand design for the foundation, they led it to make a series of substantial grants to the National Research Council "to organize Science"; to a National Bureau of Economic Research; and to the American Law Institute. Ostensibly they intended to introduce more "scientific management" into the nation's affairs. Actually, they urgently wished to block what they regarded as the growing threat of immigrants, Negroes, demagogues, laborites, socialists, and others of "inferior heredity, morals, and understanding of business and American-style democracy."

They intended the National Research Council to counter the "pacifistic" tendencies of some scientists, which they felt inhibited the development of new military technology. The National Bureau of Economic Research grew out of mounting industrial tension and violence, and an escalating concern of prominent businessmen to counteract these tendencies by using a private group of "experts."

In the field of economics, Pritchett explicitly planned to develop economic "propaganda" to counter the appeal of "popular agitators." To this end, he at one point even recommended that the Corporation purchase an independent newspaper, the *Washington Post*. (In the end they dropped the idea, not on grounds of impropriety but because Root and others thought it "a bad investment.")

In 1923 the trustees again took the initiative in creating the American Law Institute (ALI). They feared that the intrusion of immigrants and the lower classes into the legal profession constituted a national danger. Trustee Root, in a speech to the New York State Bar Association a few years earlier, had deplored the fact that "50% of the lawyers in this city are either foreign born or are of foreign born parents, and the great mass of them . . . have in their blood necessarily the traditions of the countries from which they came."

In its support for ALI and its other large initiatives in its first years, the Corporation tried to implement an underlying agenda which was not only elitist but racist—not only to help preserve the dominant position of a particular segment of American society but also to preserve its "racial purity." The trustees explicitly worried about "the alien stream flowing into our citizenship," and they made the foundation a leading supporter of eugenics studies at the time, some of which urged policies of selective breeding and forced sterilization of the "unfit."

In these various grants to set up private agencies to influence public policy—forerunners of our contemporary "think tanks"—the original Carnegie trustees not only clearly understood the potential power of private funds to shape public opinion and government policy but they had an obsession to utilize and exploit that power on behalf of the values and interests of their particular social and economic class.

In exploiting that power, they in a sense followed the kind of program Carnegie had in his libraries project and in setting up his Endowment for International Peace, for example. But with a difference: Carnegie had taken initiatives on behalf of such goals as giving opportunities for the average citizen to have access to books for self-development and for the general advancement of science, education, and world peace. He came from a poor family, he himself had immigrated, and he had lifted himself by his own boot-straps. He was descended from old Scottish radicals; he battled against unfair and unequal privilege; and he believed in the unlimited potential of the common man.

He was not saintly and benign in all his business dealings, or clear and consistent in the purposes of his philanthropies. (Indeed, like the other industrialists of his time, he fought the trade unions hard, and in his philanthropy he could give erratically and impulsively—giving pipe organs to churches even though he was not religious, and offering medals for personal acts of heroism.)

Nevertheless, the spirit of his philanthropy was always democratic, hopeful, and constructive. That within five years of his death his Corporation should have turned into a racist and reactionary machine to defend the privileges of the old WASP elite and block the advancement of immigrants and the underprivileged deformed his spirit and intent. And a group of gentlemen of high reputation and the utmost respectability perpetrated this ugly deformation.

What does this say about Carnegie's absolute trust in trustees? Did some fault, some pretentiousness, in the man himself cause him to entrust his great philanthropic creations to a group of individuals whose background and social class biases fundamentally contradicted his own?

These first years after the donor's death form the chapter of Betrayal.

The trustees' outburst of activist and politicized philanthropy lasted until 1923, when the foundation hired a personable young man, Frederick P. Keppel, a certified member of the WASP establishment, as president. He headed the Corporation for the next nineteen years. If the preceding regime had furthered a grandiose and sinister underlying agenda, Keppel chose almost effete goals. After his appointment, the Corporation added seven new trustees and the balance of forces on the board changed significantly. The Corporation then dropped its crusade to save the nation from the newcomers and shifted its emphasis to a program to uplift the cultural level of the general citizenry. Just why Keppel chose this new direction is still difficult to understand. Perhaps the choice sprang from a spirit of resignation: If the great unwashed would be always with us, then the foundation might at least try to wash them. In any case it led to rather peculiar, even quaint actual projects.

The Corporation wanted to attract the multitudes into adult education centers, the art museums, and—in at least one tie to Andrew Carnegie—the libraries. Exposing the ordinary citizenry to classical art and literature, the Corporation believed (and stated), would improve their character, judgment, and tastes—and in addition would promote social stability. In the end and by virtually every measure the effort failed miserably.

Keppel, a warm and likeable person, presided ineffectively and brought a remarkably narrow social outlook to his job as head of a major foundation. The 1920s and 1930s, when he directed the Corporation, brought severe strain and friction to American life and growing international dangers. By the early 1930s a devastating depression had struck, followed by the period of the New Deal, and when he retired World War II was already raging in Europe. Yet his gracefully written annual reports contain hardly a hint of the great issues and problems of the times. In the isolated environment of the Corporation, training for librarians, adult education conferences, and the distribution of art teaching sets continued to preoccupy. During his long tenure, the Corporation indulged in endlessly trivial pursuits.

In Keppel's final years as president, the foundation commissioned what it intended as a study of how cultural projects could address the uplift of Negroes, but by mistake chose a Swedish economist, Gunnar Myrdal, to head it. Myrdal produced a classic and highly controversial report on the general problem of race relations in America, a report that powerfully influenced later progress toward racial integration. However, the report so embarrassed and dismayed the foundation that it did everything but disavow the study it published.

For prospective donors of large foundations, several questions arise: How, in the first twenty-five years after his death, did Carnegie's keystone foundation come to focus on matters that the donor would probably have regarded in the first years as pernicious and in the later years as preposterous? And how did it happen that the Corporation hired a president of inferior capability to head the institution for the next two decades and that the trustees in that long period could not bring themselves to replace him? Where did the trustees keep faith with Carnegie's aims and values? Why did they fail utterly to bring to the foundation's programs and priorities some awareness of the sweeping changes taking place in American society and in the world? This long second chapter of the story we can charitably call the Slump.

After these two initial phases in the foundation's history—the Betrayal and Slump (which some scholars have now euphemistically designated as its periods of "scientific philanthropy" and "cultural philanthropy")—came a thirteen-year period of doldrums, 1942–55, years that brought a crucial time of war and ensuing postwar developments and problems, under three ineffective presidents.

The period of doldrums generated further questions for donors: Does such a span of years provide a reasonable turnaround time for an organization with perfect freedom to change its direction and with only a handful of staff? What about board responsibility to face a foundation's problems and address its own mistakes?

But then, after some thirty-five years, the foundation finally entered a fruitful period—vigorous programs reasonably related to the spirit and concerns of the donor and relevant to the needs of the times.

John Gardner, trained as a psychologist, joined the staff after World War II. By that time the board had ossified and the staff floundered, virtually leaderless. Gardner quickly showed his abilities by designing several promising new program initiatives in research on foreign regions of the world. He thereby became the obvious choice to succeed the ill and incapacitated John Dollard, then president, which he did in 1955.

Almost immediately thereafter the foundation moved forward in a program of "strategic philanthropy" to study and recommend changes in public policies on major national questions, especially education. Carnegie philanthropies had always proposed to use foundation funds to affect the policies and programs of other institutions, especially government. But Gardner mastered the strategy and practice of the technique. He made the goal of "excellence and equality" in American education his mission, and with the help of his able vice president, James Perkins, he pursued that goal simultaneously on a number of fronts. First, he financed a number of important educational research projects and experiments. Then he formed a prestigious commission of both laymen and experts to study the nation's educational problems and to recommend solutions. He timed the publication of their reports carefully to produce maximum impact on policy-makers.

In parallel, Gardner, through his own cogent and elegant essays and books, became important in public advocacy. By 1964, the combined impact of these activities had made Gardner a national force, and in that year President Lyndon Johnson asked him to head a task force on education—the report of which established clearly and finally the responsibility of the federal government in this crucial field. To no one's great surprise, the President called Gardner to Washington the following year to become Secretary of the Department of Health, Education and Welfare. By that point the Carnegie Corporation had finally regained the level of prestige that its founder had enjoyed as a philanthropist a half century earlier.

Another very able man, Alan Pifer, followed Gardner in 1965. Pifer had served under Gardner and quickly took firm control. Pifer ardently advocated social and economic justice and he preached eloquently and incessantly for the federal government to accept its responsibility to help achieve those goals. Unlike Gardner, who simply accepted the rather passive Establishment board he inherited, Pifer took a strong hand in selecting more liberal and more diverse members as resignations and retirements occurred.

Shortly after he took over, the foundation enjoyed a quick triumph by its sponsorship of a Commission on Public Television, which reported its findings in early 1967. Within a month President Johnson recommended passing a Public Broadcasting Act, which the Congress did in November of that same year, bringing into being a public television system supervised by an independent corporation.

As a second major initiative, Pifer created a Carnegie Commission on Higher Education to make a comprehensive study of the future financing problems of colleges and universities, which were then beginning to drown under a huge new influx of students. Ultimately the group, with $12 million of foundation funds, published scores of reports and monographs on every aspect of the problems of the nation's colleges and universities. These significantly influenced the policies of both the government and the schools themselves thereafter.

The foundation also, under Pifer, created the popular educational program *Sesame Street*, and the Children's Television Workshop, which has now become a national, and indeed international, institution.

As the years progressed, and as the nation became more troubled socially and more conservative politically, Pifer became an increasingly ardent and activist proponent of liberal policy positions. In a sense he supported the rights of the poor and disadvantaged in the United States as radically as old Andrew Carnegie attacked the English Establishment and its treatment of the Scots in the nineteenth century. Pifer also focused the grants of the foundation on support for the more promising and influential new advocates for the disadvantaged.

Fortunately for Pifer, the conversion of the board by the late 1970s from a virtually all white, male, Establishment body to a more diverse membership of women, blacks, Hispanics, and Jews protected him as his militantly stated views increasingly diverged from the country's conservative mood under Presidents Nixon and Reagan.

For prospective large donors, the Gardner and Pifer periods raise a number of interesting questions. Both led vigorously and effectively and took the foundation in directions that carried on the spirit and style of old Andrew Carnegie. Their accomplishments would surely have given him much pride and satisfaction. But did Gardner's presidency—given his elegance of style as well as the brilliance of his ideas—simply exemplify trustees passively traveling on a purposeful president's train, as they *had* for years on one going nowhere, namely Keppel's? And did Pifer not, by carefully reshaping the board in a liberal direction in accordance with his views, violate at least the theoretical concept of presidential subservience to the policy authority residing with the board?

Whatever the answers to those questions, the Gardner and Pifer period generated a renaissance in the history of the Carnegie Corporation after several uninspiring decades.

In 1982 Pifer retired. Dr. David Hamburg succeeded him. Hamburg has more quietly pursued policies generally in line with those laid down by Pifer, but focused the Corporation's attention largely on international issues and the problems of children.

So what can the history of the Carnegie Corporation teach those in the coming generation of large donors who determine to set up a general purpose grant-making foundation?

That a foundation's purposes over time will inevitably change and diverge from original intent, and that the donor should realistically understand and accept that fact?

Or that a donor should try to tie down the objectives of his foundation so tightly and specifically that no board or administration can abandon or subvert them, ever?

Or that if the foundation of a donor as wise and experienced as Carnegie can encounter such grave problems for decades at a stretch, then the foundations of donors who are more ordinary mortals face even worse prospects?

Or that time has proven the wisdom of Andrew Carnegie's faith that over the long term, and despite periods of decline, "the perpetual foundation will have a new birth of usefulness and service"?

From *The Ethics of Giving and Receiving: Am I My Foolish Brother's Keeper?* edited by William F. May and A. Lewis Soens, Jr. (Dallas: Southern Methodist University Press, 2000), pp. 96–107. Copyright © 2000 by the Cary M. Maguire Center for Ethics and Public Responsibility. Reprinted with permission from the Southern Methodist University Press.

JOSEPH LUMARDA

"Life Lessons: Making a Trust-ee"

Joseph Lumarda, currently Senior Vice President with Capital Guardian Trust Company, was for sixteen years with the California Community Foundation in Los Angeles, first as a Program Officer, later as Vice President for Development, and still later as Executive Vice President. Writing here as a laborer in the philanthropic vineyard, Lumarda describes the moment that he was transformed by feeling the weight of his vocation. The "life lesson" he learned at that privileged moment was about the meaning and importance of trust, or more precisely, about what it means to be entrusted with someone else's hopes and dreams—what it means to be, as Alfred Nobel's chief executor once called his role, "the vicar of the soul." Toward the end of his essay, Lumarda raises the large question that his experience and insight prompt: "How do we create foundations, institutions and cultures that reflect the personal and public trust required of us?" How do we put "trust" back into "trusteeship" and inspire the next generation of philanthropic leaders? Can Lumarda's report of what he learned from "Frank" do for others what Frank did for him?

There are moments in life when it all becomes clear. The jargon melts away. The strategic plans take second stage. All the meetings become moot. In terms of my personal roles in philanthropy (as trustee and professional), what motivates me and what got me where I am today, one distinctive moment with a special person comes to mind.

Several years ago, I was sitting across a kitchen table with a future donor to the California Community Foundation. We were going over the details of his philanthropic plan. Frank was a self-described small businessman, inventor, tinkerer and "string collector." This was a modest self-description for someone who built up an estate of more than $20 million.

Frank also liked to tinker with his arrangement with the community foundation. After our initial meeting, he would call me up almost monthly to see if we could "Go over this thing one more time." At this particular meeting (the last one we would have) we sat across from each other at his kitchen table surrounded by open books, half-done sculptures and other projects "in process." His breathing was labored and assisted by a stream of pure oxygen fed to him by nose-tube.

We'd been here before, but this time it was different. He usually leaned over our papers, fiddling with words or asking for my definition (and the community foundation's) of a particular concept. On this morning, he sat back and asked me to describe in detail what would happen, "When I kick off and this thing kicks in." This was the first time he wanted a presentation without interaction or questioning. I covered all the points, emphasizing both the concepts and details that we had struggled with over the past several months. His eyes, though half closed, held me throughout. After I finished and sat back in my chair, he closed his eyes and leaned his head back for what seemed to be a very long time. I hoped he wasn't falling asleep.

As my anxiety began to mount, his head snapped forward. We stared at each other for what seemed like an eternity. "Thank you, Joe," he said. This was the first time I'd heard those words. I nodded my head with what must have been a quizzical expression.

He leaned over the table, placed his hand firmly on my forearm and squeezed. He then said words I will never forget, "*I guess you'll be me—when I'm no more.*" When a donor says something that hearkens the specter of death, I often come back with a dispelling quip—but not this time. Instead, I responded, "Yes sir, I will. We will." After a few minutes of sipping our tea in reflective silence, Frank proclaimed, "Now get out of here, young man, I have work to do!"

Frank died about a month later. His estate created a fund at the community foundation that provides scholarships for disadvantaged youth pursuing vocational training. He never went to college and wished to support kids who "Liked to work with their hands." He chose the community foundation because his fund would not be tied to any one institution and would be free to support the best programs to meet his philanthropic vision.

"*I guess you'll be me—when I'm no more.*" By this Frank might have meant that he expected me to be like himself in the years to come—wise, inventive, entrepreneurial, risk-taking, stubborn, curious, and humorous. Sure, I wish I—I wish all of us at the community foundation, indeed in all foundations— could become so. But at the time I heard it as a plea, as a hope, and above all, as a longing for trust. He wasn't so much asking me to become his double as he was entrusting me with *his* mission. He was, very literally, making me his trust-ee—the eyes, ears, and spirit of his philanthropic mission. No doubt the circumstances in which we conversed conspired to make me especially alert to his meaning, but I suddenly realized—really for the first time—the awesome responsibility that being a trustee entails. And it forever changed the way I look at my role in philanthropy.

Yes, we are in our positions at foundations in order to provide support to nonprofit organizations, which we hope will improve society and cause positive social change. Yet, we are primarily here to fulfill trust—personal trust, institutional trust, public trust. One can go to schools, conferences, and institutes to learn about the science and politics of grantmaking and social change. But where does one train future workers in the philanthropic vineyard to secure and ensure trust?

Frank trained me. "*I guess you'll be me—when I'm no more.*"

My immigrant housekeeper and gardener parents prepared me. *"Work hard. Be nice. Pray often. Tell the truth."*

The convent and order of nuns my parents worked for and dedicated more than forty years of their lives to helped me. *"There is more to this world than what you see. Dedicate yourself to something beyond yourself."*

A very special United States Marine Corps drill instructor also helped me. *"At the end of the day, can I trust you scumbag future officers with a $50 million U.S. Navy aircraft? More important than that, can I trust you with my life?"*

And my friend, teacher, and mentor the late Peter Drucker instructed me, as well. *"Question everything. Strip away all assumptions. What you have left is the truth and the essential elements of innovation."*

The issue of trust begs the question: How do we create foundations, institutions, and cultures that reflect the personal and public trust required of us? We have the laws, regulations, and guidelines that guide our public trust and accountability (just ask the IRS, the Senate Finance Committee, and states' attorneys general). However, this is just the first level of legal and ethical leadership and accountability.

Beyond this, do we have the wisdom, the experiences, and, at times, the history and stories to help us fulfill the historical and moral trust given to us by the donors and founders of our foundations? How do we reach a level of accountability and leadership that inspires us to act with integrity and constancy, whether the donor is with us or not? I reached this level through Frank's firm yet hopeful gaze and words, *"I guess you'll be me—when I'm no more."*

Who are the foundation trust-ees of the future? In what training ground will we find them? Good managers? Thought leaders? Change agents? Maybe we should ask the Franks of this world. Maybe we should ask *you:* Who would you trust with your memory and agency? Who would you trust to be you—when you're no more?

Adapted from "Life Lessons and the Trust of Philanthropic Leadership," written in response to the Dialogues on Civic Philanthropy, "Philanthropic Leadership" (November 8, 2005). Reprinted by permission of the author.

ALBERT KEITH WHITAKER

"Promethean Legacy: Receptive Giving, Generous Receiving"

Albert Keith Whitaker is director of family dynamics at Calibre, Wachovia's family office, and a Research Fellow at Boston College's Center on Wealth and Philanthropy. Here, beginning with the obvious—namely, that givers need receivers—Whitaker moves quickly to the less than obvious: the character of the receiving and its effects on the consequences of the gift. Especially concerned about the legacies and bequests that parents leave their children, he argues that what is most needed is "receptive giving or generous receiving." And he turns to the mythic story of Prometheus and his "natural" son Deukalion to convey his meaning. To "give receptively," Whitaker suggests, requires allowing one's child, as Prometheus did, to witness and serve one in one's suffering; to "receive generously" requires that the child so witness and serve—and learn the lessons of humility and care. Must we parents, then, become children to our children? (Is King Lear's tragedy a caveat against this advice? See above selection.) Is there any other way of cultivating generous receiving?

ℬ

It's a commonplace, especially during Christmas-time, that 'tis better to give than to receive. A cynic might say that we repeat these wearied words to help us buck up in the face of buying bags of presents that others don't need. It's a saying that appears oddly confirmed when we have to accept many presents that we don't want.

A similar dynamic operates with bequests and legacies. Flinty old businessmen or emotionally distant grand-aunts become transformed into momentary Santas through the disposition of their wills. A great estate heralds a great man, and not only for the task of amassing it. People who receive nothing directly from large bequests still admire the bequeather. And yet no one points to receiving an inheritance with pride. It's not exactly shameful, but one doesn't talk about it in public.

But without denying the obvious—that it is good to give—I think we should give what's due to receiving. Giving forges and strengthens the ties that bind our common life together. A world that recognized only commercial transactions, tit for tat, would be a cold and heartless place. At the same time, no giver acts alone. Givers need those who receive their gifts, and the character of the receiving decisively affects the consequences of the gift. If we wish to give well, we need to inculcate in ourselves and others a deeper appreciation for receiving.

The myth of Prometheus highlights the importance of both giving and receiving.

The Western tradition identifies the Titan Prometheus as the first "philanthropist." And what a high bar he set! Prometheus fashioned the first human beings out of clay. When Zeus refused to share fire with these cold and miserable clay people, Prometheus stole the fire from Olympus and gave it to them. Human beings got warm; they also used fire to develop a thousand arts and lay the foundations for civilization.

But the consequences of Prometheus' theft were severe. Zeus chained him to a mountain and sent an eagle every day to devour his liver. His immortal liver always grew back, meaning Prometheus' torment could last forever. Zeus also punished the newly enlightened human beings, sending them a charming "gift": the beautiful Pandora with her jar of evils. Zeus meant the evils (illness, discord, and death) to humble humanity so that they would forget Prometheus' rebellion. Instead the evils stung people into a frenzy and made them wicked. Zeus then resolved to destroy the entire human race with a flood.

But Prometheus had one more trick up his sleeve. Before being chained to the mountain, he had had a mortal son, Deukalion. Deukalion was dutiful and kind, and he tried to comfort his father and keep the eagle away from his liver. Because he could see the future, Prometheus warned Deukalion of the flood and told him to build an ark and to retreat into it with his wife, Pyrrha.

Deukalion and Pyrrha did so, and they survived the inundation. Afterwards, Zeus took pity on them, who lived alone in a ravaged world. He told them to throw behind them "the bones of their mother." Deukalion realized that this command referred to their common mother the earth, and he and Pyrrha walked throwing stones behind them. The stones Deukalion threw became men, those Pyrrha threw became women. This new stoney race proved hardier than Prometheus' clay men, and so put up better with the evils and miseries that afflict our world.

Like any story about a great gift, Prometheus' tale is uplifting and noble. And like most stories about great gifts, it is filled with unintended consequences. Prometheus' evident rivalry with Zeus makes his creation of human beings not only a gift of life but also a challenge. His gift of fire sets human beings on the path to civilization, but also on a collision course with Zeus' rule. Even leaving gods aside, every modern person knows that civilization is a mixed bag: no animal is as articulate or as deceptive, as noble or as wicked, as civilized man. Zeus' gift of Pandora introduces the world to beauty, but beauty has always been a source of strife. The inundation destroys but cleanses, leads to rebirth and also a resumption of evils.

Perhaps then the first lesson we receive from this story is to be humble with respect to our giving. We cannot know all the consequences of our gifts. The intended consequence may turn out to be less important, less lasting, than unseen possibilities. Even gods such as Zeus and Prometheus, for all their power and foresight, appear caught in the web of the Fates, and the Fates share their plans with no one.

"Legacy" is unfortunately not a word that inspires humility. And yet what is Prometheus' legacy? From a certain perspective, it looks like a terrible failure. The men he so carefully makes, for whom he steals fire and to whom he teaches the arts, are doomed to destruction. Within one generation they succumb completely to Pandora's wiles, her jar of ills, their own wickedness, and then Zeus' flood. In many ways, Prometheus' story resembles that of the first few chapters of the Bible. Pride precedes a fall. Both Prometheus and Eve boast to have "made a man with the Lord." Most of their offspring destroy each other.

But not all. Prometheus' natural son turns out differently than his manufactured children. None of the clay race come to comfort their maker or chase his feathery tormenter away. None of them survive the flood to become the agent, if not the parent, of a whole new race of human beings.

Whether consciously or not, Prometheus does several things right with Deukalion. First, rather than remaining a maker of men, he submits himself to the natural process of procreation. Zeus' many liaisons with mortal wives suggest that the Greek gods had few qualms about "submitting" themselves in this way. Over time, their famous dalliances became embarrassing, when compared with the austere distance of the Jewish God. But in this case at least, their willingness to implicate themselves in nature's schemes reveals to us mortals the superior consequences of mating versus manufacturing. If nothing else, Prometheus' son seems to love him much more than his mud men do.

Deukalion wasn't around to see Prometheus as a man-maker, or to witness Prometheus' choice to have rather than mold a child. But, very importantly, Prometheus does offer his son another sort of spectacle, the spectacle of suffering. Prometheus offers his son his misery, and not just his wits or his defiance, as a crucial bequest. Seeing his father's failure and suffering, and seeing his own ability to comfort him, Deukalion learns a humility and a care that Prometheus may not have known possible.

This humility and care prepare Deukalion to outdo his famous father. Deukalion does not go on to try to make another race. He becomes the agent for the birth of a race that owes itself to powers much greater than he. These powers—the sky (Zeus) and the ground (Mother Earth), nature (Earth) and law (Zeus)—replicate, in a mythic form, the same sort of procreation that produced Deukalion. Deukalion's deeds are not as noble and grand as his father's.

Few people remember his name. And yet, knowing the whole story, without the son's actions, what would we have thought of the father's deeds?

There is much more that could be said about the story of Prometheus and Deukalion. My emphasis has rested on those parts that highlight the giver's shortcomings and his reliance on others to create his legacy. Though that emphasis may seem perverse, the story would be less powerful, enduring, and truthful without those troubling parts.

For those of us interested in giving well, the main lesson is that we must pay close attention to those who would receive our gifts—not only to who receives what but how they receive what we give. It may look odd to anyone wanting a legacy, but one of the most important gifts we may offer to our recipients is to allow them to see something of our failures and shortcomings. Life helps out in this task, gradually chaining us to a Caucasian rock of physical and mental deterioration. At least the torment won't last forever.

Like Deukalion, those we wish to benefit should have the chance to care for and comfort us in our afflictions. One of the most troubling things in life is to receive a gift that one cannot, even in the slightest way, reciprocate. How intolerable even Santa would be if he didn't eat those milk and cookies! We should do what we can to make sure our heirs and beneficiaries feel that they, like Deukalion, have done something for their benefactors. This reciprocity is a critical element in receiving well.

I have no doubt that giving will continue to shine more lustrously than receiving, even receiving well. But I hope that these reflections incline givers to humble themselves a bit more, and recipients to hold their heads a bit higher. No legacy or bequest can succeed without a combination of what we might call receptive giving or generous receiving. Prometheus' creating may inspire wonder, but his fathering deserves even more careful attention, for in it he allows himself to serve as an agent through which powers much greater than he may act. And you don't have to be an ancient Greek to understand this role. It's one that anyone who's labored on behalf of Santa knows well.

Written in response to the Dialogues on Civic Philanthropy, "Grants, Grantors, Grantees" (July 21, 2005). By permission of the author.

ELIZABETH GOUDGE

From "Christmas with the Children"

Many among us, despite enjoying privileged lives, are disinclined to be philan-thropic. Why? Even more important, what can we do about it? Aristotle taught long ago that moral education takes time, diligence, and effort: one learns to be generous, he argues, by habitually doing generous deeds, beginning early on, in the right way, at the right time, to the right people. The well-intentioned grandfa-ther, in this short story by British writer Elizabeth Goudge (1900–1984), seems to agree—at least in theory. In the first part of the story (not included here), two chil-dren, Henrietta and Hugh Anthony, are feted and showered with gifts at their family's annual Christmas day party. But the next day, the focus of this excerpt, belongs to grandfather's "annual lesson on the connection between Faith and Works." Grandfather, a retired clergyman, has the children choose toys from their collection, and he then accompanies them as they distribute their treasures among the poor. This year, however, the children encounter measles in one house and ab-ject misery and harshness in another. Grandfather wonders whether such experi-ence, especially the last, can do more harm then good. Given his ends—building the moral character of his grandchildren—are his concerns well founded? Is the annual rite—Grandfather's method and manner, or more generally, his means— sufficient to his ends?

The day after the party was the day chosen by Grandfather for the children's annual lesson on the connection between Faith and Works, and it was a black day. Faith, as understood by Henrietta and Hugh Anthony, was saying your prayers and going to church and this they had no objection to, but Works was giving away your toys to the poor and that was another thing altogether. What connection was there, they demanded indignantly of each other, be-tween kneeling in your nightgown at the side of your bed at night and saying "Our Father-witchard-in-heaven," followed by "Now-I-lay-me," and parting next day from the dolls' perambulator and the tin helmet? . . . There seemed none.

The giving away of the toys always took place in the afternoon, and in the morning, as soon as breakfast was over, Grandfather and the children with-drew to the little room half-way up the tower where the toy-cupboards were kept. They toiled up the stone stairs, carrying two large baskets and the oil-stove that was to warm them during their melancholy employment, in a de-pressing silence.

The little room had been given to the children because it was like a room in a fairy tale. It was nearly at the top of the tower and its mullioned window, set in the thickness of the wall, had a lovely view of the cathedral towers, the Tor and the jumbled roofs of the city. It was quite empty, except for the children's treasures, and in it they were never required to tidy up.

They had a cupboard each whose state, Grandfather thought, was typical of their owners. In Henrietta's cupboard her dolls, together with their garments, furniture, crockery and cooking utensils, were laid out in neat rows on the top shelf. Her books were on the second shelf and boxes of beads were on the third shelf. You could see at once where everything was, and what it was, and when you opened the cupboard door nothing fell out.

With Hugh Anthony's cupboard it was not so, for as soon as the door was opened an avalanche descended. Jumbled up among engines with their wheels off, cricket bats cracked in the middle, headless soldiers and a moth-eaten golliwog who had seen better days, were chestnuts, bits of silver-paper, birds' feathers, the skin of a defunct snake, a mangel-wurzel and, most horrible of all, a baby chicken with two heads which had been preserved in a bottle of spirits and given to Hugh Anthony by Bates two Christmases ago . . . Hugh Anthony with his scientific mind adored this chicken and could never understand why everyone else averted their eyes when it was produced.

Having lit the oil-stove Grandfather sat himself down on the old rocking-horse and proceeded to superintend. Each child was required to fill a basket but they were not required to give away anything they had received this Christmas. They chose themselves what they should give away and Grandfather only interfered when he considered the choice unsuitable.

The cupboards were opened, the avalanche fell and work began.

Hugh Anthony always started by picking out the things that he really did not want, the heads of the soldiers, for instance, and the moth-eaten golliwog, but Grandfather's voice would thunder out behind him. "No, Hugh Anthony! Rubbish must not be given to God's poor!" Then Hugh Anthony, after getting no answer to his "Why not?" which Grandfather considered a rhetorical question unworthy of answer, would be obliged to choose instead the soldiers that were very nearly intact and the least beloved of his engines, pistols and bricks. The things that he cared for most deeply, such as the two-headed chicken and the skin of the snake, Grandfather mercifully considered unsuitable.

Henrietta was the stuff of which martyrs are made, for when she had to give away she always gave what she loved best. Grandfather, as he watched her dark head bent sadly over the basket and her dainty fingers slowly placing her treasures side by side inside it, understood her and suffered agonies. Yet he never interfered with the suggestion that Gladys Hildegarde, the least-loved of Henrietta's dolls, would do just as well to give away as Irene Emily Jane the worshipped and adored . . . No . . . For who knew what spiritual strength and beauty might not pass from Henrietta to the sawdust bosom of

Irene Emily Jane, and from thence to the little girl to whom she would be given?

But the sacrifice of this lady had taken place a year ago and she was now forgotten, for time heals even the worst of wounds. Henrietta had this year, so her conscience said, to part from the snowstorm that Miss Lavender had given her on her birthday. It was an incomparable toy. It consisted of a glass globe inside which a red man in a yellow hat stood on a green field. His cottage stood in the middle distance while to the right was a fir-tree and to the left a dog. This in itself was amazing, for how in the world did the red man, his cottage, his dog, and the fir-tree get inside the globe? But there was a greater marvel yet to come for when the globe was held upside down it began to snow. First a few flakes fell, then a few more, then they fell so thick and fast that the man and his house and his dog and the fir-tree were hidden from sight. Then you turned the globe right way up again and the storm ceased . . . It was amazing . . . Henrietta took it out of the cupboard and held it in her hands, her head bent. Then for the last time she held it upside down and watched the snow fall. Then she placed it in the basket and turned her back on it.

Grandfather watched her with painful attention and her action seemed to him to take on a mystic meaning. The globe was the world itself, containing all creation, trees, animals, man and his works, the earth and the sky, and Henrietta, it seemed, was one of those rare beings who, like Catherine Earnshaw, are prepared for love's sake to see "the universe turn to a mighty stranger."

After she had parted with the snowstorm it seemed to Henrietta quite easy to part with other things; with her necklace of blue beads, her set of drawing-room furniture made by herself out of chestnuts, with pins for legs and pink wool twisted round more pins for the backs of the chairs, her toy sewing-machine and her Dolly Dimple, a cardboard person with twelve sets of cardboard underclothes and ten hats.

When the baskets were packed they went downstairs and Grandfather read to them to cheer them up, and after that there was a rather penitential dinner of boiled cod and rice pudding at which Hugh Anthony did not behave well.

"Will you have skin, Hugh Anthony?" asked Grandmother, for she did not make the children eat milk-pudding-skin if they did not want to.

"No," said Hugh Anthony shortly.

"No, what?" asked Grandmother, who was punctilious about "thank you" being inserted in the proper place.

"No skin," said Hugh Anthony.

After dinner they started out, carrying the baskets and watched with disapproval by Grandmother. It was not that she disapproved of self-sacrifice, in fact she approved of it within limits set by herself, but in this case she feared its after-results. At the worst visiting the poor led to whooping-cough and at the best it resulted in the bringing home of insect life.

It had been snowing and the children insisted upon walking behind Grandfather so as to tread in his footsteps, for he was Good King Wenceslas and they were the page who, they decided, was really a twin.

"Couldn't you walk with me?" asked Grandfather, who felt a bit lonely by himself.

"No," they said, but they did not explain why such a thing was totally out of the question so he went on feeling lonely. They looked very odd, going up the street treading in each other's footsteps, but then Torminster was used to Grandfather and the children looking odd, and took no notice.

Beyond the Close a steep street wound uphill and here lived those people referred to by the Dean as the Lower Orders and by Grandfather as God's Poor. The part of the city where they lived had a fascination for the children because in its own way it was beautiful. The street knew, as the streams know, that it looks ugly to come down a hill in a straight line, and it wound about with stream-like winding so that you never knew what was coming round the corner. The cottages on each side were old, with weather-stained walls and flights of steps leading up to their front doors, and their crinkled roofs made a lovely pattern against the sky. No street that climbs a hill can be unattractive, Henrietta used to say in after years, the irregular line of the climbing roofs sees to that, but an old street on a hillside is one of the loveliest things on earth.

Today the curious white light of snow was over the world and a stinging cleanliness was in the air. The sky, emptied now of its snowflakes, was a pale grey with jagged rents torn in it through which one saw the blue behind; aquamarine just over the hills, turquoise higher up and sapphire overhead. To their right the trees that covered the Tor showed to perfection the softness of their winter dress. The bare twigs seemed by their interlacing to create color, the brown of them melting into blue and red and purple. The Tor looked like the breast of a bird, Henrietta thought. It was hard to realize that if you came close to the trees their softness would melt into hardness and their color into stark black and brown.

Firelight shone ruddily from windows and open doors and in spite of the cold the elder children were sitting on the steps that led to them, while the babies peered over the wooden boards put across the doors to keep them from hurtling down the steps. Inside the rooms busy mothers could be seen moving backwards and forwards, their figures dark against bright-patterned wall-paper and shining pots and pans.

It was, of course, difficult to know which cottages they ought to go to, for they could not go everywhere. The only thing to do, Grandfather had said when he first started the annual lesson on Works, was to begin at the bottom of the street and stop whenever they saw children, and next year to begin where they had left off the previous year. There were bound to be complaints, of course, in the cottages where they did not go, but he was primarily concerned with the characters of his own grandchildren so he tried not to think about them.

"Last year," said Henrietta from the rear, "we stopped at the cottage halfway up on the left-hand side where the wicked little boy showed Hugh Anthony how to make a long nose."

Grandfather remembered the regrettable incident, as indeed he might, for Hugh Anthony had been making long noses ever since, no amount of spanking curing him of the habit. That was the worst of Hugh Anthony. The wrong things seemed always to make an indelible impression on him while sweet and good influences ran off him like water off a duck's back . . . Or so it seemed . . . Grandfather could only hope and pray that future years might prove it otherwise.

"We'll go and see that little boy again," said Hugh Anthony.

"We will not," said Grandfather firmly. "We will go to the first house beyond him that has respectable-looking children."

The wicked little boy seemed out and they passed the danger point in safety. Beyond were several cottages where there were no children but after that things began to happen.

They began well.

Three little tow-haired girls sat on a flight of steps one behind the other. They wore stout boots and mufflers crossed over their chests and tied in bows behind. The dirt on their faces was only surface dirt, for their necks in contrast with their black faces were white as snow, and they had the eyes of children who have been loved from the beginning. Large handkerchiefs were attached to their persons with safety-pins and they were eating bread and jam . . . A delightful family . . . A family after Grandfather's own heart . . . He smiled at them and they stopped eating bread and jam, wiped their mouths with the backs of their hands—the handkerchiefs being apparently intended for nasal use only—and smiled back at him. Then shyness seized them; they cast down their eyes and squirmed.

But Grandfather had seen behind them a clean, fire-lit kitchen, a cheerful mother and two tow-haired boys, and he led the way in, patting the heads of the girls as he climbed over them.

Inside, in an atmosphere of welcome, he was utterly happy. He sat himself down in a windsor chair, placed his hat on the floor and talked to the cheerful mother as though he had known her all his life. He felt as though the hard, happy days of his parish work were back with him again, those days when he had not felt conscious, as he was always conscious in the Close, of living a segregated life. He hated segregation, inevitable though he knew it to be. He hated the barriers of time and age and class and language. He longed for the time when all the different lights carried by man in the pageantry of life should glow into one.

But his ease was as yet impossible to Henrietta and Hugh Anthony. They stood side by side, stiff and miserable, subjected to the unwinking stare of five pairs of eyes; for the tow-headed little girls had now joined the little boys in a group as far removed as possible from their visitors. The whole width of the kitchen separated the well-dressed from the ill-dressed and it was the well-dressed, weighed down by numbers, who felt themselves at a disadvantage. What makes one feel uncomfortable, they discovered suddenly, is not what one has got or has not got, but being different.

But gradually the situation eased itself. First Henrietta took a step forward, then one of the little girls, and then before they knew where they were the chestnut chairs with the wool backs had been set out on the stone floor, becoming in a flash mahogany upon a marble pavement.

After that the giving of gifts was easy. Hugh Anthony parted almost willingly from an engine with three wheels and a box of soldiers, and Henrietta added to the chestnut chairs her blue bead necklace and Dolly Dimple.

"Isn't 'Arold going to 'ave nothink?" asked the eldest little girl.

"Who's Harold?" asked Grandfather with benign interest.

"My eldest," said the woman. "Upstairs with the measles." She sighed, glancing at the youngest little girl who was sniffling. "They'll all 'ave it now. There's Rosie sneezing already."

Grandfather's eyes popped a little behind his glasses, but he was careful to go quietly on with the conversation until the end, when he rose and thought they ought to be going. A picture book was found for Harold, mutual goodbyes were said and they departed.

"I think," said Grandfather, when they were out in the street again, "that it would be better not to mention the measles to your dear Grandmother."

"Why not?" asked Hugh Anthony.

"It would distress her," said Grandfather, "to think of the poor little boy being ill."

"Oh no, it wouldn't," said Hugh Anthony.

Henrietta privately agreed with him for she had noticed that Grandmother and Clara enjoyed hearing about other people's ups and downs. Whenever anybody's chimney caught on fire, or cook gave notice, or appendix had to come out, Clara would come running to tell Grandmother and Grandmother would say, "Dear me, Clara, you don't say so!" and look almost bright and interested.

They went on up the street, giving toys to the children whom they saw and sometimes going inside their homes, and all went well until they turned a corner and came upon a dingy-looking house from which no firelight shone. The broken window-panes were stuffed with rag, a most unusual sight in Torminster, and over the board across the door there peeped a dirty baby with a cold in its head, and no handkerchief. Grandfather, seeing the cold, would have passed on but as the children were still in single file behind him, treading in the footsteps of Good King Wenceslas, he had no control over them and before he could stop her Henrietta had darted across the pavement to the baby.

She had never seen such a pitiful baby and the sight of it made her feel dreadful. It was dirty all over, from its matted hair to its bare toes, and its poor little upper lip was terribly sore because no one had ever blown its dribbling nose. In a flash Henrietta climbed over the board and blew the nose on her own clean handkerchief, then picking up the scrap in her arms she staggered with it into the gloom beyond.

Inside were dirt and evil smells and dead ashes in the grate. A horrible-looking old woman, the grandmother perhaps, with greasy strands of grey hair escaping from a man's cap, was peeling potatoes and shouting raucously at the children who seemed swarming all over the place. Henrietta, unseen, stood still and stared, for the children had not got faces like the children she was accustomed to. They had old faces and their eyes did not seem to look at anything steadily. When the old woman hit out at two of the little ones they ducked cleverly, and without fear, but their cunning was somehow horrible. Then they saw Henrietta and came boldly crowding up to her, shouting out things that she did not understand, though she knew they were mocking things. She recoiled a little and found to her relief that Grandfather was just behind her.

"Give them some toys," he said quietly, "and then come away."

But before she had time to do anything a door burst open and a drink-sodden brute of a man was upon them, a man as repellent as it is possible for a human creature to become upon this earth. It was lucky for Henrietta that in her fright she did not see him very clearly, or understand anything of the torrent of abuse that he hurled at Grandfather, except his last shout of, "I'll have none of your damned charity."

"I have no wish to inflict it on you at the moment," said Grandfather sternly, and he moved to the door, pushing Henrietta and Hugh Anthony in front of him and quite unmoved, apparently, by the flung boot that missed his head by inches . . . This was not the first time in the course of his ministry that boots had been hurled at his head and he supposed it would not be the last, for with the vicar's permission he intended to visit this gentleman again.

Out in the street Henrietta suddenly dived under Grandfather's arm and ran back. When that terrible man had come in she had seen the children all cowering back, as they had not shrunk from their grandmother, and the sight had awakened in her some queer agony of understanding, for these were children who were not wanted. Deep down in Henrietta's mind was a half-formed memory of a time when she herself had not been wanted. It was not a real memory, like the memory of her singing mother, it was only a shadow that spread itself behind the figure of her mother, not emanating from her but from someone else, and faintly darkening those days at the orphanage when she discovered that her mother was dead and that no one would tell her anything about her father . . . Someone, at some time, had not wanted her, that was all she knew . . . The horrible man had disappeared again, but the children were still cowering in their corner. She pushed fiercely in among them and took the snowstorm from her basket. "Look!" she cried, and held it upside down. "Look at the snow falling."

Suddenly they were crowding round her, kicking and scuffling, fear and hatred forgotten and their eyes and mouths "ohs" of amazement. One of the boys seized the globe rudely from her and hit out indiscriminately at all the others so that he could have this treasure for himself. His hard fist caught Henrietta in the chest and nearly winded her, but she did not mind. Backing out from among them she ran back to Grandfather at the door, momentarily happy again.

But the swift changes of mood possible to childhood were not possible to Grandfather and he was by no means happy. He had had no idea that Torminster possessed such a family, and he was terribly sorry that the children should have seen it . . . Henrietta, he knew, would never forget . . . And he was grieved, too, that she should have parted with her snowstorm when she did, for he had not the slightest doubt that within two hours it would be at the pawnbroker's. Well, for two hours, for the first time and probably the last, those wretched children would possess for their own the world and its beauty, earth and sky, a tree, a cottage, a dog and a red man in a yellow hat.

They visited no more houses that afternoon for there was no more spirit left in them. They trailed rather sadly home, giving away the few toys that were left to the children they met.

When they got to their own garden door the light was fading and the shadows were long across the snow. The Tor woods had lost their colour and the bright patches of blue sky were swallowed up in the grey.

Henrietta and Hugh Anthony ran straight upstairs to Grandmother in the drawing-room, where the warm fire gleamed on dark paneling and coloured china and where the smell of the fresh chrysanthemums was clean and pungent. Grandfather went to his study, shut the door, fell upon his knees and prayed that the dear children might not catch the measles . . . They did not.

From *A Christmas Book* by Elizabeth Goudge (New York: Coward-McCann, 1967), pp. 143–152. By permission of David Higham Associates Limited.

ROBERT WUTHNOW

"(Not) Talking about Money: The Social Sources and Personal Consequences of Subjectivization"

Many have written about what it takes to cultivate wise adult investors and do-nors.[1] Most offer good practical advice, but few focus on why such advice may be urgently needed, especially today, not only by the wealthy few but by all families. Drawing from first-hand accounts and a national survey, contemporary sociologist Robert Wuthnow directs our attention to a now-prevalent taboo—"(not) talking about money"—which stricture, he argues, severely limits our ability to appropriately educate the next generation. Hence, money, though highly visible in the public domain, remains a murky specter—invoking part fear, part fantasy—in the private lives of many Americans. And children, having neither heard from their parents about money nor seen it transacted (thanks to high-tech mediation, such as online bank accounts, credit cards, etc.), lack the grounds for understanding why their parents behave as they do or for making financial decisions of their own. Even more important, Wuthnow observes, "It becomes especially hard for [them] to think through the relationship between money and nonpecuniary values [for example, personal, social, or sacred values] when they never hear anyone else discussing this relationship." He insists that we must consciously re-integrate these values into our lives if we are to continue to flourish. Assuming Wuthnow's diagnosis is correct, what are we to do? How do we speak about everyday financial concerns without cultivating the love of money? How do we reinfuse money talk with moral concerns? When—under what sort of circumstances—should we talk to our children about money and its better uses?

The American Taboo

. . . [I]f anthropologists are correct in arguing that all societies have taboos, we must ask where the deepest taboos in our own society are now to be found. Money is perhaps the topic that remains most subject to deep norms of stricture and taboo. More than sex, health, death, or any other aspect of personal life, it is the one most difficult for us to discuss in public.

This claim may at first glance strike some readers as peculiar. Surely anyone even casually acquainted with American culture would argue precisely the

---

1. See, for example, Charles W. Collier, *Wealth in Families* (Harvard University, 5th Printing, 2003); James E. Hughes, Jr., *Family Wealth: Keeping It in the Family* (Princeton: Bloomberg, 2004); or Jim Stovall, *The Ultimate Gift* (Mechanicsburg, Pa.: Executive Books, 2000).

opposite. Foreign visitors, for example, typically observe that buying, selling, price tags, advertising, and dollar signs seem to be everywhere. Virtually every newspaper includes a business section filled with long lists of stock quotations and discussions of currency rates. Television programs and magazines have carved out significant markets by specializing in money. The number of periodical articles dealing with money has risen steadily in recent decades, as have the number of advice books on this subject and the number of people who earn their living as brokers, accountants, and financial advisers.

The public visibility of particular topics, however, is seldom a good barometer of how much these same topics may or may not be couched in taboo. . . .

Despite the highly technical discussions of money markets, currency rates, and other financial wisdom that appear in specialized public media, the American public is almost completely mute on the subject of money. When asked if they ever discuss money or personal finances with friends, family, or anyone else, most people flatly say "no" or else qualify their answers to indicate that these discussions occur infrequently, avoid sensitive topics, and require special levels of trust. A typical response is like the one given by a Chicago insurance broker. Although he deals with money questions every day in his work, he says he never tells anybody in his personal life what he makes, how much money he has saved up, or what his investments are. Asked why not, he admits, "I don't know why; I just think it's taboo."

As people reflect on this taboo, we discover just how deeply rooted it is in our understandings of what constitutes appropriate behavior. Stuart Cummings, whose friends are mostly wealthy, says it is just plain rude to talk about money. People who do, he thinks, are trying to show how much they have. A New Jersey dentist who earns a moderate income says he gets along better with his friends when he keeps his mouth closed about any kind of financial matters. A young man in Washington, D.C., who is still struggling to get established in his profession, says he keeps quiet about money because people he associates with then think he has more than he really does. A senior banking official in Chicago says the taboo exists without exception in his company because there would be an epidemic of jealously and complaints if people knew each other's salaries. This was the same lesson Michael Lewis, author of *Liar's Poker,* learned during his short career on Wall Street: "investment bankers didn't like to talk about money."

Working women are a bit more likely than men to admit they have had conversations about money. But many say they learned very quickly to monitor themselves. A clergywoman in California, for example, admits one of her parishioners became quite offended one day when she innocently inquired about his personal finances. A Washington-based therapist says she and her fellow workers used to talk about finances when they were first starting out, but soon quit doing so because they all realized the discussions were taking a competitive turn.

The blackout on discussions of money is not absolute, of course, but what people say they *do* and *do not* talk about is also very revealing. A woman in

Philadelphia says she sometimes talks with her friends about tuition at the private school where she and her friends send their children, but this is about all she is willing to discuss. "I wouldn't talk about how much my husband makes. I wouldn't tell anybody how much we owe on credit cards or our home equity loan, or even how much our mortgage payment is. There's just a strong feeling that that's a tacky thing to do." Another woman talks occasionally with her friends about the price of automobiles or how rent costs are rising. She says the discussion, though, is usually at a very general level, like how high prices are, rather than anything touching on specific problems. A number of people say their discussions arise when they are trying to decide on a major purchase, such as an automobile or a new home. In these cases, they often feel free to seek advice from a parent or close sibling; yet it is also common for people to shield these discussions from other members of their family whom they have learned not to trust.

These examples suggest that people will talk about money when the ice has somehow been broken. They are most likely to discuss prices of consumer goods and other standard household budget items that have been advertised. In these cases, advertising makes general price levels public, so people feel they are revealing less in discussing these prices. Occasionally, people are able to discuss financial matters that might not otherwise be in the public domain because they all find themselves in the same situation. Waiting to pick children up from the same private school may be such an occasion. Another example came from a woman who found she was able to discuss home repair costs because everyone in her neighborhood happened to be making the same repairs at about the same time. What people are most reluctant to discuss are their salaries, their personal net worth, and their debts. These are more purely financial or monetary, rather than being associated with marketable goods, and as such they are protected in a cloud of secrecy. . . .

The few people who say they talk freely with friends and family about their personal finances also demonstrate that the taboo on money talk is a cultural norm rather than a kind of censorship that individuals simply develop on their own. It is a norm that most people accept, yet it is clearly a phenomenon largely of the American middle class. It is much less widespread among the underprivileged, in the working class, and among ethnic groups that retain a strong sense of family and community identity. When asked if he ever discusses his personal finances with friends and family, a Hispanic man in Los Angeles, for example, replies, "Sure, it's part of my life!" He says this is not unusual in the Hispanic community. Others who said they talked about money on a regular basis included a Minneapolis priest who discusses personal finances with others in his priests' support group, a banker who had just returned from an assignment in China where he discovered there was much more openness about personal finances, and an air force electrician who says people talk more freely about money in the military because salary levels associated with each rank are public information.

As anthropologists who study other kinds of taboo have discovered, the rules underlying deeply held social prohibitions are often best revealed when people violate these rules. Some of the examples just considered show that violations of the money taboo subject people to personal discomfort and even criticism. The people who find special circumstances in which to talk about money reveal that taboos depend on institutional arrangements. They also depend on cultural understandings that supercharge money with extra meaning, power, perhaps even a kind of sacredness. The few people who tried successfully to overcome norms against talking about money were those who consciously adopted a different stance toward it. One woman, for example, says she has been able to talk more frankly with her parents in recent years about personal finances because they have learned to joke about these issues. Bringing humor into the conversation strips money of its gravity. Another woman tries to talk openly about family finances with her children to help them understand better why she and her husband make certain decisions. The language she uses is much like the language people adopted when sex was first becoming a subject of family discussion. Money, she says, is not something special or mysterious. It shouldn't be turned into something more than it is. "It isn't so precious that it needs to be hidden or kept secret; it is just like anything else, just a fact of life."

Most parents, however, do not treat money with this degree of candor. Indeed, one of the reasons many people find it so hard to talk about money is that during their formative years they never heard their parents discuss it. Some parents intentionally shield their children from discussions of money because they fear it will generate insecurity. Others believe money, like sex, is an adult subject that children cannot understand. They talk about children being innocent and pure, whereas money is complicated and dirty, an "adult" subject.

Barb Gimelli, 40, a single mother who owns a management consulting firm, is more open about her personal finances than most people. She participates in a support group for working women that frequently gets into candid discussions of such matters. As a single woman, she also has some friends she confides in. But, like others, she sets limits on these conversations. She claims not to understand exactly why she does this, but somehow she feels such discussions are not appropriate, especially in the context of children. "My kids ask me sometimes, 'How much money do you make, mom?' And I tell them the same thing my parents always told me, 'That's not something I should share with you.' And I always think that maybe that's sort of weird. I don't know why I say that. It's sort of an automatic response, but I guess I think that it's a little crass or I don't really like talking about, oh, I make X dollars or something. Yeah, I wouldn't talk about that."

But the main reason children do not learn about money from their parents is that contemporary family patterns simply do not encourage that major financial decisions be made in the presence of children. With work being geographically separated from the home, and with mortgages being negotiated in bankers' offices and bills being paid by electronic transfers, children can grow up without having direct access to any of their parents' monetary thinking. It then becomes easier for parents to enforce the taboo against talking about money because the subject is shielded from view.

It was not always like this. In an earlier era children worked alongside parents on the family farm or in the family business. Prohibitions against idle talk about money often kept parents from discussing their deepest fears and fantasies with children. The day-to-day handling of money, however, was likely to be conducted in the presence of, and sometimes with the active participation of, children. As a result, children learned more of the reasoning behind their parents' decisions. They saw that money was not just a means of paying the bills, but an integral feature of life itself.

The significance of such interaction is clearly illustrated by an older woman, Lydia Kramer, who spoke with us about her childhood. Born in the 1920s, she lived most of her childhood during the Great Depression. . . . From the time she was nine years old, Lydia worked in the family store.

She remembers vividly one of the lessons she learned about money from this experience. "Whenever my friends came in, I felt they should have free ice cream. But my father said, 'That sounds all right if you are the only one working here and want to give free ice cream. But this is a business and you cannot make a profit if everything is free. So if you want to give something free, you put in a nickel for every ice cream you give your friends, and I'll do the same thing.'" Later, when she was a teenager, her father taught her all the other jobs in the store and gradually included her in more of the decisions he was making. She especially remembers him talking with her about the importance of knowing how hard people have to work for their money. When customers were being laid off and couldn't pay their bills, she also saw him struggling to balance compassion and keeping the business afloat. When she went away to college, she not only had skills that helped pay her way but knew how to negotiate for the best positions. She also believed firmly that helping people was more important than earning an extra dollar.

Younger people who grow up in the suburbs seldom learn what their parents think about money in such detail. They often know it is extremely important to their parents, but they have to try to guess what their parents' values are by looking at the goods they purchase or from hearing an occasional argument in the middle of the night. Sometimes they assimilate their parents' habits of spending money freely or of being extremely frugal, only to discover later that they have little understanding of *why* their parents behaved as they did. When asked what their parents actually taught them, they are caught short, realizing, as one young man in New York put it, "I'm not sure what they thought about money; I don't feel I was taught anything specific about money."

For those whose parents did talk more openly about money, the main lesson often is still that this subject should be kept under wraps. The reasons why have deep roots in American culture, linking present understandings with vestiges of ... moralist arguments ... From the ascetic moralists comes the idea that money is not as important as family, neighbors, or God. An example of this idea is given by a woman in Los Angeles who remembers seeing pictures of the saints in their robes at the Catholic church her parents attended when she was a girl and concluding that it was wrong to worry about money. From the romantic moralists the view is still prevalent in some quarters that money is crass and unsophisticated, compared with intellectual and artistic interests. Other views hark back to the aristocratic notions held by some of the founders of our society, men and women of comfortable means who thought it beneath them to discuss financial matters. In this view people who are so concerned about money that they cannot refrain from discussing it in public are shallow, boorish. In the absence of frank discussions in the home, however, these traditions have become transmuted into simple dictums that say little more than "don't talk about it." ...

The Dubious Pleasure of Money

The tendency to make money so private that we never talk about it in public has far-reaching consequences for our society and for our personal lives. We assume great responsibility for our money, but we receive little support from other people of the kind that might help us make better decisions or feel more confident about the decisions we do make. Consequently, we worry in private and feel guilty about spending too little or too much. We may live frugally, but we no longer know exactly why we do. Without the capacity to compare our thoughts and feelings with those of our peers, both our fantasies and our fears often run wild.

The ultimate indicator of how far removed our subjective sense of money is from anything concrete is the fact that people in our society seem capable of terrorizing themselves with deep-seated financial worries, no matter how much money they have. They know, perhaps from hearing about the financial misfortune of a friend, or even from personal experience, that money is always uncertain. They then turn this uncertainty into an obsession that far outweighs any material advantages they may enjoy. Karen Kelsey, [a] Washington-based therapist ... experienced this kind of fear firsthand in the life of her mother. She recalls, "I remember how Mom used to lay on her bed and sob because she thought they were going to become impoverished. But we were living in a house in Beverly Hills on Rodeo Drive, and we had horses, and we had apartment buildings, and we had nice silver and jewelry, just endless amounts of material things. But I grew up always in terror that the next day we would be out on the street, impoverished, because my mother always believed that. She had no sense of what was a reasonable amount of money, of what you needed to survive, or even of what loss was."

By the same token, our ability to fantasize about preposterous sums of money seems no longer to bear any relation to how much or how little money we actually have either. It used to be that studies of material fantasies found people reluctant to think very broadly beyond their actual standard of living. A typical example would be someone earning $10,000 a year who said it would be nice to earn $12,000. But now, as we have seen, people's minds turn to winning the lottery. Even self-styled spendthrifts say it would be nice to have "just enough," like an annual income of $200,000 or a net worth of several million.

Advertising must of course be blamed for some of the fears and fantasies that plague our imaginations. Life insurance companies play up the worst-case scenarios, while cruise companies, airlines, and game shows all provide glimpses of what it must be like to enjoy the "lifestyles of the rich and famous." We know from careful studies of the effects of advertising that most people adopt an appropriately cynical view of these appeals to their fears and fantasies. So all the blame cannot be placed on advertising alone. It is the nature of our personal lives themselves that is much more to blame. Abiding so faithfully by the taboo against discussing money with our friends and families, we are left at the mercy of our own imaginations.

Extreme fantasies and fears about money, however, represent only the least significant of the ways in which money can take possession of our personal lives. Because we have relatively few anchors in the external world for our thoughts about money, we sense that it makes incessant demands on our personal time and energy. Despite relatively high incomes, many people feel they need even more money to solve their problems. A lack of money symbolizes constraint; the way to gain freedom is thus to have more. Prosperity appears as a psychological fix, even though the desire for it magnifies our sense that things are not sufficient as they are.

Not talking about money is, in the final analysis, both a source and a consequence of the dubious pleasures we derive from it. Part of our cultural heritage tells us money can never be a source of true happiness. Handling money is just a grubby business, more detail to worry about in our personal lives. It makes no more sense to talk about it than it would to hold forth about brushing our teeth. But not verbalizing what we think about money also makes it possible to entertain private beliefs of a very different sort. We may have learned somewhere that money cannot buy happiness, but at a deeper level we believe it can. There is thus an internal contradiction in the way we think about money, one that leads us to want more and more, and yet to deny that this is what we really want at all. . . .

SUSAN TURNBULL (editor)

Selections from "Ethical Wills"

As the editor and collector of these excerpts, Susan Turnbull, Principal of Personal Legacy Advisors, explains: "Ethical Wills have their roots in Jewish tradition. Originally an oral custom, the creation of an Ethical Will was considered the final responsibility of adulthood, allowing fathers to pass on to their sons their guidelines for living a worthy life, and, in effect, to rule from beyond the grave, thereby assuring not only their own continuity but that of their faith. Contemporary Ethical Wills, by contrast, tend to be gentler in tone, less prescriptive, and not only expressive of values but also of tenderness and love. But ancient or modern, there are no set standards, regarding length or form. And, though all such Wills ultimately serve as their authors' last words, their content is generally composed in stages, allowing earlier insights to be augmented by additional perspective, and enabling authors to share them with their audience during their own lifetimes."

The excerpts from "Ethical Wills" collected here, all but one contemporary, make vivid why people so often distinguish between the goods that they bequeath and the legacies they hope to leave. Each illuminates, as well, the things closest and dearest to the author. As the writer of such a Will, what would you include and why? As recipient of such a Will, your own or one of those included here, would you welcome it? Why or why not?

Excerpts from the Ethical Will of Judah Ibn Tibbon, circa 1190, written to his son Samuel[1]

My son! Make thy books thy companions, let thy cases and shelves be thy pleasure-grounds and gardens. Bask in their paradise, gather their fruit, pluck their roses, take their spices and their myrrh. If thy soul be satiate and weary, change from garden to garden, from furrow to furrow, from prospect to prospect. Then will thy desire renew itself, and thy soul be filled with delight! . . .

Let thy expenditure be well ordered. It is remarked in the *Choice of Pearls*: "Expenditure properly managed makes half an income." And there is an olden proverb, "Go to bed without supper and rise without debt." Defile not the honor of thy countenance by borrowing; may thy creator save thee from that habit! . . .

My son! Devote thy mind to thy children as I did to thee; be tender to them as I was tender; instruct them as I instructed; keep them as I kept thee! Try to

---

1. From *Hebrew Ethical Wills*, edited by Israel Abrahams (Philadelphia: Jewish Publication Society of America, 1976), pp. 61, 79, and 80 respectively.

teach them Torah as I have tried, and as I did unto thee do thou unto them! Be not indifferent to any slight ailment in them, or in thyself (may God deliver thee and them from all sickness and plague), but if thou dost notice any suspicion of disease in thee or in one of thy limbs, do forthwith what is necessary in the case. As Hippocrates has said: Time is short and experiment dangerous. Therefore be prompt, and apply a sure remedy, avoiding doubtful treatment.

A Short Contemporary Ethical Will

My loves [three teenage children],

It is you who have been at the heart of my adult life. Choosing to be Dad's partner in your *becoming*, from conception to young adulthood, has been fundamental to most of my decisions and has been at the root of a very fulfilling life.

I expect that I will be around for a long time and that I will continue to do what I have always done with you, which is to keep the appropriate balance of holding you close and letting you go. What I have tried to do, together with Dad, is to give you the most solid base we could—of family, of home, of summer places, of schooling. Layered on top of that we have tried to give you freedom to try out life on your own terms. It has been an elastic, evolving balance of giving roots and wings, of providing freedom within a structure. Sometimes you and we have differed on the degree and nature of the structure necessary! And I suspect there still will be differences well into the future—but such is the give/take, push/pull of the whole business and of the nature of love itself.

Whether I am present or not, I hope that as you live out your own lives you can maintain the balance of the familiar and the unfamiliar by creating a solid base from which you can securely approach your options and enjoy what you have created. The most important thing that I can bequeath to you is something that I hope I have already given you: a deep conviction of your own worth that translates into personal standards and instincts that will steer you in your relationships, inspire you to believe yourself to be a fully contributing citizen of the world, and enable you to create your own version of "home."

Along these lines, I hope you each will:

Stay connected to Dad and me and with each other. You are securely part of a family, but don't take the relationships for granted. Know what is going on in each other's lives, in Dad's and my lives. Your ties to each other will be the longest ties you have—keep them well nourished; purposefully keep track of each other's emotional well being; provide support for each other in good times and difficult times.

Connect with your grandparents while they are alive—seek them out, write them, visit them, read what they have written. You will always be glad you did.

Maintain a sense of being part of an extended family of many branches. Nurture your relationships with your cousins and aunts and uncles. Tell the family stories to each other and to the next generations. Make sure the family records and writings are kept intact and passed down.

Build a web of friendships and try to keep them alive over time and distance. Old friends are wonderful.

Commit to being financially secure—don't be held hostage by debt; money = choice, debt = prison; start early because time is your ally; get professional help when you need it.

Build a base of skills and interests so you can be adaptable in the workplace.

Develop an area in which you can invest yourself with passion and go into deeply—and make money and find satisfaction.

Read a lot—continue to educate yourself; nurture your curiosity; travel.

Value the spiritual. Where do you meet the spirit? Seek it out; nurture your creativity; cultivate optimism and faithfulness.

Commit yourself to things—it is where all the rewards are: commitment to interests, people, marriage, children, work, places. Trying to keep all your options open all the time leads nowhere.

Get in the habit of good communication in all areas of your life—to keep tormenting thoughts to a minimum, to operate from light openness and not be burdened by anger, and irritation. Repair wounds quickly, with professional help if needed.

Be a citizen of the world: try to make the world a better place; one person, a small group of people can make a huge difference.

Be respectful of everyone you meet—most everyone can do something better, or knows something more than you—what is it?

Seek out those who are older and more experienced; do not be intimidated by anyone, regardless of their age or status; be respectful, interested, look them in the eye and know that you are of interest to them, also. You will better yourself through their influence; they will benefit from your interest and point of view.

My loves, I want you to have this now, to keep it with you always and if you choose to have children, to give it to them sometime, too. I may choose to add to it as the years go by.

Remember always that my love lives inside you.

Mom
June, 2004

Excerpts from Longer Contemporary Ethical Wills

The legal and financial documents may imply our values, but they do not provide a clear explanation of our motivations or a sense of the path we have taken to get to this point. Please read this document as a conversation be-tween the two of us and the two of you. Some of it will make more sense at other points in your lives than it does now, so we hope you'll keep it in a safe place and refer to it often in the future. Herein you will find information about our families and the ways our values were shaped, the financial planning that we've set up for your and your children's benefit, our non-financial assets, our intentions as they relate to charitable giving and advice on avoiding some potential pitfalls. We love you both unconditionally and want you to have a complete picture of our thinking and an explanation of the plans we have made.

Couple in their early fifties writing to their two young adult children, 2005

I have observed too many instances of people who leave this world with-out passing on their wisdom and their insights. Without the purposeful trans-fer of the riches of their accumulated experiences and knowledge, their families are robbed of the wealth that multiplies generation after generation. I want the present and future generations of this beloved family of ours to build on what has come before them, to stand on our shoulders as I am standing on those who preceded me. I want you to know where I have come from and what I have learned. I want you to know what I have worked to create and I want to share my convictions on how to live a meaningful and balanced life. I am far from being finished and far from being perfect, but I want you to have this now, knowing that what I write here is an expression of my life to the present time. I fully intend to update it as the future unfolds.

56 year old man writing to his adult children and grandchildren, 2003

We want our money to help you and not hurt you. It will help if it grants you access, flexibility and opportunity; it will hurt if it provides an easy exit from challenges and dilemmas that you need to face in order to grow into strong, successful adults.

The most important matter is not how you got your money or how you are going to spend it. It is how you are going spend your lives and what kind of peo-ple you are going to be. It is about finding your passions and pursuing them. It is striving to be excellent in whatever you do. It is also about your moral author-ity. We hope that you will always look outside yourselves and consider the per-spective of others, that you will not get so wrapped up in your own lives that you miss the people that are around you that are in need. We hope you will be aware of what is going on in your community and how events are affecting peo-ple there and all over the world. Try to take in the stranger—both physically and in your heart.

Entrepreneurial, philanthropic couple writing to adult children, 2005

The philosophy and handling of personal finances are not subjects taught in school. Therefore this letter began as a vehicle to discuss with you some ideas about financial matters and thoughts about handling money. It would sadden me if you were to conclude that finance overshadows other values of a transcending nature. Keep money in its place as a medium, as a responsibility, as power, as a means to achieve great benefit for others, as a measure of economic progress, but not as a measure of a rich and worthwhile life. The life of Scrooge is no life at all. Your relationships with others, especially your life partner and your family, are infinitely more important. These bonds are worth working hard for and sacrificing for. Marriage is worth your best efforts.

80 year old man to his seven grandchildren, 2002

I really respect how all of you, my children and children-in-law, are there for each other when times are tough. I want to encourage you to continue to be there for each other when the day comes when I am not in this life. With all my heart and soul, I encourage you to maintain your identity as brothers and sisters, because there is no one else who is better suited to be there for you, and for your wives and husbands, and all those precious grandchildren. Be aware of each other's struggles, whether it's a personal issue or a health issue, or something in business or finances. There are so many areas that can be devastating in life and you need to know that you can turn to each other to help with what needs to be done.

77 year old woman writing to her children, 2002

One of the biggest choices you make in life is the person you choose to share your life with beyond this family. That is a journey that each individual has to go through, and over time, you will experience the difference between attraction and deep love.

Our hope for each of you is that you will find someone who is good to you, and who will take care of you. You deserve to be with someone who adores you, and who will respect you and value you and who will treat you like a true equal partner. Mom and Dad do believe strongly in the formal commitment of marriage. If, as life evolved, one of you chose a same sex partner, it would be important for you to know that we would accept it as long as we knew it was one based on happiness, with the same level of commitment made.

It takes a lot of work to maintain a relationship, and what Mom and Dad saw in each other was something they hadn't experienced in their previous relationships: a commitment to a true partnership, each willing to go 110% to making it work. There are challenges in every relationship every day, of hard times of misunderstanding, of communication breakdowns, and of seeing the world differently. It is important to find a partner who is willing to go all the way with you, who is committed to seeing it through the inevitable difficulties.

Mom is still touched deeply when she remembers the night she and Dad told Grammy and Grampy that they were planning to be married:

"We took them out to dinner to talk about it. They had been waiting and hoping this would happen and Grampy immediately ordered champagne, but Grammy said, 'Wait,' and got very serious in a way we didn't often see. She adored Daddy and wanted very much for Mommy and Daddy to be together, but she needed to have a clear understanding with Dad. She took his hands and looked into his eyes and said, 'I need you to tell me right now that in this relationship, in this commitment, in this marriage, not only will you be there for Ellen, but you will never hurt her intentionally, physically, emotionally or spiritually. She is my treasure and my baby and I will entrust her to you if you can make this promise.'

"Daddy held Grammy's hands and he looked her right in the eye and said, 'I will make many mistakes, but I will never intentionally hurt her, nor could I ever think of hurting her.' That was an important contract that had tremendous meaning for me in creating trust. I felt not only valued by Dad, knowing how he felt, but by Grammy, that as a parent, she was making sure that I was going into a safe and loving place. If I am not there to make that contract with your spouse, I will hope that it happens in such a way that you feel sure, down to your toes, that you are joining with a partner who can insure those things for you."

Couple writing to their four young children, with intention of sharing letter when each reached the age of 18; written in 2002

Excerpts and permissions collected by Susan Turnbull. All rights reserved.

JOHN MAYNARD KEYNES

"Economic Possibilities for Our Grandchildren"

*Renowned British economist John Maynard Keynes (1883–1946) wrote this essay
in 1930, amidst worldwide depression. Presciently, Keynes argues in the first part
of his essay (not reprinted here) that there is no rationale for economic pessimism.
Present troubles are merely growing pains; massive accumulation of capital and
accelerated technological progress means "in the long run that mankind is solving
its economic problem." In the second part of his essay, excerpted below, Keynes
contemplates what it will mean for us to do so. He suggests that, once the struggle
for subsistence is no longer the consuming activity of human life, we will have re-
linquished our "traditional purpose"—moneymaking—and be forced to find new
activity and new purpose. Freed from the need to make a living, we will have to
cultivate "the arts of life," to value ends above means, prefer the good to the useful, and pursue enjoyment and virtue for their own sake.*

*To be sure, the "economic problem" is still far from being universally extin-
guished. But if the predicted intergenerational transfers of wealth[1] hold, there will
soon be many more children and grandchildren of wealth for whom at least some of
Keynes's concerns will become real. What are the "arts of life" we most need to cultivate? How can we encourage people to balance the pursuit of enjoyment (something unlikely to need cultivating) and the pursuit of virtue? Perhaps most important,
if we succeed in rearing young wealth holders to believe that there is more to life
than money, how do we make sure that they will continue to be responsive to the
have-nots of the world? To other worthy outlets for their philanthropic activities?*

🙢

Let us, for the sake of argument, suppose that a hundred years hence we are all
of us, on the average, eight times better off in the economic sense than we are
to-day. Assuredly there need be nothing here to surprise us.

Now it is true that the needs of human beings may seem to be insatiable.
But they fall into two classes—those needs which are absolute in the sense that
we feel them whatever the situation of our fellow human beings may be, and
those which are relative in the sense that we feel them only if their satisfaction
lifts us above, makes us feel superior to, our fellows. Needs of the second class,
those which satisfy the desire for superiority, may indeed be insatiable; for the

---

1. Estimated at between \$41 and \$136 trillion (in 1998 dollars) from 1998 to 2052 by
John J. Havens and Paul Schervish in *Millionaires and the Millennium: New Estimates of the
Forthcoming Wealth Transfer and the Prospects for a Golden Age of Philanthropy* (The Social
Welfare Research Institute at Boston College, 1999).

higher the general level, the higher still are they. But this is not so true of the absolute needs—a point may soon be reached, much sooner perhaps than we are all of us aware of, when these needs are satisfied in the sense that we prefer to devote our further energies to non-economic purposes.

Now for my conclusion, which you will find, I think, to become more and more startling to the imagination the longer you think about it.

I draw the conclusion that, assuming no important wars and no important increase in population, the *economic problem* may be solved, or be at least within sight of solution, within a hundred years. This means that the economic problem is not—if we look into the future—*the permanent problem of the human race*.

Why, you may ask, is this so startling? It is startling because—if, instead of looking into the future, we look into the past—we find that the economic problem, the struggle for subsistence, always has been hitherto the primary, most pressing problem of the human race—not only of the human race, but of the whole of the biological kingdom from the beginnings of life in its most primitive forms.

Thus we have been expressly evolved by nature—with all our impulses and deepest instincts—for the purpose of solving the economic problem. If the economic problem is solved, mankind will be deprived of its traditional purpose.

Will this be a benefit? If one believes at all in the real values of life, the prospect at least opens up the possibility of benefit. Yet I think with dread of the readjustment of the habits and instincts of the ordinary man, bred into him for countless generations, which he may be asked to discard within a few decades.

To use the language of to-day—must we not expect a general "nervous breakdown"? We already have a little experience of what I mean—a nervous breakdown of the sort which is already common enough in England and the United States amongst the wives of the well-to-do classes, unfortunate women, many of them, who have been deprived by their wealth of their traditional tasks and occupations—who cannot find it sufficiently amusing, when deprived of the spur of economic necessity, to cook and clean and mend, yet are quite unable to find anything more amusing.

To those who sweat for their daily bread leisure is a longed-for sweet—until they get it.

There is the traditional epitaph written for herself by the old charwoman:—

Don't mourn for me, friends, don't weep for me never,
For I'm going to do nothing for ever and ever.

This was her heaven. Like others who look forward to leisure, she conceived how nice it would be to spend her time listening-in—for there was another couplet which occurred in her poem:—

With psalms and sweet music the heavens'll be ringing,
But I shall have nothing to do with the singing.

Yet it will only be for those who have to do with the singing that life will be tolerable—and how few of us can sing!

Thus for the first time since his creation man will be faced with his real, his permanent problem—how to use his freedom from pressing economic cares, how to occupy the leisure, which science and compound interest will have won for him, to live wisely and agreeably and well.

The strenuous purposeful money-makers may carry all of us along with them into the lap of economic abundance. But it will be those peoples, who can keep alive, and cultivate into a fuller perfection, the art of life itself and do not sell themselves for the means of life, who will be able to enjoy the abundance when it comes.

Yet there is no country and no people, I think, who can look forward to the age of leisure and of abundance without a dread. For we have been trained too long to strive and not to enjoy. It is a fearful problem for the ordinary person, with no special talents, to occupy himself, especially if he no longer has roots in the soil or in custom or in the beloved conventions of a traditional society. To judge from the behavior and the achievements of the wealthy classes to-day in any quarter of the world, the outlook is very depressing! For these are, so to speak, our advance guard—those who are spying out the promised land for the rest of us and pitching their camp there. For they have most of them failed disastrously, so it seems to me—those who have an independent income but no associations or duties or ties—to solve the problem which has been set them.

I feel sure that with a little more experience we shall use the new-found bounty of nature quite differently from the way in which the rich use it today, and will map out for ourselves a plan of life quite otherwise than theirs.

For many ages to come the old Adam will be so strong in us that everybody will need to do *some* work if he is to be contented. We shall do more things for ourselves than is usual with the rich to-day, only too glad to have small duties and tasks and routines. But beyond this, we shall endeavor to spread the bread thin on the butter—to make what work there is still to be done to be as widely shared as possible. Three-hour shifts or a fifteen-hour week may put off the problem for a great while. For three hours a day is quite enough to satisfy the old Adam in most of us!

There are changes in other spheres too which we must expect to come. When the accumulation of wealth is no longer of high social importance, there will be great changes in the code of morals. We shall be able to rid ourselves of many of the pseudo-moral principles which have hag-ridden us for two hundred years, by which we have exalted some of the most distasteful of human qualities into the position of the highest virtues. We shall be able to afford to dare to assess the money-motive at its true value. The love of money as a possession—as distinguished from the love of money as a means to the enjoyments and realities of life—will be recognized for what it is, a somewhat disgusting morbidity, one of those semi-criminal, semi-pathological propensities which one hands over with a shudder to the specialists in mental disease. All kinds of social customs and economic practices, affecting the distribution of wealth and of economic rewards and penalties, which we now maintain at all costs, however distasteful and unjust they may be in themselves, because they are tremendously useful in promoting the accumulation of capital, we shall then be free, at last, to discard.

Of course there will still be many people with intense, unsatisfied purposiveness who will blindly pursue wealth—unless they can find some plausible substitute. But the rest of us will no longer be under any obligation to applaud and encourage them. For we shall inquire more curiously than is safe today into the true character of this "purposiveness" with which in varying degrees Nature has endowed almost all of us. For purposiveness means that we are more concerned with the remote future results of our actions than with their own quality or their immediate effects on our own environment. The "purposive" man is always trying to secure a spurious and delusive immortality for his acts by pushing his interest in them forward into time. He does not love his cat, but his cat's kittens; nor, in truth, the kittens, but only the kittens' kittens, and so on forward for ever to the end of cat-dom. For him jam is not jam unless it is a case of jam to-morrow and never jam to-day. Thus by pushing his jam always forward into the future, he strives to secure for his act of boiling it an immortality.

Let me remind you of the Professor in *Sylvie and Bruno*:—

> "Only the tailor, sir, with your little bill," said a meek voice outside the door.
>
> "Ah, well, I can soon settle *his* business," the Professor said to the children, "if you'll just wait a minute. How much is it, this year, my man?" The tailor had come in while he was speaking.
>
> "Well, it's been a-doubling so many years, you see," the tailor replied, a little gruffly, "and I think I'd like the money now. It's two thousand pound, it is!"
>
> "Oh, that's nothing!" the Professor carelessly remarked, feeling in his pocket, as if he always carried at least *that* amount about with him. "But wouldn't you like to wait just another year and make it *four* thousand? Just think how rich you'd be! Why, you might be a *king,* if you liked!"
>
> "I don't know as I'd care about being a king," the man said thoughtfully. "But it *dew* sound a powerful sight o' money! Well, I think I'll wait—"
>
> "Of course you will!" said the Professor. "There's good sense in *you,* I see. Good-day to you, my man!"
>
> "Will you ever have to pay him that four thousand pounds?" Sylvie asked as the door closed on the departing creditor.
>
> "*Never,* my child!" the Professor replied emphatically. "He'll go on doubling it till he dies. You see, it's *always* worth while waiting another year to get twice as much money!"

Perhaps it is not an accident that the race which did most to bring the promise of immortality into the heart and essence of our religions has also done most for the principle of compound interest and particularly loves this most purposive of human institutions.

I see us free, therefore, to return to some of the most sure and certain principles of religion and traditional virtue—that avarice is a vice, that the exaction of usury is a misdemeanor, and the love of money is detestable, that those walk most truly in the paths of virtue and sane wisdom who take least thought for the morrow. We shall once more value ends above means and prefer the good to the useful. We shall honor those who can teach us how to pluck the hour and the day virtuously and well, the delightful people who are capable of taking direct enjoyment in things, the lilies of the field who toil not, neither do they spin.

But beware! The time for all this is not yet. For at least another hundred years we must pretend to ourselves and to every one that fair is foul and foul is fair; for foul is useful and fair is not. Avarice and usury and precaution must be our gods for a little longer still. For only they can lead us out of the tunnel of economic necessity into daylight.

I look forward, therefore, in days not so very remote, to the greatest change which has ever occurred in the material environment of life for human beings in the aggregate. But, of course, it will all happen gradually, not as a catastrophe. Indeed, it has already begun. The course of affairs will simply be that there will be ever larger and larger classes and groups of people from whom problems of economic necessity have been practically removed. The critical difference will be realized when this condition has become so general that the nature of one's duty to one's neighbor is changed. For it will remain reasonable to be economically purposive for others after it has ceased to be reasonable for oneself.

The *pace* at which we can reach our destination of economic bliss will be governed by four things—our power to control population, our determination to avoid wars and civil dissensions, our willingness to entrust to science the direction of those matters which are properly the concern of science, and the rate of accumulation as fixed by the margin between our production and our consumption; of which the last will easily look after itself, given the first three.

Meanwhile there will be no harm in making mild preparations for our destiny, in encouraging, and experimenting in, the arts of life as well as the activities of purpose.

But, chiefly, do not let us overestimate the importance of the economic problem, or sacrifice to its supposed necessities other matters of greater and more permanent significance. It should be a matter for specialists—like dentistry. If economists could manage to get themselves thought of as humble, competent people, on a level with dentists, that would be splendid!

From "Economic Possibilities for Our Grandchildren" in *Essays in Persuasion* by John Maynard Keynes (London: Macmillan and Co., 1933), pp. 365–373. Reproduced with permission of Palgrave Macmillan.

FOUR

Effectiveness

In her memoir *Twenty Years at Hull House,* Jane Addams proudly reports the following story:

> [From the start], we were very insistent that the Settlement should not be primarily for the children, and that it was absurd to suppose that grown people would not respond to opportunities for education and social life. Our enthusiastic kindergarten teacher demonstrated this with an old woman of ninety, who, because she was left alone all day while her daughter cooked in a restaurant, had formed such a persistent habit of picking the plaster off the walls that one landlord after another refused to have her for a tenant. It required but a few weeks' time to teach her to make large paper chains, and gradually she was content to do it all day long, and in the end took quite as much pleasure in adorning the walls as she had formerly taken in demolishing them.

Assume for a moment that the time is now, and you are the benefactor of Hull House. Would you, too, proudly recount this story? Is this an example of effective philanthropy? How can you tell?

All philanthropists, large and small and whatever their goals, are interested in doing good. Hence, the effectiveness of their efforts is of prime concern. Not content with haphazard ways or impressionistic evaluations, many seek the most efficient means or procedures—strategies—to achieve their ends, as well as the most accurate quantitative measures—metrics—for assessing outcomes. As a result, a whole teaching of "strategic giving" has grown up, often neutral regarding the ends sought and therefore adaptable to most philanthropic efforts. And, while a "gold standard" for measuring philanthropic outcomes remains elusive, there are over a hundred systems of assessing philanthropic results, each vying with the next for adoption by foundations and nonprofit organizations.

But these approaches are not without their critics: Some wonder whether the goods accomplished through philanthropy really lend themselves to such tactics; others worry that their adoption may make donors risk averse, narrowing the sorts of philanthropic efforts that are undertaken and undermining the imagination, faith, and hope that often inform them.[1] Still others are concerned that the increasing rigor and expense required to measure success may discourage or disparage the thousands of small, personal charitable donations that have long constituted the major part of philanthropic largesse. Preoccupations with measurable "impact" may undervalue as well the expressions of donor ideals and personal sympathies that animate many modestly funded small foundations.

Whether or not, for example, one regards the donation of "a few weeks' time" teaching someone to make paper chains as effective philanthropy, there is little doubt that the gift made a difference, the significance of which could not be captured by head counts, flow charts, or indices of sustainability. We need to reconsider and broaden our view of philanthropic efficacy.

Concerns with strategies and metrics, popular and helpful though they may be, do not—and must not—exhaust the subject of effectiveness. Philanthropic effectiveness has its prerequisites, as well as its standards of judgment. As we already know, not all strategies are equal or equal to the task at hand; not all worthy outcomes lend themselves to quantitative measurement. The attitudes and dispositions of donors, grantmakers, and recipients all matter. So too does the quality of plans made, as well as the care and discernment with which they are executed. Expectations must be fitted to aims, as well as means to ends. Absent prudence in the selection of means suitable to the circumstances, or in the marshalling of resources, human and material, there will be little success worth measuring.

The readings in this chapter consider questions regarding both the requirements and the measures of effective philanthropy. We begin with the former:

What is required for effective philanthropy?

Heading this section is Leo Tolstoy's parable "Three Questions," which invites debate about the relative virtue of far-sighted strategy as opposed to attending to immediate concerns. The selection following, from Andrew Carnegie's "The Gospel of Wealth," sharply criticizes spontaneous relief, advocating self-help, while the next, Thomas A. Kelley's "There's No Such Thing as 'Bad' Charity," anecdotally makes vivid why the jury is still out regarding such stark alternatives.

The next two readings invite scrutiny of both the preconceptions and the attitudes we bring to our philanthropic deeds. Maeve Brennan's short story

---

1. For example, public policy professor Joel Fleishman argues that "being strategic precludes the tentative exploration and seeding of new, and sometimes conflicting, ventures that have been the source of some of our most important social innovations."

"The Joker" does so implicitly through the failed endeavor of her protagonist. Irving Kristol's speech, "Foundations and the Sin of Pride: The Myth of the Third Sector," is far more explicit, compelling us not only to take stock of the assumptions that inform the larger philanthropic culture but also to re-think what we can, or should try to, achieve.

While most philanthropists subscribe to one theory of change or another, discerning the real levers of change is still an open question, as the last four readings in this section attest. Michael A. Bailin's "Re-Engineering Philanthropy: Field Notes from the Trenches" calls for foundations that wish to effect change to first change themselves. Anton Chekov's short story "The Beggar" summons us to wonder to what extent we are important agents even in those changes we confidently think that we bring about. Nathaniel Hawthorne offers "proof," in "A Good Man's Miracle," that the goodness of a man and his intentions, not his power or wealth, produce successful change—a claim directly challenged by Daniel Akst's dictum in "Graduates, Take Heed": To make the world a better place, make money, and lots of it.

How should we judge philanthropy's effectiveness?

This is the general topic of the second set of readings in this chapter.

The first of two fictional stories is "Reb Yozifl and the Contractor," by Sholom Aleichem, which challenges us to think about the adequacy of our typical measure of philanthropic success: the utility of a venture.

Anzia Yezierska's "The Free Vacation House" invites an inside look at the trials and tribulations of evaluation as seen from the beneficiary's viewpoint, and hence encourages reflection on whether or when judging effectiveness might interfere with being effective.

The last two readings, each by an author with foundation experience, return us to more familiar grounds, though by unfamiliar paths: In "The Evaluation Wars," William A. Schambra offers an alternative to rigorous or "scientific" evaluation—most effective organizations, he claims, can be "eyeballed." Hodding Carter III in "A CEO's Perspective on Evaluation" challenges, with his journalistic eye, the rosy view philanthropists often take of their own projects: Hard evaluation is necessary, he argues, to preserve our "intellectual honesty" and to learn from our endeavors—in other words, because it promotes accountability, the subject of our next chapter.

LEO TOLSTOY

"Three Questions"

Asked to address the future role of philanthropy at a convocation of nonprofit associations, former New York Foundation executive director Madeline Lee simply identified the major issues affecting New York City, then and there in 1997, and suggested that the most "strategic" role for the nonprofit sector would entail giving priority attention to these urgent concerns. The following little parable, by renowned Russian author Leo Tolstoy (1828–1910), carries a similar message. A certain king, so that "he would never fail in anything he might undertake," seeks the answers to three questions: What is the right time to act? Who are the right people to listen to? What is the most important thing to do? Forsaking his court and counselors—the experts or professionals—he sets out to consult an old hermit, known for his wisdom. But good teacher that he is, rather than directly tell the king what to do, the hermit first demonstrates his point: live immediately—"there is only one time that is important—Now! . . . The most important man is he with whom you are . . . and the most important affair is, to do him good." So much for long-term plans and far-sighted strategies! Has the hermit's demonstration—or Madeline Lee's admonition—brought you to assent to the hermit's teaching, as it presumably did the king? Did the king ask the right questions?

ℒᎦ

It once occurred to a certain king, that if he always knew the right time to begin everything; if he knew who were the right people to listen to, and whom to avoid; and, above all, if he always knew what was the most important thing to do, he would never fail in anything he might undertake.

And this thought having occurred to him, he had it proclaimed throughout his kingdom that he would give a great reward to any one who would teach him what was the right time for every action, and who were the most necessary people, and how he might know what was the most important thing to do.

And learned men came to the King, but they all answered his questions differently.

In reply to the first question, some said that to know the right time for every action, one must draw up in advance, a table of days, months and years, and must live strictly according to it. Only thus, said they, could everything be done at its proper time. Others declared that it was impossible to decide beforehand the right time for every action; but that, not letting oneself be absorbed in idle pastimes, one should always attend to all that was going on, and then do what was most needful. Others, again, said that however attentive the

King might be to what was going on, it was impossible for one man to decide correctly the right time for every action, but that he should have a Council of wise men, who would help him to fix the proper time for everything.

But then again others said there were some things which could not wait to be laid before a Council, but about which one had at once to decide whether to undertake them or not. But in order to decide that, one must know beforehand what was going to happen. It is only magicians who know that; and, therefore, in order to know the right time for every action, one must consult magicians.

Equally various were the answers to the second question. Some said, the people the King most needed were his councilors; others, the priests; others, the doctors; while some said the warriors were the most necessary.

To the third question, as to what was the most important occupation: some replied that the most important thing in the world was science. Others said it was skill in warfare; and others, again, that it was religious worship.

All the answers being different, the King agreed with none of them, and gave the reward to none. But still wishing to find the right answers to his questions, he decided to consult a hermit, widely renowned for his wisdom.

The hermit lived in a wood which he never quitted, and he received none but common folk. So the King put on simple clothes, and before reaching the hermit's cell dismounted from his horse, and, leaving his body-guard behind, went on alone.

When the King approached, the hermit was digging the ground in front of his hut. Seeing the King, he greeted him and went on digging. The hermit was frail and weak, and each time he stuck his spade into the ground and turned a little earth, he breathed heavily.

The King went up to him and said: "I have come to you, wise hermit, to ask you to answer three questions: How can I learn to do the right thing at the right time? Who are the people I most need, and to whom should I, therefore, pay more attention than to the rest? And, what affairs are the most important, and need my first attention?"

The hermit listened to the King, but answered nothing. He just spat on his hand and recommenced digging.

"You are tired," said the King, "let me take the spade and work awhile for you."

"Thanks!" said the hermit, and, giving the spade to the King, he sat down on the ground.

When he had dug two beds, the King stopped and repeated his questions. The hermit again gave no answer, but rose, stretched out his hand for the spade, and said:

"Now rest awhile and let me work a bit."

But the King did not give him the spade, and continued to dig. One hour passed, and another. The sun began to sink behind the trees, and the King at last stuck the spade into the ground, and said:

"I came to you, wise man, for an answer to my questions. If you can give me none, tell me so, and I will return home."

"Here comes some one running," said the hermit, "let us see who it is."

The King turned round, and saw a bearded man come running out of the wood. The man held his hands pressed against his stomach, and blood was flowing from under them. When he reached the King, he fell fainting on the ground moaning feebly. The King and the hermit unfastened the man's clothing. There was a large wound in his stomach. The King washed it as best he could, and bandaged it with his handkerchief and with a towel the hermit had. But the blood would not stop flowing, and the King again and again removed the bandage soaked with warm blood, and washed and rebandaged the wound. When at last the blood ceased flowing, the man revived and asked for something to drink. The King brought fresh water and gave it to him. Meanwhile the sun had set, and it had become cool. So the King, with the hermit's help, carried the wounded man into the hut and laid him on the bed. Lying on the bed the man closed his eyes and was quiet; but the King was so tired with his walk and with the work he had done, that he crouched down on the threshold, and also fell asleep—so soundly that he slept all through the short summer night. When he awoke in the morning, it was long before he could remember where he was, or who was the strange bearded man lying on the bed and gazing intently at him with shining eyes.

"Forgive me!" said the bearded man in a weak voice, when he saw that the King was awake and was looking at him.

"I do not know you, and have nothing to forgive you for," said the King.

"You do not know me, but I know you. I am that enemy of yours who swore to revenge himself on you, because you executed his brother and seized his property. I knew you had gone alone to see the hermit, and I resolved to kill you on your way back. But the day passed and you did not return. So I came out from my ambush to find you, and I came upon your bodyguard, and they recognized me, and wounded me. I escaped from them, but should have bled to death had you not dressed my wound. I wished to kill you, and you have saved my life. Now, if I live, and if you wish it, I will serve you as your most faithful slave, and will bid my sons do the same. Forgive me!"

The King was very glad to have made peace with his enemy so easily, and to have gained him for a friend, and he not only forgave him, but said he would send his servants and his own physician to attend him, and promised to restore his property.

Having taken leave of the wounded man, the King went out into the porch and looked around for the hermit. Before going away he wished once more to beg an answer to the questions he had put. The hermit was outside, on his knees, sowing seeds in the beds that had been dug the day before.

The King approached him, and said:

"For the last time, I pray you to answer my questions, wise man."

"You have already been answered!" said the hermit, still crouching on his thin legs, and looking up at the King, who stood before him.

"How answered? What do you mean?" asked the King.

"Do you not see," replied the hermit. "If you had not pitied my weakness yesterday, and had not dug those beds for me, but had gone your way, that man would have attacked you, and you would have repented of not having stayed with me. So the most important time was when you were digging the beds; and I was the most important man; and to do me good was your most important business. Afterwards when that man ran to us, the most important time was when you were attending to him, for if you had not bound up his wounds he would have died without having made peace with you. So he was the most important man, and what you did for him was your most important business. Remember then: there is only one time that is important—Now! It is the most important time because it is the only time when we have any power. The most necessary man is he with whom you are, for no man knows whether he will ever have dealings with any one else: and the most important affair is, to do him good, because for that purpose alone was man sent into this life!"

From *What Men Live By, and Other Tales,* translated from Russian by L. and A. Maude.

ANDREW CARNEGIE

From "The Gospel of Wealth"

In his famous, still influential essay "Wealth," later republished as "The Gospel of Wealth," prototypical modern philanthropist Andrew Carnegie (1835–1919) sets forth a template for effective giving: Those of great wealth should allocate and ad-minister their surplus while alive (rather than entrust charities or bequests), give to institutions (rather than individuals), and help others who will help themselves (rather than offer relief). "Thus is the problem of rich and poor to be solved," Carnegie claims. This selection highlights Carnegie's argument for the prime importance and efficacy of promoting self-help. While "helping those who help themselves" has been updated by such terms as "empowerment" and "self-determination," it indubitably remains a powerful motif in contemporary philan-thropy. But can it effectively "solve" anyone's problem, let alone the large social problem of the disparity between the rich and poor? Is Carnegie right in claiming that a philanthropic dollar misspent does greater harm than many times that amount well spent could do good? Is there really such a thing as "bad charity" (see selection by Kelley below)?

ℛ

. . . Those who would administer wisely must, indeed, be wise; for one of the serious obstacles to the improvement of our race is indiscriminate charity. It were better for mankind that the millions of the rich were thrown into the sea than so spent as to encourage the slothful, the drunken, the unworthy. Of ev-ery thousand dollars spent in so-called charity to-day, it is probable that nine hundred and fifty dollars is unwisely spent; so spent, indeed, as to produce the very evils which it proposes to mitigate or cure. A well-known writer of philo-sophic books admitted the other day that he had given a quarter of a dollar to a man who approached him as he was coming to visit the house of his friend. He knew nothing of the habits of this beggar; knew not the use that would be made of this money, although he had every reason to suspect that it would be spent improperly. This man professed to be a disciple of Herbert Spencer;[1] yet the quarter-dollar given that night will probably work more injury than all the money which its thoughtless donor will ever be able to give in true charity will do good. He only gratified his own feelings, saved himself from annoyance,— and this was probably one of the most selfish and very worst actions of his life, for in all respects he is most worthy.

---

1. Herbert Spencer, a sociologist, is widely known as the father of Social Darwinism.—Ed.

In bestowing charity, the main consideration should be to help those who will help themselves; to provide part of the means by which those who desire to improve may do so; to give those who desire to rise the aids by which they may rise; to assist, but rarely or never to do all. Neither the individual nor the race is improved by almsgiving. Those worthy of assistance, except in rare cases, seldom require assistance. The really valuable men of the race never do, except in the cases of accident or sudden change. Every one has, of course, cases of individuals brought to his own knowledge where temporary assistance can do genuine good, and these he will not overlook. But the amount which can be wisely given by the individual for individuals is necessarily limited by his lack of knowledge of the circumstances connected with each. He is the only true re-former who is as careful and as anxious not to aid the unworthy as he is to aid the worthy, and, perhaps, even more so, for in almsgiving more injury is probably done by rewarding vice than by relieving virtue.

The rich man is thus almost restricted to following the examples of [those] . . . who know that the best means of benefiting the community is to place within its reach the ladders upon which the aspiring can rise—free librar-ies, parks, and means of recreation, by which men are helped in body and mind; works of art, certain to give pleasure and improve the public taste; and public institutions of various kinds, which will improve the general condition of the people;—in this manner returning their surplus wealth to the mass of their fellows in the forms best calculated to do them lasting good.

Originally published as "Wealth" in the *North American Review* 147 (June 1889).

THOMAS A. KELLEY

"There's No Such Thing as 'Bad' Charity"

In 1986, Thomas A. Kelly was a Peace Corps volunteer in a village of Niger. Made uncomfortable by the constant supplications he encountered when visiting the capital, and convinced such alms did no great good, he yet found a method for distributing them. Years later, in teaching a Nonprofit Law class, Kelley condemned as "bad charity" just such alms-giving, cautioning his students of its inability to relieve suffering in any meaningful way. ("Good" charity, by contrast, is strategic, he argued: it helps people "to empower themselves and challenge and reform the structures that cause them to be poor.") But in this article, thinking through the distinction he made with such confidence, he questions its reasonableness. For he recalls the chance encounter he had with one of the beggars whom he had known, on a return trip to Niger fourteen years after his tour with the Peace Corps. Kelley's experience complicates things for him. Should it do so for his students, or his readers? Is there such a thing as "bad" charity?

※

Having just finished my first year of teaching law at the University of North Carolina, I'm thinking about what I can do to be a better teacher of topics like the law of nonprofit organizations. One thing is certain: I have to resist my urge to oversimplify complex issues.

In discussing with students the nature of charity in the United States, I suggested that there are two kinds: alms to the poor that make us feel good but do little to relieve suffering, and strategic philanthropic investment that encourages individuals and communities to empower themselves and challenge and reform the structures that cause them to be poor. My point was that the first kind of charity is bad, the second kind is good, and that our country's legal system tends to promote the bad kind.

That is, of course, a ridiculously pared-down version of a complex issue. I am fully aware that the nature of charity is as much a question of spirituality and emotion as of law; but how can one fit all that into a 50-minute class period?

Looking back, I realize that I could have drawn on a story from my own recent experience that might have helped illustrate how maddeningly and wonderfully complicated the theory and practice of charity is.

The story is recent, but its roots go back to 1986 when I was a Peace Corps volunteer in the West African republic of Niger, one of the world's poorest countries. I lived in a small village in the bush, but periodically I would ride my government-issue, cherry-red motorcycle into the capital to do errands, stopping at the bank, post office, and street market.

At each of these stops a crowd of beggars, many of them grievously crippled, would limp, wheel, and skitter toward me yelling, "*C'est moi le gardien!*" They wanted to "guard" my motorcycle while I did my errands, with the understanding that the appointed "*gardien*" would collect a small payment when my shopping was complete. Like squeegee men in New York City, they were offering an unneeded service for a fee as a dignified alternative to asking for money.

In my early days in Niger, I was appalled by the commotion that the beggars caused. Giving them money, I thought, would do little good beyond furnishing them with their next meal. I could accomplish far more by using my money and energy to build wells, start vegetable gardens, and stock local schools with materials. I should focus on attacking the causes of poverty. Besides, from the perspective of an American, all that street begging was downright unseemly.

I did not yet understand that begging by the needy has an honored place in the religious and cultural traditions of Niger. Nor did I understand that people of means in Niger feel a sense of obligation to give as much as they can to the less fortunate, including those who beg on the street. Perhaps most important, I did not yet understand that it was not they but I who was causing the commotion with my ostentatious motorcycle, my Ray-Ban glasses, and my L. L. Bean backpack brimming with goods that were beyond the means of most Nigerians.

Long before I understood any of this, I solved my problem with the beggars by establishing a sort of business relationship with one or two at each of my stops. At the sound of my motorcycle, the crowd would look up and prepare to surge, but when they saw who was driving, only those with whom I did regular business would come forward. Over time, I developed an understanding that the beggars and I were playing our appropriate roles. They were needy, and it was right that they should be asking for money. From their perspective, I was ridiculously wealthy. It therefore was my legitimate role to respond to their requests generously. At some point during my stay in Niger I got over my very American discomfort and resentment at being asked for money by people on the street. When I had money, I gave freely.

In 1988, after a bit more than two years in Niger, I returned to the United States, and I then went to law school, married, had children, and bought a house. I did not often think of my *gardien* friends, though occasionally the sight of a red motorcycle or a man in a wheelchair would bring them to mind.

Then, earlier this year, I received a grant to return to Niger for a month to study African law.

On my last afternoon in the country, I visited one of the capital's tourist markets to buy gifts for friends and family. I walked slowly down a dirt lane lined with tin-shed "boutiques," poking my head into each to view the wares.

It took an hour or so of shopping and fierce bargaining to fill my bag with trinkets. I was heading for a taxi stand when a man across the road hailed me.

"My friend, you have not yet looked in my shop. Please come and see." I was about to decline, but when I glanced over I saw that he was in a wheelchair. For some reason—pity, curiosity, the faint memory that handicapped people in Niger are known for their excellent artisanship—I trotted across the lane.

In the man's shed I saw some well-made, brightly colored leather key chains. "How much?" I asked him. I did not look directly at him, partly because I was trying to convey indifference and thereby establish my bargaining position, and partly because he was still out on the lane in his wheelchair. He replied, "How much will you give me for them?" This is a typical opening gambit by West African merchants dealing with tourists. I countered by naming a price that was too low by at least half.

"Okay," he replied, "and pick out another one as a gift from me."

Jolted out of my adversarial posturing by this unusual generosity, I looked directly at him for the first time. What I saw was a sweet, bright, and faintly familiar smile.

Fourteen years earlier, he had been my regular *gardien* at the post office. I would buy my stamps inside, and then he and I would sit outside, sipping sodas and talking about the affairs of the day. Now he was a prosperous merchant dressed in expensive robes and an *el hajji* scarf worn by Muslims who have made the pilgrimage to Mecca.

After exchanging customary greetings, I asked him somewhat abruptly, "How did you become such a big man?" He spread his arms and craned his neck forward, as if to indicate "Isn't it obvious?"

"I saved the money people gave me at the post office, and when I had enough, I started my own business. Allah be praised," he said.

We talked for a few more minutes, exchanged customary blessings, and parted with the promise that we would share each other's company again.

That is where the story ends, at least for now. And if I am able to work it into my Nonprofit Law class next year, what point will it illustrate? Maybe that labeling any kind of charity as "bad" is silly. Maybe that trying to distinguish between alms and empowerment is impossible: I gave alms to my *gardien* friends, but at least one of them used the money to empower himself. Or maybe I'll just tell the story, and leave it to the students to draw their own conclusions.

MAEVE BRENNAN

"The Joker"

Isobel Bailey, the protagonist of this short story by Irish-born writer and longtime
New Yorker *columnist Maeve Brennan (1917–1993), is a believer in law, order, and*
"organized charity." Her annual Christmas supper aims to treat a handful of
"waifs"—slight acquaintances she's designated as "inexplicably separate"—to a
pleasant, elegant meal. This year breaks tradition—Isobel invites an old family
friend, Vincent, and, in a burst of enthusiastic sympathy, allows a tramp to sup in
the kitchen, overriding her "strict orders to shut the door to beggars." But the eve-
ning and its hostess begin to unravel, and seemingly fail completely when the beg-
gar acts with shocking ingratitude. Isobel is horrified as the "effect" she wishes to
produce is spoiled. Is Isobel fit to be an effective philanthropist? Is her philanthropic
effort a complete failure? Does her charity help anyone? More generally, do the dis-
positions or motives of givers necessarily determine the effectiveness of their gifts?
Who—what—is "the joker" in the story? What does the existence of "jokers" imply
for effective philanthropy?

✌

Waifs, Isobel Bailey called her Christmas Day guests. This year she had three
coming, three waifs—a woman, an elderly man, and a young man—respectable people, well brought up, gentle-looking, neatly dressed, to all appearances
the same as everybody else, but lost just the same. She had a private list of such
people, not written down, and she drew on it every year as the holiday season
descended. Her list of waifs did not grow shorter. Indeed, it seemed to lengthen
as the years went by, and she was still young, only thirty-one. What makes a
waif, she thought (most often as winter came on, always at Christmas); what
begins it? When do people get that fatal separate look? Are waifs born?

Once she had thought that it was their lack of poise that marked them—
because who ever saw a poised waif? You see them defiant, stiff, rude, silent,
but aren't they always bewildered? Still, bewilderment was not a state reserved
for waifs only. Neither was it, she decided, a matter of having no money,
though money seemed to have a great deal to do with it. Sometimes you could
actually see people change into waifs, right before your eyes. Girls suddenly
became old maids, or at least they developed an incurably *single* look. Cheerful, bustling women became dazed widows. Men lost their grip and became
unsure-looking. It wasn't any one thing that made a waif. Isobel was sure of
that. It wasn't being crippled, or being in disgrace, or even not being married.
It was a shameful thing to be a waif, but it was also mysterious. There was no

accounting for it or defining it, and over and over again she was drawn back to her original idea—that waifs were simply people who had been squeezed off the train because there was no room for them. They had lost their tickets. Some of them never had owned a ticket. Perhaps their parents had failed to equip them with a ticket. Poor things, they were stranded. During ordinary days of the year, they could hide their plight. But at Christmas, when the train drew up for that hour of recollection and revelation, how the waifs stood out, burning in their solitude. Every Christmas Day (said Isobel to herself, smiling whimsically) was a station on the journey of life. There on the windy platform the waifs gathered in shame, to look in at the fortunate ones in the warm, lighted train. Not all of them stared in, she knew; some looked away. She, Isobel, looked them all over and decided which ones to invite into her own lighted carriage. She liked to think that she occupied a first-class carriage—their red brick house in Bronxville, solid, charming, waxed and polished, well heated, filled with flowers, stocked with glass and silver and clean towels.

Isobel believed implicitly in law, order, and organization. She believed strongly in organized charity. She gave regular donations to charity, and she served willingly and conscientiously on several committees. She felt it was only fair that she should help those less fortunate than herself, though there was a point where she drew the line. She never gave money casually on the street, and her maids had strict orders to shut the door to beggars. "There are places where these people can apply for help," she said.

It was different with the Christmas waifs. For one thing, they were not only outside society, they were outside organized charity. They were included in no one's plans. And it was in the spirit of Christmas that she invited them to her table. They were part of the tradition and ceremony of Christmas, which she loved. She enjoyed decking out the tree, and eating the turkey and plum pudding, and making quick, gay calls at the houses of friends, and going to big parties, and giving and receiving presents. She and Edwin usually accepted an invitation for Christmas night, and sometimes they sent out cards for a late, small supper, but the afternoon belonged to the waifs. She and Edwin had so much, she felt it was only right. She felt that it was beautifully appropriate that she should open her house to the homeless on Christmas Day, the most complete day of the year, when everything stopped swirling and the pattern became plain.

Isobel's friends were vaguely conscious of her custom of inviting waifs to spend Christmas afternoon. When they heard that she had entertained "poor Miss T." or "poor discouraged Mr. F." at her table, they shook their heads and reflected that Isobel's kindness was real. It wasn't assumed, they said wonderingly. She really was kind.

The first of this year's waifs to arrive was Miss Amy Ellis, who made blouses for Isobel and little silk smocks for Susan, Isobel's five-year-old daughter. Isobel had never seen Miss Ellis except in her workroom, where she wore, summer and winter, an airy, arty smock of natural-color pongee. Today, she wore a black silk dress that was draped into a cowl around her shoulders, leaving her arms bare. And Miss Ellis's arms, Isobel saw at once, with a lightning flash of intuition, were the key to Miss Ellis's character, and to her life. Thin, stringy, cold, and white, stretched stiff with emptiness—they were what made her look like a waif. Could it be that Miss Ellis was a waif *because* of her arms? It was a thought. Miss Ellis's legs matched her arms, certainly, and it was easy to see, through the thin stuff of her dress, that her shoulders were too high and pointed. Her neck crept disconsolately down into a hollow and discolored throat. Her greeny-gold hair was combed into a limp short cap, betraying the same arty spirit that inspired her to wear the pongee smock. Her earrings, which dangled, had been hammered out of some coal-like substance. Her deep, lashless eyes showed that she was all pride and no spirit. She was hopeless. But it had all started with her arms, surely. They gave her away.

Miss Ellis had brought violets for Isobel, a new detective story for Edwin, and a doll's smock for Susan. She sat down in a corner of the sofa, crossed her ankles, expressed pleasure at the sight of the fire, and accepted a Martini from Edwin. Edwin Bailey was thirty-seven and a successful corporation lawyer. His handshake was warm and firm, and his glance was alert. His blond hair was fine and straight, and his stomach looked as flat and hard as though he had a board thrust down inside his trousers. He was tall and temperate. The darkest feeling he acknowledged was contempt. Habitually he viewed the world—his own world and the world reflected in the newspapers—with tolerance. He was unaware of his wife's theories about Christmas waifs, but he would have accepted them unquestioningly, as he accepted everything about Isobel. "My wife is the most mature human being I have ever met," he said sometimes. Then, too, Isobel was never jealous, because jealousy was childish. And she was never angry. "But if you understand, really understand, you simply cannot be angry with people," she would say, laughing.

Now she set about charming Miss Ellis, and Edwin had settled back lazily to watch them when the second waif, Vincent Lace, appeared in the doorway. He sprinted impetuously across the carpet and, without glancing to the right or to the left, fell on both knees before Susan, who was curled on the hearth rug, undressing her new doll.

"Ah, the grand little girl!" cried Vincent. "Sure she's the living image of her lovely mother! And what name have they put on you, love?"

"Susan," said the child coldly, and she got up and went to perch under the spreading branches of the splendid tree that blazed gorgeously from ceiling to floor between two tall windows. Beyond the windows, the narrow street lay chill and gray, except when the wind, blowing down the hill, swept before it a ragged leaf of Christmas tissue paper, red or green, or a streamer of colored ribbon.

Undisturbed by the child's desertion, Vincent rocked back on his plump behind, and wrapped his arms around his knees, and favored his host, then Miss Ellis, and, finally, Isobel with a dazzling view of his small, decaying teeth.

"Well, Isobel," he murmured, "little Isobel of the peat-brown eyes. You still have the lovely eyes, Isobel. But what am I thinking of at all!" he shouted, bounding to his feet. "Sure your husband will think me a terrible fellow entirely. Forgive me, Isobel, but the little girl took my breath away. She's yourself all over again."

"Edwin, this is our Irish poet," Isobel said. "Vincent Lace, a dear friend of Father's. I see you still wear the red bow tie, Vincent, your old trademark. I noticed it first thing when I ran into you the other day. As a matter of fact, it was the tie that caught my attention. You were never without it, were you."

"Ah, we all have our little conceits, Isobel," Vincent said, smiling disarmingly at Edwin.

Vincent's face appeared to have been vigorously stretched, either by too much pain or by too much laughter, and when he was not smiling his expression was one of dignified truculence. He was more obviously combed and scrubbed than a sixty-three-year-old man should be, and his bright-blue eyes were anxious. Twenty years ago, he had come from Ireland to do a series of lectures on Irish literature at colleges and universities all over the United States. In his suitcase, he carried several copies of the two thin volumes of poetry that had won him his contract.

"My poems drive the fellows at home stark mad," Vincent had confided to Isobel's father, the first time he visited their house. "I pay no attention to the modern rubbish at all. All that crowd thinks of is making pretty-sounding imitations of Yeats and his bunch. Yeats, Yeats, Yeats, that's all they know. But my masters are long since dead. I go back in spirit to those grand eighteenth-century souls who wandered the bogs and hills of our unfortunate country, and who broke bread with the people, and who wrote out of the heart of the people."

At this point (for it was a speech Isobel and the others were often to hear), he would leap to his feet and intone in his native Irish tongue the names of the men he admired, and with every syllable his voice would grow more laden, until at the last it seemed that he would have to release a sob, but he never did, although his small blue eyes would be wet and angry. With his wild black hair, his red tie, and his sharp tongue, he quickly became a general favorite, and when his tour was over, he accepted an offer from one of the New York universities and settled down among his new and hospitable friends. Isobel's father, who had had an Irish grandmother, took to Vincent at once, and there had been a period, Isobel remembered, when her mother couldn't plan a dinner without being forced to include Vincent. At the age of fifty, he had lost his university post. Everyone knew it was because he drank too much, but Vincent blamed it on some intrigue in the department. He was stunned. He had never thought such a thing could happen to him. Isobel remembered him shouting at her father across the dinner table, "They'll get down on their knees to me! I'll go back on my own terms!" Then he had put his head in his hands and cried, and her mother had got up and left the room in disgust. Isobel remembered that he had borrowed from everyone. After her father died, her family dropped Vincent. Everyone dropped him. He made too much of a nuisance of himself. Occasionally, someone would report having seen him in a bar. He was always shouting about his wrongs. He was no good, that was the sum of it. He never really had been any good, although his quick tongue and irreverent air had given him the appearance of brilliance.

A month before, Isobel had run into him on the street, their first meeting for many years. Vincent is a waif, she had thought, looking at him in astonishment. Vincent, the eloquent, romantic poet of her childhood, an unmistakable waif. It was written all over him. It was in every line of his seedy, imploring face. Two days before Christmas, she had invited him to dinner. He was delighted. He had arrived in what he imagined to be his best form—roguish, teasing, sly, and melancholy.

Edwin offered him a Martini, and he said fussily that he was on the wagon. "I will take a cigarette, though," he said, and selected one from the box on the table beside him. Isobel found with disagreeable surprise that she remembered his hands, which were small and stumpy, with long pared nails. Dreadful hands. She wondered what wretchedness they had brought him through in the years since she had known him. And the famous bow tie, she thought with amusement—how poorly it goes under that fat, disappointed face. Clinging to that distinctive tie, as though anyone connected him with the tie, or with anything any more.

The minute Jonathan Quin walked into the room, Isobel saw that she could expect nothing from him in the way of conversation. He will be no help at all, she thought, but this did not matter to her, because she never expected much from her Christmas guests. At a dinner party a few days before, she had been seated next to a newspaper editor and had asked him if there were any young people on his staff who might be at a loose end for Christmas. The next day, he had telephoned and given her Jonathan's name, explaining that he was a reporter who had come to New York from a little town in North Carolina and knew no one.

At first, entering the soft, enormous, firelit room, Jonathan took Miss Ellis to be his hostess, because of her black dress, and then, confused over his mistake, he stumbled around, looking for a chair to hide in. His feet were large. He wore loose, battered black shoes that had been polished until every break and scratch showed. He had put new laces in the shoes. Edwin asked him a few encouraging questions about his work on the newspaper, and he nodded and stammered and joggled his drink and finally told them that he was finding the newspaper a very interesting place.

Vincent said, "That's a magnificent scarlet in your dress, Isobel. It suits you. A triumphant, regal color it is."

Isobel, who was sitting in a yellow chair, with her back to the glittering tree, glanced down at her slim wool dress.

"Christmas red, Vincent. I think it is the exact red for Christmas, don't you? I wore it decorating the tree last night."

"And my pet Susan dressed up in the selfsame color, like a little red berry she is!" cried Vincent, throwing his intense glance upon the silent child, who ignored him. He was making a great effort to be the witty, rakish professor of her father's day, and at the same time deferring slyly to Edwin. He did not know that this was to be his only visit, no matter how polite he proved himself to be.

It was a frightful thing about Vincent, Isobel thought. But there was no use getting involved with him. He was too hard to put up with, and she knew what a deadly fixture he could become in a household. "Some of those ornaments used to be on the tree at home, Vincent," she said suddenly. "You might remember one or two of them. They must be almost as old as I am."

Vincent looked at the tree and then said amiably, "I can't remember what I did last year. Or perhaps I should say I prefer not to remember. But it was very kind of you to think of me, Isobel. Very kind." He covertly watched the drinks getting lower in the glasses.

Isobel began to think it had been a mistake to invite him. Old friends should never become waifs. It was easier to think about Miss Ellis, who was, after all, a stranger. Pitiful people, she thought. How they drag their wretched lives along with them. She allowed time for Jonathan to drink one Martini— one would be more than enough for that confused head—before she stood up to shepherd them all in to dinner.

The warm pink dining room smelled of spice, of roasting turkey, and of roses. The tablecloth was of stiff, icy white damask, and the centerpiece—of holly and ivy and full-blown blood-red roses—bloomed and flamed and cast a hundred small shadows trembling among the crystal and the silver. In the fireplace a great log, not so exuberant as the one in the living room, glowed a powerful dark red.

Vincent startled them all with a loud cry of pleasure. "Isobel, Isobel, you remembered!" He grasped the back of the chair on which he was to sit and stared in exaggerated delight at the table.

"I knew you'd notice," Isobel said, pleased. "It's the centerpiece," she explained to the others. "My mother always had red roses and holly arranged just like that in the middle of our table at home at Christmas time. And Vincent always came to Christmas dinner, didn't you, Vincent?"

"Christmas dinner and many other dinners," Vincent said, when they were seated. "Those were the happiest evenings of my life. I often think of them."

"Even though my mother used to storm down in a rage at four in the morning and throw you out, so my father could get some sleep before going to court in the morning," Isobel said slyly.

"We had some splendid discussions, your father and I. And I wasn't always thrown out. Many a night I spent on your big red sofa. Poor old Matty used to find me there, surrounded by glasses and ashtrays and the books your father would drag down to prove me in the wrong, and the struggle *she* used to have getting me out before your mother discovered me! Poor Matty, she lived in fear that I'd fall asleep with a lighted cigarette going, and burn the house down around your ears. But I remember every thread in that sofa, every knot, I should say. Who has it now, Isobel? I hope you have it hidden away somewhere. In the attic, of course. That's where you smart young things would put a comfortable old piece of furniture like that. The most comfortable bed I ever lay on."

Delia, the bony Irish maid, was serving them so discreetly that every movement she made was an insertion. She fitted the dishes and plates onto the table as though they were going into narrow slots. Her thin hair was pressed into stiff waves under her white cap, and she appeared to hear nothing, but she already had given Alice, the cook, who was her aunt, a description of Vincent Lace that had her doubled up in evil mirth beside her hot stove. Sometimes Isobel, hearing the raucous, jeering laughter of these two out in the kitchen, would find time to wonder about all the reports she had ever heard about the soft voices of the Irish.

"Isobel tells me you've started a bookshop near the university, Mr. Lace," Edwin said cordially. "That must be interesting work."

"Well, now, I wouldn't exactly say I started it, Mr. Bailey," Vincent said. "It's only that they needed someone to advise them on certain phases of Irish writing, and I'm helping to build up that department in the store, although of course I help out wherever they need me. I like talking to the customers, and then I have plenty of time for my own writing, because I'm only obliged to be there half the day. Like all decent-minded gentlemen of leisure, I dabble in writing, Mr. Bailey. And speaking of that, I had a note the other day from an old student of mine who had through some highly unlikely chance come across my name in the Modern Encyclopaedia. An article on the history of house painting, Isobel. What do you think of that? Mr. Quin and Miss Ellis, Isobel and her father knew me as an accomplished and, if I may say so, a reasonably witty exponent of Irish letters. Students fought with tooth and with nail to hear my lecture on Irish writers. . . . 'Envy Is the Spur,' I called it. But to get back to my ink-stained ex-student, whose name escapes me. He wanted to know if I remembered a certain May morning when I led the entire student body, or as many as I could lure from the library and from the steps of the building, down to riot outside Quanley's—a low and splendid drinking establishment of that time, Mr. Quin—to riot, I repeat, for one hour, in protest against their failure to serve me, in the middle hours of the same morning, the final glass that I felt to be my due."

"Well, that must have been quite an occasion, Mr. Lace, I should imagine," Miss Ellis said.

Vincent turned his excited stare on Isobel. "You wouldn't remember that morning, Isobel."

"I couldn't honestly say if I remember it or not, Vincent. You had so many escapades. There seemed to be no end to your ingenuity."

"Oh, I was a low rascal. Miss Ellis, I was a scoundrelly fellow in those days. But when I lectured, they listened. They listened to me. Isobel, you attended one or two of my lectures. I flatter myself now that I captivated even you with my masterly command of the language. Isobel, tell your splendid husband, and this gracious lady, and this gracious youth, that I was not always the clown they see before them now. Justify your old friend, Isobel."

"Vincent, you haven't changed at all, have you?"

"Ah, that's where you're wrong, Isobel. For I have changed a great deal. Your father would see it. You were too young. You don't remember. You're all too young," he finished discontentedly.

Miss Ellis moved nervously and seemed about to speak, but she said nothing. Edwin asked her if she thought the vogue for mystery stories was as strong as ever, and Vincent looked as if he were about to laugh contemptuously—Isobel remembered him always laughing at everything anyone said—but he kept silent and allowed the discussion to go on.

Isobel reflected that she had always known Vincent to be talky but surely he couldn't have always been the windbag he was now. Again she wished she hadn't invited him to dinner, but then she noticed how eagerly he was enjoying the food, and she relented. She was glad that he should see what a pleasant house she had, and that he should have a good meal.

Isobel was listening dreamily to Vincent's story about a book thief who stole only on Tuesdays, and only books with yellow covers, and she was trying to imagine what color Miss Ellis's lank hair must originally have been, when she became aware of Delia, standing close at her side and rasping urgently into her ear about a man begging at the kitchen door.

"Edwin," Isobel interrupted gently, "there's a man begging at the back door, and I think, since it's Christmas, we should give him his dinner, don't you?"

"What did he ask you for, Delia?" Edwin asked.

"He asked us would we give him a dollar, sir, and then he said that for a dollar and a half he'd sing us our favorite hymn," Delia said, and began to giggle unbecomingly.

"Ask him if he knows 'The boy stood on the burning deck,'" Vincent said.

"Poor man, wandering around homeless on Christmas Day!" Miss Ellis said.

"Get an extra plate, so that Mr. Bailey can give the poor fellow some turkey, Delia!" Isobel cried excitedly. "I'm glad he came here! I'm glad we have the chance to see that he has a real Christmas dinner! Edwin, you're glad, too, although you're pretending to disapprove!"

"All right, Isobel, have it your own way," Edwin said, smiling.

He filled the stranger's plate, with Delia standing judiciously by his elbow. "Give him more dressing, Edwin," Isobel said. "And Delia, see that he has plenty of hot rolls. I want him to have everything we have."

"Nothing to drink, Isobel," Edwin said. "If he hasn't been drinking already today, I'm not going to be responsible for starting him off. I hope you people don't think I'm a mean man," he added, smiling around the table.

"Not at all, Mr. Bailey," Miss Ellis said stoutly. "We all have our views on these matters. That's what makes us different. What would the world be like if we were all the same?"

"My mother says," said Jonathan hoarsely, putting one hand into his trouser pocket, "that if a person is bad off enough to ask her for something, he's worse off than she is."

"Your mother must be a very nice lady, Mr. Quin," Miss Ellis said.

"It's a curious remark, of Mr. Quin's mother," Vincent said moodily.

"Oh, of course you'd have him in at the table here and give him the house, Vincent!" Isobel cried in great amusement. "I remember your reputation for standing treat and giving, Vincent."

"Mr. Lace has the look of a generous man," Miss Ellis said, with her thin, childlike smile. The heavy earrings hung like black weights against her thin jaw.

Vincent stared at her. "Isobel remarks that I would bid the man in and give him the house," he said bitterly. "But at the moment, dear lady, I am not in the position to give him the leg of a chair, so the question hardly arises. Do you know what I would do if I was in Mr. Bailey's position, Miss Ellis? Now this is no reflection on you, Mr. Bailey. When I think of him, and what is going on in his mind at this moment, as he gazes into the heaped platter that you have so generously provided—"

"Vincent, get back to the point. What would you do in Edwin's place?" asked Isobel good-naturedly.

Vincent closed his mouth and gazed at her. "You're quite right, my dear," he said. "I tend to sermonize. It's the strangled professor in me, still writhing for an audience. Well, to put it briefly, if I were in your husband's excellent black leather shoes, I would go out to the kitchen, and I would empty my wallet, which I trust for your sake is well filled, and I would tell that man to go in peace."

"And he would laugh at you for a fool," Edwin said sharply.

"And he would laugh at me for a fool," Vincent said, "and I would know it, and I would curse him, but I would have done the only thing I could do."

"I don't get it," Jonathan said, with more self-assurance than before.

"Oh, Mr. Quin, Vincent is an actor at heart," Isobel said. "You should have come to our home when my father was alive. It was a one-man performance every time, Vincent's performance."

"I used to make you laugh, Isobel."

"Of course you did," Isobel said soothingly.

She sat and watched them all eat their salad, wondering at the same time how the man in the kitchen must feel, to come from the cold and deserted winter street into her warm house. He must be speechless at his good fortune, she thought, and she had a wild impulse to go out into the kitchen and see him for herself. She stood up and said, "I want to see if our unexpected guest has enough of everything."

She hurried through the pantry and into the white glare of the kitchen, where it was very hot. She rigidly avoided looking at the table, but she was conscious of the strange man's dark bulk against her white muslin window curtains, and of the harsh smell of his cigar. She wanted him to see her, in her red dress, with her flushed face and her sweet, expensive perfume. She owned the house. He had the right to feast his eyes on her. This was the stranger, the classical figure of the season, who had come unbidden to her feast.

Fat-armed Alice was petting the round brown pudding where a part of it had broken away as she tumbled it out of its cloth into its silver dish. Delia stood watching intently, holding away to her side—as though it were a matador's cape—the stained and steaming cloth.

"Take your time, Alice," Isobel said in her clear, nicely tempered voice. "Everything is going splendidly. It couldn't be a more successful party."

"That's very considerate of you, Ma'am," Alice said, letting her eyes roll meaningfully in the direction of the stranger, as though she were tipping Isobel off.

As she turned to leave the kitchen, Isobel saw the man at the table. She did not mean to see him. She had no intention of looking at him, but she did look. She saw that he had hair and hands, and she knew that he had sight, because she felt his eyes on her, but she could not have given a description of him, because in that rapid, silent glance all she really saw was the thick, filthy stub in his smiling mouth.

His cigar, she thought, sitting down again in the dining room. She leaned forward and took a sip of wine. Miss Ellis's arms, Vincent's bow tie, this boy's broken shoes, and now the beggar's cigar.

"How is our other guest getting along out there, Delia?" Isobel asked when the salad plates were being cleared away.

"Ah, he's all right, Ma'am. He's sitting there and smiling to himself. He's very quiet, so he is."

"Has he said nothing at all, Delia?"

"Only when he took an old cigar butt he has out of his pocket. He said to Alice that he strained his back picking it up. He said he made a promise to his mother never to step down off the sidewalk to pick up a butt of a cigar or a cigarette, and he says this one was halfway out in the middle of the street."

"He must have hung on to a lamp-post!" Jonathan cried, delighted.

"Edwin, send a cigar to that poor fellow when Delia comes in again, will you?" Isobel said. "I'd like to feel he had something decent to smoke for once."

Delia came in, proudly bearing the flaming pudding, and Edwin told her to take a cigar for the man in the kitchen.

"And don't forget an extra plate for his pudding, Delia," Isobel said happily.

"Oh, your mother was a mighty woman, Isobel," Vincent said, "even though we didn't always see eye to eye."

"Well, I'm sure you agreed on the important things, Mr. Lace," Miss Ellis said warmly.

"I don't like to disappoint or disillusion you, Miss Ellis, but it was on the important things we disagreed. She thought they were unimportant."

A screech of surprise and rage was heard from the kitchen, which up to that time had sent to their ears only the subdued and pleasant tinkling of glasses and dishes and silver. They were therefore prepared for—indeed, they compelled, by their paralyzed silence—the immediate appearance of Delia, who materialized without her cap, and with her eyes aglow, looking as though she had been taken by the hair and dropped from a great height.

"That fellow out there in the kitchen!" she cried. "He's gone!"

"Did he take something?" asked Edwin keenly.

"No, sir. At least, now, I don't think he took anything. I'll look and see this minute."

"Delia, calm yourself," Isobel said. "What was all the noise about?"

"He flew off when I was in here with the pudding, Ma'am. I went out to give him the cigar Mr. Bailey gave me for him, and he was gone, clean out of sight. I ran over to the window, thinking to call him back for his cigar, as long as I had it in my hand, and there wasn't a sign of him anywhere. Alice didn't even know he was out of the chair till she heard the outside door bang after him."

"Now, Delia. It was rude of him to run off like that when you and Alice and all of us have been at such pains to be nice to him, but I'm sure there's no need for all this silly fuss," Isobel said, with an exasperated grimace at Edwin.

"But Mrs. Bailey, he didn't just go!" Delia said wildly.

"Well, what did he do, then?" Edwin asked.

"Oh, sir, didn't he go and leave his dirty old cigar butt stuck down in the hard sauce, sir!" Delia cried. She put her hands over her mouth and began to make rough noises of merriment and outrage while her eyes swooped incredulously around the table.

Edwin started to rise, but Isobel stopped him with a look. "Delia," she said, "tell Alice to whip up some kind of sauce for the pudding and bring it in at once."

"Oh dear, how could he do such a thing?" Miss Ellis whispered as the door swung to on Delia. "And after you'd been so kind to him." She leaned forward impulsively to pat Isobel's hand.

"A shocking thing!" Vincent exclaimed. "Shocking! It's a rotten class of fellow would do a thing like that."

"You mustn't let him spoil your lovely dinner, Mrs. Bailey," Miss Ellis said. Then she added, to Edwin, "Mrs. Bailey is such a *person*!"

"I never cared much for hard sauce anyway," Jonathan said.

"I don't know what you're all talking about!" Isobel cried.

"We wouldn't blame you if you were upset," Vincent said. "But just because some stupid clod insults you is no reason for you to *feel* insulted."

"I think that nasty man meant to spoil our nice day," Miss Ellis said contentedly. "And he hasn't at all, has he?"

"Let's all just forget about it," Edwin said. "Isn't that right, Miss Ellis?"

"Are you people sympathizing with me?" Isobel said. "Because if you are, please stop it. I am not in the least upset, I assure you." With hands that shook violently, she began to serve the pudding.

When they had all been served, she pushed her chair back and said, "Edwin, I have to run upstairs a minute to check on the heat in Susan's room before she goes for her nap. Delia will bring the coffee inside, and I'll be down in a second."

Upstairs, in the bedroom, she cooled her beleaguered forehead with eau de cologne. She heard the chairs moving in the dining room, and then the happy voices chorusing across the hall. A moment later, she imagined she could hear the chink of their coffee cups. She wished bitterly that it was time to send them all home. She was tired of them. They talked too much. It seemed twenty years since Edwin had carved the turkey.

IRVING KRISTOL

"Foundations and the Sin of Pride: The Myth of the Third Sector"

Alluding to Oscar Wilde's famous description of the English fox hunts—"the un-speakable in full pursuit of the inedible"—one critic described foundations as "the well-intentioned in full pursuit of the not-so-relevant." This 1980 speech, by distinguished essayist and social critic Irving Kristol, goes much further, in effect describing foundations as the overreaching in full pursuit of the impossible. Addressing the annual conference of the Council on Foundations, Kristol attacks the key opinions—or "myths"—that informed and inform philanthropic culture: that philanthropy comprises a separate or separable "third sector," that foundations can and should be on the "cutting edge" of social change, and that foundation money is public money and needs to promote "the public interest." Especially relevant is Kristol's critique of the reigning passion in philanthropy, the passion for doing good. "It is a noble passion," he argues, "but it is a passion. And all passions have to be controlled. All passions are dangerous unless they are controlled." To be effective, he would have philanthropy curb its passion to do good—especially great good—with humility, discipline, and realism. Kristol thus invites us to go back to basics and rethink some fundamental ideas about philanthropy, and especially about what constitutes its effectiveness. Are the dispositions and attitudes Kristol prescribes more conducive to philanthropic efficacy than those he rejects?

Today, I want to talk about the foundation world and the sin of pride—what the Greeks called *hubris,* what the church fathers called *superbia,* namely the desire to do more good than anyone can do, a desire to do good which ends up being a form of the will to power. I think the foundation world today is suffering from the sin of pride.

Let me give you a very clear and specific instance. It is now generally said and widely thought that the foundation world (the non-profit world, as we say), constitutes a "third sector" in American society. There is, it is said, the private sector, consisting of business enterprise; the public sector, consisting of government; and then we have the third, not-for-profit sector, of which the foundations are the animating core. I would like to suggest to you that there is no third sector. Foundations are part and parcel of the private sector. They are flesh of the flesh, bone of the bone, blood of the blood of the private sector. The notion that foundations in some way constitute a sector of their own, different from, above, and superior to the other two sectors is an act of pride which will only go before a fall. That fall may consist in the fact that foundations will end up depriving themselves of their sustenance, which comes from the various parts of the private sector. Foundations are creations of the private sector.

In fact, there are only two sectors in our society: the private sector and the governmental sector. The voluntary associations in our nation do not make up a third sector; they are part of the private sector. Churches are part of the private sector. Fraternal organizations are part of the private sector. Even political parties are part of the private sector. There is no high ground which foundations can occupy and from which they can look down upon the other sectors and then try to think up policies, methods of improving the world, which are somehow disinterested in a way that those of the other two sectors are not.

The sin of pride to which I refer shows itself in many other ways. For instance, we hear it said that foundations should be setting the national agenda. But it is politics that sets the national agenda. If foundations want to get into politics, that is their privilege, but they ought to know that what they are then doing is getting into politics. They are not acting in some disinterested way; they are not representing something called "the public interest." In politics everyone represents the public interest, or rather everyone represents some conception of the public interest, for politics consists of conflicts among different conceptions of the public interest. There is no one conception of the public interest which is right as against all others. I want to emphasize that if foundations are inclined to get involved in politics this way, I think that's perfectly proper—but they ought to know what they are doing. They ought not to think that somehow they are above the political battle. They ought not to think they will not end up bearing the scars of the political battle. They ought not to think that they will be immune to political attack. Shaping the national agenda is part of the political activity of a democracy.

We also hear it said that foundations should stimulate social change, or, to use one of the favorite clichés, be on "the cutting edge" of social change. That, too, is politics. And foundations have no more perception of what is right or wrong in social change, of what is effective or what is desirable, than anyone else who is involved in politics. Foundation people are almost certainly better educated—or at least better schooled—than most people who are involved in politics. But that does not mean that they have a superior understanding of what society needs, in what directions society ought to go, or in what direction society can go.

Acts of Arrogance

There is an implicit arrogance in the notion, in the very rhetoric, that a foundation should be on "the cutting edge" of social change. First of all, it assumes you know what the cutting edge is, and you know that it cuts this way, not that way. Secondly, to be on the cutting edge of social change you have to have a complete, comprehensive, theoretical understanding of the social order—of how change is brought about and how you bring about the changes you wish as against the changes you don't wish. There is no such comprehensive theory— never has been, never will be. We do not understand ourselves that well, and we do not understand our neighbors that well. The reason we have politics at all is because the world is full of other people. Other people are never quite like us. That's the way it's always been, and that's the way it's always going to be. The notion, therefore, that any foundation or any group of scholars or any group of thinkers can have a "disinterested" conception of where society should go, one that is not open to political conflict and political argument, is an act of intellectual arrogance which can only end up creating damage to foundations. For not only can't we control social change in a disinterested way, in the end we can't control it at all. We really cannot control social change. We can try. It's very important to try. But the notion that you can come up with a master plan for social change and institute that plan and get the results that you really intended is to over-look the fact that the basic law of politics is that unanticipated consequences are always more important than the anticipated consequences of your actions.

There have been a number of such instances of intellectual arrogance over the past 25 or 30 years, some of which I have been involved in, some of which I have just witnessed. I'll mention two of them, both, as it happens, involving the Ford Foundation. Back in the 1950s, the Ford Foundation decided that the behavioral sciences were the key to the future, that the behavioral sciences, like sociology and political science, would really give us a way of controlling human destiny. They would bring about the "politics of the future," and create a better society at the least cost. And so the Ford Foundation devoted tens of millions of dollars to advancing the behavioral sciences in the universities, with great success. Unfortunately, 15 years later it turned out that the behavioral sciences were in a condition, and to this day are in a condition, of intellectual crisis; the younger scholars, whether conservative or radical, are all in rebellion against the behavioral sciences, which they find very boring, very tedious, and on the whole ineffectual. But the damage that has been done to our universities by the Ford Foundation's presumption in thinking that it knew what should be taught in the universities, that it knew exactly what it should impose on universities within the social sciences, has been enormous. Because professors don't die young. Tens of thousands of professors, with tenure, are now sitting in universities, trained in the behavioral sciences, teaching students who find them all (or most of them) thoroughly unsatisfying.

The other, more famous instance, of course, was the school decentralization fight in New York City. Being a New Yorker, that was something that came very close to the bone. There the act of arrogance was evident, because if there's one law of New York City politics it is: "Thou shalt not polarize racial and ethnic groups." That has been the overriding political law of New York City for 150 years now, but the Ford Foundation blithely went ahead and polarized the city, inflicting enormous damage on the public school system, and on the political system of the city. My impression is that having caused that damage, it has now lost interest in the subject and has gone on to something else.

Grand Designs, Sad Results

Now, I don't want to be misunderstood. It is possible to do good. It really is possible to do good. Doing good isn't even hard. It's just doing a lot of good that is very hard. If your aims are modest, you can accomplish an awful lot. When your aims become elevated beyond a reasonable level, you not only don't accomplish much, but you can cause a great deal of damage. And, in fact, I think that foundations in this country have passed up enormous opportunities to do good, simply because they have found them not sufficiently ambitious.

In my own experience, I spent several years on the Council of the National Endowment for the Humanities (NEH), and it was an organization that I was very much in favor of. In fact, I even helped persuade some of my conservative friends in Congress to vote its appropriation against their inclination. I have avoided speaking to them since. I don't know what I would now say to them. Basically, NEH did a good job; in all fairness, I think it still does half a good job. At the beginning, what NEH did was quite simple and obvious. We supported archaeological expeditions in Turkey. Someone has to support them; they're worth doing. They might discover something interesting; it seems right that NEH should do it. We supported critical editions of major texts. Again, very expensive. Again, someone has to do it, and it seems right that the National Endowment for the Humanities should do it. We went on doing all these very colorless and rather boring, but good things.

But in the end it didn't satisfy a great many people, including people in Congress, including some of the present leaders of foundations. The result is that, when you proposed something along those lines, the reaction became, "Oh goodness, come on, we don't want another edition of classical texts. Let's do something more interesting, let's do something that has an effect on the world." As a consequence, the emphasis at NEH, over these past years, has shifted. A lot of the money is now simply wasted, in my view, on all sorts of dubious "community and cultural activities." I do think that the National Endowment for the Humanities should support excellent museums. I don't think it ought to support third-rate museums. But, of course, it's now in the business of supporting third-rate ballet troupes, third-rate, fourth-rate museums, spreading the money around state-by-state, county-by-county; it has been quite politicized. It still does some good—I'd say half of what it does is still perfectly good. But it just could not be satisfied to do the good things which were not intellectually exciting. They were quite routine but worth doing and now unfortunately very few foundations are doing them.

I take a more dramatic instance. Everyone is concerned about youth unemployment in the ghetto, as I am, and I have been involved with various foundations and government as well, over the years, in trying to do something about it. It's astonishing how little has been accomplished. The reason so little has been accomplished is that no one was satisfied with doing a little; everyone wanted to do a lot. For instance, it is a scandal in this country that vocational education is in the condition it's in. It is absolutely absurd. Can you imagine a United States of America where there is a shortage of automobile mechanics, and yet there are "unemployable" kids in the ghetto who can strip an automobile in four minutes flat? It just doesn't make sense. But when you try to get a program of vocational education going—and I've tried very hard with various foundations to get a simple program of vocational education going—they say, "No! No! We don't want to train these kids to be automobile mechanics. We want to train them to be doctors, to be surgeons."

Let's be reasonable. Not everyone can be a doctor or a surgeon. Some people are going to end up as automobile mechanics. Automobile mechanics have a pretty good career. They make a great deal of money, most of it honestly. But the fact is that it has been impossible to get the resources for so limited a goal.

Foundations talk a great deal about education, and propose grand theories about education. Whenever a foundation comes to me with grand theories about education, I say: "Fine, start a school." Why not? If you have grand and novel theories about education, start a school. But it turns out that those people don't want to start a school. They want to reform the whole public education system, or whatever. But it's very hard to reform the public education system, which is populated by people with interests, ideas, and habits of their own. It's not in their interest to be reformed. So they will take your program and twist it in all sorts of ways. Whereas, a foundation can always start a school. Thus it seems reasonable to insist: if you have any good ideas about education, whether it be in the ghetto or elsewhere, *start a school*. But I have never heard of any foundation that started a school, one that would put its theories into effect. A hundred years ago that was assumed to be a very promising way to reform education. These days it is regarded as insufficiently ambitious, too modest in its intent.

Again, turning to the youth of the ghetto, if you say to a foundation: "Look, there are many bright kids in the ghetto who need help, who need scholarships, who need fellowships. Why don't you help them?" the answer to that is: "We want to help those who are really down at the bottom. That's the problem." Indeed that is the problem. Only, helping those at the bottom is not easy, whereas helping those who are at the top, or are moving up, is feasible. It works. If you suggest such a program you are accused of something called "creaming," namely, taking the most able, the most intelligent, the most ambitious, and moving them up while neglecting the rest. But that is the normal way in which all groups move into the mainstream of American life. This is true for all groups, all immigrant groups, all ethnic groups, all racial groups. You begin by moving up those who can be moved up. Their brothers, sisters, cousins, friends, see them moving up and begin to foresee that it's possible. They begin to shape their lives and their habits to *follow* them. The notion that you go directly to the hard-core unemployable, the high-school dropouts, who are "hard-core" for a reason, is utopian. They're not easy to cope with. The notion that you can cope with these people directly, and transform them overnight into willing and eager students, is childish. I'm not saying you can't do it in the case of certain individuals. And if a foundation wanted to focus enormous resources on a few such individuals, it would probably work. But it would be enormously expensive, and in the end you would just be helping a few individuals. The more sensible approach is to do what you can do—help those who wish to be helped, who can be helped, who are already motivated, and hope that others will follow in their path. It is, on the basis of experience, a realistic hope.

I'll never forget my first job, working for a fine mechanic, who was an illiterate and who owned his own factory. After I'd been there a few days, he took me aside and said, "Irving, I want you to remember two things: First, a thing worth doing is worth doing cheaply. And second, if something is too hard to do, find something easier to do." On the whole, I think that's good advice. When things get terribly hard and terribly expensive, it's a sign that—for reasons which you may never understand—it's not going to be doable. Peter Drucker—many years later I read Peter Drucker on management—ends up saying the same thing as my little machine shop owner did, namely, you pour your resources into things that work. You don't spend all your time and energy and money on things that don't work. Do what is doable, and when you do what is doable, it will affect everything else, and you then get the kind of progress in education, or in the economy, or what have you, which brings everyone into the system and from which everyone benefits.

There is a passion for doing good. It is a noble passion, but it is a passion. And all passions have to be controlled. All passions are dangerous unless they are controlled. We have had long experience in the history of Western civilization with people who spend their lives doing good. Nuns, members of religious orders, working in hospitals, in schools. All of them were under a discipline where they were on regular occasions humiliated by their institutions. That is, if you wanted to do good in the old days, say in a hospital, at some point, you emptied bedpans. Now, I'm not saying that all the professionals at the Robert Wood Johnson Foundation should spend one day a month emptying bedpans. On the other hand, it is useful to have an occasion for humility. It is very easy to sit down and devise a new health delivery service, but cleaning bedpans gives you an insight into some of the problems inherent in health delivery service. The passion for doing good, when it was restricted to religious orders, had a self-correcting mechanism in it. We have no such system of self-discipline and self-humiliation, so that the tendency toward pride and arrogance in doing good, the tendency toward an excess of passion and self-righteousness in doing good, is unchecked.

Pluralism and Private Initiative

I want to make one final point, which is really my original point. Foundations came into existence originally to do all the things that needed to be done that the government did not do in the 19th and early 20th centuries. That was the right thing for foundations to do at that time. However, the situation has changed today. We have had a reversal. There is almost nothing you can suggest which government is not eager to do. And it seems to me that foundations, therefore, have a special responsibility to be wary of government and to be a lot more solicitous of their own sector, which, I repeat, is the private sector. You're not *above* the private sector, by God, you're *in* it. I really am a little sorry, with all due respect to Landrum Bolling[1] and the city of Washington, that the Council on Foundations has decided to set up headquarters in Washington. I think that's the wrong signal to the foundation world. Foundations should not be an adjunct to government. Foundations should be an adjunct to their own, private sector. There is a tendency these days for everything to become an adjunct to government, just as there is a tendency, when foundations have a good idea, for government to take it and run away with it. My favorite example of the latter is the Meals on Wheels program. This was a marvelous program, a community program, where people got together and delivered meals to elderly people who were either house-bound or confined to their beds. And Congress heard about this and said, "That's a great idea; we'll do it." So it passed the Meals on Wheels legislation, but with all sorts of new regulations, so that the community organizations that had been delivering meals for years were all disqualified because they didn't have enough professional nutritionists, they didn't have the right number of this or enough of that, they didn't have the right inspection of their facilities, etc. So you end up with another government agency doing, in its bureaucratic and, I am convinced, in the end not very humane way, what neighbors were doing in a very pleasant and humane way.

There is clearly a tendency of government, in the name of the welfare state, to expand the conception of the welfare state so far as to be bureaucratically paternalistic. I think foundations should combat this tendency, not encourage it.

In sum, foundations should rethink their situations and their conditions. We live in a pluralistic society. Some foundations are going to be liberal, some are going to be radical, some are going to be conservative, and that's fine. That's the way it should be, as long as they realize that they are being either liberal, conservative, or radical, not somehow representing something called "the common good," which they alone are in a position to define. But I do want to emphasize, in closing, that all of those activities, whether radical, liberal, or conservative, emerge from the private sector, and are a distinctive aspect of our pluralist society. To the degree that our society becomes more centralized,

---

1. Landrum Bolling was chairman of the Council on Foundations from 1978 to 1981. —Ed.

to the degree that government becomes more intrusive in all the affairs of our lives, to that degree, foundations are going to end up in fact being adjuncts of government or being assimilated into government.

Even now it is said—and I have heard foundation executives say it, and I think most people here would probably say it—that the money you people spend is public money, and therefore you have a public responsibility. Now, in what sense is the money you spend public? Under the tax laws, the contributions made to foundations are deductible from income. If you say that that money is public money, you are saying: "Well, the government has the right to all our money, but it doesn't exercise this right at all times or in all respects. It leaves some of that governmental money for us to spend, and therefore we have a public responsibility attached to that money." I think that is socializing money in rhetoric prior to socializing it in fact. The money you people spend is *private* money. It is *not* public money. Money that the government does not take is ours. You can have whatever public responsibilities you wish to assume with that private money. But it is private money. It is the life blood of your organizations, and I think it is time foundations gave a little more thought to the source of that life blood and to what might be done to making that life blood a little more abundant and, shall we say, healthier in composition.

"Foundations and the Sin of Pride: The Myth of the Third Sector" by Irving Kristol (New York: Institute for Educational Affairs, 1980). By permission of the author.

MICHAEL A. BAILIN

"Re-Engineering Philanthropy: Field Notes from the Trenches"

During his ten-year tenure as president of the Edna McConnell Clark Founda-
tion (1996–2005), Michael A. Bailin oversaw radical changes in the foundation's
mission and modus operandi. In this speech, given at Georgetown University in
2005, Bailin outlines the transformation of the inner culture and outside deal-
ings of a foundation caught in what seemed an unavoidable status quo. As a
grant-seeker for many years, Bailin arrived at the other side of the philanthropic
table with a motor revved by one "undeniable fact: Foundations do not, in the
main, make change in this society. Grantees do." In the ensuing years, he insti-
tuted many internal changes, all directed at becoming more effective: giving pri-
orities were refocused, activities were relocated to areas within easy reach,
funding procedures were reformulated, the application process was revised, and
the foundation itself was re-staffed and re-organized. Not all the changes Bailin
helped institute may be replicable, but what about his method? Its tacit formula
is "'Foundation, know and heal thyself': Instead of forcing non-profits to change,
take stock of who you are—your limits and possibilities—puzzle out how change
happens, find already effective organizations, and work with them to become
more so." Sounds easy enough. Is it?

ço

Re-examining the Foundation's Direction

When I arrived at the Edna McConnell Clark Foundation . . . [w]e were, like
many foundations, dedicated to systems change—to reforming the great delivery systems of public service, much as the Great Society had sought to do. In
our case, the particular emphases were on systems of child welfare, middle-
school education, criminal justice, and neighborhood redevelopment. A fifth
program, in tropical disease research, was a bit more focused and enterprising—
the development of a practical, scientific approach to treating and preventing
trachoma, a disease that was needlessly blinding millions of people. We spent
some years working with a corporate partner to spin off and scale up that effort, and today it is an independent 501(c)(3) with a tested product and measurable results. It's exactly the kind of work that we're proud to be known for and
that we hope to do more of.

But when you look at the other items on that list, especially with the benefit
of six years' hindsight, you can see what made the trustees believe the time had

come for a change. The problem, in a nutshell, was this: In all of those programs—in education and justice and child welfare and neighborhood improvement—we were trying to reform huge, complex, entrenched, multibillion-dollar public systems with a staff of 25 people and around $25 million a year in grants.

Yes, the staff was terrifically talented and distinguished in their fields—something that I came to admire and value more and more, even as we completed our involvement in programs that they had created. And no, they were not making decisions on their own, but were guided by panels of first-rate advisers. And yes, other foundations also supported many of our grantees, even if not in the same activities or in a coordinated way.

But even so, we were proceeding as if we had some independent leverage over social systems that had been many decades in the making—systems that were fortified by all the ramparts of bureaucracy and regulation, and thickets of intergovernmental agreements and contracts, and moats of public dollars. We were fighting battles that had tested the power and wealth of serial U.S. Congresses and presidencies. It was a battle of Homeric proportions fought with Lilliputian resources. How could we ever imagine that we could accomplish anything so significant in our lifetimes? And how would we even know if we did?

My goal, as things evolved over the first few years, was to wind down these efforts responsibly, and in their place assemble a program that recognizes a humbling but undeniable fact: Foundations do not, in the main, make change in this society. Grantees do. That was not so clearly understood in the 1960s, but it is now—even if many who espouse that view don't act like they believe it. Today, foundations make change not primarily through the force of their own ingenuity, but on the strength of their grantees' achievements. Foundations succeed when their grantees grow stronger, achieve more, and gain stature for leadership.

And what was our foundation doing to make any of those things happen? The sad answer was *not much*. And we were far from alone.

We were, instead, trying to inject new ideas—quite often, ideas of our contrivance—into the work of grantees whose own ideas, and whose actual mission, may have been quite different from what we had in mind. We were constantly wheedling and negotiating with them, tugging here and prodding there, compromising a little on this issue, strong-arming them hard on that one. Quite often, as I learned in my years as a grant-seeker, the result was a bad fit for both the foundation and the grantee. Much of the time, the end result was not much more than the reluctant implementation of a compromised idea. Both the grantee and the foundation were essentially acquiescing in a marriage of convenience, but rarely of honesty or trust. Still, it brought some money in the grantee's door. And it produced a program that the Foundation could cite with pride (if not necessarily precision) in its annual report. So everyone was reasonably happy. And the great social systems rolled on, pretty much unaltered.

A New Way of Grantmaking

So my question became: What if, instead of focusing our energies on vast public systems, we instead concentrated on the nonprofit institutions that were doing the best work within one of those systems? Maybe their work is subversive, maybe cooperative. Maybe strategically innovative, maybe just tactically efficient. What if we just looked for organizations that seemed to be getting results, that seemed to want to do more, get better outcomes for more people, keep better tabs on what they accomplish—and help them achieve those goals? What if we stopped trying to redesign the government sector, and instead helped the best people in our own sector build what they envision?

Specifically, we imagined concentrating on a single field—we picked youth development. We imagined finding organizations within that field that are delivering effective services that want to do more, and to do it better, and to reach more people. We would not fund projects or pieces of projects; rather we would help those good organizations expand, manage themselves more effectively, track their results faster and more accurately, and in general achieve more, for more people, with more information about the outcomes. We'd be accountable not for some long-term change in a giant, amorphous system—but for how useful we were in the growth and performance of a given set of organizations, for a given population of young people.

The first reaction some people had to that idea was: *Sounds like general operating support.* Grantees will love it, people told us, but it's very expensive and risky. A good general-support grant needs to be big and unconstrained, and when you make a big bet with no strings attached, there's a decent chance you'll come up with nothing to show for it. That wasn't the approach we had in mind, but that's how the idea sounded to some people at first. (I happen to think, by the way, that general operating support is greatly undervalued at a lot of foundations. There needs to be more of it, and I applaud foundations who give their grantees more leeway. Our approach is slightly different—but it does provide a lot of leeway, and it intentionally shoulders the corresponding risks.)

The next reaction, even more negative, was: *Sounds like venture philanthropy.* The management professors and theoreticians will love it, people told us, but it's at best an interesting metaphor, not a plan of action. Follow it too far, and you'll find yourselves sitting on grantees' boards, meddling in their management, and interfering with the very things you claim to like about them: their independence, their flexibility, and their ingenuity. Plus, you'll premise the whole thing on an "exit" plan that may well never materialize. Venture philanthropy wasn't what we had in mind either, but I understand why it sounded like that to some people.

The course we actually chose is something we kind of haltingly call Institution-Building—though I'd welcome nominations for a better name. It borrows some of the best elements of the two other models, but it's not the same as either one. We felt that this approach would work well with youth development because the field—if you can call it that—has, as yet, no giant national system built around it. It has a wide but shallow network of nonprofit organizations—most of them small, many of them young and fragile—experimenting with dozens, maybe hundreds, of different ideas and approaches. It has a mission of unquestioned importance: the healthy development of young people, particularly those in low-income communities. And it has a few nonprofit institutions that seem to be accomplishing things of importance—too few that you can conclusively prove as successful, and certainly nothing that's reaching the majority of people who could benefit from it. But things that look like they have potential, that would benefit from more ambitious evaluation, and that could be reaching many more people than they now do.

Focusing on Four Outcomes

Within that relatively new and disorganized field, we decided to concentrate on organizations that run programs reaching young people in the out-of-school hours and delivering on at least one, and preferably more, of four kinds of outcomes:

- *Educational attainment or achievement.* Young people in the program would more often advance to the next grade, attend school regularly, and show measurable improvement in learning.
- *Preparation for work or self-sufficiency.* Participants would develop demonstrable skills; they would find and hold down jobs, earn income, prepare to become self-reliant and assume the other responsibilities of adulthood.
- *Civic engagement.* More young people would be participating in and contributing meaningfully to the life and development of their communities.
- *Avoiding harmful behavior.* This could include things like staying off drugs to preventing too early pregnancy, but we expect that it would be coupled with positive goals as well, at least one of the other three that I've just mentioned.

We then chose to work in New York City and Boston, geographic areas close enough to our offices so that we could pay close, competent attention to the work we were supporting. We looked for organizations at the early to middle stage of growth—with revenues somewhere between $1 million and $10 million—so that our investments would have real meaning in the context of the grantee's total budget. We then began our new work with a small allocation in what we called a "Growth Fund," where we could try out our ideas and learn quickly from mistakes and successes. We worked with a few current and former grantees that were already committed to youth development, and sought out a small number of others that shared these basic criteria:

- A demonstrated, or at least apparently effective service or product—something they produce consistently that has real value.
- Strong leadership and management.
- A financially sound and operationally viable organization.
- An ability to track its own successes and use data to make decisions.
- A general compatibility with our new style and way of doing business.

We had no illusions that we had, in-house, the expertise we would need to weigh these criteria accurately, much less to work effectively with organizations that fit the profile. Like most foundations, we had a staff with much more substantive expertise than organizational or management experience. That, too, was partly a carry-over from the old days of idea-driven philanthropy. In the old model, it wasn't important to know how to run big organizations, manage finances, create implementation teams, and the like. Foundations thought *Great Thoughts,* and other people worried about organizational charts. We were determined that that was going to change, and that eventually we would have a staff that blended substantive expertise with a solid grounding in the management disciplines. Today, we're much closer to that goal, though time will tell whether we yet have the balance right. . . .

The business of selection surprised us—first by its complexity and later by its overwhelming importance. The due-diligence approach we used was a real departure from the Request for Proposals model we had followed for most of our history, with its reliance on long, written proposals and remote, abstract criteria for selecting grantees. In our new approach, the due diligence review entailed 100 to 200 hours of work per organization, looking deeply, on-site and side-by-side with the grantee, at what they do; their financial health; their organization, their leadership and management, how they measure outcomes and use the information to improve their work; and generally how well we and they could work together.

Some of this was fact-gathering, a more extensive and more practical kind than we had ever done before. But the complexity arose not just from getting good financial statements, or from figuring out exactly how decision-making and accountability worked within a given organization. Those are always hard questions, and foundations don't ask them nearly often enough. But they can be answered fairly objectively if you do enough work.

The complexity—and in the long run, the fundamental challenge to our approach—came in the subjective decisions that we and the grantees both had to make as the process unfolds. Is this organization really ready for and committed to growth? Is this management and staff going to stick with us through the hard work ahead? Can we work together—not just deal respectfully with one another, which any grant relationship ought to entail, but actually work on some of the same things, side-by-side? Are they and we going to be able to share information and impressions, exchange advice and criticism, and be honest enough to think together, rather than dancing around one another the way most grantmakers and grantees normally do? The answers to those questions aren't on any balance sheet. You can't figure them out in a round of 20-minute interviews. It took us much longer than we thought.

But more importantly, the approach has worked well for us. We've netted a dozen organizations that show signs of real quality, a reliable product, a plausible case for effectiveness, a willingness to test and measure their work and to improve it along the way, and then, over time, a determination to grow to serve more of the young people in their communities or target areas. Getting that selection right is probably the most important thing we have done to raise the odds of success. All the right techniques applied to a fundamentally bad match would have gone nowhere. Or worse, it probably would have done real harm, certainly to the grantees, and probably to us.

The Search for Compelling Organizations

Today, after three years of testing and piloting this, we are confident enough to have placed all our chips—everything we've got—on this one bet. We have phased out the prototype Growth Fund and set up the Youth Development Fund as a full-scale program. It will soon be our only program. We will be a foundation entirely devoted to achieving performance, growth, and excellence in youth development, with a goal of more-accomplished grantees working toward a better organized, more disciplined field. We will make fewer grants to fewer grantees, but they will be in larger amounts with room for growth over time if needed.

It's worth noting that we didn't start with a prescription for how youth development should work—some preferred model that we wanted to test and refine and try to replicate. Nor did we set out with some "broken" system in our cross-hairs, and try to undo it. We didn't look for grantees whose programs conformed to our idea of what works or what tasks are most important. Most of us know less about youth development than our grantees do, and we'd be hard pressed to wow any of them with our expertise. What drew us to a given organization and its approach to youth development was, first of all, its *theory of change*. In simplest terms, that means the organization can tell you, at both a micro and a macro level, exactly what they do, with whom, at what cost; why that activity logically leads to measurable results; and how they define and recognize success when they see it. If they can't yet prove their case, they can at least make it concretely, and they can formulate it as a reasonable hypothesis that can be tested—and, if we're successful, will be tested. . . .

What We Have Discovered So Far

Doing this work effectively—everything from searching out prospects to conducting due diligence to supporting business planning—has brought about at least two major changes in the way we are staffed and organized and how we operate. The first is that our staff now includes several new senior employees with the new title Portfolio Manager. The title reflects a fundamentally new kind of job in the foundation world: someone who is helping organizations manage themselves effectively. Their job isn't to devise some ideal new way to approach youth development, it's to help organizations design and implement their own ideas for improving services, achieving more, and growing. . . .

The second big change in our organization was the invention of a fundamentally new kind of evaluation unit. Lots of foundations have staff for evaluation, and they take it seriously. But it tends to be a post-mortem exercise, more of an autopsy than a checkup on a living patient. . . .

What we now call our Office of Evaluation and Knowledge Development concentrates on diagnostics and vital signs, not post-mortems. Its job is to help grantees develop their own systems to measure what they're accomplishing in the present tense, and then use that information as soon as it's available to manage and improve the program. When these information and data systems are in place, organizations will have timely answers to questions like: How many people are participating in Program X, and how does that compare with the goal? Do young people who spend more time in component Y perform better at outcome B than those who do not? What's the rate of staffing and turnover in Program Z? Are those numbers what they were projected to be by now?

More significantly, the evaluation staff is involved in our work with grantees from the very start. The department takes part in due diligence and in business planning. Its involvement reflects how we are using all our resources at the Foundation toward achieving the twin goals of operating more effectively and adding as much value as we can to the work of our grantees.

The evaluation unit is also responsible for evaluating our work: measuring the contribution we make to our grantees and the field, the yield on our investments, the success and shortcomings of our grantmaking approach. Its overall goal is to develop useful knowledge for our grantees, the field, other parts of philanthropy, and public policymakers, based on both what our grantees accomplish and how useful we are to them. . . .

All of this rests on a *theory of change* of our own. It starts with the observation that young people get more of what they need for healthy development and constructive citizenship if they live in communities with strong institutions to guide and mentor and get them involved. There are many kinds of such institutions. But in some places, particularly low-income communities, those institutions are few, weak, small, and unsteady. Build the institutions, help them manage themselves better and smarter, give them the means to do more for more people, and you will significantly raise the odds that young people will grow up to lead healthy and stable lives. By making substantial, long-term investments in outstanding organizations with demonstrably effective programs, strong leadership, and a commitment to growth, we can eventually create better outcomes for both the young people and the communities in which they live.

But there's a further step to the theory. All of these institutions—including the strong and stable ones, and all the ones in better-off communities where resources aren't as scarce—all of them could be learning more, innovating more, improving and diversifying what they do, if they were part of a stronger, more well-knit field of youth development. The thinness and weakness of the field holds back progress as much as the weakness of particular organizations— arguably more so. Our foundation isn't big enough to build a field of youth development on its own. In fact, the field will be built not by any foundation, but by the institutions in the field. If we really find and invest in some of the best of those, and help them build their stature and ability to lead, and their opportunities to connect and work with one another, we will be influencing the formation of a better field—indirectly, but concretely. That is, in any case, the theory that guides us now, and on which we are basing our next few years' work.

"Re-engineering Philanthropy: Notes from the Trenches" by Michael A. Bailin (given as part of the Waldemar A. Nielsen Issues in Philanthropy Series, the Center for Public and Nonprofit Leadership, Georgetown University, February 21, 2003). Used by permission of the Center for Public and Nonprofit Leadership.

ANTON CHEKHOV

"The Beggar"

If social change is difficult to bring about, it is arguably more difficult to effect fundamental change in a person's heart and mind and well-established habits. Who—what?—is conducive to producing such change most effectively—most lastingly? This is the main issue to which Russian short story writer and playwright Anton Pavlovich Chekhov (1860–1904) directs our attention in this short tale. When the prosperous lawyer, Skvortsov, catches the drunken beggar, Lushkov, in a lie, he dares him to change his ways by doing some honest labor. He instructs Olga, his cook, to take the beggar to the woodshed to chop some wood. Olga shows Lushkov the shed and, apparently, much, much more. In reply to the lawyer's self-assured claim that he "saved" Lushkov, when the two happen upon each other several years later, Lushkov thanks him for his "words and deeds" but radically denies the lawyer's claim. Who—what—was the agent of change?

ॐ

"Kind sir, be so good as to notice a poor, hungry man. I have not tasted food for three days. I have not a five-kopeck piece for a night's lodging. I swear by God! For five years I was a village schoolmaster and lost my post through the intrigues of the Zemstvo. I was the victim of false witness. I have been out of a place for a year now."

Skvortsov, a Petersburg lawyer, looked at the speaker's tattered dark blue overcoat, at his muddy, drunken eyes, at the red patches on his cheeks, and it seemed to him that he had seen the man before.

"And now I am offered a post in the Kaluga province," the beggar continued, "but I have not the means for the journey there. Graciously help me! I am ashamed to ask, but . . . I am compelled by circumstances."

Skvortsov looked at his galoshes, of which one was shallow like a shoe, while the other came high up the leg like a boot, and suddenly remembered.

"Listen, the day before yesterday I met you in Sadovoy Street," he said, "and then you told me, not that you were a village schoolmaster, but that you were a student who had been expelled. Do you remember?"

"N-o. No, that cannot be so!" the beggar muttered in confusion. "I am a village schoolmaster, and if you wish it I can show you documents to prove it."

"That's enough lies! You called yourself a student, and even told me what you were expelled for. Do you remember?"

Skvortsov flushed, and with a look of disgust on his face turned away from the ragged figure.

"It's contemptible, sir!" he cried angrily. "It's a swindle! I'll hand you over to the police, damn you! You are poor and hungry, but that does not give you the right to lie so shamelessly!"

The ragged figure took hold of the door-handle and, like a bird in a snare, looked round the hall desperately.

"I . . . I am not lying," he muttered. "I can show documents."

"Who can believe you?" Skvortsov went on, still indignant. "To exploit the sympathy of the public for village schoolmasters and students—it's so low, so mean, so dirty! It's revolting!"

Skvortsov flew into a rage and gave the beggar a merciless scolding. The ragged fellow's insolent lying aroused his disgust and aversion, was an offence against what he, Skvortsov, loved and prized in himself: kindliness, a feeling heart, sympathy for the unhappy. By his lying, by his treacherous assault upon compassion, the individual had, as it were, defiled the charity which he liked to give to the poor with no misgivings in his heart. The beggar at first defended himself, protested with oaths, then he sank into silence and hung his head, overcome with shame.

"Sir!" he said, laying his hand on his heart, "I really was . . . lying! I am not a student and not a village schoolmaster. All that's mere invention! I used to be in the Russian choir, and I was turned out of it for drunkenness. But what can I do? Believe me, in God's name, I can't get on without lying—when I tell the truth no one will give me anything. With the truth one may die of hunger and freeze without a night's lodging! What you say is true, I understand that, but . . . what am I to do?"

"What are you to do? You ask what are you to do?" cried Skvortsov, going close up to him. "Work—that's what you must do! You must work!"

"Work. . . . I know that myself, but where can I get work?"

"Nonsense. You are young, strong, and healthy, and could always find work if you wanted to. But you know you are lazy, pampered, drunken! You reek of vodka like a pothouse! You have become false and corrupt to the marrow of your bones and fit for nothing but begging and lying! If you do graciously condescend to take work, you must have a job in an office, in the Russian choir, or as a billiard-marker, where you will have a salary and have nothing to do! But how would you like to undertake manual labour? I'll be bound, you wouldn't be a house porter or a factory hand! You are too genteel for that!"

"What things you say, really . . ." said the beggar, and he gave a bitter smile. "How can I get manual work? It's rather late for me to be a shopman, for in trade one has to begin from a boy; no one would take me as a house porter, because I am not of that class. . . . And I could not get work in a factory; one must know a trade, and I know nothing."

"Nonsense! You always find some justification! Wouldn't you like to chop wood?"

"I would not refuse to, but the regular woodchoppers are out of work now."

"Oh, all idlers argue like that! As soon as you are offered anything you refuse it. Would you care to chop wood for me?"

"Certainly I will . . ."

"Very good, we shall see. . . . Excellent. We'll see!" Skvortsov, in nervous haste, and not without malignant pleasure, rubbing his hands, summoned his cook from the kitchen.

"Here, Olga," he said to her, "take this gentleman to the shed and let him chop some wood."

The beggar shrugged his shoulders as though puzzled, and irresolutely followed the cook. It was evident from his demeanor that he had consented to go and chop wood, not because he was hungry and wanted to earn money, but simply from shame and *amour propre,* because he had been taken at his word. It was clear, too, that he was suffering from the effects of vodka, that he was unwell, and felt not the faintest inclination to work.

Skvortsov hurried into the dining-room. There from the window which looked out into the yard he could see the woodshed and everything that happened in the yard. Standing at the window, Skvortsov saw the cook and the beggar come by the back way into the yard and go through the muddy snow to the woodshed. Olga scrutinized her companion angrily, and jerking her elbow unlocked the woodshed and angrily banged the door open.

"Most likely we interrupted the woman drinking her coffee," thought Skvortsov. "What a cross creature she is!"

Then he saw the pseudo-schoolmaster and pseudo-student seat himself on a block of wood, and, leaning his red cheeks upon his fists, sink into thought. The cook flung an axe at his feet, spat angrily on the ground, and, judging by the expression of her lips, began abusing him. The beggar drew a log of wood towards him irresolutely, set it up between his feet, and diffidently drew the axe across it. The log toppled and fell over. The beggar drew it towards him, breathed on his frozen hands, and again drew the axe along it as cautiously as though he were afraid of its hitting his galosh or chopping off his fingers. The log fell over again.

Skvortsov's wrath had passed off by now, he felt sore and ashamed at the thought that he had forced a pampered, drunken, and perhaps sick man to do hard, rough work in the cold.

"Never mind, let him go on . . ." he thought, going from the dining-room into his study. "I am doing it for his good!"

An hour later Olga appeared and announced that the wood had been chopped up.

"Here, give him half a rouble," said Skvortsov. "If he likes, let him come and chop wood on the first of every month. . . . There will always be work for him."

On the first of the month the beggar turned up and again earned half a rouble, though he could hardly stand. From that time forward he took to turning up frequently, and work was always found for him: sometimes he would sweep the snow into heaps, or clear up the shed, at another he used to beat the rugs and the mattresses. He always received thirty to forty kopecks for his work, and on one occasion an old pair of trousers was sent out to him.

When he moved, Skvortsov engaged him to assist in packing and moving the furniture. On this occasion the beggar was sober, gloomy, and silent; he scarcely touched the furniture, walked with hanging head behind the furniture vans, and did not even try to appear busy; he merely shivered with the cold, and was overcome with confusion when the men with the vans laughed at his idleness, feebleness, and ragged coat that had once been a gentleman's. After the removal Skvortsov sent for him.

"Well, I see my words have had an effect upon you," he said, giving him a rouble. "This is for your work. I see that you are sober and not disinclined to work. What is your name?"

"Lushkov."

"I can offer you better work, not so rough, Lushkov. Can you write?"

"Yes, sir."

"Then go with this note to-morrow to my colleague and he will give you some copying to do. Work, don't drink, and don't forget what I said to you. Good-bye."

Skvortsov, pleased that he had put a man in the path of rectitude, patted Lushkov genially on the shoulder, and even shook hands with him at parting.

Lushkov took the letter, departed, and from that time forward did not come to the back-yard for work.

Two years passed. One day as Skvortsov was standing at the ticket-office of a theatre, paying for his ticket, he saw beside him a little man with a lambskin collar and a shabby cat's-skin cap. The man timidly asked the clerk for a gallery ticket and paid for it with kopecks.

"Lushkov, is it you?" asked Skvortsov, recognizing in the little man his former woodchopper. "Well, what are you doing? Are you getting on all right?"

"Pretty well. . . . I am in a notary's office now. I earn thirty-five roubles."

"Well, thank God, that's capital. I rejoice for you. I am very, very glad, Lushkov. You know, in a way, you are my godson. It was I who shoved you into the right way. Do you remember what a scolding I gave you, eh? You almost sank through the floor that time. Well, thank you, my dear fellow, for remembering my words."

"Thank you too," said Lushkov. "If I had not come to you that day, maybe I should be calling myself a schoolmaster or a student still. Yes, in your house I was saved, and climbed out of the pit."

"I am very, very glad."

"Thank you for your kind words and deeds. What you said that day was excellent. I am grateful to you and to your cook, God bless that kind, noble-hearted woman. What you said that day was excellent; I am indebted to you as long as I live, of course, but it was your cook, Olga, who really saved me."

"How was that?"

"Why, it was like this. I used to come to you to chop wood and she would begin: 'Ah, you drunkard! You God-forsaken man! And yet death does not take you!' and then she would sit opposite me, lamenting, looking into my face and wailing: 'You unlucky fellow! You have no gladness in this world, and in the next you will burn in hell, poor drunkard! You poor sorrowful creature!' and she always went on in that style, you know. How often she upset herself, and how many tears she shed over me I can't tell you. But what affected me most—she chopped the wood for me! Do you know, sir, I never chopped a single log for you—she did it all! How it was she saved me, how it was I changed, looking at her, and gave up drinking, I can't explain. I only know that what she said and the noble way she behaved brought about a change in my soul, and I shall never forget it. It's time to go up, though, they are just going to ring the bell."

Lushkov bowed and went off to the gallery.

From *The Horse Stealers, and Other Stories,* translated from Russian by Constance Garnett.

NATHANIEL HAWTHORNE

"A Good Man's Miracle"

Contemporary philanthropists are wont to speak of their "theory of change." But, as the many theories indicate, what the real levers of change are is a live question. Nathaniel Hawthorne (1804–1864), master of American fiction, here presents the story of the modestly funded benevolence of (real-life) Robert Raikes and the "miracle" it wrought—the world-wide Sunday School movement. "Proof," Hawthorne suggests, of his own theory of change: That "when the humblest person acts in the simplicity of a pure heart with no design but to do good, God may be expected to . . . adopt the action as His own." No question, something good came of something quite small. No question that by current standards Raikes' philanthropy is a model of effectiveness—it was brought to scale, its impact was wide and palpable. Still, does the subject of Hawthorne's story—or the story itself—give "proof" to such a theory? Is a "good man," or a good plan, the best harbinger of success? How really important are our intentions for our efficacy?

In every good action there is a divine quality, which does not end with the completion of that particular deed but goes on to bring forth good works in an infinite series. It is seldom possible, indeed, for human eyes to trace out the chain of blessed consequences, that extends from a benevolent man's simple and conscientious act, here on earth, and connects it with those labors of love which the angels make it their joy to perform, in Heaven above. Sometimes, however, we meet with an instance in which this wonderful and glorious connection may clearly be perceived. It has always appeared to me, that a well-known incident in the life of Mr. Robert Raikes offers us one of the most hopeful and inspiring arguments, never to neglect even the humblest opportunities of doing good, as not knowing what vast purposes of Providence we may thereby subserve. This little story has been often told, but may here be related anew, because it so strikingly illustrates the remark with which we began.

Mr. Raikes, being in London, happened one day to pass through a certain street, which was inhabited chiefly by poor and ignorant people. In great cities, it is unfortunately the case, that the poor are compelled to be the neighbors and fellow-lodgers of the vicious; and that the ignorant seeing so much temptation around them, and having no kind advisers to direct them aright, almost inevitably go astray and increase the number of the bad. Thus, though doubtless there are many virtuous poor people, amidst all the vice that hides itself in the obscure streets of a great city, like London, still it seems as if they were kept virtuous only by the special providence of God. If He should turn away His eyes for a single instant, they would be lost in the flood of evil that continually surrounds them. Now, Mr. Raikes, as he passed along, saw much to make him sad, for there were so many tokens of sin and wretchedness on all sides, that most persons, hopeless of doing any good, would have endeavored to forget the whole scene as soon as possible.

There is hardly a gloomier spectacle in the world than one of those obscure streets of London. The houses, which were old and ruinous, stood so close together as almost to shut out the sky, and even the sunshine, where a glimpse of it could be seen, was made dusky and dim by the smoke of the city. A kennel of muddy water flowed through the street. The general untidiness about the houses proved that the inhabitants felt no affection for their homes, nor took pride in making them decent and respectable. In these houses, it is to be feared that there were many people sick, suffering for food, and shivering with cold, and many, alas! who had fallen into the sore disease of sin, and sought to render their lives easier by dishonest practices. In short, the street seemed a place seldom visited by angels of mercy, or trodden by the footsteps of good men. Yet it were well that good men should often go thither, and be saddened by such reflections as now occurred to Mr. Raikes, in order that their hearts might be stirred up to attempt a reformation.

"Alas, what a spectacle is here!" thought this good man to himself. "How can any Christian remain idle, when there is so much evil to be remedied within a morning's walk of his own home?"

But we have not yet mentioned what it was that chiefly moved the heart of Mr. Raikes with sorrow and compassion. There were children at play in the street. Some were dabbling in the kennel, and splashing its dirty water over their companions, out of the mere love of mischief. Others, who had already been taught to gamble, were playing at pitch-and-toss for half-pence. Others, perhaps, were quarrelling and fighting. In a word—for we will not describe what it was so sad to witness—these poor children were growing up in idleness, with none but bad examples before their eyes, and without the opportunity of learning anything but evil. Their little, unclean faces looked already old in naughtiness; it seemed as if the vice and misery of the world had been born with them, and would cling to them as long as they existed. How sad a spectacle was this for a man like Mr. Raikes, who had always delighted in little children, and felt as if the world was made more beautiful, and his own heart the better, by their bright and happy faces! But, as he gazed at these poor little creatures, he thought that the world had never looked so dark, ugly, and sorrowful, as it did then.

"Oh, that I could save them!" thought he. "It were better for them to have been born among the wildest savages, than to grow up thus in a Christian country."

Now, at the door of one of the houses, there stood a woman, who, though she looked poor and needy, yet seemed neater and more respectable than the other inhabitants of this wretched street. She, like Mr. Raikes, was gazing at the children; and perhaps her mind was occupied with reflections similar to his. It might be, that she had children of her own, and was ready to shed tears at the thought, that they must grow up in the midst of such bad examples. At all events, when Mr. Raikes beheld this woman, he felt as if he had found somebody that could sympathize with him in his grief and anxiety.

"My good woman," said he, pointing to the children, "this is a dismal sight—so many of God's creatures growing up in idleness and ignorance, with no instruction but to do evil."

"Alas, good Sir," answered the woman, "it is bad enough on week-days, as you see;—but if you were to come into the street on a Sunday, you would find it a thousand times worse. On other days some of the children find employment, good or bad; but the Sabbath brings them all into the street together—and then there is nothing but mischief from morning till night."

"Ah, that is a sad case indeed," said Mr. Raikes. "Can the blessed Sabbath itself bring no blessing to these poor children? This is the worst of all."

And then, again, he looked along the street, with pity and strong benevolence; for his whole heart was moved by what he saw. The longer he considered, the more terrible did it appear that those children should grow up in ignorance and sin, and that the germs of immortal goodness, which Heaven had implanted in their souls, should be for ever blighted by neglect. And the earnestness of his compassion quickened his mind to perceive what was to be done. As he stood gazing at the spectacle that had so saddened him, an expression of delightful hope broke forth upon his face, and made it look as if a bright gleam of sunshine fell across it. And, if moral sunshine could be discerned on physical objects, just such a brightness would have shone through the gloomy street, gladdening all the dusky windows, and causing the poor children to look beautiful and happy. Not only in that wretched street would the light of gladness have appeared; it might have spread from thence all round the earth; for there was now a thought on the mind of Mr. Raikes, that was destined, in no long time, to make the whole world brighter than it had been hitherto.

And what was that thought?

It must be considered that Mr. Raikes was not a very rich man. There were thousands of people in England, to whom Providence had assigned greater wealth than he possessed, and who, as one would suppose, might have done far more good to their fellow-creatures than it lay in his power to do. There was a king, too, and princes, lords and statesmen, who were set in lofty places, and entrusted with the making and administration of the laws. If the condition of the world was to be improved, were not these the men to accomplish it? But the true faculty of doing good consists not in wealth nor station, but in the energy and wisdom of a loving heart, that can sympathize with all mankind, and acknowledges a brother or a sister in every unfortunate man or woman, and an own child in each neglected orphan. Such a heart was that of Mr. Raikes; and God now rewarded him with a blessed opportunity of conferring more benefit on his race, than he, in his humility, had ever dreamed of. And it would not be too much to say, that the king and his nobles, and the wealthy gentlemen of England, with all their boundless means, had for many years, done nothing so worthy of grateful remembrance, as what was now to be effected by this humble individual.

And yet how simple was this great idea, and how small the means by which Mr. Raikes proceeded to put it in execution! It was merely, to hire respectable and intelligent women, at the rate of a shilling each, to come, every Sabbath, and keep little schools for the poor children whom he had seen at play. Perhaps the good woman with whom Mr. Raikes had spoken in the street, was one of his new school-mistresses. Be that as it might, the plan succeeded, and, attracting the notice of benevolent people, was soon adopted in many other dismal streets of London. And this was the origin of Sunday-schools. In course of time, similar schools were established all over that great city, and thence extended to the remotest parts of England, and across the ocean to America, and to countries at a world-wide distance, where the humble name of Robert Raikes had never been pronounced.

That good man has now long been dead. But still, on every Sabbath-morning, in the cities and country villages, and wheresoever the steeple of a church points upward to the sky, the children take their way to the Sunday-school. Thousands, and tens of thousands, have there received instruction, which has been more profitable to them than all the gold on earth. And we may be permitted to believe, that, in the celestial world, where the founder of the system now exists, he has often met with other happy spirits, who have blessed him as the earthly means by which they were rescued from hopeless ignorance and evil, and guided on the path to Heaven. Is not this a proof, that when the humblest person acts in the simplicity of a pure heart, and with no design but to do good, *God* may be expected to take the matter into His all-powerful hands and adopt the action as His own?

Originally published 1844. Reprinted in *Nathaniel Hawthorne: Tales and Stories* (New York: The Library of America, Viking Press, 1982), pp. 868–872.

DANIEL AKST

"Graduates, Take Heed: Ignore the High-Minded Advice. Make Some Money. It's Your Moral Obligation."

With its new influx of "philanthropreneurs"—philanthropists whose preferred vehicle is for-profit enterprise—the field of philanthropy is newly investigating the capacity of capitalism, rather than altruism, to render positive change. In a different light, contemporary novelist and journalist Daniel Akst considers the same topic, addressing his short essay to graduating college students. In it he compares two graduates who want to do good in the world—"Dan," who pursues journalism hoping to write novels, and "Alex," who works in the securities industry. Fast-forwarding twenty-five years, we find Alex the philanthropist and Dan the novelist. Who has made the world a better place? Who has made a difference? Akst doesn't hesitate: Alex. Is he right? If one would do good, might it be an "outright moral obligation" to make money? Why or why not?

If you're newly graduated from college, you may be wondering right about now just how you're going to save the world.

Your commencement speech, after all, was probably delivered by a well-to-do older person who exhorted you to go out and make a difference somehow. Lots of other people will offer advice on what to do with yourself as well—rent *The Graduate* sometime and listen for that line about "plastics." Joseph Campbell, as silly as he was sage-like, might have suggested you "follow your bliss." The vastly more credible Thoreau urged you to "go confidently in the direction of your dreams."

I hope what you are dreaming of is making the world a better place, and unlike all these other kibitzers, I can tell you exactly how to do so. Just go out and make the most money you can. Then, if you still want to do more, give it away.

Contrary to your prosperous commencement speaker, anything else you do is selfishness and vanity. Don't get me wrong: It's not bad to delude yourself that you are pursuing a low-paid line of work in the name of helping others. Heck, you probably would be helping others—only not nearly as much as you could by getting rich.

Face the fact that if you embark on a career as, say, a social worker, you've done so because you like it, because it makes you feel important and because you don't have the stomach to do some really major good. That would require making piles and piles of dough.

I know this is news you don't especially want to hear. And I know it sounds callous. So instead of trying to prove the case by cold, hard logic, let me tell you a story.

This is the tale of a couple of ambitious young men who graduated from an Ivy League university in 1978. One—we'll call him "Dan"—idealistically chose a career in journalism, hoping eventually to transcend even this sainted calling in order to write novels. The other, whom we'll call "Alex," descended to the nethermost reaches of Manhattan to work in the securities industry, where he set about seeking his fortune.

Fast-forward 25 years. Our two graduates, out of touch for a while, renew their acquaintance. How have they fared since college? Dan did more or less what he set out to do. He has had a career in journalism (including some modestly edifying muckraking), has published a couple of well-received novels and now spends his days typing industriously away, undeterred by the world's indifference to his work.

Alex, meanwhile, made several hundred million dollars. In fact, Alex is retired from business and spends his time running the foundation he established with some of his wealth. When he dies, a good hunk of the rest will go the same way.

Now, my question for all you budding poets and video artists and social workers is: Who ended up doing more to make the world a better place, Dan or Alex? It's hard to argue with Alex's foundation. But Alex was improving the world long before he devoted himself and his wealth to philanthropy. How?

First, he made his money by providing an unambiguously valuable service. Trust me, become an activist or artist and sooner or later you will wonder whether what you do is really worthwhile to anyone. But Alex doesn't have to puzzle over the value of what he did, because someone clearly was willing to pay all that money for the fruits of his labor. Along the way, he treated his employees well, helping them and their families achieve better—and no doubt longer—lives, since affluence and longevity are correlated. At the end, when the business was sold, he rewarded them handsomely.

What Alex specifically did on Wall Street, moreover, helped make the securities markets more efficient, which benefits everyone—especially the present and future retirees, middle-class families, endowed colleges and other non-plutocrats who make up so much of the market by investing through pension funds, mutual funds and other institutions. Alex didn't meet a lot of widows and orphans in his work, but what he did almost certainly improved their lot.

For doing this work, Alex was magnificently rewarded, enabling him to amass a significant sum of investment capital—which makes the rest of us richer as well. Economics, remember, is not a zero-sum game. Capital is the lifeblood of the economy, fueling the productivity gains that in turn fuel expanding affluence and social progress. As if none of this were sufficient, Alex's earnings required him to pay enough income taxes over the years for the government to employ a small army of social workers. He never shirked these obligations through dubious tax-shelter schemes, either. And don't forget the foundation!

The conclusion is unavoidable: If you have a good education, you shouldn't just consider getting rich. Creating and amassing wealth is an outright moral obligation. Do so and you can take comfort not just in financing public services but in knowing that you are giving people what they need or want, generating jobs and underwriting the affluence that makes art, justice, environmental protection and other social goods possible.

Of course, making yourself a pile of money is good for you too. You'll live in a better neighborhood, drive a safer car, get to be more selective in choosing a spouse and enjoy a longer, healthier life. Your kids will get a better education, which in turn will mean more of the same for them, too—and will better equip them to improve the world still more.

From a moral standpoint, it is clear that Alex has done his part. With such an eleemosynary career under his belt—and such bulging bank accounts—he has decided to indulge himself and stop making money. The money he already has is busily reproducing itself, of course, and meanwhile he is spending most of his time figuring out how he can use it to make the world a better place. Sounds like fun, no?

Meanwhile, Dan is writing another novel—just what the world needs. The shelves at Barnes & Noble are full of them. Libraries are bursting. Yet he selfishly pours his energies into adding one more. How can he redeem himself for squandering his education in this way? Perhaps his next book should be a story about two friends and what they've learned over the years about saving the world. If it's a bestseller, he can always give the money away.

SHOLOM ALEICHEM

"Reb Yozifl and the Contractor"

In his many short stories, Russian Yiddish writer Sholom Aleichem (1859–1916) makes vivid the culture and community he knew firsthand in a small village in Eastern Europe. But the very provinciality of his setting belies his very un-provincial concerns—in this case, how to judge the effectiveness of philanthropic efforts. As the railroad is first being built through Kasrilevke, the rabbi of the town, Reb Yozifl, conceives a plan to erect a home for the poor and sick old folk because, he says, "People despise an infirm old man." Against all odds, he succeeds in raising the requisite funds from a wealthy contractor, and a luxurious moshav z'kenim ("home for the aged") is built. But while his fundraising is successful, we learn in the epilogue that his structure is not: to this day it stands unoccupied. Had Reb Yozifl done due diligence from the start, very likely he would have been able to anticipate such an eventuality. But then, again, maybe he did. Why did the wealthy contractor agree to fund the house? Is the unused home a philanthropic disaster? Might it signify a different kind of success?

Everything in the world is progressing and marching onward. So is our town of Kasrilevke.

Kasrilevke has taken a great stride ahead latterly. So much so, that you will be positively surprised if you go there now.

There is one sight in Kasrilevke especially that you will never tire of gazing at. You will see in the heart of the town, where the mud is at its deepest, a massive, yellow brick building—tall and wide—ornamented with iron, with a host of windows, a beautiful, high, carved door, and above it a marble slab bearing the following Hebrew inscription in golden letters:

MOSHAV Z'KENIM

As you look at the building you can't help thinking of a gorgeous velvet patch atop a threadbare lustrine gaberdine, green with age. How comes this luxurious Home for the Aged in the midst of poverty-stricken Kasrilevke? you ask. Was it put up to spite anybody? Or just as a practical joke? Or did somebody make a mistake? Here is the story as it was told to me the last time I was there to visit my parents' grave.

It happened at the time when the railway was being put through Kasrilevke. All kinds of curious creatures came down from Moscow: engineers, surveyors, excavators and such like, and at the head of them all a contractor—a personage of importance and a Jew into the bargain. His name is unknown to this day. Maybe he was one of Poliakov's men, or maybe he was the great financier Poliakov himself, for all anybody knows. But even a child could see that he was worth a fortune—a veritable millionaire. For how else could he afford the luxury of occupying two rooms by himself, gorge himself with chicken, swill wine on weekdays, and dally with the hotel proprietor's young daughter-in-law, the hussy? (She wears no wig even in public and despises her husband, as everybody knows.)

In those days our old friend the rabbi, Reb Yozifl, conceived a plan to erect a *moshav z'kenim* in Kasrilevke—a home for the poor and sick old folk. But why a home for the aged? you might ask. Why not a hospital? There you are again with your questions! Supposing he had set his mind on a hospital; then you'd ask: Why not a home for the aged? I can assure you of one thing, however: he certainly had no personal motive; nothing was further from his mind than the thought of a refuge for his own old age. He simply concluded that a sick old man was to be pitied more than a sick young man. To be sure, an ailing young person was in a bad way too. But if you are ill and old into the bargain, you're simply a burden to the world. Just a loathed dead weight. People despise an infirm old man—there's no gainsaying that.

In short, he made up his mind once and for all: Kasrilevke simply must have a *moshav z'kenim*. A home for the aged must take precedence over everything else. And in order to bring home to everybody how necessary it was, Reb Yozifl delivered a sermon in the synagogue on Saturday afternoon, illustrating his talk with a parable: "Once upon a time there was a king who had an only son . . ." But since I am telling you a story, I'd rather not interrupt it with another one. So we'll just defer Reb Yozifl's parable for some other time. I might tell you, however, that although the parable may not have quite fitted the moral in question, nevertheless his audience was completely carried away by it, as they were by all the parables that Reb Yozifl used to tell them. One could only wish that he had been as good at earning his daily bread as he was talented in telling parables.

On hearing his parable, one of the prominent citizens spoke up—one of the most honored, it goes without saying, for who else would dare to contradict a rabbi before a congregation of Jews?

"Yes, indeed, rabbi, there's no denying that you are right. That was a beautiful parable. The only trouble is: where do we get the cash? A home for the aged costs a lot of money, and Kasrilevke is a town of nothing but indigent, poverty-stricken, penniless, impoverished, destitute starvelings."

"Pshaw! There is a parable that applies to this case too. Once upon a time there was a king who had an only son . . ."

Anyway, the fate of the king and his only son is of no importance. What is important is that on the following day, on a Sunday, our Reb Yozifl in company of two of the most prominent householders, with a kerchief in his hand, set out for the market square and started making the rounds, going from shop to shop and from house to house—the old Kasrilevke method of "raising funds." It goes without saying that no vast fortune can be amassed in this way. Reb Yozifl, however, had plenty of time. He could well afford to wait another week. Rome wasn't built in a day either. It just couldn't be helped: a townful of poor Jews! The only hope were the outsiders—merchants that come down to Kasrilevke, or other transients putting up at the local hotels.

In Kasrilevke, if ever they lay their hands on a bird of passage, they pluck it so bare that it'll warn all and sundry to shun the town: "If ever you have to pass through Kasrilevke, go miles out of your way to stay clear of it. The town beggars there are simply intolerable!"

On hearing that a Jewish contractor had come down from Moscow, one of Poliakov's men, or maybe Poliakov himself, a multi-millionaire—Reb Yozifl donned his Sabbath best, threw his cloak over it and put his fur hat on his head. Somehow the ceremonial hat didn't go well with the big weekday stick; and he had everybody puzzled. The people argued: it's either one thing or another. If it's the Sabbath, then why a stick; if it's a weekday, why a fur hat? The problem was not solved until Reb Yozifl was seen taking along with him the two most prominent citizens and making straight for the wealthy contractor in the hotel.

I don't know what other Moscow contractors are like. But this contractor who had come to Kasrilevke to put the railway through was a curious sort. Of low stature, limber, with chubby cheeks, fleshy lips, and short arms, he was a frisky little man, running more often than walking, shouting rather than talking and bursting now and then into an explosive little laugh: He-he-he! His little eyes were always moist with tears. All his movements were brisk, hurried, precipitate, and he was dangerously nervous! Not to satisfy his every whim or to irritate him with as much as a single remark was to invite disastrous consequences. His eyes immediately caught fire and he was ready to trample you underfoot or tear you to pieces. He was a very unusual contractor indeed.

He had given instructions at the hotel that no matter who came to see him, no matter who he might be, even if it should be the Governor himself (these were his very words), he was not to be admitted without the proprietor first rapping at his door and being told by the contractor to enter. Only then the proprietor was to report to him who the caller was. Then he would either see him at once or ask him to come the next day.

Needless to say, Kasrilevke had a good laugh at this odd person and his curious ways. Surely only a Moscow contractor could conceive such outlandish notions.

Isn't it enough when a man goes to all the trouble of calling on you—so they argued—must he also stand outside your door and wait till he gets your permission to enter, or else be told to come tomorrow? No, only a Moscow contractor could do a thing like that. There can be little doubt that there isn't a greater man than Reb Yozifl the rabbi, a man of learning and a God-fearing man. Nevertheless his door is open at all times for anybody who may need him. Surely this is an established Jewish custom.

On seeing Reb Yozifl in person and, what's more, wearing his Sabbath best, the hotel proprietor, a man with a good-sized paunch, unbuttoned coat and waistcoat, and a pipe in his mouth, became all flustered:

"I bid you welcome! Welcome indeed! Such a visitor! Just imagine, the rabbi in person in my house! Such a privilege! Do be seated, rabbi! What's that? Oh, you wish to see our guest? With the greatest pleasure!"

The proprietor in his confusion forgot all about the injunction "no matter who he might be" and "even if it should be the Governor," put away his pipe, buttoned his coat, showed the rabbi and the two most prominent citizens to the guest's door, and himself disappeared.

It is hard to say what the guest was busy doing at the moment. Perhaps he was in the very act of planning the railway, figuring where to lay the tracks and where to put up the station. Or maybe he was lying down in the adjoining room and dozing. Or maybe, for all one can tell, he was just sitting there and having a chat with the proprietor's young daughter-in-law, the hussy, who wears no wig and despises her husband, as everybody knows. Who is to say what a Jewish contractor from Moscow, a personage of importance and a Jew into the bargain, might be doing—a lone man occupying two rooms? In any event, when the deputation stepped into the first room, he wasn't there. The door to the adjoining room was open and there wasn't a sound. They didn't want to step any farther. That would be bad manners; he might be sleeping. So they had a brilliant idea: the three of them gave a cough (that's a Kasrilevke custom). Hearing the noise, the contractor bolted out of his room more dead than alive. When he saw the strangers, he flared up and burst out in the true Moscow manner:

"Who are you? What do you want, you so-and-so and so-and-so? Who let you in? Haven't I told them time and again to admit no one unannounced?"

Some say that he used the word *zhidy*, kikes, although it's hard to believe that a Jew would do that. All the same, when a man's wrath is kindled, and especially a millionaire's, there's no telling what he might do.

Our readers who are acquainted with the rabbi of Kasrilevke know full well what a humble man Reb Yozifl was. Why, he'd never dream of being forward. He always preferred to be last. For it was his idea that mortal man must not be in too great a hurry; he has nothing to lose and will never miss anything. But this time he had to step forward, because those "most prominent citizens" were plainly frightened by the millionaire, who was wildly waving his hands at them and emphasizing his fury by stamping his feet. Who could say who he was? Maybe he was one of Poliakov's men, and maybe even Poliakov himself. Such being the case, they naturally had to recede a bit, get a little closer to the door. For there was no telling what might happen. Only Reb Yozifl didn't get frightened this time. He argued this way. It's one of two things: he is either a *big* man or a *little* man. If he is a big man, I don't need to be afraid of him; if he is a little man, there surely can be no occasion for fear. So he spoke right up to him in these words:

"Pardon me, you are shouting at us. Maybe you are right. Forgive us for disturbing you. But we are engaged in the performance of a good deed, and the messengers of a good deed—so our sages tell us—can suffer no injury. You see, we are collecting contributions for a great cause, a home for the aged."

The Moscow contractor stood speechless. The intrusion of the three men into his room, unannounced, like a bolt from the blue, and the conduct of this old man (the fellow with the fur hat) which struck him as both foolish and impudent, so enraged our Muscovite, so infuriated him, that he felt a tickling sensation in his nose, a sense of pressure against his brain, and all his blood rushed to his face. He was simply frantic and so completely lost control of himself that he just didn't know what he was doing. His hand was raised, as if against his own will, he swung it with all his might and dealt the old man a resounding, flaming slap.

"Take this! This is for your old folks' home!"

The slap sent the old man's fur hat and skullcap flying off his head together, and for a moment the rabbi of Kasrilevke stood with uncovered head—perhaps for the first time in his life. But this lasted no more than a second. Reb Yozifl quickly bent down, snatched up the fur hat and covered his bared head. Then he cautiously felt his cheek and looked at his hand to see if there was any blood. At the same time he said to the guest, speaking softly, sweetly, and with a curious smile on his deathly pale face:

"That's that. I take it that this was meant for me. Now, my dear man, what are you going to give for the sick old folk—I mean the home for the aged?"

What happened next can't be told. No one knows, for "the most prominent citizens," on hearing the language of Moscow from the lips of the contractor, had beaten a hasty retreat. And Reb Yozifl just wouldn't talk about the affair. This is known, however: on leaving the hotel, the old rabbi's face beamed strangely. One of his cheeks—the left—beamed even more than the other. He said with a sweet smile:

"*Mazel tov,* congratulations, fellow Jews, I have good news for you: we are going to have now, with the aid of the Almighty, a home for the aged—a home that will be a delight to God and man."

The "little folk" might have had some doubts about the rabbi's statement, if they hadn't heard with their own ears the contractor himself say, while tapping his shirt-front with his pudgy fingers:

"Men, I'm putting up a home for the aged in your town. I, I . . ."

Not only did they hear this with their own ears, but they soon saw with their own eyes the contractor walking about the town with the rabbi, then stopping to measure a plot with his stick and saying:

"This is where the building is going to stand; it'll have this frontage and this depth . . ."

Before they knew it, loads of brick, lumber, and other building materials arrived. The structure was under way.

To be sure, there were the curious who tried to question the rabbi, sound him out, get him to talk:

"Rabbi, just what did happen? Just how did this man make it up to you for his harsh words? . . . What did *you* say to *him* and what did he answer *you*? . . ."

Reb Yozifl, however, took no notice of what was said and avoided the subject, merely saying with his ever sweet smile:

"All the same, we are going to have a home for the aged, God willing. I'm telling you, it will be a delight to God and man."

Too bad—the home for the aged is unoccupied to this day. Reb Yozifl departed from this world long ago—there is no money to run the institution with.

This has ever been the fate of the little folk of Kasrilevke: when they dream of good things to eat—they haven't a spoon; when they have a spoon—they don't dream of good things to eat.

ANZIA YEZIERSKA

"The Free Vacation House"

Russian émigré Anzia Yezierska (1885–1970) wrote about the plight of people she knew too well: poor Jewish immigrants trying to make a new life for themselves on New York's Lower East Side in the first part of the twentieth century. In this short story, she also gives us a good glimpse of the problems that attend evaluation from the beneficiary's perspective. A beleaguered mother of five young children, on the verge of a "nervous breakdown," gets a visit from the Social Betterment Society, which promises a free vacation in a country house to qualified applicants. After a battery of interrogations, the mother and her children make their way to the house, where she is interrogated all over again, then beset by rules and bells that order their every movement from morning till night. At the end of her two week stay, the mother and her brood are thankful to return to their city life, now grand by comparison. The Society's attempt, simultaneously, to perform, evaluate, and promote the charitable act clearly diminishes its ability to do the good that was intended. Was this avoidable? Can one, in general, be effective and judge or demonstrate effectiveness at the same time?

ℒ

How came it that I went to the free vacation house was like this:

One day the visiting teacher from the school comes to find out for why don't I get the children ready for school in time; for why are they so often late.

I let out on her my whole bitter heart. I told her my head was on wheels from worrying. When I get up in the morning, I don't know on what to turn first: should I nurse the baby, or make Sam's breakfast, or attend on the older children. I only got two hands.

"My dear woman," she says, "you are about to have a nervous breakdown. You need to get away to the country for a rest and vacation."

"*Gott im Himmel!*" says I. "Don't I know I need a rest? But how? On what money can I go to the country?"

"I know of a nice country place for mothers and children that will not cost you anything. It is free."

"Free! I never heard from it."

"Some kind people have made arrangements so no one need pay," she explains.

Later, in a few days, I just finished up with Masha and Mendel and Frieda and Sonya to send them to school, and I was getting Aby ready for kindergarten, when I hear a knock on the door, and a lady comes in. She had a white starched dress like a nurse and carried a black satchel in her hand.

"I am from the Social Betterment Society," she tells me. "You want to go to the country?"

Before I could say something, she goes over to the baby and pulls out the rubber nipple from her mouth, and to me, she says, "You must not get the child used to sucking this; it is very unsanitary."

"*Gott im Himmel!*" I beg the lady. "Please don't begin with that child, or she'll holler my head off. She must have the nipple. I'm too nervous to hear her scream like that."

When I put the nipple back again in the baby's mouth, the lady takes herself a seat, and then takes out a big black book from her satchel. Then she begins to question me. What is my first name? How old I am? From where come I? How long I'm already in this country? Do I keep any boarders? What is my husband's first name? How old he is? How long he is in this country? By what trade he works? How much wages he gets for a week? How much money do I spend out for rent? How old are the children, and everything about them.

"My goodness!" I cry out. "For why is it necessary all this to know? For why must I tell you all my business? What difference does it make already if I keep boarders, or I don't keep boarders? If Masha had the whooping-cough or Sonya had the measles? Or whether I spend out for my rent ten dollars or twenty? Or whether I come from Schnipishock or Kovner Gubernie?"

"We must make a record of all the applicants, and investigate each case," she tells me. "There are so many who apply to the charities, we can help only those who are most worthy."

"Charities!" I scream out. "Ain't the charities those, who help the beggars out? I ain't no beggar. I'm not asking for no charity. My husband, he works."

"Miss Holcomb, the Visiting teacher, said that you wanted to go to the country, and I had to make out this report before investigating your case."

"Oh! Oh!" I choke and bit my lips. "Is the free country from which Miss Holcomb told me, is it from the charities? She was telling me some kind people made arrangements for any mother what needs to go there."

"If your application is approved, you will be notified," she says to me, and out she goes.

When she is gone I think to myself, I'd better knock out from my head this idea about the country. For so long I lived, I didn't know nothing about the charities. For why should I come down among the beggars now?

Then I looked around me in the kitchen. On one side was the big wash-tub with clothes, waiting for me to wash. On the table was a pile of breakfast dishes yet. In the sink was the potatoes, waiting to be peeled. The baby was beginning to cry for the bottle. Aby was hollering and pulling me to take him to kindergarten. I felt if I didn't get away from here for a little while, I would land in a crazy house, or from the window jump down. Which was worser, to land in a crazy house, jump from the window down, or go to the country from the charities?

In about two weeks later around comes the same lady with the satchel again in my house.

"You can go to the country to-morrow," she tells me. "And you must come to the charity building to-morrow at nine o'clock sharp. Here is a card with the address. Don't lose it, because you must hand it to the lady in the office."

I look on the card, and there I see my name wrote; and by it, in big printed letters, that word "CHARITY."

"Must I go to the charity office?" I ask, feeling my heart to sink. "For why must I come there?"

"It is the rule that everybody comes to the office first, and from there they are taken to the country."

I shivered to think how I would feel, suppose somebody from my friends should see me walking into the charity office with my children. They wouldn't know that it is only for the country I go there. They might think I go to beg. Have I come down so low as to be seen by the charities? But what's the use? Should I knock my head on the walls? I had to go.

When I come to the office, I already found a crowd of women and children sitting on long benches and waiting. I took myself a seat with them, and we were sitting and sitting and looking on one another, sideways and crosswise, and with lowered eyes, like guilty criminals. Each one felt like hiding herself from all the rest. Each one felt black with shame in the face.

We may have been sitting and waiting for an hour or more. But every second was seeming years to me. The children began to get restless. Mendel wanted water. The baby on my arms was falling asleep. Aby was crying for something to eat.

"For why are we sittin' here like fat cats?" says the woman next to me. "Ain't we going to the country to-day yet?"

At last a lady comes to the desk and begins calling us our names, one by one. I nearly dropped to the floor when over she begins to ask: Do you keep boarders? How much do you spend out for rent? How much wages does your man get for a week?

Didn't the nurse tell them all about us already? It was bitter enough to have to tell the nurse everything, but in my own house nobody was hearing my troubles, only the nurse. But in the office there was so many strangers all around me. For why should everybody have to know my business? At every question I wanted to holler out: "Stop! Stop! I don't want no vacations! I'll better run home with my children." At every question I felt like she was stabbing a knife into my heart. And she kept on stabbing me more and more, but I could not help it, and they were all looking at me. I couldn't move from her. I had to answer everything.

When she got through with me, my face was red like fire. I was burning with hurts and wounds. I felt like everything was bleeding in me.

When all the names was already called, a man doctor with a nurse comes in, and tells us to form a line, to be examined. I wish I could ease out my heart a little, and tell in words how that doctor looked on us, just because we were poor and had no money to pay. He only used the ends from his finger-tips to examine us with. From the way he was afraid to touch us or come near us, he made us feel like we had some catching sickness that he was trying not to get on him.

The doctor got finished with us in about five minutes, so quick he worked. Then we was told to walk after the nurse, who was leading the way for us through the street to the car. Everybody what passed us in the street turned around to look on us. I kept down my eyes and held down my head and I felt like sinking into the sidewalk. All the time I was trembling for fear somebody what knows me might yet pass and see me. For why did they make us walk through the street, after the nurse, like stupid cows? Weren't all of us smart enough to find our way without the nurse? Why should the whole world have to see that we are from the charities?

When we got into the train, I opened my eyes, and lifted up my head, and straightened out my chest, and again began to breathe. It was a beautiful, sun-shiny day. I knocked open the window from the train, and the fresh-smelling country air rushed upon my face and made me feel so fine! I looked out from the window and instead of seeing the iron fire-escapes with garbage-cans and bedclothes, that I always seen when from my flat I looked—instead of seeing only walls and wash-lines between walls, I saw the blue sky, and green grass and trees and flowers.

Ah, how grand I felt, just on the sky to look! Ah, how grand I felt just to see the green grass—and the free space—and no houses!

"Get away from me, my troubles!" I said. "Leave me rest a minute. Leave me breathe and straighten out my bones. Forget the unpaid butcher's bill. Forget the rent. Forget the wash-tub and the cook-stove and the pots and pans. Forget the charities!"

"Tickets, please," calls the train conductor. I felt knocked out from heaven all at once. I had to point to the nurse what held our tickets, and I was feeling the conductor looking on me as if to say, "Oh, you are only from the charities."

By the time we came to the vacation house I already forgot all about my knock-down. I was again filled with the beauty of the country. I never in all my life yet seen such a swell house like that vacation house. Like the grandest pal-ace it looked. All round the front, flowers from all colors was smelling out the sweetest perfume. Here and there was shady trees with comfortable chairs under them to sit down on.

When I only came inside, my mouth opened wide and my breathing stopped still from wonder. I never yet seen such an order and such a cleanliness. From all the corners from the room, the cleanliness was shining like a looking-glass. The floor was so white scrubbed you could eat on it. You couldn't find a speck of dust on nothing, if you was looking for it with eye glasses on.

I was beginning to feel happy and glad that I come, when, *Gott im Himmel!* again a lady begins to ask us out the same questions what the nurse already asked me in my home and what was asked over again in the charity office. How much wages my husband makes out for a week? How much money I spend out for rent? Do I keep boarders?

We were hungry enough to faint. So worn out was I from excitement, and from the long ride, that my knees were bending under me ready to break from tiredness. The children were pulling me to pieces, nagging me for a drink, for something to eat and such like. But still we had to stand out the whole list of questionings. When she already got through asking us out everything, she gave to each of us a tag with our name written on it. She told us to tie the tag on our hand. Then like tagged horses at a horse sale in the street, they marched us into the dining-room.

There was rows of long tables, covered with pure-white oil-cloth. A vase with bought flowers was standing on the middle from each table. Each person got a clean napkin for himself. Laid out by the side from each person's plate was a silver knife and fork and spoon and teaspoon. When we only sat ourselves down, girls with white starched aprons was passing around the eatings.

I soon forgot again all my troubles. For the first time in ten years I sat down to a meal what I did not have to cook or worry about. For the first time in ten years I sat down to the table like a somebody. Ah, how grand it feels, to have handed you over the eatings and everything you need. Just as I was beginning to like it and let myself feel good, in comes a fat lady all in white, with a teacher's look on her face. I could tell already, right away by the way she looked on us, that she was the boss from this place.

"I want to read you the rules from this house, before you leave this room," says she to us.

Then she began like this: We dassen't stand on the front grass where the flowers are. We dassen't stay on the front porch. We dassen't sit on the chairs under the shady trees. We must stay always in the back and sit on those long wooden benches there. We dassen't come in the front sitting-room or walk on the front steps what have carpet on it—we must walk on the back iron steps. Everything on the front from the house must be kept perfect for the show for visitors. We dassen't lay down on the beds in the daytime, the beds must always be made up perfect for the show for visitors.

"*Gott im Himmel!*" thinks I to myself; "ain't there going to be no end to the things we dassen't do in this place?"

But still she went on. The children over two years dassen't stay around by the mothers. They must stay by the nurse in the play-room. By the meal-times, they can see their mothers. The children dassen't run around the house or tear up flowers or do anything. They dassen't holler or play rough in the play-room. They must always behave and obey the nurse.

We must always listen to the bells. Bell one was for getting up. Bell two, for getting babies' bottles. Bell three, for coming to breakfast. Bell four, for bathing the babies. If we come later, after the ring from the bell, then we'll not get what we need. If the bottle bell rings and we don't come right away for the bottle, then the baby don't get no bottle. If the breakfast bell rings, and we don't come right away down to the breakfast, then there won't be no breakfast for us.

When she got through with reading the rules, I was wondering which side of the house I was to walk on. At every step was some rule what said don't move here, and don't go there, don't stand there, and don't sit there. If I tried to remember the endless rules, it would only make me dizzy in the head. I was thinking for why, with so many rules, didn't they also have already another rule, about how much air in our lungs to breathe. On every few days there came to the house swell ladies in automobiles. It was for them that the front from the house had to be always perfect. For them was all the beautiful smelling flowers. For them the front porch, the front sitting-room, and the easy stairs with the carpet on it.

Always when the rich ladies came the fat lady, what was the boss from the vacation house, showed off to them the front. Then she took them over to the back to look on us, where we was sitting together, on long wooden benches, like prisoners. I was always feeling cheap like dirt, and mad that I had to be there, when they smiled down on us.

"How nice for these poor creatures to have a restful place like this," I heard one lady say.

The next day I already felt like going back. The children what had to stay by the nurse in the play-room didn't like it neither.

"Mamma," says Mendel to me, "I wisht I was home and out in the street. They don't let us do nothing here. It's worser than school."

"Ain't it a play-room?" asks I. "Don't they let you play?"

"Gee wiss! play-room, they call it! The nurse hollers on us all the time. She don't let us do nothing."

The reason why I stayed out the whole two weeks is this: I think to myself, so much shame in the face I suffered to come here, let me at least make the best from it already. Let me at least save up for two weeks what I got to spend out for grocery and butcher for my back bills to pay out. And then also think I to myself, if I go back on Monday, I got to do the big washing; on Tuesday waits for me the ironing; on Wednesday, the scrubbing and cleaning, and so goes it on. How bad it is already in this place, it's a change from the very same sameness of what I'm having day in and day out at home. And so I stayed out this vacation to the bitter end.

But at last the day for going out from this prison came. On the way riding back, I kept thinking to myself: "This is such a beautiful vacation house. For why do they make it so hard for us? When a mother needs a vacation, why must they tear the insides out from her first, by making her come down to the charity office? Why drag us from the charity office through the streets? And when we live through the shame of the charities and when we come already to the vacation house, for why do they boss the life out of us with so many rules and bells? For why don't they let us lay down our heads on the bed when we are tired? For why must we always stick in the back, like dogs what have got to be chained in one spot? If they would let us walk around free, would we bite off something from the front part of the house?

"If the best part of the house what is comfortable is made up for a show for visitors, why ain't they keeping the whole business for a show for visitors? For why do they have to fool in worn-out mothers, to make them think they'll give them a rest? Do they need the worn-out mothers as part of the show? I guess that is it, already."

When I got back in my home, so happy and thankful I was I could cry from thankfulness. How good it was feeling for me to be able to move around my own house, like I pleased. I was always kicking that my rooms was small and narrow, but now my small rooms seemed to grow so big like the park. I looked out from my window on the fire-escapes, full with bedding and garbage-cans, and on the wash-lines full with the clothes. All these ugly things was grand in my eyes. Even the high brick walls all around made me feel like a bird what just jumped out from a cage. And I cried out, "*Gott sei dank! Gott sei dank!*"

From *Hungry Hearts and Other Stories* by Anzia Yezierska (New York: Houghton Mifflin Co., 1920).

WILLIAM A. SCHAMBRA

"The Evaluation Wars"

William A. Schambra, currently director of Hudson Institute's Bradley Center for Philanthropy and Civic Renewal, served for more than a decade as a program officer at the Bradley Foundation in Milwaukee. In "The Evaluation Wars," Schambra argues that "scientific evaluation"—evaluation that requires rigorous metrics and refined tracking and reporting procedures—is no match for "eyeballing effectiveness." Employing his experience of on-site visits with grantee organizations, Schambra suggests how such "eyeballing" can illuminate what "truly effective" grantees are: Organizations deeply committed and connected in manifold ways to the communities they serve, reflecting their "best traditions and hopes for the future." Are paper standards simply paper tigers? Does circumstantial evidence or anecdotes based on site visits make us more alive to what is really going on or to what really matters? Does trusting our own practical wisdom and intuitions, as Schambra urges, give us a pass on the need to evaluate what "deep commitment" means or which "best traditions and hopes" to look for?

ℱᴅ

"Am I doing any good by giving this money away?" is a question everyone in philanthropy should ask regularly. It is hard for funders to do good; it is all too easy for them to feel good—if they don't bother to investigate the consequences of their giving.

And so we hear much about choosing "effective" grantees and even more about "evaluating" grants given. In fact, it often sounds as if responsible philanthropy requires legions of scientists to evaluate the results of one's funding. Does that mean that small- and medium-sized foundations who lack the resources to undertake vast evaluative studies should just give up, perhaps passing their assets to some giant foundation with the scientific wherewithal to do the job right?

Wrong. First, the history of philanthropic evaluation reveals that it has certain limitations and even pitfalls for donors of all sizes. Second, a small or medium foundation can often outperform larger foundations when it comes to uncovering truly effective grantees.

Before we consider how to find the best grantees without a staff of hundreds, let's look at the long saga of evaluation.

From Charity to "Scientific Giving"

Today's effort to move beyond "sentimental charity" to "rigorous, results-oriented" giving is nothing new. It was the founding principle of large, institution-based giving that began with the Rockefeller, Carnegie, and Russell Sage philanthropies early in the twentieth century. As John Jordan reports in *Machine-Age Ideology,* these foundations searched for a mathematically rigorous social science that would give enlightened elites a way to achieve "social control" over the benighted masses. The Rockefeller Foundation declared in an early mission statement that it hoped to "increase the body of knowledge which in the hands of competent social technicians may be expected in time to result in substantial social control."

So tightly interwoven were philanthropy and the new social sciences that for all of August each summer in the 1920s, Rockefeller, Carnegie, and Sage officials would gather in the cool shade of Hanover, New Hampshire, with researchers from foundation-backed projects at the major universities and members of the National Bureau of Economic Research and the Social Sciences Research Council. They hoped to create "a vision from which new ideas may emerge," as philanthropist Beardsley Ruml put it.

After such an enthusiastic embrace of scientific, measurable outcomes by the very founders of contemporary philanthropy, how is it that, almost a century later, we still talk about the need to move from sentimental giving to rigorous, measurable outcomes *as if the idea had just occurred to us*?

As it turns out, social science underwent something of a crisis of confidence during the 1960s and '70s. Social reformers began to discover problems with the scientific, experimental method for studying the effects of social programs. This method required a donor (the government or a private entity) to design a narrowly focused social intervention, introduce it exactly the same way across a series of sites, and then compare the outcomes to "control groups"—sites with identical characteristics but not subjected to the treatment. Such efforts were cumbersome, expensive, and tended to produce results far too late to be useful to planning. Above all, experimental social science tended to show that no program ever worked. Hence evaluation expert Peter Rossi's famous Iron Law: "The expected value for any measured effect of a social program is zero." Thus some analysts became skeptics of government programs, while others persisted with their interventions, insisting they be measured in different ways.

The latter point of view was eloquently expressed by Lisbeth Schorr in two widely acclaimed books from the 1990s, *Within Our Reach* and *Common Purpose.* She argued that "the conventions governing traditional evaluation of program impact have systematically defined out of contention precisely those interventions that sophisticated funders and program people regard as most promising." To be evaluated scientifically, programs had to be narrowly defined and inflexibly applied for a limited experimental period. Truly effective programs, by contrast, tended to be "comprehensive, flexible, responsive, and persevering," and to "deal with families as parts of neighborhoods and communities." To evaluate these sorts of "comprehensive community initiatives," a new mode of measurement called "theory-based evaluation" was required. This approach, de rigueur among today's more sophisticated foundations, employs a "logic model" or "theory of change" to explain how a complex range of community elements may be brought together to produce "social change." Actual outcomes from the subsequent program can then be compared to predicted outcomes.

There is only one problem, as Gary Walker and Jean Grossman point out in their sobering and insightful *Philanthropy and Outcomes: Dilemmas in the Quest for Accountability*. Without control groups, this approach cannot show scientifically that the outcomes were produced by the program, and so "it is often difficult to know to what degree the outcomes achieved are attributable to the initiative funded." Hence the nonprofit scholar Ira Edelman found that evaluation schemes "failed to provide the kind of certainty" that experimental and statistical methods can offer. "Key players" reacted by rejecting evaluation reports and making "demands for 'hard' evidence that programs were working—evidence that was impossible to provide."

The Evaluation Wars rage on, with a bewildering variety of often conflicting approaches to measurement. . . . Small wonder that a recent survey of philanthropic leaders by the Center for Effective Philanthropy concluded, "each foundation has developed its own combination of metrics independently, described in different language, and applied in different ways . . . there is no common vocabulary to permit sharing among foundations nor any coordinated attempt to collect these measures more efficiently."

The Center also found that "even among the 225 largest foundations in the country, which have the greatest resources to evaluate grants, more than 40 percent of CEOs estimate that fewer than one-quarter of their foundations' grants are evaluated." And so, 80 years after social scientists and philanthropists gathered in New Hampshire to create a hard science of human behavior, the Center can only hope "that one day foundation leaders and trustees will have ready access to comprehensive objective performance data to guide their key decisions."

Until this hope—now almost a century old, with no fulfillment in sight— is realized, what can the family-managed or lightly staffed smaller foundation do to evaluate its programs? . . .

Wise and Effective Giving

In short, "scientific" giving is expensive and burdensome to start with, and even when these hurdles are overcome its value remains uncertain. Worst of all, the effort to evaluate grants rigorously may lead donors away from some highly effective potential grantees. Trying to discover, say, the scientifically perfect drug rehabilitation program may force a donor to ignore the most effective drug rehab programs already operating in his own city.

A purely scientific philanthropy is impossible; small foundations in particular should attempt a more intuitive style of grantmaking based on practical wisdom and keen observations close to home. Donors should recognize that their own back yards likely contain dozens of highly effective grassroots groups that should not be overlooked simply because they have never been evaluated by a phalanx of wonkish experts. Bob Woodson at the National Center for Neighborhood Enterprise and Amy Sherman at the Hudson Institute have worked with hundreds of grassroots leaders around the country who not only run solid programs themselves but are also invaluable sources of local wisdom about other programs known on "the street" to be truly effective. These local wise men and women can identify promising candidates for funding, and donors can then vet the candidates through discerning site visits. The visit is critical, for sometimes even the most effective "agents of change" can only explain what they are up to by saying, "Come and see."

Some tips for "eyeballing effectiveness" during the visit: Look first for activity. Typically, effective grassroots groups are quite busy and at times may even appear to be chaotically overwhelmed. If they are truly serving the neighborhood, they wind up pursuing not just their announced mission, but dealing with the full range of human needs brought to their doorsteps by a desperate community. For example, when children started showing up at Cordelia Taylor's Family House in Milwaukee, she could have sent them away and told them she was running a senior care facility—or she could have tried to meet their obvious need for a caring adult presence. She of course aimed for the latter. She had her son James take the kids under his wing with after-school activities and a homework club; eventually, a volunteer organized karate classes in the basement. This sort of flexible, unplanned, "off-mission" response to whatever the neighborhood needs next is a hallmark of effective grassroots work, but it plays havoc with program budgets and outcome-reporting, and makes it difficult to attract funding from larger foundations who expect to see rigid adherence to program designs and budget line-items. As Leon Watkins, director of Los Angeles's Family Helpline, told the Capital Research Center, "When someone comes in and tells me their house just burnt down, or they bring in a little girl with serious mental problems and she has no place to stay, what program do you put that under? It's hard to explain to people that concept. People who pledge support want to see programs. But that's what life is like here—whatever comes up, that's the program."

A group's busyness suggests its valued place in the neighborhood, which is also seen in another visible sign of effectiveness: the way the neighborhood shows tangible respect for the group. Cordelia Taylor had to reassure the construction company working on Family House's expansion that it needn't put fencing around its equipment at night, because the neighborhood knew it was helping her. Nothing was ever stolen from the unfenced site. Sister Jennie Lechtenberg notes that one sign of PUENTE Learning Center's importance to its East Los Angeles community is the fact that no graffiti appears on her facility's walls. (Conversely, it's easy to tell a group enjoys an uneasy relationship with the surrounding neighborhood by locked doors and elaborate security systems.)

Similarly, on a site visit to an effective grass-roots group one will see that the group genuinely respects the neighborhood, no matter how "pathological" it may seem to the experts. The group's leadership typically lives in the neighborhood it serves. (Robert Woodson calls this the "zip code test.") The leaders know the neighborhood thoroughly and can take you to its most forbidding corners without fear. . . .

A further sign of respect for the community is the way good grassroots leaders do not refer to the people they serve as "clients" and never treat them as passive, helpless victims of circumstances. Grassroots leaders know and use the names of those they are serving and are quite willing to interrupt a site visit to answer an urgent query. Visitors often see program participants washing dishes or picking up the trash during a tour, because the program shows its respect for the dignity of those it helps by asking something in return.

Grassroots groups also gain respect from neighborhoods and those they serve by having staff who themselves have overcome the problems they help others with. A former drunk with an eighth-grade education can often achieve far better results with current drunks than an entire staff of college-trained doctors, therapists, and social workers. If a nonprofit lacks any staff who can look a participant in the eye and tell him, "I beat this problem, and you can too," it's unlikely to be effective at reforming people. But if it has some of its own former participants now on staff, with or without professional credentials, it is probably turning lives around.

A site visit should also reveal evidence of good stewardship, well before you ever get to the point of examining the books. In one of my site visits for the Bradley Foundation, Sharon Mays-Ferguson pointed out a somewhat awkward window at Intercessions, her group home for teen mothers, and noted that she had wedged it in during construction because it had been donated by a supporter. When one tours Bob Coté's Step 13, a residential addiction treatment center in Denver, one learns which church donated that crucifix for his chapel and which company donated that sofa or that computer. For effective grassroots groups, nothing—not even a cast-off window—is wasted, and every donation of resources and volunteer energy is welcomed, remembered, and acknowledged.

The very method a project uses to tell you about itself says something about its effectiveness. A quality grassroots group will seldom show you into an empty conference room to view a PowerPoint presentation about abstract intervention statistics. Rather, you are usually invited to sit down with a group of people whose lives have been touched by the group. Since many grassroots groups are rooted in religious faith, to understand what they do you are asked to witness comprehensive life transformations, not superficial behavior modifications, and that can only be conveyed by listening to full stories of redeemed souls.

A final indicator of effectiveness appears when the site visit arrives at the funding pitch. From a solid grassroots group, you never hear "unless you make a grant, we cannot do anything." In fact, you may not get an explicit pitch at all.

The often implicit message is, "You have seen the fruits of our labor, not a promise about what we might do with more money. If you choose to help us, great. If not, fine. But we will be here, laboring." As Woodson argues, you should look for the groups that were already working before funding became available and that will continue to be there if it no longer is. Good groups especially do not depend on the vagaries of government funds for their existence.

One mistake foundations often make is to rush past these truly significant if subtle indicators of effectiveness, in the haste to see an audited statement, a sophisticated accounting system, or an elaborate method for tracking and reporting outcomes. A better approach would be to rely on favorable first impressions and make a small initial grant to the group. You will have the opportunity later, now as a trusted supporter, to ask for improvements in accounting and reporting—things you should be willing to help the group provide. . . .

By now, it should be clear that eyeballing effectiveness entails less what a group does than what it is. To be a transforming and healing agent in a neighborhood, a group must be embedded in the neighborhood, reflecting its best traditions and hopes for the future. It is not enough simply to deliver services, however efficiently.

While the largest foundations continue to tie themselves in knots in the Evaluation Wars, smaller foundations are free to undertake the deliberate, cumulative, intuitive process of mapping networks of effective grassroots groups in their own backyards, compiling over time their own checklists of effectiveness, based on their own local experiences. Measurable outcomes are no substitute for this deeper wisdom.

Adapted from "The Evaluation Wars," *Philanthropy Magazine* (May/June 2003), pp. 29–32. Reprinted with permission of The Philanthropy Roundtable and the author.

HODDING CARTER III

"A CEO's Perspective on Evaluation"

Hodding Carter III, former president and CEO of the Knight Foundation, and longtime journalist, applies the latter profession's standard of truth-seeking to the former's good-doing. Evaluation, as Carter describes it, acts as curative to the occupational hazards of philanthropy: the rosy gaze of good intentions, creative pride, and defensiveness. Program officers seek to protect their personal relationships with grantees, nonprofits to protect their programs, foundation executives their vision and reputation, and boards and trustees their funds. Among these players, Carter suggests, evaluation serves as a baseline—protecting truth, or "intellectual honesty." While Carter cautiously sets out the limitations of hard evaluation, he insists: "It's not okay to be ignorant, even if it is not possible to know everything." Should philanthropy seek to know as much about "everything" as it can? Does it, finally, seek "truth" in the same way journalism does? Does "eyeballing" effectiveness, as William Schambra describes it (see selection above), succumb to the native hazards of the field, or does it rather offer a new perspective to the fielder?

 ℰ

Evaluation requires a baseline, a commonly recognized starting point. Herewith is a handful of observations to establish my own baseline of preconceptions and prejudices about evaluation. . . .

Newspaper folk, in whose number I was counted until my mid-forties, learned a basic lesson about "truth" very early in their careers. Not all readers who regularly demanded that we print "the truth" actually meant what they said. What many if not most of our critics wanted to see reflected in our newspapers' pages was *their* truth.

That understanding has been of considerable solace over my five-plus years as a somewhat bemused instant foundation executive. In this world, also, it turns out that not everyone who participates in the elaborate minuet that defines relations between foundation funders and nonprofit grantees actually wants rigorous evaluation of what we fund, how we fund it, and what it produces. Unsurprisingly, often the first instinct on both sides is to seek confirmation that good intentions given life by philanthropic dollars have created tangible, lasting results.

It also turns out that the men and women who work in this field have skins almost as thin as journalists'—which is to say very thin indeed. It is more than a little strange, but something that experience convinces me is an absolute fact, that those who are professionally involved in pointing out the flaws in other people's efforts and society's workings have remarkably little tolerance for criticism of their own. When faced with probing questions, our gut reaction is hostile and defensive. We'd rather pick at the nits than deal with the fundamental differences. This admission comes from someone who in his previous life wrote about 6,500 editorials—more than a few acerbic about the failings of others—and was everlastingly unable to handle negative comments with maturity or grace.

I also worked in the U.S. Department of State for a few years and encountered (and sometimes shared) another mind-set not unfamiliar to the nonprofit and foundation worlds. Many of the foreign service officers and high-ranking political appointees responsible for the foreign policy of the United States were certain that their work was of such complexity that no outside auditor could possibly judge it with adequate sophistication. Suspicious of the motives of those in the Congress or media who demanded cause-and-effect accountability, wary of the potential for serious harm that interim judgments about long-term policies could cause, and ever mindful that some of the demands for instant assessments came from partisan politicians more interested in embarrassing the administration or a foreign government than in correcting course, they believed passionately in working behind closed doors. "We work best without being constantly second-guessed," went the refrain. Only history can judge us fairly, and then only when all the facts are in.

To put it another way, we are all human—prickly about our work and touchy about outside criticism. That translates into a high hurdle for the introduction of systematic evaluation into any undertaking, not least philanthropy. It does not help that some of evaluation's apostles make ridiculous claims for its scientific accuracy that are unsupported by the record or common sense. It is positively harmful that others tout it as a way to punish failure rather than point the way toward success.

And yet, grudgingly but with growing momentum, the movement to bring informed judgment to bear on the grand work with which we in the independent sector are engaged gathers force. Well it should. What we attempt to do matters too much to too many people to be carried forth under the banner, "What we don't know won't hurt us."

Most grants are not sought or disbursed casually, after all. Many are the end product of elaborate bureaucratic procedures that consume reams of paper and countless staff hours. Petitioners and givers initiate, respond, negotiate, elaborate, and activate, accompanied by mutual pledges of commitment and performance. Funders require bona fides, work plans, and regular reports after they fork over the cash or to keep it coming. Grantees promise results that will justify the grantors' investment and advance the meaningful work in which they are engaged. In all this, it is well understood that everyone is living up to their fiduciary, as well as programmatic, obligations.

But even when there is consensus that evaluation is a good thing, there is the untidy problem that although *evaluation* is easily definable as a word, it is anything but commonly understood as a process. And . . . even when the process is understood, there are deep divisions of opinion about how the results should be used.

Finally, the more deeply ingrained the problem that is being addressed—the more bound up it is with the muck and mire of life as it is lived by those who are not society's winners—the harder and also the more necessary the evaluation task. It is because Knight Foundation has, over the past decade, moved increasingly toward trying to deal with such problems and the social change necessary to address them that we now place so much emphasis on evaluation as an indispensable tool going in and coming out of our grants. This is a new thing for us, when measured against our fifty-four-year history. It is a new thing for me, when measured against my somewhat longer life experience, and thus I make no claim to profound insights. . . .

But for us at the Knight Foundation, after years of serious internal study and discussion, the debate is over. We have decided we owe it to everyone—from the Knight brothers, whose bequests launched us out of relative obscurity, to our grantee partners, to the larger society whose tax laws make private philanthropy possible—to gauge as accurately as possible the effects of what we do and the lessons that can be drawn from those efforts.

This is not to say that all grants require elaborate evaluation. In a number of grant categories dear to many who give and many who receive, evaluation is relatively simple. A performing arts center is proposed. Foundation K gives money toward its construction. The project is completed according to the architectural plans on the agreed-upon site. At a gala event complete with glitter and glamour, the doors are flung open. Verdict: success; money well spent.

Yet even in such straight-line projects, life is not actually that simple. Why was the new center proposed? To be an adornment? To stimulate local performing arts organizations to higher levels of achievement and financial stability? Or both? How is its debt going to be serviced? Can local organizations actually carry that load? Will taxpayers be hit with a bill they did not expect? Or will the new structure have to be filled with touring Gong Shows or their equivalent to draw more paying customers? What then of the community's artistic growth? What then is the evaluation verdict? What are the lessons learned?

If the tough questions were not asked before the project began, before baselines were established and statements of defined outcomes negotiated, there is no way to offer an informed assessment. Time will tell, but it will be telling about a constantly moving target, as the arts center's managers adapt their mission statement to changing circumstances. And the next time, in another community, when a similar opportunity presents itself, Foundation K will again be able to offer money if it wishes, but will be unable to offer informed advice about what works and doesn't work beyond how to build a civic monument that may or may not be able to justify its existence.

Now move to grantmaking whose objective is to benefit, activate, or empower people whose needs are as immense as the nation's record of failure in meeting them. Here the need for honest evaluation is matched by the difficulty in producing it. The Knight Foundation allocates a majority of its annual outlays to highly focused programs chosen by community advisory committees, in close cooperation with Knight liaisons and content specialists, in each of our twenty-six communities. Early childhood and primary and secondary education are favored targets. So are neighborhood and economic development aimed at distressed neighborhoods. Goals have been established and measurable outcomes established. The foundation has committed resources for a minimum of between three and five years for each community objective. Community work plans are living documents rather than inflexible master plans. Knight is committed to remaining involved with its partners throughout the process, measuring, offering feedback, and evaluating as we go.

At the end, we hope we will have succeeded in each and every undertaking. We know that we won't. Risk capital is what we claim to be offering, and in the world of venture capitalism, far more ventures fall on their face than make a profit. But as with venture capitalists, we want to learn from our failures and be relatively ruthless about applying the lessons learned. In the real world of public money, indeed in the more limited world of charitable dollars, our funds are very small indeed. They should not be thrown around like so many snowflakes in July. It's not okay to be ignorant, even if it is not possible to know everything.

That said, only ideologues or idiots can claim that evaluation in the arena of social change can possibly offer absolute clarity. We are not dealing with laboratory guinea pigs or mathematical formulations of elegant precision. Our communities are not hermetically sealed, uncontaminated by unanticipated variables. We are dealing with—we are ourselves—mortal humans attempting to overcome implacably difficult circumstances around which swirl a universe of contingency.

To repeat, the Knight Foundation's communities' plans of action are carefully contrived to include starting point, baselines, mutually agreed-upon objectives, systematic review, and final conclusions. But having a built-in process and having built-in certitude about what you will be able to prove are not the same thing. Our dollars are limited, even within the context of our tightly circumscribed community objectives. Those objectives are heavily dependent on a wide array of other forces and circumstances over which neither we nor our nonprofit partners have much, if any, control. The national economy may wallow; so may the local economy. Changes in local government may produce changes in emphasis or cooperation. The flight from the center city may be too advanced to reverse; a continuing flood of immigration may swamp the school in which an imaginative youth development initiative is located. A charismatic principal may suddenly quit or be transferred.

It is also quite possible that, careful as the preliminary analysis may be, as thoroughly vetted as the plan of action may be, the partner organization will not measure up to the task for any one of a wide variety of reasons. In such cases, "failure" will be as easy to assess as "success" was in the case of building a performing arts center—as easy and as meaningless. The fact that a program failed in such circumstances may well say absolutely nothing of value about the central idea.

All of this must be noted, admitted, and absorbed in ongoing evaluation work. We cannot anticipate everything in our planning process; pretense of such infallibility is long buried, I trust, with the Soviet Union's five-year plans. But the certainty of imprecision makes the case for evaluation properly understood all the more compelling.

What we can try to extract is every bit of evidence available from the data. What we don't know about how and why things work, or don't work, is the enemy. Whatever we can learn about why things work or don't work is an asset. It is feckless to worry about not knowing everything; the best is, in such cases, always the enemy of the good.

Yet even when we think we have learned everything we can from our evaluation process, it will rarely be enough to justify hard-and-fast conclusions about what works and doesn't work in each and every similar circumstance. There are no final solutions in the world of social change. For those of us who believe that evaluation is an invaluable, integral component of foundation work, humility must be the byword. Failed certainties in social science litter the landscape like so many elephant bones bleaching in the African sun. Honest hard scientists never claim final answers; good social scientists shouldn't either.

And that is my final point. The context for evaluation is no less meaningful than what evaluation can help us learn. The context is this: we set clearly defined objectives, such as preparing children to learn. Programs are the methods we adopt to achieve those objectives, but they are not the objectives and should be judged against them. A common tendency, whether in government, the private sector, or the independent sector, is to confuse one with the other. To take the political example, the tendency is to wrap the flag around failed policies and equate honest evaluation with an unpatriotic attack on national values. What honest evaluation does is to peel off the flag and let us see the difference between the ideal and the real. It is therefore the ally, rather than the enemy, of the ideal.

I began with some musings about what I think I learned about human nature from my previous vocational lives and how it relates to evaluation in my present one. Let me conclude in the same way. Investing in a particular program as though it were the be-all and end-all is well-nigh irresistible to its creators and just about guarantees losing sight of the purported goal. Having worked for two presidents, however peripherally in each case, proved that to me for all time.

Evaluation—thorough, clearly understood in its intentions, and restrained in its conclusions—helps us maintain intellectual honesty. If fundamental social change is an objective, learning must accompany doing, hand-in-hand. There are no easy answers in this field, but ignorance is a sure prescription for failure.

FIVE

Accountability

The need for "greater accountability" is an oft-heard battle cry in the field of philanthropy. Typically, it is a call for stricter adherence to current laws and regulations, promotion of new institutional policies and procedures, better fiscal probity and, above all, better reporting. It seems generally assumed that the tax advantages given to charitable institutions (unlike other tax breaks—for example, the home mortgage deduction) carry with them public obligations, and hence, public accountability. But philanthropy, in its uniquely ethical mission, claims for itself additional and more profound responsibilities, responsibilities far beyond what gets presented in its annual reports or what can be conveyed in formal ethics policies. Many a philanthropist, if asked, will claim to be accountable to entities other than the Internal Revenue Service, state attorneys general, or boards of trustees.

Take, for example, Frederick Gates. On the occasion of his retirement from the board of the Rockefeller Foundation in 1923, this long-time philanthropic advisor to John D. Rockefeller and one-time Baptist minister is reported to have made the following remarks to his fellow trustees:

> When you die and come to approach the judgment of almighty God, when you stand before St. Peter in supplication at the gates of Heaven, what do you think he will demand of you? Do you for an instant presume that he will inquire into your petty failures and your trivial virtues?—Will he ask, "How did you do as a husband for your loving and dutiful wife?" Or, "How fully did you inspire your sons, how carefully nurture and protect your daughters?"—As a captain of industry, "How did you discharge your duties to stockholders and employees?" Or to those of you who serve in the noble profession of medicine, "How did you carry out your sacred obligations to the lame, the halt, and the dying?" No! No indeed! He

will brush these matters to one side and he will ask but one question: "How did you do as a trustee of the Rockefeller Foundation?!"[1]

Not only does Gates declare philanthropists accountable to God; he insists that they must answer to Him first and most for how well they discharged their philanthropic responsibilities.

As founding director of the Rockefeller Institute for Medical Research (now Rockefeller University), Frederick Gates was on a mission to save the world through biomedicine. But as a "missionary," it seems no accident that Gates named God Almighty as the authority before whom he would have his fellow board members give account. Though few people are likely to speak as zealously as Gates, philanthropists who, like him, see themselves on a mission, especially where basic human needs and goods (such as survival or nourishment) are at stake, resonate to the need to account to something far greater than oneself. Many, like Gates, rank God first. But there are other candidates.

A list composed by Tim Walter, Director of the Association of Small Foundations, suggests the wide range of other nominees (in addition to God) to whom practitioners of philanthropy often name themselves accountable.

- Humankind (in abstract)
- People of the world, alive today
- Future generations
- Ancestors, and what they started or believed in
- Grantees, or those people the giver purports to help
- An ideal (fairness, truth, progress, justice, democracy, courage)
- The people who bought the products that generated the profits
- The country which houses the social/economic system that made it possible to generate profits from the people who bought the products
- Other donors who support your chosen goals
- The voting citizenry and their laws [the public]
- The local community
- The donor

As the list suggests, philanthropists regard themselves as responsible not only to their peers and to governmental authorities who scrutinize their practices but also to the sources of their philanthropic legitimacy or largesse—whether donor or deity or ancestors, nation or regime, local community or global humanity—and those they hope to aid—whether specific grantees or future generations. Even as philanthropists, they appear to regard themselves,

---

1. From The Frederick Taylor Gates Lecture "Making the Man" by Robert Swain Morison, M.D, reprinted in *Chapters in My Life* by Frederick Taylor Gates (New York: The Free Press, 1977). Regarding Gates' retirement speech, Morison concedes: "No manuscript exists, but its substance came to me through the vivid memories of two men who were there [including] Mr. Raymond Fosdick, later president of the foundation. . . ."

first and foremost, as human beings and citizens, embedded within a dense network of social and moral responsibilities, and accountable for far more than the bottom line. This chapter aims to lift our sights to those wider horizons. We begin with the question:

For what should philanthropy be responsible?

Acting as preface to this chapter's concerns, the story of the ring of Gyges, as told in *The Republic* of Plato, separates accountability and responsibility, challenging us to consider whether, if we had to make account to no one, we could or would act responsibly.

Ogden Nash's humorous poem, "Lines Indited With All the Depravity of Poverty," and its companion, W. S. Gilbert's lyric "If You Give Me Your Attention," prod us to consider to what degree we are responsible for our personal or professional image.

Peter Frumkin, in "Wielding Philanthropic Power Responsibly: The Problem of Legitimacy," asks us to deepen our search for "accountability" by examining the source of philanthropic "legitimacy," while Stephen G. Greene's article, "Big Fund Hits a Nerve in Vermont," presents an excellent case study for such examination. Greene's article presses us, too, to articulate philanthropy's role and responsibility vis-à-vis government's, which debate Michael S. Joyce's Letter to the Council on Foundations furthers by questioning whether and how foundations should be responsible for, and responsive to, the public interest—especially considering their obligations to private donors. In "Endowments," Jacques Turgot denies any debt to "donor intent" and champions "public utility" as the only standard by which foundations must account.

Concluding this section is "The Old Cumberland Beggar," by William Wordsworth, which describes a suppliant's relationship with his community and invites us to reassess what needs, comforts, and freedoms are most urgent to such a person, and most due.

Beyond *what* we owe, or are accountable for, to others, there is the question of *which* others and *to whom* we are responsible, as competing affections, affiliations, and duties force us, consciously or not, to choose who is most due our care, attention, or allegiance. So, second, we consider:

To whom should philanthropy be responsible?

Robert Frost's "Love and a Question" provokes, in its humble scenario, a common concern—whether we are as responsible to needy strangers as we are to our loved ones. Ralph Waldo Emerson's essay "Self-Reliance" answers the concern, as his title might suggest, by insisting that we are foremost accountable to ourselves—and, by extension, those near to us "by spiritual affinity."

The next three readings address how voluntary or philanthropic associations bind us to each other. The protagonist of Charles W. Chesnutt's "The Wife of His Youth" renews and publicly acknowledges his roots in, and responsibility to, his past, prompting his community to do the same. By contrast, in Ambrose Bierce's "The Applicant" a charity board proves unwilling to accept responsibility to their donor or his philanthropic mission. In Ralph Ellison's *Invisible Man,* a benefactor demands a rather unusual account from his beneficiary at a "site visit" to the college he helped build.

But arguably the most difficult and important question still remains: How can we encourage boards, donors, and beneficiaries—as well as members of general society—to acknowledge their responsibilities to one another? Hence, our last topical concern:

How should we educate for responsibility?

Ursula Le Guin's "The Ones Who Walk Away from Omelas" challenges us to consider how one accepts responsibility in an unjust society.

In Zona Gale's story, "Younger Generation," the eponymous subject is given a lesson in the relation between responsiveness and responsibility, the spirit of care and concern, and the conscientious action it commands. Meanwhile, in Gordon Weaver's "Haskell Hooked on the Northern Cheyenne," the protagonist reveals his education through a series of letters sparked by a fundraiser's unsolicited request; but whether Haskell has been led to a deeper understanding of his responsibilities, or led astray, is up for debate.

Benjamin Franklin's "Standing Queries for the Junto" reveal a homegrown method of inspiring and disciplining members of an association regarding their obligations to each other and to their purpose. Our last selection, Paul Pribbenow's "Are You a Force for Good?" seeks to educate professionals for these same obligations and to encourage a more rounded and robust notion of philanthropic leadership—the subject of our concluding chapter.

PLATO

From The Republic

Philanthropy, taxed with few legal obligations, operates largely outside the public eye. No wealth-holder is obliged to be philanthropic and, save for an occasional flagrant violation, few who practice philanthropy are held accountable. Yet most operate as if they were accountable, even embracing voluntary "transparency"—making public account of their activities. Why?

In this brief excerpt from The Republic, *Ancient Greek philosopher Plato (427–347 BCE) asks, more broadly, "why be just?" Glaucon, arguing with Socrates, claims that as justice is, in origin, merely human—a matter of law or convention— if one were not seen, and so judged, by others, there would be no reason to be just. Recounting the story of the shepherd Gyges, who was rendered invisible and proceeded to seduce the queen and depose the king, Glaucon concludes that all human beings, given the opportunity, would do likewise. Is Glaucon right? To whom—and for what—would you regard yourself accountable if your deeds were visible to no one? Does greater "transparency" fully correct the "invisibility" of giving and grantmaking practices?*

჻

They say that to do injustice is, by nature, good; to suffer injustice, evil; but that the evil is greater than the good. And so when men have both done and suffered injustice and have had experience of both, not being able to avoid the one and obtain the other, they think that they had better agree among themselves to have neither; hence there arise laws and mutual covenants; and that which is ordained by law is termed by them lawful and just. This they affirm to be the origin and nature of justice;—it is a mean or compromise, between the best of all, which is to do injustice and not be punished, and the worst of all, which is to suffer injustice without the power of retaliation; and justice, being at a middle point between the two, is tolerated not as a good, but as the lesser evil, and honored by reason of the inability of men to do injustice. For no man who is worthy to be called a man would ever submit to such an agreement if he were able to resist; he would be mad if he did. Such is the received account, Socrates, of the nature and origin of justice.

Now that those who practice justice do so involuntarily and because they have not the power to be unjust will best appear if we imagine something of this kind: having given both to the just and the unjust power to do what they will, let us watch and see whither desire will lead them; then we shall discover in the very act the just and unjust man to be proceeding along the same road, following their interest, which all natures deem to be their good, and are only diverted into the path of justice by the force of law. The liberty which we are supposing may be most completely given to them in the form of such a power as is said to have been possessed by Gyges the ancestor of Croesus the Lydian. According to the tradition, Gyges was a shepherd in the service of the king of Lydia; there was a great storm, and an earthquake made an opening in the earth at the place where he was feeding his flock. Amazed at the sight, he descended into the opening, where, among other marvels, he beheld a hollow brazen horse, having doors, at which he stooping and looking in saw a dead body of stature, as appeared to him, more than human, and having nothing on but a gold ring; this he took from the finger of the dead and reascended. Now the shepherds met together, according to custom, that they might send their monthly report about the flocks to the king; into their assembly he came having the ring on his finger, and as he was sitting among them he chanced to turn the collet of the ring inside his hand, when instantly he became invisible to the rest of the company and they began to speak of him as if he were no longer present. He was astonished at this, and again touching the ring he turned the collet outwards and reappeared; he made several trials of the ring, and always with the same result—when he turned the collet inwards he became invisible, when outwards he reappeared. Whereupon he contrived to be chosen one of the messengers who were sent to the court; where as soon as he arrived he seduced the queen, and with her help conspired against the king and slew him, and took the kingdom.

Suppose now that there were two such magic rings, and the just put on one of them and the unjust the other; no man can be imagined to be of such an iron nature that he would stand fast in justice. No man would keep his hands off what was not his own when he could safely take what he liked out of the market, or go into houses and lie with any one at his pleasure, or kill or release from prison whom he would, and in all respects be like a God among men. Then the actions of the just would be as the actions of the unjust; they would both come at last to the same point. And this we may truly affirm to be a great proof that a man is just, not willingly or because he thinks that justice is any good to him individually, but of necessity, for wherever any one thinks that he can safely be unjust, there he is unjust. For all men believe in their hearts that injustice is far more profitable to the individual than justice, and he who argues as I have been supposing, will say that they are right. If you could imagine any one obtaining this power of becoming invisible, and never doing any wrong or touching what was another's, he would be thought by the lookers-on to be a most wretched idiot, although they would praise him to one another's faces, and keep up appearances with one another from a fear that they too might suffer injustice.

From book II of *The Republic* by Plato. Translated from Greek by Benjamin Jowett.

OGDEN NASH

"Lines Indited with All the Depravity of Poverty"

W. S. GILBERT

"If You Give Me Your Attention"

The speaker in this humorous poem, by American poet Ogden Nash (1902–1971), seems to suggest that having wealth liberates you from care or concern, either about what you do or about what other people think of what you do. Such a state, the speaker suggests, is happiness! Nash's title, however, points to a more complicated message. The poem consists of lines, it announces, "indited with all the depravity of poverty," suggesting that they are a poor person's view of what it means to be rich. Does the poem speak truly, even if exaggeratedly? Or is the poem ironic? If you think it speaks truly, is having wealth tantamount to having the ring of Gyges (see selection by Plato above)? If, on the other hand, the poem is ironic, are wealth-holders necessarily accountable for the ways in which poor people see them?

Appended to the selection is a song, from Gilbert and Sullivan's comic opera Princess Ida, *in which a self-proclaimed philanthropist wonders at his unpopularity. Are philanthropists accountable for the way people see them or their profession?*

ৎৡ

"Lines Indited with All the Depravity of Poverty"

One way to be very happy is to be very rich
For then you can buy orchids by the quire and bacon by the flitch.
And yet at the same time People don't mind if you only tip them a dime,
Because it's very funny
But somehow if you're rich enough you can get away with spending water like
    money
While if you're not rich you can spend in one evening your salary for the year
And everybody will just stand around and jeer.
If you are rich you don't have to think twice about buying a judge or a horse,
Or a lower instead of an upper, or a new suit, or a divorce,
And you never have to say When,

And you can sleep every morning until nine or ten,
All of which
Explains why I should like very, very much to be very, very rich.

"If You Give Me Your Attention"

If you give me your attention, I will tell you what I am:
I'm a genuine philanthropist—all other kinds are sham.
Each little fault of temper and each social defect
In my erring fellow-creatures, I endeavor to correct.
To all their little weaknesses I open people's eyes;
And little plans to snub the self-sufficient I devise;
I love my fellow creatures—I do all the good I can—
Yet everybody says I'm such a disagreeable man!
     And I can't think why!

To compliments inflated I've a withering reply;
And vanity I always do my best to mortify;
A charitable action I can skillfully dissect;
And interested motives I'm delighted to detect;
I know everybody's income and what everybody earns;
And I carefully compare it with the income-tax returns;
But to benefit humanity however much I plan,
Yet everybody says I'm such a disagreeable man!
     And I can't think why!

I'm sure I'm no ascetic; I'm as pleasant as can be;
You'll always find me ready with a crushing repartee,
I've an irritating chuckle, I've a celebrated sneer,
I've an entertaining snigger, I've a fascinating leer.
To everybody's prejudice I know a thing or two;
I can tell a woman's age in half a minute—and I do.
But although I try to make myself as pleasant as I can,
Yet everybody says I'm such a disagreeable man!
     And I can't think why!

From *Princess Ida*, written by W. S. Gilbert, composed by Arthur Sullivan (1884).

PETER FRUMKIN

"Wielding Philanthropic Power Responsibly: The Problem of Legitimacy"

In this short essay, written for a dialogue among philanthropic leaders on the subject of accountability, sociologist and philanthropy scholar Peter Frumkin argues that "accountability," like "effectiveness," has become, in concept and practice, drained of its rigor: effectiveness looks solely to the performance of grantee organizations (not the performance of the donors' organizations or intentions) and accountability merely to procedural transparency (not actual accomplishments). Thus philanthropy has increasingly come to resemble a "Potemkin village"—unresponsive and irresponsible—neither seeking nor disclosing what really matters: how well philanthropists have fulfilled their own philanthropic missions. Frumkin urges practitioners to repair the damage by looking critically and carefully at the sources of their own legitimacy, legal and normative. Scrutinizing the sources of one's own legitimacy requires asking oneself questions such as these: "How do my philanthropic decisions stand with respect to the polity of which I am a part? Or, what should I do if I am operating within the law but my grants are widely perceived to be unfair or unjust?" Would addressing such questions put stronger and sharper teeth into one's effectiveness or accountability? Why or why not? (For an excellent case study with which to think about this issue, see the next selection, by Stephen Greene.)

The world of philanthropy is largely quiet, secure, and comfortable. Donors are routinely praised for being smart, insightful, and helpful, even if they possess none of these characteristics. In few fields other than philanthropy is it possible to be applauded and embraced regardless of merit and performance. While there is no one in a position to ask tough questions about philanthropic choices, some donors—particularly within the larger foundations—have in recent years begun to worry quietly about their work. They have struggled publicly to find more strategic forms of giving.

One of the most common ways in which the striving of the field for self-improvement manifests itself is the ritual recitation of two issues that are thought to be absolutely central to philanthropy's future. These issues are effectiveness and accountability. What I want to suggest here is that both of these concepts are routinely misconstrued and that they actually obscure the far more interesting concept of legitimacy.

Let's start with effectiveness. In its most commonly understood form, a donor's effectiveness has come to be associated with the performance of the vast array of grant recipients that receive the largesse. Thus, in the search to take seriously the charge of improving the field, large amounts of resources have been devoted to the evaluation of nonprofit programs. To breathe life into the concept of effectiveness, donors look out into the world of nonprofits and apply metrics of all sorts in order to come to a conclusion about effectiveness. The problem with this approach is that it overlooks a more important dimension of effectiveness in philanthropy, one that demands an inward-looking perspective. The main challenge for donors is not to track their many recipients, but to focus instead on the relative fulfillment of their own missions. The real question that donors should obsess over is whether their own philanthropic missions are being achieved, which is very different from tracking individual grants and hoping that in some way they aggregate to something larger than the sum of the parts. In reality, meaningfully addressing the effectiveness question requires a steady and daunting introspective gaze about the quality of decision-making within both institutional and individual philanthropy. Donors need to ask about how effective *they* are in achieving their objectives and in fulfilling their missions. This is very different from assuming the concept of effectiveness resides somewhere across the diffuse and distant grantee community.

If the confusion about effectiveness were not enough, philanthropy is even more muddled when it comes to the meaning of accountability. Concerns about accountability are most commonly spoken about in terms of transparency—the need to provide documents and information to the world. Thus, in the service of greater accountability, many foundations have gone to great length to make their grantmaking procedures clearer, to publish annual reports, and to meet regularly with nonprofits to explain their work. The premise of accountability as transparency is that the main problem to be overcome is one of information sharing. Donors often seem to believe that if only they could build a good web site and promulgate clear guidelines, their accountability work would be done. The problem is that accountability is not an empty vessel into which "information" about procedures can be dumped. Real philanthropic accountability demands substantive content in the form of data on the actual performance of the donor. This means that instead of sending out materials that clarify the grant-making process, donors need to actually share with the world information on whether important philanthropic objectives are really being met. Accountability, to be meaningful, must have high stakes and be grounded in disclosures about things that truly matter, namely whether philanthropic missions are being fulfilled. In this sense, it is impossible to be accountable without disclosing information about the donor's effectiveness.

In sum, it is my contention that over the past decade the field of philanthropy has been enfeebled by the notion that effectiveness involves the performance of grantee organizations (and not of the donors themselves), and that accountability is simply about communicating information about procedures (not results). What concerns me is not that this dual conceptual confusion persists, however. Lurking beneath this muddle is the bigger question of philanthropic legitimacy, an issue that rarely gets explored and debated.

Legitimacy is a touchy issue in philanthropy. Fueled by private wealth but directed at producing public benefits, philanthropy has a built-in tension. On the one hand, one is tempted to ask who has the right to say anything about how individuals and institutions carry out their philanthropic work. After all, these are private funds that supplement public programs and they should simply be welcomed as voluntary contributions to the improvement of society. On the other hand, one wonders who exactly these wealthy actors are to take it unto themselves to interpret public needs and to act as miniature and undemocratic regimes. There is a part of philanthropy, the speaking for others without their consent or consultation, that seems to require a fair amount of hubris and which is off-putting to some. It is this second line of thought that leads directly to the question of what makes philanthropy legitimate.

Legitimacy has two essential meanings. The first is straightforward: Philanthropy is legitimate when it is conducted in observance of all relevant laws and rules. Donors can claim to be legitimate when they lawfully exercise their philanthropic duties. This means avoiding some of the scandals and investigations that have recently plagued the foundation field, as made evident in the self-dealing and financial mismanagement that have surfaced in the media. The second meaning of legitimacy is much more complex. Philanthropic legitimacy can be defined as the just and fair exercise of philanthropic power. By this, I mean donors can claim to have met the test of legitimacy when they are perceived by the full range of relevant stakeholders around them as acting in a way that is just, fair, and free of caprice and ill-intent. This sets the bar considerably higher than the legal definition of legitimacy does.

My claim here is a modest one: Philanthropy has long talked about effectiveness and worried about accountability. The result of the dominant framing of the issues has been abysmal. Both concepts have been weakened and hollowed out, and a Potemkin village has sprung up around these concepts. As a counter to this approach and as a way of advancing the field, I believe that the concept of legitimacy is a far richer starting point. Rather than spend more time on tired evaluations of grantees and claim some residual effectiveness as a result of this documentation, and rather than focus on transparency as an easy solution to the call for greater accountability, I believe that donors should begin with the question of their own legitimacy, construed in both legal and normative terms. They will find that it is impossible to be legitimate without being substantively accountable for their work. They will also soon discover that it is impossible to be substantively accountable without being able to demonstrate their effectiveness at achieving their own objectives and missions. In this way, a focus on legitimacy would both elevate the quality of debate within philanthropy and, I believe, expose the poverty of the dominant conceptualization of both effectiveness and accountability.

Would this conceptual exercise be painless? Probably not. But in philanthropy as in many other domains, it remains true that where there is no pain there is no gain. I think the field of philanthropy would benefit from the pain of pondering the sources of its own legitimacy.

Adapted from "Legitimacy in Philanthropy," written for the Dialogues on Civic Philanthropy, "Accountability" (May 19, 2005). By permission of the author.

STEPHEN G. GREENE

"Big Fund Hits a Nerve in Vermont: Freeman Foundation's School Grants Seen by Critics as Slap at State Law"

Reporter Stephen G. Greene leads us to question the responsibility (or, perhaps more usefully, the legitimacy—see the previous selection) of one foundation's efforts in context of larger political concerns. In 1997, Vermont's Supreme Court ruled that Vermont's funding system for public schools was unconstitutional, and in response the legislature passed Act 60 (officially, "The Equal Educational Opportunity Act of 1997"). Act 60 established a statewide property tax and a uniform allowance for each pupil. Towns that wanted to spend more on their schools had to participate in a sharing pool with participating towns—wealthy towns would pay into the pool (and accordingly see their property taxes increase) and poor towns would draw from it (and see their tax rates decline). The new system meant that wealthy towns faced cutting their school budgets or massive tax hikes. Enter the Freeman Foundation, Vermont's most generous grantmaker. The Freeman Foundation announced a matching-grant program to support public schools statewide. Its grants enabled some schools to save valuable programs, but also helped wealthy towns escape the sharing pools by which educational equity was supposed to be established. Act 60 supporters raised the roof, calling the maneuver unjust and undemocratic. How should the Freeman Foundation have responded, either to Act 60 or to the uproar that their grant program produced? As an apolitical actor, to whom or for what is the Freeman Foundation now responsible? To whom should it be responsive?

Vermont's wealthiest foundation has committed more than $15-million in the past few months for education programs at dozens of public schools around the state—but many residents, far from being grateful, are incensed.

Critics say the Freeman Foundation, a $1.25-billion philanthropy in Stowe built with a family fortune that was made selling insurance in the Far East, is using its financial clout to derail a controversial school-financing statute that is wildly unpopular among many affluent Vermonters. Its grants, critics say, allow wealthy towns to sidestep key provisions of a 1997 law—commonly known as Act 60—that was passed in an effort to make the financing of public education more equitable.

Critics question whether a private foundation, which is barred by law from trying to influence legislation, should be making grants that have the effect, they say, of defeating the implementation of public policy.

"I'm concerned that a foundation is using its money to effectively undermine a law that was passed to fulfill a constitutional requirement," says Allen Gilbert, chairman of the school board in Worcester, Vt. "It's like a foundation telling the Birmingham schools in the 1950s, 'We'll help you set up private academies' in an effort to elude the federal mandate for public-school integration."

The Freeman fund, which primarily supports land conservation, historic preservation, and Asian studies, contends that its new program is not directed at scuttling the law but that it reflects the foundation's long-time interest in promoting educational excellence. Graeme Freeman, the fund's executive director, says the school grants respond to repeated requests from towns that faced the prospect of having to slash their school budgets—or pay much higher school taxes.

"Some communities came to us and said, 'There's this new law that's been enacted. We feel that our school is in jeopardy of having to close many of its programs. Can you help us?'" recalls Mr. Freeman, a grandson of the philanthropy's founder. "We thought long and hard about it. We understand that this is a controversial law, but we don't think that school programs should be cut. If we can help them in any way, we'd like to."

Spurred by such requests, the foundation last year announced a new, two-year matching-grant program to help support public schools. So far, some 30 towns have taken advantage of the program and have been scrambling to raise matching funds. Applications from 26 more will be considered at the foundation's spring board meeting.

Because Act 60 tinkers with several touchy issues—taxation, education, and local control—the law has become the most divisive issue in Vermont politics in years. And the Freeman grants have sparked heated debate about the proper role for foundations in helping to shape—or to confound—public policy.

Although views on Act 60 vary widely, some observers say that the proper forum for resolving the matter is in the State House in Montpelier rather than in a foundation office in Stowe.

"I elected my legislators and ask them to be very thoughtful, to consider all the complexities of different issues, and to do the best they can to solve problems," says Lorna Jimerson, who presides over the Vermont School Board Association and also has a research grant to study the influence of Act 60 on education. "A lot of people aren't happy with Act 60, but others are. I'm not sure I want a private foundation to dismantle public policy. I didn't elect them. I don't know these people."

The association has not taken a position on Act 60 or the foundation grants, Ms. Jimerson observes. But her own view, she says, is that "we depend on our elected officials to make wise decisions, and if we don't like them, we throw them out of office. This seems to circumvent that whole process."

Other critics of the Freeman grants are less outspoken, however, perhaps out of concern for alienating the state's most generous private grant maker.

"People have been almost completely unwilling to speak out," says Mr. Gilbert, the Worcester school board chairman, who also runs Concerned Vermonters for Equal Educational Opportunity. "I think it's because you don't bite the hand that feeds you."

Public-school financing has been a thorny issue in Vermont for decades. Until recently, its schools were supported entirely through local property taxes. While some towns grew rich, however, others did not, which created a widening disparity between what different towns spent on education.

A score of Vermont's 251 towns had a decided advantage over the others: Their coffers bulged with tax revenue from ski resorts or from lakefront vacation properties within their borders. That revenue enabled such towns to spend more on schooling than other towns could afford to do, while also keeping property taxes unusually low.

By the mid-1990s, the gap in per-pupil spending and residential school-tax rates between Vermont's wealthiest and poorest school districts had grown so large that the state's Supreme Court ruled in 1997 that financing education with local property taxes was unconstitutional. Annual spending per pupil ranged from less than $3,000 in some towns to more than $9,000 in others; property tax rates, meanwhile, were as low as 5 cents per $1,000 in some affluent towns, and more than $3 per $1,000 in others. The court invited the legislature to fix the problem.

The Equal Educational Opportunity Act of 1997 (commonly called Act 60) established a statewide property tax of $1.10 per $1,000 valuation, which currently generates enough revenue to provide about $5,000 per pupil in every school in the state.

The law also permits any town that wishes to spend more on its schools to participate in a sharing pool. The pool was created to ensure that any additional dollars spent on education by participating towns would affect their tax rates equally.

Wealthy towns that want to spend more money might have to raise $3, for example, for every $1 they can keep for their schools. The extra money they raise is then divided among the participating poorer towns. The law's backers intended that rich towns would pay in to the pool and see their property taxes rise accordingly, while poorer ones would draw from it and see their tax rates decline. The result, the law's advocates hoped, would be more equity statewide, insuring that students were not unfairly penalized with substandard schooling because they happened to live in poorer towns.

Those most upset by the law include residents of so-called gold towns like Ludlow, Stowe, and Stratton, who face the prospect of seeing their school tax rates increase several-fold as the law's provisions are phased in over several years.

Those towns and others have seized upon a provision in the law that excludes from sharing-pool calculations any money that towns raise privately. Act 60 supporters say that clause was included so that schools accustomed to raising a few hundred dollars from bake sales to buy band uniforms, for instance, could continue to do so.

But the Freeman grants have stimulated fund raising on a much grander scale. Coupled with the money raised to match them, they have yielded hundreds of thousands of private dollars for some schools—enough to allow wealthy towns to maintain spending levels significantly above $5,000 per pupil without having to enter the sharing pool. The matching private donations are tax-deductible—and none of the money that towns are now scrambling to raise must be shared with other towns.

In response to charges that its grants favor wealthy towns, the foundation notes that the money is available to any school district in Vermont. It points out that about half the applications so far have come from so-called "receiving" towns, which qualify for net withdrawals from the sharing pool because their tax rates are so high.

Because the grants have enabled wealthy towns to opt out of the sharing pool, however, the receiving towns that participate in that pool are finding far less money to share than they had counted on, say Act 60 supporters. What's more, they add, although all towns are eligible for Freeman grants, the wealthy ones are able to qualify for much larger grants because they have much greater success in raising matching funds. As evidence, they point to the list of the grants announced so far: $457,500 to Ludlow, for example, worth $2,434 per pupil, compared with just $3,500 ($45 per pupil) to Bridgewater and $10,000 ($9 per pupil) to Morristown.

"This is a deliberate attempt to make an end run around the law," says state Senator Mark MacDonald, who sits on the Senate Finance Committee, which helped to draft Act 60. "The requirement that there be a match virtually guarantees that wealthy school districts that have a varied and plentiful curriculum will benefit from this, and that poor districts that the law was designed to help will be adversely affected."

Thomas J. Amidon, the foundation's lawyer, points out that the Freeman grants may not be diverting any funds from the sharing pool, as some critics allege, because it is not clear that wealthy towns would have agreed to participate in the pool if it involved taxing themselves $3 for every additional $1 that goes to their school budget.

"I can't address that assumption," Mr. Amidon says. "But let's assume that the Freeman Foundation didn't do this at all. That's $15-million off the table," and therefore unavailable for any public schools.

The foundation never anticipated that its school grants would cause such a furor, Mr. Freeman says. Despite its large size, the foundation remains very much a low-profile family affair, focusing its attention on two places—Asia and Vermont—to which the family retains strong ties. Mr. Freeman's father, Houghton (Buck) Freeman, who was born in China and who speaks Chinese, chairs the board of trustees, on which he is joined by his wife, Doreen, and a long-time family associate.

All three Freemans spend much of their time reviewing grant applications and conducting site visits—including many in Asia. Graeme Freeman, with a part-time lawyer and full-time assistant, runs the foundation out of a modest office above a liquor store in a Stowe shopping center. Its investments and much of the program administration are handled by J. P. Morgan in New York.

"We have a lot of faith in many of the non-profits we work with," Mr. Freeman says, in explaining how the foundation manages with so few employees. "We feel they can do a lot of the administrative work themselves. We don't need to duplicate their efforts."

In Vermont, the foundation works closely with the Vermont Land Trust and the Preservation Trust of Vermont. Each of those statewide organizations acts almost like a program officer of the foundation, helping to recommend and monitor local grantees in the areas of land conservation and historic preservation, respectively.

"Their grants have been a tremendous boon to historic preservation," says Paul Bruhn, executive director of the Preservation Trust of Vermont, in Burlington. Freeman support has helped to save Abenaki Indian burial grounds, historic dams, and a renowned geological site, as well as libraries, museums, town halls, and other historic structures, says Mr. Bruhn.

"They have deep roots in Vermont, and care immensely about the character of this place," he adds. "They've been very open to the whole range of preservation activity that goes on in the state."

Since the Freeman Foundation began making grants in earnest six years ago, it has channeled more than $50-million to organizations and programs in Vermont. Given that kind of philanthropic commitment to the state, even some of the strongest supporters of Act 60 are cautious about doing anything that might jeopardize the flow of grant money.

Bob Gensburg, a lawyer with the American Civil Liberties Union who argued the case that led to the 1997 state Supreme Court decision on school funding, has little sympathy for the affluent towns that benefit most from the Freeman public-school grants. "The sudden shock in the gold towns that they were going to have to start paying taxes at the same level as everyone else created great consternation and distress," he says. "Privilege dies hard."

Yet even as he argues that the gold towns must share some of their wealth, Mr. Gensburg adds: "I would desperately not want this very philanthropic organization to say, 'We're going to take our marbles and go home.'"

Other foundation critics are undeterred. "The Freeman Foundation is doing all of this on our nickel," since its activities are exempt from taxes, says Mr. Gilbert. "I don't think a foundation should be subverting public policy at the public's expense."

MICHAEL S. JOYCE

Letter to the Council on Foundations

In 1980, the Council on Foundations (COF), a prominent membership organiza-
tion of grantmaking foundations and giving programs, adopted an eleven-point
statement of "Principles and Practices for Effective Grantmaking," and the follow-
ing year it made subscription to the document mandatory for all its members.
Among its endorsements was the claim that foundations should "serve the needs
and interests of the public." In this 1984 letter to the Council president, James Jo-
seph, Michael S. Joyce (1942–2006), then executive director of the John M. Olin
Foundation, announces his board's decision to discontinue its membership in the
COF, offering two reasons. First, he takes umbrage at the mandatory subscription
to outwardly imposed principles, arguing that it jeopardizes the "traditional inde-
pendence and diversity" of the philanthropic community, as well a foundation's re-
sponsibility to its own donors. Second, and for our purposes here more important,
he objects to the Council's understanding, incorporated in its principles, of the re-
sponsibility of foundations to the general public or the public interest, as well as
their relationship to the state. "If, like government, [foundations] must serve the
public interest," Joyce argues, "there is no reason why their funds should not be dis-
bursed by government itself, which is well set up to discharge the public interest."
Are foundations, or all philanthropic donors, responsible for serving "the public"
or "the public interest"? What does Joyce mean by these terms? What do you?

October 1, 1984

Mr. James A. Joseph
President
Council on Foundations, Inc.
1828 L Street, N.W.
Washington, D.C. 20036

Dear Jim:

   In my July 11 letter to you, I said that I'd let you know at the earliest opportunity the decision our Board of Trustees made concerning our membership in the Council on Foundations.

   The full Board met last Thursday for the first time since I wrote to you. We
had a lengthy discussion based on the Council's position that all its members
must subscribe to the Recommended Principles and Practices for Effective
Grantmaking. I am sorry to tell you that the Trustees concluded that we cannot
in good conscience comply with this requirement.

Please permit me to recapitulate our most important concerns, with which you are already largely familiar. These have to do both with the appropriateness of making subscription obligatory, and with the content itself of the Recommended Principles and Practices.

Several of our trustees have had distinguished careers in foundation governance and believe that it is wrong to make subscription mandatory. They do, of course, recognize the duty of trustees to govern foundations responsibly within the framework of the law and the wishes of their donors. It is precisely because we take these responsibilities so seriously that we believe it is improper to require subscription to any set of principles and practices, for to do so is to require trustees to cede judgment and to relinquish in part their responsibilities, especially to the donor, with whose wishes such principles and practices might sometimes conflict. Moreover, in considering the larger effects of obligatory subscription, it is the opinion of our trustees that such an obligation threatens to rob the foundation community of its traditional independence and diversity, on which the vitality of the philanthropic community depends.

With regard to the specifics of the document, our overriding concern among several is that the recommendations incorporate a mistaken understanding of the responsibility of foundations to the public. The document treats "the public" as a single body composed, to be sure, of various constituencies, and it strongly implies that each individual foundation should be responsive to this public and its constituent elements. In other words, each foundation is treated as analogous to the state itself, responsive to the public and representative of its various constituent groups. On this reading, each foundation should constitute itself so that it can respond quickly to the changing needs and requirements of the entire society.

This is a seriously mistaken understanding of the responsibility of foundations to the public and of their relationship to the state. Foundations are private, not public, institutions. They cannot function like governments. The responsibility of meeting the public interest is in the hands of government, not private foundations. Government has provided the tax exemption for charitable institutions in the belief that charitable activities can be better carried out by private organizations than by government itself. The government recognized, when it took this step, that there are many different kinds of charitable activities that may be carried out by many different kinds of organizations. The public interest is served not by each individual organization, but by the diversity of organizations and purposes that come into being as a result of the general encouragement provided by the tax exemption.

We believe it is wrong, then, to assert, as this document does, that each individual foundation must serve the general public or the public interest. Such a responsibility is not implied by the tax laws, nor in any event could it be carried out in a manner that would preserve foundations in their present form. The responsibility of foundations to the law is specific; the purposes they may serve consistent with the law are broad and elastic. To assert that each foundation must serve the public interest is to invite someone to define the public interest, and then to force every foundation into that defined role. More importantly, the claim deprives foundations of their legitimate reasons for existence: If, like government, they must serve the public interest, there is no reason why their funds should not be disbursed by government itself, which is well set up to discharge the public interest.

In short, we believe the Recommended Principles and Practices are informed by a philosophy which cannot be implemented and which, if it were ever widely accepted, would undermine foundations' very reasons to exist.

In closing, let me say that while we must agree to differ on the merits of the Recommended Principles and Practices and the wisdom of requiring subscription thereunto, I very much appreciate your willingness to discuss these matters with the staff and myself. I am sorry that we cannot renew our membership in the Council on Foundations.

With best regards,
Sincerely,
Michael S. Joyce.

With permission of James Piereson, Executive Director and Trustee, John M. Olin Foundation.

JACQUES TURGOT

"Endowments"

Jacques Turgot (1727–1781), a leading economist of the eighteenth century and comptroller general of France from 1774 to 1776 under King Louis XVI, wrote this essay in 1756 for the Encyclopédie, the ambitious thirty-two-volume project and major achievement of the French Enlightenment. More than a hundred years later, it was reprinted in a volume devoted to Turgot's life and writings, with this editorial note: "Much has been done since Turgot's time . . . but it is still not without some application to present-day discussions." To those who think philanthropic accountability is first and foremost to the "public," Turgot's arguments are, arguably, even more relevant today.

In beginning, Turgot argues, much like Julius Rosenwald (see selection in chapter 3), against perpetual foundations or endowments, but he does so on different grounds. According to Turgot, the sole standard for judging the worth of foundations is their public utility. But finding them at best ineffective in promoting public good, he argues that society cannot permit foundations to be accountable only to donor intent. The public, through government, must hold foundations accountable, lest the dead hand of the past throttle efforts to promote public good in the present. Would this progressive man of the Enlightenment make the same arguments against our foundations today?

To *found*, in the sense in which we are now using the word, is to assign a fund or a sum of money in order to its being employed in perpetuity for fulfilling the purpose the founder had in view, whether that purpose regards divine worship, or public utility, or the vanity of the founder—often the only real one, even while the two others serve to veil it. . . .

Our intention in this article is limited to examining the utility of *foundations* in general, in respect to the public good, and chiefly to demonstrating their impropriety. May the following considerations concur with the philosophic spirit of the age, in discouraging new foundations and in destroying all remains of superstitious respect for the old ones!

1. A founder is a man who desires the effect of his own will to endure for ever. Now, even if we suppose him to be actuated by the purest motives, how many reasons are there to question his enlightenment! How easy it is to do harm in wishing to do good! To foresee with certainty that an establishment will produce only the effect desired from it, and no effect at variance with its object; to discern, beyond the illusion of a near and apparent good, the real

evils which a long series of unseen causes may bring about; to know what are the real sores of society, to arrive at their causes, to distinguish remedies from palliatives; to defend oneself against the prestige of a seductive project, to take a severe and tranquil view of it amidst that dazzling atmosphere in which the praises of a blind public, and our own enthusiasm, show it us surrounded; this would need the effort of the most profound genius, and perhaps the political sciences of our time are not yet sufficiently advanced to enable the best genius here to succeed.

By these institutions support is often given to a few individuals against an evil the cause of which is general, and sometimes the very remedy opposed to the effect increases the influence of the cause. We have a striking example of this kind of abuse in the establishment of houses designed as asylums for repentant women. In order to obtain entrance, proof of a debauched life must be made. . . . I know well that this precaution has been made in order to prevent the *foundation* being diverted to other objects; but that only proves that it is not by such establishments, powerless against the true causes of libertinage, that it can be combated. . . .

2. But whatever utility a *foundation* might be at its conception, it bears within itself an irremediable defect which belongs to its very nature—the impossibility of maintaining its fulfillment. Founders deceive themselves vastly if they imagine that their zeal can be communicated from age to age to persons employed to perpetuate its effects. There is no body that has not in the long run lost the spirit of its first origin. There is no sentiment that does not become weakened, by mere habit and by familiarity with the objects which excite it. What confused emotions of horror, of sadness, of deep feeling for humanity, of pity for the unfortunates who are suffering, does that man experience who for the first time enters the ward of a hospital! Well, let him open his eyes and look around. In this very place, in the midst of these assembled human miseries, the ministers provided to relieve them walk about with an air careless and expressionless; they mechanically and without interest distribute from invalid to invalid the food and the remedies prescribed, and sometimes do so even with a brutal callousness; they give way to heedless conversation, and sometimes to ideas of the silliest and the grossest; vanity, envy, hatred, all the passions reigning there, as elsewhere, do their work, and the groans from the sick-bed, the cries of acute pain, do not disturb the *habitués* any more than the murmur of a rivulet interrupts an animated conversation. Such are the effects of habit in relation to objects the most capable of moving the human heart. Thus it is that no enthusiasm can be constantly sustained. And how without enthusiasm can ministers of a foundation fulfill its purpose always and with precision? What interest, in their case, can counteract idleness, that weight attached to human nature which tends constantly to retain us in inaction? The very precautions which the founder has taken in order to insure for them a constant revenue dispenses them from meriting it by exertion. Are there superintendents,

inspectors, appointed to see the work of the foundation carried out? It will be the same with these inspectors. If the obstacle to the right working comes from idleness, the same idleness on their part will prevent them from exposing it; if the abuse proceeds from pecuniary interest, they will too readily share in it. Supervisors themselves would need to be supervised. . . . Thus almost all old foundations have degenerated from their primitive institution. . . .

3. I will suppose that a foundation has had at its origin an incontestable utility, that sufficient precautions have been taken against its degeneration through idleness and negligence, that the nature of its funds has sheltered it from the revolutions of monetary changes, then I say that the very immutability which the founders have succeeded in giving it is still a great public impropriety, because time brings about new revolutions which will sweep away the utility, the foundation once fulfilled, and will render its continued operation even injurious. Society has not always the same needs; the nature and dispositions of properties, the divisions between different orders of the people, opinions, manners, the general occupations of the nation or of its different sections, the climate even, the maladies and the other accidents of human life—all experience a continual variation. New needs arise, others cease to be felt. The proportion of those remaining declines from day to day, and along with them the utility of the foundations designed to relieve them diminishes or disappears. . . .

4. I have said nothing of the splendor of the buildings and of the pomp connected with some of the grand foundations. It would be perhaps to value very favourably the utility of these objects if we estimated them at one hundredth part of the whole cost.

5. Woe to me if my object be, in presenting these considerations, to concentrate man's motives in his mere self-interest, and to render him insensible to the sufferings or the happiness of his fellow-creatures, to extinguish in him the spirit of a citizen, and to substitute an indolent and base prudence for the noble passion of being useful to mankind. In place of the vanity of founders, I desire that humanity, that the passion of the public good, should procure for men the same benefits, but more surely, more completely, and at less cost, and without the drawbacks of which I have complained.

Among the different needs of society intended to be fulfilled by means of durable establishments or foundations, let us distinguish two kinds. One belongs to society as a whole, and is just the result of the interest of each of its members, such as the general needs of humanity, sustenance for everyone, the good manners and education of children, for all families. . . . It does not require much reflection to be convinced that the first kind of social needs is not of a nature that can be fulfilled by foundations, or by any other gratuitous means, and that, in this respect, the general good ought to be the result of the efforts of each individual for his own interests. Every able-bodied man ought to procure his subsistence by his work, because if he were fed without working, it would be so at the cost of those who work. What the State owes to all its members is the destruction of the obstacles which impede them in their indus-try, or which trouble them in the enjoyment of the product which is its recom-pense. While these obstacles subsist, particular benefits will not diminish the general poverty, for the cause will remain untouched. For the same reason ev-ery family owes education to the children who are born to it, and it is only from the efforts of each in particular that the general perfection of education can arise. If you amuse yourself to endow masters and bursaries in colleges, the utility of which will be felt only by a small number of scholars, favoured by chance, who have not perhaps the necessary talents to profit by them, that will be, for the whole nation, but a drop of water spread on a vast sea, and you will have procured, at very great expense, very small results. And then you have ac-customed people to be ever applying for these endowments, and (not always) receiving them, and to owe nothing to themselves. This sort of mendacity spread over all conditions of men degrades a people and substitutes for the high impulses a character of lowness and intrigue. Are men powerfully inter-ested in that good which you would procure for them? Leave them free to at-tain it; this is the great, the only principle. Do they appear to you to be actuated by less ardor towards it than you would desire to see? Increase their interest in it. You wish to perfect education—propose prizes for the emulation of parents and children, but let these prizes be offered to whosoever can *merit* them, of-fered at least to every order of citizens; let employments and places become the recompense of merit, and the sure prospect of work, and you will see emula-tion struck up at once in the heart of all families. Your nation will soon be raised above its old level, you will have enlightened its spirit, you will have given it character, you will have done great things, and you will have done all at less expense than founding one college.

The other class of public needs intended to be provided for by foundations comprise those regarded as accidental, which, limited to particular places and particular times, enter less into the system of general administration, and may demand particular relief. It is desired to remedy the hardships of a scarcity, or of an epidemic, to provide for the support of some old men, or some orphans, for the rescue of infants exposed, for the working or maintaining works to im-prove the amenity or the salubrity of a town, for the improving of agriculture or some arts in a backward condition in a locality, for rewarding the services rendered by a citizen to the town of which he is a member, to attract to it men celebrated for their talents. Now, it is before all necessary that the means taken by public establishments or foundations should be the best in order to procure for their subjects all these benefits as fully as possible. The free employment of a part of the revenues of a community, some contribution of all its members in the case of the need being pressing and general, with a free association of, and voluntary subscriptions of some generous citizens, in the case of the need be-ing less urgent and less generally felt—here is the true means of fulfilling all kinds of schemes really useful, and this method will have the inestimable advantage over foundations, that it is subject to no great abuse. As the contribution of each is entirely voluntary, it is impossible for the funds to be diverted from their destination. If they were, their source would be soon dried up. There would be no money sunk in useless expenses, in luxury, or in building. It is a partnership of the same kind as those made for business, with the difference that its object is only the public good; and as the funds are employed only under the eyes of the shareholders, these are able to see them employed in the most advantageous manner. Resources would not be permanent for needs that are temporary; succor would be given only to the portion of society that suffered, to the branch of commerce that languished. If the need ceased, the liberality would cease, and its course would be directed to other needs. There would never be useless repetitions of schemes, because the generosity of the public benefactors would be determined only by the actual utility recognised. In fine, this method would withdraw no funds from general circulation, the lands would not be irrevocably possessed by idle hands, and their productions under the hands of an active proprietor would have no limit except that of their fecundity. Is it said that these ideas are chimerical? England, Scotland, Ireland are full of such voluntary associations, and they have experienced from them, for many years, the happiest effects. What has taken place in England can take place in France, and the English have not the exclusive right to be citizens. We have already in some provinces examples of such associations, which prove their possibility. I would cite in particular the city of Bayeux, whose inhabitants are associated in order to banish begging entirely from their town, and have succeeded in providing work for all able-bodied mendicants, and alms for all those unfit for work. This fine example deserves to be proposed for the emulation of all our towns. Nothing would be so easy, if we really willed it, as to direct to objects of certain and general utility the emulation and the tastes of a nation so sensible to honour as ours is, and so easy to lend itself to all the impressions which the Government might know how to give.

6. These reflections ought to strengthen our approval of the wise restrictions which the king, by his edict of 1749, has made to the liberty of creating new foundations. Let us add that they ought to leave no doubt on the incontestable right possessed by the Government—in the first place, in the civil order, next, by the Government and the Church, in the order of religion—to dispose of old foundations, to extend their funds to new objects, or, better still, to suppress them altogether. Public utility is the supreme law, and it ought not to be nullified by any superstitious respect for what we call the *intention of the founder*—as if ignorant and shortsighted individuals had the right to chain to their capricious wills the generations that had still to be born. Neither should we be deterred by the fear to infringe upon the pretended rights of certain bodies—as if private bodies had any rights opposed to those of the State. Citizens have rights, and rights to be held sacred, even by society—they exist independently of society, they enter into it with all their rights, only that they may place themselves

under the protection of these same laws which assure their property and their liberty. But private *bodies* do not exist of themselves, nor for themselves; they have been formed by society, and they ought not to exist a moment after they have ceased to be useful.

We conclude. No work of man is made for immortality; and since *foundations,* always multiplied by vanity, would in the long run, if uninterfered with, absorb all funds and all private properties, it would be absolutely necessary at last to destroy them. If all the men who have lived had had a tombstone erected for them, it would have been necessary, in order to find ground to cultivate, to overthrow the sterile monuments and to stir up the ashes of the dead to nourish the living.

Reprinted in *The Life and Writings of Turgot, Comptroller-General of France, 1774–6,* edited by W. Walter Stephens (London: Longmans, Green, 1895).

WILLIAM WORDSWORTH

"The Old Cumberland Beggar"

William Wordsworth (1770–1850), major English Romantic poet, wrote this ode to communal care and individual freedom in 1798, as "progress" in the form of the Industrial Revolution began indelibly to change British economic and social relations. The poem's beggar—who is not only succored by Cumberland, but an essential part of its life and spirit—daily renews, through his habitual rounds, the moral kinship among the villagers. Such relations if left to languish, Wordsworth suggests, would resign us "to selfishness and cold oblivious cares." We all need, indeed "long for," moments that assure us that we have been "the dealers-out of some small blessings" to others. The beggar thus renders service to his neighbors, and so Wordsworth beseeches those "restless" statesmen who seek to rid the world of such "nuisances," to "deem this Man not useless." Later, referring to the confined and dreary charitable work houses such reformers advocated, he says "May never HOUSE, misnamed of INDUSTRY, Make him captive!" Rather, "let him be free to wander where and when he will." What does Wordsworth's poetic argument suggest about what we owe people like the old Cumberland beggar?

Wordsworth originally prefaced the poem with a statement indicating that, as a child, he had observed such a "spectacle" with "great benefit" and warning that such men would soon be extinct. For the most part, the beggar who functions as an intrinsic part of a community is no longer in evidence, yet there are surely counterparts of such indigent, solitary wanderers still in our midst. But few of us deem the presence of such homeless people as a benefit, and few of us give benefits to them. Has the Romantic poet romanticized what such people can do for us? Or what we might do for them?

I saw an aged Beggar in my walk;
And he was seated, by the highway side,
On a low structure of rude masonry
Built at the foot of a huge hill, that they
Who lead their horses down the steep rough road
May thence remount at ease. The aged Man
Had placed his staff across the broad smooth stone
That overlays the pile; and, from a bag
All white with flour, the dole of village dames,
He drew his scraps and fragments, one by one;
And scanned them with a fixed and serious look

Of idle computation. In the sun,
Upon the second step of that small pile,
Surrounded by those wild, unpeopled hills,
He sat, and ate his food in solitude:
And ever, scattered from his palsied hand,
That, still attempting to prevent the waste,
Was baffled still, the crumbs in little showers
Fell on the ground; and the small mountain birds
Not venturing yet to peck their destined meal,
Approached within the length of half his staff.

Him from my childhood have I known; and then
He was so old, he seems not older now;
He travels on, a solitary Man,
So helpless in appearance, that for him
The sauntering Horseman throws not with a slack
And careless hand his alms upon the ground,
But stops,—that he may safely lodge the coin
Within the old Man's hat; nor quits him so,
But still, when he has given his horse the rein,
Watches the aged Beggar with a look
Sidelong, and half-reverted. She who tends
The toll-gate, when in summer at her door
She turns her wheel, if on the road she sees
The aged Beggar coming, quits her work,
And lifts the latch for him that he may pass.
The post-boy, when his rattling wheels o'ertake
The aged Beggar in the woody lane,
Shouts to him from behind; and if, thus warned,
The old Man does not change his course, the boy
Turns with less noisy wheels to the roadside,
And passes gently by, without a curse
Upon his lips, or anger at his heart.

He travels on, a solitary Man;
His age has no companion. On the ground
His eyes are turned, and, as he moves along,
'They' move along the ground; and, evermore,
Instead of common and habitual sight
Of fields, with rural works, of hill and dale,
And the blue sky, one little span of earth
Is all his prospect. Thus, from day to day,
Bow-bent, his eyes forever on the ground,
He plies his weary journey; seeing still,

And seldom knowing that he sees, some straw,
Some scattered leaf, or marks which, in one track,
The nails of cart or chariot-wheel have left
Impressed on the white road,—in the same line,
At distance still the same. Poor Traveller!
His staff trails with him; scarcely do his feet
Disturb the summer dust; he is so still
In look and motion, that the cottage curs,
Ere he has passed the door, will turn away,
Weary of barking at him. Boys and girls,
The vacant and the busy, maids and youths,
And urchins newly breeched—all pass him by:
Him even the slow-paced waggon leaves behind.

But deem not this Man useless.—Statesmen! ye
Who are so restless in your wisdom, ye
Who have a broom still ready in your hands
To rid the world of nuisances; ye proud,
Heart-swoln, while in your pride ye contemplate
Your talents, power, or wisdom, deem him not
A burden of the earth! 'Tis Nature's law
That none, the meanest of created things,
Of forms created the most vile and brute,
The dullest or most noxious, should exist
Divorced from good—a spirit and pulse of good,
A life and soul, to every mode of being
Inseparably linked. Then be assured
That least of all can aught—that ever owned
The heaven-regarding eye and front sublime
Which man is born to—sink, howe'er depressed,
So low as to be scorned without a sin;
Without offence to God cast out of view;
Like the dry remnant of a garden-flower
Whose seeds are shed, or as an implement
Worn out and worthless. While from door to door,
This old Man creeps, the villagers in him
Behold a record which together binds
Past deeds and offices of charity,
Else unremembered, and so keeps alive
The kindly mood in hearts which lapse of years,
And that half-wisdom half-experience gives,
Make slow to feel, and by sure steps resign
To selfishness and cold oblivious cares,

Among the farms and solitary huts,
Hamlets and thinly-scattered villages,
Where'er the aged Beggar takes his rounds,
The mild necessity of use compels
To acts of love; and habit does the work
Of reason; yet prepares that after-joy
Which reason cherishes. And thus the soul,
By that sweet taste of pleasure unpursued,
Doth find herself insensibly disposed
To virtue and true goodness.

               Some there are
By their good works exalted, lofty minds
And meditative, authors of delight
And happiness, which to the end of time
Will live, and spread, and kindle: even such minds
In childhood, from this solitary Being,
Or from like wanderer, haply have received
(A thing more precious far than all that books
Or the solicitudes of love can do!)
That first mild touch of sympathy and thought,
In which they found their kindred with a world
Where want and sorrow were. The easy man
Who sits at his own door,—and, like the pear
That overhangs his head from the green wall,
Feeds in the sunshine; the robust and young,
The prosperous and unthinking, they who live
Sheltered, and flourish in a little grove
Of their own kindred;—all behold in him
A silent monitor, which on their minds
Must needs impress a transitory thought
Of self-congratulation, to the heart
Of each recalling his peculiar boons,
His charters and exemptions; and, perchance,
Though he to no one give the fortitude
And circumspection needful to preserve
His present blessings, and to husband up
The respite of the season, he, at least,
And 'tis no vulgar service, makes them felt.

Yet further.—Many, I believe, there are
Who live a life of virtuous decency,
Men who can hear the Decalogue and feel
No self-reproach; who of the moral law

Established in the land where they abide
Are strict observers; and not negligent
In acts of love to those with whom they dwell,
Their kindred, and the children of their blood.
Praise be to such, and to their slumbers peace!
—But of the poor man ask, the abject poor;
Go, and demand of him, if there be here
In this cold abstinence from evil deeds,
And these inevitable charities,
Wherewith to satisfy the human soul?
No—man is dear to man; the poorest poor
Long for some moments in a weary life
When they can know and feel that they have been,
Themselves, the fathers and the dealers-out
Of some small blessings; have been kind to such
As needed kindness, for this single cause,
That we have all of us one human heart.
—Such pleasure is to one kind Being known,
My neighbour, when with punctual care, each week
Duly as Friday comes, though pressed herself
By her own wants, she from her store of meal
Takes one unsparing handful for the scrip
Of this old Mendicant, and, from her door
Returning with exhilarated heart,
Sits by her fire, and builds her hope in heaven.

Then let him pass, a blessing on his head!
And while in that vast solitude to which
The tide of things has borne him, he appears
To breathe and live but for himself alone,
Unblamed, uninjured, let him bear about
The good which the benignant law of Heaven
Has hung around him: and, while life is his,
Still let him prompt the unlettered villagers
To tender offices and pensive thoughts.
—Then let him pass, a blessing on his head!
And, long as he can wander, let him breathe
The freshness of the valleys; let his blood
Struggle with frosty air and winter snows;
And let the chartered wind that sweeps the heath
Beat his grey locks against his withered face.
Reverence the hope whose vital anxiousness
Gives the last human interest to his heart.

May never HOUSE, misnamed of INDUSTRY,
Make him a captive!—for that pent-up din,
Those life-consuming sounds that clog the air,
Be his the natural silence of old age!
Let him be free of mountain solitudes;
And have around him, whether heard or not,
The pleasant melody of woodland birds.
Few are his pleasures: if his eyes have now
Been doomed so long to settle upon earth
That not without some effort they behold
The countenance of the horizontal sun,
Rising or setting, let the light at least
Find a free entrance to their languid orbs.
And let him, 'where' and 'when' he will, sit down
Beneath the trees, or on a grassy bank
Of highway side, and with the little birds
Share his chance-gathered meal; and, finally,
As in the eye of Nature he has lived,
So in the eye of Nature let him die!

From *The Complete Poetical Works* by William Wordsworth (London: Macmillan, 1888).

ROBERT FROST

"Love and a Question"

American poet Robert Frost (1874–1963) is known for his deceptively simple narrative poems that address complex psychological and ethical concerns. Such is
"Love and a Question." In the poem, a stranger comes to the home of newlyweds,
asking "a shelter for the night." The husband, considering the weather and his
own circumstances, wonders what he should do. Rather than provide a pat answer, the poem leaves its readers with the same question, subtly shaped and
shaded: What should the bridegroom do? Should he sacrifice "the heart's desire"
of his beloved to aid a stranger? Should he condemn the needy man to face the
woes of the cold night rather than "harboring woe in the bridal house"? Whose
needs are more important? Whose more urgent? To whom should he feel most
accountable? Similarly situated, to whom would you answer?

❧

A stranger came to the door at eve,
And he spoke the bridegroom fair.
He bore a green-white stick in his hand,
And, for all burden, care.
He asked with the eyes more than the lips
For a shelter for the night,
And he turned and looked at the road afar
Without a window light.

The bridegroom came forth into the porch
With, 'Let us look at the sky,
And question what of the night to be,
Stranger, you and I.'
The woodbine leaves littered the yard,
The woodbine berries were blue,
Autumn, yes, winter was in the wind;
'Stranger, I wish I knew.'

Within, the bride in the dusk alone
Bent over the open fire,
Her face rose-red with the glowing coal
And the thought of the heart's desire.

The bridegroom looked at the weary road,
Yet saw but her within,

And wished her heart in a case of gold
And pinned with a silver pin.

The bridegroom thought it little to give
A dole of bread, a purse,
A heartfelt prayer for the poor of God,
Or for the rich a curse;

But whether or not a man was asked
To mar the love of two
By harboring woe in the bridal house,
The bridegroom wished he knew.

From *A Boy's Will* by Robert Frost (New York: Henry Holt, 1915).

RALPH WALDO EMERSON

From "Self-Reliance"

Ralph Waldo Emerson (1803–1883), American writer famous for his philosophy of Transcendentalism and doctrine of self-reliance, was candidly suspicious of gift-giving and charity. "It is not the office of a man to receive gifts. How dare you give them," he wrote once. In this selection, Emerson embeds a criticism of philanthropy and philanthropists within his argument for self-reliance (the subject, and title, of his essay). One is first and foremost accountable to oneself, he asserts, and responsible for maintaining the integrity of one's own nature. Even in branching out, he would not have us reach to any indistinct "other," but rather stay close by: "Go love thy infant; love they woodchopper," he says. "Thy love afar is spite at home." And he pointedly shuns the philanthropist who would speak to him of his responsibility to the poor—"Are they my poor?"—insisting that he has special responsibility only to those "who belong to him" and "to whom he belongs," by "spiritual affinity." To whom does he—to whom do we—mutually belong? However we answer, are these the people to whom we, as philanthropists, should be most accountable?

ℰə

Whoso would be a man must be a nonconformist. He who would gather immortal palms must not be hindered by the name of goodness, but must explore if it be goodness. Nothing is at last sacred but the integrity of your own mind. Absolve you to yourself, and you shall have the suffrage of the world. I remember an answer which when quite young I was prompted to make to a valued adviser who was wont to importune me with the dear old doctrines of the church. On my saying, "What have I to do with the sacredness of traditions, if I live wholly from within?" my friend suggested,—"But these impulses may be from below, not from above." I replied, "They do not seem to me to be such; but if I am the Devil's child, I will live then from the Devil." No law can be sacred to me but that of my nature. Good and bad are but names very readily transferable to that or this; the only right is what is after my constitution; the only wrong what is against it. A man is to carry himself in the presence of all opposition as if every thing were titular and ephemeral but he. I am ashamed to think how easily we capitulate to badges and names, to large societies and dead institutions. Every decent and well-spoken individual affects and sways me more than is right. I ought to go upright and vital, and speak the rude truth in all ways. If malice and vanity wear the coat of philanthropy, shall that pass? If an angry bigot assumes this bountiful cause of Abolition, and comes to me with his last news from Barbadoes, why should I not say to him, "Go love thy infant; love thy wood-chopper; be good-natured and modest; have that grace; and never varnish your hard, uncharitable ambition with this incredible tenderness for black folk a thousand miles off. Thy love afar is spite at home." Rough and graceless would be such greeting, but truth is handsomer than the affectation of love. Your goodness must have some edge to it,—else it is none. The doctrine of hatred must be preached, as the counteraction of the doctrine of love, when that pules and whines. I shun father and mother and wife and brother when my genius calls me. I would write on the lintels of the door-post, *Whim*. I hope it is somewhat better than whim at last, but we cannot spend the day in explanation. Expect me not to show cause why I seek or why I exclude company. Then, again, do not tell me, as a good man did to-day, of my obligation to put all poor men in good situations. Are they *my* poor? I tell thee, thou foolish philanthropist, that I grudge the dollar, the dime, the cent, I give to such men as do not belong to me and to whom I do not belong. There is a class of persons to whom by all spiritual affinity I am bought and sold; for them I will go to prison, if need be; but your miscellaneous popular charities; the education at college of fools; the building of meeting-houses to the vain end to which many now stand; alms to sots; and the thousandfold Relief Societies;—though I confess with shame I sometimes succumb and give the dollar, it is a wicked dollar which by and by I shall have the manhood to withhold.

From "Self-Reliance" in *Essays* by Ralph Waldo Emerson (London: J. Fraser, 1841).

CHARLES W. CHESNUTT

"The Wife of his Youth"

This short story, by American writer Charles Waddell Chesnutt (1858–1932), was, when it was published in 1898, the first story by an African American author to appear in The Atlantic Monthly. *Racial identity is, in fact, the most immediate subject of Chesnutt's story. But in making central the universal adage "to thine own self be true," it invites each of us to look into the mirror and ask ourselves, "Who am I? What do I owe to who I have been and where I have come from? How should the commitments I have made in my past bear on my hopes and plans for the future?"*

Mr. Ryder, the light-skinned black leader of the "Blue Vein Society," is preparing to throw a ball in honor of the woman to whom he intends to propose marriage, a woman he regards as his superior and a picture-perfect mate for the man he has so carefully groomed himself to be. But when suddenly confronted by his past and his past promises, Mr. Ryder takes the adage to heart and to his own self is true. He capitulates to no authority but his own conscience, yet he gives a public account of his decision, and in a manner by which his audience is moved to endorse his choice. Have they too awakened to their own responsibilities? To whom does Mr. Ryder acknowledge responsibility, and why? Do his actions serve as a model of the sort of promise-keeping and public accountability so prized by philanthropy?

I.

Mr. Ryder was going to give a ball. There were several reasons why this was an opportune time for such an event.

Mr. Ryder might aptly be called the dean of the Blue Veins. The original Blue Veins were a little society of colored persons organized in a certain Northern city shortly after the war. Its purpose was to establish and maintain correct social standards among a people whose social condition presented almost unlimited room for improvement. By accident, combined perhaps with some natural affinity, the society consisted of individuals who were, generally speaking, more white than black. Some envious outsider made the suggestion that no one was eligible for membership who was not white enough to show blue veins. The suggestion was readily adopted by those who were not of the favored few, and since that time the society, though possessing a longer and more pretentious name, had been known far and wide as the "Blue Vein Society," and its members as the "Blue Veins."

The Blue Veins did not allow that any such requirement existed for admission to their circle, but, on the contrary, declared that character and culture were the only things considered; and that if most of their members were light-colored, it was because such persons, as a rule, had had better opportunities to qualify themselves for membership. Opinions differed, too, as to the usefulness of the society. There were those who had been known to assail it violently as a glaring example of the very prejudice from which the colored race had suffered most; and later, when such critics had succeeded in getting on the inside, they had been heard to maintain with zeal and earnestness that the society was a life-boat, an anchor, a bulwark and a shield, a pillar of cloud by day and of fire by night, to guide their people through the social wilderness. Another alleged prerequisite for Blue Vein membership was that of free birth; and while there was really no such requirement, it is doubtless true that very few of the members would have been unable to meet it if there had been. If there were one or two of the older members who had come up from the South and from slavery, their history presented enough romantic circumstances to rob their servile origin of its grosser aspects. While there were no such tests of eligibility, it is true that the Blue Veins had their notions on these subjects, and that not all of them were equally liberal in regard to the things they collectively disclaimed. Mr. Ryder was one of the most conservative. Though he had not been among the founders of the society, but had come in some years later, his genius for social leadership was such that he had speedily become its recognized adviser and head, the custodian of its standards, and the preserver of its traditions. He shaped its social policy, was active in providing for its entertainment, and when the interest fell off, as it sometimes did, he fanned the embers until they burst again into a cheerful flame. There were still other reasons for his popularity. While he was not as white as some of the Blue Veins, his appearance was such as to confer distinction upon them. His features were of a refined type, his hair was almost straight; he was always neatly dressed; his manners were irreproachable, and his morals above suspicion. He had come to Groveland a young man, and obtaining employment in the office of a railroad company as messenger had in time worked himself up to the position of stationery clerk, having charge of the distribution of the office supplies for the whole company. Although the lack of early training had hindered the orderly development of a naturally fine mind, it had not prevented him from doing a great deal of reading or from forming decidedly literary tastes. Poetry was his passion. He could repeat whole pages of the great English poets; and if his pronunciation was sometimes faulty, his eye, his voice, his gestures, would respond to the changing sentiment with a precision that revealed a poetic soul, and disarm criticism. He was economical, and had saved money; he owned and occupied a very comfortable house on a respectable street. His residence was handsomely furnished, containing among other things a good library, especially rich in poetry, a piano, and some choice engravings. He generally shared his house with some young couple, who looked after his wants and were company for him; for Mr. Ryder was a single man. In the early days of his connection with the Blue Veins he had been regarded as quite a catch, and ladies and their mothers had maneuvered with much ingenuity to capture him. Not, however, until Mrs. Molly Dixon visited Groveland had any woman ever made him wish to change his condition to that of a married man.

Mrs. Dixon had come to Groveland from Washington in the spring, and before the summer was over she had won Mr. Ryder's heart. She possessed many attractive qualities. She was much younger than he; in fact, he was old enough to have been her father, though no one knew exactly how old he was. She was whiter than he, and better educated. She had moved in the best colored society of the country, at Washington, and had taught in the schools of that city. Such a superior person had been eagerly welcomed to the Blue Vein Society, and had taken a leading part in its activities. Mr. Ryder had at first been attracted by her charms of person, for she was very good looking and not over twenty-five; then by her refined manners and by the vivacity of her wit. Her husband had been a government clerk, and at his death had left a considerable life insurance. She was visiting friends in Groveland, and, finding the town and the people to her liking, had prolonged her stay indefinitely. She had not seemed displeased at Mr. Ryder's attentions, but on the contrary had given him every proper encouragement; indeed, a younger and less cautious man would long since have spoken. But he had made up his mind, and had only to determine the time when he would ask her to be his wife. He decided to give a ball in her honor, and at some time during the evening of the ball to offer her his heart and hand. He had no special fears about the outcome, but, with a little touch of romance, he wanted the surroundings to be in harmony with his own feelings when he should have received the answer he expected.

Mr. Ryder resolved that this ball should mark an epoch in the social history of Groveland. He knew, of course,—no one could know better,—the entertainments that had taken place in past years, and what must be done to surpass them. His ball must be worthy of the lady in whose honor it was to be given, and must, by the quality of its guests, set an example for the future. He had observed of late a growing liberality, almost a laxity, in social matters, even among members of his own set, and had several times been forced to meet in a social way persons whose complexions and callings in life were hardly up to the standard which he considered proper for the society to maintain. He had a theory of his own.

"I have no race prejudice," he would say, "but we people of mixed blood are ground between the upper and the nether millstone. Our fate lies between absorption by the white race and extinction in the black. The one doesn't want us yet, but may take us in time. The other would welcome us, but it would be for us a backward step. 'With malice towards none, with charity for all,' we must do the best we can for ourselves and those who are to follow us. Self-preservation is the first law of nature."

His ball would serve by its exclusiveness to counteract leveling tendencies, and his marriage with Mrs. Dixon would help to further the upward process of absorption he had been wishing and waiting for.

II.

The ball was to take place on Friday night. The house had been put in order, the carpets covered with canvas, the halls and stairs decorated with palms and potted plants; and in the afternoon Mr. Ryder sat on his front porch, which the shade of a vine running up over a wire netting made a cool and pleasant lounging-place. He expected to respond to the toast "The Ladies," at the supper, and from a volume of Tennyson—his favorite poet—was fortifying himself with apt quotations. The volume was open at "A Dream of Fair Women." His eyes fell on these lines, and he read them aloud to judge better of their effect:—

> "At length I saw a lady within call.
> Stiller than chisell'd marble, standing there;
> A daughter of the gods, divinely tall,
> And most divinely fair."

He marked the verse, and turning the page read the stanza beginning,—

> "O sweet pale Margaret,
> O rare pale Margaret."

He weighed the passage a moment, and decided that it would not do. Mrs. Dixon was the palest lady he expected at the ball, and she was of a rather ruddy complexion, and of lively disposition and buxom build. So he ran over the leaves until his eye rested on the description of Queen Guinevere:—

> "She seem'd a part of joyous Spring:
> A gown of grass-green silk she wore,
> Buckled with golden clasps before;
> A light-green tuft of plumes she bore
> Closed in a golden ring.
> . . . .

> "She look'd so lovely, as she sway'd
> The rein with dainty finger-tips,
> A man had given all other bliss,
> And all his worldly worth for this,
> To waste his whole heart in one kiss
> Upon her perfect lips."

As Mr. Ryder murmured these words audibly, with an appreciative thrill, he heard the latch of his gate click, and a light footfall sounding on the steps. He turned his head, and saw a woman standing before the door.

She was a little woman, not five feet tall, and proportioned to her height.

Although she stood erect, and looked around her with very bright and restless eyes, she seemed quite old; for her face was crossed and recrossed with a hundred wrinkles, and around the edges of her bonnet could be seen protruding here and there a tuft of short gray wool. She wore a blue calico gown of ancient cut, a little red shawl fastened around her shoulders with an old-fashioned brass brooch, and a large bonnet profusely ornamented with faded red and yellow artificial flowers. And she was very black—so black that her toothless gums, revealed when she opened her mouth to speak, were not red, but blue. She looked like a bit of the old plantation life, summoned up from the past by the wave of a magician's wand, as the poet's fancy had called into being the gracious shapes of which Mr. Ryder had just been reading.

He rose from his chair and came over to where she stood.

"Good-afternoon, madam," he said.

"Good-evenin', suh," she answered, ducking suddenly with a quaint curtsy. Her voice was shrill and piping, but softened somewhat by age. "Is dis yere whar Mistuh Ryduh lib, suh?" she asked, looking around her doubtfully, and glancing into the open windows, through which some of the preparations for the evening were visible.

"Yes," he replied, with an air of kindly patronage, unconsciously flattered by her manner, "I am Mr. Ryder. Did you want to see me?"

"Yas, suh, ef I ain't 'sturbin' of you too much."

"Not at all. Have a seat over here behind the vine, where it is cool. What can I do for you?"

" 'Scuse me, suh," she continued, when she had sat down on the edge of a chair, " 'scuse me, suh, I's lookin' for my husban'. I heerd you wuz a big man an' had libbed heah a long time, an' I 'lowed you wouldn't min' ef I'd come roun' an' ax you ef you'd eber heerd of a merlatter man by de name er Sam Taylor 'quirin' roun' in de chu'ches ermongs' de people fer his wife 'Liza Jane?"

Mr. Ryder seemed to think for a moment.

"There used to be many such cases right after the war," he said, "but it has been so long that I have forgotten them. There are very few now. But tell me your story, and it may refresh my memory."

She sat back farther in her chair so as to be more comfortable, and folded her withered hands in her lap.

"My name's 'Liza," she began, " 'Liza Jane. Wen I wuz young I us'ter b'long ter Marse Bob Smif, down in old Missourn. I wuz bawn down dere. W'en I wuz a gal I wuz married ter a man named Jim. But Jim died, an' after dat I married a merlatter man named Sam Taylor. Sam wuz free-bawn, but his mammy and daddy died, an' de w'ite folks 'prenticed him ter my marster fer ter work fer 'im 'tel he wuz growed up. Sam worked in de fiel', an' I wuz de cook. One day Ma'y Ann, ole miss's maid, come rushin' out ter de kitchen, an' says she, ''Liza Jane, ole marse gwine sell yo' Sam down de ribber.'

" 'Go way f'm yere,' says I; 'my husban's free!'

" 'Don' make no diff'ence. I heerd ole marse tell ole miss he wuz gwine take yo' Sam 'way wid 'im ter-morrow, fer he needed money, an' he knowed whar he could git a t'ousan' dollars fer Sam an' no questions axed.'

"W'en Sam come home f'm de fiel', dat night, I tole him 'bout ole marse gwine steal 'im, an' Sam run erway. His time wuz mos' up, an' he swo' dat w'en he wuz twenty-one he would come back an' he'p me run erway, er else save up de money ter buy my freedom. An' I know he'd 'a' done it, fer he thought a heap er me, Sam did. But w'en he come back he didn' fin' me, fer I wuzn' dere. Ole marse had heerd dat I warned Sam, so he had me whip' an' sol' down de ribber.

"Den de wah broke out, an' w'en it wuz ober de cullud folks wuz scattered. I went back ter de ole home; but Sam wuzn' dere, an' I couldn' l'arn nuffin' 'bout 'im. But I knowed he'd be'n dere to look fer me an' hadn' foun' me, an' had gone erway ter hunt fer me.

"I's be'n lookin' fer 'im eber sence," she added simply, as though twenty-five years were but a couple of weeks, "an' I knows he's be'n lookin' fer me. Fer he sot a heap er sto' by me, Sam did, an' I know he's be'n huntin' fer me all dese years,—'less'n he's be'n sick er sump'n, so he couldn' work, er out'n his head, so he couldn' 'member his promise. I went back down de ribber, fer I 'lowed he'd gone down dere lookin' fer me. I's be'n ter Noo Orleens, an' Atlanty, an' Charleston, an' Richmon'; an' w'en I'd be'n all ober de Souf I come ter de Norf. Fer I knows I'll fin' 'im some er dese days," she added softly, "er he'll fin' me, an' den we'll bofe be as happy in freedom as we wuz in de ole days befo' de wah." A smile stole over her withered countenance as she paused a moment, and her bright eyes softened into a far-away look.

This was the substance of the old woman's story. She had wandered a little here and there. Mr. Ryder was looking at her curiously when she finished.

"How have you lived all these years?" he asked.

"Cookin', suh. I's a good cook. Does you know anybody w'at needs a good cook, suh? I's stoppin' wid a cullud fam'ly roun' de corner yonder 'tel I kin fin' a place."

"Do you really expect to find your husband? He may be dead long ago."

She shook her head emphatically. "Oh no, he ain' dead. De signs an' de tokens tells me. I dremp three nights runnin' on'y dis las' week dat I foun' him."

"He may have married another woman. Your slave marriage would not have prevented him, for you never lived with him after the war, and without that your marriage doesn't count."

"Wouldn' make no diff'ence wid Sam. He wouldn' marry no yuther 'ooman 'tel he foun' out 'bout me. I knows it," she added. "Sump'n's be'n tellin' me all dese years dat I's gwine fin' Sam 'fo I dies."

"Perhaps he's outgrown you, and climbed up in the world where he wouldn't care to have you find him."

"No, indeed, suh," she replied, "Sam ain' dat kin' er man. He wuz good ter me, Sam wuz, but he wuzn' much good ter nobody e'se, fer he wuz one er de triflin'es' han's on de plantation. I 'spec's ter haf ter suppo't 'im w'en I fin' 'im, fer he nebber would work 'less'n he had ter. But den he wuz free, an' he didn' git no pay fer his work, an' I don' blame 'im much. Mebbe he's done better sence he run erway, but I ain' 'spectin' much."

"You may have passed him on the street a hundred times during the twenty-five years, and not have known him; time works great changes."

She smiled incredulously. "I'd know 'im 'mongs' a hund'ed men. Fer dey wuzn' no yuther merlatter man like my man Sam, an' I couldn' be mistook. I's toted his picture roun' wid me twenty-five years."

"May I see it?" asked Mr. Ryder. "It might help me to remember whether I have seen the original."

As she drew a small parcel from her bosom, he saw that it was fastened to a string that went around her neck. Removing several wrappers, she brought to light an old-fashioned daguerreotype in a black case. He looked long and intently at the portrait. It was faded with time, but the features were still distinct, and it was easy to see what manner of man it had represented.

He closed the case, and with a slow movement handed it back to her.

"I don't know of any man in town who goes by that name," he said, "nor have I heard of any one making such inquiries. But if you will leave me your address, I will give the matter some attention, and if I find out anything I will let you know."

She gave him the number of a house in the neighborhood, and went away, after thanking him warmly.

He wrote down the address on the flyleaf of the volume of Tennyson, and, when she had gone, rose to his feet and stood looking after her curiously. As she walked down the street with mincing step, he saw several persons whom she passed turn and look back at her with a smile of kindly amusement. When she had turned the corner, he went upstairs to his bedroom, and stood for a long time before the mirror of his dressing-case, gazing thoughtfully at the reflection of his own face.

III.

At eight o'clock the ballroom was a blaze of light and the guests had begun to assemble; for there was a literary programme and some routine business of the society to be gone through with before the dancing. A black servant in evening dress waited at the door and directed the guests to the dressing-rooms.

The occasion was long memorable among the colored people of the city; not alone for the dress and display, but for the high average of intelligence and culture that distinguished the gathering as a whole. There were a number of school-teachers, several young doctors, three or four lawyers, some professional singers, an editor, a lieutenant in the United States army spending his furlough in the city, and others in various polite callings; these were colored, though most of them would not have attracted even a casual glance because of any marked difference from white people. Most of the ladies were in evening costume, and dress coats and dancing-pumps were the rule among the men. A

band of string music, stationed in an alcove behind a row of palms, played popular airs while the guests were gathering.

The dancing began at half past nine. At eleven o'clock supper was served.
Mr. Ryder had left the ballroom some little time before the intermission, but reappeared at the supper-table. The spread was worthy of the occasion, and the
guests did full justice to it. When the coffee had been served, the toastmaster,
Mr. Solomon Sadler, rapped for order. He made a brief introductory speech,
complimenting host and guests, and then presented in their order the toasts of
the evening. They were responded to with a very fair display of after-dinner wit.

"The last toast," said the toast-master, when he reached the end of the list,
"is one which must appeal to us all. There is no one of us of the sterner sex who
is not at some time dependent upon woman,—in infancy for protection, in
manhood for companionship, in old age for care and comforting. Our good
host has been trying to live alone, but the fair faces I see around me to-night
prove that he too is largely dependent upon the gentler sex for most that makes
life worth living,—the society and love of friends,—and rumor is at fault if
he does not soon yield entire subjection to one of them. Mr. Ryder will now
respond to the toast,—The Ladies."

There was a pensive look in Mr. Ryder's eyes as he took the floor and ad-
justed his eyeglasses. He began by speaking of woman as the gift of Heaven to
man, and after some general observations on the relations of the sexes he said:
"But perhaps the quality which most distinguishes woman is her fidelity and
devotion to those she loves. History is full of examples, but has recorded none
more striking than one which only today came under my notice."

He then related, simply but effectively, the story told by his visitor of the
afternoon. He told it in the same soft dialect, which came readily to his lips,
while the company listened attentively and sympathetically. For the story had
awakened a responsive thrill in many hearts. There were some present who
had seen, and others who had heard their fathers and grandfathers tell, the
wrongs and sufferings of this past generation, and all of them still felt, in their
darker moments, the shadow hanging over them. Mr. Ryder went on:—

"Such devotion and such confidence are rare even among women. There
are many who would have searched a year, some who would have waited five
years, a few who might have hoped ten years; but for twenty-five years this
woman has retained her affection for and her faith in a man she has not seen or
heard of in all that time.

"She came to me today in the hope that I might be able to help her find this
long-lost husband. And when she was gone I gave my fancy rein, and imagined
a case I will put to you.

"Suppose that this husband, soon after his escape, had learned that his wife
had been sold away, and that such inquiries as he could make brought no information of her whereabouts. Suppose that he was young, and she much older
than he; that he was light, and she was black; that their marriage was a slave

marriage, and legally binding only if they chose to make it so after the war. Suppose, too, that he made his way to the North, as some of us have done, and there, where he had larger opportunities, had improved them, and had in the course of all these years grown to be as different from the ignorant boy who ran away from fear of slavery as the day is from the night. Suppose, even, that he had qualified himself, by industry, by thrift, and by study, to win the friendship and be considered worthy the society of such people as these I see around me to-night, gracing my board and filling my heart with gladness; for I am old enough to remember the day when such a gathering would not have been possible in this land. Suppose, too, that, as the years went by, this man's memory of the past grew more and more indistinct, until at last it was rarely, except in his dreams, that any image of this bygone period rose before his mind. And then suppose that accident should bring to his knowledge the fact that the wife of his youth, the wife he had left behind him,—not one who had walked by his side and kept pace with him in his upward struggle, but one upon whom advancing years and a laborious life had set their mark,—was alive and seeking him, but that he was absolutely safe from recognition or discovery, unless he chose to reveal himself. My friends, what would the man do? I will suppose that he was one who loved honor, and tried to deal justly with all men. I will even carry the case further, and suppose that perhaps he had set his heart upon another, whom he had hoped to call his own. What would he do, or rather what ought he to do, in such a crisis of a lifetime?

"It seemed to me that he might hesitate, and I imagined that I was an old friend, a near friend, and that he had come to me for advice; and I argued the case with him. I tried to discuss it impartially. After we had looked upon the matter from every point of view, I said to him, in words that we all know:

'This above all: to thine own self be true, And it must follow, as the night the day, Thou canst not then be false to any man.'

Then, finally, I put the question to him, 'Shall you acknowledge her?'

"And now, ladies and gentlemen, friends and companions, I ask you, what should he have done?"

There was something in Mr. Ryder's voice that stirred the hearts of those who sat around him. It suggested more than mere sympathy with an imaginary situation; it seemed rather in the nature of a personal appeal. It was observed, too, that his look rested more especially upon Mrs. Dixon, with a mingled expression of renunciation and inquiry.

She had listened, with parted lips and streaming eyes. She was the first to speak: "He should have acknowledged her."

"Yes," they all echoed, "he should have acknowledged her."

"My friends and companions," responded Mr. Ryder, "I thank you, one and all. It is the answer I expected, for I knew your hearts."

He turned and walked toward the closed door of an adjoining room, while every eye followed him in wondering curiosity. He came back in a moment, leading by the hand his visitor of the afternoon, who stood startled and trembling at the sudden plunge into this scene of brilliant gayety. She was neatly dressed in gray, and wore the white cap of an elderly woman.

"Ladies and gentlemen," he said, "this is the woman, and I am the man, whose story I have told you. Permit me to introduce to you the wife of my youth."

Originally published in *The Atlantic Monthly* 82 (1898): 55–61.

AMBROSE BIERCE

"The Applicant"

American writer Ambrose Bierce (1842–1914?), known for his especially cynical and satiric pen, lives up to his reputation in this short story. On the eve of that "blessed 365th part of the year that all Christian souls set apart for mighty feats of goodness and joy," the board of the Abersush Home for Old Men chooses to reject the application of a clearly qualified applicant. Not for lack of room, not for his lack of need, but because his presence "would—under the circumstances—be peculiarly embarrassing." True, the "circumstances" are "peculiar" but why "embarrassing"? To whom does the board regard itself accountable? To whom should any such board be accountable? Do bureaucracies—dealing with applicants, not supplicants—find it easier or more difficult to accept responsibility to those we promise to serve?

ℰℛ

Pushing his adventurous shins through the deep snow that had fallen overnight, and encouraged by the glee of his little sister, following in the open way that he made, a sturdy small boy, the son of Grayville's most distinguished citizen, struck his foot against something of which there was no visible sign on the surface of the snow. It is the purpose of this narrative to explain how it came to be there.

No one who has had the advantage of passing through Grayville by day can have failed to observe the large stone building crowning the low hill to the north of the railway station—that is to say, to the right in going toward Great Mowbray. It is a somewhat dull-looking edifice, of the Early Comatose order, and appears to have been designed by an architect who shrank from publicity, and although unable to conceal his work—even compelled, in this instance, to set it on an eminence in the sight of men—did what he honestly could to insure it against a second look. So far as concerns its outer and visible aspect, the Abersush Home for Old Men is unquestionably inhospitable to human attention. But it is a building of great magnitude, and cost its benevolent founder the profit of many a cargo of the teas and silks and spices that his ships brought up from the under-world when he was in trade in Boston; though the main expense was its endowment. Altogether, this reckless person had robbed his heirs-at-law of no less a sum than half a million dollars and flung it away in riotous giving. Possibly it was with a view to get out of sight of the silent big witness to his extravagance that he shortly afterward disposed of all his Grayville property that remained to him, turned his back upon the scene of his prodigality and went off across the sea in one of his own ships. But the gossips who got their inspiration most directly from Heaven declared that he went in search of a wife—a theory not easily reconciled with that of the village humorist, who solemnly averred that the bachelor philanthropist had departed this life (left Grayville to wit) because the marriageable maidens had made it too hot to hold him. However this may have been, he had not returned, and although at long intervals there had come to Grayville, in a desultory way, vague rumors of his wanderings in strange lands, no one seemed certainly to know about him, and to the new generation he was no more than a name. But from above the portal of the Home for Old Men the name shouted in stone.

Despite its unpromising exterior, the Home is a fairly commodious place of retreat from the ills that its inmates have incurred by being poor and old and men. At the time embraced in this brief chronicle they were in number about a score, but in acerbity, querulousness, and general ingratitude they could hardly be reckoned at fewer than a hundred; at least that was the estimate of the superintendent, Mr. Silas Tilbody. It was Mr. Tilbody's steadfast conviction that always, in admitting new old men to replace those who had gone to another and a better Home, the trustees had distinctly in will the infraction of his peace, and the trial of his patience. In truth, the longer the institution was connected with him, the stronger was his feeling that the founder's scheme of benevolence was sadly impaired by providing any inmates at all. He had not much imagination, but with what he had he was addicted to the reconstruction of the Home for Old Men into a kind of "castle in Spain," with himself as castellan, hospitably entertaining about a score of sleek and prosperous middle-aged gentlemen, consummately good-humored and civilly willing to pay for their board and lodging. In this revised project of philanthropy the trustees, to whom he was indebted for his office and responsible for his conduct, had not the happiness to appear. As to them, it was held by the village humorist aforementioned that in their management of the great charity Providence had thoughtfully supplied an incentive to thrift. With the inference which he expected to be drawn from that view we have nothing to do, it had neither support nor denial from the inmates, who certainly were most concerned. They lived out their little remnant of life, crept into graves neatly numbered, and were succeeded by other old men as like them as could be desired by the Adversary of Peace. If the Home was a place of punishment for the sin of unthrift the veteran offenders sought justice with a persistence that attested the sincerity of their penitence. It is to one of these that the reader's attention is now invited.

In the matter of attire this person was not altogether engaging. But for this season, which was midwinter, a careless observer might have looked upon him as a clever device of the husbandman indisposed to share the fruits of his toil with the crows that toil not, neither spin—an error that might not have been dispelled without longer and closer observation than he seemed to court; for his progress up Abersush Street, toward the Home in the gloom of winter evening, was not visibly faster than what might have been expected of a scarecrow blessed with youth, health, and discontent. The man was indisputably ill-clad, yet not without a certain fitness and good taste, withal; for he was obviously an applicant for admittance to the Home, where poverty was a qualification. In the army of indigence the uniform is rags; they serve to distinguish the rank and file from the recruiting officers.

As the old man, entering the gate of the grounds, shuffled up the broad walk, already white with the fast-falling snow, which from time to time he feebly shook from its various coigns of vantage on his person, he came under inspection of the large globe lamp that burned always by night over the great door of the building. As if unwilling to incur its revealing beams, he turned to the left and, passing a considerable distance along the face of the building, rang at a smaller door emitting a dimmer ray that came within, through the fanlight, and expended itself incuriously overhead. The door was opened by no less a personage than the great Mr. Tilbody himself. Observing his visitor, who at once uncovered, and somewhat shortened the radius of the permanent curvature of his back, the great man gave visible token of neither surprise nor displeasure. Mr. Tilbody was, indeed, in an uncommonly good humor, a phenomenon ascribable doubtless to the cheerful influence of the season for this was Christmas Eve, and the morrow would be that blessed 365th part of the year that all Christian souls set apart for mighty feats of goodness and joy. Mr. Tilbody was so full of spirit of the season that his fat face and pale blue eyes, whose ineffectual fire served to distinguish it from an untimely summer squash, effused so genial a glow that it seemed a pity that he could not have lain down in it, basking in the consciousness of his own identity. He was hatted, booted, overcoated, and umbrellaed, as became a person who was about to expose himself to the night and the storm on an errand of charity; for Mr. Tilbody had just parted from his wife and children to go "down town" and purchase the wherewithal to confirm the annual falsehood about the hunch-bellied saint who frequents the chimneys to reward little boys and girls who are good, and especially truthful. So he did not invite the old man in but saluted him cheerily:

"Hello! Just in time; a moment later and you would have missed me. Come, I have no time to waste; we'll walk a little way together."

"Thank you," said the old man, upon whose thin and white but not ignoble face the light from the open door showed an expression that was perhaps disappointment; "but if the trustees—if my application—"

"The trustees," Mr. Tilbody said, closing more doors than one, and cutting off two kinds of light, "have agreed that your application disagrees with them."

Certain sentiments are inappropriate to Christmastide, but Humor, like Death, has all seasons for his own.

"Oh, my God!" cried the old man, in so thin and husky a tone that the invocation was anything but impressive, and to at least one of his two auditors sounded, indeed, somewhat ludicrous. To the Other—but that is a matter which laymen are devoid of the light to expound.

"Yes," continued Mr. Tilbody, accommodating his gait to that of his companion, who was mechanically, and not very successfully, retracing the track that he had made through the snow; "they have decided that, under the circumstances—under the very peculiar circumstances, you understand—it would be inexpedient to admit you. As superintendent and *ex officio* secretary of the honorable board"—as Mr. Tilbody "read his title clear" the magnitude of the big building, seen through its veil of falling snow, appeared to suffer somewhat in comparison—"it is my duty to inform you that, in the words of Deacon Byram, the chairman, your presence in the Home would—under the circumstances—be peculiarly embarrassing. I felt it my duty to submit to the honorable board the statement that you made to me yesterday of your needs, your physical condition, and the trials which it has pleased Providence to send upon you in your very proper effort to present your claims in person; but, after careful, and I may say prayerful, consideration of your case—with something too, I trust, of the large charitableness appropriate to the season—it was decided that we would not be justified in doing anything likely to impair the usefulness of the institution entrusted (under Providence) to our care."

They had now passed out of the grounds; the street lamp opposite the gate was dimly visible through the snow. Already the old man's former track was obliterated, and he seemed uncertain as to which way he should go. Mr. Tilbody had drawn a little way from him, but paused and turned half toward him apparently reluctant to forego the continuing opportunity.

"Under the circumstances," he resumed, "the decision—"

But the old man was inaccessible to the suasion of the verbosity; he had crossed the street into a vacant lot and was going forward, rather deviously toward nowhere in particular—which, he having nowhere in particular to go to, was not so reasonless a proceeding as it looked.

And that is how it happened that the next morning, when the church bells of all Grayville were ringing with an added unction appropriate to the day, the sturdy little son of Deacon Byram, breaking a way through the snow to the place of worship, struck his foot against the body of Amasa Abersush, philanthropist.

From *In the Midst of Life: Tales of Soldiers and Civilians* by Ambrose Bierce (New York: Boni and Liveright, 1918).

RALPH ELLISON

From Invisible Man

The "site visit," in philanthropy long regarded as a positive sign of due diligence, enables each side of the philanthropic divide to learn firsthand about the responsibilities they plan to or already assume. This selection, from the classic novel Invisible Man *by American writer Ralph Waldo Ellison (1914–1994), is exactly that—a site visit. The unnamed narrator—the "invisible man"—recalls the week, while at college, that he was a driver for a white millionaire philanthropist. As they drive, the visitor, apparently a friend of the "Negro" college's founder, becomes more and more expansive about how the young man and "his people" are connected to his destiny, announcing: "[A]s you develop you must remember that I am dependent upon you to learn my fate. Through you and your fellow students I become, let us say, three hundred teachers, seven hundred trained mechanics, eight hundred skilled farmers, and so on. That way I can observe in terms of living personalities to what extent my money, my time and my hopes have been fruitfully invested. . . . Understand?" Does accountability "to" or "for" this philanthropist, or any philanthropist similarly situated, call for such an account? If "visibility," as some have argued, is not a matter of being seen but of achieving one's humanity, is such a confession likely to encourage or discourage such development? What responsibility does the young man, or any grantee so situated, have to his benefactor?*

The grass did grow and the green leaves appeared on the trees and filled the avenues with shadow and shade as sure as the millionaires descended from the North on Founders' Day each spring. And how they arrived! Came smiling, inspecting, encouraging, conversing in whispers, speechmaking into the wide-open ears of our black and yellow faces—and each leaving a sizeable check as he departed. I'm convinced it was the product of a subtle magic, the alchemy of moonlight; the school a flower-studded wasteland, the rocks sunken, the dry winds hidden, the lost crickets chirping to yellow butterflies.

And oh, oh, oh, those multimillionaires!

They were all such a part of that other life that's dead that I can't remember them all. (Time was as I was, but neither that time nor that "I" are anymore.) But this one I remember: near the end of my junior year I drove for him during the week he was on the campus. A face pink like St. Nicholas', topped with a shock of silk white hair. An easy, informal manner, even with me. A Bostonian, smoker of cigars, teller of polite Negro stories, shrewd banker, skilled scientist, director, philanthropist, forty years a bearer of the white man's burden, and for sixty a symbol of the Great Traditions.

We were driving, the powerful motor purring and filling me with pride and anxiety. The car smelled of mints and cigar smoke. Students looked up and smiled in recognition as we rolled slowly past. I had just come from dinner and in bending forward to suppress a belch, I accidentally pressed the button on the wheel and the belch became a loud and shattering blast of the horn. Folks on the road turned and stared.

"I'm awfully sorry, sir," I said, worried lest he report me to Dr. Bledsoe, the president, who would refuse to allow me to drive again.

"Perfectly all right. Perfectly."

"Where shall I drive you, sir?"

"Let me see . . ."

Through the rear-view mirror I could see him studying a wafer-thin watch, replacing it in the pocket of his checked waistcoat. His shirt was soft silk, set off with a blue-and-white polka-dotted bow tie. His manner was aristocratic, his movements dapper and suave.

"It's early to go in for the next session," he said. "Suppose you just drive. Anywhere you like."

"Have you seen all the campus, sir?"

"Yes, I think so. I was one of the original founders, you know."

"Gee! I didn't know that, sir. Then I'll have to try some of the roads."

Of course I knew he was a founder, but I knew also that it was advantageous to flatter rich white folks. Perhaps he'd give me a large tip, or a suit, or a scholarship next year.

"Anywhere else you like. The campus is part of my life and I know my life rather well."

"Yes, sir."

He was still smiling.

In a moment the green campus with its vine-covered buildings was behind us. The car bounded over the road. How was the campus part of his life, I wondered. And how did one learn his life "rather well"?

"Young man, you're part of a wonderful institution. It is a great dream become reality . . ."

"Yes, sir," I said.

"I feel as lucky to be connected with it as you no doubt do yourself. I came here years ago, when all your beautiful campus was barren ground. There were no trees, no flowers, no fertile farmland. That was years ago before you were born . . ."

I listened with fascination, my eyes glued to the white line dividing the highway as my thoughts attempted to sweep back to the times of which he spoke.

"Even your parents were young. Slavery was just recently past. Your people did not know in what direction to turn and, I must confess, many of mine didn't know in what direction they should turn either. But your great Founder did. He was my friend and I believed in his vision. So much so, that some times I don't know whether it was his vision or mine . . ."

He chuckled softly, wrinkles forming at the corners of his eyes.

"But of course it was his; I only assisted. I came down with him to see the barren land and did what I could to render assistance. And it has been my pleasant fate to return each spring and observe the changes that the years have wrought. That has been more pleasant and satisfying to me than my own work. It has been a pleasant fate, indeed."

His voice was mellow and loaded with more meaning than I could fathom. As I drove, faded and yellowed pictures of the school's early days displayed in the library flashed across the screen of my mind, coming fitfully and fragmentarily to life—photographs of men and women in wagons drawn by mule teams and oxen, dressed in black, dusty clothing, people who seemed almost without individuality, a black mob that seemed to be waiting, looking with blank faces, and among them the inevitable collection of white men and women in smiles, clear of features, striking, elegant and confident. Until now, and although I could recognize the Founder and Dr. Bledsoe among them, the figures in the photographs had never seemed actually to have been alive, but were more like signs or symbols one found on the last pages of the dictionary . . . But now I felt that I was sharing in a great work and, with the car leaping leisurely beneath the pressure of my foot, I identified myself with the rich man reminiscing on the rear seat . . .

"A pleasant fate," he repeated, "and I hope yours will be as pleasant."

"Yes, sir. Thank you, sir," I said, pleased that he wished something pleasant for me.

But at the same time I was puzzled: How could anyone's fate be *pleasant*? I had always thought of it as something painful. No one I knew spoke of it as pleasant—not even Woodridge, who made us read Greek plays.

We were beyond the farthest extension of the school-owned lands now and I suddenly decided to turn off the highway, down a road that seemed unfamiliar. There were no trees and the air was brilliant. Far down the road the sun glared cruelly against a tin sign nailed to a barn. A lone figure bending over a hoe on the hillside raised up wearily and waved, more a shadow against the skyline than a man.

"How far have we come?" I heard over my shoulder.

"Just about a mile, sir."

"I don't remember this section," he said.

I didn't answer. I was thinking of the first person who'd mentioned anything like fate in my presence, my grandfather. There had been nothing pleasant about it and I had tried to forget it. Now, riding here in the powerful car with this white man who was so pleased with what he called his fate, I felt a sense of dread. My grandfather would have called this treachery and I could not understand in just what way it was. Suddenly I grew guilty at the realization that the white man might have thought so too. What would he have thought? Did he know that Negroes like my grandfather had been freed during those days just before the college had been founded?

As we came to a side road I saw a team of oxen hitched to a broken-down wagon, the ragged driver dozing on the seat beneath the shade of a clump of trees.

"Did you see that, sir?" I asked over my shoulder.

"What was it?"

"The ox team, sir."

"Oh! No, I can't see it for the trees," he said looking back. "It's good timber."

"I'm sorry, sir. Shall I turn back?"

"No, it isn't much," he said. "Go on."

I drove on, remembering the lean, hungry face of the sleeping man. He was the kind of white man I feared. The brown fields swept out to the horizon. A flock of birds dipped down, circled, swung up and out as though linked by invisible strings. Waves of heat danced above the engine hood. The tires sang over the highway. Finally I overcame my timidity and asked him:

"Sir, why did you become interested in the school?"

"I think," he said, thoughtfully, raising his voice, "it was because I felt even as a young man that your people were somehow closely connected with my destiny. Do you understand?"

"Not so clearly, sir," I said, ashamed to admit it.

"You have studied Emerson, haven't you?"

"Emerson, sir?"

"Ralph Waldo Emerson."

I was embarrassed because I hadn't. "Not yet, sir. We haven't come to him yet."

"No?" he said with a note of surprise. "Well, never mind. I am a New Englander, like Emerson. You must learn about him, for he was important to your people. He had a hand in your destiny. Yes, perhaps that is what I mean. I had a feeling that your people were somehow connected with my destiny. That what happened to you was connected with what would happen to me . . ."

I slowed the car, trying to understand. Through the glass I saw him gazing at the long ash of his cigar, holding it delicately in his slender, manicured fingers.

"Yes, you are my fate, young man. Only you can tell me what it really is. Do you understand?"

"I *think* I do, sir."

"I mean that upon you depends the outcome of the years I have spent in helping your school. That has been my real life's work, not my banking or my researches, but my first-hand organizing of human life."

I saw him now, leaning toward the front seat, speaking with an intensity which had not been there before. It was hard not to turn my eyes from the highway and face him.

"There is another reason, a reason more important, more passionate and yes, even more sacred than all the others," he said, no longer seeming to see me, but speaking to himself alone. "Yes, even more sacred than all the others. A girl, my daughter. She was a being more rare, more beautiful, purer, more perfect and more delicate than the wildest dream of a poet. I could never believe her to be my own flesh and blood. Her beauty was a well-spring of purest water-of-life, and to look upon her was to drink and drink and drink again . . . She was rare, a perfect creation, a work of purest art. A delicate flower that bloomed in the liquid light of the moon. A nature not of this world, a personality like that of some biblical maiden, gracious and queenly. I found it difficult to believe her my own . . ."

Suddenly he fumbled in his vest pocket and thrust something over the back of the seat, surprising me.

"Here, young man, you owe much of your good fortune in attending such a school to her."

I looked upon the tinted miniature framed in engraved platinum. I almost dropped it. A young woman of delicate, dreamy features looked up at me. She was very beautiful, I thought at the time, so beautiful that I did not know whether I should express admiration to the extent I felt it or merely act polite. And yet I seemed to remember her, or someone like her, in the past. I know now that it was the flowing costume of soft, flimsy material that made for the effect; today, dressed in one of the smart, well-tailored, angular, sterile, streamlined, engine-turned, air-conditioned modern outfits you see in the women's magazines, she would appear as ordinary as an expensive piece of machine-tooled jewelry and just as lifeless. Then, however, I shared something of his enthusiasm.

"She was too pure for life," he said sadly; "too pure and too good and too beautiful. We were sailing together, touring the world, just she and I, when she became ill in Italy. I thought little of it at the time and we continued across the Alps. When we reached Munich she was already fading away. While we were attending an embassy party she collapsed. The best medical science in the world could not save her. It was a lonely return, a bitter voyage. I have never recovered. I have never forgiven myself. Everything I've done since her passing has been a monument to her memory."

He became silent, looking with his blue eyes far beyond the field stretching away in the sun. I returned the miniature, wondering what in the world had made him open his heart to me. That was something I never did; it was dangerous. First, it was dangerous if you felt like that about anything, because then you'd never get it or something or someone would take it away from you; then it was dangerous because nobody would understand you and they'd only laugh and think you were crazy.

"So you see, young man, you are involved in my life quite intimately, even though you've never seen me before. You are bound to a great dream and to a beautiful monument. If you become a good farmer, a chef, a preacher, doctor, singer, mechanic—whatever you become, and even if you fail, you are my fate. And you must write me and tell me the outcome."

I was relieved to see him smiling through the mirror. My feelings were mixed. Was he kidding me? Was he talking to me like someone in a book just to see how I would take it? Or could it be, I was almost afraid to think, that this rich man was just the tiniest bit crazy? How could I tell him *his* fate? He raised his head and our eyes met for an instant in the glass, then I lowered mine to the blazing white line that divided the highway.

The trees along the road were thick and tall. We took a curve. Flocks of quail sailed up and over a field, brown, brown, sailing down, blending.

"Will you promise to tell me my fate?" I heard.

"Sir?"

"Will you?"

"Right *now*, sir?" I asked with embarrassment.

"It is up to you. Now, if you like."

I was silent. His voice was serious, demanding. I could think of no reply. The motor purred. An insect crushed itself against the windshield, leaving a yellow, mucous smear.

"I don't know now, sir. This is only my junior year . . ."

"But you'll tell me when you know?"

"I'll try, sir."

"Good."

When I took a quick glance into the mirror he was smiling again. I wanted to ask him if being rich and famous and helping to direct the school to become what it was, wasn't enough; but I was afraid.

"What do you think of my idea, young man?" he said.

"I don't know, sir. I only think that you have what you're looking for. Because if I fail or leave school, it doesn't seem to me it would be your fault. Because you helped make the school what it is."

"And you think that enough?"

"Yes, sir. That's what the president tells us. You have yours, and you got it yourself, and we have to lift ourselves up the same way."

"But that's only part of it, young man. I have wealth and a reputation and prestige—all that is true. But your great Founder had more than that, he had tens of thousands of lives dependent upon his ideas and upon his actions. What he did affected your whole race. In a way, he had the power of a king, or in a sense, of a god. That, I've come to believe, is more important than my own work, because more depends upon you. *You* are important because if you fail *I* have failed by one individual, one defective cog; it didn't matter so much before, but now I'm growing old and it has become very important . . ."

But you don't even know my name, I thought, wondering what it was all about.

". . . I suppose it is difficult for you to understand how this concerns me. But as you develop you must remember that I am dependent upon you to learn my fate. Through you and your fellow students I become, let us say, three hundred teachers, seven hundred trained mechanics, eight hundred skilled farmers, and so on. That way I can observe in terms of living personalities to what extent my money, my time and my hopes have been fruitfully invested. I also construct a living memorial to my daughter. Understand? I can see the fruits produced by the land that your great Founder has transformed from barren clay to fertile soil."

His voice ceased and I saw the strands of pale blue smoke drifting across the mirror and heard the electric lighter snap back on its cable into place behind the back of the seat.

"I think I understand you better, now, sir," I said.

"Very good, my boy."

"Shall I continue in this direction, sir?"

URSULA LE GUIN

"The Ones Who Walk Away from Omelas"

Is giving away money a way of acknowledging and learning responsibility for others or escaping and avoiding it? This is one of the thornier questions that this parable (or "psychomyth"), by popular science fiction writer Ursula K. Le Guin, invites us to ponder. Omelas is, to all appearances, a splendid city of beauty and delight, nobility and learning; its inhabitants are as gracious and joyous as they are intelligent and cultured. Everything is pleasing, except for the dark secret of its perfection: the good fortune of the thousands of citizens of Omelas requires the abominable misfortune of one wretched child. All its citizens, on coming of age, must learn of the child's horrific misery. Almost all shed tears at the bitter injustice, but dry them "when they begin to perceive the terrible justice of reality, and to accept it." Yet some, a small number, walk away from Omelas, each one alone, and never return. Which ones—those who stay or those who leave—have learned their responsibility for others? With which group do you, as a philanthropist, identify? Or, more pointedly, are we, as philanthropists, acknowledging the terrible sight of the child or avoiding it? Does making a donation, even a most generous donation, teach us to accept responsibility for others or to proceed with our lives without guilt?

(Variation on a theme by William James)[1]

With a clamor of bells that set the swallows soaring, the Festival of Summer came to the city Omelas, bright-towered by the sea. The rigging of the boats in harbor sparkled with flags. In the streets between houses with red roofs and painted walls, between old moss-grown gardens and under avenues of trees, past great parks and public buildings, processions moved. Some were decorous: old people in long stiff robes of mauve and grey, grave master workmen, quiet, merry women carrying their babies and chatting as they walked. In other streets the music beat faster, a shimmering of gong and tambourine, and

---

1. Ursula Le Guin credits "meeting" William James, in his "Moral Philosopher and the Moral Life," with the idea for the story. The quote from James is: "Or if the hypothesis were offered us of a world in which Messrs. Fourier's and Bellamy's and Morris's utopias should all be outdone, and millions kept permanently happy on the one simple condition that a certain lost soul on the far-off edge of things should lead a life of lonely torture, what except a specific and independent sort of emotion can it be which would make us immediately feel, even though an impulse arose within us to clutch at the happiness so offered, how hideous a thing would be its enjoyment when deliberately accepted as the fruit of such a bargain?"—Ed.

the people went dancing, the procession was a dance. Children dodged in and out, their high calls rising like the swallows' crossing flights over the music and the singing. All the processions wound towards the north side of the city, where on the great water-meadow called the Green Fields boys and girls, naked in the bright air, with mud-stained feet and ankles and long, lithe arms, exercised their restive horses before the race. The horses wore no gear at all but a halter without bit. Their manes were braided with streamers of silver, gold, and green. They flared their nostrils and pranced and boasted to one another; they were vastly excited, the horse being the only animal who has adopted our ceremonies as his own. Far off to the north and west the mountains stood up half encircling Omelas on her bay. The air of morning was so clear that the snow still crowning the Eighteen Peaks burned with white-gold fire across the miles of sunlit air, under the dark blue of the sky. There was just enough wind to make the banners that marked the racecourse snap and flutter now and then. In the silence of the broad green meadows one could hear the music winding through the city streets, farther and nearer and ever approaching, a cheerful faint sweetness of the air that from time to time trembled and gathered together and broke out into the great joyous clanging of the bells.

Joyous! How is one to tell about joy? How describe the citizens of Omelas?

They were not simple folk, you see, though they were happy. But we do not say the words of cheer much any more. All smiles have become archaic. Given a description such as this one tends to make certain assumptions. Given a description such as this one tends to look next for the King, mounted on a splendid stallion and surrounded by his noble knights, or perhaps in a golden litter borne by great-muscled slaves. But there was no king. They did not use swords, or keep slaves. They were not barbarians. I do not know the rules and laws of their society, but I suspect that they were singularly few. As they did without monarchy and slavery, so they also got on without the stock exchange, the advertisement, the secret police, and the bomb. Yet I repeat that these were not simple folk, not dulcet shepherds, noble savages, bland utopians. They were not less complex than us. The trouble is that we have a bad habit, encouraged by pedants and sophisticates, of considering happiness as something rather stupid. Only pain is intellectual, only evil interesting. This is the treason of the artist: a refusal to admit the banality of evil and the terrible boredom of pain. If you can't lick 'em, join 'em. If it hurts, repeat it. But to praise despair is to condemn delight, to embrace violence is to lose hold of everything else. We have almost lost hold; we can no longer describe a happy man, nor make any celebration of joy. How can I tell you about the people of Omelas? They were not naive and happy children—though their children were, in fact, happy. They were mature, intelligent, passionate adults whose lives were not wretched. O miracle! but I wish I could describe it better. I wish I could convince you. Omelas sounds in my words like a city in a fairy tale, long ago and far away, once upon a time. Perhaps it would be best if you imagined it as your own fancy bids, assuming it will rise to the occasion, for certainly I cannot suit you all. For instance, how about technology? I think that there would be no cars or helicopters in and above the streets; this follows from the fact that the people of Omelas are happy people. Happiness is based on a just discrimination of what is necessary, what is neither necessary nor destructive, and what is destructive. In the middle category, however—that of the unnecessary but undestructive, that of comfort, luxury, exuberance, etc.—they could perfectly well have central heating, subway trains, washing machines, and all kinds of marvelous devices not yet invented here, floating light-sources, fuelless power, a cure for the common cold. Or they could have none of that; it doesn't matter. As you like it. I incline to think that people from towns up and down the coast have been coming in to Omelas during the last days before the Festival on very fast little trains and double-decked trams, and that the train station of Omelas is actually the handsomest building in town, though plainer than the magnificent Farmers' Market. But even granted trains, I fear that Omelas so far strikes some of you as goody-goody. Smiles, bells, parades, horses, bleh. If so, please add an orgy. If an orgy would help, don't hesitate. Let us not, however, have temples from which issue beautiful nude priests and priestesses already half in ecstasy and ready to copulate with any man or woman, lover or stranger, who desires union with the deep godhead of the blood, although that was my first idea. But really it would be better not to have any temples in Omelas—at least, not manned temples. Religion yes, clergy no. Surely the beautiful nudes can just wander about, offering themselves like divine souffles to the hunger of the needy and the rapture of the flesh. Let them join the processions. Let tambourines be struck above the copulations, and the glory of desire be proclaimed upon the gongs, and (a not unimportant point) let the offspring of these delightful rituals be beloved and looked after by all. One thing I know there is none of in Omelas is guilt. But what else should there be? I thought at first there were not drugs, but that is puritanical. For those who like it, the faint insistent sweetness of *drooz* may perfume the ways of the city, *drooz* which first brings a great lightness and brilliance to the mind and limbs, and then after some hours a dreamy languor, and wonderful visions at last of the very arcana and inmost secrets of the Universe, as well as exciting the pleasure of sex beyond belief; and it is not habit-forming. For more modest tastes I think there ought to be beer. What else, what else belongs in the joyous city? The sense of victory, surely, the celebration of courage. But as we did without clergy, let us do without soldiers. The joy built upon successful slaughter is not the right kind of joy; it will not do; it is fearful and it is trivial. A boundless and generous contentment, a magnanimous triumph felt not against some outer enemy but in communion with the finest and fairest in the souls of all men everywhere and the splendor of the world's summer: this is what swells the hearts of the people of Omelas, and the victory they celebrate is that of life. I really don't think many of them need to take *drooz*.

Most of the procession have reached the Green Fields by now. A marvelous smell of cooking goes forth from the red and blue tents of the provisioners. The faces of small children are amiably sticky; in the benign grey beard of a man a couple of crumbs of rich pastry are entangled. The youths and girls have mounted their horses and are beginning to group around the starting line of the course. An old woman, small, fat, and laughing, is passing out flowers from a basket, and tall young men wear her flowers in their shining hair. A child of nine or ten sits at the edge of the crowd, alone, playing on a wooden flute. People pause to listen, and they smile, but they do not speak to him, for he never ceases playing and never sees them, his dark eyes wholly rapt in the sweet, thin magic of the tune.

He finishes, and slowly lowers his hands holding the wooden flute.

As if that little private silence were the signal, all at once a trumpet sounds from the pavilion near the starting line: imperious, melancholy, piercing. The horses rear on their slender legs, and some of them neigh in answer. Sober-faced, the young riders stroke the horses' necks and soothe them, whispering, "Quiet, quiet, there my beauty, my hope. . . ." They begin to form in rank along the starting line. The crowds along the racecourse are like a field of grass and flowers in the wind. The Festival of Summer has begun.

Do you believe? Do you accept the festival, the city, the joy? No? Then let me describe one more thing.

In a basement under one of the beautiful public buildings of Omelas, or perhaps in the cellar of one of its spacious private homes, there is a room. It has one locked door, and no window. A little light seeps in dustily between cracks in the boards, secondhand from a cobwebbed window somewhere across the cellar. In one corner of the little room a couple of mops, with stiff, clotted, foul-smelling heads stand near a rusty bucket. The floor is dirt, a little damp to the touch, as cellar dirt usually is. The room is about three paces long and two wide: a mere broom closet or disused tool room. In the room a child is sitting. It could be a boy or a girl. It looks about six, but actually is nearly ten. It is feeble-minded. Perhaps it was born defective, or perhaps it has become imbecile through fear, malnutrition, and neglect. It picks its nose and occasionally fumbles vaguely with its toes or genitals, as it sits hunched in the corner farthest from the bucket and the two mops. It is afraid of the mops. It finds them horrible. It shuts its eyes, but it knows the mops are still standing there; and the door is locked; and nobody will come. The door is always locked; and nobody ever comes, except that sometimes—the child has no understanding of time or interval—sometimes the door rattles terribly and opens, and a person, or several people, are there. One of them may come in and kick the child to make it stand up. The others never come close, but peer in at it with frightened, disgusted eyes. The food bowl and the water jug are hastily filled, the door is locked, the eyes disappear. The people at the door never say anything, but the child, who has not always lived in the tool room, and can remember sunlight and its mother's voice, sometimes speaks. "I will be good," it says. "Please let me out. I will be good!" They never answer. The child used to scream for help at night, and cry a good deal, but now it only makes a kind of whining, "eh-haa, eh-haa," and it speaks less and less often. It is so thin there are no calves to its legs; its belly protrudes; it lives on a half-bowl of corn meal and grease a day. It is naked. Its buttocks and thighs are a mass of festered sores, as it sits in its own excrement continually.

They all know it is there, all the people of Omelas. Some of them have come to see it, others are content merely to know it is there. They all know that it has to be there. Some of them understand why, and some do not, but they all understand that their happiness, the beauty of their city, the tenderness of their friendships, the health of their children, the wisdom of their scholars, the skill of their makers, even the abundance of their harvest and the kindly weathers of their skies, depend wholly on this child's abominable misery.

This is usually explained to children when they are between eight and twelve, whenever they seem capable of understanding; and most of those who come to see the child are young people, though often enough an adult comes, or comes back, to see the child. No matter how well the matter has been explained to them, these young spectators are always shocked and sickened at the sight. They feel disgust, which they had thought themselves superior to. They feel anger, outrage, impotence, despite all the explanations. They would like to do something for the child. But there is nothing they can do. If the child were brought up into the sunlight out of that vile place, if it were cleaned and fed and comforted, that would be a good thing indeed; but if it were done, in that day and hour all the prosperity and beauty and delight of Omelas would wither and be destroyed. Those are the terms. To exchange all the goodness and grace of every life in Omelas for that single, small improvement: to throw away the happiness of thousands for the chance of the happiness of one: that would be to let guilt within the walls indeed.

The terms are strict and absolute; there may not even be a kind word spoken to the child.

Often the young people go home in tears, or in a tearless rage, when they have seen the child and faced this terrible paradox. They may brood over it for weeks or years. But as time goes on they begin to realize that even if the child could be released, it would not get much good of its freedom: a little vague pleasure of warmth and food, no doubt, but little more. It is too degraded and imbecile to know any real joy. It has been afraid too long ever to be free of fear. Its habits are too uncouth for it to respond to humane treatment. Indeed, after so long it would probably be wretched without walls about it to protect it, and darkness for its eyes, and its own excrement to sit in. Their tears at the bitter injustice dry when they begin to perceive the terrible justice of reality, and to accept it. Yet it is their tears and anger, the trying of their generosity and the acceptance of their helplessness, which are perhaps the true source of the splendor of their lives. Theirs is no vapid, irresponsible happiness. They know that they, like the child, are not free. They know compassion. It is the existence of the child, and their knowledge of its existence, that makes possible the nobility of their architecture, the poignancy of their music, the profundity of their science. It is because of the child that they are so gentle with children. They know that if the wretched one were not there sniveling in the dark, the other one, the flute-player, could make no joyful music as the young riders line up in their beauty for the race in the sunlight of the first morning of summer.

Now do you believe in them? Are they not more credible? But there is one more thing to tell, and this is quite incredible.

At times one of the adolescent girls or boys who go to see the child does not go home to weep or rage, does not, in fact, go home at all. Sometimes also a man or woman much older falls silent for a day or two, and then leaves home. These people go out into the street, and walk down the street alone. They keep walking, and walk straight out of the city of Omelas, through the beautiful gates. They keep walking across the farmlands of Omelas. Each one goes alone, youth or girl, man or woman. Night falls; the traveler must pass down village streets, between the houses with yellow-lit windows, and on out into the darkness of the fields. Each alone, they go west or north, towards the mountains. They go on. They leave Omelas, they walk ahead into the darkness, and they do not come back. The place they go towards is a place even less imaginable to most of us than the city of happiness. I cannot describe it at all. It is possible that it does not exist. But they seem to know where they are going, the ones who walk away from Omelas.

ZONA GALE

"Younger Generation"

Assuming responsibility for others depends on the capacity to be responsive, accountability on the ability to do some accounting. The two major representatives of the "Younger Generation," in this short story by American writer Zona Gale (1874–1938), fall short, one in each category: Margaret Larcom is unresponsive and self-absorbed; her husband Paul Larcom is generous to a fault--what he gives bears no relation to what he has. The one thinks only of her own family, the other thinks only of the "big family of all of us." Like the rest of their generation, at least those here depicted, both are self-proclaimed cynics when it comes to morals. Neither acknowledges any moral authority—nothing is "fundamental," everything is a matter of "adaptation, and climate, and convention." A wise elder, one Lucilla Bleyer, arranges for them to see differently, not by moral lesson, but by enabling them to experience, firsthand, their own capacity for care and concern, as well as their capacity to be conscientious. Witnessing the outpouring of goodwill, "Lucilla said to anybody who happened to be listening: 'They needn't worry about the younger generation, as long as that spirit can still sweep it—even once.'" Is Lucilla's optimism warranted? Are experiences like the one we witness really transformative? Are they sufficient to close the gap between responsibility and responsiveness, accountability and accounting?

ℰ

The game was over, the guests had gone, and Mrs. Bleyer in her dining-room was gathering up flowers and tulle and bonbons on the tea table. Her daughter, Mrs. Paul Larcom, and two young women who had also assisted her were still in the library. Mrs. Bleyer heard her daughter say: "What would you do that for?"

"Oh, just simply because I'm bored," said Betty Marks.

"And would that unbore you?" asked a third voice.

"Alberta, darling," said Mrs. Larcom, "let her have a gift shop, if she merely wants to. I thought she was being noble."

"Noble," said Betty. "What's noble?"

"It's nothing," Mrs. Larcom told her. "It's gone by. It's like seed pearls and sedan chairs. And yet it must have been nice to believe something—nice and old-fashioned."

"Don't you believe anything, Megs?" Betty asked her. "I don't; but you seem so depressed sometimes, I thought you must."

They laughed, and Mrs. Larcom called: "Mother! Come in and stand up for me. Even my own mother doesn't want me to believe in anything that I don't believe in; do you?"

Mrs. Bleyer, with a dish of chocolates, went in where they were, and her daughter said fondly: "Did you ever see anybody look less like a mother? She looks twenty-six, and with the most cynical eyelids!"

"I don't want you to believe in anything you don't want to believe in—no," Lucilla Bleyer said. "What don't you believe now, Megs? Her life," she added, "has been one long series of not believing in things. First, Santa Claus; then the pot of gold at the end of the rainbow; then a horsehair turning into a snake in the rain barrel. And now—"

"Now I don't believe in being good," said Mrs. Larcom calmly.

"Well, of course not," cried Betty and Alberta—exotic sisters, who had been born in New York, raised in Spain where their father was consul, and now belonged nowhere, but became it very well. "Naturally," said Betty, "living about the way we have, in half the places in Europe, you just can't have your old-fashioned morals. They're provincial; they're like wearing a bustle."

"None of them is fundamental any more," said Alberta.

"Why shouldn't there be fashions in morals?" Mrs. Bleyer asked curiously.

They stared a bit at this. And Mrs. Larcom said: "Now isn't that the un-motherest thing a mother could say? Sweetheart, don't corrupt what few we have left."

"Oh, I'm quite serious," said her mother. "It would be as foolish to keep the same old morals as it would be to wear crinoline."

"Mrs. Bleyer," cried Betty Marks delightedly, "they'll lock you up."

"But," Mrs. Bleyer continued tranquilly, "when we took off crinoline we didn't leave off everything. We changed fashions. What are your new morals? You can't just have no moral clothes at all; it wouldn't be stylish."

"Changed morals!" Margaret repeated. "But did we?"

"For example, we don't satisfy a grudge on the 'field of honor' any more. And war is unquestionably on the run. Haven't you any other new morals?"

"She wins," said Alberta languidly. "But it takes a microscope to find some of them."

"Mother," said Margaret, "since you're so keen on new things, get us up a new vaudeville stunt for the Forty."

The Forty, a dinner-dance club, was having its annual vaudeville show two weeks away. Margaret, chairman of a committee for one of the acts, indicated Betty and Alberta and said: "They don't know anything, and I don't either. Help us."

"But you want a show without any morals," Mrs. Bleyer reminded her.

She threw herself into their plans with the ardor which they loved, the ardor which never pretended to be more youthful than it was. But she cried out against all their suggestions, said that these were hackneyed and "unrepresentative."

"We want something," she held, "which shall show the spirit of the younger generation!"

It was half an hour before Betty and Alberta remembered that they were due somewhere and rushed away. And then Margaret closed the door on the two, turned to her mother, and said: "Mother—it's fussy of me. But if I could lie down and die now, I'd be glad of it."

Her mother did not go to her or touch her. If she could tide her over this, whatever it was, without the burst of tears which sympathy would bring, she wanted to do so. Mrs. Bleyer merely said: "Is it Paul again?"

"He's signed a note for five thousand this time, with an old college friend. Mother, he hasn't it to pay. We're living as if we had everything, and he gives away just about everything we have."

Mrs. Bleyer said with something like tenderness: "But after all, dear, it might be worse. Suppose he were spending it on himself, or on other women."

"I know. But it won't make bankruptcy any more honorable, nor the county house any happier for me." The laughter came now, which was not much different from tears, and she went on: "It isn't as if he were exactly generous. I don't think he really wants to give everything away; he's rather miserable about it afterward."

"Isn't it you that makes him miserable?"

"Oh, maybe. I hate to see him so impractical. He says, 'What's the difference? There's no wrong and there's no right about it. I feel like doing it, and I'm going to.' You see, mother, it isn't generosity. It's a sort of self-indulgence."

"It's a very lovable vice," said Mrs. Bleyer.

"He doesn't get much out of it, and I'm so unhappy. Mother, I hate almost everything I do and nearly everybody I see."

Her mother laughed and switched on the lights. The room burned with color, the flowers came out as if they were blooming for another spring. Mrs. Bleyer stirred the fire, moved the chairs, and said: "I hate bridge myself. I wonder why we play it."

"Well, you're left out of everything if you don't."

"If you don't play you aren't invited to play, that's true." She looked at her daughter, a slim and elegant figure in blue, and said: "You look as if you ought to be happy. I'm happy, even weighed down as I am by my old fashioned ideas that there are morals."

"Paul's coming for me," said Margaret. A pause; then she went on: "Paul doesn't think there's any right or wrong either, you know, mother. He thinks it's all adaptation, and climate, and convention, and so on."

"I remember he likes the word taboo," said Mrs. Bleyer. "It's a very handy word."

"You know that a lot of our 'must nots' are just superstition."

Mrs. Bleyer listened. Her daughter talked about conventions arising in the tribe, man's desire to appropriate a woman and to make sure that his children were his own—that was all!—a tradition which we were trying to live by now in a complicated society.

"And so you throw it all overboard," said Mrs. Bleyer, "and are happy."

"There's Paul now, I think," said Margaret. "Oh, mother, my not being happy has nothing to do with my morals. It's just Paul that makes me miserable."

Paul came in, the big, smiling fellow, well dressed, with the smooth face of a child, but blurred and sullen. He said: "Well, mother, has Megs told you that we're headed for the poorhouse?"

"You tell me," said Mrs. Bleyer, and rang for tea.

He told her, while a maid brought in the table, a dainty tea, a beautiful service. The room was large and high, the furniture old and good, the flowers, the lamps, the firelight gave it loveliness. Mrs. Bleyer looked at these two, four years married, childless, unhappy. "No program," she thought.

Margaret said, when the maid went: "New York is full of tea tables that look like this, with people around them who are miserable."

"Are you miserable?" asked Paul quickly.

"I don't have to ask you," said his wife.

Mrs. Bleyer looked in her cup. "Count me in on that," she said. "I've had to play bridge all afternoon, and to-morrow morning I have to spend at a board-of-directors meeting. New York leads you a dog's life. Go on, Paul; tell me."

"The fellow," said Paul, "used to room across the hall from me. He wanted to study law then. He was brilliant; we all thought so. He had to take a job before he could go to law school. That was four years ago. To-day he came into my office; he's been at that job ever since. He's got nowhere; he's had sickness in his family; he's got debts; he was at the end of his tether. He didn't ask for anything—all this I got out of him by questions. And suddenly while I talked to him—I don't know whether you'll understand, Mother Bleyer, but I felt as if I were in his shoes, as if I *were* Tad. It was the darndest feeling. I saw how it was with him just as if I was in his whole skin; and I knew I had only to put out my hand to save him, pick him up, set him on dry land with money to pay his debts and take his law course. And I offered to help him; that's all."

"But you didn't have the five thousand to do this with," cried Margaret. "There's the point."

"Of course I didn't," said Paul. "Did I say I did have it? But I can always borrow money in this town, and Tad can't. I signed a note with him, that's all. He didn't have the security, and I did. I wish you could have seen him—what it did for him."

Margaret turned to her mother. "It's Paul's form of a bat," she said. "It's his brand of champagne."

Paul turned on her. "Nonsense, Megs," he said shortly; "if I saw the man sinking in the middle of a river and I could borrow a rope, would it be such an almighty jag if I threw it to him?"

"But if you stood on the bank all day borrowing ropes and casting them into the stream—this is about the tenth man you've done this for—and every single time you've come home and said you felt as if you were in his shoes."

"Well, I did," said Paul. "And I'm glad I did. And why shouldn't I?"

"Because it's wrong," Margaret cried vigorously.

"But, darling!" said her mother. " 'Wrong'? What's that?"

"There's still bad judgment," said Margaret shortly, gathering up her belongings.

"If you think I'm going to live just for the kind of life your friends live, you're mightily mistaken," said Paul positively.

"Give all you like when you can afford to do it, but don't borrow to do it," cried Margaret. "It's not right, Paul."

"'Right'?" said her mother. "What's that, Margaret?"

"Oh, well," said Margaret. "Cruelty isn't right. I think Paul's charity jags are cruelty—to me."

"Get all you can and keep all you can," said Paul. "And kick off as soon as possible, if this keeps on."

"Heavens," said Margaret, "we're due at the Rods's dinner at seven o'clock."

"I'm not going," said Paul with decision.

"Come on, Paul; we're fearfully late."

"It's a dog's life, this whole thing," said her husband. "I don't know what we keep it up for. I guess I'll give away the rest I can lay hands on, and then we can have peace."

"And don't forget me," Mrs. Bleyer wailed, "with a board of directors' meeting in the morning at ten. Why will boards of directors meet at ten o'clock?"

They kissed her and went away.

"Don't be cruel or mean, darling, till we meet again," said Margaret flippantly. "You can do anything else you want to."

Next morning Mrs. Bleyer, with a basket, stepped into her car and drove to the Morning Star Bungalow. This long, low, gray building stood well up in the Bronx, its grounds were wide and green with spruces, and the curling smoke and yellow-curtained windows welcomed her. She was the first of her board of directors to arrive, and so she went up the broad stairs to the double glass doors which cut off the corridors, and entered alone, as one who knows her way.

Thirty little chairs were set in the middle of the room, a large room, with plants and canaries, and a fresco of hurrying animals in a wood of green. Some one was at the piano and thirty high voices were piping into the air the melody of:

"God's in His heaven,
All's right with the world."

Mrs. Bleyer took her basket to the table in the front of the room. The young nurse who had been at the piano nodded to the children. With a push of chairs and a scraping of feet and crutches, the thirty came towards Mrs. Bleyer—slowly, unevenly, hobbling, trying to hurry, striking iron braces against the chair legs—the thirty tiny crippled children of the Morning Star Home. She held up great loose handfuls of the flowers left from her tea. She gave them out to the children, whose eyes fastened hungrily upon them, and they seized them as they gathered about her, holding them to their faces.

There was something intolerable, unearthly about their pallor, their frailty, their eagerness, like butterflies fluttering for flowers on the brink of a chasm of death. Their voices, which had cried out in pain so often, were now in a soft babble, like the notes of the birds. They knew homelessness, loneliness, cruelty, hunger, suffering, ether, strange surroundings, but their voices were like the voices of any children, talking of flowers.

"Could I take two of them home for lunch with me?" Lucilla Bleyer said, and the nearest ones heard and shouted: "Lady, me! Teacher, take me."

She chose a little fair girl with straight thick hair, and a boy of six. They all trooped with her to the doors and cried: "Lady—me! Me! Me!" She went out by the ward where a dozen lay, too ill to go in with the rest—little legs, pressed down under great bags of sand, or figures lying motionless with closed eyes.

Into the room where the board of directors met she came shining and cried: "May I have the floor, instantly, while I am bursting to tell you of a plan?"

The tired faces of the six other women did not change much. One of them said: "Let's hear what Mrs. Bleyer has to say. Because this place here seems to me only one of a thousand despairs in the world to-day, and if she knows anything to tell us—"

"I think I do," said Lucilla Bleyer.

Two of the guests sat up very straight and prim at the luncheon table, the like of which neither of them had ever seen outside picture books. Mrs. Bleyer was coaxing them to talk, and the maid, trying to serve them and stepping over the small crutches, was frankly listening to their hesitating words. The third guest had not arrived. He had telephoned, asking her to sit down without him, and they were half done when Paul Larcom came in.

He kissed Mrs. Bleyer, bent with his big tenderness above the children, and said as he sat down: "I'm sorry to be late; it's disgraceful at such a party. But Mother Bleyer, I was with your own daughter."

"I didn't mean you to tell Megs you were coming!" she cried.

He said: "She came into the office. Seems she'd heard about a hospital bill I was mixed up in—"

"Another?"

"Well, yes. This one just happened since breakfast. The man that was cleaning our windows—he was going to lose his house, and his wife was sick. It didn't amount to much, but he spilled his gratitude onto Margaret, and she was hot. I had a dickens of a time with her."

"My name ith Betthie," remarked the little fair girl with the straight thick hair.

"You don't say. Mine's Paul." Paul looked charmed by this sudden confidence.

"Carl Auguthtuth ith hith," Bessie proceeded generously to share the limelight.

"It is not," said the other little guest crossly. "I'll say it myself: Carl Augusstuss," he hissed, to prove that he could.

Paul roared. "How old are you?"

"I'm five and heth thixth," Bessie explained.

"I'm not," Carl shouted. "I'm s-s-six!"

Endless variations of this theme were possible, and Paul became absorbed in playing upon them all. Before the ice cream came they were telling him a story, each interrupting the other in eagerness, and Carl ungallantly correcting Bessie every time she lisped.

As they rose Paul said reverently: "I wish to heaven we had two of them; then maybe Megs and I—"

"You can't afford two, Paul, the way you're adopting the crowd."

He seemed not to hear her. The two little figures had slipped down from their chairs, were holding unsteadily to the seats of the chairs, and Mrs. Bleyer was lifting the crutches.

"Good heavens," said Paul, "what's the matter—what is it?"

"Paul dear, didn't you get it, over the phone? I told you over the phone."

He groaned: "But they're so little. I didn't take it in. They're so little."

He bent to Bessie, swung her onto his shoulders, caught Carl under his arm. He sat with them in a great chair before the fire. They clung to him, even made up with each other.

"Who are they?" he cried fiercely. "I mean, where do they belong? The Home, yes, but before that? Are they having care—specialists? How many of them are there? Thirty! Forty-two! Not like this—not little, like this?"

"Like that," Mrs. Bleyer told him. "And, Paul, I wasn't thinking of them. They seem to me so helpless I wasn't even thinking of them. But I was thinking of something else, and I had a plan."

She tried to tell him of her plan, but he didn't even hear. When she was well launched and thought that she had his attention, he sprang up and said: "Look here, Mother Bleyer. May I take them down to Lawrence? He knows kids like a wizard. If he says nothing can be done for them, I'll believe him. I won't take anybody else's word. May I take them? I'll get an appointment. He's got to give me one."

He bundled the two small figures into his car. Tender as a mother he was, and strong as a father. As he went down the steps with them, Mrs. Bleyer thought: "If only Margaret could see him with children, her children."

In an hour Margaret came in. She was in something slim and gray, pale, perishable, and her hat was the hat of to-morrow, born to-day, and still carrying with it its inevitable rightness.

But she had been crying and when her mother said, "Margaret, how stunning!" her daughter wept again and said: "I'm glad you like it; it's the only dress I'll have in y-y-years. Paul has gone and bought a house for a w-w-window-washer that he never saw before." Her tone carried the implication that if only it had been a window-washer whom Paul had known intimately, all would have been forgiven.

She took off her hat, decided, since her eyes were so red, to cut two teas, and cuddled down by the fire beside her mother to be thoroughly miserable.

"Darling," said Lucilla Bleyer tentatively, "can't you get Paul's view? You two might do so much for people, might be so happy."

"If he'd only be reasonable!"

"Wouldn't you rather he'd be generous than reasonable—always?"

"He's n-n-never reasonable about giving away money." Margaret wept.

"Well," said Lucilla Bleyer, "you can always go to the devil, you know." Her daughter stared at her.

"Since there's no wrong," her mother explained, "or perhaps there isn't any devil any more. Is that why you and Betty and Alberta and all of you don't go there?"

"I'm going there," said Margaret, "if Paul doesn't stop."

Betty and Alberta dropped in presently, and one or two more with them. Again the room was warm and bright, the tea delicious; and again the cynical little voices uttered their cynical patter.

"If," Betty propounded, "by pressing an electric button that nobody would see you press, you could inherit a million by causing the death of a cruel and inhuman tyrant, and nobody would ever know, would you do it?"

"Sure!" said Margaret.

"To get rid of the tyrant or to get the million?"

"To get the million. I wouldn't have any silly qualms."

Lucilla asked: "Then why be so particular to provide that nobody would ever know you touched the button?"

"Because other people would have silly qualms," said Margaret.

Her mother said: "You dear things don't fool any one, you know. You talk like bandits, but if somebody led you in front of the button—"

"She's idealistic," Margaret murmured, in defense of her.

"There's nothing fundamental in most idealism," Alberta offered.

"What about the vaudeville act?" Margaret demanded. "You haven't thought of it again, have you, dear?"

Lucilla Bleyer was looking at them smilingly, not in the least like a shocked or disillusioned adult. "Will you leave the whole act to me," she said, "and do anything I call on you for? Anything?"

This was a sporting proposition, and they would—in a chorus.

"How many active members are there in the Forty?" Lucilla went on. "Forty? Good. I want thirty children's dresses made to measurements which

I shall give you—the daintiest, loveliest, pastel-tinted things you can devise, and shoes, socks, underthings and hair ribbons besides. Do I hold my job or do I lose it?"

She held her job and listened with a smile to the talk which followed. ". . . and some of them are smocked—and the new embroidery—and that tiny Armenian lace—and handkerchief insets. . . ."

She thought: "Where's their cynicism?"

When they had left, all but Margaret, it was Margaret who sat turning over a magazine, looking at the children's things. Her mother watched her. "It isn't her only job," she thought, "but I wish it were one of them."

She was on the point of leaving when they heard Paul's voice at the door of the apartment, and Paul running down the passage. "Mother!" he called. "He thinks he can help them both. Bessie pretty surely and Carl maybe. Oh, hello, darling. And, mother! I took them both to his hospital, but first I ran 'em out to get their little traps, and oh, my gosh, I saw the rest of 'em! Do you know what? Your board has got to let me turn Lawrence in there; he's had wonderful success with these cases. Megs, think of it—forty-two of the little beggars, or-phans and cripples, and all of 'em babies! I've told Lawrence, and he's promised. And, Megs, I'd like you to see Bessie. I wondered—there's a child I'd like to have."

"A cripple?"

Paul's eyes wavered. "Well, she needs a home a mighty sight more than if she had her legs. But Lawrence thinks she will have 'em."

"May I ask who's going to pay Dr. Lawrence?"

"Why, Megs—but—"

"And who's to pay him for this indiscriminate care of all the others? The board can't—can it, mother? Are you going to pay for this specialist's care for forty-two cases?"

Paul's look hardened. "If it's necessary—yes, I am," he said. "I've still got the summer place that's out of hock. By the great horn spoon, I can't stand it to see something like that. Megs, they're so little—"

Margaret stood up, her face quite white. "Paul," she said, "I think you're insane."

"Margaret—"

"If you had the money, I shouldn't say a word. I'd go into it with you; you know that. But you haven't the right—you haven't the *right* to take everything away from me—and my child."

His eyes and the eyes of her mother went to her face.

"I meant to tell you—so differently," she said, "when I was sure. I've planned how I'd tell it to you both—when I was sure." Her voice was lost in her weeping.

"Megs, oh, I say!" he cried, and tried to take her in his arms.

But her little figure was tense, and she did not look at him. "Go on," she said, "and take your forty-two cripples to their specialist. My baby and I will stay with mother."

"But, darling," he tried to say; and she ran weeping to Lucilla, who looked over her shoulder and shook her head at Paul.

"She has reason, you know, Paul," said Lucilla. "But oh, Margaret, if you could just work with him."

"He won't let me work with him," she sobbed. "He lends five th-thousand dollars and adopts f-f-forty-two children without ever saying a word to me."

"Megs, dearest," Paul said, "but your idea of working with me is to say, 'Don't do it.' I've stopped long ago trying to tell you about these things."

"And now I've made up my mind." said Margaret. "Either you'll give up this last crazy idea—oh, I know it's beautiful, but it's crazy, too—or I stay here, beginning *now*."

He paled at this, then he straightened and looked at her. "I've always pro- vided for you," he said quietly. "If this that you hope is true—and I hope to heaven it is—it'll make me work twice as hard and as gladly. But I don't see how it checks off what I can do—and I know I can do it—for these little kids I've promised to help."

Margaret was quiet too. "All right, Paul," she said. "You can have Milly send over my things. I'll stay here, as long as mother'll have me."

He looked at her with his pain in his eyes, and when he spoke his voice was a shade unsteady. But he said only: "Good night, Megs. Good night, mother," and went.

Margaret threw out an arm in a superb gesture; but she looked like a little girl, her mother thought.

"Mother! Wouldn't you think at such a time as this—" she began, and came and sat beside her mother and buried her face on her shoulder.

Lucilla, with her arm about her, said: "Margy, darling. This first minute of a girl alone with her mother—after she has told her—it's as wonderful as the first minute between you and Paul when you'll first look at each other over your baby's head."

Margaret sobbed: "He won't think it's w-wonderful. He'd rather have f-forty-two—"

Lucilla said: "You and I are thinking most of ourselves, of our family. What if Paul has gone a step beyond us, and is thinking of the big family of all of us?"

Margaret's stubborn head was still down, and all that she would say was: "He ought to think of me and the baby, at a time like this."

The Forty had engaged the ballroom of one of the most impressive hotels, and smilax and palms made it beautiful. The Forty and their men—"Marrieds or Hope Chests," Betty said—were in an acre of gilt chairs cut by one wide aisle on the glossy floor. Act after act went off in a clamor of appreciation—music, readings, a lion or two, a quick one-act farce, and, last, some thrilling dancing. All the acts were over save one, Margaret's mother's finale about which she was surpassingly mysterious. The intermission was long, too—apparently a vast deal of preparation was necessary. When the music ceased and the lights went down, there was a murmur of childlike expectation from that acre of gilt chairs. What if Mrs. Bleyer had actually captured a grand opera star?

The gray velvet curtains parted. On the low stage were thirty tiny children, exquisitely dressed. No one else. Then the harps began, and the children sang:

> "I sat up in my bed at night;
> I saw a stair of gold and white;
> Red birds and fairies flying there;
> I want to climb that happy stair!
> I want to live and play and run,
> I love my life like every one."

The song went on, clearly, articulately, apparently a child's happy song; and there was another like it. The applause was almost tender. No dancer, no grand opera singer could have delighted as those tiny seated figures, singing. A murmur began to run round: Why were they seated?

Then the orchestra moved, revealed a sloping floor leading down from the stage to the floor of the hall, a palm or two was shifted by the ushers, and the little figures began to get up. And now the murmur that ran round the room was one of shock and horror. Every little figure had bent forward to pick up the crutches which the palms had hidden, or else, supported by a steel brace, it came limping down the platform. These little angels, who should have had the poise of butterflies, and the grace, came slowly, haltingly, down the incline and into the aisle between the rows of gilt chairs. Now their song was a lilt about a gift, and the flowers which the children held were to be distributed among the audience. But not a child, when the time came, would give up her flower; or else it behaved like Bessie, who, having yielded a rose, burst into a storm of regretful sobs!

There was a breathless tumult now. The gilt chairs were pushed awry, the children were picked up, caressed, comforted. Lucilla Bleyer, looking on from the improvised wings, saw that ballroom of bored, cynical young people melt into a company of tender girls, gentle boys, jollying or fondling the children, their voices keyed to a new note. Down in front she saw Bessie sitting in the silver-lace lap of Margaret. Lucilla turned back and nodded to Paul: "Now," she said.

It was Paul who came down to the footlights, Paul whose voice, quite steadily, went over the room. He told the story, told more than one story, deep tragedy and black time to come, about the small persons who looked so innocently out. "Some of us," Paul concluded, "have planned to help them to specialists, to the best skill that we can command. The rest of us," he ended, "can help if we want to."

That was all, save that at a signal of music the little voices swept into that lilting tide of song which earlier Mrs. Bleyer had heard: "God's in His Heaven. . . ."

Then as Lucilla Bleyer and Paul came down the floor, they saw Margaret, with Bessie still in her lap. Margaret got up and, with her arms about the child, she came to meet them. And Bessie was far the calmer of the two.

"Paul!" cried Margaret. "We're going to do it. Betty is taking the names down. Everybody is going to help. Oh, Paul! I'd no idea! I'll go with you tomorrow, and we'll find some more."

"Margaret!" said Paul. "Margaret!"

Lucilla said to anybody who happened to be listening: "They needn't worry about the younger generation, as long as that spirit can still sweep it—even once."

But Alberta Marks observed, and patted at a tear under one eye: "Well, of course, there's nothing basic about such help. It doesn't prevent; it's just remedial. It's not fundamental."

"That spirit?" said Lucilla. "Not fundamental? Then what is?"

In the middle of the glossy floor Paul had stooped and kissed Margaret. "There's another good thing about this generation," he said. "It doesn't give a hang whether a man kisses his wife in public or not!"

From *Old-Fashioned Tales* by Zona Gale (New York: D. Appleton-Century, 1933).

GORDON WEAVER

"Haskell Hooked on the Northern Cheyenne"

How many of us take seriously the unsolicited pleas for support that arrive with the daily mail? Has such an appeal ever changed your life? It is just such an unpromising beginning that eventually gets Haskell hooked on the Northern Cheyenne, transforming his humdrum life into a mission. American fiction writer Gordon Weaver chronicles Haskell's journey in a series of letters, beginning with Haskell's first polite note to Father Cyprian, which accompanies his first perfunctory five-dollar donation to the Cheyenne Mission School in far-off Montana. Though we are never privy to the letters that Father Cyprian writes to Haskell, we know that their sustained correspondence causes Haskell to take stock of who he is and how he is living, and awakens sympathies and a sense of responsibility he never knew he had. But the account that so convinces him fails to convince his wife, his boss, or his brother. In the end, should we praise Haskell for his newly found purpose or blame him for negligence? Has he become more alert to the world and connected to others, or less so? Do we have here a model education for philanthropic accountability or a "how-not-to" guide?

March 3rd

Fr. Cyprian Hogan, OFM
Cheyenne Mission School
Broadaxe, Montana

Dear Fr. Cyprian:

　　Enclosed please find my check for five dollars ($5.00) in response to your appeal. My wife and I appreciate the gift of the little plastic teepee, and send our best wishes to you in your work among the northern Cheyenne. We're both sure the money will be put to good use, and only regret it is not more.

Yours Very Truly,
H. Haskell

March 19th

Fr. Cyprian Hogan, OFM
Cheyenne Mission School
Broadaxe, Montana

Dear Fr. Cyprian:

Enclosed find my check for $5.00 in response to your second appeal in as many weeks. From the letter of thanks you sent after the first check I feel you've gotten off on an unfounded assumption. We're not fellow Catholics. It was the "Dear Friend in Christ" salutation in your letter—or does that just mean someone who appears to feel the same way about things like charity without belonging to the same club?

My wife attended Bible camp for two summers while in junior high, so you could call us generic Protestants; anyway we're not Catholic. If we did attend a church regularly it would have to be one of the Lutheran varieties. Please don't misunderstand.

I like to call myself a liberal, and we both realize your mission helps the Cheyenne regardless of *their* religious affiliations—I remember your statement in the first appeal to the effect that only a small percentage of the tribe are practicing Catholics.

I only want the record straight. I give because I want to. Again, we send along our moral support. I know nothing about the problems you face, the daily lives of the Indians, but have some general ideas about poverty, bad nutrition, illiteracy, etc. prevailing on our federal reservations.

Yours Very Truly,
H. Haskell

P.S. You might like to know the little plastic teepee's in good hands. We have no children, but I gave it to a neighbor child, who was quite pleased. A miracle, her mother came over to thank me, and she's never done more before this than nod hello as she pulls out in her station wagon. I guess it's not the sort of toy one can buy in the stores here.

April 17th

Fr. Cyprian Hogan, OFM
Cheyenne Mission School
Broadaxe, Montana

Dear Fr. Cyprian:

What is it with you, Father? No, that's wrong. I don't want to offend, vent spleen, etc. But you're imposing, and I've got to express it. My wife warned me not to write—"Just simply ignore it," she said. "Is there a law that says you have to answer all the junk mail you get?" But you owe me a hearing.

In two weeks' time we received two appeals from you for donations to your work among the northern Cheyenne. I sent you $10.00. The canceled checks have already come back from my bank ("He didn't waste any time cashing in," my wife said when she was going over the monthly statement).

I hoped I conveyed good will, a recognition of your need, and I hoped—in vain I see now—you understood my position, that in good will you would not try to take advantage; now I get a third appeal for money. Let me be understood.

I am not wealthy. My salary is *exactly* $6,400 per annum (all right, so I get a little more each June when we work evenings on inventory). If you're interested (I doubt this), I make my living as a technical writer.

I write: technical manuals to accompany industrial air conditioning and heat transference units, explaining operation and maintenance for the layman; the text of advertising brochures used by our sales engineers; short articles on business conditions (marketing prospects, government regulations, technical developments, credit prospects for the near future) for a monthly trade magazine published by my employer.

Ye Gods, if I was rich wouldn't my checks have been larger? Wouldn't I beat the income tax with huge gifts, trust funds to see Indian orphans through graduate school? Wouldn't I sign over the deeds to properties to you, endow a chair in some university to study your problems? You abuse me.

Don't I give enough? My newsboy comes to the door in the evening to demand a contribution for summer camps for kids like himself—I give, not much, but give. College dropouts come around with magazine subscriptions to get trips to Europe. Brownies come in uniform to sell their cookies; I eat them for lunch faithfully. A neighbor (who holds loud parties we are never invited to) comes with a clipboard and informs me everyone is pledging twenty dollars for the ambulance service. I mail a buck to both political parties to keep democracy strong.

I'm not safe on the streets. Little Leaguers jump me on the way out of the bank with tin cans because they want an electric scoreboard. I get a Buddy Poppy each for wife and self. The Salvation Army surrounds me on the asphalt parking lot in the shopping center. At work, the United Fund sends me an IBM card via one of the girls in the steno pool. What is it with these people? I ask. "We've got to live here, don't we?" my wife says. I grin and give.

And now my name's on some religious sucker list. Because I've given you ten you think I'll give a hundred. I call halt. An unsolicited plastic teepee does not obligate me; I know the law. Catholics may be bound by oath or faith or mortal sin to support you. I am not.

How many of those printed formats do you have at the ready? Save it for someone else; I'm not a colored pin on a map, no target in your war to save the Red Man. I'm young, not thirty yet, owe on house and car, support a wife, heavily insured, need to hire a tree surgeon to save the one big elm on my property, suspect our furnace won't make another winter through. Give me a break.

Understand. "And then you go and write him another check," my wife says in disgust, and now pretends to be watching television too intently to hear me when I speak. "I don't want him to misunderstand is all," I say. So, $5 more, to convince you of good will, that I intend no hurt. Take it in the spirit it is given.

Sincerely,
H. Haskell

April 28th

Fr. Cyprian Hogan, OFM
Cheyenne Mission School
Broadaxe, Montana

Dear Fr. Cyprian:

I have received your long letter. You say: the force that carries you out there is the same spirit of charity you appeal to in me. Will it work to let you forgive me too?

What can I say? How kneel, sackcloth and ashes, beat the breast, how *mea culpa* from a thousand miles away via air mail? The whole thing reeks of ignorance and selfishness—all mine. Haskell thinks he understands, complains that your appeals are mass-produced, steals your time by demanding a personal reply.

I showed your letter to my wife. "I wish you'd just drop the whole thing," she said. "I should never have said those things. I didn't understand the way I do now," I said. No avail. "Just leave me out of it," she asks. Forgive her too.

When I started writing this she took the car and went over to my brother's house to visit with his wife. Have you heard anything from my brother? I gave him your address and one of the pamphlets. "What am I supposed to do with this?" he said. "Send him something." At least he folded it and put it in his pocket. "You ever heard about charity at home?" he said. Then we took turns cutting his lawn with his new electric mower.

I plead ignorance in the first place. What did I know about the northern Cheyenne, Father? The story of Thomas, the little boy abandoned in the wrecked car by his parents because they couldn't feed him, that one did me in. Literally, real tears; fortunately I happened to be home alone then too. Sure I knew the Indians had it rough, but never the details. The TB, the drunkenness, infant mortality, what did I know? What I knew I only guessed. Thomas turning blue with the cold in that rusted junker, asking how far down in the milk bottle he could drink, here I was ignorant. Can you forgive?

The same for the history pamphlets. I had ideas, broken treaties, destroying the buffalo herds, but that's all from the movies. My brother read the one about Shivington's massacre of the women and children in the village. "They had that on TV a while back, I think," he said. "This is where it happened," I said, "here, these people I'm telling you about." "I know it happened," he said. "When the program started it said it was based on an actual fact." What does he know?

I tried getting angry, the Bureau of Indian Affairs, the Secretary of the Interior (I don't even know his name), the President, affluent citizens of Montana. No good. It all came out shame in the end.

Then comes selfishness. Watch out here for self-pity.

Sometimes there's nothing to hold on to. I mean, wife, work, responsibilities, installment payments, become a little too much. I get afraid I can't hold it together for long, pieces are going to fall out, and where are we all then? Tangled up, I can't see out: it makes me selfish.

A few minutes ago (my wife still isn't back—she must be staying for the late show. Out the picture window, the last visible porch light blinked off—no parties tonight)—a few minutes ago I promised myself not to talk about my problems. But to apologize I need to be understood.

Believe it, I work hard. If I'm a success, industrial air conditioners are sold, stock dividends are voted (I don't own much yet), but where am I? I go to sleep at night promising to be ready to eat the world the next day, but it's hard to concentrate with the township's teenagers peeling the corner at the end of the block. I must dream. The resolve to be enthusiastic is sapped when the clock radio buzzes—"I suppose it won't do to heat up last night's coffee for you, it's got to be fresh-made," my wife says. How would you feel?

Do priests get up before the sun to pray? Is that me, the swollen face shaving in the bathroom mirror? The glazed eyes mine? My wife sings with the sizzling bacon in the breakfast nook, I stand dumb, looking at the sick elm in our yard. But I *do* get off to work. Do you understand me?

The days are longer now, still light when I come home, and I admit (why should I feel guilty?) to moments of peace after I greet my wife. We sit and watch the wars and speeches on film on the evening news, but who believes in that stuff? I drink a cold martini—okay, sometimes three—we talk about her day ("Did you see the moving van down towards the circle?" "Not when I came home, no. Who's moving out?" "I don't know their name, but there was a van there all day moving them out. It's the ones with the Imperial I told you about she's always driving by in." "So if you don't know their names who cares if they move?" "I didn't say I cared. I just told you.")

"Be a doll and mix one more," I say. "Two olives." All's well. I admit to moments of peace. Is it my fault they don't last?

I work in a cubicle in a large office (air conditioned). From my desk I can look out through glass panels at the busy secretaries in the steno pool, their ears plugged with dictaphones, eyes fixed on proof sheets. I never know their names until one comes around to collect donations for a wedding gift for Marie or Ardenne or Patty. I believe most of them are secret gum chewers. Engineers and marketing analysts and file clerks pass up and down aisles, say, "Here you go," when they toss a sheaf of paper into my *In* basket. Am I making sense?

I do try though. Excelsior. This Saturday I have decided to dig a small garden next to my garage. I was talking to the neighbor girl (she still has the tee-pee); she likes flowers, so I'll plant some along with a few vegetables. Back to the land.

Too tired to read it over, I hope what I've written is clear. The check, you'll see, is for ten this time, all I can do for now. Please continue to let me hear of your good work at the mission.

With sincere regard,
H. Haskell

May 29th

Fr. Cyprian Hogan, OFM
Cheyenne Mission School
Broadaxe, Montana

Dear Fr. Cyprian,

I thought I would not hear from you again. Good to know I am not forgotten. Is the little Indian chief doll authentic? I mean, are headdress, decorations on the jacket, etc., the kind the Cheyenne wear—wore once? We've put him on the mantel-piece above the fireplace. My wife thinks he's cute. She calls him Sitting Bull, though I tell her he wasn't a Cheyenne. Or was he?

Not cute though. I've been analyzing the expression on his face. At first I said: Stoic. But that's all in the folded arms. Then: Courageous. But the brown painted eyes are too pale, no steel there. Sad? His back's too stiff. Finally I knew. "He disapproves," I said to my wife. "Who what?" "He condemns." "What are you talking about, Haskell? Did I make that martootie too strong?" (She never uses my first name; nor do I—have you noticed? Hollis: my mother's maiden name—my brother got Jack, because he's the older.)

Unless I can learn to stare him (Sitting Bull) down I'm going to give him away too. "I tell you he doesn't like it," I said to my wife. "All that Indian wisdom in him disapproves." She said, "I think you're getting hooked on the northern Cheyenne, Haskell." Pure fantasy, Father, I assure you.

I wish this check could be more, but insurance all comes due at the same time: automobile, theft, fire, property, hospitalization, life.

Are there any extra pamphlets (describing the work) lying around in your office? I want to give some to friends and people at work.

Hoping to hear from you soon again,

H. Haskell

P.S. My garden progresses. Besides flowers, I planted sweetcorn, tomatoes, lettuce, beans—a landmark in this neighborhood. The little girl next door has never seen a tomato growing on a vine before in her life. "My daughter tells me you're planting regular vegetables and stuff here," her father said to me. He had come out in his slippers. "I'm Haskell," says I, hand extended. "I know who you are, I can read the writing on the mail box like anybody else, can't I? What do you want to do a thing like that for, can you tell me that?" "I like fresh corn." "You know this is gonna make my house look like hell too, don't you?" I promised to try and keep it small. "What did you expect him to say?" my wife said. Who could tell? What a world we live in, Father.

P.P.S. Next stop: public library—subject: American Indians.

June 16th

Dear Fr. Cyprian:

Pardon poor penmanship. I should be working, but who are we trying to kid? The wooden trays on my desk runneth over—copy piles up awaiting my initials (HHH—my mother's mother's maiden name was Hart). Through the glass wall around me I can see the steno I'm keeping idle. She is at a loss, buffs her nails, cleans her teeth with her tongue, changes typewriter ribbons, stacks carbons in readiness, switches off to the ladies room, returns too soon, panics, looks to me with terrified eyes, and I shake my head, pontifical as Sitting Bull on my mantel, and she slumps into her chair, defeated. The trouble is I get to thinking.

In the cafeteria a salesman said to me, "What's the use of working when the government takes a fifth of what I make before I even see it?" I swallowed my bread. "Do you know the Indians out in Montana make less a year, on the average, than you probably pay in taxes in a year?" He threw down his sandwich before he blasted me. "Oh for the Christ's sakes (he said it, Father, not me) Haskell, will you get off the goddamned boring damned Indians in Montana!" Dessert, two cupcakes under cellophane, passed in silence. What's the use?

I gave up reading the library books. "Are we doing anything tonight?" my wife asked. "Doing? I'm doing, I'm reading, right?" "If you're sticking your nose in a book all night, sure," and she turned on the television extra loud to get even. "Do you know all about Indians now?" the librarian asked when I returned them. What do I know?

Last Saturday I was weeding and cultivating my sweetcorn. Pleasant, hot sun, hands sore and back stiff, but my neighbor was watching me from his garage, pretending to putter with his son's go-kart. At last I waved and he came over. "Great day for outdoor work," says I. "Can I ask you something in a nice way? Can I ask you something simple like one gentleman to another?" "Shoot." "Will you get rid of this corn patch? Flowers I have nothing against, but you'll agree I got twenty-four thousand dollars invested in a home, I've got a right to protect it." "I'll share the sweetcorn with you. Would you and your wife come to a corn roast? I'm thinking of building a barbecue, would you like to help?" He affirms that he has tried to reason with me, now warns he will go about it in a different manner since I only want trouble. Do I need trouble, Father Hogan?

How is the work going on the dormitory? I looked around at my corn, the small green tomatoes, climbing beans, remembered the Indian children afraid to eat your school's hot lunch because they never have lunch at home, afraid to eat today because tomorrow they'll be hungry again. I checked out a book on bricklaying yesterday. My wife doesn't understand at all.

My supervisor approaches, the steno at his side. He is grim, puzzled. She wrings her hands. Must close.

In haste,
Haskell

July 27th

Fr. Cyprian Hogan, OFM
Cheyenne Mission School
Broadaxe, Montana

Dear Fr. Cyprian:
Telephoned home this afternoon. "Any mail?" I asked my wife. "Where are you calling from?" "Work, where else?" "I thought you weren't supposed to make personal calls." "What mail?" "There's one." "Are you trying to make me angry? One from where?" "Postmarked Montana." "Bring it down, I'll meet you in the parking lot." "I've got better things to do with my time." "Name one," I said, but she wouldn't, so I had to wait to get home this evening to write you.

I am honestly excited about the possibilities of the new industry as a means of helping the Cheyenne. My professional opinion of the full-color brochure layouts on the jewelry you're making is no less than good. Good. If you want I'll show them to the art boys at work and pass their judgment along. How are the orders coming in?

After sound and fury, my wife agrees to telephone all her friends and drum up a big sale for you. "How?" she says. "Have a party, I'll get out of the house, the way they do for pots and pans." Tomorrow she promises to start.

At first I pondered: Indian jewelry? But *what* doesn't matter, I see now. *Why* is all. You start with fifteen employed—how soon can you expand? You make mail order jewelry in order to remake men; I sell air conditioners. The check's only ten again, but I'll nag my wife to come up with an order for the beads that will more than make up for it.

I appreciated the personal note. Was my letter "diffuse"? It was one of those days. That set my wife off again. Am I writing letters on the sly now? I write because I need to write, I feel like writing. Am I going into the charity business? I give because I want to give. She just doesn't understand, does she. All's well now though; I agreed to go visit my brother and his wife with her.

One failure: I tried to ship you some corn and beans I harvested this week (I knew tomatoes would never make it). "Can't take it," said the little man in the blue coat at the post office. "It'd spoil." I might have said: what good's a post office that can't ship food from one man to another? People are starving out there! But he looked tired, and his blue jacket was wrinkled. Will two wrongs make a right?

Your friend,
H. Haskell

P.S. Are summers in Montana such you could use an air conditioner in the school or the new dormitory when it's done? I might be able to start something at the office to get them to contribute one. Isn't it deductible?

August 14th

Dear Father:

No letterhead stationery this time. I'm not at work, but that's all arranged. I couldn't do what I was supposed to. The steno did her best, didn't sic the supervisor on me for some time. "Mr. Haskell," she said, "if you don't give me that stuff then I've got nothing to do and Miss Lubin will be after me for sitting around." No small thing, Miss Lubin is huge and acne-scarred. What could I do. "Maybe later," says I. "Not now." She had to bring my supervisor. His name is Knauer; all my copy has to go through him. "What is it you think you're doing, Haskell?" "I told him I hadda have that stuff or Miss Lubin gets after me, Mr. Knauer," the steno said. I think she was beginning to enjoy it. "I'll do this," Knauer said. The typewriters slowed down on the other side of the glass; there hadn't been any excitement in the office since personnel hired a mousey girl named Peplinski (her name I knew!) months ago—she was a secret epileptic and threw a fit at her desk, chewed right through some bond paper one afternoon. "I can't do anything," I said.

"Are you ill, Haskell? Are you trying to pull something off on me?" "The Indians need me, Knauer," and I might have gotten snotty with him, but remembered that everyone calls him Weasel Knauer behind his back because of his narrow pointed face, so took pity and kept silence. "He's been talking funny about those Indians," he whispered to the steno, and they backed out afraid. He came back with a janitor to protect him in case I raged. "You can feel free to go home if something's wrong, Haskell," he said. The janitor carried a long-handled broom to subdue me. Am I the violent type? "Just till you feel better. Don't worry about a thing," he said, "I'll contact personnel for you."

"I'm worried about the Indians, Weasel Knauer," I said, but he kept on backing out to make sure the janitor was between us until I left the office. The girls in the steno pool tried not to stare.

My wife won't know about this letter either because she hasn't been here for three days. It could be she calls, or it could be personnel wanting to know if I'm terminating, but I don't answer the phone. I came home like they told me at the office, and I could talk to her, but she didn't quite understand.

"I'm telling you why if you'll listen to me. It was the Indians. I couldn't do what I'm supposed to do there," I said. Said she: "I don't know what's the matter with you, you talk about the Indians all the time. You never say anything except about the Indians all the time. Stay over there. Don't touch me. I don't understand you anymore. I don't want to talk about the Indians anymore." What was there left to say? But I kept on talking, and finally she cried, and she cried, so I stopped for good. So she left. I think she's with my brother and his wife. Her parents live far from here. The phone rings often, and there was someone at the door yesterday and today. I thought I recognized the broken muffler on my brother's Oldsmobile.

Why don't you write? Are you still waiting for that jewelry order I promised? Give up, Father. Nobody wants Indian-style jewelry, not my wife, not anybody. She broke her promise about holding that party to sell it. "I'd be ashamed to show cheap jewelry like that to my friends." I tried to tell her how it was to help the Cheyenne, but who understands? I think they have all the jewelry they need.

I've thought better of it too, Father. Sending out plastic teepees and Indian dolls, cheap jewelry, that's not the way, not for me anyhow. I gave Sitting Bull to the neighbor girl, but her mother brought it back. "Keep your trashy presents to yourself!" she screamed when I opened the door. I was afraid she'd have an attack of some kind. When her husband came home that night he stood in his yard and glared at my cornfield with his hands on his hips. My tomatoes are rotting on the vines. I started with a bushel basket full at the other end of the block to give them away, but when the woman (maybe it was a maid?) peeked through her curtains to see who it was she waved me off. The word must be out on Haskell.

No, the way is things like the mission school, and the free hot lunches for children who don't get them at home, and finding Thomas abandoned in the autowreck. That's the way. Build that dormitory and staff the school with teachers so you can have classes more than half a day. What kind of a world is this?

The doorbell's ringing. Maybe you've written, but I haven't gone out to see the mail. There won't be any money in this letter because my wife took the checkbook with her. I might as well answer the door, I've got to go out to mail this (if I can find a stamp). Money's not the way anyhow.

September 5th

Dear Father:

Here's Proof I no longer ignore the mail, though now all my letters are delayed a day or two because of my change of address. I've been with my brother and his family for the past few days. My wife is now with her parents, and while I'm grateful to my brother for taking me in, I will be glad to leave (he is glad our mother didn't live to see this, etc.). My sister-in-law won't stay alone in the same room with me, and their children are with her parents until I go. Can I blame them? Accept, I say to myself, they don't want to understand.

From your letter, Father Hogan, I'd almost think you didn't understand either. I'm satisfied to think that's just a problem caused by my "diffuse" expression. I comment briefly; there's much to do before I can be on my way.

Agreed, the world's as it is because we're like we are. Now concede we can change it by changing ourselves. Proof? Look in the mirror. I'm argument enough for me.

Friends, clergyman, psychiatrists? Come on now! Do I need friends with a brother like mine? I went to church last Sunday—my brother's high Episcopal these days—it's the closest one. "Excuse me, Reverend," I said (my brother says he's called Father, like you). "Would you read this little prayer and appeal for the northern Cheyenne at the end of your sermon for me today? I've got my telephone number right there if anyone wants to call in a pledge." I still have the mark on my arm where my brother grabbed me when he pulled me away to a pew. "Can't I even let you out of the house?" he said. You're the only clergy I know, and I've been consulting, not your letters, but your example. I don't see doctors because I don't have money (that's all my wife's: house, car, our small savings)—what do I need money for? I know the language of psychiatrists. They don't want to change the world.

Here I am then. We can talk all this over in detail later if you want. I wish I could say exactly when, but there are papers to be signed, arrangements—I hope for the best. Who knows, with luck I might arrive at the mission shortly after this letter.

You'll see, I'll be of use. I'll mix cement, lay bricks, teach school. I'll scour the mountains for abandoned children. I can learn. I haven't told you before this because I feared you wouldn't understand. But you'll see. It may take longer than I think. I have so little money I may have to hitchhike all the way to Montana. What does time matter when you've found your way at last, Father?

My brother shouts from downstairs that dinner is ready. The flesh must be fed. I'll close:

H. Haskell, Your Friend in Christ.

From *The Untombed Man of Thule: Stories* by Gordon Weaver (Baton Rouge: Louisiana State University Press, 1972). Copyright © 1972 by Gordon Weaver. Reprinted by permission of Louisiana State University Press.

BENJAMIN FRANKLIN

"Standing Queries for the Junto"

Benjamin Franklin (1706–1790), patriot, entrepreneur, inventor, and paradig-matic American philanthropist, was twenty-one when he formed "The Junto," a club of young Philadelphian tradesmen. This "club of mutual improvement," as Franklin called it, was an opportunity for philosophical debate, topical discussion, and professional networking. Its civic-spirited deliberations led to the creation of America's first lending library, fire department, and police force, and spurred many other philanthropic initiatives. Surely, many of the civic accomplishments of the group can be attributed to Franklin's genius, but Franklin's way of proceeding may also be responsible: As he explained in his autobiography, the debates of the Junto were "conducted in the sincere spirit of inquiry after truth, without fondness for dispute or desire of victory" and so "all expressions of positive opinions, or direct contradiction, were after some time made contra-band, and prohibited under small pecuniary penalties."

Especially interesting, for our purposes here, are the questions—given below—that members were asked to consider before attending each Junto meeting, as well as the questions they were asked and the answers they were obliged to give (under oath) to qualify for membership. Does anything in the content of the questions below, or in the required conduct of the discussants, account for the Junto's success? Could—should—such groups be formed today? Might its simple but evidently very effective system of accountability still serve as a model?

Previous question, to be answer'd at every meeting.

Have you read over these queries this morning, in order to consider what you might have to offer the Junto [touching] any one of them? viz.

1. Have you met with any thing in the author you last read, remarkable, or suitable to be communicated to the Junto? particularly in history, morality, poetry, physic, travels, mechanic arts, or other parts of knowledge.
2. What new story have you lately heard agreeable for telling in conversation?
3. Hath any citizen in your knowledge failed in his business lately, and what have you heard of the cause?
4. Have you lately heard of any citizen's thriving well, and by what means?
5. Have you lately heard how any present rich man, here or elsewhere, got his estate?

6. Do you know of any fellow citizen, who has lately done a worthy action, deserving praise and imitation? or who has committed an error proper for us to be warned against and avoid?

7. What unhappy effects of intemperance have you lately observed or heard? of imprudence? of passion? or of any other vice or folly?

8. What happy effects of temperance? of prudence? of moderation? or of any other virtue?

9. Have you or any of your acquaintance been lately sick or wounded? If so, what remedies were used, and what were their effects?

10. Who do you know that are shortly going voyages or journeys, if one should have occasion to send by them?

11. Do you think of any thing at present, in which the Junto may be serviceable to *mankind*? to their country, to their friends, or to themselves?

12. Hath any deserving stranger arrived in town since last meeting, that you heard of? and what have you heard or observed of his character or merits? and whether think you, it lies in the power of the Junto to oblige him, or encourage him as he deserves?

13. Do you know of any deserving young beginner lately set up, whom it lies in the power of the Junto any way to encourage?

14. Have you lately observed any defect in the laws of your *country*, [of] which it would be proper to move the legislature for an amendment? Or do you know of any beneficial law that is wanting?

15. Have you lately observed any encroachment on the just liberties of the people?

16. Hath any body attacked your reputation lately? and what can the Junto do towards securing it?

17. Is there any man whose friendship you want, and which the Junto or any of them, can procure for you?

18. Have you lately heard any member's character attacked, and how have you defended it?

19. Hath any man injured you, from whom it is in the power of the Junto to procure redress?

20. In what manner can the Junto, or any of them, assist you in any of your honourable designs?

21. Have you any weighty affair in hand, in which you think the advice of the Junto may be of service?

22. What benefits have you lately received from any man not present?

23. Is there any difficulty in matters of opinion, of justice, and injustice, which you would gladly have discussed at this time?

24. Do you see any thing amiss in the present customs or proceedings of the Junto, which might be amended?

Any person to be qualified, to stand up, and lay his hand on his breast, and be asked these questions; viz.

1. Have you any particular disrespect to any present members? *Answer.* I have not.
2. Do you sincerely declare that you love mankind in general; of what profession or religion soever? *Answ.* I do.
3. Do you think any person ought to be harmed in his body, name or goods, for mere speculative opinions, or his external way of worship? *Ans.* No.
4. Do you love truth's sake, and will you endeavour impartially to find and receive it yourself and communicate it to others? *Answ.* Yes.

From *The Papers of Benjamin Franklin,* Leonard W. Labaree et al., eds. (New Haven: Yale University Press, 1959), vol. 1, pp. 256–259.

PAUL PRIBBENOW

From "Are You a Force for Good?"

In this selection, Paul Pribbenow, long-time fundraiser in higher education and current president of Augsburg College in Minnesota, directs his attention to philanthropic professionals, especially those responsible for fundraising. With his eye not only on lifting their sights, here and now, but also on their responsibility for educating the next generation, Pribbenow provokingly asks, "Are you a force for good?" He thus invites professionals to look beyond their technical expertise and specific organizational objectives to the larger context of American culture and the values that ground them, and he suggests multiple lenses for doing so: vocation, stewardship, and promise keeping. But the proof of the pudding, as always, is in the eating: Do Pribbenow's categories enable you to determine whether you are or are not a "force for good"? Are they a helpful way of encouraging a more civic-spirited philanthropy in those who will replace us?

What questions do you ask to determine whether or not you, as a philanthropic fund-raiser, are a successful professional?

For most of us, those questions include:

- Have I (and my organization) met our philanthropic goals?
- Has my staff been managed as effectively as possible?
- Have we involved our board members and volunteers in meaningful ways in our philanthropic programs? Have those volunteers been trained and supported well?
- Have I helped to further the mission of my organization?
- Am I well-known among my professional colleagues and well-respected among my staff and volunteers?
- Do I earn a good salary and have a fitting title in my organization?

These are important questions for our profession. They help us to determine how well our expertise and technical knowledge have been used to further organizational objectives. They help us understand how our work and status (both as individuals and as a profession) are situated in the organizations we serve. As our profession matures, we are right to view such questions as critical to the development of a knowledge and technique base, along with the status within society, that we need to be respected as genuine professionals.

But I wonder if, after asking and answering all of these queries, we have missed the most important question in determining the meaning and role of our profession in society. Have we asked, "Am I—are we—a force for good?"

Our answers to that question, I would contend, ultimately will determine whether all of our knowledge and expertise has been used to serve the public and its goods or primarily to serve ourselves and our interests.

Are you a force for good? . . .

How Can You Be a Force for Good?

What are the strategies that allow us to begin to view our professional work as public service? How can I be a force for good? Here are three broad themes that provide a way of developing these strategies and illustrate how we might begin to reconceive the public and moral purposes of our profession and its important work.

Vocational Education

A few years ago, I convened a group of fund-raising professionals for a series of conversations related to the place of our work in American culture and the values that might ground that work. It was a fascinating six hours of discussion and testimony, one of the most provocative conversations I have participated in during my professional career.

Near the end of our sessions, as one of the senior members of the group finished an eloquent statement about his struggles to find meaning in his work, the youngest member of the group raised her hand and asked to speak. The challenge she then offered to the group still rings in my mind.

This young professional fund-raiser, still in her first position after college, said, "I have participated in, and listened to, our conversations during these sessions with great interest. I have learned much from your stories and experiences. What I have yet to understand, though, is this: You claim that these values and practices are so essential to the well-being of the fund-raising profession, but I know that there are many young and emerging professionals like me who don't have access to individuals and organizations and communities of colleagues where these values and practices are shared and passed on. Tell me this: Who do you want me to be? How do you want me to think about this work we share? What sort of professional do you hope that I will come to be? And will you help me and others like me to become that person? *Don't leave my formation as a professional to chance.*"

The silence in that room was palpable. In her profound insight, this young professional had indicted her learned and experienced colleagues. What she had challenged us to consider was how our profession helped its members to live out their vocations. She wondered how we expected her to learn and to make a part of her character the meaning and purpose of her work. She wanted to know how and where she and her fellow professionals would receive the *vocational education* needed to understand and accept the public and moral roles we expected of each other.

Vocational education is a major responsibility for our profession. The word "vocation" means to be called to a particular form of work and service. If we believe that we are called to serve the public practice of philanthropy, then educating each other about the meaning of that call seems like an essential aspect of our professional work.

How might we imagine ourselves helping to form future generations of professionals to understand the call to be public servants? How will we instill the understanding that being a force for good is the central responsibility of a successful professional? Where will we seek to provide vocational education for our profession?

I would suggest four contexts for this vocational education:

- *In the workplace*, where we spend most of our professional lives and where our most quantifiable loyalties lie. We must find ways in the midst of our everyday work lives to educate each other about our "callings."
- *In our professional associations*, through which we must do more than provide technical training and the trappings of a profession. In addition, we must help to articulate and disseminate an understanding of the "profession of faith" a true profession and professional must make.
- *In colleges and universities*, where, though we don't have the same broad-based professional education programs other professions have developed, we still must challenge these institutions to see philanthropy as a discipline worthy of exploration, research, and pedagogy; and
- *In public*, where we must model ways of being a professional in society, providing the sort of example and leadership that goes beyond organizational boundaries to serve the public good.

In each of these contexts, and others where professionals gather to work and learn together, we must be deliberate about promoting the sort of reflective practice that places the values of public service in dialogue with the knowledge and techniques of our profession. We all must learn to be forces for good. Vocational education is the first step.

Good Stewards

Stewardship is an oft-used, but also oft-abused, word in the work of our profession. We tend to delimit its power by relegating it to a description of our gift acknowledgement and recognition programs.

Another important aspect of understanding fund-raising as public service is our capacity to accept the challenge to be good stewards in our work. Stewardship—the challenge that "to whom much is given, shall much be expected"—is more than a particular program in our fund-raising department. In fact, good stewardship is a way of life.

I had a very concrete experience of stewardship as a way of life when I recently formed a stewardship task force for my institution. I asked one of my staff members to chair the group and to recruit members not simply from our development office, but from any department or office on campus that had contact with donors or volunteers or that represented our organization in some way to the wider community.

I charged the group to audit our current stewardship practices, think about whether those practices were adequate to our aspirations for enhancing our philanthropic work as an institution, and to define an expanded role (and develop a plan) for stewardship activity for the future.

The fascinating thing about the work of this group was not so much the helpful diagnosis of our current stewardship practices or its work plan for the future, but rather, the change in how both my staff, as well as the other members of the group, came to a broader understanding of what it means to be a good steward for our organization and its various constituencies. Stewardship has been raised up within our institution and the results, though still very much in process, are a more holistic and organic understanding of stewardship. We now share a more complete sense of all the gifts that are given to this organization and we have begun to practice in an integrated way what it means to be good stewards of those gifts.

As I think through the results of the work of the stewardship task force, I am struck by how expansive our understanding of stewardship activity has become. Instead of the accurate, though clearly insufficient, sense of stewardship as related simply to donor acknowledgement or endowment fund policies, we now have come to see that:

- We are first and foremost stewards of the public trust. In our mission-based organizations, we have the privilege to live up to the trust placed in us by the public. The public believes that we are working to meet their needs and serve their goods—and we must be good stewards of that trust.
- We also are stewards of the diverse organizational resources entrusted to us as staff members, including organizational image, which portrays our integrity to the wider public; organizational investments such as people, money, buildings, and relationships; and organizational infrastructure that supports relationship-building and public trust beyond our tenure.
- Finally, we also are stewards of philanthropic partnerships. We must understand that the public practice of philanthropy is not a solitary pursuit. We must pursue philanthropy together, in partnerships between donors, volunteers, board members, staff, clients and patients and students. As philanthropic fund-raisers, we must be good stewards of those partnerships.

Good stewardship defines the character of philanthropic fund-raising.

Keeping Our Promises

We live in a society that organizes its common life through contracts. We enter into contracts for just about every transaction imaginable: renting a car, buying a house, going to school, and receiving care from our doctor. Some even say we have a social contract as citizens of the U.S., paying taxes and professing loyalty in order to enjoy the protections and freedoms of citizenship.

Sometimes, however, contracts are not enough. Unfortunately, contemporary society offers few alternatives to a contract-based body politic. Our common history, though, does provide an alternative. For our founding mothers and fathers, American society was understood at least in part as a "covenant" in which they were included. Covenant denotes a set of mutual promises that bind people to each other in pursuit of common ends. We make and keep promises to each other as we negotiate our lives together.

Philanthropy is full of making and keeping promises. Every gift to my organization involves a promise made and to be kept. As philanthropic fundraisers, we have the obligation to talk about and practice philanthropy in ways that help others to understand the promises—the philanthropic covenant—to which all of us are bound.

Again, a story illustrates my point. Shortly after I arrived in my current position, I made a presentation to a group of faculty members about how I understood philanthropy and how I hoped we might work together to build a stronger philanthropic program for our institution.

I told a favorite story to the group that illustrated how I had learned to think about the necessary roles of all participants in the philanthropic community or covenant. I said that unless the donors, the recipients, the volunteers, the program experts, and the professional fund-raisers were all involved in philanthropic work, then we had lost the richness and power that comes from such joint efforts. Philanthropy, I claimed, was common work and I challenged them to join me in our common work.

After my session, a chemistry professor found me in the hallway and thanked me for my presentation. And then he uttered the phrase that will ever stand as a sign for me of how our philanthropic work has become so fragmented. He said that until he heard my talk, he always had thought of himself as "nothing more than a leech" on our organization's philanthropy—taking, but giving nothing back.

The philanthropic covenant demands that we remember that our work as professionals means nothing if we are not constantly facilitating the common work of philanthropy among all members of our communities. The covenant reminds us that making and keeping promises are the foundation of our work in building relationships, raising money, extending an image, supporting the mission of our organizations. Have you kept your philanthropic promises? Have you helped others to do the same?

Everyday, as you practice your professional duties, you have the opportunity and the privilege to serve the mission of your organization with your knowledge, your experience, and your many gifts. May you also find the wisdom and courage to be a public servant, professing faith in the public goods your work helps to secure. May your professional lives be formed by vocational education, the call to good stewardship, and the wonder of the philanthropic covenant.

May you always be a force for good.

SIX

Philanthropic Leadership

Philanthropic foundations enjoy a privileged place in American society, like in no other. According to Kenneth Prewitt, we favor them because they "mirror a central quest of the liberal society—how to attach private wealth to public goods without encroaching on individual freedom." But this is not the whole story. As much as they may exemplify and support "individual freedom," foundations, like philanthropy in general, also exemplify and support virtues necessary to sustain and perpetuate liberal society: individual responsibility and public spiritedness. As broadcast journalist Bill Moyers once put it, they address the ever-present need for "active commitment to 'live and help live.'"

These virtues and this commitment are generally acquired in homes, neighborhoods, and communities of worship, and, as Moyers recounts, often tacitly and from repeated example:

> My own father used to reminisce about growing up on the Red River, between Oklahoma and Texas. He was 14 when his own father died during the flu epidemic in 1918. Neighbors washed my grandfather's body, neighbors dug his grave and neighbors laid him in the earth. Through the years, my father was one of several men in our church who took turns sitting beside the corpse of a departed friend or fellow congregant. He often drew the midnight shift and would go directly from his vigil to his job. Shortly before his own death, as we sat talking on the front porch, I asked him: "Why did you sit up all night when you had to drive your truck all the next day?" He seemed surprised by the question, as if it had never occurred to him, and then, without hesitation, he answered: "Because it was the thing we did."[1]

---

1. From Moyers' speech to a wealth and giving forum, "Finding Justice in Charity," October 22, 2005, available online at http://www.tompaine.com/articles/2005/10/25/finding_justice_in_charity.php.

The "thing" Moyers' father did is the same thing that myriad Americans have long done—giving time, energy, and funds in abundance to efforts that promote civic well-being. But precisely because it is just the "thing we do," the vast majority of the men and women who initiate and lead such philanthropic efforts often go unsung. To some extent, this is as it must and should be: deeds speak louder than words. However, given the ever present—and growing—need for neighbors to help neighbors, we cannot take it for granted. Technology may have shrunk the size of our world, but it seems also to have increased the problem of "being alone." Arguably now more than ever, individuals must assume responsibility; now more than ever, we must note, remember, and emulate the many philanthropic leaders who summon the better angels of our nature.

The need for philanthropic leadership is widely recognized. Leadership training programs continue to proliferate, as do nonprofit management programs. No doubt such programs will equip future leaders in philanthropy—especially in organized philanthropy—with the necessary know-how to manage assets and finances, meet accountability standards, evaluate practices, do strategic planning, and master the many other techniques deemed necessary to make organizations more efficient and effective. But the technical expertise that such programs teach necessarily abstracts from the larger and richer context of philanthropic vision and moral choice. They do not teach or help others to reach the moral sensibilities and habits of the heart, the motives and passions, and the hopes and ideals that lead people to give. They may raise up able managers who will do a competent job in philanthropic foundations. But they will not raise up philanthropic leaders who will inspire others to give and serve vigorously.

The selections on philanthropic leadership that are included in this chapter are intended to help repair the deficit. Each in its own way exemplifies what such leadership may involve and addresses the general question:

What should we expect of philanthropic leaders?

Lao Tzu's reflections "On Leadership" prompt us to ask whether and how models of leadership in general might serve leaders in philanthropy.

In *Prometheus Bound,* Aeschylus introduces the first philanthropist—the god Prometheus—and gives us a picture of the aims and virtues that make him the prototypical "lover of humanity." George McCully's "The Promethean Fire—Aeschylus and the First Philanthropist" brings the prototype into modern times, encouraging us to nourish philanthropy's current enterprise with an appreciation of its rich heritage.

The next group of readings specifically considers the relationship between wealth and leadership. John Wesley, in "The Use of Money," provides us a seemingly simple formula of how we should use our wealth—"gain all you can, save all you can, give all you can"—for the benefit of others and ourselves.

Meanwhile, The Widow's Offering from the Gospel of Mark, coupled with William Plummer's "Saving Grace," provide examples, classic and contemporary, of great givers with small means, inviting reflection on what is most essential to good giving and good leadership.

The next two selections reveal great political leaders as great philanthropic leaders. Abraham Lincoln's Second Inaugural Address challenges us to determine how or whether his call for "charity for all" is still applicable, and still answerable. In "I've Been to the Mountaintop," Lincoln's philanthropic heir, Martin Luther King Jr., not only serves as an exemplary model of leadership but explicitly points to how we might become such leaders.

We turn, then, to several selections by leaders in philanthropy, beginning with Jane Addams's essay "A Modern Lear." Addams's comparison of business leader and benefactor George Pullman to Shakespeare's King Lear explicitly models how we might use stories to search for the "deep human motives" that drive philanthropists and, perhaps, determine their success or failure. Implicitly, it also points, by contrast, to Addams's own philanthropic leadership.

In his speech "The Spirit of Philanthropy and the Soul of Those Who Manage It," Paul Ylvisaker addresses himself to the "managers" of philanthropy, urging them to brood over "the custodial and the creative responsibilities" of their profession—to fully engage in its spirit, and to fight for its "soul."

John W. Gardner's "Leadership" argues that better leaders—not, indeed, better managers—are what our society lacks, and that increasingly professional and technical education will discourage the growth of leaders who accept special responsibility for civic life and "the continued vitality of this land."

We conclude with William A. Schambra's "The Ungodly Bright: Should They Lead Philanthropy into the Future?" which raises questions about the wisdom of placing philanthropic leadership in the hands of "the best and the brightest."

LAO TZU

On Leadership

Contemporary philanthropic scholar and professional Bruce Sievers gave this answer to the query, "How does one lead in philanthropy?": "With as much humility as possible." As he explains, it is "essential to be able to listen very well, engage in a continuous learning process about the field in which one works, resist the temptation to strive for uniqueness, and seek to coordinate one's efforts with the wider arena of actors in the field. Leading in philanthropy may ultimately look a lot like following in other arenas of social life." Sievers is not alone. When given an opportunity, many of his colleagues argue similarly—"servant leadership" is what some call it. As this selection makes clear, this intuition is far from new. Ancient Chinese sage Lao Tzu (570–490 BC), founder of Taoism, put the matter plainly. But unlike Sievers and his peers, Lao Tzu believes that all leaders should be humble, all leaders should serve. He thereby invites us to wonder whether there is, in fact, a difference between excellent leadership per se and philanthropic leadership in particular. Is humility, then, the one virtue essential for leadership?

డ్రా

A leader is best
When people barely know that he exists,
Not so good when people obey and acclaim him,
Worst when they despise him.
'Fail to honor people,
they fail to honor you;'
But of a good leader, who talks little,
When his work is done, his aim fulfilled,
They will say, 'We did this ourselves.'

From *Tao Te Ching,* translated from Chinese by Witter Bynner. Reprinted by permission of HarperCollins Publishers.

AESCHYLUS

From Prometheus Bound

GEORGE McCULLY

From "The Promethean Fire—Aeschylus and the First Philanthropist"

As far as we know, the Greek playwright Aeschylus (525–456 BC) coined the term "philanthropy" to describe the Titan Prometheus, in his play Prometheus Bound *(ca. 460 BC), the source of this selection. The legendary hero is said to have a "philanthropic way" (in Greek,* philanthropos tropos, *literally, a human-loving way), which spurred him to give mankind two gifts: fire, without which all the arts productive of civilization would be impossible, and blind hope, without which human beings would ceaselessly see only their doom. George McCully, president of the Catalogue for Philanthropy, noting the mutually reinforcing and empowering nature of Prometheus' gifts, as well as their "strategic significance," has suggested that this first coinage remains "a clear and potent archetype, a leading example, perfectly congruent with our modern understanding, namely, that philanthropy is private initiatives for public good, focusing on quality of life." If true, our first philanthropist may also serve as a still living model. In the excerpt that follows, we watch as Hephaestus nails Prometheus to the rock, then listen to Prometheus' self-understanding of why he rebelled against Zeus and gave humankind the gifts he did. Appended to the selection is an excerpt from George McCully's longer discussion of "The Promethean Fire—Aeschylus and the First Philanthropist." Is Prometheus's philanthropy still a potent model for ours? Why or why not?*

From *Prometheus Bound*

Enter HEPHÆSTOS, STRENGTH, *and* FORCE, *leading* PROMETHEUS *in chains*

Strength. LO! to a plain, earth's boundary remote,
We now are come,—the track as Skythian known,
A desert inaccessible: and now,
Hephæstos, it is thine to do the hests
The Father gave thee, to these lofty crags
To bind this crafty trickster fast in chains
Of adamantine bonds that none can break;

For he, thy choice flower stealing, the bright glory
Of fire that all arts spring from, hath bestowed it
On mortal men. And so for fault like this
He now must pay the Gods due penalty,
That he may learn to bear the sovereign rule
Of Zeus, and cease from his [philanthropic ways].

Heph. O Strength, and thou, O Force, the hest of Zeus,
As far as touches you, attains its end,
And nothing hinders. Yet my courage fails
To bind a God of mine own kin by force
To this bare rock where tempests wildly sweep;
And yet I needs must muster courage for it:
'Tis no slight thing the Father's words to scorn.
O thou of Themis [*to* PROMETHEUS] wise in counsel son,
Full deep of purpose, lo! against my will,[1]
I fetter thee against thy will with bonds
Of bronze that none can loose, the this lone height,
Where thou shalt know nor voice nor face of man,
But scorching in the hot blaze of the sun,
Shalt lose thy skin's fair beauty. Thou shalt long
For starry-mantled night to hide day's sheen,
For sun to melt the rime of early dawn;
And evermore the weight of present ill
Shall wear thee down. Unborn as yet is he
Who shall release thee: this the fate thou gain'st
As due reward for thy philanthropy.
For thou, a God not fearing wrath of Gods,
In thy transgression gav'st their power to men;
And therefore on this rock of little ease
Thou still shalt keep thy watch, nor lying down,
Nor knowing sleep, nor ever bending knee;
And many groans and wailings profitless
Thy lips shall utter; for the mind of Zeus
Remains inexorable. Who holds a power
But newly gained is ever stern of mood.[2]

---

1. Prometheus (*Forethought*) is the son of Themis (*Right*), the second occupant of the Pythian Oracle (*Eumen.* v. 2). His sympathy with man leads him to impart the gift which raised them out of savage animal life, and for this Zeus, who appears throughout the play as a hard taskmaster, sentences him to fetters. Hephæstos, from whom this fire had been stolen, has a touch of pity for him. Strength, who comes as the servant, not of Hephæstos, but of Zeus himself, acts, as such, with merciless cruelty.

2. The generalized statement refers to Zeus, as having but recently expelled Cronos from his throne in heaven.

Strength. Let be! Why linger in this idle pity?
Why dost not hate a God to Gods a foe,
Who gave thy choicest prize to mortal men?

Heph. Strange is the power of kin and intercourse.[3]

Strength. I own it; yet to slight the Father's words,
How may that be? Is not that fear the worse?

Heph. Still art thou ruthless, full of savagery.

Strength. There is no help in weeping over him:
Spend not thy toil on things that profit not.

Heph. O handicraft to me intolerable!

Strength. Why loath'st thou it? Of these thy present griefs
That craft of thine is not one whit the cause.

Heph. And yet I would some other had that skill.

Strength. All things bring toil except for Gods to reign;
For none but Zeus can boast of freedom true.

Heph. Too well I see the proof, and gainsay not.

Strength. Wilt thou not speed to fix the chains on him,
Lest He, the Father, see thee loitering here?

Heph. Well, here the handcuffs thou mayst see prepared.

Strength. In thine hands take him. Then with all thy might
Strike with thine hammer; nail him to the rocks.

Heph. The work goes on, I ween, and not in vain.

Strength. Strike harder, rivet, give no whit of ease:
A wondrous knack has he to find resource,
Even where all might seem to baffle him.

Heph. Lo! this his arm is fixed inextricably.

Strength. Now rivet thou this other fast, that he
May learn, though sharp, that he than Zeus is duller.

Heph. No one but he could justly blame my work.

Strength. Now drive the stern jaw of the adamant wedge
Right through his chest with all the strength thou hast.

Heph. Ah me! Prometheus, for thy woes I groan.

---

3. Hephæstos, as the great fire-worker, had taught Prometheus to use the fire which he afterwards bestowed on men.

Strength. Again, thou'rt loth, and for the foes of Zeus
Thou groanest: take good heed to it lest thou
Ere long with cause thyself commiserate.

Heph. Thou seest a sight unsightly to our eyes.

Strength. I see this man obtaining his deserts:
Nay, cast thy breast-chains round about his ribs.

Heph. I must needs do it. Spare thine o'ermuch bidding;
Go thou below and rivet both his legs.[4]

Strength. Nay, I will bid thee, urge thee to thy work.

Heph. There, it is done, and that with no long toil.

Strength. Now with thy full power fix the galling fetters:
Thou hast a stern o'erlooker of thy work.

Heph. Thy tongue but utters words that match thy form.

Strength. Choose thou the melting mood; but chide not me
For my self-will and wrath and ruthlessness.

Heph. Now let us go, his limbs are bound in chains.

Strength. Here then wax proud, and stealing what belongs
To the Gods, to mortals give it. What can they
Avail to rescue thee from these thy woes?
Falsely the Gods have given thee thy name,
Prometheus, Forethought; forethought thou dost need
To free thyself from this rare handiwork.

Exeunt HEPHÆSTOS, STRENGTH, *and* FORCE, *leaving* PROMETHEUS *on the rock.*

Prometheus.[5] Thou firmament of God, and swift-winged winds,
Ye springs of rivers, and of ocean waves
That smile innumerous! Mother of us all,
O Earth, and Sun's all-seeing eye, behold,
I pray, what I, a God, from Gods endure.
    Behold in what foul case
    I for ten thousand years

---

4. The words indicate that the effigy of Prometheus, now nailed to the rock, was, as being that of a Titan, of colossal size.

5. The silence of Prometheus up to this point is a touch of supreme insight into the heroic temper. In the presence of his tortures, the Titan will not utter even a groan. When they are gone, he appeals to the sympathy of Nature.

Shall struggle in my woe,
    In these unseemly chains.
Such doom the new-made Monarch of the Blest
    Hath now devised for me.
Woe, woe! The present and the oncoming pang
    I wail, as I search out
The place and hour when end of all these ills
    Shall dawn on me at last.
What say I? All too clearly I foresee
The things that come, and nought of pain shall be
By me unlooked-for; but I needs must bear
My destiny as best I may, knowing well
The might resistless of Necessity.
And neither may I speak of this my fate,
Nor hold my peace. For I, poor I, through giving
Great gifts to mortal men, am prisoner made
In these fast fetters; yea, in fennel stalk
I snatched the hidden spring of stolen fire,
Which is to men a teacher of all arts,
Their chief resource. And now this penalty
Of that offence I pay, fast riveted
In chains beneath the open firmament.
    Ha! ha! What now?
What sound, what odour floats invisibly?
Is it of God or man, or blending both?
And has one come to this remotest rock
To look upon my woes? Or what wills he?
Behold me bound, a God to evil doomed,
    The foe of Zeus, and held
    In hatred by all Gods
    Who tread the courts of Zeus:
    And this for my great love,
    Too great, for mortal men.
    Ah me! what rustling sounds
    Hear I of birds not far?
    With the light whirr of wings
    The air re-echoeth:
All that draws nigh to me is cause of fear.[6]

Enter Chorus of Ocean Nymphs, *with wings, floating in the air*

---

6. The words are not those of a vague terror only. The sufferer knows that his tormentor is to come to him before long on wings, and therefore the sound as of the flight of birds is full of terrors.

Chorus. Nay, fear thou nought: in love
    All our array of wings
    In eager race hath come
To this high peak, full hardly gaining o'er
    Our Father's mind and will;
And the swift-rushing breezes bore me on:
For lo! the echoing sound of blows on iron
Pierced to our cave's recess, and put to flight
    My shamefast modesty,
And I in unshod haste, on winged car,
    To thee rushed hitherward.

Prom. Ah me! ah me!
Offspring of Tethys blest with many a child,
Daughters of Old Okeanos that rolls
Round all the earth with never-sleeping stream,
    Behold ye me, and see
    With what chains fettered fast,
I on the topmost crags of this ravine
Shall keep my sentry-post unenviable.

Chor. I see it, O Prometheus, and a mist
Of fear and full of tears comes o'er mine eyes,
    Thy frame beholding thus,
    Writhing on these high rocks
    In adamantine ills.
New pilots now o'er high Olympos rule,
    And with new-fashioned laws
    Zeus reigns, down-trampling Right,
And all the ancient powers He sweeps away.

Prom. Ah! would that 'neath the Earth, 'neath Hades too,
Home of the dead, far down to Tartaros
Unfathomable He in fetters fast
    In wrath had hurled me down:
    So neither had a God
Nor any other mocked at these my woes;
But now, the wretched plaything of the winds,
I suffer ills at which my foes rejoice.

Chor. Nay, which of all the Gods
Is so hard-hearted as to joy in this?
Who, Zeus excepted, doth not pity thee
    In these thine ills? But He,
    Ruthless, with soul unbent,

Subdues the heavenly host, nor will He cease
Until His heart be satiate with power,
Or some one seize with subtle stratagem
The sovran might that so resistless seemed.

Prom. Nay, of a truth, though put to evil shame,
    In massive fetters bound,
    The Ruler of the Gods
Shall yet have need of me, yes, e'en of me,
    To tell the counsel new
    That seeks to strip from Him
His sceptre and His might of sovereignty.
    In vain will He with words
    Or suasion's honeyed charms
    Soothe me, nor will I tell
    Through fear of His stern threats,
    Ere He shall set me free
From these my bonds, and make,
    Of His own choice, amends
    For all these outrages.

Chor. Full rash art thou, and yield'st
In not a jot to bitterest form of woe;
Thou art o'er-free and reckless in thy speech:
    But piercing fear hath stirred
    My inmost soul to strife;
For I fear greatly touching thy distress,
As to what haven of these woes of thine
Thou now must steer: the son of Cronos hath
A stubborn mood and heart inexorable.

Prom. I know that Zeus is hard,
And keeps the Right supremely to Himself;
    But then, I trow, He'll be
    Full pliant in His will,
    When He is thus crushed down.
    Then, calming down His mood
    Of hard and bitter wrath,
    He'll hasten unto me,
    As I to Him shall haste,
    For friendship and for peace.

Chor. Hide it not from us, tell us all the tale:
For what offence Zeus, having seized thee thus,

So wantonly and bitterly insults thee:
If the tale hurt thee not, inform thou us.

Prom. Painful are these things to me e'en to speak:
Painful is silence; everywhere is woe.
For when the high Gods fell on mood of wrath
And hot debate of mutual strife was stirred,
Some wishing to hurl Cronos from his throne,
That Zeus, forsooth, might reign; while others strove,
Eager that Zeus might never rule the Gods:
Then I, full strongly seeking to persuade
The Titans, yea, the sons of Heaven and Earth,
Failed of my purpose. Scorning subtle arts,
With counsels violent, they thought that they
By force would gain full easy mastery.
But then not once or twice my mother Themis
And earth, one form though bearing many names,[7]
Had prophesied the future, how 'twould run,
That not by strength nor yet by violence,
But guile, should those who prospered gain the day.
And when in my words I this counsel gave,
They deigned not e'en to glance at it at all.
And then of all that offered, it seemed best
To join my mother, and of mine own will,
Not against His will, take my side with Zeus,
And by my counsels, mine, the dark deep pit
Of Tartaros the ancient Cronos holds,
Himself and his allies. Thus profiting
By me, the mighty ruler of the Gods
Repays me with these evil penalties:
For somehow this disease in sovereignty
Inheres, of never trusting to one's friends.
And since ye ask me under what pretence
He thus maltreats me, I will show it you:
For soon as He upon His father's throne
Had sat secure, forthwith to divers Gods
He divers gifts distributed, and His realm
Began to order. But of mortal men
He took no heed, but purposed utterly
To crush their race and plant another new;

---

7. The words leave it uncertain whether Themis is identified with Earth or distinguished from her. The Titans as a class, then, children of Okeanos and Chthôn (another name for *Land* or *Earth*), are the kindred rather than the brothers of Prometheus.

And, I excepted, none dared cross His will;
But I did dare, and mortal men I freed
From passing on to Hades thunder-stricken;
And therefore am I bound beneath these woes,
Dreadful to suffer, pitiable to see:
And I, who in my pity thought of men
More than myself, have not been worthy deemed
To gain like favour, but all ruthlessly
I thus am chained, foul shame this sight to Zeus.

Chor. Iron-hearted must he be and made of rock
Who is not moved, Prometheus, by thy woes:
Fain could I wish I ne'er had seen such things,
And, seeing them, am wounded to the heart.

Prom. Yea, I am piteous for my friends to see.

Chor. Didst thou not go to farther lengths than this?

Prom. I made men cease from contemplating death.[8]

Chor. What medicine didst thou find for that disease?

Prom. Blind hopes I gave to live and dwell with them.

Chor. Great service that thou didst for mortal men!

Prom. And more than that, I gave them fire, yes, I.

Chor. Do short-lived men the flaming fire possess?

Prom. Yea, and full many an art they'll learn from it.

Chor. And is it then on charges such as these
That Zeus maltreats thee, and no respite gives
Of many woes? And has thy pain no end?

Prom. End there is none, except as pleases Him.

Chor. How shall it please? What hope hast thou?
      Seest not
That thou hast sinned? Yet to say how thou sinned'st
Gives me no pleasure, and is pain to thee.
Well! let us leave these things, and, if we may,
Seek out some means to 'scape from this thy woe.

---

8. The state described is that of men who "through fear of death are all their life time subject to bondage." That state, the parent of all superstition, fostered the slavish awe in which Zeus delighted. Prometheus, representing the active intellect of man, bestows new powers, new interests, new hopes, which at last divert them from that fear.

Prom. 'Tis a light thing for one who has his foot
Beyond the reach of evil to exhort
And counsel him who suffers. This to me
Was all well known. Yea, willing, willingly
I sinned, nor will deny it. Helping men,
I for myself found trouble: yet I thought not
That I with such dread penalties as these
Should wither here on these high-towering crags,
Lighting on this lone hill and neighbourless.
Wherefore wail not for these my present woes,
But, drawing nigh, my coming fortunes hear,
That ye may learn the whole tale to the end.
Nay, hearken, hearken; show your sympathy
With him who suffers now. 'Tis thus that woe,
Wandering, now falls on this one, now on that.

Chor. Not to unwilling hearers hast thou uttered,
 Prometheus, thy request,
And now with nimble foot abounding
 My swiftly rushing car,
And the pure æther, path of birds of heaven,
I will draw near this rough and rocky land,
 For much do I desire
To hear this tale, full measure of thy woes. . . .

Prom. Think not it is through pride or stiff self-will
That I am silent. But my heart is worn,
Self-contemplating, as I see myself
Thus outraged. Yet what other hand than mine
Gave these young Gods in fulness all their gifts?
But these I speak not of; for I should tell
To you that know them. But those woes of men,
List ye to them,—how they, before as babes,
By me were roused to reason, taught to think;
And this I say, not finding fault with men,
But showing my good-will in all I gave.
For first, though seeing, all in vain they saw,
And hearing, heard not rightly. But, like forms
Of phantom-dreams, throughout their life's whole length
They muddled all at random; did not know
Houses of brick that catch the sunlight's warmth,
Nor yet the work of carpentry. They dwelt
In hollowed holes, like swarms of tiny ants,
In sunless depths of caverns; and they had

No certain signs of winter, nor of spring
Flower-laden, nor of summer with her fruits;
But without counsel fared their whole life long,
Until I showed the risings of the stars,
And settings hard to recognize. And I
Found Number for them, chief devise of all,
Groupings of letters, Memory's handmaid that,
And mother of the Muses. And I first
Bound in the yoke wild steeds, submissive made
Or to the collar or men's limbs, that so
They might in man's place bear his greatest toils;
And horses trained to love the rein I yoked
To chariots, glory of wealth's pride of state;
Nor was it any one but I that found
Sea-crossing, canvas-wingèd cars of ships:
Such rare designs inventing (wretched me!)
For mortal men, I yet have no device
By which to free myself from this my woe.

Chor. Foul shame thou sufferest: of thy sense bereaved,
Thou errest greatly: and, like leech unskilled,
Thou losest heart when smitten with disease,
And know'st not how to find the remedies
Wherewith to heal thine own soul's sicknesses.

Prom. Hearing what yet remains, thou'lt wonder more,
What arts and what resources I devised:
And this the chief: if any one fell ill,
There was no help for him, nor healing food
Nor unguent, nor yet potion; but for want
Of drugs they wasted, till I showed to them
The blendings of all mild medicaments,
Wherewith they ward the attacks of sickness sore.
I gave them many modes of prophecy;[9]
And I first taught them what dreams needs must prove
True visions, and made known the ominous sounds
Full hard to know; and tokens by the way,
And flights of taloned birds I clearly marked,—
Those on the right propitious to mankind,

---

9. The lines that follow form almost a manual of the art of divination as then practiced. The "ominous sounds" include chance words, strange cries, any unexpected utterance that connected itself with men's fears for the future. The flights of birds were watched by the diviner as he faced the north, and so the region on the right hand was that of the sunrise, light, blessedness; on the left there were darkness and gloom and death.

And those sinister,—and what form of life
They each maintain, and what their enmities
Each with the other, and their loves and friendships;
And of the inward parts the plumpness smooth.
And with what colour they the Gods would please,
And the streaked comeliness of gall and liver:
And with burnt limbs enwrapt in fat, and chine,
I led men on to art full difficult:
And I gave eyes to omens drawn from fire,
Till then dim-visioned. So far, then, for this.
And 'neath the earth the hidden boons for men,
Bronze, iron, silver, gold, who else could say
That he, ere I did, found them? None, I know,
Unless he fain would babble idle words.
In one short word, then, learn the truth condensed,—
All arts of mortals from Prometheus spring.

From "The Promethean Fire—Aeschylus and the First Philanthropist"

Very few people today, even professionals, know what the word "philanthropy" means, or how it relates to charitable giving. A few years ago a survey was conducted in Minnesota, asking people to define the term, and their answers ranged from the mystified—"I don't know, some sort of gastro-intestinal disorder?" and "Sexual promiscuity?"—to the confident but incomplete: "Rich people helping poor people." When the question arises at meetings of professionals there are often as many definitions as there are people in the room. The cause and result of this broadly shared vagueness and confusion is that the word is rarely used; many people consider it too fancy and even pretentious for ordinary purposes, so they frequently opt for the much simpler word and concept, "giving."

This is how great ideas die, and it is in this case tragic, because in truth "philanthropy" has a clear, powerful, inspiring, and donor-friendly meaning and history, which would be beneficial to revive. . . .

The first recorded use of the expression was by Aeschylus, the first great playwright and tragedian of ancient Greece, in his *Prometheus Bound* (ca. 460 B.C.). There Prometheus himself, the Titan who had created Man from clay, out of his *philanthropos tropos*—"mankind-loving character"—gave humanity two gifts: fire, symbolizing all knowledge and practical skills that distinguish civilization from living in caves; and "blind (i.e., unknowing) hope," or optimism. . . .

We can derive some valuable lessons from his usage:

- The name "Prometheus" meant "forethought" or what we call "foresight"—the ability to think ahead, or see into the future—an essential attribute of donors, but in the story only Prometheus and his mother, Earth, had it, which was significant.

· The word "philanthropic" was at first an adjective not a noun; and it modified not the gift, nor even the giving, but the personal attitude, character, or disposition of the donor.

· The remarkable phenomenon for which Aeschylus may even have coined this expression was a feeling and act of general benevolence on the part of the donor, not just to help himself, his family, neighbors, tribe, or even nation, but all humanity—*anthropos*—which Prometheus had created as one.

· The "love" referred to—*philos*—was not merely felt or thought, but expressed—acted upon, in benefaction—doing good.

· The benefaction was freely voluntary—not obliged as a duty (moral or otherwise), nor extracted from the donor/benefactor by any outside influence (e.g., aggressive fundraising); it was "initiated" by the donor himself, and was partly for that reason morally respectable.

· The gifts were not just "good" for the beneficiaries, but empowering— increasing their competencies and improving their prospects as human beings.

· This empowerment by philanthropy was profound—changing the course of human history. The gifts of fire and optimism were civilizing and ennobling, enabling humans, as Aeschylus himself put it, to emerge from caves, to fulfill their uniquely human potential. . . . [T]he gifts were also mutually reinforcing—the "fire" and "blind hope" or optimism, and progress, went hand-in-hand, each nourishing the others in what we might today call "positive feedback loops."

· Zeus had no such respect or love for the cave-dwellers, and had apparently planned to destroy them. He therefore regarded Prometheus' philanthropy as a rebellion against his rule (which Prometheus had also helped establish), so he punished Prometheus (apparently no good deed went unpunished even in ancient Greece) by having him chained to a rock in the Caucasus, and sending an eagle to devour his liver daily (Titans being immortal, it grew back at night). This gruesome ordeal lasted 30,000 years—not very donor-friendly— but for our purposes, as well as for the Greeks, this key part of the story yoked philanthropy with freedom and democracy, against tyranny. . . .

This combination of associations—of philanthropy, or love of humankind, with *freedom* against slavery, with *democracy* against tyranny, with *education* as self-development and empowerment, with *civilization* as against primitiveness, and with *optimism* and *progress* in history—and the assertion that they are mutually interdependent and mutually reinforcing—is what we

[can] call the Classical concept of philanthropy. It is strikingly rich and profound, very far above and beyond our relatively dessicated modern interpretations of philanthropy as "rich helping poor" or "caring" or just "giving."

Text and footnotes from *Prometheus Bound* by Aeschylus, translated by E. H. Plumptre, in vol. 8, part 4 of The Harvard Classics, edited by Charles W. Eliot. (New York: P. F. Collier and Sons, 1909–1914).

From *Philanthropy: An Overview* by George McCully (unpublished manuscript). By permission of the author.

JOHN WESLEY

"The Use of Money"

In this sermon, John Wesley (1703–1791), theologian, powerful orator, and founder of Methodism, interprets Christ's charge to "Make unto yourselves friends of the mammon of unrighteousness" to urge Christians to educate themselves about the proper use of money. Wesley promulgates (his still famous) three simple rules by which one might do so to best effect: "Gain all you can. Save all you can. Give all you can." Gain all you can without harm to mind or body, your own or your neighbor's, by honest industry and by common sense. Save all you can to keep yourself, as well as your children, from prodigal desires—for food, apparel, ornament, furnishings, or other superfluities. And, finally, as God "placed you [on earth] not as a proprietor, but a steward," give all you can, "by employing all on yourself, your household, the household of faith, and all mankind, in such a manner, that you may give a good account of your stewardship when you can be no longer stewards." For Wesley, we are all, primordially, undeserving recipients of God's bounty and, hence, we should act not as prideful owners but as humble servants or stewards. Though he writes to and for Christians, and his prime concern is the salvation of Christian souls, many would agree that how one comports oneself with respect to money—making it, saving it, and giving it away—matters. And among the virtues high on the list of many laborers in the philanthropic vineyard are the virtues extolled here—thrift, generosity, prudence, and, most especially, humility. Can this message be separated from its theological moorings? Should all philanthropic leaders—Christian and non-Christian—take it to heart?

"I say unto you, Make unto yourselves friends of the mammon of unrighteousness; that, when ye fail, they may receive you into the everlasting habitations."
—Luke 16:9

Our Lord, having finished the beautiful parable of the Prodigal Son, which he had particularly addressed to those who murmured at his receiving publicans and sinners, adds another relation of a different kind, addressed rather to the children of God. "He said unto his disciples," not so much to the scribes and Pharisees to whom he had been speaking before,—"There was a certain rich man, who had a steward, and he was accused to him of wasting his goods. And calling him, he said, Give an account of thy stewardship, for thou canst be no longer steward" (Luke 16:1, 2). After reciting the method which the bad steward used to provide against the day of necessity, our Saviour adds, "His lord commended the unjust steward" namely, in this respect, that he used timely precaution; and subjoins this weighty reflection, "The children of this world are wiser in their generation than the children of light" (Luke 16:8). Those who seek no other portion than this world "are wiser" (not absolutely; for they are one and all the veriest fools, the most egregious madmen under heaven; but, "in their generation," in their own way; they are more consistent with themselves; they are truer to their acknowledged principles; they more steadily pursue their end) "than the children of light;"—than they who see "the light of the glory of God in the face of Jesus Christ." Then follow the words above recited: "And I,"—the only-begotten Son of God, the Creator, Lord, and Possessor of heaven and earth and all that is therein; the Judge of all, to whom ye are to "give an account of your stewardship," when ye "can be no longer stewards;" "I say unto you,"—learn in this respect, even of the unjust steward,— "make yourselves friends," by wise, timely precaution, "of the mammon of unrighteousness." "Mammon" means riches or money. It is termed "the mammon of unrighteousness," because of the unrighteous manner wherein it frequently procured, and wherein even that which was honestly procured is generally employed. "Make yourselves friends" of this, by doing all possible good, particularly to the children of God; "that, when ye fail,"—when ye return to dust, when ye have no more place under the sun,—those of them who are gone before "may receive you," may welcome you, into the "everlasting habitations."

An excellent branch of Christian wisdom is here inculcated by our Lord on all his followers, namely, the right use of money—a subject largely spoken of, after their manner, by men of the world; but not sufficiently considered by those whom God hath chosen out of the world. These, generally, do not consider, as the importance of the subject requires, the use of this excellent talent. Neither do they understand how to employ it to the greatest advantage; the introduction of which into the world is one admirable instance of the wise and gracious providence of God. It has, indeed, been the manner of poets, orators, and philosophers, in almost all ages and nations, to rail at this, as the grand corrupter of the world, the bane of virtue, the pest of human society.

Hence nothing so commonly heard, as:

Nocens ferrum, ferroque nocentius aurum.
And gold, more mischievous than keenest steel.

Hence the lamentable complaint,

Effodiuntur opes, irritamenta malorum.
Wealth is dug up, incentive to all ill.

Nay, one celebrated writer gravely exhorts his countrymen, in order to banish all vice at once, to "throw all their money into the sea":

In mare proximum,
Summi materiem mali!

But is not all this mere empty rant? Is there any solid reason therein? By no means. For, let the world be as corrupt as it will, is gold or silver to blame? "The love of money," we know, "is the root of all evil;" but *not* the thing itself. The fault does not lie in the money, but in them that use it. It may be used ill: and what may not? But it may likewise be used well: It is full as applicable to the best, as to the worst uses. It is of unspeakable service to all civilized nations, in all the common affairs of life: It is a most compendious instrument of transacting all manner of business, and (if we use it according to Christian wisdom) of doing all manner of good. It is true, were man in a state of innocence, or were all men "filled with the Holy Ghost," so that, like the infant Church at Jerusalem, "no man counted anything he had his own," but "distribution was made to everyone as he had need," the use of it would be superseded; as we cannot conceive there is anything of the kind among the inhabitants of heaven. But, in the present state of mankind, it is an excellent gift of God, answering the noblest ends. In the hands of his children, it is food for the hungry, drink for the thirsty, raiment for the naked: It gives to the traveller and the stranger where to lay his head. By it we may supply the place of an husband to the widow, and of a father to the fatherless. We may be a defence for the oppressed, a means of health to the sick, of ease to them that are in pain; it may be as eyes to the blind, as feet to the lame; yea, a lifter up from the gates of death!

It is therefore of the highest concern that all who fear God know how to employ this valuable talent; that they be instructed how it may answer these glorious ends, and in the highest degree. And, perhaps, all the instructions which are necessary for this may be reduced to *three plain rules*, by the exact observance whereof we may approve ourselves faithful stewards of "the mammon of unrighteousness."

I. "Gain all you can."

The first of these is (he that heareth, let him understand!) "Gain all you can." Here we may speak like the children of the world: We meet them on their own ground. And it is our bounden duty to do this: We ought to gain all we can gain, without buying gold too dear, without paying more for it than it is worth.

But this it is certain we ought not to do; we ought not to gain money at the expense of life, nor (which is in effect the same thing) at the expense of our health. Therefore, no gain whatsoever should induce us to enter into, or to continue in, any employ, which is of such a kind, or is attended with so hard or so long labour, as to impair our constitution. Neither should we begin or continue in any business which necessarily deprives us of proper seasons for food and sleep, in such a proportion as our nature requires. Indeed, there is a great difference here. Some employments are absolutely and totally unhealthy; as those which imply the dealing much with arsenic, or other equally hurtful minerals, or the breathing an air tainted with steams of melting lead, which must at length destroy the firmest constitution. Others may not be absolutely unhealthy, but only to persons of a weak constitution. Such are those which require many hours to be spent in writing; especially if a person write sitting, and lean upon his stomach, or remain long in an uneasy posture. But whatever it is which reason or experience shows to be destructive of health or strength, that we may not submit to; seeing "the life is more" valuable "than meat, and the body than raiment." And if we are already engaged in such an employ, we should exchange it as soon as possible for some which, if it lessen our gain, will, however not lessen our health.

We are, Secondly, to gain all we can without hurting our mind any more than our body. For neither may we hurt this. We must preserve, at all events, the spirit of an healthful mind. Therefore we may not engage or continue in any sinful trade, any that is contrary to the law of God, or of our country. Such are all that necessarily imply our robbing or defrauding the king of his lawful customs. For it is at least as sinful to defraud the king of his right, as to rob our fellow subjects. And the king has full as much right, to his customs as we have to our houses and apparel. Other businesses there are, which however innocent in themselves, cannot be followed with innocence now at least, not in England; such, for instance, as will not afford a competent maintenance without cheating or lying, or conformity to some custom which not consistent with a good conscience: These, likewise, are sacredly to be avoided, whatever gain they may be attended with provided we follow the custom of the trade; for to gain money we must not lose our souls. There are yet others which many pursue with perfect innocence, without hurting either their body or mind; And yet perhaps you cannot: Either they may entangle you in that company which would destroy your soul; and by repeated experiments it may appear that you cannot separate the one from the other; or there may be an idiosyncrasy,—a peculiarity in your constitution of soul, (as there is in the bodily constitution of many) by reason whereof that employment is deadly to you, which another may safely follow. So I am convinced, from many experiments, I could not study, to any degree of perfection, either mathematics, arithmetic, or algebra, without being a Deist, if not an Atheist: And yet others may study them all their lives without sustaining any inconvenience. None therefore can here determine for another; but every man must judge for himself, and abstain from whatever he in particular finds to be hurtful to his soul.

We are, Thirdly, to gain all we can without hurting our neighbour. But this we may not, cannot do, if we love our neighbour as ourselves. We cannot, if we love everyone as ourselves, hurt anyone in his substance. We cannot devour the increase of his lands, and perhaps the lands and houses themselves, by gaming, by overgrown bills (whether on account of physic, or law, or anything else) or by requiring or taking such interest as even the laws of our country forbid. Hereby all pawn-broking is excluded: Seeing, whatever good we might do thereby, all unprejudiced men see with grief to be abundantly overbalanced by the evil. And if it were otherwise, yet we are not allowed to "do evil that good may come." We cannot, consistent with brotherly love, sell our goods below the market price; we cannot study to ruin our neighbour's trade, in order to advance our own; much less can we entice away or receive any of his servants or workmen whom he has need of. None can gain by swallowing up his neighbour's substance, without gaining the damnation of hell!

Neither may we gain by hurting our neighbour in his body. Therefore we may not sell anything which tends to impair health. Such is, eminently, all that liquid fire, commonly called drams or spirituous liquors. It is true, these may have a place in medicine; they may be of use in some bodily disorders; although there would rarely be occasion for them were it not for the unskillfulness of the practitioner. Therefore, such as prepare and sell them only for this end may keep their conscience clear. But who are they? Who prepare and sell them only for this end? Do you know ten such distillers in England? Then excuse these. But all who sell them in the common way, to any that will buy, are poisoners general. They murder His Majesty's subjects by wholesale, neither does their eye pity or spare. They drive them to hell like sheep. And what is their gain? Is it not the blood of these men? Who then would envy their large estates and sumptuous palaces? A curse is in the midst of them: The curse of God cleaves to the stones, the timber, the furniture of them. The curse of God is in their gardens, their walks, their groves; a fire that burns to the nethermost hell! Blood, blood is there: The foundation, the floor, the walls, the roof are stained with blood! And canst thou hope, O thou man of blood, though thou art "clothed in scarlet and fine linen, and farest sumptuously every day;" canst thou hope to deliver down thy fields of blood to the third generation? Not so; for there is a God in heaven: Therefore, thy name shall soon be rooted out. Like as those whom thou hast destroyed, body and soul, "thy memorial shall perish with thee!"

And are not they partakers of the same guilt, though in a lower degree, whether Surgeons, Apothecaries, or Physicians, who play with the lives or health of men, to enlarge their own gain? Who purposely lengthen the pain or disease which they are able to remove speedily? Who protract the cure of their patient's body in order to plunder his substance? Can any man be clear before God who does not shorten every disorder "as much as he can," and remove all sickness and pain "as soon as he can?" He cannot: For nothing can be more clear than that he does not "love his neighbour as himself;" than that he does not "do unto others as he would they should do unto himself."

This is dear-bought gain. And so is whatever is procured by hurting our neighbour in his soul; by ministering, suppose, either directly or indirectly, to his unchastity, or intemperance, which certainly none can do, who has any fear of God, or any real desire of pleasing Him. It nearly concerns all those to consider this, who have anything to do with taverns, victualling-houses, opera-houses, play-houses, or any other places of public, fashionable diversion. If these profit the souls of men, you are clear; your employment is good, and your gain innocent; but if they are either sinful in themselves, or natural inlets to sin of various kinds, then, it is to be feared, you have a sad account to make. O beware, lest God say in that day, "These have perished in their iniquity, but their blood do I require at thy hands!"

These cautions and restrictions being observed, it is the bounden duty of all who are engaged in worldly business to observe that first and great rule of Christian wisdom with respect to money, "Gain all you can." Gain all you can by honest industry. Use all possible diligence in your calling. Lose no time. If you understand yourself and your relation to God and man, you know you have none to spare. If you understand your particular calling as you ought, you will have no time that hangs upon your hands. Every business will afford some employment sufficient for every day and every hour. That wherein you are placed, if you follow it in earnest, will leave you no leisure for silly, unprofitable diversions. You have always something better to do, something that will profit you, more or less. And "whatsoever thy hand findeth to do, do it with thy might." Do it as soon as possible: No delay! No putting off from day to day, or from hour to hour! Never leave anything till to-morrow, which you can do to-day. And do it as well as possible. Do not sleep or yawn over it: Put your whole strength to the work. Spare no pains. Let nothing be done by halves, or in a slight and careless manner. Let nothing in your business be left undone if it can be done by labour or patience.

Gain all you can, by common sense, by using in your business all the understanding which God has given you. It is amazing to observe, how few do this; how men run on in the same dull track with their forefathers. But whatever they do who know not God, this is no rule for you. It is a shame for a Christian not to improve upon them, in whatever he takes in hand. You should be continually learning, from the experience of others, or from your own experience, reading, and reflection, to do everything you have to do better today than you did yesterday. And see that you practice whatever you learn, that you may make the best of all that is in your hands.

II. "Save all you can."

Having gained all you can, by honest wisdom and unwearied diligence, the second rule of Christian prudence is, "Save all you can." Do not throw the precious talent into the sea: Leave that folly to heathen philosophers. Do not throw it away in idle expenses, which is just the same as throwing it into the sea. Expend no part of it merely to gratify the desire of the flesh, the desire of the eye, or the pride of life.

Do not waste any part of so precious a talent merely in gratifying the desires of the flesh; in procuring the pleasures of sense of whatever kind; particularly, in enlarging the pleasure of tasting. I do not mean, avoid gluttony and drunkenness only: An honest heathen would condemn these. But there is a regular, reputable kind of sensuality, an elegant epicurism, which does not immediately disorder the stomach, nor (sensibly, at least) impair the understanding. And yet (to mention no other effects of it now) it cannot be maintained without considerable expense. Cut off all this expense! Despise delicacy and variety, and be content with what plain nature requires.

Do not waste any part of so precious a talent merely in gratifying the desire of the eye by superfluous or expensive apparel, or by needless ornaments. Waste no part of it in curiously adorning your houses; in superfluous or expensive furniture; in costly pictures, painting, gilding, books; in elegant rather than useful gardens. Let your neighbours, who know nothing better, do this: "Let the dead bury their dead." But "what is that to thee?" says our Lord: "Follow thou me." Are you willing? Then you are able so to do.

Lay out nothing to gratify the pride of life, to gain the admiration or praise of men. This motive of expense is frequently interwoven with one or both of the former. Men are expensive in diet, or apparel, or furniture, not barely to please their appetite, or to gratify their eye, their imagination, but their vanity too. "So long as thou dost well unto thyself, men will speak good of thee." So long as thou art "clothed in purple and fine linen, and farest sumptuously every day," no doubt many will applaud thy elegance of taste, thy generosity and hospitality. But do not buy their applause so dear. Rather be content with the honour that cometh from God.

Who would expend anything in gratifying these desires if he considered that to gratify them is to increase them? Nothing can be more certain than this: Daily experience shows, the more they are indulged, they increase the more. Whenever, therefore, you expend anything to please your taste or other senses, you pay so much for sensuality. When you lay out money to please your eye, you give so much for an increase of curiosity,—for a stronger attachment to these pleasures which perish in the using. While you are purchasing anything which men use to applaud, you are purchasing more vanity. Had you not then enough of vanity, sensuality, curiosity before? Was there need of any addition? And would you pay for it, too? What manner of wisdom is this? Would not the literally throwing your money into the sea be a less mischievous folly?

And why should you throw away money upon your children, any more than upon yourself, in delicate food, in gay or costly apparel, in superfluities of any kind? Why should you purchase for them more pride or lust, more vanity, or foolish and hurtful desires? They do not want any more; they have enough already; nature has made ample provision for them: Why should you be at farther expense to increase their temptations and snares, and to pierce them through with more sorrows?

Do not leave it to them to throw away. If you have good reason to believe that they would waste what is now in your possession in gratifying and thereby increasing the desire of the flesh, the desire of the eye, or the pride of life at the peril of theirs and your own soul, do not set these traps in their way. Do not offer your sons or your daughters unto Belial, any more than unto Moloch. Have pity upon them, and remove out of their way what you may easily foresee would increase their sins, and consequently plunge them deeper into everlasting perdition! How amazing then is the infatuation of those parents who think they can never leave their children enough! What! cannot you leave them enough of arrows, firebrands, and death? Not enough of foolish and hurtful desires? Not enough of pride, lust, ambition, vanity? Not enough of everlasting burnings? Poor wretch! thou fearest where no fear is. Surely both thou and they, when ye are lifting up your eyes in hell, will have enough both of the "worm that never dieth," and of "the fire that never shall be quenched!"

"What then would you do, if you were in my case? If you had a considerable fortune to leave?" Whether I would do it or not, I know what I ought to do: This will admit of no reasonable question. If I had one child, elder or younger, who knew the value of money; one who I believed, would put it to the true use, I should think it my absolute, indispensable duty to leave that child the bulk of my fortune; and to the rest just so much as would enable them to live in the manner they had been accustomed to do. "But what, if all your children were equally ignorant of the true use of money?" I ought then (hard saying! who can hear it?) to give each what would keep him above want, and to bestow all the rest in such a manner as I judged would be most for the glory of God.

III. "Give all you can."

But let not any man imagine that he has done anything, barely by going thus far, by "gaining and saving all he can," if he were to stop here. All this is nothing, if a man go not forward, if he does not point all this at a farther end. Nor, indeed, can a man properly be said to save anything, if he only lays it up. You may as well throw your money into the sea, as bury it in the earth. And you may as well bury it in the earth, as in your chest, or in the Bank of England. Not to use, is effectually to throw it away. If, therefore, you would indeed "make yourselves friends of the mammon of unrighteousness," add the Third rule to the two preceding. Having, First, gained all you can, and, Secondly saved all you can, then "give all you can."

In order to see the ground and reason of this, consider, when the Possessor of heaven and earth brought you into being, and placed you in this world, he placed you here not as a proprietor, but a steward: As such he entrusted you, for a season, with goods of various kinds; but the sole property of these still rests in him, nor can be alienated from him. As you yourself are not your own, but his, such is, likewise, all that you enjoy. Such is your soul and your body, not your own, but God's. And so is your substance in particular. And he has told you, in the most clear and express terms, how you are to employ it for him, in such a manner, that it may be all an holy sacrifice, acceptable through Christ Jesus. And this light, easy service, he has promised to reward with an eternal weight of glory.

The directions which God has given us, touching the use of our worldly substance, may be comprised in the following particulars. If you desire to be a faithful and a wise steward, out of that portion of your Lord's goods which he has for the present lodged in your hands, but with the right of resuming whenever it pleases him, First, provide things needful for yourself; food to eat, raiment to put on, whatever nature moderately requires for preserving the body in health and strength. Secondly, provide these for your wife, your children, your servants, or any others who pertain to your household. If when this is done there be an overplus left, then "do good to them that are of the household of faith." If there be an overplus still, "as you have opportunity, do good unto all men." In so doing, you give all you can; nay, in a sound sense, all you have: For all that is laid out in this manner is really given to God. You "render unto God the things that are God's," not only by what you give to the poor, but also by that which you expend in providing things needful for yourself and your household.

If, then, a doubt should at any time arise in your mind concerning what you are going to expend, either on yourself or any part of your family, you have an easy way to remove it. Calmly and seriously inquire,

(1) In expending this, am I acting according to my character? Am I acting herein, not as a proprietor, but as a steward of my Lord's goods?
(2) Am I doing this in obedience to his Word? In what Scripture does he require me so to do?
(3) Can I offer up this action, this expense, as a sacrifice to God through Jesus Christ?
(4) Have I reason to believe that for this very work I shall have a reward at the resurrection of the just?

You will seldom need anything more to remove any doubt which arises on this head; but by this four-fold consideration you will receive clear light as to the way wherein you should go.

If any doubt still remain, you may farther examine yourself by prayer according to those heads of inquiry. Try whether you can say to the Searcher of hearts, your conscience not condemning you,

"Lord, thou seest I am going to expend this sum on that food, apparel, furniture. And thou knowest, I act herein with a single eye as a steward of thy goods, expending this portion of them thus in pursuance of the design thou hadst in entrusting me with them. Thou knowest I do this in obedience to the Lord, as thou commandest, and because thou commandest it. Let this, I beseech thee, be an holy sacrifice, acceptable through Jesus Christ! And give me a witness in myself that for this labour of love I shall have a recompense when thou rewardest every man according to his works."

Now if your conscience bear you witness in the Holy Ghost that this prayer is well-pleasing to God, then have you no reason to doubt but that expense is right and good, and such as will never make you ashamed.

You see then what it is to "make yourselves friends of the mammon of unrighteousness," and by what means you may procure, "that when ye fail they may receive you into the everlasting habitations." You see the nature and extent of truly Christian prudence so far as it relates to the use of that great talent, money. Gain all you can, without hurting either yourself or your neighbour, in soul or body, by applying hereto with unintermitted diligence, and with all the understanding which God has given you;—save all you can, by cutting off every expense which serves only to indulge foolish desire; to gratify either the desire of flesh, the desire of the eye, or the pride of life; waste nothing, living or dying, on sin or folly, whether for yourself or your children;—and then, give all you can, or, in other words, give all you have to God. Do not stint yourself, like a Jew rather than a Christian, to this or that proportion. "Render unto God," not a tenth, not a third, not half, but all that is God's, be it more or less; by employing all on yourself, your household, the household of faith, and all mankind, in such a manner, that you may give a good account of your stewardship when ye can be no longer stewards; in such a manner as the oracles of God direct, both by general and particular precepts; in such a manner, that whatever ye do may be "a sacrifice of a sweet-smelling savour to God," and that every act may be rewarded in that day when the Lord cometh with all his saints.

Brethren, can we be either wise or faithful stewards unless we thus manage our Lord's goods? We cannot, as not only the oracles of God, but our own conscience beareth witness. Then why should we delay? Why should we confer any longer with flesh and blood, or men of the world? Our kingdom, our wisdom is not of this world: Heathen custom is nothing to us. We follow no men any farther than they are followers of Christ. Hear ye him. Yea, to-day, while it is called to-day, hear and obey his voice! At this hour, and from this hour, do his will: Fulfil his word, in this and in all things! I entreat you, in the name of the Lord Jesus, act up to the dignity of your calling! No more sloth! Whatsoever your hand findeth to do, do it with your might! No more waste! Cut off every expense which fashion, caprice, or flesh and blood demand! No more covetousness! But employ whatever God has entrusted you with, in doing good, all possible good, in every possible kind and degree to the household of faith, to all men! This is no small part of "the wisdom of the just." Give all ye have, as well as all ye are, a spiritual sacrifice to Him who withheld not from you his Son, his only Son: So "laying up in store for yourselves a good foundation against the time to come, that ye may attain eternal life!"

The Sermons of John Wesley, 1872 edition, Sermon 50, on Luke 16:9.

MARK 12:41–44

The Widow's Offering

WILLIAM PLUMMER

"Saving Grace: A Washerwoman Donates $150,000 to Give Students a Chance She Never Had"

In this biblical account, here paired with a recent story, Jesus' praise goes to a poor widow, who gives but a farthing to the treasury, over those who donate far more, for she gave "of her want," not plenty, "even all her living." Osceola McCarty, a Mississippi washerwoman, also gave away her "living"—her lifelong savings—but to a local university, and thus serves as a contemporary example of the widow. Not from Jesus but from the national press (and President Clinton) did she receive praise, and her offering has been referred to as the gift. *Clearly, we do not regard all philanthropic giving as equal. Clearly, the widows and the Osceola McCartys among us are regarded as leaders of the pack. Why? What matters most in philanthropic leadership? Motive? Means? Disposition? Something else?*

The Widow's Offering

41 And Jesus sat over against the treasury, and beheld how the people cast money into the treasury: and many that were rich cast in much.

42 And there came a certain poor widow, and she threw in two mites, which make a farthing.

43 And he called *unto him* his disciples, and saith unto them, Verily I say unto you, That this poor widow hath cast more in, than all they which have cast into the treasury:

44 for all *they* did cast in of their abundance; but she of her want did cast in all that she had, *even* all her living.

"Saving Grace: A Washerwoman Donates $150,000 to Give Students a Chance She Never Had"

For most of her 87 years, Osceola McCarty of Hattiesburg, Mississippi, took in the wash of the local gentry—and did it by hand. McCarty, who tried a washer and dryer but found them woefully inadequate, scrubbed her clothes on a washboard in the backyard of the wood-frame house she once shared with her mother and grandmother. She boiled the whites in a big black pot and hung them on the line to dry and sparkle. The bankers and doctors and lawyers of Hattiesburg (population 45,000) considered McCarty a treasure.

What they did not know was that McCarty, who retired in December, was quietly amassing her own treasure. In fact nobody would ever have known, except that last month the University of Southern Mississippi (USM) in Hattiesburg announced that the tiny washerwoman was leaving some $150,000 to finance scholarships for the area's African-American students. "I want them to have an education," says McCarty, who never married and has no children of her own. "I had to work hard all my life. They can have the chance that I didn't have."

McCarty lost her chance in the sixth grade when an unwed aunt came out of the hospital unable to walk. McCarty left school to care for her; she also helped her mother and grandmother with their backyard laundry business. "Even when I was little," says McCarty, "I was always getting into the wash, till my mama got a switch." By the time her aunt got back on her feet a year later, McCarty thought she was too far behind to return to school. "I was too big," she says. "So I kept on working."

Most of McCarty's days followed a simple routine. She got up with the sun, started the washing and ironing and stopped when the sun went down. "She had a bench in the backyard with three tubs on it," says Helen Tyre, 89, who hired McCarty back in 1943. "She and her mother and grandmother carried the water from a hydrant." Tyre remembers a time when McCarty charged just 50 cents a bundle (a week's worth of laundry for a family of four). Eventually her fee climbed to $10 a bundle, still not all that much. McCarty's needs are few. She does not have a car. She has one TV that works and an air conditioner that she rarely turns on. Mostly, she reads her Bible.

McCarty thought for years about leaving money to the local university. But it was only this past June, shortly after arthritis forced her to stop taking in wash, that she reached out to the school. "Frankly, I didn't believe it at first," says Bill Pace, executive director of the USM Foundation, which handles the school's donations. "I was amazed that someone who made their money that way could save that much and then would give it away."

Though the scholarships were not supposed to go into effect until after McCarty's death, Pace and other USM officials wanted her to see one of her beneficiaries graduate. So they awarded the first Osceola McCarty Scholarship of $1,000 (tuition is $2,400 a year) to Stephanie Bullock, 18, whose mother teaches school in Hattiesburg and whose father supervises a water-treatment plant. Stephanie has a twin brother, Stephen, and the Bullocks were worried about sending both kids to school. "When we heard about the scholarship," says Stephanie, "my mama was smiling from ear to ear."

Word of McCarty's gift has, in fact, caused a good many people to smile— and open their pocketbooks. Local businesspeople have pledged to match

McCarty's $150,000 contribution, and checks are coming in from all over. Mc-Carty, meanwhile, is a bit bewildered by the fuss—and by the question she hears over and over: Why didn't you spend the money on yourself? "I am spending it on myself," she answers with the sweetest of smiles.

From *The Holy Bible,* King James Version (New York: American Bible Co.).

ABRAHAM LINCOLN

Second Inaugural Address

*Our sixteenth president, Abraham Lincoln (1809–1865), widely held to be Amer-
ica's greatest political leader, may be regarded as well as America's quintessential philanthropic leader. He summoned us not only to dedicate ourselves to
freedom and equality (as, for example, in the Gettysburg Address). Here, in his
Second Inaugural, the wounds of war still wide open, Lincoln calls upon the citizens of the Union also to treat their defeated brethren "with malice toward none,
with charity for all." He thereby summons us to actively practice charity, understood not only as helping those in need, but even more broadly, as showing lov-
ingkindness towards all human beings, including our enemies. In this summons,
Lincoln evokes, too, another more expansive notion of equality—the equality of
all human beings as stained by original sin. Lincoln accepted the brutal war that
came and valiantly led us through it, firmly believing that the war was a test of
whether our nation, or any nation conceived in liberty and dedicated to equality, can long endure. But now, in 1865, with the end of the war in sight, he looked
to bind up the wounds, suggesting that the test of our nation's mettle would hereafter be charity. Can Lincoln's leadership, as evidenced in this speech, still bring
light to our nation in our own troubled and violent times? Does it carry any lessons for philanthropy and philanthropic leadership?*

March 4, 1865
Fellow Countrymen:

At this second appearing to take the oath of the Presidential office there is
less occasion for an extended address than there was at the first. Then a statement somewhat in detail of a course to be pursued seemed fitting and proper.
Now, at the expiration of four years, during which public declarations have
been constantly called forth on every point and phase of the great contest
which still absorbs the attention and engrosses the energies of the nation, little
that is new could be presented. The progress of our arms, upon which all else
chiefly depends, is as well known to the public as to myself, and it is, I trust,
reasonably satisfactory and encouraging to all. With high hope for the future,
no prediction in regard to it is ventured.

On the occasion corresponding to this four years ago all thoughts were
anxiously directed to an impending civil war. All dreaded it, all sought to avert
it. While the inaugural address was being delivered from this place, devoted
altogether to *saving* the Union without war, urgent agents were in the city

seeking to *destroy* it without war—seeking to dissolve the Union and divide effects by negotiation. Both parties deprecated war, but one of them would *make* war rather than let the nation survive, and the other would *accept* war rather than let it perish, and the war came.

One-eighth of the whole population were colored slaves, not distributed generally over the Union, but localized in the southern part of it. These slaves constituted a peculiar and powerful interest. All knew that this interest was somehow the cause of the war. To strengthen, perpetuate, and extend this interest was the object for which the insurgents would rend the Union even by war, while the Government claimed no right to do more than to restrict the territorial enlargement of it. Neither party expected for the war the magnitude or the duration which it has already attained. Neither anticipated that the *cause* of the conflict might cease with or even before the conflict itself should cease. Each looked for an easier triumph, and a result less fundamental and astounding. Both read the same Bible and pray to the same God, and each invokes His aid against the other. It may seem strange that any men should dare to ask a just God's assistance in wringing their bread from the sweat of other men's faces, but let us judge not, that we be not judged. The prayers of both could not be answered. That of neither has been answered fully. The Almighty has His own purposes. "Woe unto the world because of offenses; for it must needs be that offenses.come, but woe to that man by whom the offense cometh." If we shall suppose that American slavery is one of those offenses which, in the providence of God, must needs come, but which, having continued through His appointed time, He now wills to remove, and that He gives to both North and South this terrible war as the woe due to those by whom the offense came, shall we discern therein any departure from those divine attributes which the believers in a living God always ascribe to Him? Fondly do we hope, fervently do we pray, that this mighty scourge of war may speedily pass away. Yet, if God wills that it continue until all the wealth piled by the bondsman's two hundred and fifty years of unrequited toil shall be sunk, and until every drop of blood drawn with the lash shall be paid by another drawn with the sword, as was said three thousand years ago, so still it must be said "the judgments of the Lord are true and righteous altogether."

With malice toward none, with charity for all, with firmness in the right as God gives us to see the right, let us strive on to finish the work we are in, to bind up the nation's wounds, to care for him who shall have borne the battle and for his widow and his orphan, to do all which may achieve and cherish a just and lasting peace among ourselves and with all nations.

The text can be found in *The Collected Works of Abraham Lincoln,* edited by Roy P. Basler (New Brunswick, N.J.: Rutgers University Press, 1953), vol. 8, pp. 332–333.

MARTIN LUTHER KING Jr.

"I've Been to the Mountaintop"

Dr. Martin Luther King Jr. (1929–1968), leader of the modern civil rights move-
ment, traveled to Memphis in the spring of 1968 to support the 1,300 striking
sanitation workers protesting low wages and unfit working conditions. On the
night of April 3, he gave this sermon to a crowd gathered in the Bishop Charles
Mason Temple Church of God. He was assassinated the next day.

King frames this address with an account of his own leadership, beginning
with the assertion that he would choose no other time in which to live or lead,
and ending with the affirmation that he has "seen the promised land." Envious
of neither past nor future, he was consummately the right man at the right
time—a visionary in step with his own generation. Philanthropic leader par ex-
cellence, King counsels, as well as models, how to be a better brother to our
fellow men. Near the end of his speech, he solicits his listeners to "develop a dan-
gerous kind of unselfishness." Applying the parable of the Good Samaritan to
contemporary circumstances, he states: "The question is not, 'If I stop to help this
man in need, what will happen to me?'" Rather, it is this: "If I do not stop to help
the sanitation workers, what will happen to them?" Like the king of Tolstoy's
"Three Questions" (see selection in chapter 4), King invites all of us to under-
stand ourselves as the "right" person in the "right time": for the right time is now,
and the right thing is to help the man in need. Is King's model imitable? Is King's
question the question of philanthropy?

April 3, 1968

Thank you very kindly, my friends. As I listened to Ralph Abernathy in his eloquent and generous introduction and then thought about myself, I wondered
who he was talking about. It's always good to have your closest friend and associate say something good about you. And Ralph is the best friend that I have
in the world.

I'm delighted to see each of you here tonight in spite of a storm warning.
You reveal that you are determined to go on anyhow. Something is happening
in Memphis; something is happening in our world.

As you know, if I were standing at the beginning of time, with the possibility of general and panoramic view of the whole human history up to now,
and the Almighty said to me, "Martin Luther King, which age would you like
to live in?"—I would take my mental flight by Egypt through, or rather across
the Red Sea, through the wilderness on toward the promised land. And in spite

of its magnificence, I wouldn't stop there. I would move on by Greece, and take my mind to Mount Olympus. And I would see Plato, Aristotle, Socrates, Euripides and Aristophanes assembled around the Parthenon as they discussed the great and eternal issues of reality.

But I wouldn't stop there. I would go on, even to the great heyday of the Roman Empire. And I would see developments around there, through various emperors and leaders. But I wouldn't stop there. I would even come up to the day of the Renaissance, and get a quick picture of all that the Renaissance did for the cultural and aesthetic life of man. But I wouldn't stop there. I would even go by the way that the man for whom I'm named had his habitat. And I would watch Martin Luther as he tacked his ninety-five theses on the door at the church in Wittenberg.

But I wouldn't stop there. I would come on up even to 1863, and watch a vacillating president by the name of Abraham Lincoln finally come to the conclusion that he had to sign the Emancipation Proclamation. But I wouldn't stop there. I would even come up to the early thirties, and see a man grappling with the problems of the bankruptcy of his nation. And come with an eloquent cry that we have nothing to fear but fear itself.

But I wouldn't stop there. Strangely enough, I would turn to the Almighty, and say, "If you allow me to live just a few years in the second half of the 20th century, I will be happy." Now that's a strange statement to make, because the world is all messed up. The nation is sick. Trouble is in the land. Confusion all around. That's a strange statement. But I know, somehow, that only when it is dark enough can you see the stars. And I see God working in this period of the twentieth century in a way that men, in some strange way, are responding—something is happening in our world. The masses of people are rising up. And wherever they are assembled today, whether they are in Johannesburg, South Africa; Nairobi, Kenya; Accra, Ghana; New York City; Atlanta, Georgia; Jackson, Mississippi; or Memphis, Tennessee—the cry is always the same—"We want to be free."

And another reason that I'm happy to live in this period is that we have been forced to a point where we're going to have to grapple with the problems that men have been trying to grapple with through history, but the demands didn't force them to do it. Survival demands that we grapple with them. Men, for years now, have been talking about war and peace. But now, no longer can they just talk about it. It is no longer a choice between violence and nonviolence in this world; it's nonviolence or nonexistence.

That is where we are today. And also in the human rights revolution, if something isn't done, and in a hurry, to bring the colored peoples of the world out of their long years of poverty, their long years of hurt and neglect, the whole world is doomed. Now, I'm just happy that God has allowed me to live in this period, to see what is unfolding. And I'm happy that He's allowed me to be in Memphis.

I can remember, I can remember when Negroes were just going around as Ralph has said, so often, scratching where they didn't itch, and laughing when they were not tickled. But that day is all over. We mean business now, and we are determined to gain our rightful place in God's world.

And that's all this whole thing is about. We aren't engaged in any negative protest and in any negative arguments with anybody. We are saying that we are determined to be men. We are determined to be people. We are saying that we are God's children. And that we don't have to live like we are forced to live.

Now, what does all of this mean in this great period of history? It means that we've got to stay together. We've got to stay together and maintain unity. You know, whenever Pharaoh wanted to prolong the period of slavery in Egypt, he had a favorite, favorite formula for doing it. What was that? He kept the slaves fighting among themselves. But whenever the slaves get together, something happens in Pharaoh's court, and he cannot hold the slaves in slavery. When the slaves get together, that's the beginning of getting out of slavery. Now let us maintain unity.

Secondly, let us keep the issues where they are. The issue is injustice. The issue is the refusal of Memphis to be fair and honest in its dealings with its public servants who happen to be sanitation workers. Now, we've got to keep attention on that. That's always the problem with a little violence. You know what happened the other day, and the press dealt only with the window-breaking. I read the articles. They very seldom got around to mentioning the fact that one thousand, three hundred sanitation workers were on strike, and that Memphis is not being fair to them, and that Mayor Loeb is in dire need of a doctor. They didn't get around to that.

Now we're going to march again, and we've got to march again, in order to put the issue where it is supposed to be. And force everybody to see that there are thirteen hundred of God's children here suffering, sometimes going hungry, going through dark and dreary nights wondering how this thing is going to come out. That's the issue. And we've got to say to the nation: we know it's coming out. For when people get caught up with that which is right and they are willing to sacrifice for it, there is no stopping point short of victory.

We aren't going to let any mace stop us. We are masters in our nonviolent movement in disarming police forces; they don't know what to do. I've seen them so often. I remember in Birmingham, Alabama, when we were in that majestic struggle there, we would move out of the 16th Street Baptist Church day after day; by the hundreds we would move out. And Bull Connor[1] would tell them to send the dogs forth and they did come; but we just went before the dogs singing, "Ain't gonna let nobody turn me around." Bull Connor next would say, "Turn the fire hoses on." And as I said to you the other night, Bull Connor didn't know history.

---

1. Theophilus Eugene "Bull" Connor (1897–1973), a police official and a member of the Ku Klux Klan in Alabama, actively opposed the American civil rights movement.—Ed.

He knew a kind of physics that somehow didn't relate to the transphysics that we knew about. And that was the fact that there was a certain kind of fire that no water could put out. And we went before the fire hoses; we had known water. If we were Baptist or some other denomination, we had been immersed. If we were Methodist, and some others, we had been sprinkled, but we knew water.

That couldn't stop us. And we just went on before the dogs and we would look at them; and we'd go on before the water hoses and we would look at it, and we'd just go on singing, "Over my head I see freedom in the air." And then we would be thrown in the paddy wagons, and sometimes we were stacked in there like sardines in a can. And they would throw us in, and old Bull would say, "Take them off," and they did; and we would just go in the paddy wagon singing, "We Shall Overcome." And every now and then we'd get in the jail, and we'd see the jailers looking through the windows being moved by our prayers, and being moved by our words and our songs. And there was a power there which Bull Connor couldn't adjust to; and so we ended up transforming Bull into a steer, and we won our struggle in Birmingham.

Now we've got to go on to Memphis just like that. I call upon you to be with us Monday. Now about injunctions: We have an injunction and we're going into court tomorrow morning to fight this illegal, unconstitutional injunction. All we say to America is, "Be true to what you said on paper." If I lived in China or even Russia, or any totalitarian country, maybe I could understand the denial of certain basic First Amendment privileges, because they hadn't committed themselves to that over there. But somewhere I read of the freedom of assembly. Somewhere I read of the freedom of speech. Somewhere I read of the freedom of the press. Somewhere I read that the greatness of America is the right to protest for right. And so just as I say we aren't going to let any injunction turn us around. We are going on.

We need all of you. And you know what's beautiful to me, is to see all of these ministers of the Gospel. It's a marvelous picture. Who is it that is supposed to articulate the longings and aspirations of the people more than the preacher? Somehow the preacher must be an Amos, and say, "Let justice roll down like waters and righteousness like a mighty stream." Somehow, the preacher must say with Jesus, "The spirit of the Lord is upon me, because he hath anointed me to deal with the problems of the poor."

And I want to commend the preachers, under the leadership of these noble men: James Lawson, one who has been in this struggle for many years; he's been to jail for struggling; but he's still going on, fighting for the rights of his people. Rev. Ralph Jackson, Billy Kiles; I could just go right on down the list, but time will not permit. But I want to thank them all. And I want you to thank them, because so often, preachers aren't concerned about anything but themselves. And I'm always happy to see a relevant ministry.

It's alright to talk about "long white robes over yonder," in all of its symbolism. But ultimately people want some suits and dresses and shoes to wear down here. It's all right to talk about "streets flowing with milk and honey," but God has commanded us to be concerned about the slums down here, and his children who can't eat three square meals a day. It's all right to talk about the new Jerusalem, but one day, God's preacher must talk about the new New York, the new Atlanta, the new Philadelphia, the new Los Angeles, the new Memphis, Tennessee. This is what we have to do.

Now the other thing we'll have to do is this: Always anchor our external direct action with the power of economic withdrawal. Now, we are poor people, individually, we are poor when you compare us with white society in America. We are poor. Never stop and forget that collectively, that means all of us together, collectively we are richer than all the nations in the world, with the exception of nine. Did you ever think about that? After you leave the United States, Soviet Russia, Great Britain, West Germany, France, and I could name the others, the Negro collectively is richer than most nations of the world. We have an annual income of more than thirty billion dollars a year, which is more than all of the exports of the United States, and more than the national budget of Canada. Did you know that? That's power right there, if we know how to pool it.

We don't have to argue with anybody. We don't have to curse and go around acting bad with our words. We don't need any bricks and bottles, we don't need any Molotov cocktails, we just need to go around to these stores, and to these massive industries in our country, and say, "God sent us by here, to say to you that you're not treating his children right. And we've come by here to ask you to make the first item on your agenda—fair treatment, where God's children are concerned. Now, if you are not prepared to do that, we do have an agenda that we must follow. And our agenda calls for withdrawing economic support from you."

And so, as a result of this, we are asking you tonight, to go out and tell your neighbors not to buy Coca-Cola in Memphis. Go by and tell them not to buy Sealtest milk. Tell them not to buy—what is the other bread?—Wonder Bread. And what is the other bread company, Jesse? Tell them not to buy Hart's bread. As Jesse Jackson has said, up to now, only the garbage men have been feeling pain; now we must kind of redistribute the pain. We are choosing these companies because they haven't been fair in their hiring policies; and we are choosing them because they can begin the process of saying, they are going to support the needs and the rights of these men who are on strike. And then they can move on downtown and tell Mayor Loeb to do what is right.

But not only that, we've got to strengthen black institutions. I call upon you to take your money out of the banks downtown and deposit your money in Tri-State Bank—we want a "bank-in" movement in Memphis. So go by the savings and loan association. I'm not asking you something that we don't do ourselves at SCLC. Judge Hooks and others will tell you that we have an account here in the savings and loan association from the Southern Christian Leadership Conference. We're just telling you to follow what we're doing. Put your money there. You have six or seven black insurance companies in Memphis. Take out your insurance there. We want to have an "insurance-in."

Now these are some practical things we can do. We begin the process of building a greater economic base. And at the same time, we are putting pressure where it really hurts. I ask you to follow through here.

Now, let me say as I move to my conclusion that we've got to give ourselves to this struggle until the end. Nothing would be more tragic than to stop at this point, in Memphis. We've got to see it through. And when we have our march, you need to be there. Be concerned about your brother. You may not be on strike. But either we go up together, or we go down together.

Let us develop a kind of dangerous unselfishness. One day a man came to Jesus; and he wanted to raise some questions about some vital matters in life. At points, he wanted to trick Jesus, and show him that he knew a little more than Jesus knew, and through this, throw him off base. Now that question could have easily ended up in a philosophical and theological debate. But Jesus immediately pulled that question from mid-air, and placed it on a dangerous curve between Jerusalem and Jericho. And he talked about a certain man, who fell among thieves. You remember that a Levite and a priest passed by on the other side. They didn't stop to help him. And finally a man of another race came by. He got down from his beast, decided not to be compassionate by proxy. But with him, administered first aid, and helped the man in need. Jesus ended up saying, this was the good man, this was the great man, because he had the capacity to project the "I" into the "thou," and to be concerned about his brother. Now you know, we use our imagination a great deal to try to determine why the priest and the Levite didn't stop. At times we say they were busy going to a church meeting—an ecclesiastical gathering—and they had to get on down to Jerusalem so they wouldn't be late for their meeting. At other times we would speculate that there was a religious law that "One who was engaged in religious ceremonials was not to touch a human body twenty-four hours before the ceremony." And every now and then we begin to wonder whether maybe they were not going down to Jerusalem, or down to Jericho, rather to organize a "Jericho Road Improvement Association." That's a possibility. Maybe they felt that it was better to deal with the problem from the causal root, rather than to get bogged down with an individual effort.

But I'm going to tell you what my imagination tells me. It's possible that these men were afraid. You see, the Jericho road is a dangerous road. I remember when Mrs. King and I were first in Jerusalem. We rented a car and drove from Jerusalem down to Jericho. And as soon as we got on that road, I said to my wife, "I can see why Jesus used this as a setting for his parable." It's a winding, meandering road. It's really conducive for ambushing. You start out in Jerusalem, which is about 1,200 miles, or rather 1,200 feet, above sea level. And by the time you get down to Jericho, fifteen or twenty minutes later, you're about 2,200 feet below sea level. That's a dangerous road. In the days of Jesus it came to be known as the "Bloody Pass." And you know, it's possible that the priest and the Levite looked over that man on the ground and wondered if the robbers were still around. Or it's possible that they felt that the man on the ground was merely faking. And he was acting like he had been robbed and hurt, in order to seize them over there, lure them there for quick and easy seizure. And so the first question that the Levite asked was, "If I stop to help this man, what will happen to me?" But then the Good Samaritan came by. And he reversed the question: "If I do not stop to help this man, what will happen to him?"

That's the question before you tonight. Not, "If I stop to help the sanitation workers, what will happen to all of the hours that I usually spend in my office every day and every week as a pastor?" The question is not, "If I stop to help this man in need, what will happen to me?" "If I do not stop to help the sanitation workers, what will happen to them?" That's the question.

Let us rise up tonight with a greater readiness. Let us stand with a greater determination. And let us move on in these powerful days, these days of challenge to make America what it ought to be. We have an opportunity to make America a better nation. And I want to thank God, once more, for allowing me to be here with you.

You know, several years ago, I was in New York City autographing the first book that I had written. And while sitting there autographing books, a demented black woman came up. The only question I heard from her was, "Are you Martin Luther King?"

And I was looking down writing, and I said yes. And the next minute I felt something beating on my chest. Before I knew it I had been stabbed by this demented woman. I was rushed to Harlem Hospital. It was a dark Saturday afternoon. And that blade had gone through, and the X-rays revealed that the tip of the blade was on the edge of my aorta, the main artery. And once that's punctured, you drown in your own blood—that's the end of you.

It came out in the *New York Times* the next morning, that if I had sneezed, I would have died. Well, about four days later, they allowed me, after the operation, after my chest had been opened, and the blade had been taken out, to move around in the wheelchair in the hospital. They allowed me to read some of the mail that came in, and from all over the states, and the world, kind letters came in. I read a few, but one of them I will never forget. I had received one from the President and the Vice-President. I've forgotten what those telegrams said. I'd received a visit and a letter from the Governor of New York, but I've forgotten what the letter said. But there was another letter that came from a little girl, a young girl who was a student at the White Plains High School. And I looked at that letter, and I'll never forget it. It said simply, "Dear Dr. King: I am a ninth-grade student at the White Plains High School." She said, "While it should not matter, I would like to mention that I am a white girl. I read in the paper of your misfortune, and of your suffering. And I read that if you had sneezed, you would have died. And I'm simply writing you to say that I'm so happy that you didn't sneeze."

And I want to say tonight, I want to say that I too am happy that I didn't sneeze. Because if I had sneezed, I wouldn't have been around here in 1960, when students all over the South started sitting-in at lunch counters. And I knew that as they were sitting in, they were really standing up for the best in the American dream. And taking the whole nation back to those great wells of democracy which were dug deep by the Founding Fathers in the Declaration of Independence and the Constitution. If I had sneezed, I wouldn't have been around here in 1962, when Negroes in Albany, Georgia, decided to straighten their backs up. And whenever men and women straighten their backs up, they are going somewhere, because a man can't ride your back unless it is bent. If I had sneezed, I wouldn't have been here in 1963, when the black people of Birmingham, Alabama, aroused the conscience of this nation, and brought into being the Civil Rights Bill. If I had sneezed, I wouldn't have had a chance later that year, in August, to try to tell America about a dream that I had had. If I had sneezed, I wouldn't have been down in Selma, Alabama, to see the great movement there. If I had sneezed, I wouldn't have been in Memphis to see the community rally around those brothers and sisters who are suffering. I'm so happy that I didn't sneeze.

And they were telling me, now it doesn't matter now. It really doesn't matter what happens now. I left Atlanta this morning, and as we got started on the plane, there were six of us, the pilot said over the public address system, "We are sorry for the delay, but we have Dr. Martin Luther King on the plane. And to be sure that all of the bags were checked, and to be sure that nothing would be wrong with the plane, we had to check out everything carefully. And we've had the plane protected and guarded all night."

And then I got into Memphis. And some began to say the threats, or talk about the threats that were out. What would happen to me from some of our sick white brothers?

Well, I don't know what will happen now. We've got some difficult days ahead. But it doesn't matter with me now. Because I've been to the mountaintop. And I don't mind. Like anybody, I would like to live a long life. Longevity has its place. But I'm not concerned about that now. I just want to do God's will. And He's allowed me to go up to the mountain. And I've looked over. And I've seen the promised land. I may not get there with you. But I want you to know tonight, that we, as a people, will get to the promised land. And I'm happy, tonight. I'm not worried about anything. I'm not fearing any man. Mine eyes have seen the glory of the coming of the Lord.

JANE ADDAMS

"A Modern Lear"

Renowned American social reformer and political activist Jane Addams (1860–1935) here focuses on the bloody 1894 Pullman Strike, a major social upheaval at the time. Looking to understand the "deep human motives, which, after all," she says, "determine events," she turns to The Tragedy of King Lear *for help and illumination. The reasons the striking workers broke with their one-time beloved benefactor and philanthropic employer, George Pullman, were similar, she argues, to those responsible for Cordelia's break with her one-time too-loving father, King Lear. Pullman, then, is for her "a modern Lear." Addams readily acknowledges the "lavish goodness and generosity" that Pullman showed his employees, as well as the "extraordinary benefits" the old king heaped upon his daughter. But she faults both for being overly paternalistic, so absorbed in carrying out their personal plans of improvement that they failed to notice the blossoming moral impulses, the independent growth, the many desires, new concerns, and common experiences of the very people they intended to help. The virtues of these two leaders were inseparable from their vices, hence, the source of their respective tragedies. Modern philanthropists, beware, Addams concludes: "So long as [you] are 'good to people,' rather than 'with them,' [you] are bound to accomplish a large amount of harm." Keep before you, she advises, "the old definition of greatness: that it consists in the possession of the largest share of the common human qualities and experiences." Does Addams correctly understand the "deep human motives" that cause beneficiaries to become resentful? Is the analogy of rebellious children apt? Does she, tacitly or explicitly, point to principles that could inform better, stronger, and more just philanthropic leadership?*

ℱ𝒶

Those of us who lived in Chicago during the summer of 1894 were confronted by a drama which epitomized and, at the same time, challenged the code of social ethics under which we live, for a quick series of unusual events had dispelled the good nature which in happier times envelops the ugliness of the industrial situation. It sometimes seems as if the shocking experiences of that summer, the barbaric instinct to kill, roused on both sides, the sharp division into class lines, with the resultant distrust and bitterness, can only be endured if we learn from it all a great ethical lesson. To endure is all we can hope for. It is impossible to justify such a course of rage and riot in a civilized community to whom the methods of conciliation and control were open. Every public-spirited citizen in Chicago during that summer felt the stress and perplexity of the situation and asked himself, "How far am I responsible for this social disorder? What can be done to prevent such outrageous manifestations of ill-will?"

If the responsibility of tolerance lies with those of the widest vision, it behooves us to consider this great social disaster, not alone in its legal aspect nor in its sociological bearings, but from those deep human motives, which, after all, determine events.

During the discussions which followed the Pullman strike, the defenders of the situation were broadly divided between the people pleading for individual benevolence and those insisting upon social righteousness; between those who held that the philanthropy of the president of the Pullman company had been most ungratefully received and those who maintained that the situation was the inevitable outcome of the social consciousness developing among working people.

In the midst of these discussions the writer found her mind dwelling upon a comparison which modified and softened all her judgments. Her attention was caught by the similarity of ingratitude suffered by an indulgent employer and an indulgent parent. King Lear came often to her mind. We have all shared the family relationship and our code of ethics concerning it is somewhat settled. We also bear a part in the industrial relationship, but our ethics concerning that are still uncertain. A comparative study of these two relationships presents an advantage, in that it enables us to consider the situation from the known experience toward the unknown. The minds of all of us reach back to our early struggles, as we emerged from the state of self-willed childhood to recognition of the family claim.

We have all had glimpses of what it might be to blaspheme against family ties; to ignore the elemental claim they make upon us, but on the whole we have recognized them, and it does not occur to us to throw them over. The industrial claim is so difficult; the ties are so intangible that we are constantly ignoring them and shirking the duties which they impose. It will probably be easier to treat the tragedy of the Pullman strike as if it were already long past when we compare it to the family tragedy of Lear which has already become historic to our minds and which we discuss without personal feeling.

Historically considered, the relation of Lear to his children was archaic and barbaric, holding in it merely the beginnings of a family life, since developed. We may in later years learn to look back upon the industrial relationships in which we are now placed as quite as incomprehensible and selfish, quite as barbaric and undeveloped, as was the family relationship between Lear and his daughters. We may then take the relationship of this unusually generous employer at Pullman to his own town full of employees as at least a fair one, because so exceptionally liberal in many of its aspects. King Lear doubtless held the same notion of a father's duty that was held by the other fathers of his time; but he alone was a king and had kingdoms to bestow upon his children. He was unique, therefore, in the magnitude of his indulgence, and in the magnitude of the disaster which followed it. The sense of duty held by the president of the Pullman company doubtless represents the ideal in the minds of the best of the present employers as to their obligations toward their employees, but he projected this ideal more magnificently than the others. He alone gave his men so model a town, such perfect surroundings. The magnitude of his indulgence and failure corresponded and we are forced to challenge the ideal itself: the same ideal which, more or less clearly defined, is floating in the minds of all philanthropic employers.

This older tragedy implied maladjustment between individuals; the forces of the tragedy were personal and passionate. This modern tragedy in its inception is a maladjustment between two large bodies of men, an employing company and a mass of employees. It deals not with personal relationships, but with industrial relationships.

Owing, however, to the unusual part played in it by the will of one man, we find that it closely approaches Lear in motif. The relation of the British King to his family is very like the relation of the president of the Pullman Company to his town; the denouement of a daughter's break with her father suggests the break of the employees with their benefactor. If we call one an example of the domestic tragedy, the other of the industrial tragedy, it is possible to make them illuminate each other.

It is easy to discover striking points of similarity in the tragedies of the royal father and the philanthropic president of the Pullman Company. The like quality of ingratitude they both suffered is at once apparent. It may be said that the ingratitude which Lear received was poignant and bitter to him in proportion as he recalled the extraordinary benefits he had heaped upon his daughters, and that he found his fate harder to bear because he had so far exceeded the measure of a father's duty, as he himself says. What, then, would be the bitterness of a man who had heaped extraordinary benefits upon those toward whom he had no duty recognized by common consent; who had not only exceeded the righteousness of the employer, but who had worked out original and striking methods for lavishing goodness and generosity? More than that, the president has been almost persecuted for this goodness by the more utilitarian members of his company and had at one time imperiled his business reputation for the sake of the benefactions to his town, and he had thus reached the height of sacrifice for it. This model town embodied not only his hopes and ambitions, but stood for the peculiar effort which a man makes for that which is misunderstood.

It is easy to see that although the heart of Lear was cut by ingratitude and by misfortune, it was cut deepest of all by the public pity of his people, in that they should remember him no longer as a king and benefactor, but as a defeated man who has blundered through oversoftness. So the heart of the Chicago man was cut by the unparalleled publicity which brought him to the minds of thousands as a type of oppression and injustice, and to many others as an example of the evil of an irregulated sympathy for the "lower classes." He who had been dined and feted throughout Europe as the creator of a model town, as the friend and benefactor of workingmen, was now execrated by workingmen throughout the entire country. He had not only been good to those who were now basely ungrateful to him, but he felt himself deserted by the admiration of his people.

In shops such as those at Pullman, indeed, in all manufacturing affairs since the industrial revolution, industry is organized into a vast social operation. The shops are managed, however, not for the development of the workman thus socialized, but for the interests of the company owning the capital. The divergence between the social form and the individual aim becomes greater as the employees are more highly socialized and dependent, just as the clash in a family is more vital in proportion to the development and closeness of the family tie. The president of the Pullman Company went further than the usual employer does. He socialized not only the factory but the form in which his workmen were living. He built and, in a great measure, regulated an entire town. This again might have worked out into a successful associated effort, if he had had in view the sole good of the inhabitants thus socialized, if he had called upon them for self-expression and had made the town a growth and manifestation of their wants and needs. But, unfortunately, the end to be obtained became ultimately commercial and not social, having in view the payment to the company of at least 4 per cent on the money invested, so that with this rigid requirement there could be no adaptation of rent to wages, much less to needs. The rents became static and the wages competitive, shifting inevitably with the demands of trade. The president assumed that he himself knew the needs of his men, and so far from wishing them to express their needs he denied to them the simple rights of trade organization, which would have been, of course, the merest preliminary to an attempt at associated expression. If we may take the dictatorial relation of Lear to Cordelia as a typical and most dramatic example of the distinctively family tragedy, one will asserting its authority through all the entanglement of wounded affection, and insisting upon its selfish ends at all costs, may we not consider the absolute authority of this employer over his town as a typical and dramatic example of the industrial tragedy? One will directing the energies of many others, without regard to their desires, and having in view in the last analysis only commercial results?

It shocks our ideal of family life that a man should fail to know his daughter's heart because she awkwardly expressed her love, that he should refuse to comfort and advise her through all difference of opinion and clashing of will. That a man should be so absorbed in his own indignation as to fail to apprehend his child's thought; that he should lose his affection in his anger, is really no more unnatural than that the man who spent a million of dollars on a swamp to make it sanitary for his employees, should refuse to speak to them for ten minutes, whether they were in the right or wrong; or that a man who had given them his time and thought for twenty years should withdraw from them his guidance when he believed them misled by ill-advisors and wandering in a mental fog; or that he should grow hard and angry when they needed tenderness and help.

Lear ignored the common ancestry of Cordelia and himself. He forgot her royal inheritance of magnanimity, and also the power of obstinacy which he shared with her. So long had he thought of himself as the noble and indulgent father that he had lost the faculty by which he might perceive himself in the wrong. Even when his spirit was broken by the storm he declared himself more sinned against than sinning. He could believe any amount of kindness and goodness of himself, but could imagine no fidelity on the part of Cordelia unless she gave him the sign he demanded.

The president of the Pullman company doubtless began to build his town from an honest desire to give his employees the best surroundings. As it developed it became a source of pride and an exponent of power, that he cared most for when it gave him a glow of benevolence. Gradually, what the outside world thought of it became of importance to him and he ceased to measure its usefulness by the standard of the men's needs. The theater was complete in equipment and beautiful in design, but too costly for a troupe who depended upon the patronage of mechanics, as the church was too expensive to be rented continuously. We can imagine the founder of the town slowly darkening his glints of memory and forgetting the common stock of experience which he held with his men. He cultivated the great and noble impulses of the benefactor, until the power of attaining a simple human relationship with his employees, that of frank equality with them, was gone from him. He, too, lost the faculty of affectionate interpretation, and demanded a sign. He and his employees had no mutual interest in a common cause.

Was not the grotesque situation of the royal father and the philanthropic employer to perform so many good deeds that they lost the power of recognizing good in beneficiaries? Were not both so absorbed in carrying out a personal plan of improvement that they failed to catch the great moral lesson which their times offered them? This is the crucial point to the tragedies and may be further elucidated.

Lear had doubtless swung a bauble before Cordelia's baby eyes that he might have the pleasure of seeing the little pink and tender hands stretched for it. A few years later he had given jewels to the young princess, and felt an exquisite pleasure when she stood before him, delighted with her gaud and grateful to her father. He demanded the same kind of response for his gift of the kingdom, but the gratitude must be larger and more carefully expressed, as befitted such a gift. At the opening of the drama he sat upon his throne ready for this enjoyment, but instead of delight and gratitude he found the first dawn of character. His daughter made the awkward attempt of an untrained soul to be honest, to be scrupulous in the expressions of its feelings. It was new to him that his child should be moved by a principle outside of himself, which even his imagination could not follow; that she had caught the notion of an existence so vast that her relationship as a daughter was but part of it.

Perhaps her suitors, the King of France or the Duke of Burgundy, had first hinted to the young Cordelia that there was a fuller life beyond the seas. Certain it is that someone had shaken her from the quiet measure of her insular existence and that she had at last felt the thrill of the world's life. She was transformed by a dignity which recast her speech and made it self-contained, as is becoming a citizen of the world. She found herself in the sweep of a notion of justice so large that the immediate loss of a kingdom seemed of little consequence to her. Even an act which might be construed as disrespect to her father was justified in her eyes because she was vainly striving to fill out this larger conception of duty.

The test which comes sooner or later to many parents had come to Lear, to maintain the tenderness of the relation between father and child, after the relation had become one between adults; to be contented with the responses which this adult made to the family claim, while, at the same time, she felt the tug upon her emotions and faculties of the larger life, the life which surrounds and completes the individual and family life, and which shares and widens her attention. He was not sufficiently wise to see that only that child can fulfill the family claim in its sweetness and strength who also fulfills the larger claim, that the adjustment of the lesser and larger implies no conflict. The mind of Lear was not big enough for this test. He failed to see anything but the personal slight involved; the ingratitude alone reached him. It was impossible for him to calmly watch his child developing beyond the strength of his own mind and sympathy.

Without pressing the analogy too hard may we not compare the indulgent relation of this employer to his town to the relation which existed between Lear and Cordelia? He fostered his employees for many years, gave them sanitary houses and beautiful parks, but in their extreme need, when they were struggling with the most difficult question which the times could present to them, when, if ever, they required the assistance of a trained mind and a comprehensive outlook, he lost his touch and had nothing wherewith to help them. He did not see the situation. He had been ignorant of their gropings toward justice. His conception of goodness for them had been cleanliness, decency of living, and above all, thrift and temperance. He had provided them means for all this; had gone further, and given them opportunities for enjoyment and comradeship. But he suddenly found his town in the sweep of a world-wide moral impulse. A movement had been going on about him and through the souls of his workingmen of which he had been unconscious. He had only heard of this movement by rumor. The men who consorted with him at his club and in his business had spoken but little of it, and when they had discussed it had contemptuously called it the "Labor Movement" headed by deadbeats and agitators. Of the force and power of this movement, of all the vitality within it, of that conception of duty which induces men to go without food and to see their wives and children suffer for the sake of securing better wages for fellow-workmen whom they have never seen, this president had dreamed absolutely nothing. But his town had at last become swept into this larger movement, so that the giving up of comfortable homes, of beautiful surroundings, seemed as naught to the men within its grasp.

Outside the ken of this philanthropist, the proletariat had learned to say in many languages that "the injury of one is the concern of all." Their watchwords were brotherhood, sacrifice, the subordination of individual and trade interests to the good of the working class; and their persistent strivings were toward the ultimate freedom of that class from the conditions under which they now labor.

Compared to these watchwords the old ones which the philanthropic employer had given his town were negative and inadequate.

When this movement finally swept in his own town, or, to speak more fairly, when in their distress and perplexity his own employees appealed to the organized manifestation of this movement, they were quite sure that simply because they were workmen in distress they would not be deserted by it. This loyalty on the part of a widely ramified and well-organized union toward the workmen in a "scab shop," who had contributed nothing to its cause, was certainly a manifestation of moral power.

That the movement was ill-directed, that it was ill-timed and disastrous in results, that it stirred up and became confused in the minds of the public with the elements of riot and bloodshed, can never touch the fact that it started from an unselfish impulse.

In none of his utterances or correspondence did the president of the company for an instant recognize this touch of nobility, although one would imagine that he would gladly point out this bit of virtue, in what he must have considered the moral ruin about him. He stood throughout pleading for the individual virtues, those which had distinguished the model workman of his youth, those which had enabled him and so many of his contemporaries to rise in life, when "rising in life" was urged upon every promising boy as the goal of his efforts. Of the new code of ethics he had caught absolutely nothing. The morals he had taught his men did not fail them in their hour of confusion. They were self-controlled and destroyed no property. They were sober and exhibited no drunkenness, even though obliged to hold their meetings in a saloon hall of a neighboring town. They repaid their employer in kind, but he had given them no rule for the higher fellowship and life of association into which they were plunged.

The virtues of one generation are not sufficient for the next, any more than the accumulations of knowledge possessed by one age are adequate to the needs of another.

Of the virtues received from our fathers we can afford to lose none. We accept as a precious trust those principles and precepts which the race has worked out for its highest safeguard and protection. But merely to preserve those is not enough. A task is laid upon each generation to enlarge their application, to ennoble their conception, and, above all, to apply and adapt them to the peculiar problems presented to it for solution.

The president of this company desired that his employees should possess the individual and family virtues, but did nothing to cherish in them those social virtues which his own age demanded. He rather substituted for that sense of responsibility to the community, a feeling of gratitude to himself, who had provided them with public buildings, and had laid out for them a simulacrum of public life.

Is it strange that when the genuine feeling of the age struck his town this belated and almost feudal virtue of personal gratitude fell before it?

Day after day during that horrible suspense, when the wires constantly reported the same message, "The president of the company holds that there is nothing to arbitrate," one longed to find out what was in the mind of this man, to unfold his ultimate motive. One concludes that he must have been sustained by the consciousness of being in the right. Only that could have held him against the great desire for fair play which swept over the country. Only the training which an arbitrary will receives by years of consulting first its own personal and commercial ends could have made it strong enough to withstand the demands for social adjustment. He felt himself right from the *commercial* standpoint, and could not see the situation from the *social* standpoint. For years he had gradually accustomed himself to the thought that his motive was beyond reproach; that his attitude to his town was always righteous and philanthropic. Habit held him persistent in this view of the case through all the changing conditions.

The diffused and subtle notion of dignity held by the modern philanthropist bears a curious analogy to the personal barbaric notion of dignity held by Lear. The man who persistently paced the seashore, while the interior of his country was racked with a strife which he alone might have arbitrated, lived out within himself the tragedy of King Lear. The shock of disaster upon egotism is apt to produce self-pity. It is possible that his self-pity and loneliness may have been so great and absorbing as to completely shut out from his mind a compunction of derelict duty. He may have been unconscious that men were charging him with a shirking of the issue.

Lack of perception is the besetting danger of the egoist, from whatever cause his egoism arises and envelops him. But, doubtless, philanthropists are more exposed to this danger than any other class of people within the community. Partly because their efforts are overestimated, as no standard of attainment has yet been established, and partly because they are the exponents of a large amount of altruistic feeling with which the community has become equipped and which has not yet found adequate expression, they are therefore easily idealized.

Long ago Hawthorne called our attention to the fact that philanthropy ruins, or is fearfully apt to ruin, the heart, "the rich juices of which God never meant should be pressed violently out, and distilled into alcoholic liquor by an unnatural process; but it should render life sweet, bland and gently beneficent."

One might add to this observation that the muscles of this same heart may be stretched and strained until they lose the rhythm of the common heartbeat of the rest of the world.

Modern philanthropists need to remind themselves of the old definition of greatness: that it consists in the possession of the largest share of the common human qualities and experiences, not in the acquirements of peculiarities and excessive virtues. Popular opinion calls him the greatest of Americans who gathered to himself the largest amount of American experience, and who never forgot when he was in Washington how the "crackers" in Kentucky and the pioneers of Illinois thought and felt, striving to retain their thoughts and feelings, and to embody only the mighty will of the "common people." The danger of professionally attaining to the power of the righteous man, of yielding to the ambition "for doing good," compared to which the ambitions for political position, learning, or wealth are vulgar and commonplace, ramifies throughout our modern life, and is a constant and settled danger of philanthropy.

In so far as philanthropists are cut off from the influence of the *Zeit-Geist*, from the code of ethics which rule the body of men, from the great moral life springing from our common experiences, so long as they are "good to people," rather than "with them," they are bound to accomplish a large amount of harm. They are outside of the influence of that great faith which perennially springs up in the hearts of the people, and re-creates the world. . . .

The new claim on the part of the toiling multitude, the new sense of responsibility on the part of the well-to-do, arise in reality from the same source. They are in fact the same "social compunction," and, in spite of their widely varying manifestations, logically converge into the same movement. Mazzini once preached, "the consent of men and your own conscience are two wings given you whereby you may rise to God." It is so easy for the good and powerful to think that they can rise by following the dictates of conscience by pursuing their own ideals, leaving those ideals unconnected with the consent of their fellow-men. The president of the Pullman Company thought out within his own mind a beautiful town. He had power with which to build this town, but he did not appeal to nor obtain the consent of the men who were living in it. The most unambitious reform, recognizing the necessity for this consent, makes for slow but sane and strenuous progress, while the most ambitious of social plans and experiments, ignoring this, is prone to the failure of the model town of Pullman.

The man who insists upon consent, who moves with the people, is bound to consult the feasible right as well as the absolute right. He is often obliged to attain only Mr. Lincoln's "best possible," and often have the sickening sense of compromising with his best convictions. He has to move along with those whom he rules toward a goal that neither he nor they see very clearly till they come to it. He has to discover what people really want, and then "provide the channels in which the growing moral force of their lives shall flow." What he does attain, however, is not the result of his individual striving, as a solitary mountain climber beyond the sight of the valley multitude, but it is underpinned and upheld by the sentiments and aspirations of many others. Progress has been slower perpendicularly, but incomparably greater because lateral.

He has not taught his contemporaries to climb mountains, but he has persuaded the villagers to move up a few feet higher. It is doubtful if personal ambition, whatever may have been its commercial results, has ever been of any value as a motive power in social reform. But whatever it may have done in the past, it is certainly too archaic to accomplish anything now. Our thoughts, at least for this generation, cannot be too much directed from mutual relationships and responsibilities. They will be warped, unless we look all men in the face, as if a community of interests lay between, unless we hold the mind open, to take strength and cheer from a hundred connections.

To touch to vibrating response the noble fibre in each man, to pull these many fibres, fragile, impalpable and constantly breaking, as they are, into one impulse, to develop that mere impulse through its feeble and tentative stages into action, is no easy task, but lateral progress is impossible without it.

If only a few families of the English speaking race had profited by the dramatic failure of Lear, much heart-breaking and domestic friction might have been spared. Is it too much to hope that some of us will carefully consider this modern tragedy, if perchance it may contain a warning for the troublous times in which we live? By considering the dramatic failure of the liberal employer's plans for his employees we may possibly be spared useless industrial tragedies in the uncertain future which lies ahead of us.

Originally published in *Survey* 29 (November 2, 1912), pp. 131–137.

PAUL YLVISAKER

"The Spirit of Philanthropy and the Soul of Those Who Manage It"

Paul Ylvisaker (1939–1992) enjoyed a distinguished career in philanthropy and public service, as an executive at the Ford Foundation, New Jersey's first Commissioner of Community Affairs, Dean of Harvard University's Graduate School of Education, and senior consultant at the Council on Foundations. In this 1987 speech, Ylvisaker addresses himself specifically to the managers of philanthropy— those "who don't own the money but make their living giving it away" and to the trustees who shoulder "the fiduciary responsibilities involved in running foundations." Such managers, he writes, are stewards not only of philanthropic funds, but of the philanthropic spirit, which is equally indebted to two traditions—the older tradition of "charity" and the more recent one, "philanthropy." As these traditions are more competitive than they are complementary, Ylvisaker contends, "we are tested by how creatively we balance and resolve their contending logics and meld them into a concept and code of behavior that honor the imperatives of both traditions." While he acknowledges that each practitioner must resolve the tensions in his or her own way, he concludes by offering eleven "commandments" to help guide the way, maxims that have enabled him to keep alive the spirit of philanthropy and, not inconsequentially, his own soul. As noted, Ylvisaker speaks to (and of) managers, not leaders. Do you regard Ylvisaker himself as a manager or as a leader? More generally, is whatever it is that makes a good philanthropic manager the same as or different from what is required for good philanthropic leadership? In eulogizing Ylvisaker shortly after his death, Pablo Eisenberg called him a "master of the art of inducing epiphanies." Is there anything that Ylvisaker says here to or about philanthropy's managers that earns him this title?

> *"Philanthropy is not just another institution. It stands for something distinctive and special, with a tradition and necessarily a spirit which represent to society the nobler motives of altruism and the more humane considerations so characteristically missing in the worlds of business and politics."*

Stewardship is a term that is healthily disciplining, but it is also too passive: it does remind us of the specific trusts we have accepted, but it does not suggest the creative roles we inescapably play. We are stewards not merely of money, but of a tradition—a tradition [that] is still evolving. And that makes us accountable not only for what we preserve but for what we create.

I'd like to brood with you over both the custodial and the creative responsibilities of philanthropic managers.

I'll be making some generalizations that suffer all the liabilities of half-truths. Fair warning à la Robert Wood,[1] who once introduced me with the mischievous alert: "I want you to listen carefully to Paul Ylvisaker. He's always persuasive but not always right." Still, how else than by generalizing do we human beings communicate insights—or keep an audience awake?

Who are the managers of philanthropy? To start with, the seven or eight thousand who don't own the money but make their living giving it away (the "philanthropoids"), plus another nearly equal number of trustees who manage organized philanthropy without benefit—some would say, without burden—of paid staff, but essentially are responsible for discharging the fiduciary responsibilities involved in running foundations.

Even at that, we're talking about a meager fraction of Americans: only six out of 100,000 who are trustees of foundations, and only three out of 100,000 who are paid staff.

Philanthropy is not easy to generalize about, despite those meager numbers. There can't be a more esoteric human activity, nor one more extraordinarily diverse—especially given the vast assortment of trusts that exist and therefore of the responsibilities involved.

But it is not enough to take refuge in diversity. We have a name, and therefore an identity; we have a function, and therefore a set of personal and public responsibilities. In searching for the spirit of philanthropy, that quintessential that instructs us in how we should behave and what values we ought to symbolize, there are two traditions to explore.

First, that of charity, the older and better understood; it has become almost instinctive in ours and other cultures in its presuppositions if not always its practice. Its "pure theory" builds upon six elements:

1. Altruism, the subordination of self-interest.
2. Compassion and empathy as the best avenues to understanding.
3. Taking the perspective of "the least among us." John Rawls built this into his theory of justice: the just society is one which tests its actions by their impact on the condition of its least powerful members.
4. A readiness to affirm and to act alone.
5. A quest for a better human condition, sometimes in its sense of perfection reminiscent of the search for the Holy Grail.
6. Giving as a one-to-one human encounter in a microworld of personal relationships.

---

1. Robert C. Wood (1923–2005) was a noted political scientist, presidential adviser, Secretary of Housing and Urban Development, Massachusetts Institute of Technology professor (1959–1966), and president of the University of Massachusetts (1970–1977).—Ed.

In juxtaposition to this tradition of charity, another has evolved, [which] we now call modern (organized) philanthropy. It has developed its own set of presumptions, adapted from and adapting to, another environment:

1. The environment in which it works is the one in which institutions, rather than individuals, are the key actors. We have moved from the world of the one-on-one to that of institutionalized interaction.
2. There is a separation of donor and beneficiary into a world of intermediaries. The original donor, if still involved, acts through trustees, who act through staff, who act through one or more layers of nonprofit agencies, who act through staff, who act through a filter of representatives of the class, or problems, ultimately being dealt with. And further distancing occurs with the growth of specialization.
3. A look past the immediate condition of persons to what we call root causes and systemic reform.
4. A tilt toward reason and dispassion as the best route to systemic understanding and change.
5. A consciousness of institutional image and self-concern, ranging from tax considerations and the explicit rationalization by corporations of self-interest in their charity, to the incessant search all of us are engaged in for a distinctive mission and focus.
6. A recognition of a public responsibility, with accompanying public disciplines and restraints—and the redirection of that search for the Holy Grail toward an even more elusive concept called the public interest.
7. A conscious engineering of power, not only through grants and leveraging but through processes such as convening in which the gift plays only a part. Also, an explicit recognition of playing a social role, not simply a personal one.
8. A shift from gift to negotiated contract. We do this to both provide discipline and an assurance of effectiveness by watching carefully the terms of the grant. We also, by that method, allow reciprocity and participation. It is not the Lady Bountiful, unilateral act, and therefore it is consistent with the nature of our time. But have the very words "gift" and "grant" become archaic? Think about the way you deal with applicants. It is a negotiated contract that we have come to, rather than a gift or grant.
9. A search for consensus in approach and resolution. Consensus is an institutional imperative in our times, simply to minimize the friction generated by institutions moving through a crowding social and political environment.
10. A bias in favor of excellence and a meritocratic elite, both as justifications in themselves for philanthropy, but also as the preferred vehicle for helping the less advantaged.

Let's be clear: each of these elements has its own rationalizing logic. I am not putting these things down, but describing them. Each has made its own contribution to the evolving tradition of philanthropy. Without what they represent, charity could never have developed into the equilibrating and distinctive social force it has become. Charity could not have adapted to the social, economic, and political transformations that have taken place in modern society.

But the change has produced an institution and a profession with internal tensions, if not outright contradictions. Philanthropy has evolved, as Joseph Schumpeter[2] once analyzed capitalism to have evolved, to produce a routinization of progress. Good works in our time have become routine, which partly explains the paradox of organized philanthropy routinely turning out worthy grants with gray-flannel-suit regularity and rhetoric—just read all those foundation annual reports.

Have we moved from flesh-and-blood giving to dispassionate and depersonalized philanthropy?

Which of these two traditions—the charitable or the more recent—are we the custodians of? The answer is both. We are tested by how creatively we balance and resolve those contending logics and meld them into a concept and code of behavior that honor the imperatives of both traditions. This may seem, and partly is, just another version of the contemporary dilemma: how do we remain human in an institutional environment?

But it's not that; philanthropy is not just another institution. It stands for something distinctive and special, with a tradition and necessarily a spirit which represent to society the nobler motives of altruism and the more humane considerations so characteristically missing in the worlds of business and politics.

Each of us will find his or her own way of living with these tensions—each one's own resolution, each one's own way of contributing creatively to the evolving practice of philanthropy. But there are some guiding maxims and imperatives I would urge on you, though clearly they reflect my own biases and pieties. (You'll note there are eleven commandments. Anything to outdo Moses.)

1. Guard your own humanity. The first ethical commandment, taught to me by a distinguished professor of ethics, is to take care of yourself. This is not acting for number one; it means taking care of what you are or should be, so that you can radiate that out to others. If you lose your own soul—whether to arrogance, insensitivity, insecurity or the shield of impersonality—you diminish the spirit of philanthropy. The goal to aspire to is that you will be a

---

2. Joseph Schumpeter (1883–1950), noted economist, was credited, among other things, with the idea of "creative destruction," which describes the process of industrial transformation that accompanies radical innovation.—Ed.

distinguished human being who gives to the foundation as much an identity as you derive from it, and far more than the money you give or negotiate away. In a very real sense, you are philanthropy, even if you don't own the money.

2. Guard the soul of your own organization, even from your own pretensions. Those of you lucky enough to be part of an institution that has a soul know what a precious environment it is. It's a secure environment within which distinctive personalities complement rather than compete with each other; it's an open environment in which hierarchy is respected but not imposed, and where posturing and game-playing are unnecessary; it's an institution in which values are explicitly and easily discussed, and there is a consistency between values stated and values played out; it's an organization [that] demonstrates its humanity equally in its responsiveness to the needs and sensibilities of its external constituencies and in the care with which it nourishes and grows in its own personnel.

3. Be ready to speak out and act on your own on those hopefully rare occasions when principle is at stake or the unspoken needs to be aired.

4. Constantly assess your own motivation, whether what you're arguing for reflects your own power-drive and personal predilections or a measured evaluation of public need and foundation goals. This goes for trustees as well as staff, and ranges well beyond the more apparent realm of conflicts and interest.

5. Scan the whole gamut of your foundation's activities to make certain they are consistent with the goals and spirit of the philanthropic tradition. Are the values that peek through the back-page listing of your investments the same as those featured in the pious opening pages of your annual report? In your convening function, are you more intent on demonstrating influence than on catalyzing and releasing community energies?

Do your personnel policies and board compositions jibe with the affirmative action expectations directed at your applicants? Does the care with which you consider public needs and foundation policy match the exhaustive scrutiny you give to applicant proposals and budgetary attachments? Compile your own checklist of such questions; you'll find it an instructive and sometimes chastening exercise.

6. Constantly traverse the lengthening distance between the words used in foundation docket items and press releases and the ultimate impact and beneficiaries of the grants once made. Have the intended beneficiaries really benefited? Who are they, and how many of them are from among the least advantaged? Has the quest for a better human condition dissipated in the chase after some abstraction? Have verbalizations and the mere recital of good grants made substituted for demonstrable attainment of tangible goals?

7. Be willing to open the black box of philanthropy to share with others the mysteries of values and decision-making. They may seem disadvantageous to you as a protective mechanism, but in reality they're a breeding place for

personal and institutional botulism. An anaerobic environment is not a healthy one for the spirit of philanthropy, nor for the soul of a manager.

Be ready and willing to mix with the community, and with those closer to real life than you are. Engage in dialogue with others who have legitimate interest in what you're doing and who may provoke you into insights that seclusion may have kept you from. Consider another ethical commandment: always be ready to explain publicly your decision and your reasons for your actions. Don't wind up your organization so tight that competing ideas can't filter through.

8. Never stop affirming. When you find your battery of hope, excitement, and even idealistic naiveté so drained that you don't let an applicant finish a presentation without pointing out why it can't be done, it's time you departed for another profession. Philanthropy builds on the hope of rising generations; it lights fires rather than snuffs them out.

9. Follow both routes to understanding, the compassionate as well as the analytical. No one can comprehend the universe who does not understand and care for the sparrow.

10. Don't ever lose your sense of outrage. Bill Bondurant[3] can't forget, nor can I after he related it, the wondering comment of an applicant who looked about Bill's comfortable office and lifestyle: "How, Bill, do you keep your sense of outrage?" There has to be in all of us a moral thermostat that flips when we're confronted by suffering, injustice, inequality, or callous behavior.

11. Don't ever lose your sense of humor. Organized philanthropy so easily dulls into pretentious drabness, and we all need the revitalizing spark of a good laugh, mostly at ourselves.

My own chastening reminder is the memory of a cocktail party at which I, Mr. Big Bucks from the Ford Foundation, was pontificating to all within earshot. To make a point even more impressive, I paused to pick up an olive. But what my bad eyes had missed was that it was actually a cigar butt. Any of you who has ever tasted one knows the abrupt and ignominious end of that pious performance.

Philanthropy—in the degree to which it fulfills the aspiration of its spirit and tradition—is a rare element in our social firmament, a salt that cannot be allowed to lose its savor. It is a distinctive function that, like religion, relies eventually and essentially on its moral power.

We diminish that force when we get absorbed in a mistaken quest for power of another sort, be it money or social and political influence. Philanthropic influence derives more from spirit than from social positioning or monetary domination. The love of that money is undoubtedly the most corrupting element in the grantmaking enterprise.

There is enough of an alien spirit already attaching itself to philanthropy—self-interest being an ancient example and partisanship and political manip-

---

3. Executive Director, Mary Reynolds Babcock Foundation, 1974–1993.—Ed.

ulation a more recent one—without our failing to recognize and honor the spirit and tradition of which we are stewards.

The power of organized philanthropy can indeed corrupt. But conducted in a humane spirit, and with soul, it can also ennoble.

I was once asked to work for Joe Clark, then mayor of Philadelphia. When I inquired of him what the job was, really, he thought a minute and replied, "To help fight the battle for my mind." It was an irresistible challenge.

But what I'd ask of someone about to join us as a foundation manager would be quite another dimension: "Help fight the battle for our soul."

"The Spirit of Philanthropy and the Soul of Those Who Manage It" by Paul Ylvisaker, a speech given before the Thirty-Eighth Annual Conference of the Council on Foundations, Atlanta, Ga., March 1987. Reprinted by permission of the Council on Foundations.

JOHN W. GARDNER

"Leadership"

*A leader in education, philanthropy, and politics, John W. Gardner (1912–2002)
has been called, among other things, a "renaissance man," the "quintessential
American hero," and "the citizen of his era." A psychologist by training, he
joined the Carnegie Corporation in 1946 and was appointed president in 1955.
After serving as President Johnson's Secretary of Health, Education, and Welfare, Gardner founded both Common Cause (a citizen advocacy group), and Independent Sector (a national coalition of nonprofits), and served, as well, as
trustee and professor at Stanford University. In all his many activities, Gardner
advocated civic responsibility and community building, fearing most that history might pass this judgment on our nation: "It was a great nation full of talented people with enormous energy who forgot that they needed one another."*

*In this chapter on "Leadership," Gardner acknowledges the importance of
educating people as specialists—scholars, scientists, or professionals—but re-
grets that such education encourages only the kind of leadership "which follows
from the performing of purely professional tasks in a superior manner," not
"leadership in the normal sense." Against the latter, he argues, young people
have been deliberately inoculated with an "antileadership vaccine." What we
need, he suggests, is an antidote—a renaissance of moral leadership: men and
women who "express the values that hold the society together," who can "conceive and articulate goals that lift people out of their petty preoccupations," and
who are able to "unite [people] in pursuit of objectives worthy of their best efforts." Though Gardner does not speak specifically about philanthropy, the fast-
growing industry of nonprofit management and other allied programs may
testify to the fact the philanthropy, too, is creating professionals, not leaders. But
is Gardner right? Do technical and professional expertise necessarily make one
unfit for leadership, philanthropic or otherwise? What kind of education would
make one more fit for the requisite civic leadership he outlines? Where do we
find—how should we educate—the future Gardners?*

We are immunizing a high proportion of our most gifted young people against
any tendencies to leadership. The process is initiated by the society itself. The
conditions of life in a modern, complex society are not conducive to the emergence of leaders. The young person today is acutely aware of the fact that he is
an anonymous member of a mass society, an individual lost among millions of
others. The processes by which leadership is exercised are not visible to him,
and he is bound to believe they are exceedingly intricate. Very little in his

experience encourages him to think he might someday exercise a role of leadership.

This unfocused discouragement is of little consequence compared with the expert dissuasion the young person will encounter if he is sufficiently bright to attend a college or university. In some institutions today the best students are carefully schooled to avoid leadership responsibilities.

Most of our intellectually gifted young people go from college directly into graduate school or into one of the older and more prestigious professional schools. There they are introduced to—or, more correctly, powerfully indoctrinated in—a set of attitudes appropriate to scholars, scientists and professional men. This is all to the good. The students learn to identify themselves strongly with their calling and its ideals. They acquire a conception of what a good scholar, scientist or professional man is like.

As things stand now, however, that conception leaves little room for leadership in the normal sense; the only kind of leadership encouraged is that which follows from the performing of purely professional tasks in a superior manner. Entry into what most of us would regard as the leadership roles in the society at large is discouraged.

In the early stages of a career there is a good reason for this: becoming a first-class scholar, scientist or professional requires single-minded dedication. Unfortunately, by the time the individual is sufficiently far along in his career to afford a broadening of interest, he often finds himself irrevocably set in a narrow mold.

The antileadership vaccine that the society administers to our young people today has other subtle and powerful ingredients. The image of the corporation president, politician or college president that is current among most intellectuals and professionals today has some decidedly unattractive features. It is said that such men compromise their convictions almost daily, if not hourly. It is said that they have tasted the corrupting experience of power. They must be status-seekers, the argument goes, or they would not be where they are.

Needless to say, the student picks up such attitudes. It is not that professors propound these views and students learn them. Rather, they are in the air and students absorb them. The resulting unfavorable image contrasts dramatically with the image these young people are given of the professional, who is almost by definition dedicated to his field, pure in his motives and unencumbered by worldly ambition.

My own extensive acquaintance with scholars and professionals on the one hand and administrators and managers on the other does not confirm this contrast in character. In my experience, each category has its share of opportunists. Nevertheless, the negative attitudes persist.

As a result the academic world appears to be approaching a point at which everyone will want to educate the technical expert who advises the leader, or the intellectual who stands off and criticizes the leader, but no one will want to educate the leader.

We have all seen men with lots of bright ideas but no patience with the machinery by which ideas are translated into action. As a rule, the machinery defeats them. It is a pity, because the professional and academic man can play a useful role in practical affairs. But too often he is a dilettante. He dips in here or there; he gives bits of advice on a dozen fronts; he never gets his hands dirty working with one piece of the social machinery until he knows it well. He will not take the time to understand the social institutions and processes by which change is accomplished.

The curse of citizen action is the glancing blow—a little work on this committee and on to the next one; a little work on that committee and on to something else. Too often the citizen active in community affairs is essentially a dabbler, never getting in deep enough to have any effect; never getting far enough below the surface to understand how the machinery works in whatever activity he is trying to change; just lingering long enough to sign the committee report, not staying long enough to see what the consequences of the report are.

That is not good enough in a society designed to depend on citizen concern and action.

We will never have effective leadership in our cities until we persuade the ablest and most influential members of the community that they must take personal responsibility for what happens to their city. It is one of the anomalies of our national life today that such persuasion is necessary. One might argue that when our ablest people evade the responsibility of leadership, the society is far gone in decadence. But we're not decadent. We're the victims of specialization. The able individual who doesn't lead is not just standing idle. He is a highly trained lawyer, busy pursuing his profession. Or a college professor busy writing books. Or a corporation executive busy with his business.

He has never been led to believe that the problems of the city are really his problems. But he must now learn that lesson. He must no longer believe that membership on the board of one distinguished hospital plus earnest participation in the Community Fund defines the limits of his civic duties. He must plunge with both feet into the city's toughest, grimiest and most complex problems, both short—and long—term: the question of today's riot and the question of whether the city itself has any tolerable future.

The plain fact is that all over this country today trouble is brewing and social evils accumulating while our patterns of social and professional organization keep able and gifted potential leaders on the sidelines.

Federal laws, dollars and programs don't teach children nor heal the sick. Teachers teach children and doctors heal the sick—individual teachers and doctors in the schools and clinics of Atlanta and Seattle and Phoenix. In other words, everything depends upon increased vitality out where the action is.

We must find ways of bringing together in some kind of working relationship the varied leadership elements in the community—the elected and appointed political leadership, business leaders, union leaders, educators, ministers, minority group leaders and the press.

What every city needs is a loose coalition of responsible leadership elements, willing to work together on a nonpartisan basis to resolve urgent civic problems. I have watched many cities struggle with their problems, and I can assure you that such a coalition is necessary. City Hall can't go it alone. The business leaders can't go it alone. Minority leaders can't go it alone.

Of course, the coalition must be sufficiently fluid to permit the inclusion of all significant elements of community life; a coalition that excludes or suppresses important elements of potential community leadership is self-defeating.

One of the maladies of leadership today is a failure of confidence. Everyone who accomplishes anything of significance has more confidence than the facts would justify. It is something that outstanding executives have in common with gifted military commanders, brilliant political leaders and great artists. It is true of societies as well as of individuals. Every great civilization has been characterized by a sublime confidence in itself.

Lacking such confidence, too many leaders add ingenious new twists to the modern art which I call "How to reach a decision without really deciding." Require that the question be put through a series of clearances within your organization, and let the clearance process settle it. Or take a public-opinion poll and let the poll settle it. Or devise elaborate statistical systems, cost-accounting systems, information-processing systems, hoping that out of them will come unassailable support for one course of action rather than another.

The confidence required of leaders poses a delicate problem for a free society. We don't want to be led by Men of Destiny who think they know all the answers. Neither do we wish to be led by Nervous Nellies. It is a matter of balance. We are no longer in much danger, in this society, from Men of Destiny. But we *are* in danger of falling under the leadership of men who lack the confidence to lead. And we are in danger of destroying the effectiveness of those who have a natural gift for leadership.

We can have the kind of leaders we want, but we cannot choose to do without them. It is in the nature of social organization that we must have them at all levels of our national life, in and out of government—in business, labor, politics, education, science, the arts and every other field. Since we must have them, it helps considerably if they are gifted in the performance of their appointed task. The sad truth is that a great many of our organizations are badly managed or badly led. And because of that, people within those organizations are frustrated when they need not be frustrated. They are not helped when they could be helped. They are not given the opportunities to fulfill themselves that are clearly possible.

In the minds of some, leadership is associated with goals that they regard as distasteful—power, profit, efficiency and the like. But leadership, properly conceived, also serves the individual human goals that our society values so highly, and we shall not achieve those goals without it.

So much of our leadership energies have been devoted to tending the machinery and to keeping our complex society running that we have neglected even the possibility of moral leadership.

Leaders have a significant role in creating the state of mind that is the society. They can serve as symbols of the moral unity of the society. They can express the values that hold the society together. Most important, they can conceive and articulate goals that lift people out of their petty preoccupations, carry them above the conflicts that tear a society apart, and unite them in the pursuit of objectives worthy of their best efforts.

We don't need leaders to tell us what to do. That's not the American style of leadership in any case. We do need men and women in every community in the land who will accept a special responsibility to advance the public interest, root out corruption, combat injustice and care about the continued vitality of this land.

We need such people to help us clarify and define the choices before us.

We need them to symbolize and voice and confirm the most deeply rooted values of our society. We need them to tell us of our faithfulness or infidelity to those values.

And we need them to rekindle hope. So many of us are defeated people—whatever our level of affluence or status—defeated sometimes by life's blows, more often by our own laziness or cynicism or self-indulgence.

The first and last task of a leader is to keep hope alive—the hope that we can finally find our way through to a better world—despite the day's bitter discouragement, despite the perplexities of social action, despite our own inertness and shallowness and wavering resolve.

WILLIAM A. SCHAMBRA

"The Ungodly Bright: Should They Lead Philanthropy into the Future"

Taking his bearings from Warren Buffet's decision (summer 2006) to bequeath his billions to the "ungodly bright" leaders of the Bill and Melinda Gates Foundation, William A. Schambra, director of The Bradley Center for Philanthropy and Civic Renewal, raises a general question about the form of grantmaking leadership that this bequest represents: Are the purposes of philanthropy best served if it looks to the few, ungodly bright among us—especially those with scientific and technical expertise—to identify and solve our most fundamental problems? Using the example of eugenic approaches to the "root causes" of human troubles, Schambra warns of the dangers of a top-down, expert-driven philanthropy. Echoing Tocqueville's view of what makes American civil society strong, Schambra calls for a new approach to philanthropy—"civic renewal philanthropy"—that would directly address the immediate needs of suffering humanity, rely more on the leadership and engagement of ordinary individuals, and promote public-spirited citizens. Can this "Tocquevillean" approach to philanthropy work today? Who is better situated to address today's social problems, the expert elite or everyday citizens? How can the enormously wealthy—and the ungodly bright—best satisfy their desire to "make a difference"?

૪ઽ

When Warren Buffett announced his multi-billion-dollar bequest to the Bill and Melinda Gates Foundation in the summer of 2006, he explained his generous if unconventional act of charity by claiming that "if your goal is to return the money to society by attacking truly major problems that don't have a commensurate funding base—what could you find that's better than turning to a couple of people who are young, who are ungodly bright. . . ."

American philanthropy's romance with the "ungodly bright" has a long, if not always noble, pedigree. After all, the first large foundations—Carnegie, Rockefeller, Russell Sage—were established during, and fully reflected the predilections of, America's progressive era at the beginning of the twentieth century. The progressives were persuaded that, just as disease was rapidly being conquered by modern science and medicine, so "social pathogens"—the ultimate source of our social ills—could be tracked down and eradicated once and for all, given new sciences of human behavior like sociology, psychology, and public administration. But this would require that the management of human affairs be taken out of the hands of the benighted many and put into the care of the enlightened few, trained and credentialed in the new social sciences. Not coincidentally, this was precisely the direction history itself wished to take. As their name suggests, progressives were convinced that history was the story of inexorable progress from the selfish individualism and parochial localism of the past to a new era of social-minded brotherhood. But only the ungodly bright *avant garde* had the historical and scientific insight to break with the parochial allegiances of the past, and persuade or compel the many to follow them into a more promising, socially conscious, collective future.

The first large foundations eagerly bought into progressivism's view that new, professionally trained elites were trailblazers into a brighter future. And so they invested massively in the rationalization, standardization, and modernization of old professions like law, education, and medicine. To bring a new order and discipline to public affairs, they also funded the development of new professions like social work and public administration. These updated old and new professions would find their home in the modern research university—another favorite funding target for Carnegie and Rockefeller—where genuinely objective research could be conducted free from the distorting pressures of politics and markets, and where the next generation of elites would be trained.

Even the way these foundations organized themselves—existing in perpetuity, with highly abstract statements of purpose—reflected an abiding faith in the progressive accumulation of intelligence in the hands of the few. As long-time Rockefeller Foundation president Raymond Fosdick noted, only open-ended, perpetual giving was able to accommodate the optimistic conviction that "the dead hand should be removed from charitable bequests," leaving grantmaking decisions entirely "in the hands of living men," because "the wisdom of living men will always exceed the wisdom of any man, however wise, who has long since been dead."

This overarching faith in the new sciences of society lies behind one of the most frequently repeated justifications for modern philanthropy, uttered first by John D. Rockefeller himself: "The best philanthropy is constantly in search for finalities—a search for cause, an attempt to cure the evils at their source." The old, discredited approach of charity, in this view, responded too emotionally and directly to the immediate problems of individuals before them. It did not use its head. It lacked the steely, detached scientific knowledge to see *through* the bewildering, distracting, superficial manifestations of social ailments, down to the final, root causes of those ailments, which we now had the power to cure once and for all.

But only the ungodly bright few are able properly to exercise scientific discipline. Quoting Oliver Wendell Holmes, Fosdick made this link explicit: "If notwithstanding the apparent confusion and welter of our life, we are able to find a steadiness of purpose and quiet dominating intelligence, it is largely because of [those] who have been trained to a considerable extent in the scientific method."

It might seem today that we no longer look to social science with such naïve, utopian expectations. Nevertheless, the language and practice of modern American philanthropy still reflect an abiding faith in the ungodly bright to lead us into a new, more rational world. As recently as 2006, the new president of the Rockefeller Foundation took office with an unabashed reaffirmation of the vision of 1910: "The focus of this wonderful foundation on the root causes of social ills is very powerful and very compelling."

Hence, foundations invariably describe themselves as innovators and experimenters, relentlessly pursuing "social change" through new and imaginative projects that will conclusively reveal the hidden workings of underlying social forces. Their programs are designed according to cutting edge academic theories about social behavior and carried out by staff with impressive professional credentials. Foundations know that they are tapping into root causes because their programs produce concrete outcomes analyzable by sophisticated scientific metrics. Philanthropy is peculiarly positioned to play this pioneering role in social change, it is often argued, because it is mercifully insulated from market forces, political demands, and other bothersome pressures of the everyday world, and so can come at public problems from a uniquely objective, detached point of view. In other words, foundations still provide a perch from which the ungodly bright can steer social change in a progressive direction.

It is hardly surprising, then, that Warren Buffett should have surveyed the perplexing variety of charitable needs and projects clamoring for his attention, and concluded that it was better to "attack truly major problems" by turning his fortune over to the intelligent few. For all the changes the twentieth century wrought, its philanthropy closed the century as it began, with leadership by the ungodly bright still regarded as the only progressive and enlightened path for grantmaking.

After a full century of insisting that their peculiar value to society is the ability to get to root causes of, and decisively solve, social problems, how have foundations performed? For a field so insistent that its grantees show demonstrable outcomes, philanthropy in fact has precious little to show for itself. One hundred years ago, at a time when the federal government's presence in social policy was insignificant, foundations did in fact play a major role in establishing the institutions and professional structures of medicine and public health, with considerable pay-off when it came to combating diseases like yellow fever and hook worm. Later, scientific developments in agriculture supported by the large American foundations produced the "Green Revolution," saving millions from starvation. But when it comes to social—not medical or agricultural—problems, the record of philanthropy is abysmal.

Here, philanthropy has largely tinkered around the edges of the delivery systems of the social welfare state, fine tuning this program, replicating that one, and rearranging existing services into new combinations. That may be commendable work, but it's hardly how philanthropy justifies itself. It claims rather that the ungodly bright deserve the privileged position of grantmaking leadership because they *don't* tinker, but rather cut directly to the source of significant social problems, grasp their cause, and solve them once and for all—just as hookworm was decisively eradicated in large parts of the South. And this is precisely where philanthropy has such a feeble record. It would be difficult, if not impossible, to name a single social problem—even an insignificant one—the roots of which philanthropy has laid bare and solved.

Even worse, philanthropy has on at least one occasion followed what looked like a root cause in a particularly monstrous direction. Early in the twentieth century, the new science of eugenics recommended itself to Andrew Carnegie, John D. Rockefeller, and his son "Junior," precisely because it appealed to their "root causes" aspirations. Just as tracking physiological diseases back to germs had begun to eliminate root causes of medical ailments, so tracking social pathology—crime, pauperism, dypsomania, and moral laxity—back to defective genes would allow us to attack it at its roots. Indeed, suggested prominent progressive scholar Charles Van Hise, "We know enough about eugenics so that if the knowledge were applied, the defective classes would disappear within a generation." They would disappear because the eugenicists had set out to persuade the state to confine and sterilize the unfit. As Junior noted, this was the only "scientific way of escape from the evils" to which bad genes gave rise.

From the perspective of philanthropic eugenics, the old practice of charity—that is, simply alleviating human suffering—was not only inefficient, it was downright harmful. As birth control heroine Margaret Sanger (another Rockefeller grantee) put it, America's charitable institutions are the "surest signs that our civilization has bred, is breeding, and is perpetuating constantly increasing numbers of defectives, delinquents, and dependents."

Efforts to develop and apply eugenics to eliminate the defective classes were undertaken with Rockefeller and Carnegie support at the Eugenics Record Office at New York's Cold Spring Harbor. Rockefeller funds would also go toward research institutions in Germany that were seeking ways to discourage the propagation of inferior individuals and races, drawing their inspiration from the techniques proving themselves in the United States. By the time Cold Spring Harbor's eugenics program ended in the late '30s, tens of thousands of "defectives" in America had been institutionalized or sterilized, and the ground had been laid for the most unspeakable horrors of the twentieth century.

It might be possible to dismiss the eugenics episode as a wrong turn on the road to progress, as indeed, it is treated in the few histories that mention it at all. But it is also possible to look at eugenics as illustrative of the central danger posed by commissioning the ungodly bright to drive relentlessly to the root causes of social problems. Modern philanthropy asks our foundation elites—already well insulated from the rest of us by credentialed expertise, professional detachment, and privileged tax status—to look past or to deliberately ignore the immediate and diverse needs of those immediately in front of them. Those needs are, after all, mere symptoms, attention to which was the old, discredited approach of charity.

But once the ungodly bright steel themselves sufficiently to see sufferers not as unique individuals, but rather as insubstantial manifestations of underlying pathologies, it becomes easy to pursue solutions that at first ignore, and finally violate, innate human dignity. Indeed, the bright may well conclude that the most merciful way to alleviate suffering is to prevent anyone from becoming a sufferer in the first place—by cutting off suffering at its genuine root. They become vulnerable to British socialist Havelock Ellis's view, that "the superficially sympathetic man flings a coin to the beggar; the more deeply sympathetic man builds an almshouse for him; but perhaps the most radically sympathetic of all is the man who arranges that the beggar shall not be born."

Today, of course, our knowledge of the human genome and our growing capacity to manipulate it at will present us unparalleled opportunities to see to it that beggars—or "undesirables" of any sort—shall not be born. The fact that we are now able to do so without resort to the crude, messy eugenics of sterilization makes it all the more tempting to view this as a purely scientific act of "radical sympathy." As late as 1952, Raymond Fosdick would praise Rockefeller's investments in its natural sciences program as a way to "develop so sound and extensive a genetics that we can hope to breed in the future superior men." That temptation is compounded by the fact that the eugenics episode has been airbrushed entirely from the relentlessly upbeat historical account of American philanthropy. At the precise moment when we need more than ever to grapple with the subtle moral pitfalls of genetics-driven, root-causes philanthropy, we are too embarrassed or too ashamed even to acknowledge that we have faced and failed the test before.

Whether the philanthropy of the ungodly bright takes a monstrous turn, or—as it has for over a century—merely conceals its futility with lofty rhetoric, it would be useful today to rethink philanthropy, given the likely arrival of considerable amounts of philanthropic dollars as wealth passes from one generation to the next.

What might a new approach to philanthropy look like? It would start by challenging the central premise of twentieth-century philanthropy that the ungodly bright are somehow better equipped to solve society's problems than are everyday citizens. The notion that citizens themselves could and should play a central role in solving their own problems is, of course, reflected in Alexis de Tocqueville's understanding of American democracy. The great danger of the new age of democracy, in his view, was that citizens would become too absorbed with narrow, materialistic pursuits to pay attention to public affairs, and would be willing to turn over their affairs to management by bright, benevolent elites. That might result in a smoothly operating and efficient social service delivery system. But it would also mean an ominous concentration of power in a few hands, as well as a gradual impoverishment of the spirit or soul of the democratic citizen, as he lost the capacity or the desire to engage with—and to be enlarged by—vigorous encounters with other citizens of differing backgrounds and opinions.

Curiously, American foundations today frequently fund studies and conferences anxiously pondering precisely this problem of citizen disengagement and the decline of the democratic spirit in America. But they seldom look critically at their own practices, to consider whether their clear preference for public management by the ungodly bright might not in itself convey a dispiriting message to democratic citizens, and feed the cycle of disengagement.

How might it be otherwise? Tocqueville suggested that Americans had avoided the central problem of democracy by leaving considerable authority to solve problems in the hands of small, local, decentralized institutions and voluntary associations of all sorts, within which citizens would be expected to thrash out their differences and come up with their own, albeit often rough-and-ready, solutions to their problems. This is more than seeking "feedback" from citizens about programs designed for them by others. It is, rather, genuine self-government, with final decisions left to citizens themselves.

Perhaps foundations wishing to pursue an alternative to leadership by the ungodly bright could build their giving instead squarely on Tocqueville's insight. They could redirect funding to programs that originate with the views of citizens at the grassroots, with their understanding of the problems they face, and how they wish to go about addressing them. Solutions tailored by citizens who actually live with the problems are more likely to be effective for their own neighborhoods. Community ownership insures that these approaches will be supported and sustained over the long haul, rather than provoking the sort of resistance that often greets programs designed by remote experts and "parachuted" into neighborhoods. Perhaps most important, the process of formulating and proposing solutions to their own problems cultivates in citizens the skills essential to democratic self-governance—the ability at first to endure, but finally perhaps to relish, the messy, gritty process of deliberating, arguing, and compromising demanded by American democracy's conviction that all citizens are to be treated with dignity and respect. This is at some remove, indeed, from Warren Buffett's preference for a kind of philanthropy that would insulate him from being "too involved with a lot of people I wouldn't want to be involved with and [having] to listen to more opinions than I would enjoy."

Tocquevillian or civic renewal philanthropy would reach out quietly but actively into the communities it wishes to assist, harvesting "street wisdom" about which groups genuinely capture a community's self-understanding of its problems. Such groups will more than likely have duct tape on their industrial carpeting and water stains on their ceilings. They will not be able to draft clever, eye-catching fundraising brochures or grant proposals. They will not have sophisticated accounting systems, or be able to lay out a schedule of measurable outcomes. They will not speak the language of the social sciences, but more often than not, the language of sin and spiritual redemption. They will not be staffed by well-paid credentialed experts, but rather by volunteers whose chief credential is that they themselves have managed to overcome the problem they are now helping others to confront. No matter what the group's formal charter states, it will minister to whatever needs present themselves at the door, even if it means being accused of inefficiency or mission drift. For each person is treated not as an inadequately self-aware bundle of pathologies, but rather as a unique individual, a citizen possessed of a soul, demanding a respectful, humane response to the entire person.

This approach turns completely on its head the still-entrenched orthodoxy of progressive philanthropy. Indeed, it looks suspiciously like charity—the antiquated, discredited approach which nonetheless honored and ministered personally to the individual before it. Charity does indeed deal with "mere symptoms" because they are what people themselves consider important, rather than with root causes visible only to experts who can "see through" the client. Because civic renewal philanthropy tackles social problems individual by individual, neighborhood by neighborhood, and because it relies on and entrusts ordinary, public-spirited citizens, familiar with the communities of which they are a part, to lead the way—to identify and resolve their own problems in their own way—this approach will not appeal to the ungodly bright.

It is hardly surprising that the immensely wealthy today should find appealing the century-old vision of putting massive funding into cutting-edge technology in order to deliver the decisive, "knock-out punch" to some vexing social problem. Perhaps a handful, however, will come to appreciate the lesson of the past century, that there are no knock-outs in the effort to improve society, and the search for them can readily take ugly turns. By funding more concrete, immediate, community-based efforts of the sort described by Tocqueville, however, it would be possible to make modest headway against social ills. It would also contribute to a much loftier purpose, the revival of civic engagement and democratic self-governance in America, perhaps thereby helping to insure the survival of our democratic republic. But to appreciate the importance of that goal, it is necessary to transcend the narrow, scientific knowledge of the ungodly bright. It requires instead a kind of prudence or wisdom that aims at an attainable good, while accepting and working with, rather than trying to see through, the bewildering variety of human needs. It thus fully respects and helps to preserve democratic citizenship and human dignity. This would be the philanthropy, not of the ungodly bright, but rather of the godly wise.

Written in response to the Dialogues on Civic Philanthropy, "Philanthropic Leadership" (November 8, 2005). By permission of the author.

INDEX

PHILANTHROPIC AND NONPROFIT STUDIES

Dwight F. Burlingame and David C. Hammack, general editors

Thomas Adam, editor. *Philanthropy, Patronage, and Civil Society: Experiences from Germany, Great Britain, and North America*

Albert B. Anderson. *Ethics for Fundraisers*

Peter M. Ascoli. *Julius Rosenwald: The Man Who Built Sears, Roebuck and Advanced the Cause of Black Education in the American South*

Karen J. Blair. *The Torchbearers: Women and Their Amateur Arts Associations in America, 1890–1930*

Eleanor Brilliant. *Private Charity and Public Inquiry: A History of the Filer and Peterson Commissions*

Dwight F. Burlingame, editor. *The Responsibilities of Wealth*

Dwight F. Burlingame and Dennis Young, editors. *Corporate Philanthropy at the Crossroads*

Charles T. Clotfelter and Thomas Ehrlich, editors. *Philanthropy and the Nonprofit Sector in a Changing America*

Ruth Crocker. *Mrs. Russell Sage: Women's Activism and Philanthropy in Gilded Age and Progressive Era America*

Marcos Cueto, editor. *Missionaries of Science: The Rockefeller Foundation and Latin America*

William Damon and Susan Verducci, editors. *Taking Philanthropy Seriously: Beyond Noble Intentions to Responsible Giving*

Gregory Eiselein. *Literature and Humanitarian Reform in the Civil War Era*

David C. Hammack, editor. *Making the Nonprofit Sector in the United States: A Reader*

Jerome L. Himmelstein. *Looking Good and Doing Good: Corporate Philanthropy and Corporate Power*

Warren F. Ilchman, Stanley N. Katz, and Edward L. Queen II, editors. *Philanthropy in the World's Traditions*

Warren F. Ilchman, Alice Stone Ilchman, and Mary Hale Tolar, editors. *The Lucky Few and the Worthy Many: Scholarship Competitions and the World's Future Leaders*

Thomas H. Jeavons. *When the Bottom Line Is Faithfulness: Management of Christian Service Organizations*

Amy A. Kass, editor. *The Perfect Gift*

Ellen Condliffe Lagemann, editor. *Philanthropic Foundations: New Scholarship, New Possibilities*

Daniel C. Levy. *To Export Progress: The Golden Age of University Assistance in the Americas*

Mike W. Martin. *Virtuous Giving: Philanthropy, Voluntary Service, and Caring*

Kathleen D. McCarthy, editor. *Women, Philanthropy, and Civil Society*

Marc A. Musick and John Wilson, editors. *Volunteers: A Social Profile*

Mary J. Oates. *The Catholic Philanthropic Tradition in America*

Robert S. Ogilvie. *Voluntarism, Community Life, and the American Ethic*

J. B. Schneewind, editor. *Giving: Western Ideas of Philanthropy*

William H. Schneider, editor. *Rockefeller Philanthropy and Modern Biomedicine: International Initiatives from World War I to the Cold War*

Bradford Smith, Sylvia Shue, Jennifer Lisa Vest, and Joseph Villarreal. *Philanthropy in Communities of Color*

David Horton Smith, Robert A. Stebbins, and Michael A. Dover, editors. *A Dictionary of Nonprofit Terms and Concepts*

David H. Smith. *Entrusted: The Moral Responsibilities of Trusteeship*

David H. Smith, editor. *Good Intentions: Moral Obstacles and Opportunities*

Jon Van Til. *Growing Civil Society: From Nonprofit Sector to Third Space*

Andrea Walton. *Women and Philanthropy in Education*

For more than thirty years, **Amy A. Kass** has been an award-winning teacher of classic texts in the College of the University of Chicago, where she serves as Senior Lecturer in the Humanities. Beyond the academy, using similar literary materials, she has for many years directed nationwide seminars on civic leadership and philanthropic practice, beginning with the "Tocqueville Seminars on Civic Leadership" at the University of Chicago and continuing, most recently, in the "Dialogues on Civic Philanthropy" at the Hudson Institute in Washington, D.C., where she is also Senior Fellow. Amy Kass is the author of numerous articles and books on cultural, philanthropic, and related topics, including *The Perfect Gift: The Philanthropic Imagination in Poetry and Prose* (Indiana University Press, 2002) and *Wing to Wing, Oar to Oar: Readings on Courting and Marrying* (with Leon Kass). She currently works with the philanthropic community—donors, foundation and nonprofit leaders, scholars, and trustees—to help develop more responsible, responsive, and civic-spirited philanthropy. She has served on the National Council on the Humanities of the National Endowment for the Humanities, the Council of Scholars of the American Academy of Liberal Education, and as a consultant on American history and civic education for the Corporation for Public Broadcasting, the Corporation for National and Community Service, and the USA Freedom Corps.